SPOTLIGHT ON PARAGRAPH AND ESSAY SKILLS

CAROLE ANNE MAY

Camosun College

Toronto

National Library of Canada Cataloguing in Publication

May, Carole Anne, 1948–
    Spotlight on paragraph and essay skills / Carole Anne May.

Includes index.
ISBN 0-13-120247-2

    1. English language—Paragraphs. 2. Essay—Authorship. I. Title.

PE1439.M39 2004   808'.042   C2003-906068-3

Copyright © 2004 Pearson Education Canada Inc., Toronto, Ontario

All rights reserved. This publication is protected by copyright, and permission should be obtained from the publisher prior to any prohibited reproduction, storage in a retrieval system, or transmission in any form or by any means, electronic, mechanical, photocopying, recording, or likewise. For information regarding permission, write to the Permissions Department.

ISBN 0-13-120247-2

Vice President, Editorial Director: Michael J. Young
Acquisitions Editor: Marianne Minaker
Marketing Manager: Toivo Pajo
Signing Representative: Carmen Batsford
Developmental Editor: Matthew Christian
Production Editor: Richard di Santo
Copy Editor: Ann McInnis
Production Coordinators: Heather Bean, Patricia Ciardullo
Page Layout: Christine Velakis
Permissions Research: Nicola Winstanley
Art Director: Julia Hall
Cover and Interior Design: Gillian Tsintziras
Cover Image: Nonstock

1 2 3 4 5   08 07 06 05 04

Printed and bound in Canada.

dedication

This book is dedicated to the memory of my kind and loving parents—Annie and Harry.

brief contents

Preface   xv

Part 1   Understanding Paragraphs   1

Chapter 1   Preparing and Planning to Write   3
Chapter 2   Analyzing Paragraph Development   19
Chapter 3   Analyzing Detail Organization   35
Chapter 4   Time-Order, or Process, Development   51
Chapter 5   Comparison and Contrast Development   63
Chapter 6   Classification and Division Development   75
Chapter 7   Cause and Effect Development   87
Chapter 8   Definition Development   97
Chapter 9   Beginning Essays   109

Part 2   Sentence Foundations   129

Chapter 10   Nouns, Pronouns, and Verbs   131
Chapter 11   Subjects and Verbs   165
Chapter 12   Punctuation and Capitalization   195
Chapter 13   Modifiers   223
Chapter 14   Patterns of Sentences   253
Chapter 15   Sentence-Level Errors   285

Part 3   Readings   329

Chapter 16   Paragraph Readings   331
Chapter 17   Longer Readings   347

Answer Key   379

Index   407

detailed contents

Preface xv

Part 1 Understanding Paragraphs 1

Chapter 1 Preparing and Planning to Write 3

Introduction 3
What Is a Paragraph Composition? 4
Pre-test: What Is a Paragraph? 4
Preparing to Write 7
ESL Pointer: Count and Non-Count Nouns 15

Chapter 2 Analyzing Paragraph Development 19

Introduction 19
Five Basic Modes of Paragraph Development 20
ESL Pointer: The Use of Articles A, An, *and* The 30

Chapter 3 Analyzing Detail Organization 35

Introduction 35
Locating the Topic Sentence 35
Developing an Effective Topic Sentence 37
The Body of the Paragraph 41
The Conclusion of the Paragraph 44
ESL Pointer: Expressions of Quantity 47

Chapter 4 Time-Order, or Process, Development 51

Introduction 51
Useful Transitions in Time-Order, or Process, Development 52
Reading Time-Order Development 52
Topic Sentences Reveal Development 54
Setting Up Clear Paragraph Organizatio 55
The Drafting Process 55
Marking Scheme for Paragraph Compositions 55
Proofreading Marks 57

Setting Up a Title Page for Paragraph Composition Assignments 59
ESL Pointer: Understanding Time Transitions 60

Chapter 5   Comparison and Contrast Development   63

Introduction   63
Comparison Development   65
Contrast Patterns of Development   66
Reading Comparison and Contrast Development   68
ESL Pointer: Special Comparison and Contrast Words   71

Chapter 6   Classification and Division Development   75

Introduction   75
About Classification and Division in Academic Writing   76
Reading Classification and Division Development   78
ESL Pointer: Working with Classification and Division Transitions   81

Chapter 7   Cause and Effect Development   87

Introduction   87
Thinking about Cause and Effect Relationships   88
Tips for Constructing Cause and Effect Organization   88
Reading Cause and Effect Patterns   90
ESL Pointer: Cause and Effect: Using Since, Because, So, *and* Therefore   94

Chapter 8   Definition Development   97

Introduction   97
Using a Formal Definition   97
Generating Ideas for the Definition Mode   98
Reading Some Definition Paragraphs   101
ESL Pointer: Subordination   106

Chapter 9   Beginning Essays   109

Introduction   109
About the Academic Essay   109
Why Am I Asked to Write an Essay?   110
An Overview of the Parts of an Essay   111
How Do I Begin to Write an Essay?   112
Tips for Constructing an Argument   117

Transitional Devices   120
ESL Pointer: Passive and Active Voice   124

Part 2   Sentence Foundations   129

Chapter 10   Nouns, Pronouns, and Verbs   131

Introduction: Learning about Grammar   131
Self-Test   131
Nouns   135
Concrete and Abstract Nouns   135
Subjects and Objects   137
Pronouns   141
Verbs   144
Review Test   156
ESL Pointer   Verb Tenses   161

Chapter 11   Subjects and Verbs   165

Introduction   165
Self-Test   165
The Functions of Grammatical Terms   168
Subjects and Verbs   169
To Be and *To Have*   169
More about Verb Phrases   171
Prepositional Phrases in Sentences   173
Prepositions and Prepositional Phrases   173
Prepositional Phrases and Subjects   175
Compound Subjects   178
Understood Subjects   179
Compound Verbs   180
Subject—Verb Agreement   180
Subject—Verb Agreement with Pronoun Cases   180
Subject—Verb Agreement: *One* and *Each*   181
Inverted Order: The Subject Is Not Always First   181
Review Test   187
ESL Pointer: Indefinite Pronouns and Verb Agreement   189

Chapter 12   Punctuation and Capitalization   195

Introduction   195
Self-Test   195
Punctuation   198
Capitalization   212
Review Test   217
ESL Pointer: The Use of Quotation Marks in Direct Speech   219

Chapter 13   Modifiers   223

Introduction   223
Self-Test   223
Adjectives   226
Adverbs   231
Prepositional Phrases   236
Adverb and Adjective Usage   241
Review Test   246
ESL Pointer: Prepositions of Place and Time   249
ESL Pointer: Adjective + Preposition Arrangements   250

Chapter 14   Patterns of Sentences   253

Introduction   253
Self-Test   254
Simple Sentences   256
Compound Sentences   257
Complex Sentences   262
More about Clauses   262
Compound and Complex Sentences   278
Review Test   279
ESL Pointer: Conditional Sentences Using the Conjunction If   283

Chapter 15   Sentence-Level Errors   285

Introduction: Six Types of Sentence Faults   285
Self-Test   286
Sentence Fragments   291
Tips: How to Correct Fragment Errors   292
Run-on Sentences   295

Comma Splice   298
Pronoun Reference Problems   303
Pronoun Agreement   304
Shifts in Sentences   306
Parallelism Problems   310
Hints to Finding Parallelism Faults   311
Review Test   319
ESL Pointer: Verbals and Parallelism   325

Part 3   Readings   329

Chapter 16   Paragraph Readings   331

Introduction   331

Time-Order, or Process, Mode   331

Reading 1: A Pill to Make You Thin   331
Jacqueline Swartz

Reading 2: Keeping Your Sanity   332
Desirée Stevens

Reading 3: Optical Microscope and Electron Microscope   333
Dr. R. C. Brooks

Reading 4: Site Preparation, Planting and Care   333
The Canadian Rose Society

Reading 5: Mackenzie House, Historic Buildings of Toronto   334
Sandra Alexandra

Reading 6: The Devil in Ms. Griffiths   335
R. M. Vaughan

Comparison and Contrast Mode   335

Reading 7: The Liontamer   335
David Elliott

Reading 8: Winter Tick on Different Host Species   336
F. A. Leighton

Reading 9: General Overview, Research: Theoretical Chemistry   336
Joshua Wilkie

Cause and Effect Mode   337

Reading 10: Give Girls a Chance   337
Cheryl Embrett

Reading 11: Halifax, Nova Scotia's Eclectic Ol' Capital by the Sea   338
Allan Lynch

Reading 12: A Look at Barrier-free Design   338
Maureen Sherlock-Glynn and Brenda Millar

Reading 13: Caring for Wildlife Habitat at Home   339
Susan Campbell and Sylvia Pincott

Definition Mode   339

Reading 14: Letter to the Editor   339
Kevin Neish

Reading 15: Dracula Without Kitsch   340
John Arkelian

Reading 16: What Is a Megathrust Earthquake?   341
Ralph G. Currie

Classification and Division Mode   341

Reading 17: Tomatoes, Tomatoes   341
Lois Hole

Reading 18: Participation, Participants, and Providers   342
Gordon Selman, Mark Selman, Michael Cooke, and Paul Dampier

Reading 19: Chosen Peoples: Aboriginals Are Now Being Courted by Universities Across the Country   342
Brian Bergman

Reading 20: Engineering Rice Plants with trehalose-Producing Genes Improves Tolerance to Drought, Salt, and Low Temperature   343
Ray Wu and Ajay Garg

Reading 21: Urban Oil Spills as a Non-Point Pollution Source in the Golden Horseshoe of Southern Ontario   344
James Li and Peter McAteer

Chapter 17   Longer Readings   347

Introduction   347

Family and Relationships   347

Reading 1: Bad Boys   347
Mordecai Richler

Reading 2: A Personal Journey through Genetics and Civil Rights   350
David Suzuki

Reading 3: Betrayal of Trust   354
Sharon Butala

Environment and the Outdoors   354

Reading 4: The Worst Kind of Ice-Breaker   356
Judy Plaxton

Reading 5: Sonar Surveillance Despite Whale Injuries   359
Peter Carter

Reading 6: Whose Trail Is It Anyway?   361
Tom Cruickshank

Business and Marketing   363

Reading 7: The Trouble with "How's it going, ladies?"   363
Richard Rotman

Reading 8: Reinventing Our Food for Fun and Profit   365
Pam Freir

Reading 9: Cirque du Soleil   367
Jason Kirby

Reading 10: CD Pirates Drive Down the Music Volume   368
Edward Helmore

Culture and Communications   371

Reading 11: Phone Calls Are Futile   371
Charles Whaley

Reading 12: The Simplification of Culture   372
Neil Bissoondath

Reading 13: Rink Rage   375
The Economist

Reading 14: Intellectual Property: A Different Kind of Inuit Ownership   376
Denise Rideout

Answer Key   379

Index   407

Longer Readings Organized by Rhetorical Mode

Time-Order, or Process, Mode

A Personal Journey through Genetics and Civil Rights   350
David Suzuki

The Worst Kind of Ice-Breaker   356
Judy Plaxton

Cirque du Soleil   367
Jason Kirby

Comparison and Contrast Mode

The Trouble with "How's it going, ladies?"   363
Richard Rotman

Reinventing Our Food for Fun and Profit   365
Pam Freir

The Simplification of Culture   372
Neil Bissoondath

Cause and Effect Mode

Betrayal of Trust   354
Sharon Butala

Sonar Surveillance Despite Whale Injuries   359
Peter Carter

Rink Rage   375
The Economist

Definition Mode

Phone Calls Are Futile   371
Charles Whaley

Intellectual Property: A Different Kind of Inuit Ownership   376
Denise Rideout

Classification and Division Mode

Bad Boys   347
Mordecai Richler

Whose Trail Is It Anyway?   361
Tom Cruickshank

CD Pirates Drive Down the Music Volume   368
Edward Helmore

preface

Welcome to *Spotlight on Paragraph and Essay Skills*. This is a text that I have written to help encourage student writers, through its philosophy and structure, to become capable, confident, and eager to handle higher-level challenges in their writing. *Spotlight on Paragraph and Essay Skills* teaches paragraph structure, organization, and rhetorical patterns through the reading and analyzing of paragraphs, and it then develops the composition of paragraphs based on five rhetorical patterns. Many college composition textbooks develop the idea of writing in terms of a top-down or a bottom-up approach. This book takes a different tack by emphasizing the conception of writing as a complex process, as a recursive undertaking, and as an individual project having phases or stages.

The materials on which this text is based (especially the pre-tests, exercises, group activities, and writing assignments) have been very popular with both teachers and students over the course of my three decades of teaching at four community colleges. Students consistently reported their enjoyment with the approach and the nature of the exercises and assignments, along with their satisfaction over the improvement they saw in their abilities to analyze, organize, and construct written material.

Spotlight on Paragraph and Essay Skills has been designed with a clear sequence that builds application with varied exercises—both individual and collaborative—from the prewriting phases, to richly layered three-point paragraphs, to the basic college essay while also paying close attention to assisting students with their fundamental knowledge of grammatical and mechanical aspects of English. I have included challenging exercises which develop critical thinking and many opportunities to practise and apply foundational concepts. For college and university composition classes that include many students whose native language is not English, *Spotlight on Paragraph and Essay Skills* presents a special section for ESL students in each of its fifteen teaching chapters. These are called *ESL Pointers* and present ideas and practice in areas of common difficulty for ESL students. Instructors and ESL students should find these sections particularly useful.

In addition, *Spotlight on Paragraph and Essay Skills* offers an important element—readings—both at paragraph and multi-paragraph levels. The paragraph readings in Chapter 16 develop students' analysis of organization through rhetorical mode and specific questions, encouraging and enlarging critical thinking. Chapter 17 contains longer readings, covering current issues of high interest. *Spotlight on Paragraph and Essay Skills* asks students to pay particular attention to specific vocabulary, to examine rhetorical modes, and to use their critical analysis in response to key questions.

Key Features

Spotlight on Paragraph and Essay Skills has several useful and important features:

It provides students with practice in analysis of paragraph form and design. This practice not only assists critical reading skills but also prepares an effective background for paragraph composition construction. Key ideas in this book are reinforced to provide students with a consistent and helpful framework for thinking about their written expression so they have a clear and unified approach to their writing.

It offers a selection of paragraph and longer readings that reflect a diversity of topics. Students with widely different backgrounds and experiences should find the topics interesting and informative.

It offers intense and varied opportunities for students to practise. Ideas are not merely introduced. Students work through practices designed to develop critical thinking via a series of steps and strategies that encourage engagement and reflection. The structure of the exercises encourages collaborative work among students.

Many of the exercises have been keyed to an Answer Key found at the end of the text. The reviews in the grammar chapters, however, do not have answer keys provided. Instructors or professors may choose to use the reviews as chapter tests in their classes. Answers to the review tests are found in the Instructor's Manual.

It provides students with strong grammar reinforcement. Students may complete the grammar self-tests themselves and mark them. In consultation with their instructors, they can determine which areas of grammar study need particular attention. This method provides both instructor and student with an individualized approach to grammar study. In addition, the grammar study also supplies a conceptual framework that goes beyond rote learning and seeks a level of understanding not usually exacted in grammar study sections of work texts.

Faculty Supplements

Spotlight on Paragraph and Essay Skills is accompanied by an Instructor's Manual, available for download at **www.pearsoned.ca/instructor**, that will be an invaluable resource to anyone using this textbook. Included in the Instructor's Manual are answers to the review tests, a set of suggested activities for each chapter, and additional tests with answers.

Acknowledgements

I am especially grateful to Pearson Education Canada for the opportunity to bring this book forward. Marianne Minaker, Matthew Christian, Richard di Santo, and Carmen Batsford have been outstanding in their encouragement and support. I wish also to acknowledge my students who have been the source of inspiration and instruction over my years as a college instructor. They have afforded me with many opportunities for meaningful learning experiences and joyful interaction. I am deeply indebted to them. Finally, I must thank my wonderful family for their caring and support during the writing of this book. I sincerely hope that *Spotlight on Paragraph and Essay Skills* helps college writing students to become competent in their skills as they engage in the sheer delight of learning.

part 1

understanding paragraphs

chapter 1

Preparing and Planning to Write

Chapter Objectives
What will you have learned when you have completed this chapter? You will be able to

1. recognize what a paragraph composition is.
2. recognize a number of prewriting and organizing strategies.
3. apply some prewriting and organizing strategies.
4. complete a review test on the concepts in the chapter.

Introduction

In your daily life as an adult, most of the time you write because you need to explain or remember something. You might jot a note or two in a week, write a list of things to remember, or send a short letter or email to someone, but unless you are taking a course, you probably do not write compositions. Most adults do not expect to write much every day unless they are journalists, writers, or professionals who do a lot of writing as part of their work. However, you may be surprised at how much and how often you are expected to communicate in writing, both in your future courses and in the workplace.

Like most people, you may feel afraid of doing some writing for a number of reasons. It may have been a long time since you have written anything in "formal" English. You might also feel unsure of the rules of formal grammar. You may be uncertain just exactly where to start in the process of writing a college- or university-level paper.

This section is designed to help you learn to build confidence in your writing by starting with smaller compositions called *paragraph compositions*. This work will help prepare the way for longer pieces of writing called *essays*.

As you learn to write for academic courses, you will be introduced to some rules and conventions for composition. The chapters that follow will provide exercises to prepare you for formal writing. The written work you will do in college and university courses is called *academic writing* and has its own rules, often different from those of other types of writing. Usually, the writing you see in newspapers and magazines, for instance, is not academic writing. Not all writers are required to follow the same conventions in their work. However, as an academic writer, you will learn about the standards of writing practice expected of you.

Most of the time, academic writing is judged and graded. You, your instructors, professors, other students, friends, and even family may all play a part in evaluating your written assignments. As you know, sometimes writing is evaluated or judged—"good," "poor," or "excellent." Perhaps you will see differing opinions about exactly what makes some writing "good"; however, you will notice there is close agreement on what can help make academic writing effective.

As an academic student writer, you must educate yourself on standards of practice. There are guidelines of practice called *conventions* in academic writing that you should know about. Grammar, spelling, punctuation, formatting, structure of arguments, presentation, and organization are all parts of academic writing conventions.

Although some may argue that judgments about writing are a matter of taste, others maintain writing in university and college is evaluated on the basis of accepted standards. They claim conventions exist in academic writing for reasons. First, writing conventions help ideas become clear through providing a focussed organization and structure. Rules of essay writing help writers express complicated thoughts more clearly and assist readers to grasp what the writer is expressing. Complex, abstract ideas, using the conventions of paragraph and essay writing to assist the development of such ideas, need careful construction on the part of the writer.

Most of the time when you write for academic purposes, you will write in order to persuade or convince your reader that your point of view is worth considering. Therefore, you will want your writing to be forceful but not too pushy or egotistical. You hope your writing is interesting and informative, not boring. In a way, you want to educate your reader to your viewpoints, but you do not want to sound like a dull textbook or a self-appointed expert. Above all, you want your writing to be clear.

Remember: instructors are looking for certain aspects of good writing, including the application of standard writing conventions in your papers. Your professors or instructors will be looking at how your writing develops over a semester, how you apply principles of academic writing, and how your writing works to make meaning clear. *Spotlight on Paragraph and Essay Skills* begins with an overview of what a paragraph composition is, along with some ideas for preparing to write.

What Is a Paragraph Composition?

A paragraph composition is usually a short piece of writing on one general topic. It begins with a *topic sentence*, or a sentence that contains the *main idea* of the paragraph. Next, it contains separate *points* about the topic. After each point, you should elaborate or explain the point. You can provide examples, reasons, facts, or other *ideas that support* the point. You should end the paragraph composition in a sentence that brings the discussion to a close.

To write a good paragraph composition, you will need to plan carefully. You will need to include some convincing ideas and a logical construction. Writing paragraph compositions will help prepare you for longer forms of academic writing such as the essay and term paper. Using paragraph compositions as an entry point to academic writing, you will have the opportunity to practise without having to write pages and pages to start. You will also gain experience with editing, revising, and preparation of a paper to be graded or evaluated by someone else.

PRE-TEST: WHAT IS A PARAGRAPH?

In your own words and on a separate piece of paper, write down what you think makes up a good paragraph. Tell what parts a paragraph must have. Talk about how paragraphs should be the same, but also mention how they can differ. Be prepared to share your answers with the class.

Exercise 1   Reading Examples of Paragraph Compositions

Below you will see some examples of paragraph compositions. Read each one.

Can you spot the topic sentence in each paragraph?

Can you find the points each writer is making?

Can you find support or explanation for each point?

Did you notice the closing sentence?

Did you notice differences between the paragraphs?

PARAGRAPH 1 Buying a new mattress may be one of the most stressful situations for couples. First of all, partners have to agree on what type of mattress they are going to purchase. They must agree on the price, the size, the quality, and the construction. Getting agreement on all four points may not be easy. As a matter of fact, couples may enter the store with the intention of purchase but with no agreement at all in connection to the nature of their purchase. Next, once in the store, partners must assess what the salesperson tells them and then must seek negotiation with their partners. This business is a tricky one because as they negotiate with each other, partners often feel they must not reveal too many personal secrets to the salesperson. They might even be guarding the price they are willing to pay in order to try to negotiate a better price. Perhaps the most difficult, even embarrassing, part of the whole scene is revealing sleep preferences to a perfect stranger. Usually the salesperson will ask questions like "Which side of the bed do you prefer to sleep on? Are you a restless sleeper?" He or she may then invite couples to "try out the bed," so couples may find themselves lying stiffly side-by-side while a salesperson smiles down on them. Since most couples only buy two or three mattresses in their lifetime together, it is probably worth it to discuss not just what they will purchase but also how they plan to go about it once they are in the store: a little more planning might turn stress into an adventure.

PARAGRAPH 2 The columbine, a wildflower native to Western Canada, is easy to identify. Hikers may recognize any of the five species of columbine by noticing a particular feature common to all varieties. Each species has a hornlike spur that protrudes from the back of each petal of the flower. This wildflower is also distinctly coloured. It may possess blue, lavender, red, yellow, or white blossoms that flourish from Ontario to British Columbia. Finally, nature lovers may be able to distinguish the columbine by its leaves. They are divided into three distinct leaflets. The columbine provides quiet, beautiful elegance in unexpected places in the wild, and walkers can discover the flower by paying attention to these details.

PARAGRAPH 3 The Canadian Wildlife Service (CWS) is a unique department in the Government of Canada. First, it began as a unit responsible for monitoring migratory birds in Canada and protecting them. Both Canada and the United States signed The Migratory Birds Convention in 1916, regulating the hunting of game birds and protecting other non-game birds. Later the government expanded CWS's mandate to manage all wildlife found in Canada's national parks. This responsibility included looking after game and fur animals through planning and scientific study. Over the years under the direction of the CWS, 40 national wildlife areas and 80 nesting sites for birds have been placed under preservation. The CWS's work in these areas became world renowned. Today, the CWS is part of Environment Canada, and its distinguished history has become largely invisible to the average Canadian.

Exercise 2 Group Activity: What Makes Up a Good Paragraph?

Form a group of three to five people. Discuss the answers to each of the following questions. One member of the group should write the group's response in the spaces provided. You should be prepared to share your answers with the rest of the class.

1. In your own words, describe what a paragraph is.

   _____

   _____

2. Look over the previous exercise. What reasons can you give to tell what makes the paragraphs effective?

   a. _____

   b. _____

   c. _____

3. How can paragraphs differ?

   a. _____

   b. _____

   c. _____

4. In what ways must paragraphs be the same?

   a. _____

   b. _____

   c. _____

Preparing to Write

What Is Prewriting?

Prewriting is what you do as a writer to prepare for the writing task. There are many ways to prepare; you may find some work more effective than others. Various writing experts call these *strategies* for prewriting. Others prefer to view prewriting as a *series of stages*. In any case, it is important for you to remember that the preparation for writing is equally as important as the actual writing itself.

Think of prewriting as a crucial part of *composing*. When you are composing, you are setting down ideas on the page. You are trying to discover what you know about something or what you think of something. You are attempting to discover your ideas. When you compose, try to let ideas flow without stopping or censoring them. Set out ideas as they occur to you. Try to work in a free and flowing way with your ideas. It is not important to correct errors in spelling, grammar, punctuation, or usage at this stage. In fact, if you do stop to correct something, you will interfere with the stream of ideas that are coming to mind.

Think of this little rule when you start prewriting for a project: Write now; fix later! For the purposes of this book, think of prewriting and organizing as the following:

1. brainstorming and freewriting
2. clustering ideas
3. arranging ideas into a logical order (different ways of outlining: formal outlines, informal outlines, mapping, spokes and wheels, box charts)

Brainstorming

Brainstorming is the activity of writing down all the ideas that pop into your mind when you think about a particular topic. It is a technique for generating or creating ideas. There are no right answers or wrong answers; instead, you will find a rush of ideas that you want to put down on the page. Just let the ideas flow.

This activity has three purposes: first, it lets you know what you know about a topic. If after a few minutes you find you have written down very little in your brainstorming session, you may decide that you need to change your topic. The second purpose of brainstorming is that it helps unblock ideas; it gets the creative juices flowing, so to speak. Finally, the sudden rush of ideas is an excellent method of overcoming the dreaded writer's block—a stoppage of writing thoughts.

Exercise 3 *Individual Brainstorming Activity*

Find a quiet space to work in—one that allows you to work without interruption. Have a clean sheet of paper to use for this exercise.

1. Quickly look over the topics suggested on the following page.
2. Quickly choose one topic.
3. Scribble down as many ideas, words, or phrases that come into your mind in connection with the topic. Continue brainstorming for several minutes.

4. When you feel you have exhausted what you have to say about the topic, stop writing.

5. Now look over your scribbles. Did you have quite a lot to say? Could you organize your ideas in some way? Did you notice if the exercise went well for you or not? Did you change your topic at all?

Topics for Brainstorming

tea	cars
watching television	fashion
backpacking	vacations
insomnia	soap operas
snow sports	smoking
studying	relaxation
restaurants	keeping fit
	playing baseball

Exercise 4 Group Brainstorming Activity

Part A

Your instructor will divide the class into five or six groups. Together your group will brainstorm for ideas. You may use the board in the classroom, large sheets of paper, or note sheets to do the exercise. The person who is the fastest writer in the group should take notes in fairly large letters so that everyone in the class can see them from different parts of the room. Another person should keep the group focussed on their task by asking questions and by making sure the note-taker has enough time to take down each note. Write down everything the group suggests, no matter how silly.

The instructor will tell you when to begin. Everyone will brainstorm, using the same topic: *bargains*.

Part B

The instructor will tell the groups when to stop. When you have finished, you should post your group's notes somewhere in the classroom where everyone can see them. Be sure to give your group a name and write it at the top of your page or at the top of the board so that your group's work can be distinguished from another's. Next, the instructor will ask everyone to go around the room to each set of notes and read them over. Then all of the groups will meet as a class to discuss how the brainstorming session went, what was effective, and what was not. You will also discuss how the sets of notes are different and how they might be the same.

Part C

Each group should take another group's notes and try to organize them so that ideas are clustered around how they relate to each other. Each group should use other large sheets of paper or the board to do the organizing. The organizing group should write its name and the original group's name on the organized set of notes. Post the new organized notes somewhere in the classroom where everyone can see them. Then groups should go to the new organized notes to see what the other group has done with their ideas. The class should then get back together and each group should discuss how it organized the notes and why. Groups can debate why some notes may have been left out and others included.

Freewriting

Freewriting means writing on a topic for a set time without stopping. Freewriting is a way to gather ideas, to focus on what you might think of a topic, and to write without stopping yourself to check on spelling, grammar, or punctuation. When you freewrite, you should think of it like "free-falling with words." You simply want to experience the flow of your own ideas and thoughts. You do not want to interrupt them or you in any way. In fact, try writing without lifting your pen or pencil from the page. Write and write, even if you happen to be repeating the same words; write your name, the date, or whatever else you can think of to keep the flow of words coming.

Usually, freewriting works best if you limit the time of the activity. It is difficult to freewrite for more than several minutes. For example, a writer could not freewrite for hours—it would be too difficult to accomplish. However, you can freewrite at any time, in virtually any place, as long as you have a pen or pencil and notepaper or a computer.

It is also important to limit distractions when you freewrite, if you can. You must intensely concentrate on the activity as you do it. You cannot have someone talking to you or interrupting your flow of ideas. Try to choose a place to freewrite that is private and without possible interruption. You will freewrite for a short time, so you need not arrange a whole evening to do it.

Here is what you can do to freewrite when you want to get ideas flowing. Just take five to ten minutes for the activity. Your instructor may have given you a topic already. If you do not have one, you can always look through a magazine or newspaper for some topics. Write five or six of these topics on a clean sheet of paper. Take another clean sheet of paper, a pen or pencil, and a timer. Start the timer and set it for five minutes. Choose one of your topics and write, without stopping, for the full five minutes. Do not let the pen or pencil come away from the page.

When the timer sounds, look over what you have written. Are you surprised that you had so much to say? Could you organize your ideas in order to write a paragraph composition, for example? What did you like about the exercise? What did you not like?

Exercise 5 Freewriting in Class

Your instructor will provide you with a topic for freewriting. He or she will give you a set time to freewrite, possibly five minutes or more. Afterward, be prepared to discuss what happened to you and your writing during the exercise. Your instructor will ask you to look over your writing to see if it can be organized into a paragraph form. You may wish to add ideas during the class discussion. It is interesting to hear the wide variety of ideas students can come up with during a freewriting session. Pay attention to what others in the class say. You may learn just how many different points of view can emerge from one topic.

Clustering Ideas

Another method to get ideas flowing is a technique called *clustering*. Clustering is a way of *mapping out ideas* by using associations or connections.

To begin, write a single word (usually a thing or idea) in the centre of a clean sheet of paper. Put a circle around it. Now think of an idea that associates with your central idea. Connect it with a line and put a smaller circle around it. As another idea occurs to you, add it, but make sure that the idea connects with one of the other ideas on your page. Put all new ideas in circles.

Now that your clustering or mapping is done, look over your page. Do you see one cluster that you might be able to develop even more? Do you see associations between any of the clusters? Do any of the clusters really interest you more than others?

Exercise 6 Clustering

Choose one of the topics below that interests you. Place it in the centre of your page and begin adding related ideas, circling them, and connecting associated ideas. Use circles and lines: circles signify the ideas; lines represent the connections. Your instructor may ask to see your work on clustering.

Topics for Clustering

movies	friendship
lunches	families
hobbies	work
accidents	trends

Organizing Ideas: Outlining

After you have decided what you want to say, use *outlining* to arrange your ideas. An outline is an organized way of fitting ideas together. There are many ways to outline ideas. In the next pages, you will learn how to outline or arrange your ideas for a paragraph composition.

An outline is like a blueprint for a paragraph. In most cases, making an outline is very important for writers. The outline makes clear to writers what they are going to say and how they are going to say it. An outline arranges the topic sentence (main idea) and the supporting details, often using *point form*. Point form means you will write notes rather than full sentences for the points and proof. Some instructors prefer that outlines be written in sentence form. Check with your instructor to see which she or he prefers. The next few pages will provide you with some extra practice in outlining.

Outline in Point Form for a Paragraph Composition

Topic sentence: Indoor plants require a good deal of care.

Major Points:

    A) Watering Needs

    Proof: Explanation, Examples

    1. overwatering a problem

        a. check dampness, insert finger into soil

        b. find out from nursery

    2. different needs for different plants

        a. growing medium

            i. cacti

            ii. African violets

        b. different conditions

            i. ferns

            ii. large-leafed

        c. fertilizing

    3. sunlight

        a. different species:

            i. mosses, ferns

            ii. compared to cacti

        b. rotating the plant pot

Wrap-up (concluding) sentences: Plant owners must pay attention to the proper watering of their house plants, their varying needs, and their sunlight requirements if they wish to have beautiful, healthy plants in their homes.

Paragraph Coming from the Outline

Indoor plants require a good deal of care. The first concern is the watering needs of different plants. Many plant owners make the mistake of overwatering their plants. It is always important to check the dampness of the soil by pressing a finger down into the soil about half an inch. All house plants do not require the same amount of watering. A nursery can advise customers how much water is enough for each variety of plant. Another factor to remember is that, like people, plants have varying needs. For example, the growing medium for a cactus contains almost no soil at all: instead, it is a grit, sand, and light peat moss combination. An African violet, on the other hand, prefers a rather rich, light humus to grow in. Ferns prefer a moist, rather dark situation, whereas broad-leafed plants generally grow well in airy, bright positions. Each species of plant will also have differing needs when it comes time to fertilizing. Some, like cacti, require very little fertilizer while broad-leafed plants must be given fertilizer on a regular basis. Finally, indoor plants differ in the amount of sunlight they require. Some plants, like mosses and ferns, do not like direct sunlight. Many other plants seem to thrive in direct sun. If plant owners pay particular attention to these basic needs of their household plants, they will find their plants will respond by thriving and continuing to provide pleasure for several years.

Exercise 7 Creating Outlines from Paragraphs

Below you will find some paragraph compositions. After each one, you will see the form for an outline. Write in the topic sentence. In note form, write in the major points and the proof (explanation or supporting details for the points). Also write in the wrap-up or concluding sentence. Check your answers in the Answer Key at the back of the book.

PARAGRAPH 1 People should not be allowed to smoke in public places. Many non-smokers find the smoke from tobacco irritating and offensive. Some people suffer from respiratory health problems. A few may be hypersensitive or allergic to tobacco smoke, for example. Non-smokers who seem to have a better sense of smell than smokers find their clothing absorbs and holds the unpleasant stench of cigarette smoke. Furthermore, smoking can cause damage to physical property. In some cases, furniture and rugs have been burned from the cigarette of a careless smoker. Rooms become stuffy and stale, while even wallpaper and paint can be discoloured by heavy tobacco smoke. Finally, smoking could lead to serious public risk. Fires might easily start in chairs and sofas from a carelessly tossed, lit cigarette. Drapery or fabric in a room can readily and quickly catch into flames. Large, crowded public places could become a disaster area if someone were to drop a lit cigarette. People should show respect for other patrons and their safety by not smoking in public places.

Topic sentence: _____

Major point 1: _____

Proof (explanation or example): _____

Proof (explanation or example): _____

Proof (explanation or example): _____

Major point 2: _____

Proof (explanation or example): _____

Proof (explanation or example): _____

Major point 3: _____

Proof (explanation or example): _____

Proof (explanation or example): _____

Proof (explanation or example): _____

Wrap-up sentence: _____

PARAGRAPH 2 Consumers can "food-shop" wisely. The first idea for shoppers to think about is planning. It is important to prepare a weekly menu and then base the shopping trip on what is needed for the menu. Besides, many stores feature "specials," which can be bought in bulk, and are cheaper. Having a grocery list in hand stops consumers from "impulse buying" along the aisles. The next objective is for consumers to avoid convenience foods. Premixed and convenience foods are costly and non-nutritional. Most of these items are high in fat, salt, and food additives. Most convenience foods leave people feeling hungry because they do not satisfy healthful needs. Finally, shoppers should think about what food item packs the most nutritional "bang for the buck." Whole-grain foods like whole wheat, unprocessed rice, beans, lentils, and other grains, for example, are rich in complex carbohydrates but are inexpensive to purchase. Also, many cheaper cuts of meat can be prepared to make delicious, wholesome meals if consumers are ready to spend extra time on preparation. Shoppers should pay attention to the freshness of the produce they buy. Overripe produce, for instance, should not be purchased as it will soon spoil. With some planning and attention, consumers can do some careful shopping in the grocery store, while saving money and avoiding unnecessary trips to the store.

Topic sentence: _____

Major point 1: _____

Proof (explanation or example): _____

Proof (explanation or example): _____

Proof (explanation or example): _____

Major point 2: _____

Proof (explanation or example): _____

Proof (explanation or example): _____

Proof (explanation or example): _____

Major point 3: _____

Proof (explanation or example): _____

Proof (explanation or example): _____

Proof (explanation or example): _____

Proof (explanation or example): _____

Wrap-up sentence: _____

Exercise 8 Group Activity: Adding Major Points and Proof

Form groups of five to seven people. For each of the following topic sentences, think of three major points and proof in the way of examples or explanations. One person in the group should write down the group's responses. Another should be prepared to report on the group's answers. Your instructor will advise you how much time you will have to work in your group. Try to use the best points and proof your group can come up with. Choose three of the following.

Topic sentence 1:   Moving house can be very stressful.

Topic sentence 2:   Sharks are highly adapted predators.

Topic sentence 3:   A hobby can make someone money.

Topic sentence 4:   Finding good student accommodation is difficult.

Topic sentence 5:   The latest movie I saw was terrible.

Topic sentence 6:   What is "comfort food"?

Topic sentence 7:   Travelling by bus has its advantages.

ESL POINTER

Count and Non-Count Nouns

A noun names a thing, whether it is real (*concrete*) or imagined or felt (*abstract*).

Think of a *count* noun as a thing you can count or number.

Juanita has a cat with yellow-green eyes.

She paid a tax on the shoes.

Georges made a suggestion.

Can you count cats? Can you count taxes? Can you count or number suggestions?

A *non-count* noun refers to a noun that cannot be counted. In the English language, think of non-count nouns as *whole* concepts which cannot be enumerated or divided into parts.

The weather was bad today.

Can you count weather? If you say "a weather," you are intending to say it is countable.

The furniture was expensive.

Can you count furniture without dividing it up? In this case, *furniture* is a collective noun. You can count *pieces* of furniture, but not *furniture*.

The warmth of the fire felt good to Roman.

Can you count warmth? If you say "a warmth," you are using the word *warmth* in a different sense—you are implying it can be counted.

Here are other examples of non-count nouns.

Some Non-Count Nouns

courage	stress	machinery
anger	homework	equipment
knowledge	leisure	clothing
work	traffic	milk
love	progress	advice

However, some non-count nouns can become countable if they are used in different contexts.

Work is difficult on the farm. (non-count)

He enjoys *works* of art. (countable)

Phillipa found the *stress* in her life overwhelming. (non-count collective)

Everyone endures the *stresses* and strains in life. (countable in general ways)

Tea can be good for your health. (non-count collective)

The store carries 16 different *teas*. (countable, referring to varieties)

Wine tastes delicious with this fish dish. (non-count collective)

This restaurant serves six German *wines* and seven French *wines*. (countable, referring to varieties or separate types of wines)

Maurice is having *difficulty* with his computer. (non-count)

Several *difficulties* on the job led to his firing. (countable)

Exercise 1 Count and Non-Count Nouns

Decide if the noun is a count or non-count noun. Write **C** or **NC** in the blanks.

1. news _____
2. assistance _____
3. course _____
4. building _____
5. fish _____
6. guidance _____
7. punctuation _____
8. research _____
9. trust _____
10. software _____
11. information _____
12. intelligence _____
13. luxury _____
14. curtain _____
15. truth _____
16. laundry _____

Exercise 2 Count and Non-Count Nouns

Decide if there is an error in count and non-count use in each of the following sentences. Correct the errors. Check the Answer Key when you have completed the exercise.

1. Paulo wanted to have his freedoms when he was a little boy at school.
2. I don't think the supervisor knows about the new works we are expected to do.
3. He had to control his anger and many fears.
4. They were stopped on the freeway for 15 minutes because the traffics held them up.
5. She takes out the garbages every second day on her way out to work.
6. The farm machinery stood by the side of the road.
7. I enjoy popcorns with butter when I go to the movies.
8. Do not buy new equipment for the office until we check the price.
9. Marcella hates doing houseworks on the weekends.
10. It takes courage to do what you think is right.

CHECKOUT

What is a one-paragraph composition? A paragraph composition has these parts:

- topic sentence
- explanation (major points that support the topic sentence)
- proof (examples and explanation that support each major point)
- wrap-up sentence

Prewriting helps prepare you for writing using

- brainstorming
- freewriting
- clustering
- outlining

chapter 2

Analyzing Paragraph Development

Chapter Objectives
What will you have learned when you have completed this chapter? You will be able to

1. recognize modes of paragraph development.
2. apply five basic modes of organization.
3. find the rhetorical mode through reading paragraphs.

Introduction

Writers organize their ideas because a clear arrangement can help readers understand what writers have to say. Academic writing, in particular, must be clearly organized, and most often, composition experts and textbooks advise using *rhetorical modes*, methods of organizing paragraphs and essays. Not everyone agrees on just how many rhetorical modes are possible. *Spotlight on Paragraph and Essay Skills* will introduce you to five basic methods of paragraph development, that is, five rhetorical modes.

This chapter will present you with five methods frequently used by academic writers to organize their thoughts on paper. First, you will be introduced to each method, or rhetorical mode. Then you will read a paragraph composition that uses the particular method, and then you will do some related exercises. Finally, you will learn how to construct a summary paragraph. Although summary paragraphs are not strictly considered a rhetorical mode, they are important and are introduced in this chapter to help you understand basic paragraph construction and to deepen your understanding of the reading in your course work. Later on, in other chapters, you will write paragraph compositions based on each rhetorical mode. After working through all of these chapters, you will be comfortable with recognizing methods of development in other people's writing and with constructing your own paragraph compositions.

As you develop writing skills, you will learn to appreciate that sometimes one method or mode is more effective in a particular context or with a specific topic than another. As you read, you will begin to recognize rhetorical modes when they are used by writers of articles and textbooks. You will see that thinking about ways of developing ideas in writing can help you conceptualize abstract thoughts. As you practise writing, you will begin to acknowledge that paying attention to how someone else writes will help you to become a better writer. Rhetorical modes will provide a framework for your writing, so that you do not feel as if you have nothing to "hang onto" as you write. Remember, the more practice you have using a method, the more effective and inventive you can become in its application.

Five Basic Modes of Paragraph Development

Mode One: Time-Order, or Process, Development

This mode, sometimes called *chronological order*, is used to describe a process or explain how something works. You clearly set out ideas as steps or stages, and by doing so, you take readers either through a process of how to do something, the order of events, or the explanation and analysis of a process. For example, accounts from history or stories from your own life often use time-order. Recipes, for instance, use time-order to describe to the reader what to do first, second, and so on. Instruction manuals use time-order to describe a process. You can use time-order when you write about anything from your life, like raising children, fixing a car, playing a game, or planning a wedding. If you wish to inform the reader about how something works, you can also use this mode. You might want to explain how the tax system in local or municipal government works, how the anti-locking mechanisms on a car's breaking system operate, or how an insect uses natural chemicals to battle its enemies.

The steps you talk about in time-order must be arranged in a specific order. Details are arranged in the order they occur, that is, chronological order. A step-by-step sequence is vital. Your reader will become confused if you present steps or stages in an incorrect order of presentation. After all, your explanation is being imagined as your reader reads. Therefore, you must pay close attention to logical connections and progression of steps, stages, or events.

A famous Canadian actor, Kate Reid, had a memorable career in theatre and film. She was born in London, England, and first went on the stage during the 1950s. She then moved to Canada. Kate Reid's acting career really began in 1959, when she played in Canada's famous Stratford Shakespearean Festival. Soon her skills as an actor became recognized by critics, theatre directors, and the public. By 1958 her reputation was growing, and in 1962 she was featured in the main role in *Who's Afraid of Virginia Woolf?* on Broadway. By 1974 she had received a great honour—she was made an Officer of the Order of Canada because of her contribution to the performing arts in Canada. She went on to do major parts in movies, including *The Andromeda Strain* (1971), *Equus* (1977), *Atlantic City* (1980), *Sweethearts Dance* (1988), *Bye Bye Blues* (1990), and *Deceived* (1991), her last film. She continued to promote the arts and Canadian actors throughout her lifetime. She died of cancer in 1993. Because of her distinguished career, Kate Reid will always be remembered for her rich performances as one of Canada's great character actors.

Notice that the above paragraph uses a sequence of dates to reveal information. Also, you may have noticed that the *topic sentence* is the *first sentence* of the paragraph.

Mode Two: Comparison and Contrast Development

Writers can make clear how things are the same or different. A *comparison* piece discusses how things are similar. *Contrast* explains how things are different. Often, writers will use details to present likenesses (comparison) and differences (contrast) in order to establish elaborate ideas. Each approach provides a particular focus. Writers may employ both comparison and contrast as a single mode in one paragraph, while others may use only comparison or only contrast.

You may choose to use comparison and contrast together in a single piece of writing, or you may decide to develop your ideas by using either one. For example, you can discuss all the similarities first and then move through the differences. Or you may choose to discuss one thing first, and then compare and contrast it to something else. For instance, if you want to discuss how coaching hockey was different when you were a child, you might begin with a discussion of coaching today in the first part of the composition, and following that, you might discuss what coaching was like some years ago. In so doing, you could highlight differences for your reader as you draw the discussion to a close. Using *block form*, you might cluster all the points connected to one thing. In *point-by-point form*, you discuss one idea or point between the two items and then discuss it in more detail. There are many ways to develop ideas using comparison and contrast, so depending on the purpose and length of the paper you must write, look for different, fresh ways to use this method.

Journalism, as the saying goes, is "history in a hurry"; photography, by contrast, is "history in an instant." Journalists try to capture a scene, a moment, or an event through carefully chosen words so that the public can get a feel for it quickly. Photography, however, registers an image more indelibly in the public's heart and imagination than the printed word. Moreover, words take time to read and understand. If someone does not understand the language, he or she might not benefit from the journalist's story. A picture, in contrast, needs no words. A viewer can take in the image whether he or she speaks the journalist's language or not. In addition, in an "instant" world, what is faster and perhaps easier, seems to be preferred. Since so much in advertising and the media compete for the public's attention, to stop and read may lose out to the rapid glance. Pictures and images are simply faster and more convenient. Despite these subtle differences, both print journalism and photography are closely linked to bring the public what contemporary news reporting has become today.

You can tell that the writer is showing the differences between journalism and photography as they relate to the news. The author has chosen contrast in details to get this idea across to the reader. The writer provides three distinctions between the two things and talks about what makes the distinction interesting.

Mode Three: Classification and Division Development

Classification is a method that uses a clustering analysis as a framework. In classification, you group or cluster ideas, concepts, or items into categories. Let's suppose, for instance, that you wanted to discuss salmon as a topic. One way of organizing information about salmon is to arrange the varieties into groups or categories—pink, chum, and coho. You could then discuss the characteristics of each group. Classification becomes the tool for thinking, organizing, and writing.

You can use a classification method of development for almost any topic. Your classification clusters can be of your design, but you must have reasons for clustering the groups as you do. Make sure that in the body of your paragraph you can distinguish the categories for your reader. Vehicle drivers, for example, may be classified in many ways, depending on how you view them. However, it is important to keep your categories clear because you must be able to distinguish them for your reader.

Division is somewhat different. You do not think in terms of clusters or groups; instead when you use division, you consider a subject, topic, or idea by breaking it into component parts. Usually you will state the parts or divisions in your topic sentence, and you will follow by examining each part in turn, by providing supporting details. For example, you might discuss the parts of a computer, a stereo, a debate, a real estate contract, or whatever seems to suit a discussion of parts. This mode is often used in scientific writing. You may notice in your biology textbook, for instance, a discussion of the parts of an ecosystem, a bird's wing, or the respiratory system of a mammal. These explanations all divide a larger topic into constituent parts.

Classification and division are generally placed together as one rhetorical method, but you will usually see each used separately. The reason may be the difficulty of including both in a short piece of writing since talking about groups of things and talking about component parts can be complex. They are kept together in composition textbooks because the two have a common ground: in different ways, they separate items or ideas into groups (categories) or parts.

> Three kinds of bus riders—the shy, the curious, and the aggressive—seem to belong to every city. The shy bus passenger tends to try to make herself invisible. She will often wait at the end of the line to get on board and then will move to the back of the bus. Once there, she will often look out the window or read a book to avoid eye contact. The second type, the curious bus rider, seems to want to look around. She will climb on the bus, take the first available seat, and then have a good look around at her comrades in ridership. She might smile and say hello to the passenger next to her as she begins taking in the sights, sound, and smells around her. Perhaps the most noticeable is the aggressive rider. She will make her way to the head of the line, trod on other passengers' toes, elbow her way to the best seat, and generally strike out like a person with a mission. She will make eye contact with almost all the passengers she meets on board, but she does not give a friendly greeting. Often you will see her staring around in a grimace with her belongings spilling into the aisle or the seat next to her. She seems to be saying, "Stay away from me!" Bus riders may come in many sorts or types, but these three are unmistakeable.

This author has used classification; the topic sentence shows what the method of development will be. The writer has classified bus riders into three types and then discusses what each type is like. In the same fashion, you can classify or divide your topic in any manner that seems reasonable to you. You might name three or four types of things or ideas as in classification, or you might discuss four or five parts that make up something, employing a division method of arrangement of ideas. How you classify or divide is your choice, but you must develop your classification or division so that it is convincing to your reader and logical in its design.

Mode Four: Cause and Effect Development

Cause and effect is a rhetorical mode that describes a close relationship between two ideas or events. You must link how something causes something else and clearly establish the effects that a thing has. Scientific writers, for instance, might use this method to explain the significance of an experiment which supports their research results. Suppose that they investigated how fertilizers of different types affect plant growth—corn, for example. Their findings, written in an article, would then present evidence of the outcomes of their experiment. They may describe the conditions under which a particular fertilizer would or would not produce the best crop. In other words, they would describe results.

Social scientists also examine the relationships between things and use the cause and effect method of development in their writing. They might, for instance, be studying the effects of television watching, stress, drug abuse, partnerships, and so on. They may also choose to examine the causes of something rather than the effects. Cultural anthropologists, for example, might be interested in why people use certain products, like computers. They might want to consider what reasons humans have for using convenience foods, buses, services, and so forth.

The cause and effect method of development is complicated because you cannot rely on your personal impressions and experience alone to guide you when you write. It is more abstract than a process, or a comparison and contrast method. In using cause and effect, you must reason your way through. Your reasons must be convincing, and the relationship between ideas must be clear. If you develop a piece of writing using this mode, you establish verifiable or reasonable connections between causes and effects. Sometimes, you may have to rely on the results of documented research to "back up" your assertions in order to provide first-hand evidence for your points. This method of development is perhaps the most difficult to use because a clear cause (reason) must be convincingly related to effects (results).

You can use details to show the effect or effects of some cause stated in the topic sentence. In other words, details are arranged to convince readers that there is the relationship of a cause to a result. For example, you may choose to talk about smoking and health. You may wish to show this relationship in a topic sentence that says smoking is very harmful to your health. In support, you must establish that smoking is the cause which results in bad effects. A cause–effect development in details or examples is used then to establish reasons for or the results of something. In any situation, there may be more than one cause, and the effects may be given as details or examples in the paragraph. On the other hand, you might name an effect in the topic sentence, and provide the causes as details in the paragraph. It is up to you to decide on the arrangement you wish to use, but you must provide a plausible connection between your ideas for readers. You must also consider your purpose in writing. Choice of mode and purpose are closely related.

Caffeine has come under suspicion as contributing to one disorder or another. It stimulates the body in a number of ways. First, it speeds up the nervous system. It also increases heartbeat and basal metabolic rate. In addition, it promotes secretion of stomach acid and steps up production of urine. Furthermore, in some cases, drinking too much caffeine may cause lumps to form in the breast. Many doctors advise women against drinking beverages high in caffeine for this very reason. Finally, excessive intake of caffeine can cause physical dependence. Some individuals have experienced "withdrawal" symptoms if foods like coffee, tea, cola drinks, or chocolate have been taken out of their diets. These people experience withdrawal symptoms such as tiredness, headaches, and muscle pain. Caffeine, therefore, must be considered to be a powerful drug having definite and damaging effects.

This paragraph shows a cause and effect pattern. The cause is stated in the first sentence, the topic sentence—that caffeine produces certain negative effects in the body. The details that follow are the effects of caffeine in the body. Notice that examples and an explanation are included in the discussion of the effects.

Mode Five: Definition Development

The *definition* method of development is more complex than the others. Writers must define or tell what something is. Although this method might seem simple at first glance, it is complicated to accomplish.

You must carefully construct how the ideas relate together to form a definition. Its development should answer these questions: "What is *x*?" and "What are the characteristics of *x*?" To begin, you can situate your idea in a general class of things, so it can be understood as a concept. Then, you must explain the distinguishing features of the thing or idea you wish to define and examine its characteristics. Consider the following example.

Suppose you choose definition as the rhetorical mode to write about friendship. You must first decide what friendship is by thinking about what things it might resemble—about what general class of things it belongs to. Perhaps you decide to place it in the class of things called "human relationships." Next, you must determine how friendship can be distinguished from something else in that class—love, for instance. Then, you must explain the distinguishing features of friendship. In other words, ultimately, you must bring out the special features of the idea in order to define it.

In another example you might be examining what a good hockey player is. You might spend time thinking over the context in which a player functions. That context might be described by "street hockey," for instance. From this specific context, determine the distinguishing player qualities you want to include in your definition. In the case of a good street hockey player, you could set out the qualities or characteristics you believe to be defining ones; accordingly, you would establish that the qualities you have described are relevant to your choice of context. In other words, you would connect the characteristics with the context in order to form your definition.

You will see definition paragraphs in a variety of sources. A journalist, for example, could be writing about what it means to be a French Canadian living abroad today. Another writer may be working to define what it means to be a good writer for a rural community newspaper, or perhaps a philosopher may explain what is entailed by the definition of "good citizen." Doctors describe the healthy person, psychologists label human behaviours, and other experts work to explain what it means to be something.

What is a memory? A psychologist may look at the idea of memory by thinking about how people act and how the brain processes experience. Ralph W. Gerard suggests that memory is "the modification of behaviour by experience." A cognitive psychologist tries to link experience and the mind, examining the relationship between recognition and recall in the study of human memory. A musician may consider memory in a different way: what the hand, eye, ear, and voice can do together is memory. An athlete may talk about memory in terms of a moment frozen like a photograph, the play forever there to be studied or glimpsed. To a writer, memory may be many things. Perhaps like Proust, a writer hopes to make the past into a series of tangible objects through the remembering, using involuntary memory rather than deliberate recollection. Memory can thus be perceived differently depending on the point of view.

In the above paragraph, the writer uses four different perspectives to create the definition of memory. You can see it is useful to think about definition by considering what it might mean from various points of view or perspectives like the ones in the example paragraph. Of course, memory is viewed as a complicated, problematic issue. To get at a complex idea, you may sometimes want to explore the ways other writers or theorists have defined it.

Practise what you have learned about rhetorical patterns by completing the following exercise.

Exercise 1 Group Activity: Reading for Modes

Form a group of three to five people. Read each of the paragraph compositions below. Together decide what mode of development has been used to organize each paragraph. Discuss why you believe the method is successful. Suggest other modes of development the writer could have used. Write down your answers. Be prepared to share your answers.

PARAGRAPH 1 My happy childhood has influenced me as an adult. When I was little, I was taught to share. Sometimes that was hard to do because there were six children in my family. Even though it was difficult, we learned to co-operate. Today I remember that sharing, and I think I am a more generous person because of it. In addition, although we were poor, we respected ourselves and each other. We never went hungry, and we were always cleanly dressed. As an adult, I think that experience taught me that money had nothing to do with self-respect. Finally, the good parenting I had really helps me today because I have children of my own. Even though my parents were busy people, they took time to talk to us kids and took us everywhere with them. They taught us a number of skills and values; they gave us discipline. Learning all of that as a child helps me now as I struggle to raise my own family. Remembering positive things about my childhood, I realize how these experiences helped shape me as an adult and parent.

PARAGRAPH 2 Delicious homemade soup is easy to prepare. First, you should buy some plump, meaty short ribs, cheap cuts of chicken, or extra vegetables if you are a vegetarian. Then assemble your ingredients: garlic, onion, celery stalks and leaves, green cabbage, carrots, one large can of tomatoes, lentils or buckwheat, peas, one bay leaf, one beef bouillon cube, parsley, salt, and pepper. Now follow these cooking steps. Cut the short ribs into four-inch pieces, removing the extra fat. Heat a large soup kettle and add a dash of cooking oil. Add chopped onions, celery stalks and leaves, and minced garlic. Sear these vegetables, stirring rapidly to prevent any burning. After two to three minutes, add the short ribs to the vegetables in the kettle. Sear the meat on all sides. Add 6–8 cups of water or enough to cover the meat. Add one bay leaf and a few peppercorns. Cover the kettle and turn the stove to medium to low heat. As the stock is simmering, skim off the excess fat with a large, slotted metal spoon. After two to three hours, add two cups of chopped cabbage, one cup of carrots, the can of tomatoes, one-half cup of washed lentils or buckwheat, a bouillon cube, 1/3 cup of parsley, and additional celery leaves. Mix the soup thoroughly. Let the soup simmer for about forty-five minutes. Then remove the short ribs and strip off the meat from the bones. Return the meat to the soup. Finally, add peas, salt and pepper. Taste the soup and adjust the seasoning. This hearty soup is ready to serve. It is especially nutritious with thick slices of heavy rye or brown bread. A nourishing meal for four to six people, this soup is inexpensive, delicious, and easy to freeze.

PARAGRAPH 3 Is female handwriting different from that of males in western society? Some handwriting experts claim that it is easy to spot female handwriting because it is "tidier" than that of males. Although both genders can have a tendency to "open" handwriting, most females tend to tolerate fewer handwriting botch-ups and will clean them up for the reader. Secondly, some experts say a reader can recognize that handwriting has been done by a male because it is even and uses a smaller form. Some samples studied showed that the small, even writing seemed to be created by males three out of five times. Finally, most female handwriting tends to be somewhat fancier than that of males. Special loops and curlicues, along with particular care applied to punctuation marks and the formation of capital letters, seem to be the hallmarks of the female hand. Of course, many disagree and claim this is an oversimplified view; however, when you read handwriting, see if you can judge whether the writing was done by a male or female. You might believe you are able to recognize certain differences.

PARAGRAPH 4 What is "realism" in fiction? Writers became interested in "writing from the real" because they found romantic literature boring and unhelpful. Romantic literature referred to writing which depicted people, places, and situations in the ideal. Heroes were noble and greater than the average person could ever hope to be. Characters struggled with issues which were great universal themes. Their anguish was larger than life, and they were more beautiful and strong—beyond ordinary. Eventually, writers began to try to get at some kind of truth in the world by using realistic material from it. They tried to incorporate accuracy and detail in their writing, including providing precise background information. Details became almost like a photograph. In addition, realist writers became concerned with social and psychological issues so that characters suffered and saw some of life's ugliness, disorder, and disharmony. Readers may gain a sense of authenticity when they read realist fiction, something the writers hoped to achieve—a closer glimpse at the "truth" and an experience.

PARAGRAPH 5 Three components make up a first-rate community theatre. The first necessary element is a co-operative group of people who are enthusiastic and energetic. Most people who work in community theatre are volunteers, willing and able to give up their time. Since few people are paid, it becomes important for all contributing members to feel valued and respected. Next, community theatres require a home base. In other words, to flourish in a community, a theatre needs a designated space or building. The local government can then provide tax reduction support, special grants, and so on to the group. Also, the place itself can become important to the community. Advertising becomes easier. Word-of-mouth, community newspapers, and passers-by all become good sources for telling about the theatre's shows. The final ingredient is skill. Good community theatres can attract knowledgeable people who are willing to contribute voluntarily. Many may know about directing, writing, marketing, carpentry, and technical theatre knowledge such as lighting, sound, and set design. In addition, good community theatres help give young people a start in theatre, a career often difficult to break into. These aspects make community theatre the special thing that it is.

PARAGRAPH 6 The company offers its customers three types of billing. "Direct Account" billing allows customers not to have to be reminded of payment. The company debits customers' accounts directly. The second form of billing is "E-Billing." This billing is all done electronically. The company emails customers when their account is due, giving the amounts and payment due dates. Customers then respond by sending their credit card numbers directly to the Web site of the company. The third type of billing is called "Prepayment Plan." This plan allows customers to pay in advance. The company gives a 5 percent discount to those customers who choose the third billing plan. All of the plans are flexible and can be changed in favour of one of the others; however, the company requires 30 days' written notice of customers' intentions to change their type of plan.

PARAGRAPH 7 Learning to play a musical instrument is like taking a vacation. First of all, if a person has not played the instrument before, the experience is like going to a new place. There are many new things to discover about the place and about the person who travels or is learning to play. Secondly, just as a vacation takes someone's mind off their troubles, so does learning to play an instrument like the piano. Each person knows how refreshing it is to be able to forget stresses and problems and concentrate deeply on how his or her fingers are moving on the keyboard; reading the music and trying to keep time really is like a "time-out," similar to the feeling of a short, enjoyable trip. Most important is the satisfaction a person feels at doing and succeeding at something new. Vacations can offer a sensation of well-being because something new may have been tried—a new place visited, a new challenge accepted, perhaps. The musical student can also feel a similar satisfaction of achieving a new and difficult set of skills. In these three ways, and perhaps more, learning to play a musical instrument can be like a little holiday.

Exercise 2 Identifying Rhetorical Mode in Paragraphs

Read and examine the following paragraphs. Decide if the mode is time-order, comparison or contrast, cause and effect, division or classification, or definition. Write the mode after the paragraph. Check your answers in the Answer Key.

PARAGRAPH 1 What is the "underground economy"? Some experts define it as business transactions between people trying to escape paying taxes or to escape government control. Skilled workers can take advantage of "under the counter deals." Usually transactions take place in cash with no paper trail or means of tracing the work or—payment. The underground economy includes all illegal activities, too. Prostitution, drug trafficking, tax evasion, smuggling, and stealing are some examples. Interestingly enough, any average citizen can participate without knowing it. Canadians who do not report income become part of the underground economy. Some experts believe that the underground economy is part of the growing disrespect for the law, while others say it is simply a response to tough economic times.

Mode: _____

PARAGRAPH 2 The artistic tradition and community of the Northwest Coast Aboriginal peoples uniquely differed between the genders. In the past, villages and patrons supported a special group of male artists who were exempt from the everyday chores of the tribe. Some members of this artistic group made items for individuals or families within the tribe, while others were specialists who created outstanding objects that were meant to be preserved and cherished, like special carved totems, for example. From a young age, these specialists were apprenticed to master artists. Women had a different tradition. Although women did not share membership in this select group, many wove baskets and textiles. Many women became specialists in their own right in the artistic forms that were traditional to women: basketry, weaving, clothing design, and the creation of ceremonial regalia. Haida women, for example, were renowned for their amazing basketry made from the bark of the huge coastal cedars. While the role of the male artist was more visible in traditional Northwest Coast Aboriginal culture, both genders had a role in artistic development for the community.

Mode: _____

PARAGRAPH 3 Fish hawks, or ospreys, and bald eagles have some interesting differences. Both birds are predators, although bald eagles are much larger, reaching a wingspan of 1.8 metres. Ospreys, while smaller, are swifter when attacking prey. The two birds vary in size. Ospreys have crested heads, while bald eagles have smooth, white head feathers. Nesting habits also differ. Both birds build their nests out of sticks, but bald eagles tend to return to the same nest site year after year. Thus, the nests of bald eagles

Chapter 2   Analyzing Paragraph Development   29

are built up over the years and can become quite huge. The two birds have distinctly different feeding behaviours. Ospreys feed exclusively on fish. Bald eagles, however, include fish like salmon in their diet along with other small prey such as ducks, rabbits, snakes, and even turtles. Ospreys are much more cosmopolitan birds than bald eagles; ospreys with their piercing cries can be seen hunting in and around waters close to human settlement. Bald eagles tend to be somewhat wary of people. Finally, the two birds vary in their migration habits. Ospreys migrate to South America in the winter months, but bald eagles remain in residence year round. For many reasons, ospreys and bald eagles, two of Canada's largest avian predators, have striking distinctions.

Mode: _____

PARAGRAPH 4   If you are a hiker who likes to find adventure along the forest trails of southern Canada, you are probably already familiar with a native plant that can cause great discomfort to you if you touch it. A member of the Sumac family and having shiny leaves and whitish berries, poison ivy grows along the gravelly or sandy slopes of forests. The plant prefers to grow in lime-based soils, but it can thrive virtually anywhere in woody habitat. Poison ivy causes a painful contact dermatitis to a hiker anywhere it touches bare skin. This rash results in watery skin blisters which tend to last several days. Of course, poison ivy causes tremendous itching, and scratching a poison ivy rash will spread it.

Mode: _____

PARAGRAPH 5   Significant changes during the 1970s in North America can be said to have transformed attitudes. First, views of marriage changed. Marriage and birthrates fell, but there was a sharp rise in the number of unwed couples of all ages. Gay couples began to rally for their rights to same-sex marriages. Therefore, the public began to think about the traditional view of marriage almost as a thing of the past. In addition, customary views of religion changed because some say there was a "loss of faith." Many young men renounced the faith of their fathers, and many priests forsook pulpits. Yet as the decade came to a close, churchgoing was on the rise again. Some explain this reconnection with faith in the late 1970s as the expansion of the moral majority and the attempt to re-establish what were called "family values." Although the 1970s have been referred to as the time of the "me generation," many strong grassroots movements were formed that protested social injustice and corporate expansion and development. Thousands of gays and lesbians went public to demand their rights; other groups espoused the causes of minority groups—immigrants, senior citizens, environmentalists, non-smokers, and women. All in all, the decade of the 1970s in North America was a strange blend of conflicted values and a compilation of forces, impacting on one another.

Mode: _____

PARAGRAPH 6 Experts divide rumours into two species: spontaneous and premeditated. Most spontaneous rumours appear in periods of stress, such as a fuel crisis. They seem to thrive in an atmosphere of anxiety, mistrust, repression, or chaos and spread quickly. The second type, premeditated rumours, do not develop in an unprompted fashion. Instead, they are often planted for dubious purposes, particularly in highly competitive business environments. Both types of rumours die when they become irrelevant or when stressful conditions do not prevail.

Mode: _____

Exercise 3 Group Activity: Finding Examples of Rhetorical Modes

In this exercise, you will work as a group. Form a group of three to five people who want this extra practice. Each of you should find an example of each method of development in writing from newspapers, magazines, or the Internet. One group member can find an example of contrast; another person can find an example of comparison and so forth. Your group will meet to share the pieces of writing and to discuss the mode of development. Your group should discuss what each method of development is and why it is effective or not. You should also find the topic sentence in each of the pieces of writing, the points the writer establishes, and the evidence the writer gives. Be prepared to share your answers with the whole group.

ESL POINTER

The Use of Articles A, An, and The

In the English language, words such as *a*, *an*, and *the* are words used to point out whether something is specific, to name a definite one, or whether something is used in the general sense, to name any, or an indefinite. *The* is called a *definite* article, while *a* and *an* are called *indefinite* articles.

Look over these examples:

A man delivered these flowers for you.

The man delivered these flowers for you.

Can you tell the difference in meaning between these two sentences?
In the first sentence, *a* man, not specific or known, delivered flowers. In the second sentence, the definite article *the* implies a particular, or definite, man made the delivery.

A teacher can make a good salary.

The teacher can make a good salary.

In the third sentence, the meaning is a general one. In this sentence, the writer is implying that teaching is a good profession because a teacher can make a good salary. In the last sentence, the writer is referring to a specific, or definite, teacher—*the teacher*. This sentence might mean that the teacher has promise in his or her profession. Perhaps the writer is pointing out that the teacher here—a definite one—has the possibility of earning a good salary for a number of reasons.

Use *an* when the noun or word after it begins with a vowel or vowel sound. (In English, it is too difficult to pronounce *a* with an immediate vowel sound after it.)

> an expression, an hour, an iceberg, an army, an umbrella, an honest person, an eagle, an Irish terrier, an obstacle

However, some words may begin with a vowel, but sound like they begin with a consonant.

> a useful tool
>
> a European trip
>
> a Ukrainian dance

Use *a* or *an* when you are referring to a person's being a member of a professional or political group, a particular religion, or a nation.

> Chieko is an engineer.
>
> Marco is a federalist.
>
> René is a Liberal.
>
> Miguella is a Catholic.

Use the definite article in the singular or plural to refer to a specific or particular one or group. Use the indefinite article *a* in the singular and use *some* in the plural when you wish to generalize.

Note

However, if you are referring to species, then sometimes non-count nouns can become countable. For example, **the fish**, **a fish**, **fishes**.

Fishes *refers to the variety of species, as in this sentence:* **There are many fishes in the sea affected by the spawn of fish farms**.

Some nouns do not usually take articles, for example, some sports and academic subjects.

> hockey, baseball, basketball, biology, history

Some nouns of nationality, when used as adjectives, do not use articles. When you are using a nationality as an adjective, do not use an article. Do not make these nouns plural by adding *-s* or *-es*.

> He is Chinese. (*not* He is a Chinese; *compare with* The Chinese do not want war.)

Emile is French. (*not* Emile is a French; *compare with* The French were absent from the talks.)

Hakata is my student; she is Japanese. (*not* She is a Japanese; *compare with* The Japanese import wood from Canada.)

However, other nouns of nationality can be used with articles and can be made plural by adding *-s* or *-es*.

He is German.

He is a German.

The Germans are having a national election.

Remember, certain nouns of nationality are not made plural by adding *-s* or *-es*. Here are some examples:

British, Polish, Scottish, Danish, Spanish, Russian, English

Exercise 1 Indefinite Articles

Write *a* or *an* before each of the following nouns. Check your answers in the Answer Key.

1. _____ hockey game
2. _____ organ transplant
3. _____ field of daisies
4. _____ piece of cheese
5. _____ used car
6. _____ enraged customer
7. _____ few ounces of gold
8. _____ loud noise
9. _____ walk on the beach
10. _____ egg carton
11. _____ unusual job
12. _____ endangered species
13. _____ young child
14. _____ plate of cookies
15. _____ intelligent woman
16. _____ orange from Japan

Exercise 2 Articles

Complete each sentence, using *a*, *an*, or *the*. Do not fill the space if you do not think an article is needed. Check your answers in the Answer Key.

1. Jose wants to take _____ orange from the ones in the fridge.

2. _____ dog in the hallway belongs to my friend.

3. Lucia wants to study _____ Spanish.

4. _____ Canadians love their national sport.

5. She purchased _____ eggplant for the curry.

6. My friend Gordon really enjoys the game of _____ curling.

7. The children found _____ lost cat and don't know who it belongs to.

8. My teacher speaks _____ Danish.

9. Eduardo wants to study _____ molecular biology.

10. Because _____ professor was absent, _____ students had to work by themselves on the assignment.

11. He wants to play _____ volleyball on the university team.

12. He went to catch _____ airplane, but _____ irport was closed.

13. _____ engineer can earn extra money for original designs.

14. Her uncle is _____ priest in South America.

15. Please hand me _____ fork that is on the table next to you.

16. I love to have _____ apple in my lunch every day.

17. _____ manager of the hotel is not available to talk to the patron.

18. Have you got _____ money to pay for _____ new computer?

19. We spoke to _____ man who had saved the boy from drowning.

20. Ottawa is _____ capital city of Canada.

CHECKOUT

To develop paragraph compositions, you can use rhetorical modes of development as a tool to arranging ideas:

- mode one: time-order or process

- mode two: comparison and contrast

- mode three: classification and division

- mode four: cause and effect

- mode five: definition

As a writer, you use different methods to suit different circumstances. You learn to use these methods to help map out your thinking, so that your writing becomes clear for you and for your reader.

chapter 3

Analyzing Detail Organization

Chapter Objectives

What will you have learned when you have completed this chapter? You will be able to

1. understand a paragraph's organization.
2. find topic sentences in paragraphs.
3. write effective topic sentences, showing the rhetorical mode.
4. add points and supporting details to topic sentences.
5. write concluding, or wrap-up, sentences to paragraphs.

Introduction

As you recall, in Chapters 1 and 2, you examined five rhetorical modes—tools for you to use when you want to think about *how* you wish to develop your ideas. Once you have decided on the rhetorical mode, however, you must then consider what points you want to talk about, what details you will use to support your points, and what arrangement to use. In other words, you have discovered a paragraph will be organized around its topic sentence, main ideas or major points, and supporting details. It is important for you to recognize that writers may choose different arrangements. Reading other writers' work, you can examine how they have chosen to arrange their ideas. Doing so will help make you both a better writer and a better reader.

Locating the Topic Sentence

As you read the following paragraphs, you will notice that the topic sentence will be located in various places in different paragraphs: you may see it at the beginning, middle, or end of paragraphs. In some cases, the topic sentence may be simply implied and not directly stated. Often writers locate the topic sentence at the beginning of each paragraph, because it is then relatively easy to develop the ideas that flow from it.

Using a clear topic sentence is vital to you as a developing academic writer. *Spotlight on Paragraph and Essay Skills* recommends that, as a developing writer, you place your topic sentence at the beginning of your paragraph. As you gain more confidence, experience, and skill in your writing, you may decide to position the topic sentence in other places in your paragraphs.

35

Exercise 1 Locating the Topic Sentence

Underline the topic sentence in each of the following paragraphs. Remember: the topic sentence contains the main idea of the paragraph. Bear in mind that, in some cases, a writer may leave out the topic sentence entirely: in such cases, readers must infer the topic sentence. Check your answers in the Answer Key at the back of the book.

PARAGRAPH 1 F. H. Varley was a member of the Group of Seven. He was born in 1881 and died in 1969. In 1912, he emigrated from England to Canada where he found work in commercial art. Varley was celebrated as a Canadian portrait painter. His most famous works include illustrations of the war in Europe in 1918 and many portraits. He spent years travelling between points in Canada and in the Arctic, sketching, photographing, and painting dramatic landscapes. He worked mostly in watercolours and oils. Many of his works now hang in prominent galleries in Canada and throughout the world and in the homes of art collectors as far away as Hong Kong.

PARAGRAPH 2 The United Nations was established in 1945, with its headquarters in New York City, New York, USA, and Geneva, Switzerland. Its mandate is to promote world peace and economic and social justice, along with the development of human rights and freedoms. The UN has some new concerns since 1945—science and technology. It is extremely difficult for the UN to resolve problems within nations because, in order to do so, all member nations of the UN must pull together in a diplomatic manner on a given agenda; in other words, all member nations must agree. Though the UN has suffered some severe financial problems in the past 15 years, it is beginning to regain world respect and confidence. Surprisingly, Canada is one of the largest contributors to the finances of the UN.

PARAGRAPH 3 In the first days of lumbering, the tree trunks on first-growth trees were huge, and cuts had to be made higher up on the trunk. Doing such cutting was a dangerous business. Before the introduction of the crosscut saw, lumbermen used the timber axe, a heavy, awkward tool. Lumbermen stood on a platform or springboard that was built around the tree, one man on either side of the tree. The progress in cutting was slow, and three times the usual number of oxen and, later, horses were used to haul the timber from difficult inland terrain. Skid roads had to be built out of logs to get the timber out of the forests. Tree cutters and the lumber industry in Canada have had to cope with many technical problems throughout their history.

PARAGRAPH 4 Rowing is a sport that is gaining in popularity. In Canada, rowing events have been reported as early as 1816 in St. John's Harbour. In the 1840s, rowing clubs began in Quebec and Ontario. In 1867, four Canadian rowers won a race in Paris, France. Between 1954 and 1960, Canadian rowing became even more commonplace because of the Commonwealth Games. In 1976, several Canadian rowers took medals at the Olympics. In the milder southern Canadian climate, hundreds of people now enjoy rowing as the major sport in their lives, and several key areas have become the training grounds for future Canadian champion rowers.

Developing an Effective Topic Sentence

Paragraph compositions are relatively short pieces of writing. Therefore, you should choose a topic that can be handled effectively—one that does not require a lengthy development. Because you cannot deal with complex issues in a single one-paragraph composition, you should begin by selecting a topic which seems appropriate to a composition of 150 to 250 words. Once you decide on a suitable topic, you shape a sentence having two purposes:

1. to contain the main idea or focus of the paragraph; and

2. to show the rhetorical mode you will use to work through your ideas: time-order, comparison or contrast, cause and effect, classification and division, or definition.

After you have shaped this important topic sentence, ask yourself the following questions:

1. Is the topic sentence I have developed "too big"? Is it too broad? Am I trying to deal with too much in a limited number of words? Is my statement so general that it might cause me to wander around my topic?

2. Is the topic sentence "too small"? Is it too narrow? Am I only going to be making one point? Am I restricting myself so much that I will be left with too little to say?

3. Is the statement "just right"? Does it show my general direction without being too ambitious or too restrictive? Does it indicate what method I will be using to organize my ideas? Does it seem interesting enough for me to write about and for my readers to read?

If your topic sentence seems "just right," you are ready to begin. Now you will practise by doing some work with shaping topic sentences.

Exercise 2 Shaping Topic Sentences

Following are some topic sentences. Read them and decide what you think—are they too broad, too narrow, or "just right"? Imagine that someone has given you each of them as a topic sentence for a paragraph composition. Would you be able to use them? Why or why not? Some possible answers appear right after the exercise.

1. His dog is disgusting.

2. I failed my computing test.

3. Green is Melanie's favourite colour.

4. Scientists are discovering new ways of treating cancer.

5. Highways are dangerous.

6. The criminal was a 15-year-old from Saskatchewan.

7. Puppy love can be divided into three types.

8. Email programs consist of seven basic features.

9. Children, unlike adults, should not play contact sports.

10. Swimming and hockey have certain similarities.

What have you decided? Read the explanations below to see how your answers compare.

1. This statement is too narrow. It is really an opinion—someone's dog is disgusting. It does not invite discussion. The writer does not indicate how he or she will handle the topic: there is no clear rhetorical mode indicated.

2. This statement is also narrow. It says that a person has failed a computing test, but beyond that, it does not indicate what the discussion will be about. Had the writer suggested that there were "four reasons for failing my computing test," then he or she would have more to talk about. The writer could generalize and discuss why people fail tests or why some people fail tests and others don't.

3. This sentence is too narrow to be an effective topic sentence. Although green may not be someone's favourite colour, this fact cannot provide enough to write about. Secondly, there is no clear mode indicated by the statement. Not having a clear mode can lead to just as many problems as not having enough to say.

4. At first glance, this topic sentence seems "just right"; however, a writer would probably soon learn that it is too broad—it tries to take in too much. Remember that a paragraph composition is short. This topic might make a good thesis statement for an essay, but in a short composition, it will not be explained well enough to be satisfying to both the writer and the reader.

5. This statement is too broad. Everyone knows that some highways can be dangerous, but it does not indicate which ones and why. It might be effective for the writer to discuss the different dangers on two highways (contrast) or the types of dangerous highways (classification). The topic sentence lacks focus because it does not direct how the writer will develop ideas.

6. The statement is too narrow to be a good topic sentence. It is a fact that the criminal is 15 years old, but unless the topic sentence is opened up for more discussion, there is little left for the writer to say. Besides, youth and crime is too complex a topic to try to deal with in such a short paragraph composition. Furthermore, there is no clear development for ideas indicated by this statement.

7. This topic sentence seems "just right." The writer uses a clear indication of mode—classification—in order to discuss the topic of puppy love. The topic also seems manageable and suitable for a shorter piece of writing.

8. This topic sentence also seems "just right." The writer uses a division method—what seven parts make up an email program. The topic seems suitable for a shorter composition.

9. This topic sentence also seems "just right." The writer indicates a contrast mode. He or she will explain the differences in the suitability of contact sports for the two age groups. The topic is manageable in a one-paragraph composition, too.

10. This topic sentence seems "just right." The writer uses a comparison mode. He or she will discuss in what ways swimming and hockey are the same. The topic is suitable for a shorter composition.

How did you manage in your answers to the shaping exercise? As a writer, you will find the topic sentence is very important to your writing task. You will use the topic sentence as an obvious starting point from which to write. You will have a clear direction, because a good topic sentence provides it. You can then sketch out what your paragraph will be about. From it, you can move to the body of your discussion.

Exercise 3   Group Activity: Recognizing Patterns in Topic Sentences

Effective topic sentences may show one of the following modes:

1. time-order, or process

2. comparison and contrast

3. classification and division

4. cause and effect

5. definition

Form a group of three to five people. Read each of the topic sentences below. Decide what rhetorical mode you think the writer would use. Write your group's answer after each sentence. Be prepared to share answers with the class.

1. Foreign-made cars are more economical to operate than North-American-built vehicles. _____

2. A garage sale can be easy to organize if a person follows a few simple steps. _____

3. Adult learning is different from youth learning. _____

4. When I was 17, I learned what love meant. _____

5. The history of computers is entertaining to read about. _____

6. Some elderly drivers can cause accidents on the road. _____

7. Television commercials are unlike advertisements in magazines. _____

8. Canada's climate may be divided into five regional types. _____

9. The wetlands of Ontario and Manitoba are unique in four ways. _____

10. Here's how to restore an antique chair. _____

11. Both card games and chess can be educational. _____

12. Repairing a bicycle tire is easy to do. _____

13. Judging others can lead to some serious problems. _____

14. How can someone learn to keep a secret? _____

15. What is a bargain? _____

Exercise 4 Group Activity: Developing Topic Sentences Together

Form a group of three to five people. Choose one person to lead the group. Choose another to write down the group's responses. Choose another to report responses to the class. Follow these steps. Agree on each topic sentence you construct.

Below you will see several topics. After each topic you will see a suggested rhetorical mode. Choose 10 of the following. Write a topic sentence for each of the 10 according to the suggestion requested. Discuss any aspect of the topic. For example, if the topic is "driving," you may choose to discuss an aspect of the topic, like ambulance driving, professional driving, highway driving, and so forth.

1. Christmas (time-order)

2. pets (definition)

3. parenting (contrast)

4. shopping (classification)

5. safety (division)

6. fashion (time-order)

7. stress (cause and effect)

8. recreation (comparison)

9. condominiums (contrast)

10. travel (division)

11. marriage (definition)

12. radar traps (time-order or process)

13. hockey (classification)

14. bread making (division)

15. beer (classification)

16. photography (comparison)

17. diets (cause and effect)

18. camping (time-order or process)

19. happiness (cause and effect)

20. jokes (classification)

Exercise 5 Group Activity: Finding Effective Topic Sentences

Form a group of five people. Each member of the group is responsible for finding a single paragraph in a magazine or newspaper that has an effective topic sentence. Group members will come together to share the paragraphs they have found. Group members should be prepared to discuss why paragraphs have been selected and why topic sentences are effective. If the group disagrees, the members should set aside those paragraphs. The instructor may wish to collect the paragraphs and distribute them.

Now that you have practised shaping the topic sentence, consider the body of the paragraph. What points will you make? What evidence will you use?

The Body of the Paragraph

The explanation part of the paragraph composition makes up the content of the writing. Often called the *body* of the paragraph or essay, the explanation is made up of points. Each point has support or evidence for it, too. In other words, you establish a point that follows from the topic sentence. Then you give proof for the point. The proof might be an example, a reason, a statistic, an anecdote, an explanation, or an illustration.

Exercise 6 Finding the Points in the Body

Read each of the following paragraph compositions. Underline the topic sentence for each one. Then number each point the writer is making. Then indicate the sentences that provide proof for each point. Write *proof* over these sentences. Be prepared to share your answers with the rest of the class.

PARAGRAPH 1 Papier mâché is a fun and inexpensive craft for children of all ages. The materials are cheap and easy to come by. Collect a stack of old newspapers, a square pan with sides that are about 25 cm high, about 500 ml of all-purpose flour, string, a small paintbrush, poster paint, and bits of wire to make a form. The steps are simple. Tear the newspaper into long, thin shreds. This is a job most young children love to do! Place the paper shreds into the square pan and cover them with water. Let the mixture soak for several minutes until the paper is soft and pliable. Add the flour and blend the ingredients together until all of the flour has been well incorporated into the strips of paper. Children will love this step too, because they can dig in and enjoy the fun. Let the mixture rest for about 30 minutes. While the mixture is curing, shape a form with the wire. String may be added as well. Children may decide to make masks, jewellery, baskets, boxes, toys, or whatever pleases them. After 30 minutes, apply the first layer to the form. Keep adding more layers and wetting the mixture down if it becomes too dry or stiff. Let the shape dry overnight. The next step—decorating—holds lots of creative potential. More layers can be added if needed. The piece should be perfectly dry before paint is applied. Mix bright colours of poster paint and then decorate the piece. Use string or plastic beads or small objects to add interest. Paint over these so that the piece has texture. You can add glitter or lacquer to give the piece a glossy effect. Children will proudly display their creations for everyone to see. So, with a few simple steps and materials, anyone can have fun making papier-mâché projects.

PARAGRAPH 2 Commuting can be relaxing. First, the commuter can enjoy watching the scenery while someone else does the driving. Many people do not enjoy driving themselves from home to work and back again because they hate battling the traffic and the rush hour grids. Another reason commuting can be enjoyable is the cost. It is much cheaper to take public transit than to pay for car insurance, gas, and maintenance on a vehicle. Commuters can save money. Finally, many people find commuting fun. They enjoy meeting new people, reading a book, or just calming their nerves while they occupy themselves with their own thoughts. Some people even claim that commuting is the only time of the day they have to themselves. All of these reasons provide convincing evidence that commuting can be a positive experience.

Exercise 7 Adding Points

Add three major points to each of the following topic sentences. Remember: you want to add ideas that relate to the topic sentence. Your ideas should be convincing.

1. Vacations can be a disaster.

   a. _____

   b. _____

   c. _____

2. Rabbits and skunks have three main differences.

   a. _____

   b. _____

   c. _____

3. Car accidents can have serious effects on young drivers.

   a. _____

   b. _____

   c. _____

4. What is a good listener?

   a. _____

   b. _____

   c. _____

5. Doing laundry is easy if you follow these steps.

   a. _____

   b. _____

   c. _____

Exercise 8 Group Activity: Providing Proof or Evidence

Form a group of three to five people. For each of the following points, provide proof. You can use examples, facts, reasons, statistics, or more explanation. Be prepared to share your answers with others in the class.

1. Working and going to school is a difficult situation.

   a. Time management

   Proof: _____

b. Getting enough rest

Proof: _____

c. Getting to know others isn't easy.

Proof: _____

2. Women are better at some sports than men.

a. Synchronized swimming

Proof: _____

b. Floor gymnastics

Proof: _____

c. Figure skating

Proof: _____

3. What makes up a nutritious diet?

a. Whole foods

Proof: _____

b. Fresh ingredients

Proof: _____

c. Careful preparation

Proof: _____

The Conclusion of the Paragraph

The *wrap-up* concludes the paragraph composition. It is often called the *conclusion*, but this name tag can be deceiving to a developing writer. A conclusion in this sense is not always something that logically concludes from a written argument. For example, a narrative paragraph which tells a story or anecdote does not necessarily have a logical conclusion. Rather, a conclusion, or wrap-up, in a paragraph completes the paragraph, so that the reader feels satisfied that it has ended somehow.

Concluding, or wrap-up, sentences will depend on the rhetorical mode and the writer's purpose. In the case of a paragraph composition that uses a time-order method of development, for example, the paragraph composition may not actually have a conclusion: it may simply require a closing statement of some sort, telling the reader the process description is complete. A comparison or contrast mode may require a wrap-up sentence that mentions similarities or differences. On the other hand, a cause–effect mode will call for a statement that draws a probable conclusion from the points presented. In this case, it is really important to have a conclusion that follows from the arguments—points and evidence—presented in the composition. If you do not provide a clear and logical conclusion, then the paragraph composition will not have been very convincing to the reader.

In all your paragraph composition writing, you should try to leave the reader with some sense of satisfaction: each piece should end reasonably and clearly. The wrap-up sentence should help the paragraph come to a logical and pleasing ending.

Exercise 9 Adding Wrap-up Sentences

Add a good wrap-up sentence to each of the following paragraphs. Add your sentence to the line provided. Your instructor may ask to see your work, or you may be asked to share your answers with others.

PARAGRAPH 1 Kitchen magnets became a fad in the early 1960s. They came about because refrigerators became widely available in the 1950s, when most people wanted to switch from the traditional iceboxes to major electric appliances. As householders began to use the fridge door as a place to post notes for members of the family, marketers noticed that the fridge had become a kind of bulletin board. They invented and developed "fridge magnets" in charming shapes and colours.

Wrap-up sentence: _____

PARAGRAPH 2 Foxes will eat anything. Foxes have become raiders of more than just the chicken houses in people's backyards. They love junk food, like noodles, potato chips, and jam, but are equally at home with cattle feed or mash. They seem to be constantly hungry and are always on the search for new edible delights. Half-grown pups, too small to hunt real game, forage in the woods for berries and roots, beetles, grubs, or even flying insects. The larvae in a dead stump or a wasp's nest can provide them with an ample meal.

Wrap-up sentence: _____

PARAGRAPH 3 Everyone enjoyed watching the first 3-D movies in the 1950s. At the door, patrons were handed strange-looking cardboard glasses. The glasses were to be worn when viewers were watching the movie. The glasses were included in the price of the admission ticket. One eyeglass was red-tinted plastic, the other, green. In the theatre, all viewers, young and old, put on their weird equipment in order to see the spectacular visual effects that were advertised on every billboard.

Wrap-up sentence: _____

PARAGRAPH 4 According to psychologists, taking a short nap is good for you. When you feel sleepy in the afternoons or after eating, you should lie down for a short snooze. You should not sleep more than 20 minutes because you do not want your body to reach deep REM sleep, the deepest of the sleep stages. It can be startling to be pulled out of the REM stages of sleep. After all, you want to feel refreshed after a nap, not groggy and grumpy.

Wrap-up sentence: _____

Exercise 10 Group Activity: Putting Skills Together

Form a group of four or five people. Complete the exercise below. Be prepared to share your answers with the rest of the class.

1. Underline the topic sentences; indicate if no topic sentence is given.

2. Tell what rhetorical mode has been used: time-order; comparison, contrast; cause and effect; division, classification; or definition. Although the organization may seem to have a mixed pattern in some paragraphs, try to find one that seems dominant.

3. Examine the points provided in each paragraph. Number them.

PARAGRAPH 1 Blood pressure, the force exerted by blood against the inner walls of the blood vessels, fluctuates as the heart beats. The highest pressure, occurring when the heart contracts, is called systolic pressure; the lowest pressure, when the heart dilates, is called diastolic pressure. Blood pressure is designated as a ratio, with systolic pressure over diastolic. In people, blood pressure can vary according to a person's age, the level of exertion being applied to the body, and the level of excitement a person is feeling.

PARAGRAPH 2 Among the most insidious hazards is that of smoking during pregnancy. In 1976 more than 36 percent of Canadian women in the childbearing ages of 15 to 44 years were smokers. Yet a study by Quebec's Laval University found that smoking in pregnancy increased the risk of prenatal death by 24 percent, and 12 studies cited by the Public Health Service have revealed a "significant elevated mortality risk among the infants of smokers." In Sweden, which has the lowest infant mortality rate in the world, researchers have computed the "total death risk" in stillbirths, and in deaths occurring before one year of age, as an astonishing 60 percent higher for babies of smoking mothers. Despite these startling findings, many women continue to smoke while they are pregnant.

PARAGRAPH 3 What is the history of printmaking in Canada? Printmaking is the art of making images using several techniques. Woodcuts were the first printmaking images made, and these images were used mostly for advertising purposes in the 18th century. Then artists' sketches were etched or engraved on copperplates, and these prints became a popular art form. A rolling press, or intaglio press, was first brought to Canada in 1790, and prints became more sophisticated. The next development came with the intaglio press and aquatint etchings. For many years after that, lithography became the main form of printmaking. Finally, colour screen printing, or serigraphy, became the predominant form of printmaking.

PARAGRAPH 4 The Thunderbird is an important creature in Aboriginal mythology. First, the Thunderbird is a powerful, supernatural being that produces and controls lightning and thunder. The Aboriginal stories say that when the Thunderbird flaps its wings, it produces thunder. When the Thunderbird opens and closes its powerful eyes, it produces lightning. Furthermore, the power of the Thunderbird as a hunter is told of in many Aboriginal stories and songs. This wonderful creature is said to hunt whales and shoot arrows, using its wings like arms. It is said that humans can inherit the gifts of the Thunderbird. A person who is hit by lightning and survives becomes the shaman of the tribe; it is believed the person then has the power of the Thunderbird. In many Aboriginal legends, the Thunderbird is described as one of the most powerful creatures of all.

ESL POINTER

Expressions of Quantity

Most count nouns form their plural by adding *-s* or *-es*.

dog	→	dogs
calendar	→	calendars
melon	→	melons
church	→	churches
fox	→	foxes

Non-count nouns do not have a plural form.

Some Non-Count Nouns		
furniture	education	work
equipment	information	homework
traffic	knowledge	courage

weather	research	warmth
leisure	progress	news
transportation	advice	music

Singular count nouns can use *the*, *this* (close to you), *that* (away from you).

the banana, this banana (close by), that banana (farther away)

Plural count nouns can use *the*, *these* (close to you), *those* (away from you)

the bananas, these bananas (close by), those bananas (farther away)

Quantity Words with Count and Non-Count Nouns

Some words show quantity and go with nouns. Some quantity words that go with singular count nouns are *each*, *every*, *any*, and *one*.

each person, every boy, any dog, one banana

Some words show quantity and go with plural count nouns: *some, any, most, more, all, a lot (of), many, several, a few, a couple of,* and *both*. Use *few* or *fewer* with plural count nouns.

some people, any boys, most dogs, more bananas, all trees, a lot of vegetables, many shoppers, several men, a few children, a couple of cars, both women

Some words show quantity and go with non-count nouns: *a little, some, any, much, more, all, less, a lot of, very little,* and *no*.

Exercise 1 Expressions of Quantity

Complete each expression with an appropriate quantity word. Some may take several answers; choose one. Check your answers in the Answer Key at the back of the book.

1. _____ apples
2. _____ intelligence
3. _____ sheep
4. _____ weather
5. _____ plums
6. _____ work
7. _____ people

8. _____ rain

9. _____ furniture

10. _____ workers

11. _____ transportation

12. _____ child

13. _____ glasses

14. _____ magazine

Exercise 2 Nouns with Quantity Words

Each sentence contains errors that relate to *quantity words* and count and non-count nouns. Find the errors. Then correct each sentence. Write your corrections above each sentence.

1. Several heavy traffics were outside my apartment today.

2. A couple of student were talking about the assignment.

3. A lot of orange were spoiled in the bin at the store.

4. Lee had a lot of troubles with his new car this week.

5. Was there many informations at the orientation session today?

6. Both child wanted to go out to the park to enjoy the sunny afternoon.

7. Less sandwiches were available at the cafeteria after five o'clock.

8. More girl wanted to play on the beach than boy.

9. He has a lot of energies for such a small man!

10. More educations is needed in today's world.

11. Several knowledges about diving is important for a couple of person on the trip.

12. She has decided to put fewer furnitures in her bedroom this semester.

13. Every women in the bakery knows Giorgio, who always comes to buy a couple of bun each morning.

14. A few equipment was broken when we bought them.

15. These advices does not help me get a few informations I need.

CHECKOUT

Now that you have completed the exercises in the chapter, try the review that follows to see if you can provide full, clear answers to the questions.

1. What is a paragraph?

2. What is a topic sentence?

3. Where can topic sentences be found in paragraphs?

4. If a reader cannot find a topic sentence, what does the reader usually do?

5. Name five methods by which details can be organized in paragraphs.

6. How can a reader make use of key words or phrases in paragraphs?

7. Give a reason why knowing about paragraph organization is important.

chapter 4

Time-Order, or Process, Development

Chapter Objectives
What will you have learned when you have completed this chapter? You will be able to

1. recognize time-order, or process, development through reading paragraphs.
2. shape topic sentences using time-order, or process, development.
3. write a paragraph composition using time-order, or process, development.
4. set up a title page for presentation.

Introduction

If you want to write about how to do something, use time-order, or process, development, often called *chronological* order. Outline and then clearly explain each step of the process. The order in which you present the steps is critical, because you are describing a sequence. Let's suppose, for example, you wish to tell the reader how to make a perfect breakfast for someone on a special day. The order of preparation is important: after all, you want the food to be ready and hot at the same time. You don't want to have to backtrack in order to do a step, leading to confusion and a cold breakfast, in this case.

In addition, time-order can be used if you wish to report on a series of events or a process. For instance, you might tell a story from your life, describe an incident you witnessed, tell someone else's story, or relate a chronicle from history. In these examples, you are reporting a narrative or story, having a chronological order to it. Using time-order effectively, you make a story sensible to readers. You may also wish to use time-order to explain a process of some sort. Perhaps you are taking a nursing course and are assigned to write about how the body produces and uses insulin. A time-order mode would be the most appropriate way to organize your explanation of the process.

This chapter discusses time-order, or process, organization in detail. You may find that time-order is a relatively easy mode to adopt, because you are working with experience and observation as the content of your writing. After all, everyone has a story to tell or knows how to do something. You do not need to rely strictly on abstract ideas; instead, you can go though the events as you observe or remember them. You can tell your reader what happened in a step-by-step manner.

To begin, in this chapter, you will do some practice with the mode. Then you will complete your first paragraph composition, using time-order, or process, development.

Useful Transitions in Time-Order, or Process, Development

Transitions are words or phrases that act as connectors between ideas. The function of transitions is to show a reader that a new aspect or point of the topic is about to be discussed. Transitions are cues for the reader: they signal a turn in the explanation. You might want to think about them as connecting bridges between ideas.

Different rhetorical modes of development use different transitions. When you use time-order, or process, development, you should employ specific transitions that show a chronological or step-by-step relationship.

Useful Time-Order Transitions

first	secondly, thirdly
to begin with	following that
in the first place	next
before	after that
presently	in due time
now	then
meanwhile	soon
when	until
after a while	later
afterward	finally

Reading Time-Order Development

It is often useful for you to examine how another writer has put together his or her ideas. Analyzing another writer's development of ideas and studying the use of devices such as transitions can assist you in your writing.

Exercise 1 Time-Order Development

Read the following paragraph, paying attention to the specific transitions the writer uses.

My friend Paula plans and organizes picnics that are inexpensive as well as entertaining for family and friends. To begin with, she decides how many people she will invite and what they like to eat. Next, she calls her closest friends to help with food preparation and expense. She includes the children at this stage, too. Her picnics include potato salad—two types—one for vegetarians and one for meat-eaters, roasted chicken legs, green salad, corn salad, bean salad, hot dogs for the children, potato chips, and devilled eggs. We all show up the day before the picnic with a number of selected food items. We form a production line of cooks, each of us having several tasks to perform. For example, someone peels and cooks the potatoes, another person chops vegetables, usually two people chop onions for the salads and hot dogs, and another friend devils the eggs and puts the salad ingredients together for three salads. Paula usually roasts the chicken legs in her special sauce. Then we each take something home to store in our refrigerators. Paula also appoints people who are non-cooks to do other things: one person brings games and sports equipment, another brings a couple of large coolers, another gets together blankets, napkins, paper plates, and plastic cutlery. Someone else might arrange the entertainment at the picnic. There is always what Paula calls "the last minute person." His or her job is to bring or go buy whatever we need that we have forgotten when we get to the park. Groups usually bring their own beverages. Paula says that is the best idea, because it is difficult to please all of us when it comes to what we want to drink. When it is the day of the picnic, we all show up at the designated place and time, ready to dig in and have a good time. Without Paula's organizational skills and energy, all of her friends and family would miss some great summer festivities.

First, notice that the topic sentence implies that a process, or some steps, will be described: "My friend Paula *plans* and *organizes* picnics that are inexpensive as well as entertaining for family and friends." The two words in italics tell you some sort of arrangement will be explained.

Next, notice the transitional words and phrases the writer chooses to introduce the ideas and shape the mode. "To begin with," "next," "the day before the picnic," "then," and "when it is the day" all show time-order, or sequence. Inside the paragraph, you will also see other transitions, such as "for example" and "also": these help add one idea to another. Such expressions not only assist in developing ideas by a time-order method, but they also help the ideas to be coherent and clear; they signal the reader, and they make ideas fluid.

Finally, look at the wrap-up, or closing, sentence of the paragraph. Does it bring the writer's ideas together? You begin to notice that, if you write an effective wrap-up sentence, you will leave your reader with a feeling of closure and satisfaction.

Exercise 2 Group Activity: Reading Time-Order, or Process, Development

Get together in a small group. Read the following paragraph. Pay attention to the topic sentence and the wrap-up sentence. Also notice the transitions the writer uses. Then examine how many steps or stages in the process development the writer provides. Let the example above guide you in your analysis. Be prepared to share ideas with others.

With the costs of food going higher and higher, many people are banding together to learn to organize neighbourhood food co-operatives. The first step is for a group of interested people to get together. Usually one or two people get the idea and start talking to neighbours and friends to see if there are enough people who want to make worthwhile plans. Organizers can place notices on bulletin boards in churches, nearby schools, community centres, and public libraries. The group might decide to take advantage of the free advertising cable companies and small, local newspapers offer. Then, after a number of people show interest in the project, the group sets the first meeting. They decide the scope of their co-operative and begin to discuss the kind of policies and practices their association would like to have. There are numerous questions to sort out—How large should their co-operative get? Should the group work out of someone's home, or should they rent a small space somewhere? Should the group hire some part-time help? Are there legal problems to consider? After these decisions have been made, they can discuss how to finance the co-op, what the ongoing responsibilities of each member will be, who should be in charge of various duties, and where to buy the goods and produce. After the initial planning stages, the new co-op can begin its work of saving money for its members and providing an excellent service at the same time.

Topic Sentences Reveal Development

You will recall that your topic sentence should indicate what rhetorical mode—time-order, comparison and contrast, classification and division, cause and effect, or definition—you will use when you are developing your writing. Of course, you don't say, "I will use contrast to develop this topic." Instead, key words or phrases in your topic sentence show the manner in which your paragraph will be developed.

However, shaping a topic sentence takes practice. The following exercise should assist you in learning to develop clear topic sentences based on a *time-order* mode.

Exercise 3 Writing Some Time-Order Topic Sentences

Read the topics below. Choose 12 topics to work with. For each one, develop a topic sentence that indicates a time-order, or process, mode of development. You may use any aspect of the topic for your topic sentence. Use separate paper. Your assignment should show your name, the date, and the assignment number at the top of the page. Your instructor may ask you to hand in this assignment.

Topics for Time-Order, or Process, Topic Sentences

fires	gambling
laundry	photography
decisions	skateboarding
microwaves	meditation
travel	shopping
parks	wines
pizza	sailing
baseball	neighbours
parties	toast
bikes	apartments

Setting Up Clear Paragraph Organization

Rhetorical modes such as time-order can greatly assist you in developing the ideas of your paragraph. However, you must still arrange your ideas in a clear manner. A simple method of setting up your ideas in a time-order mode is as follows:

1. Establish each step in a separate sentence. Tell the reader what the step is. Use transitions to help you do so.

2. Discuss the step. In a sentence or two, tell why the step is important, or explain what you think is important information connected to the step.

3. Establish your next step in a separate sentence. Use a transition to introduce the next step. The transition lets your reader know you are bridging one idea and the next.

4. Discuss the next step in a separate sentence. Provide relevant information about the step in another sentence or two.

5. Continue establishing steps and discussion.

6. Wrap up the discussion in the last sentence. Provide closure to the piece for the reader.

Exercise 4 Following the Writer's Organization

Go back to the paragraph about Paula and the picnic. Using the six-step formula above, trace how the writer developed points in the paragraph.

The Drafting Process

Because writing is a process, you will learn to produce several attempts, called *drafts*. Your first draft should never be your final draft; in other words, you should find ways you can improve your first draft. Perhaps you will detect problems in the organization. Perhaps you will see that your point has not been clearly established. You will probably also observe errors in proofreading—that is, errors in spelling, punctuation, grammar, and usage.

Your instructor may ask to see your first completed draft. He or she will make comments on the draft and then ask you to make revisions, clean up errors, improve the style, and so forth. In the second draft, you will be expected to pay closer attention to such details. In addition, your instructor may ask to see you for a *writing conference*. The conference is really a short meeting between you and your instructor to discuss your draft.

Your instructor will mark and make comments on your paper. Furthermore, he or she may provide you with a marking scheme sheet. This sheet shows you what your instructor will be looking for in your paper. Below is an example of a marking scheme sheet an instructor might use to mark a paragraph composition.

Marking Scheme for Paragraph Compositions

A marking scheme is a plan showing what writing features your instructor or professor will consider in order to assign a grade to a piece of written work. You will notice the following marking scheme sheet provides you with a lot of information. It shows you the areas your instructor may consider when he or she evaluates your paragraph composition. Take some time to look over it carefully. You may want to hone your proofreading skills according to the marking scheme sheet. It can be very disappointing to lose marks in an assignment because of careless mistakes.

Check with your instructor to find out whether he or she uses a marking scheme sheet similar to the one following.

Marking Scheme for Paragraph Compositions

Content: .... /10
(Clear points; good evidence; good examples; good explanations)

Organization: .... /15
(Clear, directing topic sentence; clear points and proof; conclusion)

Style: .... /15
(Sentence variety; some use of semicolons or colons; effective word choice; level of vocabulary; syntax; diction)

Mechanics: .... /10
(Sentence grammar; word usage; spelling; punctuation)

Total: .... /30

| A+ = 29 | B+ = 26 | C+ = 23 |
| A = 27–29 | B = 24–25 | C = 21–23 |

Comments:

_____

_____

_____

_____

Proofreading Marks

Every instructor has his or her own method of evaluating compositions. However, there is a common point: each is concerned about what you say in your writing and how you say it. Most instructors use specific marks called *proofreading marks* when reading and commenting on student papers. The following is a list of common proofreading marks, according to the accepted standards of academic practice.

Proofreading Marks

Symbol/Abbreviation	Meaning
ℓ	delete or remove this
∧	insert a mark or something here
P	punctuation
s.s.	sentence sense or structure
s-v agr	subject–verb agreement problem
frag	fragment error
r.o. or c.s.	run-on sentence or comma splice
∧	something needs to be inserted
w.w.	wrong word
w.c.	word choice
?	what does this mean?
tense	problem with verb tense
¶	start a new paragraph
sp	spelling
p.o.v.	shifting the point of view

Writing Assignment 1 Time-Order Paragraph

Choose a topic sentence you have written which has been checked by your instructor and write a paragraph composition using a time-order or process method of development. There are more topics available in the next section. To complete the assignment, bear in mind the following:

1. The assignment should be 150–300 words long.

2. The assignment should have a title page.

3. The assignment should be double-spaced.
4. Check over spelling, grammar, and punctuation before you hand in your assignment.
5. Complete the work using a computer, available on your campus. Most instructors expect all assignments to be done using a word-processing program. If you are unable to comply with this requirement, please talk to your instructor.

More Topics for Time-Order Paragraph

how to plan a wedding
how to change the oil in a car
how to make a complaint
how to set up a tent
how to wallpaper a room
how to apologize to your lover
how to use the Internet
how to stop someone from snoring
how to hold a garage sale
how to play a game (or sport)
how to use a fax machine
how to shop for bargains
how to dye your hair
how to prepare for a test or exam
how to build a go-cart
how to catch a mouse without a trap
how to pickle eggs
how to buy a used bicycle (or car)
how to organize a meeting
how to purchase a computer
how to overcome shyness
how to be an effective negotiator
how to write a song
how to start a small business
how to can peaches
how to ask someone to marry you
how to saddle a horse
how to decorate a basement room
how to stop a fight
how to stop gossiping
how to catch a trout
how to investigate your credit rating
how to polka
how to play a trick

Setting Up a Title Page for Paragraph Composition Assignments

Presentation is very important when you are handing in assignments in academic courses. Presentation means the following:

1. The assignment is clearly typed (word-processed) on clean paper using a serif font of 11 or 12 points. Do not use smaller or larger fonts.

2. The assignment has been well edited. It has been read several times for errors (proofread). In other words, the writer has gone over the organization and content, along with spelling, punctuation, and sentence grammar, before handing in the paper.

3. The writer uses standard white bond and not a coloured paper that is difficult to read.

4. The writer sets up a title page. Centre the title of your assignment. The title should show the focus of the paper: it does not have to be a sentence. An example of a title page follows.

Example of a Title Page

Paragraph Composition Assignment 1: Time-Order

Title—Subtitle

Your name

The course

The date of handing in

Your instructor's name

Course section number

ESL POINTER

Understanding Time Transitions

In the previous section, you read about transitional words and phrases commonly used when you wish to write using a time-order mode. These transitions are used in English to help your reader follow your ideas from point to point. You will use transitions and other connectors for two main reasons: first, you want your ideas to relate in some reasonable way, and secondly, you want your ideas to "stick together," or cohere. Transitions can help give your writing *coherence*.

Useful Transitions in Time-Order Mode		
first	later	before
to begin with	following that	next
meanwhile	afterward	until
after a while	then	when
finally	soon	secondly, thirdly
after that	now	presently
in the first place	in due time	last

In the English language, you will find some transitions that indicate a process is just beginning. Transitions like *first*, *to begin with*, *now*, and *in the first place* are good examples.

Other transitions show that another step or stage will be introduced. Transitions such as *next*, *then*, *after that*, *later*, *secondly*, *thirdly*, and *later* tell your reader you are about to explain or describe another step.

Some transitions indicate what happened in a sequence first—*before*, *to begin with*, *in the first place*, *first*, and *now*. Other transitions tell the reader what happened in a sequence immediately after the first stage or step—*next*, *afterward*, *following that*, and *after that*.

If you are explaining a process that happened over time, use transitions that indicate a duration of time has elapsed: *following that*, *after a while*, *when*, *in due time*, and *later*.

To describe the end of your process, you can use the transitions *finally* or *last*.

Exercise 1 Transitions

Choose transition words which could fit into each of the following short passages. Check your answers in the Answer Key.

1. Alejandro and Emile were planning a meeting. _____, they decided their agenda. _____ they had to book a room. _____ they had to inform members of the community where and when the meeting was to be held.

Chapter 4   Time-Order, or Process, Development   61

2. My grandmother and I always prepared pickles together. _____, we would go out to the garden and gather the freshest, ripest cucumbers and onions we could find. _____ we washed the cucumbers carefully and scrubbed them with a soft brush. _____ we set them in a cool place, and _____ we began to peel and chop the onions. _____, we would prepare the brine for the cucumbers.

3. Kiyoshi got tired of waiting for his girlfriend. _____ he called her on his cell phone. _____ he tried calling her at work. _____, he gave up and went home for the evening, annoyed that she had not turned up.

4. Bathing your dog can be quite simple. _____ assemble all of the things you will require, like towels, dog shampoo, leash, and a large plastic container. _____ fill the tub with warm water, but be careful not to fill it to the top. _____, call your dog sweetly and nicely, so he won't suspect what you have planned for him. _____ clip on his leash and lead him to the bathing area, speaking softly to him in a friendly manner.

5. _____ fill these orders and _____ pack them into these boxes.

6. Follow these procedures in an earthquake. _____ seek protection from falling objects. _____ try to shelter your body from injury by moving away from windows. _____, act quickly because earthquakes give you little time to think.

7. To play this game, _____ put your game piece on the game board in the box marked "start." _____ roll the dice. _____ count the number of squares you will move on the board according to the number on the dice. _____, move your game piece the number of squares.

8. To stirfry this delicious vegetable, _____ wash it, _____ dry it, and _____, cut it into bite-sized pieces.

CHECKOUT

1. Appropriate transitional words and phrases can show the time-order, or process, method of writing development.

2. You can use key words and phrases in a topic sentence to show which mode of writing development you are using.

3. You must arrange all required information on the title page of each writing assignment before handing it in to the instructor.

4. The drafting process will give you essential writing practice and sharpen your editing skills.

5. Describe a simple way of setting up ideas in a time-order sequence.

chapter 5

Comparison and Contrast Development

Chapter Objectives

What will you have learned when you have completed this chapter? You will be able to

1. recognize the comparison and contrast mode through reading paragraphs.
2. practise working with similarities and differences between two ideas.
3. recognize a block form or point-by-point arrangement of ideas.
4. write a paragraph composition using comparison and contrast development.

Introduction

The next mode is used when you want to write about two things or ideas to show what the similarities (comparison) or differences (contrasts) are between them. When you compare two items, you look for ways in which the items are the same. When you contrast two items, you look for differences between them. You can also combine these approaches and use both comparison and contrast in your development. For example, imagine you wanted to discuss visiting your home town after several years of being away from it. You might begin your discussion with a comparison, looking at the way the town has stayed the same. You might then move your analysis to a contrast—what is different about the town then and now.

In the comparison and contrast mode, you will notice two main ways of arranging your points and supporting details: *block form* and *point-by-point*. In block form, you arrange all the ideas about each item in a block and then discuss the ideas in that block. For example, if you wanted to discuss bees and wasps, you might arrange all of your ideas about bees together in a block and place the ideas on wasps in another block. If you choose a point-by-point arrangement, you could arrange your discussion by points and discuss the two items in relation to each point. For example, if you consider the topic of bees and wasps once more, you might decide to talk about these three points: methods of food gathering, flight mechanisms, and body structures. In a point-by-point arrangement, you would write about the method of food gathering in bees and then discuss the habits of wasps in collecting their food. Then, you would discuss the next point—the flight mechanisms of both insects. Finally, you would talk about your last point in connection with both—the features of the body structure of each animal.

A comparison and contrast mode can be an effective one if you plan your composition carefully. You must spend time thinking about the two items. Think about how they are different and how they are the same. Try to think of ways that are interesting, because it is easy to point out the obvious about the two items. Do not tell the reader what everyone already knows about the two items; instead, think about distinguishing features that will be appealing to read about.

Working through an example may help to clarify use of the mode. Imagine, for example, you want to contrast your hockey experiences as a child with your adult experiences. It would be too obvious simply to say, "As a child, there was not as much violence in the game of hockey." Readers would probably already know that most kids' hockey games have fewer fights in them. What is there to say that would be more interesting to read about?

As you dig down and think hard about your experiences, try to select out what has particular meaning to you. Then ask yourself a question: what makes the experience different? Sometimes, drawing a chart with one item on one side and the other item on the other side can help you think more clearly. You can then consider what the two items have in common and what sets them apart in your experience or in your interpretation.

Example of a Comparison and Contrast Chart

Peewee Hockey	**Adult Hockey**
Often played on outdoor rinks	Mostly played on indoor rinks
Players just learning	Players experienced but sometimes out of shape
Mostly played just for fun	Often competitive
In leagues	Often associated with community events
Supervised by adults	Independent
Coached	Not necessarily coached

You can see that laying the two lists side-by-side may help you to think creatively about them. Using this "chart" method can also help you generate new ideas. Think about particular aspects of two things and tease out what makes them the same or different. Now you can decide whether you wish to use block form—discuss the peewee ideas first and then discuss the adult experiences—or a point-by-point arrangement in which you take three of your strongest points and discuss peewee and adult experiences in relation to each point.

When you use a comparison and contrast method of development, therefore, you will consider what two items have in common and what differences seem to exist between them. The next section will discuss comparison and contrast separately.

Comparison Development

As mentioned, this mode is useful when you wish to consider what is similar between two things, ideas, processes, and so forth. Often you can learn a good deal about something when you juxtapose it, or place it side by side with another item. Remember: in a comparison development, you are looking for how two items are the same.

Consider an experience from your life in which you actually use a comparison and contrast mode. Let's suppose, for example, you go out for a meal with your friends. Perhaps you choose an Italian restaurant for your dinner. After the meal is over, you begin to discuss what you think of the food. You might find yourself comparing or contrasting the food you just ate with another favourite restaurant's, with your own cooking, or with a family member's recipe. You might use examples from your own experience to help convince your listeners, or you might use what you have read in a food review. You are using a comparison and contrast mode to develop ideas about your experiences.

Examining similarities is a useful tool to enrich your understanding. It can provide a different perspective. For example, you may wish to examine what features two writers have in common. You could start with themes that appear in both authors' works. From there, you could begin to investigate why these themes are of interest to them. As you begin your comparative study, you might begin to recognize ideas or facts which you had not discovered until now. Looking over the similarities helps you classify or organize information in a way that highlights features. Perhaps you gain a greater knowledge of each writer's works by examining what makes his or her works the same as the other's. Your discussion may then develop around finer and finer points. As your discussion unfolds, you might notice how specific your ideas become.

Comparison helps you in two ways. First, as a writer and thinker, you make use of comparison in order to establish criteria, values, judgments, standards, or other measurements. Furthermore, you utilize this manner of development to extend your knowledge about something. After all, you know from experience you can learn a lot when you examine ideas or things in new ways, perhaps by looking at them in juxtaposition and by organizing your thoughts differently. Not everyone interprets comparisons in the same way.

Comparisons of one special kind are called *analogies*. You might employ these in situations in which you want to make an association between two items that do not seem to have much in common. Placing two items together in an unusual relationship and then considering what is similar about them is an interesting and revealing way of thinking. Analogies are most useful because they help you to examine things in a manner that varies from your normal way of thinking. Consider this statement, for instance: "Preparing a term paper is like going for a visit to the dentist."

Suddenly, you are asked to think, "How in the world can these be the same?" You might choose to organize your seeing in new ways and ask, "What parts of each process could associate with the other—the anticipation, the ordeal itself, the evaluation, the relief of tension?" Before long, you will find yourself analyzing one idea in relation to the other through examining the commonalities.

Make your analysis convincing. In academic writing, your interpretations must be reasonable, clear, and effectively laid out for your reader. Your reader needs to see that your argument is clear.

It is also important to recall that your ideas must cohere, or "stick together." Use transitions that show comparison to bridge ideas and make them flow.

Useful Transitions for Comparison

similarly	in the same fashion
also	still
likewise	like
in the same way	both

Exercise 1 Finding Similarities

Items are paired in the following list. Think of how these two items can be related. Write down at least three links between the two.

- a candle and a flower
- a comic book and a greeting card
- a Canadian and an American
- the games Bingo and Lotto
- deer and mice
- goblins and devils
- values and judgments
- a coat and a shawl
- lacrosse and ice hockey
- pennies and diamonds

Contrast Patterns of Development

On the other hand, you may want to consider the differences between two things or ideas. This mode is called *contrast*. You can use this as a tool, too, for analysis to help expand and develop your thinking and writing.

In contrast methods of development, you think in terms of what makes two things different from one another. To do so, you must have some clear understanding of or point of view on each item. If you wished, for instance, to contrast modelling with clay to modelling with paper, you would have to be acquainted with each type. Often this how-to knowledge comes from experience, but there are many ways of knowing about something.

You may also be able to talk in more abstract, interpretive terms when you speak of concepts. Wisdom, to illustrate, is defined differently in different cultures. It might be said that living in one culture may help you to understand what it is like to live in another. People quickly become aware of the differences in practice or tradition between cultures. You may gain knowledge that you do not even recognize you have until you need to call upon it or interpret it. In this fashion, writers often discover what they know about something when they write about it. Differences may be invisible, deeply-set ideas which require the light of good, analytic writing to make them visible.

Consider an example here for clarity's sake. There are differences between you and your father or mother, but you may not have thought about what they might be. In fact, you have knowledge of the differences, although you may not have articulated that knowledge in any way. If someone were to ask you, "How are you different from your mother or your father?" you might have to stop for a few minutes to think it over. Before long, though, you would be able to provide some answers to the question. In fact, you might be surprised by your own response. This type of experience is probably familiar. You have been asked a question and then have answered. Afterward you may have said to yourself, "I didn't know I knew that." In a similar way, writing can be an act of recognition.

You can use a contrast method of development to assist you to sort out what you know. You can consider two things that you think typically share many similarities: contrast will force you to consider their qualities in detail to determine if the two items really are alike at all. In fact, the examination may highlight differences. For example, you might say that two items—"school" and "education"—are alike, but are they? If you stop to think more deeply about the two items, you might find they have striking differences.

You could argue that school is unlike education because it is compulsory, whereas education could be seen as embracing all learning. In addition, you could imagine that education is a process that brings you some kind of wisdom, unlike school, which works from a set of social and curricular standards. These school standards may not bring you wisdom in the same sense. You could continue to think about what ways the two things are sharply distinct from one another. You would be sorting out what you think and what you learn from your examination.

It may be true that writers must search for differences in order to discover them. You will find that this task is sometimes not as easy as it looks. It will require you to think intensely in new ways. It will take some practice and research on your part. Deep learning involves engagement and intellectual work.

Exercise 2   Group Activity: Thinking of Difference

Form a group of three to five people. Choose five of the paired items below. List as many differences between each pair of items as you can think of. One person should record the group's ideas. Another group member should be prepared to report on the group's ideas. Be prepared to share your imaginative ideas.

Topics for Thinking of Difference

adult students and child students   gates and fences
unemployed and employed workers   teacher and parent

misdemeanours and crimes	driving a car and driving a motorcycle
jealousy and envy	bats and birds
theatre and film	tea and coffee
hobbies and work	flattery and glibness
order and authority	mysticism and the supernatural
apprehension and fear	collecting and hoarding
apricots and peaches	good and evil

When you write using the contrast mode, remember to add transitions of contrast to help your ideas cohere in your paragraphs:

Useful Transitions for Contrast

although	however
on the other hand	unlike
even so	despite
yet	nevertheless
on the contrary	though

Reading Comparison and Contrast Development

Exercise 3 Reading for Comparison and Contrast

Each of the paragraph compositions below uses either comparison or contrast development. Read each, paying attention to the development: point-by-point or block form. If the paragraph uses comparison, think about the similarities being discussed. If the paragraph uses contrast, think about the differences being discussed. Also notice the topic sentences and how they are structured. Finally, look at the wrap-up sentences. In other words, read these examples analytically, like a writer.

PARAGRAPH 1 Knitting and crocheting are very similar. Both crafts use techniques that are easy to learn. Someone who has never learned to crochet or knit can learn within a few minutes by watching someone else or by following basic instructions from a book or the Internet. Besides, materials used for both hobbies are very much the same: they require yarn and tools like needles or hooks. These supplies are available at department stores, at craft or hobby shops, and at specialty stores. Perhaps the most significant similarity is that the items created from knitting or crocheting are relatively inexpensive and are most useful. Sweaters, hats, gloves, mittens, and scarves, easily produced by these crafts, are always welcomed by family or friends. Homemade items are often cherished and passed from one generation in a family to another. All in all, since knitting and crocheting are quite easy to learn, share similar equipment, and produce useful and economical items, either can be easily adopted by any handcrafter or hobbyist.

PARAGRAPH 2 Plant cells and animal cells have important differences. First, plant cells have a rigid, non-living wall made from a material called cellulose. Animal cells, on the other hand, have walls made from a living, thin membrane. Furthermore, plant cells have small green bodies called chloroplasts, which help to manufacture food. Chloroplasts are absent in animal cells. Finally, plant cells have pouch-like bodies called vacuoles which retain water. Animal cells do not possess these features. These distinctions in structure make plant and animal cells easily distinguishable under the microscope.

PARAGRAPH 3 Do only children feel differently about their upbringing than children from larger families? Some adults who were sole children report a feeling of isolation. These adults said that as children they felt lonely because they did not have brothers and sisters to relate to. Others said that they felt their parents' expectations of them as only children were too high. They felt that their parents were putting all their hopes into them alone. At times, this expectation was seen as a difficult burden to carry. Some adults also reported that in later life they felt somewhat cheated. They would have liked to have had brothers or sisters to share or play with. Yet others reported being an only child as a positive experience because they did not have to share and thus received many more privileges than they would probably have gotten in a larger family. Although the evidence is still being gathered, it is clear that sharing and expectations are different for children who are the only child in their immediate families.

Exercise 4 *Group Activity: Similarities and Differences*

Part A

Each person should bring two objects from home. Form groups of three to five people. Each person should display the items he or she brings from home. The group should discuss what is the same about each set of items and what is different. The group can then select one pair of items and list the similarities or the differences.

Part B

The same groups should get back together. Using the list of similarities or differences, the group should construct a comparison or contrast chart. One member of the group should be the recorder. The group should then compose a paragraph together. The recorder should give a copy of the paragraph to the instructor.

Part C

The same groups should get back together. The instructor will provide each group member with a copy of the paragraph that was written by the group in Part B. Now, the group should look over the paragraph and discuss how it can be improved. The group should correct errors in spelling, punctuation, and grammar. One group member should be the recorder. The group should supply the instructor with a final, corrected copy of the group's paragraph composition.

Writing Assignment 2 Contrast Paragraph

Choose one of the topics below to write a paragraph composition using contrast development. If none of these topics appeals to you, you may choose your own after you have discussed it with your instructor. To complete the assignment, bear in mind the following:

1. The assignment should be 150–300 words long.
2. The assignment should have a title page. For more information on setting up a title page, see Chapter 4.
3. The assignment should be double-spaced.
4. Check over spelling, grammar, and punctuation before you hand in your assignment.
5. Complete the work using a computer, available on your campus. Most instructors expect all assignments to be done using word processing, on a computer. If you are unable to comply with this requirement, please talk to your instructor.

Topics for Contrast Paragraph

father and grandfather	heartbreak and frustration
workers and employers	watching videos and going to a movie
baseball and soccer	lacrosse and soccer
dreaming and fantasizing	morning and evening
cars and trucks	pears and apples
writing and talking	jokes and tricks
spending and saving	quails and partridges
oak and willow trees	toads and frogs
homemade and commercial ice cream	produce and create
comfort and love	mother and grandmother
reading and watching television	

Writing Assignment 3 Comparison Paragraph

Choose one of the topics below to write a paragraph composition in a comparison pattern. If none of these topics appeals to you, you may choose your own after you have discussed it with your instructor. To complete the assignment, bear in mind the following:

1. The assignment should be 150–300 words long.
2. The assignment should have a title page. For more information on setting up a title page, see Chapter 4.
3. The assignment should be double-spaced.
4. Check over spelling, grammar, and punctuation before you hand in your assignment.
5. Complete the work using a computer, available on your campus. Most instructors expect all assignments to be done using word processing, on a computer. If you are unable to comply with this requirement, please talk to your instructor.

Topics for Comparison Paragraph

friendship and work	oysters and mussels
novels and life	seesaws and careers
winning and losing	cameras and eyes
video games and trees	bogs and swamps
punishment and discipline	yesterday and today
playing a musical instrument and walking a duck	wish and want
killer and beluga whales	hockey and football
drawing with ink and with graphite	desserts and dreams
bicycling and hiking	antiques and gardens
committees and networking	sisters and brothers
pomegranates and oranges	swallows and finches

ESL POINTER

Special Comparison and Contrast Words

In the English language, some words are commonly used to show differences. Sometimes they are called *conjunctions*, or joiner words. A *coordinating conjunction* joins two equal elements together. The two elements may be different, and the coordinating conjunction *but* indicates difference. Notice that, in a compound sentence, you should *use a comma* in front of coordinating conjunctions.

I walked to work, but my husband took the car.

He wanted to speak, but the words would not come. (Notice the comma in front of *but*.)

Another expression also indicates difference. The expression *different from* usually appears in a sentence in which two items have been named.

Bob is different from his brother.

A rat is different from a mouse.

Her work is different from her home life.

Two common expressions in English used to show similarity are *the same as* and *similar to*. These expressions are used when you want to indicate that two things are the same. However, *the same as* means the two items are identical, whereas *similar to* implies some qualities are the same while others are not.

> For Lian, a shopping trip is similar to a vacation. (In some ways, the two items have similarities.)
>
> For Lian, a shopping trip is the same as a vacation. (Lian sees both items in exactly the same way.)
>
> His smoking is similar to his drinking. (In some ways, the two items have similar qualities.)
>
> His smoking is the same as his drinking. (In some sense, the two habits are exactly the same.)
>
> Her dress is the same as her mother's. (They are identical items.)
>
> Her dress is similar to her mother's. (In some ways, the two dresses are alike, but they are not identical.)

Exercise 1 Writing Sentences

Write sentences according to the instructions given below. Use separate paper. Your instructor may ask to see your sentences.

Example: Write a sentence in which you tell that your car and your brother's car have some characteristics that are the same.

Answer: My car is similar to my brother's.

or

My car and my brother's are similar.

1. Write a sentence in which you tell about your work and your partner's work and how they are similar.

2. Write a sentence in which you tell about your computer and Maj's computer and how they are different.

3. Write a sentence in which you tell about one meal yesterday and one meal today and how they are the same.

4. Write a sentence in which you tell about your dog and Hoshi's dog and how they share some of the same characteristics.

5. Write a sentence in which you tell about your suitcase and Max's suitcase and how they are identical.

6. Write a sentence in which you tell about your neighbourhood and your sister's neighbourhood and how they are different.

7. Write a sentence in which you tell about Tony's sweater and Guy's sweater and how they share some of the same characteristics.

8. Write a sentence in which you tell about Misu's lawnmower and your lawnmower and how they are identical.

9. Write a sentence in which you tell about your father's microwave and your microwave and how they share some of the same characteristics.

Exercise 2 Expressions of Comparison and Contrast

Use *but*, *different from*, *the same as*, or *similar to* in each of the following sentences. Check your answers in the Answer Key.

1. My briefcase is _____ yours because it has the same colour and lock.

2. After some years, Kim realized he was _____ his brother, so he began to appreciate their differences.

3. The instructor wanted to finish her marking, _____ she was just too tired to do it.

4. The table that Lars bought is _____ the one I bought, because it does not have the extra leaf.

5. The news story you told me is _____ the one I heard earlier, except I understood the incident happened today.

6. Her singing is _____ it was when she was my student; I think if she practises more, she will improve.

7. Miguel wanted to quit smoking, _____ he could not break the habit.

8. Turkish coffee is _____ Greek coffee.

9. My grade in the English course is _____ Joan's, _____ I did more work.

10. Her umbrella is _____ mine, even though we purchased our umbrellas at different stores.

CHECKOUT

1. You can use the chart method to examine similarities (comparison) and differences (contrast) in order to generate writing ideas.

2. Transitional words used in a piece of writing are clues to its method of development.

3. One special kind of comparison is called the *analogy*.

4. You can improve your ability to spot the type of writing development by reading and analyzing the work of many writers.

chapter 6

Classification and Division Development

Chapter Objectives
What will you have learned when you have completed this chapter? You will be able to
1. recognize the classification and division mode through reading paragraphs.
2. practise working with the concept of classification and division.
3. write a paragraph composition using classification and division development.

Introduction

A more complicated pattern for developing ideas in academic writing is classification and division. Classification and division are linked here for discussion because they have some commonalities. Use a classification method of organization when you wish to group or categorize ideas or things. For example, if you want to discuss the game of soccer, you could cluster ideas—styles of play, home countries of players, or levels of skill. You would give readers a view of soccer by classifying some important aspects of it, perhaps achieving a new way of looking at the topic. Use a division method when you wish to partition a topic into component parts. For example, you might want to study and discuss what makes up a good transit system in a large Canadian city. You would consider the parts of the system and then discuss each part: you might decide that a good transit system must be attractive, accessible, and friendly to the public. You could discuss each component and how the component contributes to the whole.

Classification is a tool used in organizing human knowledge. In the natural sciences, such as biology or zoology, systems of cataloguing are used. Scientists cluster plants or animals from the particular to the largest groups, like this: species, genera, families, orders, classes, phyla, and kingdoms. Geologists classify the earth's layers according to specified time periods, or earth history. Other scientists, like physicists, employ laws to categorize scientific knowledge. Social scientists also classify and divide human knowledge. Psychologists, anthropologists, educators, and sociologists look at human behaviour, culture, history, and artefacts using either one or a combination of more than one method of organizing. Classification, therefore, provides a way of looking at something, whether complex or simple, by grouping or clustering, helping you to manage a way of seeing and understanding.

Division may be a mode you see more often in such areas as philosophy, literary criticism, anthropology, sociology, linguistics, economics, history, and art. In these disciplines, scholars are interested in systems, fields, operations, meanings, concepts, representations, and so forth. They find division a powerful tool in their analysis.

About Classification and Division in Academic Writing

As a student writer in an academic program at a college or university, you will be expected to understand and use classification and division to organize your thinking and writing. There are many ways to think about classification and division as methods of organizing thought. You'll be surprised at how much information from one area in your studies will intersect with another.

Knowledge in language studies might cross into history, sociology, psychology, or ethics. Literature study might be grouped by genres or types, by historical context, by region, by date, by author, by theme, or in other ways. It is important to recognize how and why these categories have been established. Let's consider an example.

Suppose the course you choose to take is one in Canadian literature. The course syllabus might show Canadian literature as social artefact through stories, poems, and novels that centre around important social issues or events: perhaps WW I and WW II, women and suffrage, Aboriginal land claims, industrialization in Canada, agrarian issues, or the relationship between communication and development. Generally speaking, the process of classification or division will very much depend on the course designer's perspective or purpose, so for the sake of the example, imagine that the course designer for the Canadian literature course you have chosen wants students to recognize some of the social practices in Canada. He or she would select literature pieces that would represent some of those practices. Then he or she might decide to arrange them in a chronological order to facilitate the idea of development of such practices. Another course designer might use classification and division another way. Thus, how you classify or divide a topic depends on your purpose.

Bear in mind that you must carefully choose transitions that will convey a mode of classification and division to your reader. Transitions also help your writing flow and make your paragraphs much more coherent. Here are some common transitions you can use.

Useful Classification and Division Transitions

for example	specifically
besides that	the first type
another part	one category
accordingly	a further category
in addition to	for instance
one component	to illustrate
next	another group
furthermore	also
as well as	such as

Chapter 6   Classification and Division Development   77

Exercise 1 *Classifying and Dividing*

Look at the page below. One side of the page shows how ideas can be classified into types or groups. The other side of the page shows how the same subject can be divided into component parts. Complete the page with another person from the class. Decide together whether your answers are good ones or not. Be prepared to share answers with other members of the class. Check with your instructor if you are in doubt about any of the answers you and your partner come up with.

Classify:

What types or groups?

1. Subject: Health food

Types: non-fat; organic; not modified; locally-grown

2. Subject: Fishing

Types: _____

3. Subject: Music

Types: _____

4. Subject: Cooking

Types: _____

5. Subject: Jokes

Types: _____

6. Subject: Outdoor recreation

Types: _____

7. Subject: Computers

Types: _____

8. Subject: Shopping malls

Types: _____

Divide:

What component parts?

1. Subject: Health food

Parts: no additives; organic ingredients; clear labelling; no animal fat or by-products

2. Subject: Fishing

Parts: _____

3. Subject: Music

Parts: _____

4. Subject: Cooking

Parts: _____

5. Subject: Jokes

Parts: _____

6. Subject: Outdoor recreation

Parts: _____

7. Subject: Computers

Parts: _____

8. Subject: Shopping malls

Parts: _____

Reading Classification and Division Development

Today, organization of information is everywhere. When you are researching in the library or on the Internet, you will recognize how ideas have been classified or divided. Methods of organizing can be powerful tools for you to acquire. Remember that knowledge and information are often organized in relation to perspective and purpose.

Exercise 2 Reading for Classification and Division Patterns

Read each of the following paragraphs below. Decide whether the paragraph is a classification pattern, a division pattern, or a combination of the two patterns.

PARAGRAPH 1 Sea slugs, or nudibranchs (NOO-da-branks), are common in the northwest Pacific Ocean, but three types are of interest. The first type is the red sponge nudibranch. It blends in easily with the colour of the sponge on which it sits and eats. It actually takes the pigment of the sponge into its own body and so can camouflage itself. Another type is the sea lemon. It gets its name from its shape and colour and has bumpy skin with black dots like pepper. The sea lemon lays long strings of yellow eggs which can be found on the moist undersides of rocks. The third type of sea slug is called the frosted nudibranch. This animal is beautifully decorated and can be seen in the intertidal zone. It feeds on sponges and sea anemones and can store the stinging cells of its prey for its own defence. While these sea slugs may not be as showy as other marine life, they are fascinating and gorgeous in their own way.

PARAGRAPH 2 Most bean salads are made up of three particular types of beans because they are nutritious and relatively cheap to purchase. The first main bean ingredient is a popular dried bean called the *kidney bean*. Kidney beans, which get their name from their shape, provide some protein and vitamins. These beans can be soaked and cooked before using. The second main dried bean has a number of different names. Some people use the term *garbanzo* while others call them *chickpeas*. Garbanzos are not peas at all, but are special beans used by millions of people on earth because of their high nutritive value. These beans are round and, when cooked, rather chewy. As well as adding nutrition to the salad, they are visually appealing with an interesting texture. The last bean ingredient is a snap bean like a green or a yellow wax bean commonly grown in the garden for freezing or canning. These snap beans add a delicate flavour all their own. They are best when they are fresh, lightly cooked, and added to the bean salad right away. Beans comprise a nutritious alternative ingredient for salads and provide an economical and welcome change for most people.

PARAGRAPH 3 Of particular interest to Canadian biologists is the work being done by their American counterparts in the wildlife management of wolves. Wildlife biologists are monitoring wolf mortalities in Yellowstone National Park in the United States to determine what makes up the mortalities. They developed a study of the numbers of wolf deaths within the packs in the park from 1995–1998. In total, 44 wolves died: 13.6% died of natural causes; 29.5% were shot, mostly illegally within the park's boundaries; 13.6% were killed by vehicles on the road; and two, or 4.5%, died in natural disasters—one in an avalanche and the other in a thermal accident. The causes of the remaining wolf mortalities are unknown. Without this careful monitoring, scientists would not be able to determine how and why the wolf population is growing or decreasing in Yellowstone. At the same time, Canadian biologists consider how this study will impact on their work with wolves within Canadian national parks.

PARAGRAPH 4 What are the symptoms of concussion in an athletic injury? An athlete may display one or more of the symptoms. First, he or she may have a vacant stare and be slow in responding to questions or following directions. Next, the person may have incoherent or slurred speech. He or she may report feeling sick to the stomach and having waves of nausea. Also, the athlete may experience some temporary memory loss or deficits. He or she may be unable to recall simple information such as the score, the team's name, a person's name, and so forth. The injured athlete may also have blurred or double vision and describe not being able to focus clearly on an object in the distance. Ringing in the ears, loss of consciousness, and headache are also significant symptoms. Concussion is serious, and everyone involved in team sport or management should be aware of the telltale signs.

PARAGRAPH 5 Almost all drivers want a good sound system in their car. Basically there are two types of stereo: the factory radio and the aftermarket stereo. Factory radios are usually adequate for most purposes and perform well. They offer reasonably good sound quality, but the drawback is that there are no connections for enriching the bass. A special line-output converter must be purchased to add bass and deepen tone. The aftermarket stereo is a car stereo that is manufactured by a different company from the automobile manufacturer. These stereos must be purchased separately, from companies such as Sony, Alpine, Pioneer, and so on. Deciding which sound system to choose will depend on the owner's taste and budget.

Exercise 3 Investigating Classification and Division Mode

Part A

Your classification and division method of development can be improved by talking about your ideas with another person. For this exercise, you will work in pairs. Together, using the Internet, do some basic research on one of the following in order to learn either what groups or categories exist in the field (classification) or what parts make it up (division).

Topics for Research

anthropology	Canadian literature
astronomy	hockey
botany	dogs
chemistry	physics
marketing	early childhood education
soil science	shellfish
computing	retailing

Part B

You should present your findings to the rest of the class and be prepared to answer questions. Be certain to say whether you discovered a classification or division pattern in your research, and what you discovered about the method.

Writing Assignment 4   Classification Paragraph

Choose one of the topics from below and write a paragraph composition in a classification pattern. If none of these topics appeals to you, you may choose your own after you have discussed it with your instructor. To complete the assignment, bear in mind the following:

1. The assignment should be 150–300 words long.

2. The assignment should have a title page. For more information on setting up a title page, see Chapter 4.

3. The assignment should be double-spaced.

4. Check over spelling, grammar, and punctuation before you hand in your assignment.

5. Complete the work using a computer, available on your campus. Most instructors expect all assignments to be done using word processing, on a computer. If you are unable to comply with this requirement, please talk to your instructor.

Topics for Classification Paragraph

weddings	theatre
cooking	reunions
contact sports	renovations
birds	desserts
hobbies	restaurants
movies	games
construction	magazines
childhood problems	crafts
travel	festivals

Internet searches	skiing
cars	beer
fashion	lotteries
gardening	money

Writing Assignment 5 Division Paragraph

Choose one of the following topics and write a paragraph composition using a division method of development. To complete the assignment, bear in mind the following:

1. The assignment should be 150–300 words long.

2. The assignment should have a title page. For more information on setting up a title page, see Chapter 4.

3. The assignment should be double-spaced.

4. You should check spelling, grammar, and punctuation before you hand in your assignment.

5. You should complete the work using a computer, available on your campus. Most instructors expect all assignments to be done using a word-processing program. If you are unable to comply with this requirement, please talk to your instructor.

Topics for Division Paragraph

relaxation	a good boss
driving	a good worker
a good cook	a good movie
a successful small business	a good book
family	an unusual habit
a joke	personal style
a union	an enemy
an excellent workplace	a habit
a relationship	marriage
a friend	partnership

ESL POINTER

Working with Classification and Division Transitions

In the English language, transitions give your writing coherence. They make the ideas stick together. They make little bridges between ideas, too. Your reader is able to understand how you have arranged your points because the transitional word or phrase has a specific meaning, according to the mode. It is important to think about the meaning of transitions and how they work.

Useful Transitions in Classification Modes

one category	the first type (of)
a further category	the second type (of)
as well as	another sort (of)
in addition to	one sort (of)
another group	one kind (of)
furthermore	the second kind (of)

Useful Transitions in Division Modes

accordingly	the first component
besides that	the second component
next	another component
the first part	the first element
the second part	the second element
another part	the first ingredient
one component	another ingredient

Useful Transitions for Giving Examples

for example	such as
for instance	specifically
to illustrate	also

Study these examples showing the use of transitions:

One sort of sports car is the R-class. The Porsche Boxster, *for example*, has a specific design patented by Porsche International.

Three types of chemicals are dangerous and should be kept out of reach of small children. The *first kind* is corrosive chemicals. These can do harm on contact with a person's skin. Chemicals which unclog a drain, *for instance*, are extremely harmful when added to water.

The *first component* of a good speaker is complete control over tonality of voice and modulation.

Another group of cereals that is taking a high share of the market is the microwaveable type, *such as* instant oats.

A *third part* of the system includes a sophisticated fibreoptic cable.

The *first ingredient* for a good cake is a fresh egg.

One element of an elementary school education is caring instruction; *another element* is lively "talk."

Note that in English you say *one kind of* + *singular noun, one part of* + *singular noun, one component of* + *singular noun*. Be careful of count and non-count nouns! One exception is the expression *one type of* + *noun*. The noun is seen as generic, representing a class of things, so you should consider it as a non-count noun.

One type of car runs on batteries. (generic)

One component of work is purpose. (one component + non-count noun)

One part of transportation is planning. (one component + non-count noun)

One type of animal that lives in the jungle is the sloth. (generic)

Exercise 1 Transitions

Complete each sentence with *one type of, one component of, one part of,* or *one kind of*. Check your answers in the Answer Key found at the back of the book.

1. Rada bought herself _____ chocolate.

2. My mother-in-law will only wash with _____ soap.

3. _____ the game is tricking your opponents.

4. The customer wanted to exchange _____ software.

5. She claimed that _____ the toaster had been damaged in shipment.

6. _____ the concert will be dedicated to the early music of Mozart.

7. Sylvestine tried to purchase _____ pop at the corner store, but the store did not carry the product.

8. Misha says that _____ her housework includes mopping.

9. _____ weather sailors really hate is hail.

10. _____ the civil engineering program is calculus.

You should also note that when you use *such as*, you do not require commas. When you use *for example*, put a comma in front of the expression and after it.

Services such as home support are being cut from the provincial budget.

Services are being cut from the provincial budget, for example, home support.

Exercise 2 Practice with Transitions

Choose a transition from one group—classification, division, or example—to fit into each of the following. Check your answers in the Answer Key found at the back of the book.

1. There are three basic types of crucifers. _____ of crucifer is broccoli.

2. _____ of the interview begins as you enter the interview room.

3. The government's ferry schedule consists of four categories. _____ of category is the holiday schedule.

4. The menu was separated into six parts. _____ contained appetizers. _____, a diner could choose from 15 appetizers, either hot or cold. _____ contained main dishes.

5. Roscoe, my dog, is _____ of terrier.

6. The equipment room contained _____ of steamer.

7. A mosquito deterrent, _____ Deet, will keep these insects away for several hours.

8. The company has decided to reorganize its information technology section. Company executives have decided to create five groups. They say that _____ will be responsible for budget and marketing directives.

9. My grandfather is an avid fly fisherman. He claims there are seven types of flies you can tie and _____ fly is capable of catching a lake trout.

10. Canadians prefer _____ of winter sport.

11. One _____ of screwdriver, _____, the Robertson, is important to have in your household tool kit.

12. Marmalade, _____ of condiment found on the breakfast table, is often served with muffins, scones, or toast.

13. As well as _____ of copier, our company can _____ offer you _____ that is far more efficient for your business needs.

14. Nels has three types of shoe in his closet: _____ is for good wear when he needs to dress up; _____ is for walking; and _____ is for casual wear around the house.

15. The engineer has designed a system with three components. _____ it is different from our design.

CHECKOUT

1. A chart is useful for organizing classification and division writing ideas.
2. A method of writing organization can advance the perspective and purpose of the writer.
3. Before handing your writing assignment in for evaluation, be sure to follow the conventions of presentation recommended by your instructor.

chapter 7

Cause and Effect Development

Chapter Objectives
What will you have learned when you have completed this chapter? You will be able to
1. recognize cause and effect through reading paragraphs.
2. practise working with the idea of cause and effect.
3. write a paragraph composition using cause and effect development.

Introduction

You should use cause and effect development when you wish to discuss how *something influences or affects something else*. You may also use this mode when you are considering *the causes of something*. It is important to recognize that the function of the cause and effect mode is to establish the relationship between ideas, making it necessary for you to think out how ideas are connected or why they might be connected in particular ways.

Sometimes you may also have to consider what other relationships may be possible; in other words, you may have to *predict possible connections*. Think about this example. During the past few years, communities have become concerned over the safety of their water supplies. Thinking as a writer and using a cause and effect mode, you might begin to link what has happened to make people so cautious about their drinking water, what people are doing because of water safety scares, and what predictions can be made about water in local communities in the not too distant future.

Often cause and effect development is used in the natural sciences, particularly in regard to the environment. You might read about how some natural phenomenon occurs and what effects the phenomenon might have on its surroundings. Let's suppose, for example, that a biologist wants to think about the impact of lack of rainfall on particular wildlife in a region. He or she might study how the animal's behaviour changes, how its life cycle is changed, or how its new behaviour impacts other animals in its community or environment. Much of scientific writing is either process oriented or causally related (cause and effect).

As a writer, you may use three cause and effect techniques. First, you might analyze by giving a description of an event or some occurrence. Then you might express the effect or effects the event has had or may have in the future. In another technique, you might describe an event and then, afterward, write about the possible causes of that event. As a final approach, you might consider two events and then write about how they may relate in a cause and effect manner; for example, is one the cause of the other, or is one the effect or result of the other?

Of course, all of these techniques are somewhat complex: each demands that you pay strict attention to your arguments, observations, and conclusions. Some events are complicated and cannot be explained simply. Some events have several effects. Some effects are not yet known or recognized. In all cases, you must work to make the link between relationships plausible for readers. You must pay even closer attention to naming causes.

If you use cause and effect as a means of developing your ideas, you might find you need to do some research on your topic. In order to prepare college-level papers, you can expect to do background reading specifically in regard to your topic. Since this book does not ask you to write long essays or research papers, you will not necessarily be expected to research your topic. However, should you choose a topic that has more complexity to it, you must check with your instructor to be sure you have enough information to structure a reasoned cause and effect piece.

Thinking about Cause and Effect Relationships

Consider the statements below:

> Being late for work constantly, being uncooperative with other employees, and not following directions led to Elmer's firing.
>
> Inhaling 20 or more cigarettes on a daily basis can lead to irritation of the lining of the nose, throat, and lungs; shortness of breath; heart over-stimulation; emphysema; lung cancer; or heart attacks.
>
> Learning to drive at an earlier age may help make you a better driver.

Notice that the first statement describes possible reasons or causes for one effect—Elmer's firing. Notice that the second statement describes the possible results of one behaviour—smoking (inhaling 20 cigarettes daily). The third statement tries to establish a link between learning to drive early and becoming a better driver. It uses the third cause and effect development technique: it considers two events and discusses how they may be linked. Of the three statements, it is the most difficult to develop because it will require evidence or proof (research).

Tips for Constructing Cause and Effect Organization

Here are some hints to help you when you are constructing cause and effect as a mode of development in your writing:

A. Watch out for oversimplification. Don't try to make something complex too simple. Don't say that just one cause leads to just one effect—that could lead to some faulty conclusions. Consider the following example:

> Watching television creates violence.

In this statement, the writer has overgeneralized in two ways. First, he or she has said that sitting in front of a television and just watching the programs, anything from the news to cooking shows, leads to some sort of violence. What sort of violence does he or she mean? How can the connection be made? Does the same apply to funny shows—the more comical shows watched, the more humour created in the viewer? Secondly, the writer claims a single cause for violence. How can the writer say that such a complicated thing as violence can come from a single cause—television viewing? How is this possible?

B. Do not connect two unrelated events together to form a wrong conclusion. Don't jump to the wrong conclusion after something has happened. Consider the following statements:

> I failed the course because someone hates me.
>
> Buying an SUV is a stupid thing to do because my friend bought two, and he said they were both lemons.
>
> I had a horrible day today because it was Friday the 13th.

Can you see how illogical these statements are? Did everyone who failed the course fail because someone "had it in for them"? What if you consider those who passed—did they all pass because they were popular? Is it probable? Is buying an SUV stupid because only one person says it is? Would most people who own SUVs believe this statement? Did everyone have a bad day on Friday the 13th? If not, is it probable that the date was the reason for your bad day?

C. Examine the causes and effects. Study what you are saying. Start by asking, "*Why?*" Frame your topic or subject into a *why* question; then you can begin to trace or unravel some of its essential ideas. Follow the example given below.

Examining Causes and Effects

Topic: Failure in school

Refined Topic: Failure of younger children in school

Why Question: Why do some young children fail in elementary school?

Possible Causes and Effects:

1. cannot read and understand the printed materials—leads to—confusion and inaccuracy—called "failure" of the student

2. cannot understand written directions—leads to—doing wrong things—getting wrong answers—called "failure" of the student

3. cannot follow teacher's directions—may have a first language interfering with understanding a second language—teacher may use a different vocabulary—teacher may be unclear in giving specific directions—teacher may speak too softly or may not get the child's attention—leads to—confusion—the child's doing the wrong thing at the wrong time or not following directions at all—called "failure" of the student

4. may have a learning disability—may not perceive the same as others—leads to—misinterpretation—called "failure" of the student

5. may be bored with materials or task—child may already be able to perform the task—already understands the concept or skill—leads to confusion and inaccuracy—called "failure" of the student

You can see that once you begin to investigate possible reasons for why failure may occur in school, you begin to uncover the complexity of the topic. No one single answer is better than another, and you may not be able to elaborate all possible reasons.

Secondly, you might want to ask a different type of question: "What changed because of something else?" You may not be so interested in the reasons something occurred as the changes that came about because of some event or action. In other words, you may want to examine the impact of something on something else. You can discover many examples of such examinations: sociologists and lawyers frequently want to consider what influence a particular law is having in the courts; governments may want to study the impact of a new policy; a college or university may want to investigate what influence new admissions policies are having on its student population. Every day experts are studying the influences of something on something else in order to determine what is working effectively and what is not and to examine unexpected outcomes as well.

In using the cause and effect mode, you must pay strict attention to the transitions you are using. They are key to helping your reader follow your reasoning. They are critical to coherence, too.

Useful Cause and Effect Transitions

as a result	hence
consequently	since
for these reasons	due to
because	then
therefore	as a consequence
thus	so

Reading Cause and Effect Patterns

Read each of the following paragraphs. Each develops ideas using a cause and effect pattern. Notice the transitions used to show this method of development. Examine what effects or what causes the writer is discussing. Be prepared to share your analysis with the rest of the class.

PARAGRAPH 1 Because of several factors, young children today are very conscious of their appearance. First, young children tend to watch many long hours of television. They are bombarded with advertising that tells them what to wear and how to look. Children may then ask their parents to buy particular clothes or shoes that will make them look just like the "kids on TV." In turn, others see how their peers are dressed and then want to look like their classmates who look like the television advertisements. Another reason for the sudden interest in personal appearance is the influence from the schools themselves.

PARAGRAPH 2 Many teachers today are instructing children in personal hygiene. Dental care, bathing, and grooming may actually be taught in the daily curriculum. Because these instructions come from an "official" like a teacher or a public health nurse, children tend to treat these instructions seriously. They may not want to disobey the school or teacher, but instead, they want to fit in and be pleasing to others. For these reasons, young children today seem concerned about how they look.

PARAGRAPH 3 Cutting down large tracts of forest indiscriminately has disastrous results. First, the soil is lost. Trees have deep roots that help to anchor other small plants and the soil. As trees are cut down, this anchoring is lost. Heavy rainfall then carries off the top layer of soil, which is often the richest. Along with this soil erosion, banks of streams and rivers where large numbers of trees have been forested begin to wash away. Moreover, the plant and animal life are destroyed in the forested region. The natural homes for many creatures are gone or diminished with the trees. Plants that require the shade and benefits of the forest can no longer grow. Brutal logging practices can leave the land sterile and incapable of sustaining new life. The government is now becoming aware of these terrible consequences and is demanding that logging companies change their methods of tree cutting and removal.

Exercise 1 Group Activity: Imagining Causes and Effects

Form groups of three to five people. Provide answers for each of the following. Write down your answers and be prepared to report them to the rest of the class. You do not need to research any of the topics. Instead, put as many ideas together as your group can imagine. Then, choose four topics for your discussion.

1. What are three causes of insomnia?
2. What are three effects of gambling?
3. What are three causes of overachievement?
4. What are three effects of stealing?
5. What are three causes of tooth decay?
6. What are three causes of homelessness?
7. What are three effects of homelessness?
8. What are three causes of forest fires?
9. What are three negative effects of erosion?
10. What are three causes of computer crashes?
11. What are three beneficial effects of stretching?
12. What are three causes of obesity in young children?

Exercise 2 Group Activity: Finding the Cause and Effect Mode

Part A

Each member of the group should find an article that contains a paragraph or two using a cause and effect development. The article should be short. Each group member should bring the paragraph or paragraphs to class.

All of the paragraphs will be placed on one table. Each pair of students should select one of the articles. The pair should read the article and discuss how the author develops his or her ideas by cause and effect. Then each pair should write five sentences as follows:

1. What is the topic sentence (or main idea sentence) of the paragraph?
2. Does the author write about causes or effects?
3. What relationship does the author say exists between the ideas?
4. Name the effects or the causes mentioned.
5. Does the author convince you through the cause and effect development? Why or why not?

After completing the questions, the pair should staple their answers to the article selected. The instructor will collect the answers from all of the groups.

Part B

At the next class session, the instructor will place all of the answers and articles on a table. Working in pairs, select one of the articles. Be sure you find a set of student answers stapled to the article you select.

Read the article and the student answers. Do you agree or disagree with the answers on the student sheet? The class will share responses in a larger group session.

Writing Assignment 6 Cause and Effect Paragraph

Choose one of the topics from below to write a paragraph composition using a cause and effect development. If none of these topics appeals to you, you may choose your own after you have discussed it with your instructor. To complete the assignment, bear in mind the following:

1. The assignment should be 150–300 words long.
2. The assignment should have a title page. For more information on setting up a title page, see Chapter 4.

3. The assignment should be double-spaced.

4. Check over spelling, grammar, and punctuation before you hand in your assignment.

5. Complete the work using a computer, available on your campus. Most instructors expect all assignments to be done using word processing, on a computer. If you are unable to comply with this requirement, please talk to your instructor.

Topics for Cause and Effect Paragraph

1. Why is unemployment so high?
2. What are the causes of divorce?
3. What effects does cold have on hibernating animals?
4. What reasons are there for considering some things "pornographic"?
5. What effects is the digital camera having on photography?
6. Why is the Internet so popular?
7. Why is stress considered a problem?
8. Why are some drugs outlawed in North America?
9. What influences our ideas of beauty?
10. Why are recreation vehicles so popular?
11. What effects do video games have?
12. Why do lovers quarrel?
13. What results does debt have on an individual?
14. Why do sports cars attract many people?
15. Why are professional athletes paid so much?
16. What effects can be achieved with lighting?
17. Why does the military choose specific helicopters?
18. Why do many species of birds migrate each year?
19. What results do cuts to social security programs have in a small city?
20. Why are Canadian farmers in trouble?

ESL POINTER

Cause and Effect: Using Since, Because, So, *and* Therefore

You may know that *since* and *because* are called *subordinate conjunctions*. You may also know that *so* is a *coordinating conjunction*. The word *therefore* is not a conjunction, but acts as a *conjunctive adverb* in a sentence.

A subordinating conjunction works in a complex sentence to join dependent clauses to independent clauses in order to show a relationship between these two clauses.

George took a taxi home *because* he was too tired to walk.

Since it was raining, Stella took her umbrella.

The word *so* is a coordinating conjunction because it joins two independent clauses to form a *compound sentence*.

Abdul walks to work, *so* his wife can use the car.

The guest arrived early at the hotel, *so* he could have a rest before dinner.

Notice that in each compound sentence, you should place a comma in front of the coordinating conjunction unless the sentence is very short.

In English, the word *therefore* is a conjunctive adverb. It usually appears in a compound sentence. However, it does not join two independent clauses. Instead, you should use a semicolon (;) to join the clauses. Put the semicolon in front of *therefore*.

He was absent from work; therefore, he lost pay.

Notice, too, that you should place a comma after *therefore* in a compound sentence.

In all of the example sentences, you should pay attention to which part of the sentence can be considered the cause and which part can be considered the effect (or result).

George took a taxi home *because* he was too tired to walk.

    effect (result)   cause (reason)

Since it was raining, Stella took her umbrella.

    cause (reason)   effect (result)

Abdul walked to work, *so* his wife could use the car.

    effect (result)   cause (reason)

The guest arrived early at the hotel, *so* he could have a rest before dinner.

    effect (result)   cause (reason)

He was absent from work; *therefore*, he lost pay.

    cause (effect)   effect (result)

> *Note*
> *If the subordinate clause comes first in a complex sentence, put a comma after it:*
>
> Since it was raining, Stella took her umbrella.

Exercise 1 Punctuating Sentences with Commas

Supply commas where you think they belong in each of the following sentences. Be careful: some sentences may not require commas.

1. Because the chef was sick the meal was delayed.
2. The young soldier sent a letter to his girlfriend so he could say goodbye.
3. He was afraid of the dogs since he had been bitten by one previously.
4. We ordered a pizza because we were hungry and in a hurry.
5. Donna loved the movie therefore she plans to buy the DVD.
6. Because our house is up for sale we must keep it very tidy.
7. Since the princess was lost she sat down and cried.
8. The shoes were too tight for Angelo therefore he returned them to the store.
9. His parents worked hard so Igor could get a good education.
10. Because the dinner was delicious we all applauded the cook.

Exercise 2 Distinguishing Causes and Effects

Write *cause* (reason) and *effect* (result) over the appropriate part of each sentence.

1. Since the children are not going to school today, let's go on a picnic.
2. The factory closed; therefore, many families were in turmoil.
3. Some snakes make bad pets because they do not relate to humans.
4. Several managers invented a new management strategy, so the workers felt better appreciated.
5. Since it is so sunny in the summer, we should wear sunscreen.
6. Herbert's drinking was out of control, so he lost his job.

7. Candles are easy to make because materials are easy to get anywhere.

8. Her Aunt Mazy insisted on arriving late to dinner because she thought it was dramatic.

9. Because the office is closed on Saturdays, we will have to pay the account today.

10. Lemons and oranges were colourful in the fruit punch; therefore, Jody added more.

11. Beavers are mammals because they nurse their young with milk.

12. The little girl waited along the street, so she could watch the parade.

13. I wait for you after class because I have a crush on you.

14. Since you do not like turnips, I won't put any in the pie.

15. The roses thrived because there was so much sunlight.

CHECKOUT

1. The cause and effect method of writing organization establishes a special relationship between ideas.
2. Predictions of possible cause and effect connections can be supported by plausible argument and research outcomes.
3. By using appropriately chosen transitional words and phrases, you let your reader see the cause and effect method of writing development.

chapter 8

Definition Development

Chapter Objectives
What will you have learned when you have completed this chapter? You will be able to
1. practise working with the idea of definition as development.
2. recognize definition development through reading paragraphs.
3. write a paragraph composition using definition development.

Introduction

You might ask: How is a definition pattern different from a division pattern? This is a fair and useful question. You will recall that, in formulating a division pattern, you have to think about what constitutes or comprises something; in other words, you must think about what parts make it up. A definition pattern is somewhat similar, but it differs in relation to its purpose.

A definition provides a necessary explanation of what something is. This explanation may consist of only a few words or phrases; however, if you were to write about a complex idea or concept, you would expect to write a good deal more. Sometimes definitions stipulate what a speaker or writer means by a word or term—many words and terms have multiple meanings or shades of meaning, as the dictionary shows. For example, if you looked up *freedom* in any dictionary, it might say: "choice" or "independence" or "autonomy." If you wished to use the idea of freedom with an emphasis on a person's choice, then you would have to stipulate that sense in your definition. You would have to say to your reader or listener that you mean "freedom" in the sense of having choices. You would then have to provide further explanation for your *stipulative* definition, one that stipulates your sense of a term or idea.

At other times, you may wish to write *extended definitions*, which take a lot more explanation and careful thought. Extended definitions can run for several pages. As a writer, you might choose to consider what something means to you—your views on what that idea or concept is. By so doing, you are writing a definition: you are thinking about an idea by adding your views and research on an idea in order to answer the question, "What is it?"

Using a Formal Definition

A formal definition has three parts: the term or idea that you are going to define, the class of things the term or idea belongs to, and the distinguishing characteristics (what distinguishes it from others in its group). Consider the following two formal definitions:

      1   2   3
A peavey is a tool with a long handle with a sharp hook at one end used by loggers for handling logs in the water.

Part 1 names the term or idea. (peavey)

Part 2 names the group it belongs to. (tool)

Part 3 names distinguishing features. (long handle, sharp hook, used by loggers, used for handling logs, used on logs in the water)

      1   2   3
A problem is a situation requiring action but in which the required action is not known. (Nickols, 2000)

Part 1 names the term or idea. (problem)

Part 2 names the group it belongs to. (situation)

Part 3 names the distinguishing features. (requires action, but required action is not known)

  You may choose to use a formal definition as your topic sentence. Then you might discuss or explain your definition in the paragraph. You may discuss aspects of the distinguishing features. You may provide examples as well.

Exercise 1 Writing Some Formal Definitions

Work in pairs for this exercise. Together write clear sentence definitions for five of the following terms. Be prepared to share your answers with the rest of the class.

hot dog	goat	party	elevator
model	pizza	spy	faith
work	guide	slave	tuna
duty	blueprint	profit	sled
shelf	sheriff		

  The formal definition works well if you already have a fairly clear idea of what your definition will be. Sometimes, however, you must work through ideas to develop a definition you are comfortable with for your discussion.

Generating Ideas for the Definition Mode

  How do writers "get at" what they think something is? A useful way to begin is by asking a direct question and using this question as a launch to thinking. For example, imagine you were going to do a paper in a course on human behaviour. Perhaps you are interested in reading, researching, thinking, and writing about human emotion—let's say, fear. You would begin by asking, "What is fear?"

  In such a case, you attempt to define fear. You could look at the parts that make it up (division) to help with the initial outline of ideas. Then you might add or stipulate what sense of the word *fear* you will use. Your purpose, then, in writing a definition mode may be quite different from one using division. In definition, a writer's purpose is to explain or elaborate what something is.

Another approach is to look at what something is unlike. You first need to consider what you think about the topic itself. One way you could begin your thinking process is to think about what fear is not like.

Look at the example below. The notes you see are "thinking notes"—what someone might have written down as he or she worked through an idea.

Example of "Thinking Notes"

1. What is fear?

2. What is fear unlike?

It is unlike confidence. It is unlike certainty. It is unlike calmness. It is unlike happiness.

3. Why is fear unlike confidence?

Confidence is feeling secure about what will happen or what you know. Fear is not like that because fear seems to imply some sense of not knowing, not being able to tell what will happen.

4. Why is fear unlike certainty?

Certainty makes you think you know something. Fear makes you feel you do not know something. You trust certainty; you do not trust fear.

5. Why is fear unlike calmness?

Calmness means a relaxed state of mind and body. You feel in control when calm. Fear, on the other hand, makes your heart beat faster, your thoughts race, your palms sweat, and your feelings go out of control.

6. Why is fear unlike happiness?

Happiness makes you feel comfortable and accepting. Fear makes you feel alert and guarded.

Can you see how you are building a progression of thought or a chain of ideas by investigating in such a manner? Of course, there is much more to say about each one of these contrasting pairs, but you now understand that you have created something like a *map* of the idea called *fear*.

At this stage in your thinking, you might begin to investigate and research what others have to say about fear. You might read poetry that expresses a fearful situation. You might read articles in professional journals that discuss or describe ideas about fear. You might go to texts or articles written by experts in the field. You could search the Internet. You could utilize a wide range of investigative possibilities, in other words.

How deeply and how long you investigate a topic depends upon the course you are taking, the nature of the assignment, your audience, your purpose, and how much time you have to give to it. In any case, once you have decided the limits of your investigation, you could begin to write about what fear is.

What the "Thinking Notes" Revealed

unlike confidence

seems to imply some sense of not knowing

not being able to tell what will happen

unlike certainty

makes you feel you do not know something

do not trust it

unlike calmness

makes your heart beat faster, your thoughts race, your palms sweat, and your feelings go out of control

---

You can also see that if you continued your investigation in this way, you would be able to write a paper that provides a definition of fear. At any stage of the investigation, you would be able to stipulate the sense of what you mean. You can use your own experiences to help give a special sense to the term. You could help project your own views of what fear is based on by living, reading, and researching "in the world."

Exercise 2 Getting the Sense of a Word

Choose someone else from the class to work on this exercise with you. It will help to have someone else who will help you think through the assignment. Work together and hand in the assignment as a group project.

In this exercise, look at the topic below. Then take each idea listed and write down how each idea is unlike the topic. Write your ideas in note form and follow the same procedure as you saw used in the investigation of fear. Use separate paper and hand in your work for checking.

1. Topic: *school* (Start: What is a school?)

    a. home (Ask: How is a school unlike a home?)

    b. parent (Ask: How is a school unlike a parent?)

    c. friend (Ask: How is a school unlike a friend?)

2. Topic: *memory*

   Start: What is memory unlike?

   List three things or ideas memory is unlike.

   Take each idea and ask: How is memory unlike this? or that?

   List the ways in which they differ.

   Then, using your "thinking notes," write about what memory is like.

The following transitions will help make your piece of writing "stick together." In other words, they will assist the coherence and flow of your writing.

Useful Definition Transitions

for example	in addition
furthermore	also
besides	for instance
further	moreover
specifically	accordingly
at the same time	in other words
certainly	indeed
of course	

Reading Some Definition Paragraphs

Read the paragraphs of definition given below. You will notice that the topics selected are not as complex or abstract as those you will use for essays.

PARAGRAPH 1 What is a good car? A good car is reliable. There is nothing worse than getting in a car only to find out it will not start. Drivers must feel confident that, no matter the situation, their cars will get them to where they want to go—day or night. A good car is comfortable. Sitting in a car for long ferry waits or in traffic gridlock can be more unpleasant if the vehicle is cold and has hard seats. Finally, the key attribute of a good car is that it is economical. Because gas prices are rising day by day, some drivers may find they are not able to afford to run their own cars because they are too expensive to operate. A good car, then, besides being dependable and comfortable, is relatively cheap to own and operate.

What is the writer's definition of a good car? Name the points.

PARAGRAPH 2 What is a good hockey game? To answer the question, you need to decide from whose point of view you are considering it. From the owner's point of view, a good hockey game is one in which his team wins. Winning means staying on top and being popular in the media. It also means getting the value the owner is paying for since some players make millions in their contracts. The owner might say a good hockey game is one that has high ticket sales. Making money might be the most important feature of a good game to a team owner. Fans might have different definitions. Some might say a good hockey game is exciting to watch, with plenty of fast skating, passing and pressing in the end zones, and excellent plays. Others might say a good game is based only on the excellent plays. Players, on the other hand, might see a good game differently. They may say that a defining element is how well the team worked together on offence and defence. They may also simply consider the number of errors made during play or the number of penalties their team committed. Since a game is viewed by people in different ways in order to decide on a good definition, you would have to consider more than one point of view.

How does this writer define a good hockey game? How does he or she develop the ideas?

PARAGRAPH 3 What is a good cup of coffee? To a Canadian, a great cup of coffee has a rich, full taste. It is strong, but not bitter. It has an aroma that can wake up the senses and say, "Hey—let me get you going!" To an American, to be good, the coffee has to be somewhat strong, very hot, and really fresh. Most Americans would agree that good coffee should be available from almost any location, whether it be from a service station, a restaurant, or an upscale coffee shop. To a Greek, a good cup of coffee must be very strong. It should be served in a demitasse that has at least a layer of sugar in the bottom. The coffee should never be served in a paper cup because good coffee has to be savoured. For a Greek, a good cup of coffee takes time to drink—it should not be gulped. It could be said, then, that the definition of a good cup of coffee becomes a matter of taste and tradition: no one culture seems to have the "right" answer.

What does this writer say about the definition of a good cup of coffee? How does the writer develop his or her definition?

For the purposes of this book, you will be asked to write a paragraph of definition. Since a paragraph composition is relatively short (compared to an essay), it is important to leave more complex and abstract topics for a definition essay, where you will have enough space to explore more complicated ideas. Use simpler, more manageable topics in your paragraphs of definition.

Exercise 3 Collecting Ideas in the Definition Mode

From a newspaper or magazine, bring in one or two articles in which a writer attempts to define what something is. Be prepared to talk about what you have found.

Answer these questions in regard to the article or articles you find:

1. Who is the writer?

2. What is the source?

3. What is the topic?

4. How does the writer define his or her subject? What points does he or she make?

5. Does he or she use a formal definition in his or her paragraph?

6. Do you agree or disagree with the writer's definition? If you disagree, why do you feel this way? How could you improve the definition?

Exercise 4 Writing More Definitions

Without using a dictionary, complete each of the following. (Answer in three sentences.)

1. In your opinion, what is a good teacher?

_____
_____
_____

2. In your opinion, what is grace?

_____
_____
_____

3. In your opinion, what is greed?

_____
_____
_____

4. In your opinion, what is a mystery?

_____
_____
_____

5. In your opinion, what is a good student?

___

6. In your opinion, what is a good job?

___

7. In your opinion, what is a miracle?

___

Writing Assignment 7 Definition Paragraph

Choose one of the following topics and write a paragraph composition using a definition method of development. To complete the assignment, bear in mind the following:

1. The assignment should be 150–300 words long.

2. The assignment should have a title page. For more information on setting up a title page, see Chapter 4.

3. The assignment should be double-spaced.

4. You should check over spelling, grammar, and punctuation before you hand in your assignment.

5. You should complete the work using a computer, available on your campus. Most instructors expect all assignments to be done using a word processing program. If you are unable to comply with this requirement, please talk to your instructor.

Topics for Definition Paragraph

1. What is a good chef?
2. What is a poor writer?
3. What is a good party?
4. What is an excellent wine or beer?
5. What is a perfect pet?
6. What is a fun movie?
7. What is a good kindergarten?
8. What is a good witch?
9. What is a good burger?
10. What is a peer?
11. What is a shooting star?
12. What is a tourist?
13. What is safety?
14. What is a tall ship?
15. What is a disaster?
16. What is an actor?
17. What is an Ipsos-Reid poll?
18. What is duty?
19. What is a delicacy?
20. What is a glacier?
21. What is a good joke?
22. What is a bad joke?
23. What is a good piece of furniture?
24. What is relaxation?
25. What is the perfect game of golf?
26. What is a mistake?
27. What is a partnership?

ESL POINTER

Subordination

In English a complex sentence usually contains two clauses. One clause is called the *independent clause*. It can stand alone. The other clause is called a *dependent clause* and cannot stand alone. Despite the fact that it has a subject and a verb, it does not complete a whole thought. Sometimes the dependent clause is called a *subordinate clause*.

It is important for you to recognize that the clauses relate to one another in a number of ways. Sometimes the clauses show *time*, *condition*, *place*, or *reason* because of a conjunction called the *subordinating conjunction* that begins the dependent or subordinate clause.

Some Subordinating Conjunctions

after	if
when	although
since	whenever
as	unless
where	because
until	wherever
before	though
while	

Exercise 1 Clauses

Identify each of the clauses in each of the following complex sentences as independent or dependent clauses. Notice that a comma is used when the dependent or subordinate clause comes first in the sentence. Check your answers in the Answer Key.

1. After the students left the classroom, the teacher organized the bookshelves.
2. She has hardly spoken to me since we had our argument.
3. Tulips and daffodils are cheery spring flowers because they provide bright splashes of colour in the landscape.
4. Whenever Thomas goes out to eat, he takes his cocker spaniel along with him.
5. Shelly ordered a new washing machine before she left the store.
6. Unless you give me a raise, I will quit this job!
7. I notice happiness wherever I go.
8. Magda studies hard as she wants to be a doctor.
9. While Stephen tossed the salad, Monique set the table.

10. The report is on Lou's desk although he has not read it yet.

11. If Eda arrives late, she will miss the speaker's presentation.

12. Wherever Mim goes, her little white poodle follows.

13. Because the tablecloth is stained with tea, we will have to bleach it.

14. Jamal will partition the new hard drive after I back up my data on CD.

15. In the late summer afternoon, Dell and his family sailed on the small lake until the sun went down.

Exercise 2 Clauses

Identify if the clauses relate by *time*, *condition*, *place*, or *reason*. Your instructor may ask you to work in pairs and come up with the correct answers.

1. Before you wash the car, please buy the groceries for our supper.

2. Ngozi wishes to take a break while the other students work.

3. If bears scare you, would you go into the woods?

4. Whenever we are in Ottawa, we like to visit the National Gallery.

5. The dentist worked quickly as the small child was quite anxious.

6. Several members of the theatre community stay at my house whenever they are in town for a performance.

7. The Association for Animal Rights was boycotting the pet food factory because it was in violation of several by-laws.

8. Do you enjoy eating vegetables because they are good for you?

9. The receptionist jumped up with a start when the fire alarm rang.

10. Since the roofer will not be able to complete the job this week, Yasha will hire a new roofing contractor.

11. Do you enjoy eating cotton candy whenever you go to the fall fair?

12. Although Yasuo spoke with an accent, he spoke very good English.

13. My brother Royce loves to go out for dinner before he goes to a movie.

14. The bird sang sweetly on the fence while its mate bathed energetically in a little pool of water between the rocks in the garden.

15. When I give you the signal, everyone should laugh hysterically.

Exercise 3 Clauses

Combine the pair of clauses to form a complex sentence, using the subordinate conjunctions suggested. Use separate paper. Check your answers in the Answer Key found at the end of the book. Remember: if you use a dependent (subordinate) clause at the beginning of a sentence, use a comma after it.

1. Salim writes his own songs. He is shy about performing publicly. (although)
2. The owl sat silently watching from the highest branch of the tree. The mouse scurried through the grasses below. (while)
3. Does Yasmina visit you? Is Yasmina in town? (when)
4. Slice the mushrooms. Heat the butter. (after)
5. The choreographer spends his time rehearsing. The show starts. (until)
6. Her relatives arrived from India. Harpreet was delighted. (because)
7. Marina is having a baby in April. She is looking at baby clothing in the flyers. (since)
8. Zoe hates cooking. She won't admit it. (though)
9. The cat goes. Her kittens follow. (wherever)
10. He went to Cuba. He went to Spain. (before)
11. Do not turn off the computer. You will be away for more than one day. (unless)
12. Kira went to the marketplace. She bought eggplant for the stew. (where)

CHECKOUT

1. There are similarities between the division and the definition modes of writing development; however, each serves a different purpose.
2. An extended definition may comprise several written pages.
3. Asking yourself useful questions about your definition topic can be a helpful way to start writing.
4. You can create "thinking notes" which, like a map of your ideas, can help you navigate through a preliminary investigation of your topic.

chapter 9

Beginning Essays

Chapter Objectives
What will you have learned when you have completed this chapter? You will be able to
1. recognize the basic parts of an academic essay.
2. shape thesis statements.
3. structure a simple outline for an essay.
4. write a beginning essay (optional).

Introduction

What is an essay? An *essay* is a written composition centring around one idea or theme. It presents a particular point of view, attempting to convince or persuade the reader. A short essay can be 500 words long, but typically college or university students are asked to write essays from 800 to 1500 words in length. Essays can be much longer, however.

Writers have inherited the form called "the essay." It has been accepted by the experts and by scholars as a writing "convention" for many years, but there are points of disagreement. Some English instructors prefer a specified structure to the essay which students must follow. Other instructors allow a more flexible form. Some instructors demand that the thesis statement be placed in a particular position in the introductory paragraph of an essay, while others do not make that request. Most instructors insist that writers take a particular point of view and defend it through the essay. On the whole, instructors expect students to know how to revise and proofread. All instructors expect to receive written work that is thoughtful and carefully edited. Some instructors place less importance on mechanical skills than on content. To some composition instructors, the form is just as important as the ideas. All in all, you should not count on every English instructor to have the same expectations. Recognize that different instructors have their own preferences and ideas. Be smart: find out what writing requirements each instructor in each of your courses has.

About the Academic Essay

Conventionally, an essay has three parts: the *introduction*, the *body*, and the *conclusion*. Essays written for academic or scholarly purposes also have these same components. Specifically, academic essays have an introduction consisting of one paragraph and a *thesis statement that focuses the whole essay*. The introduction is an important feature of the essay because it frames what the essay will be about and opens the topic for your reader.

The *body* of a basic academic essay consists of *a minimum of three separate paragraphs*. It can, however, have more than three body paragraphs; in fact, it can have as many as a writer wants it to have. But it must have at least three body paragraphs to be considered a basic essay. Each body paragraph discusses a major idea of the thesis and develops points and evidence to support claims made by the thesis. An essay has a *conclusion* which sums up major ideas in the essay and leaves the reader with a general thought on the topic.

Essentials of the Essay

An academic essay must have the following:

1. Introductory paragraph containing a thesis statement (focus idea)
2. Body paragraphs (at least three that support the claims of the thesis)
3. Conclusion (summing up and providing a general thought)
4. Strong evidence
5. Excellent editing
6. Clear presentation (word processed with title page, 11 or 12 point serif font, good spacing)

Why Am I Asked to Write an Essay?

Most students would argue that there is only one purpose in writing an essay—to please an English teacher and pass a course. This claim may be partially true; however, there is more to it than that. Writing an essay helps develop thinking, but it also assists in other ways.

An essay can provide you with opportunities. First, it can be a challenge. An essay can test skills of written expression and organization. It can become a test of your intellectual powers and of your abilities to use language effectively. Moreover, it provides the chance to work with abstraction, using language. It provides the prospect of working through some intellectual puzzle like nothing else can. As college or university students know, being able to write good arguments is often crucial to passing courses in the humanities.

Next, an essay can be a tool. You can use it to convince or persuade someone of a particular point of view. It is writing that unwraps a writer's opinions to public view. Moreover, an essay can be discovery. Essays and other forms of writing help you to discover your thoughts on a subject. It is true that you sometimes do not know what you think about something until you try writing about it. As a writer, you learn what you think about a specific topic or idea as you work your way through the writing process. In addition, your reader may learn from what you have to say.

Finally, an essay can be entertainment. Good discussion is entertaining, after all. You may choose a particular tone—light, casual, serious, amusing and so forth—in order to create a mood in a reader. You may actually have fun doing the writing, too.

In all of these ways, essay writing allows you many learning opportunities. You probably are aware, of course, that it is only through the drafting and writing stages that you can develop as a writer. You can read a lot about essay writing, that is perfectly true, but it is through your writing experiences that you will learn the most.

An Overview of the Parts of an Essay

The Introduction

The introduction of an essay is contained in a paragraph by itself. First, try to make the introduction interesting to read. Begin in the most engaging way you can imagine. Next, provide some background that helps to restrict the topic in some way. This is called the *controlling idea* because it helps narrow the focus of discussion. Lastly, the introduction should contain a sentence which indicates what the essay is going to be about. This sentence, called the *thesis statement*, shows the reader where you are going to take the discussion. It focuses in on the narrowed topic, the controlling idea, to discuss a specific aspect. Then the thesis statement angles the particular aspect to show your point of view and the method, or mode, of development.

Although the thesis statement may, in fact, be placed anywhere in the introductory paragraph, *Spotlight on Paragraph and Essay Skills* suggests that you place the thesis statement as the last sentence of your introduction. As you become more experienced and confident in your writing, you may decide to place it in other positions. For the time being, however, it is more manageable for you to have the thesis statement as the last sentence of the first paragraph of your essays.

The Body of the Essay

The body of an essay contains the points and discussion of the points you want to establish. The body should contain *a minimum of three paragraphs*, but it can contain more. Each paragraph should contain a topic sentence which controls the ideas in each paragraph. The discussion for each point should be thorough. You should set out a point; then you should provide proof and explanation for the point. This process is called *elaborating your ideas*. When you elaborate ideas, you make them full and convincing. The proof or support you provide could consist of examples, quotations, illustrations, or specified reasons. You may also provide some commentary as well. Furthermore, paragraphs throughout the body of the essay should be balanced; that is, some paragraphs should not be five lines long, while others are seventy.

Occasionally, at the end of a body paragraph, except the last, a writer will use sentences called *transitional sentences*. These lead-in sentences, found at the ends of body paragraphs, help bridge ideas between the paragraphs. They review ideas and then suggest new ones to be found in the next paragraph. Transitional sentences are not concluding sentences. They do not sum up or conclude anything. Instead, they are sentences with a dual function: they look back and draw a key word or phrase from the paragraph, and then they look ahead to draw a key word or phrase from the next paragraph. In so doing, they develop coherence between the body paragraphs. Transitional sentences are particularly useful in lengthy essays.

The Conclusion

The conclusion *wraps up the ideas of an essay*. First, you may restate or rephrase your thesis statement. Next, you can summarize the points made in the piece so that the ideas are refreshed for the reader. Then, you end the essay by leaving the reader with a general thought on the topic. Try to have a forceful ending that eases the reader out of the topic.

Flat endings leave flat impressions. Note that you should not introduce new ideas in the conclusion but should use the conclusion to tie up the ideas in the essay.

Exercise 1 The Terms of Essay Writing

You can see that essay writing has a vocabulary of its own. Here are some of the terms used in connection with essay writing. As you think of each term, write down a definition for each one. Work in pairs. Each pair should then check their answers with another working pair in the class.

essay	introduction
body	conclusion
support	controlling idea
thesis statement	topic sentence
unity	organization
expository	narrative
mode of development	editing
draft	transitional sentence
coherence	persuasive
elaborating ideas	

How Do I Begin to Write an Essay?

Getting Started and the Introductory Paragraph

One of the most difficult activities for all writers is getting started. Even the most experienced writers can have trouble just putting the first words down on the page. You, too, may find this happening when you write, but you should not worry about the situation for too long. It is natural in the writing process to have difficulty getting started. Have a course of action you follow. Try some of the prewriting strategies mentioned in Chapters 1 and 2 of this book. Try using questions to get started:

1. What do I know about this topic?
2. What do I like about this topic?
3. What do I dislike about this topic?
4. What aspects of the topic seem clear?
5. What aspects of the topic seem unclear?
6. Where have I read about this topic before?
7. What sources proved useful after I searched the Internet?
8. Do I have any strong opinions on this topic?

Try writing your answers to these questions as you are responding to them. You will find by writing to a focus—the questions—you may suddenly start to "unblock" a lot of ideas. Moreover, just the act of writing helps us write. Getting something on the paper, even writing your responses to the previous eight questions, is much more satisfying than writing nothing at all.

The Controlling Idea

Once you have settled on a satisfactory topic, you are ready to consider the *controlling idea*. The controlling idea is a narrower aspect of the topic. Sometimes, you must work and think your way through to getting something that can work as a controlling idea.

You can use some of the prewriting strategies you learned about in previous chapters of this book. Although these strategies were set out for paragraph compositions, they are just as useful when you are preparing to write essays. You might begin with brainstorming.

After you have selected your topic, take a few minutes and brainstorm for ideas. As you recall, to brainstorm simply means to take a pen and paper in order to think about your topic, jotting down whatever occurs to you. Do this activity for five to ten minutes, and then stop to read what you have written. Using your notes, try writing one or two more narrowed ideas. You are looking for a controlling idea in the topic. Consider the following example.

Imagine that you choose early childhood education as your subject. You can see immediately that the topic is far too broad to handle. Instead, you must give some thinking time to what aspect of the topic early childhood education you wish to discuss. You might brainstorm for a few minutes and then recognize an aspect of the topic that appeals to you. To illustrate, perhaps you become aware that in your brainstorming you are mentioning gender-related issues. You might attempt putting together early childhood education and gender issues to see if a controlling idea develops.

Broad Subject	**Controlling Idea**
early childhood education	gender issues in early childhood education

Do you think this controlling idea is helping you to narrow your topic down so that a clear and effective thesis can emerge?

Exercise 2 The Controlling Idea

Choose five of the following topics. Imagine a more specific aspect of the topic. Write it down as your controlling idea. Be prepared to share your answers.

Topics for Developing the Controlling Idea

comic books	apartments
travelling	poverty
movies	books
essays	jokes
recreation	cars
music	celebrations
media	art

The Thesis Statement

For a student writer, most written course assignments will include some *expository* writing. In other words, you will be asked to *explain* or *inform* your reader about a specific aspect of a topic. It is very important, then, that you choose a topic that you know something about. Later on when you do research papers, you may find yourself investigating a topic which is unfamiliar to you. In most composition courses, though, you will have the opportunity to write from quite a large selection of topics. Therefore, select a topic which interests you and which you know something about. Otherwise, you will quickly get bogged down because you may run out of things to say.

After you have determined your controlling idea you can then think about a specific aspect of the controlling idea—the thesis statement. Remember: a *thesis statement* is a sentence that shows what specific aspect of a topic your paper will discuss; it often also shows your particular view.

The thesis statement should be clear and concise. Not all of the notes you made in your brainstorming session will be useful, but some of them will be. Look over your notes. Are there any that could be included in your essay? Which ones are useful? Why?

It is also important to recognize *overgeneralizations*. These are statements which, although appearing to be factual, are unsupported conclusions. For example, "Women love shopping" is an overgeneralization. Not all women love shopping. In fact, some hate it. Overgeneralizations should be avoided, particularly when it comes to thesis statements.

Exercise 3 Examining Overgeneralizations

Read each of the following statements. Each is an overgeneralization. Write down what in particular makes the statement false or an overgeneralization. Be prepared to share your answers.

1. Foreign students spend too much money.

2. In Canada children are independent by age 12.

3. Everyone in Canada loves hockey.

4. Left-handed people are more intelligent.

5. All Canadian teenagers watch too much television.

6. Women are more verbal than men.

7. Snack foods are bad for your health.

8. Playing sports develops character.

Exercise 4 Group Activity: Recognizing Effective Thesis Statements

Form a group of three to five people. Read each of the following thesis statements. Then decide if each statement would be a workable thesis statement or not. Tell why the thesis statement is effective or ineffective. Is it too broad in scope? Is it an overgeneralization? Is it too narrow in scope? Does it seem manageable for a basic essay? Also decide what rhetorical mode you might expect the writer to use. Someone in the group should record your answers. Be prepared to share your responses with the rest of the group.

1. The world is a cruel place.
2. Sparring is an important part of the martial arts.
3. Names reveal everything about a person.
4. One aspect of reading literature is analyzing characters.
5. The fishing industry on the east coast of Canada needs revitalization.
6. Cable television has changed the way viewers watch television.
7. Women play hockey differently from men.
8. The CFL should be closed down for three reasons.
9. Unions should support women's groups.
10. Younger parents make better parents.
11. Not everyone should be protected by the law.
12. Fashion design has a surprising history in Canada.
13. Children should be seen and not heard.
14. Today credit unions are very much like banks.
15. The Olympics are a waste of money.

Exercise 5 Shaping Thesis Statements

Imagine that each of the following topics will be developed into an essay. Your task is to take each topic and shape it into a clear thesis statement. Your thesis statement should show the mode of development for your paper. Your instructor may wish to see the work from Exercise 5; otherwise, he or she may ask you to share answers in your class.

Topics for Thesis Statements

skiing	magazines
curing snoring	biking
part-time jobs	communication
networking	clubs
family recipes	gifts

Writing the Introduction

The introduction has three plain purposes: to get your reader interested in the topic; to provide some background information to your reader and get to the controlling idea of the essay; and to provide the thesis statement for the whole essay. The introduction should be at least five sentences long. If it is too short, it will not fulfill the three purposes. On the other hand, do not make the introduction too lengthy.

Start the introduction with an interesting statement of some sort: a "grabber." Next, in a general way, provide some background information about the topic that helps to narrow the discussion: the controlling idea. Finally, shape your thesis statement and place it as the last sentence of your introduction. Be sure that the thesis statement shows a clear method of development. Your reader should be able to tell what your paper is going to be about and how it will be developed simply by reading your thesis statement.

Remember that, for a student, academic writing usually means writing for a course. Instructors and markers do not want to wade through cluttered introductions. They do not want to struggle to find out what the thesis is or where it has been placed. In short, be clear and direct in the introductory paragraph of your essay.

Writing the Body of an Essay

When you write essays, you try to convince your reader of a few things. To be convincing, you must have organized and clear ideas. Realize just how important spending time organizing your essay is.

First, you want to show your reader that you have thought ideas through, in other words, you have given thought to your topic. Your reader can tell when an essay has been slapped together without attention to detail, good evidence, conventional essay format, and clear organization. You want your essay to be thoughtfully and carefully arranged for best presentation.

Next, you must work to connect ideas to convince your reader. Ideas should not appear to be "splashed" onto the page nor to fit randomly with the topic. You must establish the relationship between the ideas. You must make the "fit." The reader will depend on that connection.

Furthermore, you must select your evidence or arguments wisely. The examples or pieces of evidence you select must support the topic or point you are establishing. This proof must be convincing; otherwise, your reader will not take your ideas seriously. You might think of structuring your essay in a different way. Consider an analogy.

You can think of writing an essay somewhat like playing a card game. When you have decided what topic to write about and when you have formulated a thesis, it is like the first approach to the card table. You know basically what the game is that you are about to play. You understand the ground rules of the game, just as you understand the ground rules of essays, but you do not know precisely how the game will work out, just as you do not know exactly how your essay will turn out. You are dealt a hand just as you deal yourself ideas. In order to win a hand, you must use your best cards. To win a point or to convince your reader, you must use the best ideas or strongest examples you can find. Otherwise, if you play the first hand you get, without thinking it through, you will lose the hand, and you may lose the game. In this case, you may lose the reader and suffer the consequences.

Let's consider what makes up a good argument.

Choosing Evidence

Think first how a person wins an argument or how someone is convincing. Imagine a convincing person. What situation is this person in? How does the person behave? What sort of language does the person use? How does the person win?

Think of salespeople as examples of those who can win when they want to. Most effective salespeople and most effective sales training courses use a great deal of psychology in the process. First, salespeople are taught to be clear in their own objectives. They are taught that they can sell anything to anyone if they are clear about their purpose. So, first of all, as a writer, you must use the same technique. When you are establishing a point, ask yourself, "What am I really trying to write about? What point is it that I am trying to establish?"

The next thing a salesperson might be taught is how to get the customer to buy what it is the salesperson is trying to sell. In other words, how can the goal be reached? You too must think of how you are going to achieve your purpose. As a writer, once you have established the point you are trying to make, you should ask yourself, "How am I going to convince someone that my point could be true?"

Making something convincing lies in selecting powerful examples. Think of at least two reasons why your point may be valid. Three reasons are even more attractive. A good salesperson can think of a whole flock of reasons why you should buy his or her product. In sales, you are taught not to stand there wasting a customer's time while you desperately try to think of good reasons the customer should buy your product. Often a salesperson will rehearse dialogue with an imaginary customer many times and may even have anticipated possible arguments or questions the customer may have. In a similar way, when you construct an argument, you must also anticipate questions and arguments. You must think of or find several real examples or illustrations or facts to support the point you are trying to establish. Here are some tips to help you construct the argument.

Tips for Constructing an Argument

1. **Establish a point.** For example, if you were writing about television program content, you might begin with a point like this:

   Most television programs have a poor level of content, and viewers are insulted.

2. **Provide proof or evidence for your point.** You might use examples, statistics, explanations, anecdotes, or facts. For example, you might say this:

   A good example of such programming is the "reality show" and the "challenge" that many networks now broadcast. These shows depict people doing utterly stupid things for money. Most of the time the characters' behaviour displays the worst in people. In one show, one character was asked to cheat and steal from another in order to "knock the person out of the game."

3. **Explain how the proof connects with your point.**

4. **Keep the point you are trying to establish separate from the proof.** Do not mix the two in the same sentence.

The news anchor, the "hero" of the supper hour, is a person who is not really genuine because he or she must create a persona for the camera and the viewers, pretending to be an expert in all things and at all times.

Notice that the writer has mixed the point being established with the proof. What is the point the writer wants to make? What is the proof he or she uses?

The point: "The news anchor is really not genuine."

First piece of evidence to support the point: "he or she must create a persona for the camera and the viewers, pretending to be an expert in all things and at all times." The reader will find this statement confusing to follow because it has blended the point with something else.

5. **Choose the most convincing evidence you can find or think of.** A weak example does not convince anyone.

6. **Be confident in your statements.** Say things like, "The politician was selfish in his actions, causing the ruin of several important people in his life." Don't say, "Some may not agree with me, but I sort of think that the politician might have been just a little selfish." Make a bold, clear statement as your point. Then find good evidence to back up your claim. Then comment if you wish.

7. **Use transitional devices (a word, a phrase, or a whole sentence) to bridge ideas.** Transitions indicate to the reader that you are adding to the idea, contrasting it, comparing it, or modifying it in some way, or that you are changing to a new point. You will find more about transitional devices in the next few pages.

8. **Allow yourself to write freely.** As Henriette Anne Klauser tells us in *Writing on Both Sides of the Brain: Breakthrough Techniques in Writing*:

   When you edit and write at the same time, the result is often a disaster: a disaster for you as a writer and eventually for your reader. Purple patches come from the unrestricted pen. Go back and edit later. Later is when you invite the logical sequential strength side of you to come forward and apply all the techniques of good grammar and construction that have been drilled into you since the beginning of your school days. (15)

Exercise 6 *Evaluating Evidence*

Find another person in the class to work with on this exercise. Together evaluate each pair of statements. The first statement is supposed to provide a clear point. The second statement is supposed to provide evidence or proof for the point.

After statement 1, write **C** if you believe the statement clearly establishes a point. Write **O** if you think the statement is an overgeneralization. Write **P** if you think the statement is an opinion and not a fact. Write **V** if you think the statement is too vague.

Then consider statement 2. Does it provide good supporting evidence? If it does, write **YES**. If it does not, write **NO**. Be prepared to explain and share your answers.

Pair A

Statement 1: Owners of pets are irresponsible people.

Statement 2: The other day I noticed a dog owner who did not pick up after his dog.

Pair B

Statement 1: Some safety features of our roadways need to be improved.

Statement 2: According to a survey in *Safe Driving*, 62 percent of drivers do not shoulder-check when they pull out from the curb.

Pair C

Statement 1: All math anxiety stems from poor self-esteem.

Statement 2: Practising positive "self-talk" can improve math scores on tests.

Pair D

Statement 1: Something needs to be done about the crime rate in this city.

Statement 2: Crimes are on the increase.

Pair E

Statement 1: I believe Tanya is the best person for president of the student council.

Statement 2: She is well organized and a hard worker.

Pair F

Statement 1: Children should be protected from violence on television.

Statement 2: My children get aggressive after they watch cartoons.

Concluding an Essay

The last paragraph of your essay is called a *concluding paragraph*, or a *conclusion*. The conclusion is also an important paragraph because it is the last section your reader will meet. You want to leave the reader feeling satisfied after he or she has read your essay, feeling "eased out" of the writing in an effective manner.

Your concluding paragraph should provide three things for the reader:

1. **It should be a restatement of the thesis.** Write the thesis again, but use different words. This technique reminds the reader of what you had set out to discuss in your essay. In long essays, such a restatement is particularly useful.

2. **It should highlight the main points of the essay.** Look at each body paragraph and summarize each in a few words. Your summary statement may be only one sentence long, but in a lengthy essay, you may need two or more sentences to recap the major points you have made.

3. **It should end by leaving the reader with a general thought on the topic.** Instead of simply summing up your ideas and leaving the reader there, add a global thought on the topic. This general thought provides closure in the reader's mind. However, do not add new ideas to the essay in the conclusion. A conclusion is not the place to introduce new ideas or points that have not been mentioned previously in the essay. Instead, the last paragraph is the closing stage of a presentation—a place where you as a writer sum up and then uplift the reader. You want the reader to leave your piece thinking about what you have said in your conclusion.

Essentials for the Body of the Essay

The body of the essay and the support should have these characteristics.

- The body of the essay should have a clear organization.
- Points should be clearly established and laid out in separate sentences.
- Points should be supported by strong examples, reasons, or facts.
- The arguments should be as convincing as you can make them.
- You should use transitions selectively.
- You should have a confident style, convincing but not arrogant.
- You should be concise in your sentence structure.

Keep these hints in mind when you write. Review them from time to time. Remember: the work you do in advance of the actual writing will make the writing itself a much easier task.

Transitional Devices

When you write, you must show connections or relationships between ideas. Words, phrases, and sentences called *transitions*, or *transitional devices*, help make connections between ideas in sentences and between sentences themselves.

What transitional device you use may depend on what rhetorical mode you are using. For example, if you were going to be contrasting ideas (a contrast mode), then you would expect to use transitional devices showing contrast. If you were using cause and effect pattern, you would select transitions that conveyed a cause and effect relationship.

Examples of Transitional Words and Phrases

To add ideas:

furthermore	in addition
another	moreover
also	and

To show process:

first	next
when	to begin with
finally	during
second	before
as soon as	initially
while	afterward
third	after
then	at last
after that	until

To add examples:

for instance	for example
a case in point	to illustrate

To show cause/effect relationships:

of course	for
thus	hence
therefore	due to
consequently	as a result
since	then

To show contrast:

on the other hand	whereas
although	unlike
in contrast	but
yet	conversely
however	a differing

To show similarity (comparison):

similarly	the same
just as	also
in addition	as well as
like	in the same way

In a paragraph, you use transitional words between major points or as a bridge to examples or explanations. If you were using transitional sentences, at the end of a body paragraph you would place a sentence that quickly summarizes the main gist of the paragraph, but opens up the possibilities of other ideas. This transitional sentence bridges ideas from one paragraph to the next. However, it is not necessary to place a transitional sentence at the end of the last body paragraph because you do not require a link to a conclusion.

Example of a Process, or Time-Order, Essay

Read the following student essay. It uses a process mode. As you read, pay attention to the parts of the essay. Look at how Kerry-Anne has structured her introduction. Notice how clearly she lays out each stage of the process. You should also know the writing circumstances: Kerry-Anne wrote this essay under timed conditions in the classroom.

Settling an Argument

Kerry-Anne Doole

When as humans we have an argument or disagreement with a friend, it can take time to come to a peaceful resolution, but it is well worth the effort involved. Settling an argument involves admitting to not being perfect. The steps to settling an argument are many. Most of the time a resolution can be found, but there are times when more help is needed.

The first step to settling an argument is talking one-on-one with the other person. It is important not to go to anyone else at this point. When we go to another person and tell them about our argument, this action causes people to take sides. The person we talk to about our argument is going to tell others about the problem, leading to rumours. As the rumours spread, the story can be twisted: our words may end up being misunderstood. The person we originally argued with may find out through the grapevine that we are upset with him or her. Hearing such a story second hand can lead to hurt feelings and a possible end to a great friendship. We risk breaking up long-established relationships if we do not try to deal with issues more directly, including the person involved. Often we may find the problem more easily resolved by going to him or her first. In fact, most of the time, going to anyone else can cause greater problems in the relationship. The second reason meeting face-to-face is important is to try to clear up misunderstandings. It is crucial to go back to the person we argued with and ask for clarification on any issues that we do not understand. We may have heard the person say one thing, when in reality he or she said something entirely different. Furthermore, the friend we argued with may not realize that we are upset with him or her. Meeting face-to-face would also allow for apologies on both sides. The third reason for a meeting is common courtesy. The polite thing to do is to talk to the person who has offended us. If we do not go back to the original person, how can the relationship be repaired in all honesty? If we go to the person that we originally argued with, it eliminates the number of other people who can take sides and reduces possible misunderstandings. However, it can sometimes be difficult to meet another person when both parties feel angry or hurt.

If the person refuses to listen, the second step is to take someone else with us. This person must be neutral. Neutral means that the person will not take sides in the argument. A neutral person is like a mediator who has no connection with either party. It is important for the person to be neutral because nothing productive will be accomplished at a meeting if he or she starts to take sides. Moreover, the purpose of having someone else go with us is to allow for reasonable, calm conversation. The mediator can help to keep tempers under control. When things start to get out of hand, he or she can stop the discussion until everyone has cooled down. In addition, the mediator allows each party to have a say, eliminating the possibility of one person taking over the conversation. Both people in the conflict feel as if their version of the argument has been heard. The mediator, therefore, creates the space where each party has a voice and where neither person feels frustrated by not being able to express their side of the story. In these ways, the mediator helps to bring the two opposing sides to a peaceful resolution, but the mediator's work still involves one last stage.

The final step involves a plan of action. The mediator helps the people involved in the argument to draft a plan of action. A plan of action means what the parties are willing to do to work out their differences. To draft such a plan, they need to sit down with the mediator and put in writing what they will do to solve their disagreement. They must agree to follow through, or the plan will not work. One example of following through is getting together once a week over coffee to talk about their differences. Furthermore, there must be a desire to change or the reconciliation will not succeed. If one of the people involved in the argument refuses to make an effort, the relationship will not succeed. The two parties need to stay focused on their goal of friendship. If the parties have agreed to work together, then they must be committed to what they need to do. The plan of action makes clear what needs to be done in order to get the relationship working again; more importantly, the plan of action is a negotiated agreement between the two people—each one must make a commitment to move forward in a positive way.

The steps to solving an argument can be painful and difficult. Participants must be willing to be direct with one another, get the assistance of a neutral person or mediator, and draft a plan of action which both parties agree to follow. Negotiating a conflict between friends is a risky business. It may mean losing a friendship. It may also mean that a stronger relationship develops. No one really knows for certain. If the people involved in the argument are willing to work together, their relationship has a fighting chance. If they are not capable of working out their differences, it may be time to go their separate ways. However, learning to settle an argument in a reasonable fashion using clear steps may be one of the most important lessons any person can have.

Writing Assignment 8 A Beginning Essay (Optional)

Your instructor may ask you to try writing a beginning essay. Choose one of the following topics. Write an essay of about 700–800 words that has an introduction, three body paragraphs, and a conclusion. Your first essay will be using something from your own experience in a time-order, or process, method of development.

Use these suggestions:

1. Double space your work.
2. Provide a clear title page as suggested in Chapter
3. Check over spelling, grammar, and punctuation before you hand in your assignment.
4. Complete the work using a computer, available on your campus. Most instructors expect all assignments to be done using a word-processing program. If you are unable to comply with this requirement, please talk to your instructor.

Topics for Time-Order, or Process, Essay

how to make a celebration feast
how to teach a dog a trick
how to make downtown living more enjoyable for residents
how to make the morning commute more pleasant
the process of selecting a university or college
the process of choosing a partner
the process of reading for enjoyment
how to win an argument
how to order from the Internet
how to file a tax return
how to curl
how to manage a bar
how to diet
how to eat vegetarian
gardening
playing a sport or . . .

ESL POINTER

Passive and Active Voice

Voice is an expression used in relation to verbs. If a verb is in the *active voice*, it means the subject does the action. If a verb is in the *passive voice*, it means the subject is the recipient of the action indicated by the verb.

You will notice that the print media (newspapers and magazines) sometimes use the passive voice. You will see the passive voice used frequently in science and technical writing.

Here are some tips about the passive voice:

1. **You cannot use the passive voice with these common verbs:**

stay	walk	sleep	arrive
appear	come	cry	
go	happen	die	

2. **Usually the passive voice consists of a form of *to be* plus the past participle of the main verb.**

3. **Only transitive verbs (those that take objects) can be written in the passive voice.**

   Here are some examples of the active and passive voice:

   Monica loves good poetry. (active voice)

   Good poetry is loved by Monica. (passive voice)

   The company employees enjoy a spring break. (active voice)

   A spring break is enjoyed by the company employees. (passive voice)

   Use the active voice whenever you can.
   There are some particular circumstances in which you can use the passive voice:

1. **Use the passive voice when the object of the action seems to be more important than the subject.**

   Active: We instituted a new sexual harassment policy at the college.

   Passive: A new sexual harassment policy was instituted at the college. (The policy is more important in this case than who instituted it.)

2. **Use the passive voice when the subject is unknown.**

   Passive: The car was hit on the front passenger side. (It is not clear who hit the car.)

3. **Use the passive voice if you wish to blur agency or responsibility.**

   Passive: Several shots were fired. (You may not wish to name who did the shooting.) Sometimes the subject or agent of an action may be protected by having a statement reported in the passive voice. It removes responsibility from the subject or agent.

Exercise 1 *Voice*

Identify whether each statement is in the active or passive voice. Check your answers with the Answer Key found at the end of the book.

1. French is spoken in many parts of Canada. _____

2. The lieutenant studied for his exams. _____

3. Lemon sauce will complement the fish. _____

4. His wallet was stolen on Tuesday night. _____

5. The guests were invited to dine on the deck of the ship. _____

6. Morgan was not pleased by the arrangement. _____

7. Brushing your teeth helps prevent cavities. _____

8. The orchestra conductor was interpreting the passage of music in a new way. _____

9. The gift was boxed and ready for shipment. _____

10. Hockey sticks are made in Quebec. _____

11. The doctor appeared tired after surgery. _____

12. An unusual occurrence is happening in the southwest. _____

13. Groober was elected to Parliament on June 24th. _____

14. The prisoner was escorted from the court by a guard. _____

Exercise 2 Voice

Change each of the following passive constructions into active voice. Rewrite each sentence on the lines provided. Check your answers in the Answer Key.

1. The poodle was leashed to the bike rack by its owner.

   _____

2. A feast was prepared by Chef Bonhomme.

   _____

3. The umbrella was found by the station master.

   _____

4. The novel was written by Margaret Atwood.

   _____

5. The saddle was placed on the horse by the ranch hand.

6. The murder was solved by Detective Goodley.

7. He was held responsible by the board.

8. My party was arranged by my children.

9. She was made upset by the accident.

10. I was convinced to quit smoking by my brother.

CHECKOUT

1. Academic essay writing has specific requirements and follows useful conventions.
2. There are many intellectual opportunities provided by essay writing.
3. Following a course of action can help overcome the difficulties of getting started writing an essay.
4. With the help of your instructor you can formulate an organizational plan before beginning to write an essay.
5. Developing a workable thesis statement in advance of beginning to write the essay can help to avoid the disappointment of much wasted effort.
6. Clear writing organization, cogent rational argument, and convincing supporting evidence will invite the serious consideration of your reader.

part 2

sentence foundations

chapter 10

Nouns, Pronouns, and Verbs

Chapter Objectives

What will you have learned when you have completed this chapter? You will be able to

1. recognize some basic grammatical terms.
2. classify words according to their function.
3. distinguish between the object of a verb and the object of a preposition.
4. identify the correct forms of nouns, pronouns, and verbs.

Introduction: Learning about Grammar

Grammar is a set of rules or guidelines applied to a language which enables the relationship between words in sentences to be understood. Studying grammar is an exercise in thinking. Your study of grammar will help you analyze and solve problems, using words as the tool.

Go step by step through this grammar study. It is most important that each idea is understood. Remember: always be sure you understand everything clearly. Chapter 10 will teach you about terms and functions.

In the following section, you will find a self-test that asks questions about the grammar ideas in Chapter 10. Each of the grammar chapters that follows also begins with a self-test to help you to determine what you know about grammar. Try writing the self-test before you do the work in the chapter. In this way, you will begin to understand how the tests can help you learn what you need to study. You will find the answers in the Answer Key at the back of the book.

Chapter 10: Self-Test

Part 1: Nouns

Underline all nouns in the following sentences. (10 points)

1. Mr. Miller bought property on the lake.
2. The representative will be back in a moment.

3. Several workers did not sign the petition.

4. The doctor gave her pills for her depression.

Part 2: Nouns as Subjects or Objects

All nouns have been underlined. Write **S** above the nouns that work as subjects in the sentences. Write **O** above the nouns that work as objects of verbs in the sentences. Be careful: some nouns are acting as objects of prepositions and not objects of verbs. (10 points)

1. Mary Jane and Peter are planning to be married in the spring.

2. A fax machine sat in the hall.

3. Malcolm invited Bob to the club dinner.

4. High in the trees noisy crows squawked at us.

5. The group ordered French fries, sandwiches, and coffee for their meeting.

Part 3: Verbs

Underline all verbs in the following sentences. (5 points)

1. We had been waiting for over two hours for our plane.

2. Marcus will be singing a duet with Patty.

3. Have you ever worked for the government?

4. Rita is sick today.

5. His uncle started the business several years ago.

Part 4: Verb Tenses

Write **P** if the verb shows present action. Write **PT** if the verb shows past action. Write **F** if the verb shows future action. (10 points)

1. Oatmeal makes a good breakfast. _____

2. Will he stay for dinner? _____

3. Several chickens were wandering on the road. _____

4. Am I supposed to go, too? _____

5. Walter emptied the trash. _____

6. Butterflies are beautifully patterned. _____

7. Jocelyn hates snakes. _____

8. Had Rob forgotten his promise? _____

9. My supervisor was telling us what to do. _____

10. Ernest knew everything about computers. _____

Part 5: Verb Forms

Give the correct form of the verb as indicated. (2 points each, 20 points)

1. The children have _____ (eat) their lunches.
2. The man had _____ (swear) under his breath.
3. Yesterday I _____ (see) a golden eagle.
4. Five weeks ago they _____ (begin) their divorce.
5. Rodd has _____ (do) his best work this year.
6. No one had _____ (bring) any paper cups for the picnic.
7. We were _____ (choose) a bright wallpaper for the bathroom last week.
8. Clare has _____ (work) for the mobile phone company for 15 years.
9. Helen and Norm have _____ (write) a report to the Ministry of Education.
10. I may _____ (drive) to Port Townley on the weekend.

Part 6: Identification

Identify whether each underlined word is a noun, pronoun, or verb. Write your answers in the spaces. (½ point each, 5 points)

1. They were afraid of him. _____
2. The union was upset by the offer. _____
3. I am flying to Reno. _____
4. Were you interested in the meeting? _____
5. Does Bennie like kale? _____
6. The officer gave her some advice. _____
7. The garden lost its colour. _____
8. Ivan is mixing the dough. _____
9. Mary Ruth loves dancing. _____
10. We gave it to Nicole. _____

Part 7: Verb Identification

(5 points)

A. Underline all verbs. (½ point)

B. Identify whether each verb is action or non-action. Write your answers in the spaces. (½ point)

1. Ray decided to leave. _____

2. They are hot in the sun. _____

3. The cyclists stopped for a break. _____

4. I thought about it. _____

5. Leslie is certain about the answer. _____

Exercise 1 Classifying

In order to understand grammar, you must first be aware of how words are classified. Then you can begin to look at how classes of words function in sentences. Classify the following terms.

Example: wrench, pliers, screwdriver, hammer, chisel   <u>tools</u>

Terms	**Class**
1. poodle, cocker spaniel, German shepherd, Doberman pinscher	_____
2. knife, fork, spoon, scoop, spatula, pie lifter	_____
3. Volkswagen, Chevrolet, Chrysler, Mazda, Ford	_____
4. chair, table, stool, couch, bookshelf, bed	_____
5. mouse, rat, rabbit, bear, wolf, kangaroo	_____

How did you classify?
What process did you go through? If you understood classes of things, you recognized characteristics or traits the items had in common. Then you had to think of the name of the class.
Check your answers in the Answer Key.

Nouns

Grammar consists of much the same sort of classifying. You will most often be able to determine the class of words in grammar not by shape, or colour, or size as you did with some of the items above, but rather, by what each class of words does. In grammar, then, it is important to remember the term or *part of speech* (the name of the class of words) and *function* (what the words in this classification do in sentences).

Exercise 2 Nouns

A word is a *noun* if you can place *the*, *a*, or *an* in front of it, and if the addition makes sense. A noun names a person, place, or thing. Underline all the words below that can be classed as nouns. Check your answers in the Answer Key.

foot	wagon	rum	rare
apricot	joke	sauce	examination
planet	magnificent	create	hate
main	love	moist	harbour
end	paint	retire	community
law	tent	hero	sit
hour	skip	person	
television	kitchen	ghetto	

Concrete and Abstract Nouns

In grammar, the words *abstract* and *concrete* are used to classify nouns. The term *concrete* designates the class of nouns which name tangible material things. Words like *gate* or *truck* are concrete nouns. Here are some examples of concrete nouns:

cigarette, building, barn, dinner, pen, Andy

The term *abstract* designates the class of nouns which name such things as ideas, emotions, and situations. A word like *safety* is an abstract noun because it refers to a state or condition. An abstract noun like *anger* refers to an emotion. Here are some examples of abstract nouns:

fear, tension, accident, argument, worry

Exercise 3: Concrete and Abstract Nouns

Underline all the nouns in the following sentences. Check your answers in the Answer Key. Write **A** above every noun that is abstract. Write **C** above every noun that is concrete.

          C   A   C
The small **child** toddled off in the **direction** of its **mother**.

1. The passengers waited for the bus in the pouring rain.

2. Ronnie bought two more models for his collection.

3. The artist used coloured paper, scissors, glue, and a soft pencil.

4. Many children hate games if they cannot be boss.

5. The rusty ship waited for a new coat of grey paint.

6. The smiling prince bowed to the guests at the dinner party.

7. Outside the hotel gunshots and cannon fire broke the silence.

8. The carpenter pounded finishing nails into the trim around the window.

9. The eggs fell to the pavement and smashed.

10. The television program was too long.

11. The company will send the order by delivery van.

12. The juvenile skunk wandered out of the bushes and stood on the path to the shed.

13. The wasp stung the old woman.

14. Paul brought his father's truck back to the farm.

15. The fight in the bar was over a rule in hockey.

Exercise 4 Concrete and Abstract Nouns

List 10 concrete nouns and 10 abstract nouns. Do not use any from the lists or your practice exercises. Ask another class member to evaluate your answers.

Concrete Nouns

1. _____
2. _____
3. _____
4. _____
5. _____
6. _____
7. _____
8. _____
9. _____
10. _____

Abstract Nouns

1. _____
2. _____
3. _____
4. _____
5. _____
6. _____
7. _____
8. _____
9. _____
10. _____

Chapter 10 Nouns, Pronouns, and Verbs   137

Subjects and Objects

To name a person, place, or thing is a function of the noun. However, that definition does not clarify how a noun functions in a sentence. For example, nouns can function as subjects or as objects of sentences. In order to figure out how a word functions, you have to study the whole sentence in which the word is found.

The subject of the sentence is the *doer of the action* or *what the sentence is about.*

The frog hopped across the path. (*Frog* is the subject because it did the action.)

To determine what the subject in a sentence is, think about what it is that the sentence is all about. If you consider that the sentence above is about a frog, you can then say that the subject of the sentence is probably the word *frog*.

Exercise 5 Subject Nouns

Write down which noun is the subject noun, or the doer of the action. All nouns have been underlined, but not all nouns are functioning as subject nouns. Check your answers in the Answer Key.

1. Marie prepared a fresh, green salad. _____

2. The small dog barked at the postman on the street. _____

3. The boxer threw a left-handed punch at his opponent's jaw. _____

4. Terry erased her math mistakes with a large, pink eraser. _____

5. Sylvia interrupted the meeting to announce some news. _____

6. The workers stopped for lunch. _____

7. Wally scrubbed the floor with a brush. _____

8. Seven dancers entertained people in the streets. _____

9. The wolf hunted the shaggy, sick moose. _____

10. The car skidded from the intersection. _____

11. The soccer team won the match. _____

12. The train halted near the tunnel. _____

You can see that all of the subject nouns did the action in each of the sentences in the exercise above. How can you tell which noun is the subject if a sentence shows no action?

If a sentence possesses no action, it will be a sentence of description. The subject noun in this type of sentence will be the main noun that is described; in other words, it is best to begin by asking, "What is this sentence all about?"

There is a girl in the hallway.

There is no action word in this sentence. So, you must figure out which noun the sentence is mainly centred on. Is this sentence about a hallway or about a girl? Because the sentence is all about the girl, *girl* is the subject noun of the sentence.

Exercise 6 Subject Nouns

All of the sentences below show no action; they are sentences of description. All nouns have been underlined. Write down which noun is the subject noun. Check your answers in the Answer Key.

1. The actor was absent for rehearsal. _____
2. For 24 years, Margaret was a secretary. _____
3. The paper was dotted with specks of paint. _____
4. My dog Kady loves to play with a tennis ball. _____
5. Yesterday at nine o'clock, Tom was in the cafeteria. _____
6. Yogurt is easy to find at any store. _____
7. The soup was made from fresh vegetables and chicken. _____
8. The lawn near the swimming pool was healthy and green. _____
9. There are cookies on the shelf in the pantry. _____
10. Here is the lamp from Sears. _____
11. Philip was in the library at lunchtime. _____
12. There were no children in the school yard. _____

Nouns can also function as an object in a sentence. An object is the *receiver of the action* of the verb. It answers *what?* after the action verb.

Annie bought some beautiful yellow roses.

Annie is a noun and functions as the subject of the sentence; *Annie* did the action of buying *roses*. *Roses* is also a noun, but it is not functioning as the subject of the sentence because *roses* did not do the action—Annie did. Roses are what Annie bought. *Roses* receive the action.

Exercise 7 Subject Nouns and Object Nouns

All nouns have been underlined. Write **S** above every noun that acts as a subject. Write **O** above every noun that is functioning as an object of the verb in the sentence. Some sentences can have more than one object; others may not have any at all!

Do not write **O** above objects of prepositions. In phrases like "with a light motion," *with* is a preposition or word of direction. *Motion* is the object of the preposition *with*. If you ask the question "With what?" *motion* is the answer. Therefore, *motion* is the object of the preposition *with*; it is not the object of the verb. It is not what got sanded. Check your answers in the Answer Key.

1. <u>Rodd</u> sanded the <u>plywood</u> with a light <u>motion</u>.
2. The <u>students</u> set the <u>rules</u> for the psychology <u>classroom</u>.
3. The fat <u>man</u> hid his <u>money</u> underneath the <u>floorboards</u>.
4. The <u>puppy</u> grabbed the <u>rag</u> on the floor and <u>tugged</u>.
5. Mrs. <u>Pobsby</u> rolled up the <u>rug</u> in the living <u>room</u>.
6. The <u>chef</u> tossed the <u>salad</u> into the <u>air</u>.
7. The young <u>boy</u> sprained his <u>ankle</u> in the <u>fall</u>.
8. Her <u>cousin</u> ate a whole, giant <u>pizza</u> last <u>night</u>!
9. <u>Ozzie</u> collects <u>rocks</u> and <u>stones</u> from the <u>beach</u>.
10. Last March <u>Madame Lem</u> predicted a <u>disaster</u> in <u>California</u>.

Exercise 8 Subject Nouns and Object Nouns

Underline all nouns; write **S** above all nouns which work as subjects, and write **O** above all nouns which work as objects of the verbs.

           S   O
The **tourists** bought **souvenirs** from the **pedlars** near the **wharf.**

1. The child drew a picture of his home.
2. The coffee from the restaurant tasted sour and burned.
3. A crow was digging our garbage from the bins.
4. Near the stream beside an old oak a girl was reading a novel.
5. The supervisor threw a surprise party for her staff.
6. On the weekend the family had a picnic at Fairview Hill Park.
7. Francis bought a parrot from a travelling salesman.
8. Charlie spent too much time on his project.

9. The gentleman ordered a ham sandwich and a beer.

10. Harvey cooked a delicious spaghetti sauce for last night's supper.

You now know nouns can be of two types: *concrete* and *abstract*. Nouns can function as *subjects* or *objects* within sentences. You should also know that a sentence can contain more than one subject or more than one object. This means that two or more people or things could be doing the action. In grammar, you call having more than one subject a *compound subject* and having more than one object a *compound object*.

Alexander, Phillip, and Terry were rowing the boat.

Three people are the subjects or doers of this sentence; therefore, this sentence contains a compound subject (more than one).

Jessie bought scissors, fabric, bias tape, and a pattern for her new summer outfit.

Notice that Jessie bought a number of items. In other words, *scissors*, *fabric*, *tape*, and *pattern* are all functioning as objects of the verb. Compound objects work to share the same action or description.

Exercise 9 Subject Nouns and Object Nouns

First underline all nouns. Then find all subjects and objects in the sentences below. Write **S** above subject nouns and **O** above object nouns. Be careful: not all sentences contain objects. Do not write **O** above objects of prepositions.

1. The real estate agent and the owner negotiated the price of the land.

2. Maxwell built a small, wooden bridge over the ravine.

3. The astronauts measured the temperature of the atmosphere outside the module.

4. The kittens were abandoned in the old house.

5. Several pilots were removed from active duty.

6. Many people like smaller foreign cars and trucks.

7. Gasoline and water do not mix.

8. Hot blueberry muffins are delicious with butter.

9. The players and the coach were overjoyed with the victory.

10. Four teenagers pushed the dune buggy to the service station.

11. Stella's eyes were irritated by the dust.

12. Sound and light travel in waves.

13. The early explorers reached the coast of Canada hundreds of years ago.

14. The honeybee landed on a bright, purple wildflower.

15. The students of Halifax Elementary and their teachers visited Gloaming Park.

Pronouns

Pronouns are another class of words in grammar. Because pronouns can *take the place of nouns*, they can do the same work as nouns (*pro = for*); in other words, they can work as subjects or objects.

Any noun can have a pronoun substitute. Instead of saying a person's name, you might say *he* or *she*, or *you*. Consider the two sentences below. The first one contains all nouns; the second sentence substitutes pronouns for the nouns.

Iris told Bill that Iris was wrapping the gift for Bill.

She told him that she was wrapping it for him.

Pronouns take on the same functions in sentences as nouns.

         subject   object of the verb

The young **supervisor** was finishing the **project.**

However, there is a difference between noun use and pronoun use. The subject form of a pronoun is not the same as the object form.

Consider these sentences:

subject   object of the preposition *to*
He gave it to **me.**

subject   object of the preposition *to*
I gave it to **him.**

The subject form of the pronoun *he* changes to the form *him* when used as an object. Notice, too, that the subject form of the pronoun *I* changes to *me* when used as an object.

Pronoun Changes of Form

Subject Case	Object Case
I	me
he	him
she	her
it	it
we	us
you	you
they	them

142 Part 2 Sentence Foundations

Exercise 10 Pronouns

Substitute pronouns for nouns. Check your answers in the Answer Key.

Noun	**Pronoun Substitutes**
1. the watch	_____
2. Mark and Jane	_____
3. the dog	_____
4. an instructor	_____
5. the government	_____
6. the television	_____
7. Mr. Feldman	_____
8. children	_____
9. The worker drank the tea.	_____
10. Mrs. Grabowski and Mr. Fisher are here to see Mrs. Gallant.	_____
11. The chicks and hens were pecking for worms.	_____
12. The landlady talked to the city councillor.	_____
13. Ross doesn't mind work.	_____
14. Ruth's son went to see the show.	_____
15. The books sold quickly.	_____

Exercise 11 Subject and Object Nouns and Pronouns

Underline all nouns; put all pronouns in parentheses (pronoun), write **S** above the nouns or pronouns which are working as subjects, and write **O** above the nouns or pronouns which are working as objects of the verbs. Check your answers in the Answer Key.

    S   S   O   O
Valerie and **Stan** enjoy their **children** and their **home.**

             S   O
(They) received a **call** about the **shipment.**

     S   O
The **trees** in the **forest** have been attacked by spruce **budworm.**

1. We whipped the cream for the icing.
2. Rhonda wrote a poem about Daisy's childhood.
3. The mayor opened the new art gallery.
4. After the meeting, he took the reports to his home.
5. I watched the parade for two hours.
6. Books and papers were missing from the room.
7. During the night, we heard voices in the backyard.
8. John and I will investigate the charge.
9. She broke it.
10. Al left the meat on the counter.
11. You caught a cold and the chills from the rain.
12. I taught Joe and her to play tennis.
13. We broadcast the program.
14. The dogs and the cat chased the squirrel up the tree.
15. He shut the window to his office.
16. They flew the kite in the open field.
17. I hit the rocks.
18. The doctor and nurse were discussing the patient's progress.
19. She froze the strawberries for jam.
20. Several students were smoking outside the coffee room.

Exercise 12   Review of Nouns

Use separate paper. Clearly label the exercise. Your instructor may ask to see this review.

1. Write three sentences. Each sentence should contain at least one concrete noun. Underline each concrete noun.
2. Write three sentences. Each sentence should contain at least one abstract noun. Underline each abstract noun.
3. In three separate sentences, use the following three words as nouns working as subjects.

    a. Mark   b. the designer   c. walk

4. In three separate sentences, use these three words as nouns working as objects of verbs.

   a. cash   b. doctor   c. nails

5. Make up two sentences of your own that have compound subjects. Underline the compound subjects.

6. Make up two sentences of your own that have compound objects of verbs. Underline the compound objects.

7. Use three pronouns working as subjects in three, clear sentences.

8. Use three pronouns working as objects in three, clear sentences.

Verbs

Verbs are another class of words in grammar. You can see how verbs function in sentences by considering what the subject is doing or by viewing how the subject is linked to the rest of the sentence.

There are two types of verbs, each having a different task:

1. **Action verbs tell what subjects do in sentences.** They tell what action was performed by the subject.

2. **Non-action verbs link the parts of the sentence together.** They do not tell what subjects do. Instead, they tell about the state of the subject.

Action Verbs

Think of an action verb as a word that shows what someone or something can do; ask yourself: "Could I do this?"

Actions can be either a mental or a physical process.

I walk to work. (physical action)

I think about it. (mental action)

I annoyed him. (mental action)

I laughed at the joke. (physical action)

Exercise 13 Action Verbs

Underline all of the action verbs in the sentences below. Remember that some verbs do not work to show action. Check your answers in the Answer Key.

1. The alarm clock rang at six this morning.
2. Sparky caught a mouse.
3. My son is very tall for a 14-year-old.
4. Monique swims every Saturday.
5. The gardener seeded the lawn.
6. We cooked hamburgers for supper last night.
7. Each year for seven years we went to Long Beach to camp.
8. She stopped near the shopping centre to check out her car.
9. Eleanor traded in her stereo.
10. I understood his meaning.
11. They wrote about the contest.
12. He fixed the transmission in his car.
13. Alice bought some bricks to construct a barbecue.
14. The customers read magazines at the counter.
15. You saw him only yesterday.

Non-Action (Linking) Verbs

Some verbs do not show action at all. If a sentence is one of description, it contains a non-action verb. These non-action verbs can also be called *linking verbs*. They link parts of the sentence together. Here are some sentence examples of linking verbs:

No Action: I am tall.

No Action: Phyl is efficient.

No Action: The book was good.

There is no action in any of the three sentences above. All are descriptive. Non-action verbs are called linking verbs when they appear alone in sentences. Linking verbs link the parts of sentences together; they also tell about the state of the subject. The subjects in these sentences do not do anything; the sentence merely describes them.

Monica is afraid.

In this sentence, Monica is being described. She is not doing any action.

> **Examples of Non-Action Verbs**
>
> | | |
> |---|---|
> | am | appear |
> | look | become |
> | is | was |
> | taste (no object) | are |
> | were | feel |
> | seem | smell (no object) |
> | sound (no object) | |

Exercise 14 Action and Non-Action Verbs

Underline all verbs, write **ACT** above those showing actions, and write **NO ACT** above those not showing action. Check your answers in the Answer Key.

1. The dog lay in the sun.
2. Ralph is my brother.
3. The student has 40 dollars for a book.
4. The dinner smells good.
5. We were in the store for a few minutes only.
6. Grammar is fun!
7. The newspaper reporters interviewed the premier.
8. Here are the missing sets of keys!
9. The husband and wife purchased a tent trailer.
10. Martin will be there.
11. Susan was afraid of bugs.
12. The English instructor is absent from class.
13. The children felt sick from overeating.
14. Arnold smokes and drinks too much.
15. The idea sounded like fun.

Auxiliary Verbs

Non-action verbs can be combined with action verbs. When you combine action verbs with non-action verbs, you are being very exact about the time of the action or about the condition of the action. Non-action verbs used in connection with action verbs are called *helping verbs* because they help the action to be complete or exact. They are also referred to as *auxiliary verbs*. Together they form verb phrases.

We will be sewing our own clothes this fall.

Sewing is the action verb. *Will* and *be* are the non-action, or helping, verbs. These helping verbs show that the action will take place in the future.

Nora should be earning a good wage.

Earning is the action verb. *Should* and *be* are the helping verbs. These helping verbs help to set the condition on earning: Nora ought to be earning a good wage; perhaps she isn't, and someone is concerned about that. In another sense, you might be wondering how much money Nora is making these days, and you might be saying that at this time in her working life, "Nora should be earning a good wage."

Typical Helping, or Auxiliary, Verbs

can	am	did
has	might	would
been	be	had
must	may	does
were	are	shall
was	could	do
will	have	
should	is	

Notice that some auxiliary verbs indicate time while others indicate condition.

He can walk. (meaning he is able to—shows condition)

She might sing. (she hasn't quite decided yet—shows condition)

I was paddling the canoe. (shows time—was indicates the past).

Often you will see non-action verbs added to action verbs. In grammar, this is done to show the complete time of the action or the condition of the action. Remember: the non-action verbs (NA) added to action verbs (AV) are often called helping (auxiliary) verbs because they help the action to be complete. Together they are called the *verb phrase*.

    NA   AV
I **am walking** to work.

     NA   AV
She **was bending** the rules.

     NA   AV
Rod **has swept** the garage.

Sometimes auxiliary verbs (those that do not show action) show time in sentences. In the following examples, verbs have been underlined.

He <u>is sleeping</u>. (*Is* shows that the action of sleeping is occurring in the present.)

I <u>am falling</u> in love. (*Am* shows that the action of falling occurs in the present.)

He <u>did know</u>. (*Did* shows that the action of knowing occurred in the past.)

The cat <u>was creeping</u> along the ground on its belly. (*Was* indicates past.)

They <u>were choosing</u> a colour for the bathroom. (*Were* indicates past.)

We <u>are leaving</u> for Ottawa. (*Are* indicates present.)

I <u>did knit</u> this sweater by myself. (*Did* indicates past.)

Mark <u>will steer</u> the boat. (*Will* indicates future.)

I <u>am beginning</u> a new book. (*Am* indicates present.)

Sometimes helpers set up a special condition for the action verb. These verbs are called *modals*, or *modal auxiliaries*. In the following examples, verbs have been underlined.

I <u>can skate</u>. (*Can* shows that you have the ability to do the action of skating.)

Fran <u>may leave</u> now. (*May* shows that there is permission to do the action of leaving.)

The welder <u>might quit</u> his job. (*Might* shows that there is a choice to do the action of quitting.)

He <u>must stop</u>. (*Must* shows no choice.)

The baby <u>should sleep</u> well tonight. (*Should* indicates a condition—the baby ought to do this.)

Ken <u>can draw</u> very well. (*Can* indicates that Ken has the ability to do the action.)

The social worker <u>would know</u> what to do. (*Would* indicates a condition—this person will probably be able to do the action.)

The puppy <u>could learn</u> quickly. (*Could* indicates the past of can; in other words, whenever you tried to teach the pup, he was able to learn.)

Randy <u>might decide</u> against it. (*Might* indicates a condition; Randy has the option to choose to do the action.)

Exercise 15 Action and Non-Action Verbs

Underline all verbs in the following sentences. Look for both action and non-action (linking or auxiliary) verbs. Consider modals as well.

1. Malcolm is coming for dinner tonight.

2. She has seen you before.

3. The flowers and vegetables have grown well this season.

4. Will you be needing the car?

5. We have drunk too much.

6. I was going to meet him on Saturday.

7. Must you snore so loudly?

8. Did they teach you anything?

9. Would you mind that?

10. The women were losing some benefits on the job.

11. She can stay here tonight.

12. Could you ever strike it rich on Lotto 6/49?

13. He is always forgetting things.

14. Lucille did know the answer.

15. I have been given the wrong instructions.

Basic Verb Tense

The form of the verb that shows time is called *verb tense*. Verbs can have three basic tenses: past, present, and future.

I walk to the college campus. (*Walk* indicates **simple present** tense. The sentence means that the person who is the speaker of the sentence walks to campus often, perhaps each day, and that he or she continues to walk.)

I walked to the college campus. (*Walked* indicates the **simple past** tense. The sentence means that the person who is the speaker of the sentence has just finished walking. It may be that the speaker walks to campus once in a while; we are not certain, but we do know that the speaker has completed the action for the time being.)

I will walk to the college campus. (*Will walk* indicates the **simple future** tense. The sentence means that the person who is the speaker has the intention of walking. He or she has not yet done the action; the speaker is telling us of an action that will take place in the future.)

Note that the simple tenses usually contain only one verb.

I run to the store each day. (simple present)

I ran to the store each day. (simple past)

I will run to the store each day. (simple future)

Progressive and Perfect Tenses

PROGRESSIVE TENSE

I am walking to the college campus. (*Am walking* indicates the **present progressive** tense. The sentence means that the person is in the process of walking. The action is in progress: the action continues over a period of time.)

I was walking to the college campus when I saw a deer. (*Was walking* indicates the **past progressive** tense. The sentence means the person was in the process of walking in the past when he or she noticed a deer.)

I will be walking to the college campus this week. (*Will be walking* indicates the **future progressive** tense. The sentence means the person will perform the action of walking in the future. The sentence indicates the action will happen over time—one week.)

Here are more examples of progressive tense:

I am learning to play the guitar in the evenings.

Esther is waiting for her bus right now.

The neighbour was painting his garage door during the weekend.

My friends are having coffee with their supervisor from three until four today.

Our chickens were escaping from their pen when I saw them in the morning.

We will be expecting you for dinner at seven o'clock.

PERFECT TENSE

I have walked to the college campus every day for five years. (*Have walked* indicates **the present perfect** tense. The sentence means that the action you started five years ago continues to this day.)

Sometimes the present perfect tense is used when you do not know exactly when an action happened in the past. For example, you could say, "His brother has resigned his position," indicating an action occurred at an unspecified time. You are not exactly sure when his brother did the action.
However, if you use the past perfect tense, it means that an action you started in the past is now over. Another action or habit might begin after that.

I had walked to the college campus before I moved away. (*Had walked* indicates the **past perfect** tense. An action you started in the past no longer continues today.)

Generally speaking, when you use a past perfect action in a sentence that contains another action, the past perfect happens first.

Sheila had wanted some peace and quiet, so she wandered off by herself. (Sheila's wanting peace and quiet occurred before she wandered off.)

When you use the future perfect tense, it means that you expect an event to conclude before a specified time.

I will have walked to the campus by eight o'clock. (*Will have walked* indicates the **future perfect** tense. This sentence means that you predict an action to be completed by a certain future time; it also implies another future action will take place.)

Here are more examples of the perfect tense:

He has wanted to marry her for a long time. (present perfect)

They have tried to convince him to quit smoking. (present perfect)

Marvin had worked for the company for 12 years. (past perfect)

Note the difference in meaning between these two sentences:

Eagles have nested in that tree for four seasons. (present perfect—The eagles started the habit of nesting in a particular tree and are expected to continue their habit of nesting there.)

Eagles had nested in that tree for four seasons. (past perfect—The eagles no longer nest there. Their habit of nesting in that particular tree is over.)

PERFECT PROGRESSIVE TENSE

When the perfect tense is placed with the progressive tense, the form is called the *perfect progressive*. This form is used when you want to emphasize an action over time.

Tyron has been practising his karate since he was six. (*Has been practising* is the **present perfect progressive** tense. It indicates that Tyron's activity has occurred over a long period of time and is continuing into the present.)

Tyron had been practising his karate since noon when he was interrupted by a phone call. (*Had been practising* indicates the **past perfect progressive** tense. It indicates that Tyron was completing an action over time in the past; now the action is over.)

Tyron will have been practising his karate for the Olympic tryouts. (*Will have been practising* indicates the **future perfect progressive** tense. The sentence indicates that Tyron will perform an action over time in the future. The future perfect progressive tense emphasizes a length of time over which an action occurs. Usually a second action or a reason for the first action is implied. In this case, Tyron will practise in order to compete.)

Exercise 16 *Identifying Verb Tense*

Read each sentence. Identify the verb by underlining it. Then write whether the verb is simple present, past, or future, or if it is present, past, or future progressive, or if it is present, past, or future perfect, or if it is present perfect progressive, past perfect progressive, or future perfect progressive. Check your answers in the Answer Key.

1. Olivia has been wanting to buy a house in Calgary for several years now.

2. Several of the voters had left before the candidate arrived.

3. Have you been standing there all this time?

4. Montrose had loved the opera all his life.

5. If the bus is not running on time, Marcella expects to be late.

6. No one knew the handsome stranger who was drinking alone at the bar.

7. Twelve kittens had been sold before we selected one.

8. Mannequins can be so lifelike that customers will often ask them for directions.

9. Were the restaurant owners fighting the new ban on smoking?

10. The Count de la Roy will have written his book by the time we arrive at his castle.

11. Have Daniella and Peter ever gone out on a date together?

12. The chief of police suspected the person who was sitting next to him at the banquet.

Regular and Irregular Verbs

Verbs are called *regular verbs* if they form the past tense by adding *ed* to their past participles or past forms. Verbs are called *irregular* if they do not form the past tense by the addition of *ed* to the past participle

Some Regular Verbs

Present	Past
work	worked
cry	cried
look	looked
fix	fixed

Some Irregular Verbs

Present	Past
become	became
begin	began
break	broke
bring	brought
catch	caught
choose	chose
come	came
do	did
draw	drew
drink	drank
drive	drove
eat	ate
fall	fell
feed	fed

Chapter 10   Nouns, Pronouns, and Verbs   153

fly	flew
forgive	forgave
freeze	froze
give	gave
go	went
grow	grew
know	knew
ride	rode
ring	rang
rise	rose
run	ran
see	saw
sing	sang
speak	spoke
spin	spun
steal	stole
swear	swore
swim	swam
take	took
throw	threw
wear	wore
write	wrote

Exercise 17 Verb Forms

A. Fill in the form of the verb that is requested in each sentence.

B. Then at the end of each sentence, indicate if the verb is in the past, present, or future.

I was <u>reading</u> (read) a book all day. (past)

1. The young birds are _____ (feed) from our backyard feeder this morning. _____

2. She must _____ (write) a note to her old friend. _____

3. We _____ (worry) about the baby last year. _____

4. Last week Harold _____ (fly) to Kamloops. _____

5. Did she _____ (freeze) the fish he caught? _____

6. I will _____ (forgive) Arnold soon. _____

7. Can you _____ (speak) louder. _____

8. Marvin _____ (take) lots of chances. _____

9. They were _____ (throw) out the old TV. _____

10. Every winter I _____ (catch) a cold. _____

11. Tina does _____ (drive) a truck for a living. _____

12. The children will _____ (become) cranky if they get too tired. _____

13. The crew _____ (stop) work at eleven last night. _____

14. Are you _____ (eat) supper at home? _____

15. Last October my elderly neighbour _____ (fall) on an icy patch. _____

16. The sailors are _____ (wear) dress uniforms. _____

17. Does your brother _____ (grow) his own vegetables? _____

18. Mrs. Upton _____ (rise) each day at five a.m. _____

19. The clerk _____ (swear) under his breath. _____

20. The Clarks _____ (go) to the prairies last summer. _____

Has, *Have*, and *Had* as Auxiliary Verbs

When you add *has*, *have*, or *had* to some verbs, they form an irregular past participle. Choose the correct form when you are writing.

Irregular Past Participles

Present	Past	Past Participle
become	became	has, have, had become
begin	began	has, have, had begun
break	broke	has, have, had broken
bring	brought	has, have, had brought
catch	caught	has, have, had caught
choose	chose	has, have, had chosen
come	came	has, have, had come
do	did	has, have, had done
draw	drew	has, have, had drawn
drink	drank	has, have, had drunk
drive	drove	has, have, had driven

eat	ate	has, have, had eaten
fall	fell	has, have, had fallen
feed	fed	has, have, had fed
fly	flew	has, have, had flown
forgive	forgave	has, have, had forgiven
freeze	froze	has, have, had frozen
give	gave	has, have had given
go	went	has, have, had gone
grow	grew	has, have, had grown
know	knew	has, have, had known
ride	rode	has, have, had ridden
ring	rang	has, have, had rung
rise	rose	has, have, had risen
run	ran	has, have, had run
see	saw	has, have, had seen
sing	sang	has, have, had sung
speak	spoke	has, have, had spoken
spin	spun	has, have, had spun
steal	stole	has, have, had stolen
swear	swore	has, have, had sworn
swim	swam	has, have, had swum
take	took	has, have, had taken
tear	tore	has, have, had torn
throw	threw	has, have, had thrown
wear	wore	has, have, had worn
write	wrote	has, have, had written

Exercise 18 Adding Verb Forms

Add the correct form of the verb to each of the following sentences. Check your answers in the Answer Key.

1. Cecilia has _____ (write) a cheque for a down payment on the car.

2. Has he _____ (forgive) you for it?

3. Margaret had _____ (take) out a loan.

4. Have the students _____ (break) the alarm?

5. We have _____ (throw) out the old sofa.

6. I had _____ (know) him a short time.

7. We _____ (see) the premier last week.

8. Raisins and almonds had _____ (give) me energy.

9. Have you ever _____ (ride) a camel?

10. Last night it _____ (begin) to get chilly.

11. Rita and Elsie have _____ (speak) to me.

12. Has Eddie _____ (fall) off the wagon?

13. The children _____ (become) silent because they were frightened.

14. A bald eagle has _____ (take) over the Douglas fir next to our house.

15. Have they _____ (choose) their new leader?

16. Last night I _____ (see) him at the pub.

17. The wire fence has _____ (tear) a hole in my shirt.

18. How many times have you _____ (write) your essay?

19. He has _____ (go) to Ontario to look for work.

20. The RCMP have _____ (give) out some information.

Chapter 10: Review Test

Your instructor may wish to see your test.

Part 1: Nouns

Underline all nouns in the following sentences. (10 points)

1. Clifford bought snacks from the convenience store.

2. The investigator will generate a special report.

3. Several chips of wood flew off the saw.

4. Her anger interrupted her concentration.

Part 2: Nouns as Subjects or Objects

All nouns have been underlined. Write **S** above the nouns that work as subjects in the sentences. Write **O** above the nouns that work as objects in the sentences. Some nouns are acting as objects of prepositions and not objects of verbs. (10 points)

1. The <u>demonstration</u> lasted for 20 <u>minutes</u>.

2. The <u>hill</u> was too high for the <u>cyclist</u>.

3. <u>Neil</u> searched the <u>cupboards</u>.

4. Our <u>group</u> will miss <u>Julie</u>.

5. <u>Mistletoe</u> and <u>holly</u> are used at <u>Christmas</u>.

6. <u>Tanya</u> wore a red <u>vest</u> to the <u>opera</u>.

Part 3: Verbs

Underline all verbs in each of the following sentences. (5 points)

1. The fish were swimming to the shallow end of the pond.

2. I did see Wayne yesterday.

3. Were they going to recover their losses?

4. First aid is an important treatment to administer.

5. Her friend customized her van.

Part 4: Verb Tenses

Write **P** if the verb shows simple present tense. Write **PT** if the verb shows simple past tense. Write **F** if the verb shows future action. (10 points)

1. Floods cause enormous damage. _____

2. Will Mike repair the motorcycle for us? _____

3. The floor show was boring. _____

4. Am I expected to attend? _____

5. The shortstop threw the ball. _____

6. Had you made a mistake? _____

7. Furniture costs a lot of money. _____

8. Are you sure about it? _____

9. The copy was hard to read. _____

10. She was telling me about her ordeal. _____

Part 5: Verb Forms

Give the correct form of the verb as indicated. (2 points each, 20 points)

1. The townspeople have _____ (give) time to the festival every summer.

2. Ruby has _____ (wear) her red shoes to the party.

3. My neighbour and I were _____ (freeze) several dozen cobs of corn from her garden.

4. Today the sun has _____ (rise) at 5:20 a.m.

5. The artist had _____ (draw) a sketch of the rocks.

6. Most of the children did _____ (swim) in the new pool yesterday.

7. The pitcher is _____ (catch) the throw from left field.

8. Monique has _____ (fly) on Air Japan previously.

9. The neighbourhood children had _____ (grow) some sunflowers last summer.

10. Has Brad _____ (feed) the ducks?

Part 6: Identification

Identify whether each underlined word is a noun, pronoun, or verb. Write your answers in the spaces. (½ point each, 5 points)

1. Sheila called them about it. _____

2. The examination was difficult. _____

3. Rose felt happy. _____

4. The house seemed too quiet. _____

5. Marvin gave him a ride. _____

6. Coriander is a spice. _____

7. The class took a break. _____

8. Marnie has been sick. _____

9. The police are unable to come. _____

10. It was missing. _____

Chapter 10   Nouns, Pronouns, and Verbs   159

Part 7: Verb Identification

(5 points)

A. Underline all verbs. (½ point)

B. Identify whether each verb is action or non-action. Write your answers in the spaces. (½ point)

1. They climbed the small mountain. _____

2. He is sorry about the argument. _____

3. The coach instructed the team. _____

4. She slept in the sun porch. _____

5. Tony seemed upset. _____

Try the following reviews to see what you remember. Your instructor may ask you to hand in both reviews for checking.

Exercise 19   Review

Part A

Use the following words as action verbs in good sentences. You may change the form of your action verb to suit your sentence.

watch   write   slide
salt   peak   camp

Part B

Underline all verbs, write **AV** above all action verbs, and write **NA** above all non-action verbs in the following sentences.

1. They were planning and talking about the next day.

2. The students and the helpers arranged the papers into stacks and put them on proper shelves.

3. During the storm one of the doors broke off its hinges.

4. Will you make some coffee now?

5. The movie was action-packed and fun!

6. Did he finish his assignment?

Part C

Underline all verbs and tell the tense—what time the action in the sentence is taking place—by writing **F** (future), **P** (present), and **PT** (past) on each of the blanks.

1. Louise was filing the record sheets. _____

2. Ann did not receive her cheque this week. _____

3. Will you take the dictionary? _____

4. The student figured out the answer to the algebra problem. _____

5. She must pass this course. _____

Exercise 20 *Review of Subjects, Verbs, and Objects*

Find the subjects, verbs, and objects: write **S** over the subject or subjects; write **O** over the object or objects of the verbs, and underline the verb or verb phrases in each sentence.

1. Vicky and Ralph planted the potatoes and then weeded the garden.

2. I was telling them about my experiences.

3. Would she write a note to me about this?

4. The baby was biting his toes.

5. Fresh cookies and milk make a satisfying snack.

6. She drew a line, studied it, and then erased it.

7. I should go to the play tonight.

8. My sister and her husband often take trips in their camper.

9. They catch salmon every spring.

10. The child fought for the toy and hit his friend with it.

11. Have they seen the new building yet?

12. Are you looking for work?

13. Squawking seagulls rested on the rocks.

14. A spider spins a web and catches other insects.

ESL POINTER

Verb Tenses

Exercise 1 Working with Verb Tenses

Change each verb tense as indicated. Check your answers in the Answer Key.

1. They will not listen. (past perfect)

2. Felicia went on Tuesday. (simple future)

3. The dog barks all day. (simple past)

4. Those roses died. (future progressive)

5. He invited me. (simple present)

6. Sandra played the accordion. (present perfect progressive)

7. The clown does card tricks. (simple future)

8. Vicky will cut her hand. (simple present)

9. The cat catches mice. (past progressive)

10. I took my time. (present progressive)

11. Lisa will not tolerate it. (past progressive)

12. I cleared my desk on Thursday. (simple future)

13. Pamela inflates the story. (simple past)

14. We collected bottles. (simple future)

15. Terry closed the case. (present perfect)

16. The schedule was out of date. (simple present)

17. Joanne scans the headlines. (simple future)

18. The sheriff will note your new address. (simple present)

19. The child tears her jacket. (past perfect progressive)

20. He spun the wheel. (simple present)

Exercise 2 Sentences and Tenses

On a separate sheet of paper, make sentences according to the directions given below. Your instructor may have you hand in your work.

1. Use *fish* as a noun in a sentence containing a past progressive verb.
2. Use *sail* as a future perfect progressive verb in a sentence.
3. Use *worry* as a noun in a sentence containing a present simple verb.
4. Use *plant* as a past progressive verb in a sentence.
5. Use *stage* as a simple past verb in a sentence.
6. Use *work* as a noun in a sentence containing a past perfect verb.
7. Use *sour* in a sentence containing a present progressive verb.
8. Use *shop* as a noun in a sentence containing a future perfect progressive verb.
9. Use *juice* as a noun in a sentence containing a simple future verb.
10. Use *fly* as a present progressive verb in a sentence.

CHECKOUT

1. Grammar enables the relationship between words in sentences to be understood.
2. The study of grammar can sharpen thinking skills.
3. If there is no action word in the sentence, determine the sentence subject by asking what the sentence of description is all about.
4. Some typical examples of classes of words are: subject nouns, object nouns, concrete nouns, abstract nouns, action verbs, non-action verbs, regular verbs, irregular verbs, and auxiliary verbs.
5. The members of a class of words have characteristics in common. For example, some auxiliary verbs indicate time, while others indicate condition.

chapter 11

Subjects and Verbs

Chapter Objectives
What will you have learned when you have completed this chapter? You will be able to
1. understand grammatical terms by looking at their context.
2. decide what part of speech a word is by taking note of its function.
3. spot modal verbs.
4. know the correct forms of *to be* and *to have.*
5. recognize subject–verb agreement.
6. distinguish verb phrases and prepositional phrases.
7. identify compound subjects and compound verbs.

Introduction

It is important for you to understand what grammar terms mean by considering the context in which a word is used rather than by trying to apply to every sentence situation a definition you have memorized. By looking at how a word functions, you will understand its part of speech.

This chapter has as its main focus subject and verb agreement, since many students often have difficulty matching subjects and verbs in number and gender when they write. Try writing the self-test below first in order to determine what you remember about subjects, verbs, and their agreement. Check your answers in the Answer Key found at the end of the book.

Chapter 11: Self-Test

Part 1: Subject and Verb Identification

Write **S** above each subject. Write **V** above each verb. (½ point each, 10 points)

1. Amy and Lowell booked a flight to Toronto for the holidays.
2. The druggist filled the prescription and then left for lunch.
3. Lucinda comes from a very small African country.

4. The flies were buzzing around the fruit salad.
5. Several of the customers were upset by the poor meal.
6. The child seemed afraid of the water.
7. Have you had your break?
8. Under the sign, we spotted our missing keys.
9. Chocolate ice cream is too rich for me.

Part 2: Subject–Verb Agreement

Make the verbs agree with their subjects. Underline the correct verbs. (10 points)

1. Kimberly or Mitchell (want, wants) a new video game.
2. Crumpled paper and dirty plastic (was, were) rolling in the windy street.
3. The mayor or his secretary (is, are) going to speak on television tonight.
4. A steady stream of customers (pour, pours) into the new supermarket.
5. The choirmaster and his students (perform, performs) on Thursdays.
6. The tax on tobacco products (is, are) high.
7. Gilbert and Roy (is, are) going to cater the party.
8. A bowl of soup and a slice of fresh bread (make, makes) a wholesome lunch.
9. (Are, Is) Janice or Maureen going to answer the phone?
10. (Has, Have) the truckers formed a blockade?

Part 3: Identification of Subjects

Write **S** above each subject in each of the following sentences. (10 points)

1. Dawn and her niece will take a course together.
2. One of the students wasn't feeling well.
3. A case of fresh peaches fell from the truck.
4. The manager of the theatre spoke to the attendant.
5. Do Marcus and Leo take karate lessons here?
6. The hoot of an owl came from the tall Douglas fir.
7. After a long semester, the instructor felt exhausted.
8. Only one of those chairs is a genuine antique.

Part 4: Subject–Verb Identification

Write **S** above each subject in each sentence; write **V** above each verb in each sentence. (18 points)

1. The judge and the jury looked worried about the testimony.
2. Snap your fingers.
3. There are 10 children waiting for the gym teacher.
4. Machines buzzed and hummed in the huge office.
5. A burst of applause came from the audience.
6. Bonnie was writing her final exam in nursing.
7. Randy clipped the hedge and weeded the flower garden.

Part 5: Subject–Verb Agreement

Read each sentence carefully. If the sentence contains a subject–verb agreement error, circle the error, and write the correction in the space provided. If the sentence does not contain a subject–verb error, write CORRECT in the space provided. (30 points)

1. Each of the tomatoes were ripe. _____
2. Here is the newspaper and the magazine from the drugstore. _____
3. Have Marilyn or Cheryl ever sung a solo before? _____
4. One of those kittens are promised to my neighbour. _____
5. Where is the answer key for my math questions? _____
6. Vanessa or her sister go water skiing on Clear Lake. _____
7. The toast and the jam was tasteless. _____
8. There is the set of missing papers. _____
9. Each of the girls were trying to get the job. _____
10. One of the men in my department own a farm. _____
11. The group of campers were too noisy last night. _____
12. The supervisor or the clerk check for errors in accounting. _____
13. Nina and Peggy has chosen an interesting hobby. _____
14. An appointment book and a calculator is missing from her desk. _____
15. Each of the colours in the garden harmonize with those of the house. _____

The Functions of Grammatical Terms

Understanding what various terms do, that is, how they function in sentences, requires you to analyze the context, usually whole sentences.

The *rock* fell onto the road.
I will *rock* the baby to sleep.
He enjoys *rock* music.
The child threw a *rock* at the shed.

To understand what part of speech *rock* is in all four sentences, you must determine how it functions in each sentence. Is *rock* a noun in the second sentence? Is it a noun in the third sentence? If it is a noun in the first sentence, how is it functioning?

The *rock* fell onto the road.

In this sentence, *rock* is what did the action in the sentence; it is the subject, or doer, of the action. Because the sentence states *the rock*, you know it refers to a thing.

I will *rock* the baby to sleep.

In this sentence, on the other hand, the doer, or subject, of the sentence is not *rock*. The subject of the sentence is the pronoun *I*. *Rock* is an action word in this sentence; it tells what the *I* (subject) is about to do—*rock*.

He enjoys *rock* music.

He is the doer of the action, or the subject of the sentence, and *enjoys* is the action he does—the action verb. *Music* is the thing he enjoys—it is an abstract noun. Because *music* tells what he enjoys and is the receiver of the action, it is a noun functioning as the object. Now, how does *rock* function?

Rock describes what sort of music he enjoys. You do not know if he enjoys classical music or gospel music, but you do know he enjoys the type of music called rock. Thus, *rock* functions as an adjective because it describes the noun *music*.

The child threw a *rock* at the shed.

In this sentence, the doer, or subject, of the sentence is *child*, a noun. The action the child performed is *threw*. But how does *rock* function in this sentence? *A rock* indicates a noun, and it is what the child threw. Therefore, it functions as an object.

Use a step-by-step breakdown of each sentence in order to know how the parts of the sentence function together. You will deepen your understanding of the meaning of the sentence. *Using analysis* is what grammar study is all about.

Grammar study may pleasantly surprise you by sharpening your problem-solving and thinking abilities. As you hone your powers of analysis, you can benefit by an improvement in your reading and language performance. Besides these benefits, you will learn to become a better editor of your writing and others' writing.

Remember, read each sentence carefully. In order to gain meaning from the sentence think of **S-V (subject–verb:** a subject is doing something) or **S-V-O (subject–verb–object:**

a subject is doing something to an object). Then use analysis to figure out how words in the sentence function in relation to one another.

Subjects and Verbs

You will recall that a subject of the sentence is the *doer, or performer,* of the action. You will also remember from the previous chapter that a verb can *show action or link parts of the sentence.* Sentences should have *both subjects and verbs* and *complete a whole thought.*

The mule kicks hard.

Mule is the subject, and *kicks* is the action the mule expresses.

The mayor is rich.

This sentence is a description telling what the mayor (subject) is. The linking verb shows no action and links *mayor* to *rich.*

Exercise 1 Subjects and Verbs

Write **V** above each verb. Some verbs show action; some are linking verbs. Write **S** above each subject. Check your answers in the Answer Key at the back of the book.

1. The children are at the movie all afternoon.
2. We whispered to each other about the secret email.
3. Her daughter is tall for a girl of six.
4. Maxwell worked for the insurance company during the late 1990s.
5. I phoned for an appointment with the orthopedist.
6. She is nervous because of the noise of the fireworks.
7. You are silly some of the time.
8. Pat's friend was an architect from western Ontario.
9. They drank iced tea in the shade of the rose trellis.
10. Margaret lives in St. John's only during the weekends.

To Be and *To Have*

The forms of the verb *to be* do not show action; they tell what something is. The forms of the verb *to have* do not show action either; they tell what something or somebody has.

Forms of the Verb *To Be*	Forms of the Verb *To Have*
I am a person.	I have a cold.
He is an electrician.	He has a Firebird.
She is a carpenter.	She has two sisters.
We are on campus.	We have a garden.
You are my friend.	You have made a mistake.
They are excited.	They have coffee at ten.
She was in Winnipeg.	She had a fever.
We were at the beach.	We had a fight.

Some non-action verbs, called *linking verbs* or *state-of-being verbs*, are generally based on the verb *to be*.

Linking Verbs

am	sound	appear
is	grow	smell
were	are	remain
become	was	

Remember: when non-action verbs are placed with action verbs, they are called *auxiliary* (*helping*) verbs; together they make *verb phrases*.

My father *is* an alderman. (linking verb)
Ronald *has* four children. (non-action verb)
Their mother *has planned* a party for them. (auxiliary with action verb)
The crowd *was gathering* outside the arena. (auxiliary with action verb)

Exercise 2 Subjects and Verbs

Write **V** above each verb. Write **S** above each subject.

1. The monk in the red cloak is the leader of the group.

2. Several students were at the office of the registrar early this morning.

3. The team and their coach have lunch at 12:30 each day of practice.

4. The antique buttons are not in the box.

5. He was the manager of the theatre for over 11 years.

6. I am sorry about the whole sad affair.

7. Surprisingly, the missing key was on the bedroom bureau.

8. That clock in the bedroom is wrong.

9. Last week Tom had the flu, a cough, and chills.

10. The bird in that rare Japanese painting is stunningly beautiful.

More about Verb Phrases

A *phrase* is a group of two or more words working together to do a task. There are many different types of phrases. A *verb phrase* works to show the complete action or state of the subject and contains one or more auxiliary (helping) verbs and often one action (main) verb.

Here are some examples of verb phrases. Notice how the verbs in the phrases work together.

Ted *will be waiting* a long time for his cab.

You *could have been studying* for your exam.

The employees *may have left* the office early.

Mr. Mallory *will be checking* on the baggage.

Does Arlene *want* another cup of coffee?

Other Common Auxiliary Verbs

am	was	has
had	could	would
might	*may*	*can*
be	do	is
were	have	*should*
will	*must*	been
did	does	

Sometimes a helping verb is called a *modal* because it sets a specific mode, or condition, on the action verb. Modals are shown in italics in the above group.

He *could* work harder.

Could is the modal. It implies the subject has the ability to work harder if he so wishes.

The professor *might* visit France.

Might is the modal; it indicates that the professor has not yet decided. There is the possibility of going.

I *must* remember to change the baby soon.

Must is the modal; it indicates a duty or obligation.

Exercise 3 Verb Phrases

Underline each verb phrase. Check your answers in the Answer Key.

1. Malcolm is working for the company from Sault Ste. Marie.
2. He has been driving the same car for 10 years.
3. It might rain today.
4. Alex must write to her father before the deadline date.
5. I should go with you to the opening of the new theatre.
6. They are deciding what to do over their son's disability.
7. The raccoon was noisily picking through our garbage.
8. The rookie police officer can leave soon.
9. Marta has had bad luck for the last few years.
10. We may have been writing to the wrong person about the complaint.

Exercise 4 Verb Phrases and Subjects

Underline each verb or verb phrase. Write **S** above each subject.

1. The general reviewed the troops and then dismissed them.
2. Chef Mimi stirred the soup and then tasted it.
3. Misty could have been answering the question.
4. Phillip hurriedly ordered a hamburger and then ate it quickly.

5. My mother worries about me and always gives me advice.

6. They searched the woods but found no traces of the lost man.

7. Eddie will sweep the floor and dust the furniture.

8. A pill bottle, an old shaver, and several empty boxes were in the bottom drawer.

9. Mr. and Mrs. Tripper were shopping at MayTime Mall yesterday evening.

10. The dockworkers were yelling at the speaker and were demanding some answers.

Prepositional Phrases in Sentences

You will recall that a phrase is a group of words that works together to do a specific job. One type of phrase that you have examined is a verb phrase. The verb phrase works to show a complete action or state. Another type of phrase is a phrase that works to show a particular detail in a sentence. This type of phrase is called a *detail*, or *prepositional*, *phrase*. The job of the prepositional phrase is to give details of *how*, *where*, *when*, *what sort*, or *why*.

Most prepositional phrases begin with a little word of direction called a *preposition* and end in a noun or sometimes a pronoun. They have objects called *objects of the preposition* because they answer *what* after the preposition.

Consider these examples:

Karena ate her lunch and read her book in George Hill Park.

Karena is the subject of the sentence. *Ate* and *read* (compound verbs) are the action verbs. *Lunch* is an object of the verb—what she ate. *Book* is an object of the verb—what she read. *In George Hill Park* is a prepositional phrase telling where she completed the action. *George Hill Park* is the object of the preposition *in*. (in what? In George Hill Park.)

His team had won the hockey tournament in last year's winter games.

Team is the subject of the sentence. *Had won* is the verb phrase. *Tournament* is the object of the verb—what the team won. *In last year's winter games* is a prepositional phrase that tells when the team won the tournament. *Games* is the object of the preposition *in*.

Jasbir went to the store for some onions.

Jasbir is the subject of the sentence. *Went* is the action verb. *To the store* is a prepositional phrase telling us where Jasbir went. *Store* is the object of the preposition *to*.

For some onions is a prepositional phrase telling us why Jasbir went in the first place. *Onions* is the object of the preposition *for*.

Prepositions and Prepositional Phrases

Prepositional phrases are introduced by common introductory words of direction. These introductory words are called *prepositions*.

Common Prepositions

about	despite	over
outside	above	down
through	across	during
to	after	except
toward	against	for
under	along	from
underneath	around	in
until	at	inside
with	before	into
within	behind	near
without	below	of
beneath	off	beside
on	between	
by	out	

Prepositional phrases end in nouns or pronouns. Sentences can contain several prepositional phrases. Here are some more examples of prepositional phrases.

Some Prepositional Phrases

without happiness	around it
above the crowd	toward them
except Freddy	between classes
on the tray	against you
by the rocks near her	for the children
through the window	underneath the bridge
off the record	

Do not choose the prepositional phrase as part of the subject. Often the prepositional phrase separates the subject from the verb as in these examples.

The members of the board are meeting tonight.

Members is the subject of the sentence. *Are* is the linking verb. *Of the board* is a prepositional phrase describing which members are meeting. *Of the board* is not part of the subject.

The flock of starlings was circling the large tree.

Flock is the subject of the sentence. *Was circling* is the verb that agrees with *flock*. *Of starlings* is a prepositional phrase describing what was in the flock. *The tree* is the object; it is what the flock was circling.

Notice that you could easily make a mistake in subject–verb agreement by selecting *board* as the subject of the first sentence and selecting *starlings* as the subject of the second sentence. Thinking these sound "right," you might mistakenly write:

The members of the board is meeting tonight.
A flock of starlings were circling the large tree.

These two sentences contain *subject–verb agreement errors* because the verbs do not match with their true subjects. Watch for sentences that contain prepositional phrases, separating subjects from verbs.

Exercise 5 *Prepositional Phrases*

Underline each prepositional phrase. Check your answers in the Answer Key.

1. Across the valley lies a beautiful ranch.
2. The family had a picnic along the river near some rocks.
3. A group of bears was eating wild berries at the park gate.
4. We found the missing letter among the papers.
5. He shouted with a loud voice.
6. The dancers on the stage are part of the show.
7. The runner won the race against the odds.
8. Near the swamp beside a clump of weeds the dog rested.
9. The couple walked through the crowd of protesters.
10. The cups behind the counter are valuable antiques.

Prepositional Phrases and Subjects

Most often the prepositional phrase in a sentence comes after a subject, but occasionally, the prepositional phrase is found at the beginning of a sentence.

During the storm on that hot August night, the baby was born.

The subject of the sentence is *baby*. The linking verb is *was*. *During the storm* and *on that hot August night* are two prepositional phrases which tell when the baby was born.

Between the two towns the government built a new bridge.

Note that *between the two towns* is a prepositional phrase which begins the sentence. *Government* is the subject of the sentence. *Built* is the action verb. *Bridge* is the object—what was built.

Exercise 6 Subjects, Verbs, and Verb and Prepositional Phrases

Underline each verb or verb phrase. Write the letter **S** above the subject(s) of each verb. Place each prepositional phrase in parentheses ( ).

1. In the middle of the third act, the author of the play left the auditorium.

2. The doctor will be performing the operation on Mrs. Lambert this evening or tomorrow morning.

3. During this morning, someone entered the garage and took several sets of tools.

4. From the front balcony of the professor's house, he could see the entrance to the bank.

5. The earthquake destroyed most of the buildings in the town and caused considerable damage to nearby farms.

Exercise 7 More about Prepositional Phrases

Prepositional phrases tell us *when, why, where, how,* or *what*. Underline each detail phrase. Over each phrase write *when, where, how, what,* or *why*. Check your answers in the Answer Key.

                     where   when
Come to my **house after seven**.

1. He bought the boat from a dealer in Edmonton.

2. The Boy Scouts pitched their tents in the woods.

3. This wallet is made of snakeskin.

4. Wayne and Reeves walked against the strong winter wind.

5. After the game, the students drank beer.

6. Sheila's aunt from Jamaica is visiting until Sunday.

7. The jacket on the floor was extremely dirty.

8. A flock of magpies chattered high in the trees.

9. My monkey knocked over the tall vase of flowers.

10. The man and his dog slept under the bridge.

Exercise 8 Verbs, Verb Phrases, and Subjects

Underline each verb or verb phrase. Write **S** above each subject. Place parentheses ( ) around the detail (prepositional) phrases. Check your answers in the Answer Key.

1. At the party, I met an old friend from Yellowknife.

2. One of the horses escaped from the corral.

3. The driver of the commercial truck fell asleep at the wheel.

4. His raise of $30 was quite a surprise.

5. A bunch of flowers arrived for you today.

6. The winners of the race stayed at the racetrack.

7. His marks for his mechanics exams were not very high.

8. After the storm, the baseball game continued.

9. The ducks and the loons were feeding near the shore.

10. The master of ceremonies tripped on his way to the podium.

Exercise 9 Subject–Verb Agreement and Detail Phrases

Underline the verb that matches each subject. Place parentheses ( ) around the detail (prepositional) phrase. Check your answers in the Answer Key at the back of the book.

1. There (is, are) two pens on the desk.

2. The key to the doors (is, are) on the wall.

3. Marvin from Flin Flon (drive, drives) home each weekend.

4. The group of men (is, are) expecting a raise in pay.

5. All of the students (has, have) left the campus.

6. There (is, are) some cupcakes in the fridge.

7. Up the hill and over the bridge (was, were) a long hike.

8. In the mornings she (prepare, prepares) breakfast for her family.

9. The odour of cigarettes (irritate, irritates) me.

10. The prices of those items (go, goes) up weekly.

Compound Subjects

Sometimes sentences may contain *two or more subjects* that share in the "doing" of the action.

Todd and *Ralph* are working on their car in the garage.

In the above sentence, two subjects are doing the action.

Frieda or *Jim* is working at the garage.

In the above sentence, one or the other subject is doing the action. Notice that a compound subject may be connected by *and* or by *or*. If *and* is used as the conjunction, or joiner, both subjects are the doers of the action. If *or* is used as the conjunction, then both subjects are given, but only one is the doer of the action. The conjunction *or* indicates a choice. The verb must agree with one or the other.

Roger or *his girlfriend* is going to be in charge of the show tonight.

Use *is* as the verb because it agrees with *Roger* or *his girlfriend*—not both.

Exercise 10 Verb Phrases and Compound Subjects

Underline each verb or verb phrase. Write **S** above each subject.

1. Janet or Tina goes out each Wednesday for choir practice.

2. Kibibe and her cousin love to rent foreign videos.

3. The postman and the insurance agent have stopped by today with special documents.

4. Hawaii or Miami is an excellent vacation spot during January and February.

5. Mr. and Mrs. Tully are leaving for Quebec for at least two months.

6. The magazine and the dictionary belong to Marie.

7. The girls or their mother should be visiting you soon.

8. The wrench or the screwdriver is missing from my tool box.

9. The movies and live theatre are interesting forms of entertainment.

10. The class and the instructor will go on a field trip to the art gallery.

Understood Subjects

Find the verb in the following sentence, and then try to figure out what the subject is in the sentence.

Give Mrs. Jenkins a copy of this book.

The verb in the above sentence is *give*. The sentence is a *command*. The sentence is actually saying: You give Mrs. Jenkins a copy of this book. However, when you give orders, you leave out the word *you*. The word *you*, which is the subject of the sentence, is understood by the reader or listener. Here is another sentence. Find the verb; then figure out what the subject is.

Bring me a cup of coffee.

The verb in the above sentence is *bring*. The subject is *you* (understood).

Exercise 11 Verbs and Commands

Write the letter **V** above each verb. Write the subject of the sentence. Check your answers in the Answer Key at the back of the book.

      V
Return the book to the library. (*You* is understood.)

1. Stack the empty cartons by the garbage cans in the backyard.

2. After dinner, offer the guests coffee and liqueurs.

3. Distribute copies of these letters among the members of all departments.

4. Before the end of the week, remove all signs from the walls of the building.

5. After sweeping the floor, arrange the books on the shelf.

6. Please stop the guests at the door and introduce yourself.

Compound Verbs

Sentences express more than one action when they contain compound verbs.

Pete washed and waxed his car.

Pete has done two actions—*washed* and *waxed*.

The teacher was talking to the class, (was) writing notes on the board, and (was) laughing.

The teacher has done three actions—*was talking*, *writing*, and *laughing*.

When you are considering sentences, remember that sentences may contain more than one subject or more than one verb—compound subjects or compound verbs.

Subject–Verb Agreement

Written English can be more formal than verbal English. You cannot always rely on what you might use in your speech. When you use written language, especially formal written language, you must be certain that what you have written is regarded as standard, correct English. Generally, an academic student is expected to avoid use of informal, non-standard English in her or his assignments.

In English grammar, subjects of sentences must match or agree with their verbs. For example, you would not say: "They is coming to the party." You know that *they* and *is* do not go together. It is important, then, to practise making subjects agree with their verbs.

Subject–Verb Agreement with Pronoun Cases

You will recall that pronouns *take the place of* or *can substitute for nouns*. Case refers to the number and gender of pronouns.

Case (Pronoun Number and Gender)

I refers to a single or singular person—first person.

She refers to a singular female person—third person singular.

He refers to a singular male person—third person singular.

It refers to a singular thing or animal—third person singular.

We refers to more than one person—first person plural.

You refers to one or more than one person—second person singular or plural.

They refers to more than one person—third person plural.

Here are examples of alternative pronoun subjects:

The teachers (they) are at a conference.

Randy (you), please close the door.

The gerbil (it) gets new toys each week.

Yolanda (she) works as a realtor.

The technician (he) is training at the local community college.

Subject–Verb Agreement: *One* and *Each*

The *indefinite pronouns one* and *each* are singular. They are called *indefinite* because they do not refer to a specific person. These pronouns are often used as the subjects of sentences. When they are used as subjects, they are frequently separated from the verbs by other words or prepositional phrases. Remember: *always make the verb agree with the subject*. Do not be confused by words that come between the subject and the verb.

One of those books *is* mine. (not *are*)

One of my brothers *plays* hockey. (not *play*)

Each of those glasses *is* cracked. (not *are*)

Each of the guests wants more wine. (not *want*)

Exercise 12 One *and* Each

Write the correct word in the blank. Check your answers in the Answer Key.

1. (goes/go) One of those buses _____ to Prince George.

2. (was/were) Each of the contestants _____ given five minutes to work out the answer.

3. (gives/give) One of these books _____ information about summer vacations in Europe.

4. (is/are) One of those houses _____ for sale.

5. (needs/need) Each of the workers _____ new safety boots.

6. (has/have) One of her children _____ a cold.

Inverted Order: The Subject Is Not Always First

Most of the time the subject comes before the verb. Sometimes, however, the verb can come before the subject in particular circumstances.

SITUATION 1

There is, there are, there were, here is, here are, here were, where is, where are, or *where were* begin the sentence:

There are two pens on the table.

The subject is *pens*, not *there*. Try changing the sentence around and saying: *Two pens are there on the table.*

Here is your hat.

The subject is *hat*, not *here*. Try saying: *Your hat is here.*

There are some cookies on the table in the kitchen.

The subject is *cookies*. Say: *Some cookies are there on the table in the kitchen.*

Was there any money in his wallet?

The subject is *money*. Try this as a statement: *Any money was there in his wallet.*

Where was the truck parked?

The subject is *truck*. The verb is *was parked*. Say: *The truck was parked where?*

SITUATION 2

Prepositional phrases start the sentence and the subject comes last:

In the middle of the forest was an old cabin.

The sentence starts with two prepositional phrases: *in the middle* and *of the forest*. Say: *An old cabin was in the middle of the forest.*

In the top drawer of his desk was a photograph of his former wife.

Say: *A photograph of his former wife was in the top drawer of his desk.*

SITUATION 3

In questions, the subject will often come between an auxiliary verb and the main verb.

Has he finished his work?

The verb is *has finished*. The subject *he* is between the auxiliary verb *has* and the main verb *finished*.

Will she be seeing him today?

The subject is *she* and the verb is *will be seeing*.

Have her parents sold their house?

The subject is *parents*; the verb is *have sold*.

Did you watch the program about South America?

The subject is *you* and the verb is *did watch*.

Chapter 11   Subjects and Verbs   183

Exercise 13   Subjects and Verbs

Write the letter **S** above each subject and the letter **V** above each verb (including auxiliary verbs).

1. Will he be running for election this fall?
2. There are two books by this author in the library on William Avenue.
3. Were there any pineapples in the last shipment of fruit and vegetables?
4. Where is the stapler that I just bought?
5. Here are his coat, gloves, and scarf.
6. In a paper bag at the bottom of the trunk was an old revolver.
7. During the past few weeks, there have been several accidents at the intersection.
8. Have Mrs. Pepin and Miss Meredith been working on their report?
9. Where were those birds flying?
10. Has the manager cancelled his appointment with Dr. Ross?

Exercise 14   Subject–Verb Agreement

Underline the correct verb for each sentence. Be careful to match subjects with verb forms when you are making your selection.

1. Edna or Sharon (is, are) typing the minutes from the meeting.
2. The papers and the folders (was, were) sitting on the filing cabinet.
3. The author of the book or her publisher (is, are) speaking there tonight.
4. Verna or her friend (go, goes) to the school to do volunteer work.
5. A monkey or a dog (make, makes) a good pet.
6. Smoking and eating too much (is, are) bad for your health.
7. Christopher and I (have, has) been going to sales.
8. The cat and the dog (have, has) fleas.
9. The child and his brother (was, were) watching the firemen.
10. The library or city hall (is, are) closed on Mondays.

Exercise 15 Subject–Verb Agreement

Write the correct word in the blank.

1. (play/plays) Their three sons _____ softball.

2. (make/makes) That colour _____ the room seem larger.

3. (visit/visits) Ralph or Rick _____ the museum every summer.

4. (make/makes) Loud noises _____ him feel nervous.

5. (cost/costs) A bucket of ice cubes _____ six dollars.

6. (enjoy/enjoys) My sister and her husband _____ their children.

7. (was/were) Allen or Sally _____ elected to student council.

8. (goes/go) My mother and father _____ to visit my brother in Toronto.

9. (was/were) The fruit and the vegetables _____ not fresh.

10. (look/looks) His mother or his brother _____ after his children.

11. (visits/visit) Friends or relatives _____ every Christmas.

12. (needs/need) The curtains in this room _____ to be washed.

13. (has/have) Another shipment of electrical parts _____ just arrived.

14. (receive/receives) The workers at the Fairmont _____ good wages.

15. (are/is) The hotels or the restaurants _____ popular in Charlottetown.

16. (goes/go) A bag of potato chips _____ well with a bottle of cold beer.

17. (was/were) A carton of cigarettes _____ missing from our order.

18. (is/are) The weight of those stones _____ too heavy for the floor.

19. (is/are) The cupboards in the kitchen and the large chair in the dining room _____ made of maple.

20. (agrees/agree) The members of the legislature _____ on very few topics.

Chapter 11   Subjects and Verbs   **185**

Exercise 16   Review

Read each of the following sentences carefully. If the sentence contains an error, underline the error and write the correction. If the sentence does not contain an error, write the word **CORRECT.**

One of those bicycles <u>are</u> hers.   _____is_____

Mary and Fred commute to Richmond by bus.   __correct__

1. We was asked to leave the auditorium.   _____
2. Mr. Jones owns two restaurants.   _____
3. Her brother and sister works at Home Depot.   _____
4. Several copies of this book is now available.   _____
5. Mr. Jackson is waiting for you in your office.   _____
6. Sheila or Ron make the coffee every morning.   _____
7. This pack of cards has only one joker.   _____
8. One of my sons deliver papers on his block.   _____
9. The manager or her assistant works late every Friday. _____
10. Her parents has just returned from Vancouver.   _____
11. Each of the three apple trees were damaged during the storm. _____
12. Dr. Drobny, Mrs. Roberts, or Mr. Bauer are going to attend the conference in Cape Town.   _____
13. Helen and Sam arrived from Medicine Hat.   _____
14. The flavour of these vegetables are excellent.   _____
15. Her two brothers goes fishing every weekend.   _____
16. One of my friends has bought a new car.   _____

Exercise 17   Review of *Is* and *Are* with *Here*, *There*, *and* *Where*

Read each of the following sentences carefully. Decide whether the word *is* or the word *are* should be used in the blank. Fill in the blank with the correct word.

1. Here _____ the books that you wanted.

2. Where _____ the coffee and the milk?

3. Here _____ the pack of cookies that you left on my desk.

4. There _____ several people in the auditorium.

5. Here _____ the pencil and the eraser that I borrowed from you.

6. There _____ a man waiting to see you.

7. _____ there any doughnuts in the kitchen?

8. Where _____ the calculators that we used yesterday?

Exercise 18 Review of *Has* and *Have*

Read each of the following sentences carefully. Decide whether the word *has* or the word *have* should be used in the blank. Fill in the blank with the correct word.

1. _____ the children come home from school yet?

2. _____ the real estate agent telephoned yet?

3. _____ Miss Wilcox and Mr. Block been introduced to each other?

4. _____ the shipment of men's shoes arrived yet?

5. _____ my son and daughter-in-law visited you recently?

Exercise 19 Review of Errors in Sentences

If the sentence contains an error, underline the error and write the correction in the space provided. If the sentence does not contain an error, write the word **CORRECT** in the space provided.

One of those computers <u>are</u> hers.	is
The twins work at the fast-food restaurant.	correct

1. Mrs. Magnum or he are generally in the office by eight o'clock. _____

2. Uncle Ted and Aunt Martha feel happy to be home again. _____

3. One of your sisters resembles my cousin. _____

4. Is there any crackers left in the box? _____

5. These writing pads was all that he ordered. _____

6. There are the shovel and the rake that I was looking for. _____

7. Don't the faucets in the bathroom work properly? _____

8. Has the plumbers gone on strike? _____

9. Each of the members of our club were given a complimentary ticket. _____

10. Here is the dictionary and the novel that you ordered. _____

11. The noise of those engines have given him a headache. _____

12. Has the instructor finished writing his report? _____

13. He and she usually walks to work. _____

14. The waiters in this hotel were trained by an expert. _____

15. Jerry Johnson, his wife, or his sister works at the community club on Saturday morning. _____

Chapter 11: Review Test

Part 1: Subject and Verb Identification

Write **S** above each subject. Write **V** above each verb. (½ point each, 10 points)

1. The sportscaster and the producer are going to Montreal for the World Series.

2. A throng of customers was waiting for the doors to open.

3. Put the stamps and the letter on the kitchen counter.

4. My travel agent will make all the arrangements for us.

5. The hero of the play was only 11 years old.

6. Will you need a bus pass this month?

7. Yvonne and Russ celebrated their tenth wedding anniversary this weekend.

8. One of the executives of the company has been talking to the journalist.

9. A sting from a bee can be quite painful.

Part 2: Subject–Verb Agreement

Make verbs agree with their subjects. Underline the correct verbs. (10 points)

1. Rudolph and Comet (is, are) expected to win the favourite-reindeer contest this Christmas.

2. The target and the scores (was, were) taken down after the shooting tournament was over.

3. A basket of plump plums (is, are) sitting out on display.

4. (Was, Were) Joe or Bob supposed to hose down the horse stalls?

5. The trail and the climb (was, were) too difficult for a novice.

6. The plane and the crew (was, were) grounded by the terrible wind storm.

7. The cashier and the clerks (work, works) late shifts to get the stock ready for the annual sale.

8. A boatload of tourists (stop, stops) at the village to see the artisans' work.

9. (Has, Have) the children put their duffel bags into the school bus?

10. (Do, Does) Kevin or Jill take minutes at the meetings?

Part 3: Identification of Subjects

Write **S** above each subject in each of the following sentences. (10 points)

1. Women and children in colourful clothing filled the fields near the festival grounds.

2. Each of the computers needed to be serviced.

3. One of the old bicycles belonged to the old gentleman from Halifax.

4. The winner of the snooker tournament gave an interview to *City Magazine*.

5. Do Freddie and Arlette shop at Superstore or Loblaws?

6. The sound of the dentist's drill made me nervous.

7. Kathleen or Anne will plan the trip to England.

Part 4: Subject–Verb Identification

Write **S** above each subject in each sentence; write **V** above each verb in each sentence. (17 points)

1. The lawyer and her new secretary carefully prepared the briefs for the court case.

2. Play ball with your children in the summer.

3. The cougar roared and threatened the rancher.

4. A gust of wind flipped the sign into the ditch.

5. Rodney was stapling the vapour barrier over the insulation.

6. Here are the containers of cream cheese for the icing.

7. The gardener planted the pole beans in May and harvested them in early July.

Chapter 11　Subjects and Verbs　189

Part 5: Subject–Verb Agreement

Read each sentence carefully. If the sentence contains a subject–verb agreement error, circle the error, and write the correction in the space provided. If the sentence does not contain a subject–verb agreement error, write **CORRECT** in the space provided. (30 points)

1. One of the photocopiers contains coloured paper. _____
2. There are three astronauts on the space mission. _____
3. Have Donna or Stephen found a good campsite? _____
4. Each of those cars sell for $50 000. _____
5. Where is the calculator and briefcase from my office? _____
6. Monica or her sister love to share an apartment. _____
7. The fireworks and the music were thrilling. _____
8. There are the bunch of grapes. _____
9. Each of the animals appear frightened. _____
10. One of the trainees was afraid to ask questions. _____
11. The organization are arranging a conference in Victoria. _____
12. The electrician or the apprentice wire each house according to the code. _____
13. Del and Maureen wants to make a pizza. _____
14. The witness and the prosecutor were both out of order in the courtroom. _____
15. Each of the tourists were given a small flag of Canada. _____

ESL POINTER

Indefinite Pronouns and Verb Agreement

Some words called *indefinite pronouns* usually take singular verbs. Remember: they are called *indefinite* because they do not refer to a specific person or thing.

Indefinite Pronouns

anyone	everybody	most
somebody	neither	none
one	any	someone
each	more	nothing
some	anything	everything

all	nobody	another
anybody	everyone	few
no one	either	

Indefinite pronouns such as *all*, *few*, *some*, *more*, and *most* may be singular or plural depending on what they are referring to.

All of the paper was ruined when I spilled my coffee on it. (refers to a single page)

All of the men were upset by their new marching orders. (refers to men)

Most of the banana was good. (refers to a single banana)

Most of the bananas were good. (refers to a bunch of bananas)

Some of the cheese was spoiled. (refers to a single piece of cheese)

Some of the cheeses were spoiled. (refers to a variety of cheeses)

Exercise 1   Agreement and Indefinite Pronouns

Read the following sentences. Find subject–verb agreement errors having to do with indefinite pronouns. Repair the errors. Some sentences may be correct as shown. Pay attention to count and non-count nouns. Check your answers in the Answer Key.

1. A few of the people was buying extra bread on sale.
   _____

2. Some of the movie were really funny.
   _____

3. Most of the children loves to play in the water of the splash pool.
   _____

4. One of his marriages were successful.
   _____

5. None of the wine in the antique bottle taste good.
   _____

6. Both of my partners want to stay in business.
   _____

7. All of the furniture were destroyed in the fire.
   _____

8. Alistair and most of his friends drinks too much on the weekends.

9. I feel sad because no one want to come to my party.

10. Most of the questions were difficult to answer on the nutrition exam.

11. All of the paint were used up for the barn.

12. Some of the evidence are unconvincing.

Exercise 2 More Subject–Verb Agreement

Read the following sentences. Find subject–verb agreement errors. Repair the errors. Some sentences may be correct as shown. Check your answers in the Answer Key.

1. The audience at the concert were throwing insults at the stage.

2. Under the counter there was piles of free samples for customers.

3. A case of carbonated juices was donated by Safeway.

4. Neither the dictator nor his henchmen were held responsible for the crimes.

5. Students or the professors votes in the coming campus election.

6. Someone on the rooftops was shooting at police.

7. Most of the photographs is memorable.

8. Nobody question his authority.

9. Do you know whether there is extra computers for student use?
   _____

10. The manager of the stores and his three assistants are developing a new marketing plan.
    _____

11. No one from these two campuses have been notified.
    _____

12. Each of the missing reports have been recovered by police.
    _____

13. Neither of the departments we contacted have a student rep.
    _____

14. The committee make its recommendations to the dean.
    _____

15. None of the conference were worthwhile.
    _____

16. The CD or the memos contains the needed information.
    _____

17. Nearly two-thirds of the town were destroyed by floods.
    _____

18. A loud flock of starlings were gathering in the cornfield.
    _____

CHECKOUT

1. Reduce memorization; analyze the whole sentence.
2. Complete sentences contain both subjects and verbs.
3. Auxiliary verbs help action verbs.

4. Verb phrases contain two types of verbs.
5. Modals set conditions on the action verb.
6. Compound subjects and compound verbs appear in some sentences.
7. Academic students should know the conventions of standard English.

chapter 12

Punctuation and Capitalization

Chapter Objectives

What will you have learned when you have completed this chapter? You will be able to

1. use punctuation correctly—the comma, the semicolon, the colon, the apostrophe, and quotation marks.

2. recognize conjunctive adverbs.

3. capitalize words as required.

Introduction

Punctuation means the use of marks like commas, periods, semicolons, and so on in writing to make meaning clear. Punctuation can be a matter of style, but as an academic English student, you still need to know about the standard use of rules of punctuation when you edit or proofread your written work for mistakes. You also must know about the rules of capitalization for your academic writing. *English handbooks*, which deal with the rules of punctuation, capitalization, spelling, grammar, usage, and specific writing forms like the essay or research paper, will provide a useful reference for you when you are working on your writing.

Try the following self-test to see what you remember about comma, semicolon, colon, and capital use. Check your answers in the Answer Key at the back of the book.

Chapter 12: Self-Test

Part 1: Comma Use

Insert commas wherever you think they are necessary in the following sentences. Be careful: some sentences may not require commas. (½ point each, 12 points)

1. The beaver the eagle the bulldog and the koala are all animals used as national symbols by four countries.

2. Before the play was finished Rita left the auditorium.

3. Ten of the horticulture students were turning the soil breaking up lumps and adding compost; four of the others were sorting seedlings checking labels and reviewing the garden plan; the last students were loading the plants into wagons moving them to the garden site and planting them in raised beds.

4. On November 10 1871 British Columbia joined the new federation of provinces called Canada.

5. Their wedding day will be 9 June 1998.

6. A loud bang I understand startled everyone in the movie theatre.

7. The last cigarette I had was in August 2000.

8. Walking briskly each day working in the garden and doing chores around the house improve a person's fitness levels.

9. Arlette joined the military on August 12 1988 and she left the service on October 16 1994.

10. Of course his remark was sarcastic stupid and rude.

Part 2: Semicolon Use

Add semicolons wherever you think they are necessary in the following sentences. Be careful: some sentences do not require semicolons. (1 point each, 14 points)

1. The children's rabbit escaped from its hutch fortunately, the neighbour found him and brought him home.

2. The crow wanted the handout from the tourist however, it was afraid of the tourist's dog which watched carefully.

3. We were afraid of the damage that the storm might do.

4. The clothes dryer was broken Monica had to hang the wash on the line.

5. During the heat, one of the workers was taken to hospital she was attended to immediately.

6. I think you look nice in green you may not agree with me about it.

7. Please allow me to introduce myself I am Count Dracula.

8. The family called the RCMP because they heard shots coming from down the street.

9. Sony is a well-known brand name in electronics it was the first company to develop a portable cassette player for individual use.

10. No one knew what had happened to the treasure everyone had a theory about it.

11. Many farmers prefer to work their fields at night they enjoy the peacefulness and the cool air.

12. *Pinocchio* and *Snow White* are two Disney classics my children love both of them.

13. The minister swayed in the pulpit the congregation sang a rousing hymn.

14. Do these packages include instructions with the software?

Part 3: Colon Use

Add colons wherever you think they are necessary in the following sentences. Be careful: some sentences do not require colons. (1 point each, 7 points)

1. Be sure to order the following parts the halogen bulb, the bolts, and the tap fittings.
2. He told us his secret he cherished every moment of his life.
3. Paul and Francine received some lovely wedding gifts a DVD player, a new set of china, and a trip to Tahiti.
4. The reason the rocket had not launched was ridiculous the door of the module had been left open.
5. The remedy consisted of peppermint leaves, lemon, and stout.
6. City hall sent out the following material property tax notices, schedules of council meetings, and notification of new zoning laws.
7. He was told to obey the following orders check all passports, question travellers about their destinations, and inspect hand luggage for weapons.

Part 4: Commas, Colons, and Semicolons

Add commas, colons, and semicolons wherever you think they are necessary in the following sentences. Some sentences may not require commas, colons, or semicolons. (½ point each, 10 points)

1. Grade 12 students met with first-year Mohawk College students they discussed courses at the post-secondary level demands of their schedules and careers in chemistry.
2. Steven was an energetic child who found every opportunity to get into mischief.
3. Having a car payment high rent and extra food costs stretched the family's budget to the limit no one had much extra personal spending money.
4. Most animals use some sort of communication exactly what the communication is how it functions and why a particular species uses it are questions scientists are trying to answer.
5. He on the other hand told the audience about his campaign platform however he forgot to tell them about his government's latest scandal.
6. Canadian poets like P. K. Page Margaret Atwood and Susan Musgrave still live and write in Canada other modern Canadian writers are leaving Canada to find opportunities in places like the United States Britain and France.
7. The children formed a circle the music began.
8. Wayne told Maureen his secret he had never loved her.

Part 5: Capitalization

Read each sentence carefully. Underline each letter which should be capitalized. (1 point each, 30 points)

1. Last monday uncle robert stopped at the four roads motel.
2. He consulted with several doctors in toronto.
3. The royal canadian mounted police were called in to investigate the robbery in port renfrew.
4. we ordered swiss steak and french fries.
5. The Alberta credit union is closed on saturdays and most evenings except Fridays.
6. mrs. walsh talked to a woman from the department of mines and resources.
7. Some of the students bought four safeway cheesecakes and a case of coke for the meeting at lansdowne junior high school.

Punctuation

The Comma

The comma *separates* items or *encloses parts of a sentence* to clarify meaning. There are two main categories of comma use.

CATEGORY 1

1. **Commas to Separate Words, Phrases, Letters, or Figures in a Series**

   Separate distinct items in a series because doing so helps keep meaning clear. Use a comma between the last item and the word *and* or *or*.

Unclear:	The children played cat and mouse, snakes and ladders and cops and robbers. (The meaning is unclear because the last comma in the series was omitted.)
More clear:	The children played cat and mouse, snakes and ladders, and cops and robbers. (The meaning is made more clear because the last comma is included.)
Unclear:	The students bought red, green, blue, mauve and pink notebooks. (The number of categories of notebook is unclear because the last comma is missing. There could be four or five.)
More clear:	The students bought red, green, blue, mauve, and pink notebooks. (The meaning is made more clear because the last comma is included. You can now tell the students have purchased five colours of notebooks.)

2. **Commas between Adjectives in a Series**

   Use commas to *separate adjectives in a sequence*. Be sure the adjectives are all describing the noun separately. If you can say "and" between the adjectives, you can use a comma.

   Rita used an old, clean, baby diaper to wash the windows. (Do not use a comma between the last adjective in a series and the item it describes.)

3. **Semicolons with Commas**

   When items in a series contain commas already, use semicolons to separate the larger items or units of meaning.

   Some of the workers sorted letters, bills, and pamphlets; others called people from the voters' lists, survey list, and telephone book; several other people helped the volunteers, food vendors, and caterers set up tables.

4. **Commas in a Date**

   Use a comma to separate parts of a date.

   Sheila left for her new job on Thursday, March 27, 2005.

   The celebration was to be held in October 2006. (No comma is used between the month and year when the day of the month is missing.)

   They announced their engagement on 5 February 2005. (No comma is used when the day of the month is given first.)

   They visited us at Easter 2004. (No comma is used between dates and holidays.)

   Their trip was in spring 1912. (No comma is used between dates and seasons.)

5. **Commas and Place Names**

   Use a comma to separate names of places.

   Calgary, Alberta   Moncton, New Brunswick
   Hull, Quebec   Sarnia, Ontario

   She received mail at the hotel, Centennial Square, Yorkton, Saskatchewan.

   Mona will see him in Abbotsford, British Columbia, at Christmas. (Two commas are used to set off the name of a province after a city has been named.)

6. **Commas and Parts of Letters and Memos**

   Use commas to set off the greeting in letters or memos and the closings of letters or memos.

   Dear Luigi,
   Dear Cousin Hobnob,

Sincerely yours,

Yours truly,

7. **Commas after Introductory Phrases or Clauses**

   During the hockey game, a fan threw a beer can at the ref.

   By the way, never call me again.

   Because he felt sorry for himself, Spike pouted.

   In a flash, Superman was on the roof.

Exercise 1   Using Commas

Place commas wherever you think they are necessary in the following sentences. Check your answers in the Answer Key at the back of the book.

1. At the largest music store in town Bob Dylan Leonard Cohen and Michael Jackson are all available on CD at sale prices.

2. After bathing the baby doing the wash returning some phone calls and cooking dinner Bob was exhausted.

3. She is looking for a copy of *National Geographic* from May 1998.

4. Election day in the province is 23 June 2005.

5. Alberta British Columbia Saskatchewan and Manitoba are considered the West in Canada.

6. Christmas 2003 and Easter 2004 were not as prosperous for the merchants as was predicted.

7. Have you ever visited Santa Barbara California or Portland Oregon?

8. The students were planning to bring cakes cookies juice and pop to the picnic.

9. Each hospital patient got cream and sugar bread and butter and a cup and saucer on his or her dinner tray.

10. Jennifer prepared the dough batter and pastry; Stella shaped the buns breads and cookies; Alicia baked sorted and stacked all the items.

11. We knitted pink red orange blue and yellow scarves and toques for the children.

12. For breakfast Mr. Stanton ordered a boiled egg light toast sugarless jam and puffed rice with skim milk.

13. Maria worked in Baden Baden Germany from February 22 1997 to July 6 2003.

14. We will tour Winnipeg Manitoba Edmonton Alberta and Swift Current Saskatchewan for the Small Business Association of Canada.

15. Rice whole wheat lentils and beans are all good sources of protein.

Exercise 2   Group Activity: Using Commas

Form a group of three to five. Together agree where to place commas in the following sentences.

1. Amy Ann Jamie and Frank will of course help set up the tables for bingo.

2. On February 14 2005 Jane and Robert Tony and Maggie and Louis and Cheryl will all take a trip together to Banff Alberta.

3. Sidney puzzled over his writing assignment wrote down several ideas for his essay and then began to write the first draft.

4. Tomatoes oranges lemons grapefruit and limes contain large amounts of vitamin C.

5. Mrs. Allonzo on the other hand voted against the motion at the meeting.

6. Worried about her student loan tired after a hard day's work and frustrated in the traffic Shirley began to cry.

7. Ilsa bought two loaves of fresh bread several grams of salami dill pickles hot mustard and crispy lettuce for the picnic sandwiches.

8. Farley's quote that was from the Bible seemed appropriate.

9. The last time I saw him was spring 1999.

10. A terrible earthquake occurred in Lima Peru in March 1952.

11. Uncle Maxwell dozing in his chair during the meeting suddenly fell with a loud crash.

12. The long lonely cries of the pup attracted the small curious children to the cage.

13. The letter stated that as you are aware the rent is past due.

14. Sweet potatoes curly endive oyster mushrooms and Japanese eggplant seem like exotic vegetables to me.

15. Elmo painted the figures cut them out and pasted them; Sam arranged them on the layout sheet pasted them in place and tacked them down; Helen photographed them placed them in a pile and removed them from the studio.

Exercise 3 Using Commas

Insert commas in the following sentences wherever you think they are necessary. Check your answers in the Answer Key.

1. Ronald needed glue nails drill bits and wood for his woodworking project.
2. Many of the students worried about test anxiety low marks and peer pressure when they were youngsters in school.
3. Her relatives will arrive from Sydney Australia on Tuesday August 23 2006.
4. The article was published in January 2003.
5. Squirrels chipmunks rats and mice are all considered rodents.
6. The cafeteria offered eggs and ham eggs and bacon and eggs and hash browns on its breakfast menu.
7. Two of the children were playing with beads blocks and boxes; five children were drawing painting and colouring; others were whispering listening and watching.
8. Antonio wanted to study psychology philosophy and music in his further studies.
9. The test flight was scheduled for 7 May 2004.
10. We will buy onion and jalapeño salt and vinegar and cheddar and bacon potato chips for the party.
11. Sarah arrived in Hamilton Ontario in fall 1991.
12. He enjoys rock and roll rhythm and blues and jazz on his car stereo.
13. Do you take cream and sugar milk or sugar in your coffee?
14. Maureen Alice Amanda and Terry are all applying for the job.
15. The new shopping mall will open on Saturday December 1 2007.
16. Don was born in Vancouver British Columbia; his son was born in Oshawa Ontario.
17. Apples quinces and crab apples are high in pectin content.
18. The book was interesting informative and current.
19. The puppy ran up the stairs into the bedroom through the patio doors and onto the deck.
20. He was concerned that we get a fair wage have good working conditions and know about safety on the job.
21. Poodles terriers spaniels and retrievers are popular breeds of dogs.

22. Arnold will fix the refrigerator repair the basement steps paint the fence and build a new deck this summer during his vacation.

23. The green grocer stocks Valencia Mandarin and Seville oranges.

24. November 11 1918 was a significant date in world history.

25. The employment agency helps clients write résumés prepare for interviews select appropriate interview techniques and do follow-ups.

CATEGORY 2

Use commas *to enclose information that explains, emphasizes, or interrupts.*

1. **Use commas to surround information that is non-essential.**

    Mr. Gaines, who is a coach, commented on the game for the radio listeners.

    He was worried, one might say, about his new position as manager.

    A clause that is not needed to define essential meaning is called *a non-restrictive clause*. The commas indicate it is non-essential information. *Who is a coach* is incidental information. You do not need it to identify the subject since his name is specifically given. It is information that may add interest, but it is *non-essential*. *Who is a coach* is called a *non-restrictive clause*. (A clause contains a subject and verb set.)

    One might say is called an *interrupter*, or *parenthetical expression*. It divides up the main idea, but it does not actually add information. It is considered a *non-restrictive*, or *non-essential*, element. It is not a clause because it usually does not contain a subject or verb.

Common Parenthetical Expressions

of course	therefore
it seems	no doubt
however	after all
on the other hand	for example
as a matter of fact	

Here are some common interrupters, or parenthetical expressions, used in sentences:

He will, after all, accept the new position.

Toni, on the other hand, does not agree with the policy.

Bears, as a matter of fact, are rather shy and solitary creatures.

The newscaster and the editor, it seems, were at odds over the issue.

2. **If the information is essential to the sentence, do not use commas.**

The woman who spoke with such passion impressed the audience.

Who spoke with such passion is needed to identify the speaker. If you use commas around the clause (a unit containing a subject and verb set), you will be saying that it is not needed (non-essential) in the sentence to identify the speaker. However, since the sentence requires the information for its intended meaning, you do not use commas. A clause that is needed to define or provide essential meaning is called a *restrictive clause*. *Who spoke with such passion* is a restrictive clause—no commas are used.

The student who invented the product won a prize.

Who invented the product is essential. You need to have the clause in order to identify which student has won the prize. *Who invented the product* is a restrictive clause.

Exercise 4 Using Commas

For this exercise, form a group of three to five people. Together agree where to place commas in the following sentences.

1. Timothy Findley's only mystery novel *The Telling of Lies* is set in a hotel in a vacation spot.

2. A circus on the other hand might be more fun for the children.

3. The people who waited outside the classroom were studying intensely for their upcoming exam.

4. Mr. Jones who runs the hardware store has decided to seek a seat in the next provincial election.

5. His excuse as a matter of fact was ridiculous and insulting.

6. The older children however tend to want to play games that require more interaction.

7. The meeting you understand was cancelled because of her lateness.

8. The bank more importantly knew about the error for some time.

9. The couple who vacationed in Mexico became terribly ill on their return.

10. Her story was in my opinion simply silly.

11. The priest who was working with the farmers in the fields became faint from the heat.

12. His dog which waits for him by the gate is well trained and loving.

13. Anna who is in training in the RN program has always enjoyed helping others.

14. The television show dreadful as it was was loved by millions.

15. Alfonso becoming braver by the minute interrupted the director to give his own viewpoint on the matter.

USING COMMAS IN COMPLEX SENTENCES

Complex sentences are made up of two or more clauses. Each clause has a subject–verb set. One clause can stand alone; it is called the *main clause*, or *independent clause*. The other clause cannot stand alone; it is called the *dependent clause*.

    main clause   dependent clause
Arnold won (because he was strongest).

      main clause   dependent clause
They slept in the tent (until a storm approached).

If a dependent clause comes first in a sentence, use a comma after it.

   dependent
    clause   main clause
(If I am late,) I will miss the meeting.

Exercise 5 *Complex Sentences*

Work in pairs to decide the answers to this exercise. Underline the main clauses. Put the dependent clauses in parentheses ( ), and then place commas wherever you think they are needed in the following sentences. Check your answers in the Answer Key.

1. Since he fought with his sister little Edward was sent to his room.

2. While Ronald was baking the bread we prepared the salad.

3. You can clean the windows after you have your lunch.

4. Some of the animals of the forest were frightened because the wind was so strong.

5. Unless I win the chess game I will be disappointed.

6. She waited at the campus until her boyfriend picked her up.

7. As Mario opened the library book a $20 bill fell to the floor.

8. Since my uncle is a nervous fellow the doctor has advised him to avoid driving in rush hour traffic.

9. The dog couldn't decide if she wanted to bury the bone or not.

10. While her parents were on vacation the teenager threw a wild party at the house.

11. The supervisor will call you if there is any work.

12. As Rodney turned to get the box of cereal from the store shelf a mouse scampered across the floor and disappeared under the bulk bins.

13. Because the snowstorm blew down some heavy trees power was lost in most of the city.

14. Max was elected president of the club because he is a tremendous organizer.

The Semicolon

A semicolon has *one main purpose*—to *join* two complete ideas (*independent*, or *main*, *clauses*) or simple sentences together.

> John loves to watch hockey; he particularly enjoys the playoff series.

Notice that the semicolon joins one sentence—*John loves to watch hockey.*—to another sentence—*He particularly enjoys the playoff series.* The semicolon in this example works like the conjunction *and*.

CONJUNCTIVE ADVERBS

Be sure that the word you think is a conjunction really is one. *However, moreover, otherwise, consequently, therefore, likewise, nevertheless, furthermore,* and *indeed* are not conjunctions. They do not join. They are called *conjunctive adverbs*. Always use correct punctuation, usually a semicolon, with these words.

> Matthew was leaving for Europe; consequently, he felt rushed.
>
> You must secure the lock firmly; otherwise, the door swings open easily.
>
> The veterinarian warned the cat owner not to give the kitten feather toys; nevertheless, the owner disregarded the advice.

One way to check if a word is functioning as a conjunction in a sentence is to *try to move the word to another position* in the sentence. If the word does not make sense in another position, then it is a conjunction because *conjunctions are fixed* in a particular position.

On the other hand, *if you are able to move the word* into any other position, then you have probably discovered a *conjunctive adverb*. If you move the word, you will see that nothing remains to join the clauses or simple sentences together.

> Samuel wanted to buy a new car however the payments were too high.

Try moving *however* to another position in the second clause. Can you do it?

Because you can move the word, it cannot be a conjunction. After you move it, you will see that there is no word or punctuation mark to join the two clauses.

> Samuel wanted to buy a new car ?? the payments were too high however.
>
> Samuel wanted to buy a new car ?? the payments however were too high.

Use a semicolon to join the two main clauses. Use a comma after the conjunctive adverb.

> Samuel wanted to buy a new car; however, the payments were too high.

Exercise 6 Group Activity: The Semicolon

Form a group of three to five students. Together correct the semicolon use in the following sentences. If the sentence is correct, write **OK** after it. Check your answers with some of the other groups. Answers can also be checked in the Answer Key.

1. Tony was afraid of dogs, therefore, he would not consider a job as a postman. _____

2. After a long night of tossing and turning, Elrod made up his mind about accepting the promotion; the decision made him happy. _____

3. Arnold, a considerate person, offered to stay after the dance and help clean up the social director did not hear his kind offer and walked past him without speaking. _____

4. He tried raising patio tomatoes; that was an expensive disaster. _____

5. Please be seated; the doctor will be with you in a moment. _____

6. The students worked very hard to complete the project, however, they were unable to meet the deadline. _____

7. The contractor was unsure of removing the large tree from the front of the lot; and he consulted with an architectural landscaper to help sort things out. _____

8. The dance pair was dazzling in their finery; as they swept across the floor to the beat of the samba. _____

9. Unfortunately, Mr. Costanos cannot come to the phone; because he is in conference. _____

10. The explorers dove into the icy waters; hoping to find examples of blue-green algae, they were determined in their quest. _____

11. At three, call Mrs. Penman about the shipment of Crazy Glue; at four, call our Toronto office about the Hula Hoops. _____

12. The Cat Fanciers' Club of Regina met in the basement of the church; and the meeting was to plan the annual cat show to be held in the Memorial Arena. _____

13. The letter lay on the front porch; it seemed ominous to Teddy because it bore the seal of the RCMP. _____

14. The small boy pouted and shouted his demands; moreover, he instructed his parents on what they were to order for him in the restaurant. _____

15. California is a beautiful state, but it is running out of fresh drinking water. _____

The Colon

A colon has two major uses. The most common use is to show your reader that you will be giving a list of some sort.

> Eleanor gathered her equipment: camera, tripod, lens case, and light meter.

Notice that when you choose to use a colon, you do not separate your verb and object with a colon.

> **Misuse of colon:** Eleanor gathered: camera, tripod, lens case, and light meter.

Do not separate the verb *gathered* from its objects—*camera, tripod, lens case,* and *light meter.*

A second major use of the colon is to add a second sentence which explains the first sentence.

> Nat knew that the preparation work for the wedding cake was complicated: she had baked the fruitcake months in advance and had to have at least a week prior to the wedding before she iced it.

Notice that the second idea is a complete sentence that adds explanation to the first sentence. Using a colon every now and then in your writing helps to enrich and enliven your writing style. However, don't overuse it because, like anything used too often, it can become boring and predictable.

Exercise 7   Colon Use

Check the colon use in each of the following sentences. If you think the sentence is right as given, write **OK** after the sentence. If you think the sentence has a colon error, repair the error. Check your answers in the Answer Key.

1. The campers were told to bring: pots, tents, hatchets, and matches to the camp. _____

2. Several features of a successful relationship include: trust, humour, communication, and concern. _____

3. Being an engineer was not what he expected: the piles of paperwork he faced made him feel more like a clerk. _____

4. Please include the following in my order: toothpicks, live bait, six artichokes, a large can of Reddi-whip, and a bag of ice. _____

5. Her job consisted of: inspecting the site plan, reviewing the septic site, and checking perc tests. _____

6. We learn to give love: it is a gift that costs little but means a great deal. _____

7. Murphy, my crazy cocker spaniel, was known for: chewing furniture, messing on the rugs, stealing the children's toys, and barking at the drop of a pin. _____

8. Tell them to: open the mail, fax me important messages, and send out the orders to Waterloo. _____

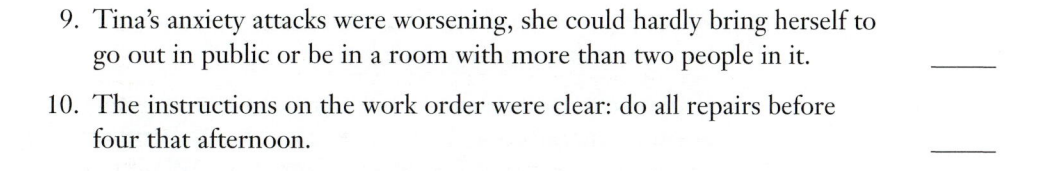

9. Tina's anxiety attacks were worsening, she could hardly bring herself to go out in public or be in a room with more than two people in it. _____

10. The instructions on the work order were clear: do all repairs before four that afternoon. _____

Exercise 8 Adding Colons and Commas

Add colons and commas wherever you think they are necessary in the following sentences. Be careful: some sentences may not require colons or commas at all.

1. His answer was always the same it protected him from the truth.
2. Many woodworking hobbies require expensive tools power saws electric drills lathes sanders and routers.
3. Meteorites are not stars at all they are pieces of metal or stone that fall toward the earth.
4. Yanni cancelled her dancing lessons she did not like her instructor.
5. Some languages are easier to learn than others although some are less commonly used.
6. Robins towhees and blackbirds are noisy birds that have a rich vocabulary of sound.
7. The group will discuss the following topics parenting nutrition discipline and games.
8. Since he had left his hospital job Norman had gotten a string of jobs car washer janitor dishwasher and hamburger chef.
9. Basket weaving is not as simple to do as people think it requires a great deal of patience finger dexterity and knowledge of patterns and materials.
10. The church committee elected the following people Mr. Biggs Mrs. Bannish Mrs. King and Ms. Merihue.

Exercise 9 Group Activity: Comma, Semicolon, and Colon Use

Form a group of three to five people. Add commas, semicolons, or colons to each of the following sentences wherever the group thinks they are necessary.

1. South Korea sometimes called the Republic of Korea has a population of approximately 45 million.
2. No one listened to Rebecca's excuses they had heard them all before.
3. The college hired an ombudsperson who would hear the complaints of both students and faculty the ombudsperson would try to represent all issues without bias.
4. When you are sending your children to camp please include the following items extra socks extra underwear a flashlight with extra batteries rain boots and a raincoat.

5. Although we enjoyed the dinner expensive as it was we did not appreciate the humour of the stand-up comedian.

6. Rapée pie a favourite in Quebec contains simple ingredients chicken pork rabbit potatoes and onions.

7. The chairperson of the committee gave the following directives to the committee meet deadlines attend every meeting and refrain from smoking.

8. Wallace opened a small craft stand at the ferry terminal he sold many items handcrafted belts quilted goods seashell ornaments and handmade soaps.

9. At one time the Inuit used the igloo when travelling it was a dome-shaped shelter made from snow blocks which protected the traveller from biting winds.

10. Everyone arrived on time Terry Randy Maxine and Marge.

11. Because Irene was sick she missed three of her math classes.

12. Stop shaking the table I am trying to draw a picture!

13. Police dogs specially trained police and mediators were sent into the hostage-taking area.

14. The DVD player the television the stereo the computer and the answering machine were damaged by the power surge.

The Apostrophe

Use an apostrophe in two cases: when you want to show that someone owns something (*possession*) or when you are using a shortened form of two words, called a *contraction*.

SHOWING POSSESSION

Simon's dog, the children's lunches, the rabbits' warren, her friend's address

Rather than learning complicated rules for the use of an apostrophe, remember this: start from your meaning—the root word. For example, if you were going to write about a town and its decision to change its water protection policy, then work from the root word—*town*—out to the possessive form:

town ⟶ town's ⟶ town's policy

If, on the other hand, you intend to talk about several towns and their policies, start with the new root word—*towns*—and work out to the possessive:

towns ⟶ towns' ⟶ towns' policies

As you know, some nouns in English do not form their plural in a regular way. Look at these examples:

men, women, children, mice, deer, sheep, feet, curricula, antennae, alumni, analyses, teeth

In such cases, these are the root words. It would make no sense for you to add an additional *-s* or *-es* to each one like this: *mens, womens, teeths, deers,* and so forth because these are not the plural forms. They are nonsense words. To make irregular plural nouns possessive, use the same procedure: work out from the root word (which is already in the plural):

Correct: men's hats

Incorrect: mens' hats

(There is no root word *mens*. Always *look to the immediate left of the apostrophe for the root word*. You can see that immediately to the left of the apostrophe is *mens*, which is not a word.)

Correct: women's clubs

Incorrect: womens' clubs

Correct: children's toys

Incorrect: childrens' toys

A special situation arises in connection with two people and ownership. If you wanted them to share ownership of something, then you would write the last person's name in the possessive case by using an apostrophe. If, however, you wanted to show that each person owned something separately, you would make each person's name in the possessive case.

Bill and Sharon's restaurant (jointly owned—a single restaurant shared)

Bill's and Sharon's restaurants (Each person owns a restaurant.)

the cat and kittens' blanket (They share the same blanket.)

the cat's and kittens' blankets (The cat has a blanket. The kittens share one blanket.)

the cat's and kitten's blankets (The cat has a blanket. Now there is only one kitten with its own blanket.)

CONTRACTIONS

The second major use of apostrophes is in *contractions—when two words are shortened into one*. The apostrophe takes the place of the missing letters.

Common Contractions

here is	here's
you are	you're
he will	he'll
she is	she's
it is or it has	it's
there is	there's
I am	I'm

will not	won't
can not (or cannot)	can't
they will	they'll
I will	I'll

Exercise 10 Using Apostrophes

Read each sentence. Think carefully whether you will need to use apostrophes or not. Add apostrophes wherever you think they are necessary. Check your answers in the Answer Key at the back of the book.

1. None of Zoes flowers survived the winter, and shes upset about it.
2. Two of the childrens socks are missing from the dryer.
3. One of the mens complaints was about overtime pay.
4. The golfers swing was so poor that everyone ducked to avoid being hit.
5. His cats name tag was missing from its collar.
6. Tom and Annas card shop was sold last week.
7. The ships whistle blew and the passengers lunch was disturbed by the noise.
8. Theyll be over to talk with you in a minute.
9. The hospitals surgeon told us hed be assisting in Dads operation.
10. Were afraid youre too late to save the sheeps life.

Capitalization

Use 1

Always use a capital letter at the beginning of every sentence.

>Mr. Woods lifts weights.
>Fish are animals.

Use 2

Always capitalize a person's name and any title that goes with that name.

>I watched Patty and Nell in the contest.
>Have you met Professor Ko?

I introduced Dr. Brim.
Mrs. Wippinski is my aunt.

Do *not* use capitals to identify occupations or professional rank unless they are part of a person's title.

Wendy is an electrician.
Who is the new lawyer?
Bob is now manager of the department.
How pleased we were to meet Premier Allen!

Use 3

Always capitalize names of relatives when you are using them as a kind of title.

I decided to ask Mother.

Have you spoken to my mother? (You need no capital here. You are not addressing your mother by her title.)

I think Uncle Bob is a card.
My friend's uncle is a farmer.

Use 4

Always capitalize the word *I*.

I want to know why.
I can't go.

Exercise 11   Capitalization

Put in capital letters where they are needed. Check your answers in the Answer Key.

1. has uncle fred taken the job with doctor robinson?
2. did i tell you that my mother knows your uncle seth?
3. the supervisor told mr. eng to talk to his doctor.
4. early in the afternoon the teacher talked to superintendent davis.
5. inspector gladeau discussed the incident with chief beckley.

Use 5

Always use capital letters to distinguish specific cultures, nationalities, and languages.

Do you speak French?
We are Canadian citizens.
Her friend is Jewish.

Use 6

Always use capital letters for days of the week, months of the year, and special holiday names.

> I'll visit you on Boxing Day.
>
> Ralph will be in Ontario on Monday.

Do *not* capitalize the names of seasons: fall, winter, spring, summer.

Use 7

Always capitalize the first word and the important words in the titles of books.

> I enjoyed reading *A Bend in the River*.
>
> Our English class is reading *The Fall of the Sparrow*.

Exercise 12 Capitalization

Put in capital letters where necessary. Check your answers in the Answer Key.

1. *a whale for the killing* is the title of a book by farley mowat, the famous canadian author.

2. many indo-canadian members of the community will be visiting india this summer.

3. my mother and i will spend christmas together in halifax.

4. last tuesday the manager of the department told us that march and april would have sales in spring fashions.

5. did you know that gwen speaks fluent english, italian, and spanish?

6. mark read *twelve days to a better body*.

7. a well-known scientist talked to dr. johnson at the convention in red deer.

8. new year's day is a statutory holiday for canadian workers.

9. the notice reported free french lessons to the residents of the city of moncton.

10. chef schneider prepares delicious german dishes.

Use 8

Use capital letters in the names of places in addresses.

> They live at 22 Alder Way.
>
> The newest movie theatre is on Johnson Street near Broad Avenue.

Use 9

Use capital letters for geographical names.

> They canoed on the Sooke River.
> June moved to Swift Current, Saskatchewan, from Grande Prairie, Alberta.
> My sister-in-law used to live in Thunder Bay, Ontario.

Use 10

Capitalize words like *river*, *lake*, and *mountains* when they are in the name of the place.

> North Saskatchewan River
> Lake Erie
> Rocky Mountains

Use 11

Use capital letters for the names of organizations or institutions.

> She works for the Ministry of Health.
> We went to Coldale High School.
> Mariette works for the Ontario Hydro Commission.

Use 12

Use capital letters for the names of specific buildings.

> They met at Oxford Towers.
> That hotel is the Dominion Hotel.

Use 13

Use capital letters for brand names or product names with registered trademarks.

> Phillip organized a workshop with Microsoft technicians.
> My aunt loves Diet Coke on ice in the summer.
> Buy two boxes of Kleenex at the drugstore, please.

Exercise 13 Capitalization

Put in capital letters where they are necessary.

1. the niagara peninsula is known by canadians and americans alike.

2. does the fraser river flow into the pacific ocean?

3. we attended a seminar at the holiday inn in nanaimo, british columbia.

4. morgan has a savings account at island credit union in the herald building.

5. while vivian was on james island, she met some people from montreal, quebec.

6. The union of public employees talked to representatives from the ministry of labour.

7. my aunt laverne sold her house on fernie street and bought a condominium in sydney, n.s.

8. i told her to talk to ms. macdonald, the minister of employment.

9. arlette bought the book *best restaurants in canada* at the gift shop.

10. the burlington recreation centre hosted hockey teams from across canada and the united states.

11. we will make german potato salad for supper on saturday.

12. a german shepherd dog is an intelligent, trainable, and loyal breed.

13. i knew him when he attended mount royal secondary school.

14. on mother's day, i'll send my mother a bouquet of carnations and roses.

15. the students of edmonton college organized a skiing trip to the cascade mountains.

16. for the city, a french poodle or a welsh terrier makes a friendly family pet.

17. i bought a box of christie's cookies and a can of sunrype apple juice as treats for the kids i babysit in oak bay.

18. my honda lawnmower has lasted for more than six years.

19. the boy scouts had a carwash at the petrocan station on shelbourne street.

20. the university of victoria had a guest speaker in the clearihue building last thursday evening.

21. she wears jordache jeans, zanny tee-shirts, and bongo shoes.

22. my brother-in-law is the manager of the toy shop on yates street.

23. uncle john's toyota corolla station wagon runs better than his volkswagen.

24. the president of the alberta government employees union was quoted in wednesday night's calgary herald.

25. the teenager bought a bottle of pepsi and a package of hostess chips.

Chapter 12: Review Test

Part 1: Commas

Insert commas wherever you think they are necessary in the following sentences. Be careful: some sentences may not require commas. (½ point each, 12 points)

1. The dogwood the wild rose the crocus and the trillium are all flowers used as provincial emblems.
2. Maxwell left his shift early because he felt feverish.
3. Five of the employees were collecting the mail sorting the addresses and checking the postal codes; two of the others were checking addresses on parcels sorting packages and checking labels; one employee was feeding the letters into the scanner checking addresses and monitoring the computer.
4. On December 8 1991 the Soviet Union became the Commonwealth of Independent States.
5. The deadline for project proposals is 7 May 2005.
6. The meeting was of course interrupted by the same individual.
7. The last trip I had was in July 2000.
8. Chewing furniture stealing food and pestering the cat made the new pup rather unpopular.
9. Frederick Ormstead joined the college on February 17 1989 and he retired from teaching on August 26 2003.
10. For your information misunderstandings can be avoided by using clear communication focussed goals and understandable language.

Part 2: Semicolons

Add semicolons wherever you think they are necessary in the following sentences. Be careful: some sentences do not require semicolons. (1 point each, 14 points)

1. Marilyn applied for the job as technician she believes her experience qualifies her for the job.
2. The teenagers longed to go to the concert therefore, they were prepared to spend the night in line waiting for tickets.
3. She was certain that his answer would be disappointing.
4. Mediterranean cooking is very flavourful and healthful many cooks are experimenting with some of the classic recipes.
5. After the summer storm, six of their rose bushes were broken Lewis has managed to save two of them.

6. The doctor made a decision you may not agree with her.
7. The master carpenter studied his blueprints he puzzled over a set of difficult stairs.
8. Martine was frustrated because she had not won the prize.
9. There are three rattlesnakes found in Canada one called the western rattlesnake can be found in the southerly parts of three western provinces.
10. Paulina and Vincent broke off their engagement no one is certain what happened between them.
11. Ruffed grouse are chicken-like birds of the woodlands the males make a distinct drumming sound.
12. Politics and government gossip don't interest Carla in the least.
13. Helmut coaches soccer at the university his son is on the team.
14. Her illness left her feeling restless and moody.

Part 3: Colons

Add colons wherever you think they are necessary in the following sentences. Be careful: some sentences do not require colons. (1 point each, 7 points)

1. Don't make the mistake of giving out credit card numbers over the phone or telling strangers what your bank account number is.
2. Finally, the plan was revealed everyone was to get a cut in personal taxes.
3. The children received many gifts from their grandparents books, dolls, painting sets, and video games.
4. His excuse for arriving late for the important meeting seemed suspicious thieves had stolen his car.
5. Her recipe for good health was exercise, good nutrition, plenty of sleep, and lots of humour.
6. Jill and April made the following costumes for the play one platypus, three penguins, four cats, and one toad.
7. Good hockey players require certain skills and talents they must be fast on the ice, agile on skates, and quick-thinking.

Part 4: Commas, Colons, and Semicolons

Add commas, colons, and semicolons wherever you think they are necessary in the following sentences. Be careful: some sentences may not require commas, colons, or semicolons. (1/2 point each, 10 points)

1. The captain of the hockey team met with management they discussed training time contract demands and endorsement rights.

2. Emile proved to be a wonderful juggler who could entertain crowds of all sizes.

3. Eating patterns family values and parenting skills may begin at home in our early years we continue to modify these beliefs during our life times.

4. The reporter on the other hand would not reveal his sources he believed in protecting his informant.

5. We worried of course in spite of ourselves however, we did not reveal our anxiety.

6. Sports such as boxing kick-boxing and wrestling are considered to be too violent some groups are openly opposing them lobbying for new laws against them and speaking out against the sponsors.

7. Do not forget your dental appointment the dentist must check your sore tooth and repair the filling.

8. The rainy evening was to be different for Howard he was to meet the woman of his dreams.

Part 5: Capitalization

Read each sentence carefully. Underline each letter which should be capitalized. (1 point each, 30 points)

1. Last tuesday aunt lisa stayed at the pacific princess hotel.

2. I converse with a group on the internet.

3. the canadian cancer society sells daffodils every april to raise money for cancer research.

4. We prepared swiss fondue and german chocolate cake.

5. the bank of montreal is closed most evenings, except thursdays and fridays.

6. mr. eriksen talked about the situation with his neighbour, mr. yinh, who works for the department of fisheries.

7. Some of the parents brought thrifty's nacho chips, mexicale salsa and a case of pepsi for the ball game at spectrum high school.

ESL POINTER

The Use of Quotation Marks in Direct Speech

Quotation marks look like this: " ". They are used *to surround the words a speaker says directly*. Open quotation marks show the beginning of the speaker's words like this: ". Closed quotation marks show the end of the speaker's words like this: ".

In the English language quotation marks are essential when you are directly quoting what someone says. In other words, use quotation marks in direct speech.

Stephano said, "I will never love anyone the way I love you!"

Notice that the quotation starts with a phrase identifying who the speaker is and a verb—*Stephano said*. Then you will see a comma used to separate the speaker identification from his or her words. Then you will see open quotation marks, followed by the speaker's actual words. Then you will notice a closing mark of punctuation at the end of the speaker's sentence. Then you will see closed quotation marks.

If the speaker's words are interrupted because the identifying phrase is placed in the middle of the sentence, then do not use a capital letter for the second part of the speaker's words unless the beginning word requires it (a name, the pronoun *I*, or a specific place).

"I will never love anyone," Stephano said, "the way I love you!"

or

"I will never love anyone," said Stephano, "the way I love you!"

Do not use quotation marks if you are reporting speech indirectly. In these cases, you will notice that what the speaker said is a fact you are reporting. You will usually introduce the indirect quotation with *that*.

Stephano said that he will never love anyone the way he loves you.

Notice that you are indirectly reporting what Stephano has said; therefore, no quotations marks are needed.

Exercise 1 Using Quotation Marks in Direct Speech

Add correct punctuation to each of the following quotations. Work in pairs. Try to determine the correct answers together.

1. The small child whined I want another cookie!
2. Through the action of the waves the teacher explained the shore line is ever-changing.
3. I don't want to walk by myself said Milla it is too dark outside.
4. The mechanic said he would not be able to fix my car until Thursday.
5. No one can predict the economy accurately mused Professor Plumply.
6. When I arrived, no one was at the party explained Mrs. Garr.
7. Tell them to stop making that terrible racket ordered the frustrated writer.
8. Alain exclaimed all my emails are lost!
9. The chief surgeon told the patient you will have to stop smoking.
10. What does it matter asked Marie if I finish this on time or not.

Exercise 2   Practice with Direct and Indirect Speech

Change the form of each sentence as requested. Check your answers with the Answer Key at the back of the book.

1. The clerk replied, "The cost of mailing the package is $20.00." (change to indirect speech).

2. My sister-in-law said she is afraid of mice and spiders. (change to direct speech)

3. One television reporter said that he was shocked by the damage to the building. (change to direct speech)

4. "In about two months' time," Chula explained, " I will be on a train in the Sudan." (change to indirect speech)

5. "One of the things I dislike the most," the president stated, "is being misquoted by the press." (change to indirect speech)

6. The two students complained to Professor Nguyen that their marks were incorrect on the economics exam. (change to direct speech)

7. Tara remarked, "I won't work on week nights any longer unless I get a raise." (change to indirect speech)

CHECKOUT

1. Academic English students need to acquire and use exemplary writing skills.

2. An English handbook can provide a useful reference to help with your writing work.

3. If a dependent clause comes before the main clause in a sentence, use a comma after the dependent clause.

4. *However, moreover, consequently, therefore, likewise, nevertheless, furthermore, otherwise,* and *indeed* are not conjunctions. They are conjunctive adverbs.

5. The correct use of standard punctuation and capitalization in academic writing helps to make meaning clear to the reader.

chapter 13

Modifiers

Chapter Objectives
What will you have learned when you have completed this chapter? You will be able to
1. distinguish between the forms of adjectives used to compare things.
2. recognize adverbs which tell *how*, *where*, *why*, or *when*.
3. use adjective and adverb prepositional phrases.
4. avoid misuse of *good*, *well*, *bad*, *badly*, *real*, and *really*.

Introduction

Modifiers are words that describe other words. They are used to provide detail and colour to sentences. You can use them to show what kind or sort of noun you are discussing, and when, where, why, or how something occurred. Basic modifiers in English are *adjectives*, *adverbs*, and *prepositional phrases*.

To check out your knowledge of modifiers, try the following self-test. Check your answers in the Answer Key found at the back of the book.

Chapter 13: Self-Test

Part 1: Finding Adjectives

Read the following sentences. Underline all adjectives that you read. Note: not all sentences contain adjectives. (1 point each, 18 points)

1. They were ashamed of the fact that they had been very greedy.
2. The impatient customer left the convenience store in a huff.
3. I recommend fresh lemons for the recipe and not lemon extract.
4. The historic lighthouse had the most wonderful view of the beautiful bay at sunset.
5. Hubert warned the excited tourists about the light-fingered thieves that roamed the bustling streets of Cairo.
6. Madelaine quietly spoke to the young children as they entered the imposing doors of the dinosaur exhibit.

7. He cut himself a thick slice of blueberry pie.

8. A shaggy moss partially covered the stone statue.

9. Turpentine has a very strong odour.

10. He usually waits until seven in the evening.

Part 2: Finding Adverbs

Read the following sentences. Underline all adverbs that you read. Note: not all sentences contain adverbs. (1 point each, 20 points)

1. With a shy smile, the supervisor quietly thanked his workers for the retirement gift.
2. Today we are expecting Joanne to bring the green salad to the potluck supper because she usually does.
3. The rescue team desperately tried to save the hikers who had fallen quite dangerously close to the rapids.
4. Anna is intensely watching the skating competition because her daughter is performing now.
5. He will certainly call you if a position unexpectedly opens tomorrow.
6. The hockey announcer talks excitedly when he is not on the air.
7. Many students are extremely happy with just one course in English; however, I believe students need more work than a single course provides.
8. The opposite page has clear diagrams.
9. She tied her hair tightly into a ponytail; then she began her exercise routine.
10. A tiger lily is a commonly grown plant which can do rather well in poor soils.

Part 3: Finding Prepositional Phrases

Read the following sentences. Put parentheses ( ) around every prepositional phrase you read. Note: not all sentences contain prepositional phrases. (1 point each, 12 points)

1. Despite the weather, the ball game continued in the rain.
2. We were worried about the exam on Monday, but we did not discuss our fears with anyone.
3. Do you have fresh vegetables in your garden?
4. Helen did not appreciate the joke in the lunch room, but I found it funny.
5. The workers invited their old supervisor for a beer at the hotel.
6. Please relax; the flight will be over in a short time.
7. A crowd of students gathered just as the speaker arrived on the platform.

Part 4: Identifying Adjective and Adverb Prepositional Phrases

Read the following sentences. Put parentheses ( ) around each prepositional phrase you read. Then write **ADJ** above the prepositional phrase if it is an adjective prepositional phrase. Write **ADV** above the prepositional phrase if it is an adverb prepositional phrase. (1 point each, 10 points) (½ point for finding, ½ point for identifying **ADJ** or **ADV**)

1. The woman from Brazil talked to immigration officials.
2. A container of pumpkins and a large vase of sunflowers decorated the stage of the hall.
3. One of the planks is missing from the deck.
4. They wandered through the mall while the children talked about their plans.
5. Maria gathered the clothes in her arms.

Part 5: Using Comparisons

Underline the correct comparative form of the forms given in parentheses. (1 point each, 10 points)

1. The circus ride we had at the PNE was (good, better, best) than the Ferris wheel at the fair.
2. Ron was the (more, most) ambitious engineer I have ever met.
3. The (bad, worse, worst) film we saw was *Freddie Got Fingered.*
4. Of the two flavours, grape is the (good, better, best).
5. That job is the (little, less, least) complicated of the four I have to do.
6. Carey was the (much, more, most) energetic of the recruits in the class.
7. That is the (more, most) sensible of the two solutions.
8. Sol is (good, better, best) at cooking than his wife is.
9. (Many, More, Most) tourists visited the display than the organizers had expected.
10. This restaurant is (good, better, best) at presenting food than the average place.

Part 6: Your Own Sentences

Make up your own sentences according to the directions given below. Follow instructions carefully. (2 points each, 10 points) (to be marked by the instructor)

1. Use the word *sell* in a sentence that contains one adverb prepositional phrase. Underline the adverb prepositional phrase.

_____

_____

2. Use the word *pretty* in a sentence that contains two adverbs. Underline the adverbs.
_____
_____

3. Use the word *game* in a sentence that contains one adjective prepositional phrase.
_____
_____

4. Use the word *party* in a sentence that contains two adjectives. Underline the adjectives.
_____
_____

5. Use the word *child* in a sentence that contains one adjective and one adverb.
_____
_____

Part 7: Usage

Correct the following sentences by crossing out the incorrectly used adjective or adverb. Write in the correct form above the incorrect form. (5 points)

1. Amy is a real talented actor.
2. The puppy was behaving bad.
3. Francis and Rob danced good together.
4. Several loaves of bread were not baked good enough.
5. Stella felt badly about telling her boyfriend their relationship was over.

Adjectives

Creating Interesting Sentences

You know every sentence contains at least one subject–verb (S-V) set or subject–verb–object (S-V-O) set.

    S   V
The boy studies.

  S   V
Dogs growl.

   S   V   V
A woman is reading.

   S   V   O
The child builds models.

```
      S     V      O
```
Hillary knits tams.

The sentences above are "bare bones"; there is no detail in them. To make sentences more interesting to read and more exact in meaning, you can add words of description. Suppose you were to describe every noun in each of the sample sentences. The sentences then might look like this:

```
                  N
The redheaded boy studies.
     describer
```

```
          N
Wild dogs growl.
describer
```

```
                   N
A tall, young woman is reading.
   describers
```

The energetic child builds interesting models.
    describer   describer

```
   N                              N
Hillary knits crazy, colourful tams.
              describers
```

The added describer words help to distinguish what kinds of nouns you are talking about. *Words that describe nouns* are called *adjectives*.

Exercise 1   Group Activity: Adjectives

Form a group of three to five people. Complete the following activity together. Below is a list of nouns. Add two adjectives to the front of each noun. Place a comma between your adjectives. Be prepared to share your answers.

Example: a tiny, efficient kitchen

1. a _____, _____ beach

2. the _____, _____ restaurant

3. some _____, _____ geese

4. a _____, _____ course

5. two _____, _____ children

6. the _____, _____ dessert

7. a _____, _____ dog

8. one _____, _____ apple

9. the _____, _____ bus

10. some _____, _____ sentences

228   Part 2   Sentence Foundations

11. several _____, _____ people

12. the _____, _____ shoes

13. a _____, _____ liquid

14. _____, _____ garbage

15. the _____, _____ horse

Exercise 2 Sentences with Adjectives

Work in pairs. Use each of the following nouns in sentences. Use three adjectives in each of your sentences. Be prepared to share your answers with the rest of the group.

1. friend _____
_____

2. party _____
_____

3. furniture _____
_____

4. ocean _____
_____

5. breakfast _____
_____

6. park _____
_____

7. garden _____
_____

8. inspector _____
_____

9. storm _____

_____

10. grandmother _____

_____

11. mouse _____

_____

12. news _____

_____

13. trouble _____

_____

14. onions _____

_____

Forms of Adjectives

Adjectives are often used when we compare things.

> Eunice makes a good hamburger; Arnie's is better, but Mel's is the best.

In the sample sentence, you see three *adjectives of comparison*—*good*, *better*, and *best*.

Good is used to describe one item. *Better* is used to talk about the differences between two things. *Best* refers to the differences among three things.

Using Regular Adjectives to Compare

Positive (One)	Comparative (Two)	Superlative (Three+)
tall	taller	tallest
great	greater	greatest
happy	happier	happiest
friendly	friendlier	friendliest

Using Irregular Adjectives to Compare

Positive (One)	Comparative (Two)	Superlative (Three+)
good	better	best
bad	worse	worst
little	less	least
much	more	most
many	more	most

ADJECTIVES USING MORE AND MOST

You can show comparison using adjectives by simply adding *more* or *most* to a single form. Below are some examples.

Using *More* and *Most* to Compare

Positive (One)	Comparative (Two)	Superlative (Three+)
fortunate	more fortunate	most fortunate
silly	more silly	most silly
heavy	more heavy	most heavy
shady	more shady	most shady
graceful	more graceful	most graceful
plump	more plump	most plump
satisfied	more satisfied	most satisfied

There are different ways of making comparisons:

Instead of saying: plump—more plump—most plump
You could say: plump—plumper—plumpest

But not all adjectives can use this regular form.

You cannot say: graceful—gracefuler—gracefulest

Mixed Adjective Forms

It is important not to mix adjective forms when using adjectives that compare. A common mistake is to mix *more* and *most* with the regular adjective form; an error results like this:

Incorrect: more friendlier
Incorrect: more better
Incorrect: more drier

Exercise 3 Adjectives That Compare

From any of the lists on the previous pages select adjectives which correctly complete the following sentences. Check your answers in the Answer Key.

1. Although this year's statistics for child poverty are _____, last year's were _____.

2. I think Valerie's is the _____ restaurant in town.

3. Tom felt horrible because he thought he had given the _____ speech of his life.

4. Of the two arguments, the first is _____.

5. Mary Ruth remarked that the new hotel had the _____ service in the city, and she would not return to the place.

6. Uncle Clifford said, "That was the _____ enjoyable time I ever had!"

7. It is _____ important of all that you check the pressure gauge.

8. The movie was _____ interesting than the book.

9. Cougars are _____ dangerous when food is scarce.

10. Today's announcement was _____ welcome than last week's.

11. Of the two brothers, Quigley is the _____ charming.

12. I seldom think about which are the _____ exciting fashions today.

13. Has she become _____ serious about her work than she used to be?

14. That house plan is _____ expensive than this one.

15. The baby's cold is _____ today than yesterday.

Adverbs

Adjectives describe nouns. They give details about nouns. Other words, called *adverbs*, describe *verbs, adjectives,* or *other adverbs.* Adverbs tell *why, when, where, how,* or *how much.*

      adv   V
Carrie **suddenly** stopped for a break.

Here *suddenly* is an adverb; it describes the verb *stopped.* The adverb tells how Carrie stopped.

                     adv   adj
Manuela was **perfectly** happy with the idea.

Here *perfectly* is an adverb; it describes the adjective *happy*. The adverb tells how happy Manuela was.

                    adv adj
The supervisor was **very** ill.

Here *very* is an adverb; it describes the adjective *ill*. *Very* tells how ill the supervisor was.

Exercise 4 *Adverbs*

Most of the time, adverbs have *-ly* as an ending (suffix). Here are some typical adverbs. Form a group of three to five people and use each of these *-ly* adverbs in good sentences. You should end up having 15 separate sentences.

nervously	finally	stubbornly
silently	basically	rapidly
frankly	financially	happily
coldly	immediately	truly
hopelessly	discreetly	unusually

Many adverbs do not end in *-ly*. Here is a list of some of them.

Some Adverbs Not Ending in *-ly*	
not	somewhat
just	soon
then	there
so	almost
less	always
very	too
also	much
here	quite
now	never
often	seldom
rather	

Exercise 5 *Adverbs*

Underline all the adverbs you read in the following sentences. (You can include prepositions, too.) Check your answers in the Answer Key.

1. Often George speaks really freely at public meetings.

2. My dog sleeps lazily in the sun whenever she can position herself just right.

3. My wife and I seldom go to restaurants because we find the food is too greasy.

4. The teenagers sadly said goodbye, parted slowly on the steps, and then waved weakly.

5. On very damp Saturdays, Marco usually sleeps in, happily snuggled in his warm bed.

6. The politician never swears unless he is quite alone.

7. The family usually goes camping there almost every holiday in the summer.

8. Walter and Frieda often dance in contests, but they are somewhat shy about it.

9. Mushrooms always taste very good with butter and lemon sprinkled generously on top.

10. We scarcely know her, yet she seems strangely familiar to us.

11. Ada understands German perfectly, but she is unable to speak it fluently.

12. Luke was unhappily married for 12 years and was just too miserable over it.

13. They shook their heads furiously at the suggestion and then agreed.

14. Cacti grew beautifully in his sunny backyard although he almost never tended them.

15. Francisco was somewhat dismayed that he had gotten rejected so loudly.

Adverbs Telling When

Adverbs tell us *how*, *where*, *why*, or *when*. Here is a list of some of the adverbs that can tell when an action takes place. Adverbs can also be used to describe people's habits.

Some Adverbs Telling When

always	usually	often
hardly	sometimes	frequently
never	scarcely	occasionally
hardly ever	rarely	seldom

Here are a few of these adverbs used in sentences:

He usually reads before he goes to sleep.

The children seldom eat fish.

He is often at the office by 7:00 a.m.

The elderly frequently rest after meals.

Adverbs of Time

Other adverbs refer to time specifically. Here are some examples:

then, yesterday, tomorrow, today

Exercise 6   Adverbs

Read each sentence and underline each adverb. Check your answers in the Answer Key.

1. Alvin did his assignments really carefully yesterday.
2. They discovered the neatly folded note outside.
3. The children fought noisily over there in the play lot.
4. The colt clumsily stumbled to its feet.
5. The most beautiful cake at the fair was Sabrina's.
6. Here are the reports recently received by our department.
7. Seldom will Donald respond unless he is provoked intentionally.
8. The angry bear ferociously charged the two hunters.
9. Yesterday the baby slept quietly in the sun porch while Cheryl happily read her latest magazine.
10. Sean rarely goes anywhere.
11. Bravely, the boy fought back his tears.
12. We will leave early, but we will call you later to hear the news.
13. The two children smiled shyly at one another.
14. Immediately, you must apologize for your rude remark.
15. Slowly, Fernie opened his eyes, and quietly, he spoke in a low, but steady voice.
16. Heather is a less experienced secretary than Estelle.
17. Today the sun shone brightly over the lake.
18. The tiny deer is too frightened to move.
19. They were more afraid of the water than the wasps.
20. His coach was extremely suspicious of the player's excuse.
21. Honestly, Jans did not take advantage of the situation; he rarely does.
22. What was more upsetting to the teacher was the parent's insistence that the child was always right.

Chapter 13 Modifiers **235**

23. Please sit down, and tell me calmly and clearly what happened.
24. A young salesman was arguing softly with the resident of the old building.
25. Tomorrow we will be quite happy to help you.
26. The back door banged loudly, and Kerry stomped angrily through the kitchen.
27. She was so worried about the car that she stared blankly at the service manager.
28. The management is certainly sorry that you strongly disliked your meal.
29. He casually informed her that she was fired immediately.
30. We hardly recognized him when he was extremely well dressed.

Exercise 7 Finding Adverbs

Underline all the adverbs you read in the following sentences. Note: some sentences also contain adjectives. Do not underline adjectives.

1. The restless students were really anxious about the test results from yesterday.
2. The work went smoothly today except for one small delay.
3. Some toffee is too chewy for my old fillings.
4. A red snapper tastes delicious when it is lightly baked with lemon sauce and fresh dill.
5. The city workers systematically tore up the pavement in front of the park.
6. The librarian helpfully directed me to the CD-ROM on the second floor of the building.
7. Indian corn called maize is used extensively in Mexican cooking.
8. Sometimes drug companies add codeine to cough syrups.
9. Yesterday there was an outburst of anger from a taxpayer's group.
10. Mandy seldom takes a taxi, but tomorrow she plans to take one to the airport.
11. The examination went poorly for Clark because he had not studied thoroughly.
12. Do you always do as you are instructed?
13. Frequently, André was too late to get any real bargains.
14. The circle of friends was suddenly broken by an unexpected death.
15. Bacon and eggs are rather high in fat, but surprisingly, they remain a popular breakfast food.

Prepositional Phrases

You may recall that phrases are groups of two or more words working together to perform a certain task. One type of phrase you examined is called a verb phrase. Another type of phrase mentioned earlier in this book is called a detail phrase or a prepositional phrase.

A prepositional phrase works in the same way as an adjective or an adverb. The phrase adds detail to a sentence. Like an adjective, a prepositional phrase can describe a noun as in this sentence.

The girl in the white hat is my cousin.

In the white hat is a prepositional phrase. It describes the girl. Since *girl* is a noun and adjectives describe nouns, the phrase works just like an adjective.

The cake on the bottom shelf of the fridge is stale.

On the bottom shelf and *of the fridge* are two separate prepositional phrases. The first phrase, *on the bottom shelf*, describes the cake. The second phrase, *of the fridge*, describes the shelf. Both phrases describe nouns; therefore, both phrases are *adjective prepositional phrases*.

A prepositional phrase *can also work like an adverb to tell how, where, when, or why an action takes place*. These sample sentences show prepositional phrases acting like adverbs:

He was working for better grades.

For better grades is a prepositional phrase. It adds why the person was working. The prepositional phrase describes working (a verb); the phrase works like an adverb.

She faced her opponent with a snarl.

With a snarl is a prepositional phrase. It describes how she faced her opponent. The phrase works like an adverb.

Hugh swims in his neighbour's pool.

In his neighbour's pool describes where Hugh swims. It is a prepositional phrase, working like an adverb.

We eat at six.

At six tells when we eat. This small prepositional phrase works like an adverb.
Prepositional phrases often come between the subject–verb set.

       S   V
The **president** (of the corporation) **was** only thirty.

Notice *of the corporation* is a prepositional phrase which interrupts the subject–verb set, *president—was*.

Remember: prepositional phrases begin with words of direction. These introductory words are called prepositions. You will recall you learned about these words in Chapter 11. Go back to review the list of prepositions found there if you wish.

Notice that prepositional phrases end in nouns or pronouns: you may also recall these are called *the objects of the prepositions*. They answer *what?* after the preposition.

Here are some examples of prepositional phrases.

Examples of Prepositional Phrases

without a trace	except Bernice
on the campus	above the people
by the main building	near them
around the city	through the ordeal
between meals	against me
off the edge	toward her
underneath the deck	

Exercise 8 Prepositional Phrases

Read the following sentences. Underline all prepositional phrases you read. Check your answers in the Answer Key.

1. Between you and me, I think Molly and Rich are planning a special dinner in honour of their parents' wedding anniversary.

2. The volcano was an inferno of flames and melted rock.

3. Traditional forms of embroidery can be found in many cultures of the world.

4. A rare wasp was discovered in a bog near Copetown, Ontario.

5. In case of an emergency, call 9-1-1.

6. Have you ever seen any killer whales in the waters around Vancouver Island?

7. Kindergarten is a special time for children because they leave the security of their homes and parents behind them.

8. Inside the tunnel, the workers could see a light that was coming from beneath them.

9. Peacocks are loved for their great beauty despite their irritating voices.

10. The potter plopped the lump of clay in the centre of her wheel and then kicked the wheel with her foot.

11. Along the edges of the field, we found deposits of a red-brown mineral.

12. The pouch of jewels disappeared without a trace.

13. Across the open meadows and through the thickets and forests, the travellers hiked to safety.

14. I have written in my notebook that there will be an exam on Wednesday.

15. Below the surface of the water was a school of tiny blue fish.

16. We all took an interest in the scene except Vicki who was bored with the nature hike.

17. Please uncork this bottle of wine for me.

18. The crane was caught in a tangle of old fishing line below the wharf.

19. She is prying into my business and asking my neighbours questions about me.

Exercise 9 Group Activity: Prepositional Phrases

Form a group to complete this exercise. Add prepositional phrases to the following sentences as indicated by the blanks. Be prepared to share answers.

1. _____ the dog barked _____.

2. The teenager _____ is my cousin.

3. The van _____ was customized _____.

4. _____ I read a book _____.

5. _____ the girl sewed a skirt _____.

6. The animals _____ are hungry.

7. Several crows landed _____.

8. The clamp _____ broke.

9. _____ Michael worked _____.

10. A painting _____ sold _____.

11. We roamed _____ and _____.

12. The cathedral _____ holds mass _____.

Exercise 10 Adjective or Adverb Prepositional Phrases

Earlier you learned that prepositional phrases could act like adjectives (describing nouns) or adverbs (describing verbs, adjectives, or other adverbs). Read the following sentences. First, underline the prepositional phrases. Then write **ADJ** above the phrase if you think the prepositional phrase describes a noun, or write **ADV** if you think the prepositional phrase describes a verb, adjective, or another adverb. Check your answers in the Answer Key at the back of the book.

1. On Sunday afternoon, the family gathered on the grounds for a reunion.
2. Several of the dogs were running loose in the playground and terrifying two small girls on tricycles.
3. Workers in the city were striking for better wages.
4. The woman in the sun hat just won a prize for the finest carnations.
5. Inside the house the cats were yowling around the kitchen and asking for their dinner.
6. Thousands of salmon were dying from the chemical spill of garden fertilizer.
7. Mrs. Lum, who was seated at the large, decorated table, was happy about the celebration of her 80th birthday.
8. The sailors from the American ship visited several shops and a large restaurant on Government Street.
9. People from that region of the globe do learn the customs of their new Canadian home.
10. The weapons had been tested during the Gulf War by various countries.
11. We saw Gabrielle on the upper deck of the large ferry.
12. Help us with this heavy couch; we want it moved to the other side of the room.
13. Joshua was not frightened by the other man's threats, but he left within a few minutes.
14. The baby in the little blue sneakers is eating his first bowl of chocolate ice cream.
15. That tin of biscuits is imported from Britain.
16. On an evening during the winter, the scientist saw the asteroid in the fourth quadrant of the galaxy.
17. On Laugh Night on Tuesday at the downtown bar, a young comedian nervously told his bad jokes to a silent audience.
18. The group of campers wandered along the beach at low tide.
19. A flock of blackbirds was singing high in the treetops.
20. The fat puppy ate his plate of crunchies and a large saucer of milk.
21. Take this box of books up the stairs, down the hall, and into my room; put it on the shelf over my bed.
22. He sent his girlfriend a basket of roses; inside the basket, he had tucked a small box of chocolates.
23. Despite my protests, Charlotte went on the trip.

Exercise 11 Group Activity: Sentences with Adjective or Adverb Prepositional Phrases

Form a group. Together compose sentences according to the directions given below. Be prepared to share your answers with the rest of the class.

1. Use the word *treasure* in a sentence that contains at least one adjective prepositional phrase.

2. Use the word *recording* in a sentence that contains at least one adverb prepositional phrase.

3. Use the word *party* in a sentence that contains at least one adjective prepositional phrase.

4. Use the word *trapped* in a sentence that contains at least one adverb prepositional phrase.

5. Use the words *melt* and *lab* in a sentence that contains one adjective prepositional phrase and one adverb prepositional phrase.

6. Use the word *expert* in a sentence that contains one adjective prepositional phrase and one adverb prepositional phrase.

7. Use the word *expense* in a sentence that contains two adjective prepositional phrases.

8. Use the words *shoe* and *rip* in a sentence that contains one adjective prepositional phrase and two adverb prepositional phrases.

9. Use the words *sleep* and *fly* with one adverb prepositional phrase and two adjective prepositional phrases.

10. Make up a single sentence that contains as many adjective or adverb prepositional phrases as you can think of!

Exercise 12 Mixed Practice

The following sentences may contain adjectives, adverbs, or prepositional phrases. Follow the instructions given below. Check with others in the class for answers.

A. Underline all adjectives.
B. Highlight all adverbs.
C. Put all prepositional phrases in parentheses ( ).
D. Write **ADJ** above all adjective prepositional phrases.
E. Write **ADV** above all adverb prepositional phrases.

1. The sound of a distant drum rolled across the valley as the soldiers slowly advanced through the forest.

2. The adventurous boys intercepted a letter in an official-looking envelope and excitedly imagined that it had arrived from a master spy.

3. The inventive young cook used a mixture of raisins, bread crumbs, and nuts for the stuffing and blended cucumber, chervil, white wine vinegar, and olive oil for the dressing.

4. Despite the heavy rain, the enthusiastic players continued in their designated positions.

5. A very tired employee finished the last of the financial reports that her demanding boss had requested earlier.

6. He inherited a string of stables from his mother and a chain of drugstores from his father.

7. The pure water originated from springs and collected in mountain hollows.

8. Their huge mortgage created a terrible burden in their busy lives and made them so anxious about the payments that the young couple sold the property.

9. Uncle Wilfred is a distinguished musician who really enjoys giving benefit concerts to sick or elderly residents of the city.

10. The border collie herded the reluctant sheep back to their pens for the night.

Adverb and Adjective Usage

An adverb should be placed as close as possible to the word it describes; otherwise, the meaning of the sentence might be different from what the writer intended.

Consider these examples using the adverb *only*.

Only Lucia loved Nestor. (Only one person loved Nestor.)

Lucia only loved Nestor. (Perhaps she really did not like him but loved him.)

Lucia loved Nestor only. (At this time, Lucia is concentrating on Nestor alone.)

Here are some examples which show how meaning in sentences can go wrong if the adverb is misplaced.

He got almost killed.

They fell just into the river.

He walks his dog hardly down this street.

Peggy spends money seldom on herself.

Morton ate just the pizza.

Just Morton ate the pizza.

Good and *Well*

Good is an adjective; you should use it to describe nouns. *Well* can be either an adjective or an adverb. You must be careful to choose the right word for correct usage in sentences.

Misuse:	Delbert sings good.
Correct use:	Delbert sings well.
Misuse:	Baldev is doing good after his operation.
Correct use:	Baldev is doing well after his operation.
Correct use of *well* as an adjective:	I visited your aunt; she is well. (*Well* describes the aunt.)
Correct use of *well* as an adverb:	The performer danced well in the play. (*Well* describes how the person danced.)

Real and *Really*

Real is an adjective. *Really* is an adverb.

Misuse:	Sheila is a real good friend.
Correct use:	Sheila is a really good friend.
Misuse:	This cake is real sweet.
Correct use:	This cake is really sweet.
Correct use of *real* as an adjective:	He has never seen real snow.

Bad and *Badly*

Bad is an adjective. *Badly* is an adverb.

Misuse:	The accident victim is hurt bad.
Correct use:	The accident victim is hurt badly.
Misuse:	Melissa plays tennis bad.
Correct use:	Melissa plays bad tennis.
Correct use:	Melissa plays tennis badly.

However, if a sentence contains a linking verb (no action), you use the adjective form *bad* in the sentence.

> Aaron felt bad about the news.
>
> The food was bad at the restaurant.
>
> My puppy is being bad in the playroom.
>
> The soup tasted bad to me.
>
> Those flowers smell bad.
>
> Some new music sounds bad.
>
> The weather looks bad.

Remember linking, or non-action, verbs.

Some Linking Verbs			
feel	was	being	is
taste	smell	am	were
be	are	sound	look
seem	appear	become	

Exercise 13 Adjective and Adverb Usage

Add *good, well, real, really, bad,* or *badly* to each of the sentences below. Check your answers in the Answer Key.

1. The dockyards have been _____ disturbed by all of the recent cutbacks.

2. Indra loves creating with stained glass; her works are _____ beautiful.

3. Those cupboard doors fit _____; I think we should call the contractor back and let him have a _____ look at them.

4. The meeting went _____; fights broke out over the least contentious issues.

5. My feet feel _____ after I had that long walk wearing those tight shoes.

6. The choir sang _____ at the concert.

7. Did you know she got a _____ offer to act in that Hollywood film?

244 Part 2 Sentence Foundations

8. The _____ tooth was _____ aching.

9. Dylan has a _____ good friend who helps him with his essays.

10. A pack of dogs was making a _____ mess of the garbage in the cans down in the back alley.

11. Behind our hedge we saw a nest full of _____ small, speckled hummingbird eggs.

12. The goalie played _____, but I think the team's defence was poor.

13. Are you a _____ expert cook, or are you a novice whose meals usually turn out _____?

14. Don tried making a _____ box kite, but it flew _____.

15. The young fellow felt so _____ about the incident that he offered to do some _____ community work.

16. The graph indicates that car sales have gone _____ in the summer months.

17. The soldiers were not treated _____ during the hostage taking.

18. How _____ can you ride a horse?

19. A true friend will help in times of _____ trouble.

Intensifiers

When *adverbs* (adv) *describe adjectives* (adj), they tend to *heighten or intensify the qualities* of the adjectives.

adv   adj
very polite

adv   adj
too weary

  adv   adj
extremely upset

   adv   adj
happily married

When *adverbs describe other adverbs,* they tend to *heighten or intensify the qualities of how something was done.*

Wendy works quite well under stress.

Quite is an adverb that describes another adverb, *well. Quite* tells how well the subject works.

Watch for adverbs that intensify the meanings of other modifiers. They deepen the meaning of modifiers in sentences.

Exercise 14 Mixed Practice for Review: Dividing Sentences into Parts of Speech

Identify the parts of speech in each sentence by writing **N** above all nouns, by writing **P** above all pronouns, by writing **S** above nouns or pronouns which are subject nouns or pronouns, by writing **O** above object nouns or pronouns, by writing **V** above all verbs, by writing **A** above action verbs, by writing **L** above linking, or non-action, verbs, by writing **ADJ** above all adjectives, by writing **ADV** above all adverbs, and by enclosing preposition phrases in parentheses ( ).

1. The huge cougar roared at the tourists.

2. Mr. Feldman conducted the symphony orchestra.

3. Suddenly, the ridiculous actor burst into tears.

4. The shrewd criminal is secretly devising a clever scheme of escape.

5. In the winter, Austin walks through heavy snows and seldom misses days of work.

6. They were happily camping on the banks of the rushing river.

7. The hotel is serving sugar-coated doughnuts, hot coffee, and buttered toast in its main foyer.

8. One of the pigeons can do cute tricks for tasty snacks.

9. In the morning, we will take Edgar to the Victoria International Airport.

10. Mary Jane was carefully washing the cotton fabric for the patchwork quilt.

11. Surprisingly, no one suspected Richard of the petty theft despite his motive.

12. We are quite sorry about the unfortunate incident.

13. In the frigid darkness, the soldiers waited impatiently for their orders.

14. The umpire ejected the veteran ballplayer during the last inning of the game.

Chapter 13: Review Test

Part 1: Finding Adjectives

Read the following sentences. Underline all adjectives that you read. Be careful: not all sentences contain adjectives. (1 point each, 21 points)

1. Alexander seemed sorry about the missing report.
2. We remembered the funny incident that had happened when we were silly children.
3. The toasted marshmallows and hot chocolate certainly tasted wonderful around the fire.
4. The negligent driver was speeding through a school zone like a maniac.
5. The raspberry juice thoroughly stained Jessica's favourite cotton dress.
6. The autumn months can be chilly and gloomy, but I rather enjoy the rain.
7. Duncan prepared baked apples with ginger sauce for our dessert tonight.
8. We were somewhat afraid to enter the darkened basement.
9. The patient cannot eat solid foods while he is slowly recovering from surgery.
10. Sharon will adapt quickly to the changes in her office.

Part 2: Finding Adverbs

Read the following sentences. Underline all adverbs that you read. Be careful: not all sentences contain adverbs. (1 point each, 20 points)

1. The scientist carefully conducted the delicate experiment.
2. Yesterday they were anxiously calling the newsroom and talking confidentially to the veteran reporter.
3. The most recent study proves conclusively that the virus is deadly.
4. There at the edge of the very old forest a stately Douglas fir grew.
5. The young man was not closely related to the victim, but he knew her very well.
6. The most experienced skydiver warned the nervous beginners who were tightly gathered in a small group.
7. Her uncle exported specialty food products that were made in Canada.
8. The speaker was visibly upset by the damaging remarks that had been recently printed in the local newspaper.
9. The party was quite successful and was surprisingly economical.
10. Miles is a rather respected writer who certainly can become argumentative about neutral topics.

Part 3: Finding Prepositional Phrases

Read the following sentences. Put parentheses ( ) around every prepositional phrase you read. Identify each phrase as **ADJ** (adjective) or **ADV** (adverb). Be careful: not all sentences contain prepositional phrases. (½ point for finding the phrase and ½ point for identifying it as either an **ADJ** phrase or an **ADV** phrase) (12 points total)

1. During the campaign, the candidate lost his best friend.
2. The bowl of fresh flowers filled the room with a sweet, spicy scent.
3. For 15 years, the satellite had been making its orbit around the earth.
4. They were certainly not sorry that the budget cuts had not affected any of the departments in their institution.
5. Montgomery had been elected to Parliament when he was about 30 years old.
6. In a fury, Greg turned on his heel and was gone.
7. A herd of Canadian elk blocked the Yellowhead Highway.

Part 4: Identifying Adjective and Adverb Prepositional Phrases

Read the following sentences. Put parentheses ( ) around each prepositional phrase you read. Then write **ADJ** above the prepositional phrase if it is an adjective prepositional phrase. Write **ADV** above the prepositional phrase if it is an adverb prepositional phrase. (1 point each, 10 points) (½ point for finding, ½ point for identifying it as **ADJ** or **ADV**)

1. An excited group from Morioka arrived on the Seattle ferry.
2. A bouquet of red roses and a bottle of wine arrived by special messenger on Friday.
3. The reel of fishing line cost $14.
4. At the beep, please leave your message for Gail or Tanya.
5. Surprisingly, Richard swims at the new Commonwealth pool.

Part 5: Using Comparisons

Underline the correct comparative form of the forms given in parentheses (1 point each, 10 points)

1. The recipe we got from Gertie for tourtière is (good, better, best) than the one we have.
2. Marina is the (more, most) skilled dancer that I have ever seen.
3. The (bad, worse, worst) meal we had on our trip was in Washington state.
4. Of the two poems, yours is the (good, better, best).

5. That technician is the (little, less, least) experienced of the five new employees.
6. The Belle Princess is the (much, more, most) luxurious cruise ship in the whole fleet.
7. That is the (more, most) mature of the two plants.
8. Susan is (good, better, best) at finding out the truth than I am.
9. (Many, More, Most) applicants applied for the job than the company expected.
10. This cola is (good, better, best) tasting than that one.

Part 6: Your Own Sentences

Make up your own sentences according to the directions given below. Follow instructions carefully. (10 points, to be marked by the instructor or the marker)

1. Use the word *repair* in a sentence that contains one adverb prepositional phrase. Underline the adverb prepositional phrase.

   _____

   _____

2. Use the word *angry* in a sentence that contains two adverbs. Underline the adverbs.

   _____

   _____

3. Use the word *mansion* in a sentence that contains one adjective prepositional phrase. Underline the adjective prepositional phrase.

   _____

   _____

4. Use the word *letter* in a sentence that contains two adjectives. Underline the adjectives.

   _____

   _____

5. Use the word *feel* in a sentence that contains one adjective and one adverb. Underline the adjective; circle the adverb.

   _____

   _____

Chapter 13 Modifiers 249

Part 7: Usage

Correct the following sentences by crossing out the incorrectly used adjective or adverb. Write the correct form above the incorrect form. (5 points)

1. Lisa is a real honest friend.
2. The steak was burning bad.
3. Eileen and I travel good together.
4. The microwave does not work good on high power.
5. Jane felt badly about missing the opportunity.

ESL POINTER

Prepositions of Place and Time

In the English language, some prepositions are commonly used to indicate time. These prepositions are *on*, *at*, and *in*.

I will arrive in Germany *on* December 12, 2005.

Jenny will have her interview *on* Friday afternoon. (Use *on* to indicate a particular date or day.)

The choir is singing *at* 8 o'clock this evening.

At midnight, the church bell will ring. (Use *at* to indicate the hour something is expected. It is also used with *midnight*, *noon*, or *night*.)

Her students will meet with her *in* 10 minutes. (Use *in* to indicate the number of minutes or hours something is expected.)

My grandmother loves to rest *in* the afternoons in the summer. (Use *in* to indicate a part of the day, a month, a season, or a year.)

Exercise 1 Prepositions of Place and Time

Use *in*, *on*, or *at* in each of the following sentences. Check your answers in the Answer Key.

1. Kiley is expected to arrive _____ 35 minutes.
2. We think the plane will arrive _____ 5:00 a.m. today.
3. _____ six o'clock, I am going to visit an old friend in the city.

4. He must be going to his meeting _____ nine this morning.

5. The family loves to vacation _____ the winter.

6. _____ late evening, Hyston loves to read murder mysteries.

7. My aunt's social club meets _____ noon every second Tuesday downtown.

8. Tavi said he would join us for a drink _____ 50 minutes.

9. One of the passengers will wait for a flight _____ August.

10. _____ Sunday I will bring you some parcels.

11. May I call you at home this evening _____ eight?

12. Daffodils and tulips bloom _____ spring.

13. _____ Thursday, my uncle is having surgery on his knee.

14. _____ fall many species of birds leave Canada for warmer climates.

15. The restaurant manager called to say you have a reservation _____ Saturday, March 12th.

Adjective + Preposition Arrangements

Some common adjectives often have particular prepositions following them. You will notice these combinations frequently in speech and in writing.

Here are some common combinations:

Common Adjective + Preposition Arrangements

Adjective + *of*:	Adjective + *to*:	Adjective + *with*:
quality of	accustomed to (used to)	pleased with
aware of	similar to	popular with
capable of	suitable to (*or* for)	satisfied with
suspicious of	related to	
afraid of	opposed to	
proud of	attached to	

Exercise 2 Adjectives + Prepositions

Fill each blank with the appropriate preposition. Check the your answers in the Answer Key at the back of the book.

1. Fernand is pleased _____ his new decorating job.
2. The priest is opposed _____ the policy on fundraising.
3. Are these green sweatshirts popular _____ younger teenagers?
4. A tiger is capable _____ eating half its weight in food every two days.
5. I think the new supervisor is suspicious _____ our plan to develop the area.
6. The mayor and city council are not aware _____ our group's proposal.
7. Some children feel closely attached _____ favourite toys.
8. Do you think the criminal is capable _____ such a violent act?
9. The house is suitable _____ a family of four.
10. I believe Saeed's argument is similar _____ his brother's.
11. My friend Joy is related _____ a famous opera singer.
12. Was the customer satisfied _____ the repair we did?
13. His mother is very proud_____ her children's accomplishments.
14. The little boy is afraid _____ dogs.
15. Vito is not yet accustomed _____ the harsh Canadian winters.

Exercise 3 Adding Modifiers

Work in pairs. Use separate paper. Add adjectives, adverbs, adjective prepositional phrases, or adverb prepositional phrases as instructed in each of the following. Be prepared to share your answers.

1. Make up a sentence about a dog. Your sentence should contain two adjectives and one prepositional phrase of your own choosing.
2. Make up a sentence about a dream. Your sentence should contain three prepositional phrases of your own choosing.

3. Make up a sentence about a news story. Your sentence should have two adverbs, three adjectives, one adverb prepositional phrase, and one adjective prepositional phrase.

4. Make up a sentence about tea. Your sentence should contain one adjective prepositional phrase, two adverbs, and one adjective.

5. Make up a sentence about a child. Your sentence should contain five modifiers of your own choosing.

CHECKOUT

1. To make sentences more interesting to read and more exact in meaning, you can add words of description.

2. There are different ways of making comparisons.

3. Adjectives describe nouns; adverbs describe verbs, adjectives, or other adverbs.

4. Prepositional phrases work in the same way as adjectives or adverbs.

chapter 14

Patterns of Sentences

Chapter Objectives

What will you have learned when you have completed this chapter? You will be able to

1. identify simple, compound, complex, and compound-complex sentences.
2. recognize how to connect independent clauses in compound sentences.
3. recognize coordinating conjunctions.
4. understand the use of dependent and independent clauses in complex sentences.
5. decide whether the special relationship between ideas in a complex sentence is based on time or condition.
6. recognize subordinate conjunctions.
7. use relative clauses.
8. write various patterns of sentences.

Introduction

English has four basic patterns of sentences: simple, compound, complex, and compound-complex. Each sentence pattern can be recognized by the number of ideas it contains and by how the ideas relate to one another.

Each sentence pattern contains at least one clause. A *clause* is a unit of meaning with a subject–verb set in it. What makes sentence patterns different from one another is how the clauses in each pattern relate.

Try the self-test to see what you remember about sentence patterns. Then check your answers in the Answer Key found at the end of the book.

Chapter 14: Self-Test

Part 1: Identifying Patterns of Sentences

Read each sentence carefully. Write **SIMPLE** after each simple sentence. Write **COMPOUND** after each compound sentence. Write **COMPLEX** after each complex sentence. (2 points each, 30 points)

1. Write to me if you have time. _____
2. Several people were hurrying to catch the bus, but they were too late. _____
3. Hamsters are popular pets for kids. _____
4. The airport was crowded; I couldn't find my friend. _____
5. Is your brother-in-law a qualified electrician? _____
6. Please wait here until she returns. _____
7. Although he was young, he was wise for his age. _____
8. Gene tried to row across the lake, but he tired after an hour. _____
9. The supervisor wanted her staff to be more productive and cooperative. _____
10. Many hours were spent in talking about the project, and, at last, the plans were finalized. _____
11. Because Arlene couldn't swim, she was not allowed to go. _____
12. She has been a member of the Peel Regional Police Service for 10 years. _____
13. The radio and the television were on at the same time. _____
14. While I got a haircut, my son read a book. _____
15. You can buy this used book from me, or you can pay a lot more at the bookstore. _____

Part 2: Identifying Clauses

Underline every main clause (simple sentence). Put parentheses around every dependent clause. (½ point for each part, 20 points)

1. While you were at the store, the office supervisor called you.
2. Although the wind was strong, no property was damaged.
3. Please ask Meg if she is coming with us.
4. Ronald played the violin until he was 12 years old.

5. Call me when you get home.

6. We're having a celebration after our last exam is over.

7. Since she left, I've been lonely.

8. The fisherman caught some fish when he went out yesterday.

9. As the child walked, he whistled.

10. When we were away last weekend, the power was off at our house.

Part 3: Combining Sentences

Combine these simple sentences into one good complex sentence. (5 points each, 20 points, to be marked by your instructor or marker.)

1. The soup was cold.

   The soup was salty.

   We complained about the soup.

   _____

   _____

2. She yelled at her son.

   She was sorry for yelling.

   She apologized to her son.

   _____

   _____

3. The green dress was expensive.

   The blue dress was cheaper.

   I bought the blue dress.

   _____

   _____

4. The sea was rough.

   We did not take the boat out.

   The boat was 12 feet long.

   _____

   _____

Part 4: Your Own Sentences

In the spaces provided, write your own sentences, but be sure to follow directions carefully. (5 points each, 30 points, to be marked by the instructor or the marker.)

1. Write a good compound sentence using the word *storm* in your sentence.

   _____
   _____

2. Write a good simple sentence using the word *desk* in your sentence.

   _____
   _____

3. Write a good compound sentence using the word *bank* in your sentence.

   _____
   _____

4. Write a good simple sentence using the word *magic* in your sentence.

   _____
   _____

5. Write a good compound sentence using the word *violence* in your sentence.

   _____
   _____

6. Write a good compound sentence using the word *groceries* in your sentence.

   _____
   _____

Simple Sentences

A simple sentence contains *one complete idea, a single subject–verb set*. It is a *one-clause sentence*. A clause that can stand on its own is called a *principal, main,* or *independent clause.*

   S   V
The **tree bends** in the wind. (The sentence has one S-V set; the whole idea is that the tree bends.)

      S   V   V

The **tree bends** and **groans** in the wind. (The sentence has one S-V set [S-V-V]; it remains a one idea sentence—a tree can bend and groan.)

      S   S   V

The **tree** and the **shrubs bend** in the wind. (The sentence has one S-V-V set; one idea is expressed in the sentence—certain things [called trees and shrubs] can bend in the wind).

Compound Sentences

A compound sentence, on the other hand, is really a double sentence. It expresses *two simple, complete ideas*. It contains two separate S-V sets, two completely separate ideas or *independent clauses*. To create a compound sentence, write one simple sentence, and then add another simple sentence to it. Think of a compound sentence as one (independent clause) + one (another related independent clause) = compound.

    The tree bends in the wind, but it does not break.

    First simple sentence: The tree bends in the wind.

    Second simple sentence: The tree does not break in the wind.

The two simple sentences have been joined with *but*. In addition, the noun *tree* has been changed to the pronoun *it*, and the phrase *in the wind* has been dropped to make smoother reading.

Joiner words, or *conjunctions*, join simple sentences together to make compound sentences. Conjunctions that work in compound sentences are called *coordinating conjunctions* because they coordinate two independent clauses:

Coordinating Conjunctions			
and	but	yet	
or	for	so	nor

The punctuation mark called the *semicolon* can join related clauses (the two independent clauses) to make compound sentences.

    I love to eat ice cream; I buy it every shopping trip.

Exercise 1 Compound Sentences

All of the following sentences are compound sentences. Write **1** above the first complete idea (simple sentence) in the sentence; write **2** above the second complete idea (simple sentence) in the sentence.

1. I studied hard, but I did not pass the test.

2. She must have left, or she would be in the office right now.

3. Eileen wrote to the company, but she did not get an answer.

4. Susan was tired, and she wanted to go home.

5. Most of the houses in our area were built in the 1950s, but some new ones are being built up on the hill.

6. The meeting was cancelled, but it will be rescheduled for next week.

7. Sherry filled in an application for the job, and she mailed it on her way to class.

8. Would you like to come with us, or would you prefer to stay here?

9. My mother won a contest last week, and she's delighted with the prize.

10. The boys did the dishes, and then they mowed the lawn.

Exercise 2 Compound Sentences

Work in pairs. Add another complete idea (simple sentence) to each of the following simple sentences so that you have formed good compound sentences. Use either one of the coordinating conjunctions *and, but, or, for, nor, yet,* or *so,* or use a semicolon to connect your ideas. Write the new compound sentences in the spaces provided. Check with other teams to correct your answers.

1. Groceries are expensive today.
   _____

2. The movie was exciting.
   _____

3. His course was boring.
   _____

4. Some of the customers were angry.
   _____

5. I lost 20 dollars.
   _____

6. Arnie bought a new car.
   _____

7. Her daughter is a doctor.

   _____

8. It is raining hard.

   _____

9. The unemployment rate is high.

   _____

10. His wife attends Valley College.

    _____

Exercise 3 Compound Sentences

Combine these simple sentences into compound sentences. Use *or*, *and*, *but*, *nor*, *so*, *yet*, or *for* or use a *semicolon* to join the sentences. Rewrite your sentences in the spaces provided. Check your answers with other students in the class.

   The day was sunny. (simple sentence)

   The day was not hot. (simple sentence)

   The day was sunny, but it was not hot. (compound sentence)

1. The fans cheered.

   The fans got to their feet.

   _____

   _____

2. The coffee is strong.

   The coffee is not hot.

   _____

   _____

3. Margaret worked hard all her life.

   Margaret raised four children on her own.

   _____

   _____

4. The back of the lawn chair is broken.

   The chair needs to be fixed.

   _____
   _____

5. The cat caught a mouse in the backyard.

   The cat did not kill the mouse.

   _____
   _____

6. We planted tulip bulbs last fall.

   None of the tulips came up this spring.

   _____
   _____

7. A terrific storm blew down the shack.

   The greenhouse beside the shack was not harmed.

   _____
   _____

8. Several people were lined up at the bank.

   Several people seemed angry.

   _____
   _____

9. I bought a toy for my son.

   The toy was really expensive.

   _____
   _____

10. Lightning flashed across the lake.

    A hard rain began to pour down.

    _____
    _____

11. My uncle owns a delicatessen.

    The delicatessen is not doing a good business.

    _____

    _____

12. They went trout fishing last week.

    They caught four large rainbow trout.

    _____

    _____

13. Alice worked in her father's hardware store.

    Alice found the work dull.

    _____

    _____

14. Dogs can be a tremendous nuisance.

    This fact does not prevent people from owning them.

    _____

    _____

15. Children from the school went for a picnic at the beach.

    The picnic was a wonderful success.

    _____

    _____

Exercise 4 Simple and Compound Sentences

Read the following sentences. Write **S** after each simple sentence, and write **C** after each compound sentence. Check your answes in the Answer Key.

1. Margot and Antonio make the best cappuccino coffee at a restaurant on the wharf.   _____

2. After driving through the storm, Michelle was tired, hungry, and nervous.   _____

3. Certainly children need plenty of exercise and fun in their lives.   _____

4. At the festival, a few merrymakers were swimming in the city fountain, and the police were called to remove them.   _____

5. A clown was talking to the cashier in the beauty shop, and she was smiling and laughing at his remarks. _____

6. Nadia will have to go to the store to buy some anchovies for the Caesar salad. _____

7. Workers did not ratify the agreement; they decided to walk off the job at midnight the next day. _____

8. Their cottage industry was making scented candles and soap. _____

9. We will drive through the Okanagan to pick up some peaches for canning, and we have also decided to tour around Kelowna at the same time. _____

10. The watch is broken, or it needs a new battery. _____

11. Collecting rare glass and old jazz records are two of Felicia's interests. _____

12. A student in my class, Raymond, can speak four languages fluently. _____

13. The hostess had prepared for all eventualities, but she was not prepared for the Duke's sudden arrival at dinner. _____

Complex Sentences

Now you know a *compound* sentence is really a double sentence made up of two simple (one idea) sentences and a coordinating conjunction (*and, but, or, so, nor, for,* or *yet*) used to join the two main clauses. *Complex* sentences are also two-idea sentences, but they have an important difference.

In a complex sentence, *how the two ideas relate to one another* is most important. *One clause* is called the *independent* (or main or principal) clause while the other is called the *dependent* (subordinate or fragment) clause. The *dependent clause* needs the main, or independent, clause in order to make sense in the sentence.

He would not eat his Brussels sprouts because he hated the taste.

The first clause is *He would not eat his Brussels sprouts*. The second clause is *because he hated the taste*. Although the second clause contains a subject–verb set, it cannot stand by itself. It is *a fragment*. The first clause can stand alone; it is independent.

More about Clauses

The ideas in a complex sentence are called *clauses*. Complex sentences have at least *one independent clause* (simple sentence) and *one dependent clause;* the clauses have a special relationship based on *time* or *condition*. The independent clause is like a simple sentence and the second clause is like a fragment or piece of a sentence. All clauses contain subject–verb sets.

He would not eat his Brussels sprouts because he hated the taste.

The second clause gives a reason why he would not eat the vegetables. The relationship between the two clauses is based on a *condition*—a causal one. The dependent clause serves as the condition.

You could keep changing the condition. Conditions and time factors change the meaning of sentences. The independent clause can be kept the same, but by adding different times or conditions, you can change the meaning of the sentence.

independent clause	dependent clause
(simple sentence)	**(adding a new condition)**

He would not eat his Brussels sprouts until she ate hers.

He would not eat his Brussels sprouts because they were overcooked.

He would not eat his Brussels sprouts although his parents threatened him.

He would not eat his Brussels sprouts if you paid him.

All of the dependent clauses add a condition to the independent clause, or they show a time relationship with the independent clause:

independent clause	dependent clause
(simple sentence)	**(adding a new condition)**

He would not eat his Brussels sprouts after they were cooked. (Perhaps he likes to eat them raw.) (time)

He would not eat his Brussels sprouts when suppertime arrived. (time)

He would not eat his Brussels sprouts before he went out. (time)

He would not eat his Brussels sprouts as he was watching TV. (at the same time as)

Exercise 5 *Two Types of Clauses*

Write **I** above the part of the sentence that is the independent clause. Write **D** above the clause that is the dependent clause. Check your answers in the Answer Key.

1. Because we had a party last night, we're exhausted today.

2. A salesperson will help you if you ring the bell.

3. When Joan was in Europe, she visited Rome.

4. The kids were watching television as we were playing cards.

5. Although Maxine is a qualified welder, she can't find work.

6. Before you go to bed, let the cat out.

7. After his family telephoned, Bob was depressed.

8. Since Aileen won't be able to be in class tomorrow, I'll collect the assignment for her.

9. The plant died because it was left in the hot sun.//
10. If I tell you about it, will you keep it a secret?
11. Because her son had the measles, Dorothy missed a week of classes.
12. When he went for the interview, he lost his glasses.
13. He twisted his ankle while he was waterskiing.
14. If the baby cries, pick her up.
15. I wanted to go to Montreal although I couldn't afford the trip.
16. The game was exciting because the two teams were very competitive.
17. I can't go home until I finish this work.
18. After the new manager was appointed, the employees became suspicious.
19. Most of the students were nervous because they'd been away from school for a long time.
20. While I was driving down Blakely Road, I saw a family of deer near the roadside.

Conjunctions

As you will remember, special words called *conjunctions* hook the two clauses (ideas) together in a complex sentence. These are called *subordinate conjunctions* in complex sentences: they show a time or conditional relationship. They are powerful because they control meaning.

Consider this complex sentence.

Wanda screamed as the dentist extracted her tooth.

The subordinate conjunction *as* shows a special time relationship between the two ideas. You get a picture in your mind of Wanda screaming just as the dentist is pulling her tooth. In other words, *as* shows ideas happening at the same time or simultaneously.

Next, take the same two ideas, but change the conjunction.

Wanda screamed after the dentist extracted her tooth.

After shows a time relationship. Which idea happened first? First, the dentist extracted Wanda's tooth. Second, Wanda screamed.

Change the conjunction again.

Wanda screamed because the dentist extracted her tooth.

Because shows a reason and, therefore, it indicates a condition exists between the two ideas. Wanda screamed (why?) because the dentist extracted her tooth.

It is most important to recognize the meaning *through the relationship of clauses in a complex sentence*. To do that, you must consider whether time or condition plays a part. You'll notice, too, that reading with this awareness of the relationship between ideas will increase your overall reading ability tremendously.

Below you will find a list of subordinate conjunctions and their functions.

Subordinate Conjunctions	
To establish a time relationship:	**To establish a condition:**
after	if
as	since
before	because
until	although
while	when

Here are example sentences using subordinate conjunctions:

After the concert, we went to Bob's Place for steak and beer. (time)

As Roland was working the tiller, we rowed the boat. (time)

Before the winner was announced, the contestant fainted. (time)

Until the old person got a seat, he had to stand on the bus. (time)

While I was boiling the pasta, you prepared the salad. (time)

When Stephanie finished singing, the audience burst into applause. (time)

If the fire alarm rings, leave by the nearest exit. (condition)

Since Jacob was a small boy, he wanted to fly a plane. (time)

Because rent is expensive in Toronto, she decided to leave. (condition)

Although most people are cautious, accidents still happen. (condition)

The clauses can change position, too. In other words, all of the above sentences could start with the independent clause and end in the dependent clause; meaning would remain the same. To experiment, let's take three sentences and exchange the position of the clauses.

Jacob wanted to fly a plane since he was a small boy.

She decided to leave because rent in Toronto is expensive.

Accidents still happen although most people are cautious.

As you can see, the meaning does not change. However, *when the dependent clause is placed first* in a sentence, it is *followed by a comma*. When an independent clause is placed first, the sentence does not usually require a comma.

Exercise 6 Clauses and Complex Sentences

Work in pairs. Decide if there is a time relationship or a conditional relationship between the clauses. Write **TIME** or **CONDITION** after each sentence once you have made your decision. Check your answers in the Answer Key found at the end of the book.

1. My friends called today because they wanted my advice. _____

2. I was sorry after I said it. _____

3. When the buzzer goes off, take the buns out of the oven. _____

4. Because he was too old, he was not accepted. _____

5. He wanted to stay in school until he'd achieved his goal. _____

6. Children will be good if you are good to them. _____

7. Although they made a mistake, they didn't apologize. _____

8. She laughed as Randy told her the joke. _____

9. We were afraid because we had made the wrong choice. _____

10. If the plant gets too tall, pinch it back. _____

11. Because Laurie can fix her own car, she saves a lot of money. _____

12. I saw an old friend when I was out last night. _____

13. The hall looked colourful after it had been decorated. _____

14. Hockey is popular since fans find it an exciting game to watch. _____

15. When he was 17, he was a cadet. _____

16. If it rains, the game will be cancelled. _____

17. After she came to Canada, she worked in a grocery store. _____

18. He kept on drinking until there was a crisis in his family. _____

19. After I cleaned the eavestroughs, I painted them. _____

20. Although he appeared to be calm, he was very angry. _____

Exercise 7 Clauses and Complex Sentences

Make each dependent clause into a good complex sentence by adding words to make it complete. Be sure to add at least one independent clause along with your dependent clause in each of your complex sentences.

since he was laid off

Tony has been very worried since he was laid off.

1. because the sun was hot

_____

2. when the tide comes in

_____

3. as we arrived

_____

4. since going to the movies was fun

_____

5. although she wanted to help

_____

6. before my watch broke

_____

7. if she can

_____

8. although the room was messy

_____

9. as the meeting was going on

_____

10. while I sleep

_____

11. because Mr. Beggs has a bad temper

_____

12. until the lights went out

_____

13. after we watched the parade

_____

14. when Sal won't talk to me

_____

15. before the settlement was reached

_____

Sentence Fragments

A *sentence fragment is a piece of a sentence*. Although it may contain an S-V set, it does not make sense by itself. Here are some examples of sentence fragments:

> Because I was sick.
>
> Wendy dusting the shelf.
>
> Dark and stormy clouds.
>
> Since the coach was angry.
>
> Forgetting my assignment on the table.

Note that none of these make sense by themselves. Each fragment is relying on the sentence before it or after it in order to complete its meaning.

Sentence fragments are generally considered serious errors in academic writing. They can make reading difficult and meaning ambiguous. Although you may use fragments when speaking with another person, fragment errors are *sentence-level errors in formal writing*.

Exercise 8 Recognizing Fragments and Sentence Patterns

Read each of the following word groups. If the word group is a fragment (piece of a sentence), write **FRAGMENT** after it. If the word group is a simple sentence, a compound or a complex sentence, write **SIMPLE**, **COMPOUND**, or **COMPLEX** after it.

1. She was afraid to go.   _____

2. Running too hard and breathing with difficulty.   _____

3. Reuben wanted to keep track of his hours, but he forgot to write
   them down.   _____

4. Unusual animals can be found living in the tropics, and some
   species are particular to that zone only.   _____

5. After the celebration is over.   _____

6. She is learning to operate a motorcycle.   _____

7. The vegetable garden needs to be watered daily.   _____

8. Although Allen is afraid of snakes, he won't admit it. _____

9. Ralph and Steve jog every morning before work. _____

10. Many wonderful things to eat! _____

11. We sang and paddled our canoe. _____

12. The young woman was a gifted pianist. _____

13. Since the water heater had broken. _____

14. The papers, blowing all over the floor. _____

15. Eating too many rich foods and sleeping too much can create health problems. _____

Exercise 9 Simple, Compound, and Complex Sentences

Remember: a simple sentence contains a single idea, a compound sentence is made up of two simple sentences or independent clauses, and a complex sentence involves a special relationship between an independent and dependent clause. Identify each of the following sentences by writing **SIMPLE**, **COMPOUND**, or **COMPLEX** after each. Check your answers in the Answer Key.

1. Ted and Mark have lived in the same neighbourhood for 20 years. _____

2. I went to the concert alone because my friend wouldn't come with me. _____

3. Since Rita arrived in York, she's been really busy. _____

4. Norman did not finish the job. _____

5. Many fish died in the river, but a cause could not be found. _____

6. The baby giggled and giggled. _____

7. The postal workers went on strike since a settlement could not be reached. _____

8. Would you like more coffee with your toast? _____

9. The music was low, but it bothered me anyway. _____

10. When were you in New Brunswick? _____

11. We went for a beer after work. _____

12. Tell me the truth, or I'll be angry with you! _____

13. Add one cup of flour and two fresh eggs to the pancake recipe. _____

14. We talked, and then we took a long stroll along the beach. _____

15. The wedding party was a success; everyone enjoyed it. _____

16. He loses his temper if he can't have his way. _____

17. When you drive south on Allan Road, turn left at Finch Avenue. _____

18. The office was closed, and I couldn't wait for it to open again. _____

19. Stop lying to me! _____

20. Two of the students were discussing some of the difficulties of coming back to college. _____

Relative Clauses

Relative clauses are *special dependent clauses found in complex sentences*. They begin with *who, that,* or *which* and sometimes *whose* or *whom*. They are called *relative clauses* because they start with relative pronouns; these clauses must be placed next to the words they describe. Relative clauses often split the independent clause because they are often placed in the middle.

The man who passed me looks familiar.

The man looks familiar [independent clause] who passed me. [dependent clause (relative clause)].

Who passed me is a clause pointing out which man you are talking about. The clause must be placed right after *man*.

If you do not place relative clauses next to the things they define, funny things can happen.

The little boy bought the dog who wore glasses and a Blue Jays baseball cap. (Where should the relative clause *who wore glasses and a Blue Jays baseball cap* be placed correctly?)

The portrait belonged to the City of Halifax that was sold. (What's wrong with this? How would you fix it so that the meaning is clear?)

The answer was found at the back of the book which was wrong. (Is it the answer or the book that is wrong?)

Mr. Altman that had fleas found an old, shaggy dog. (Who had fleas in the above sentence?)

Mike lost his cat in the park that was orange and three-legged. (This information is quite silly when it is arranged in this way.)

Cathy that was a brown tabby and wearing a blue collar lost her cat in the park. (Doesn't it sound as if Cathy is wearing a collar and is lost?)

These sentences are ridiculous, aren't they? It is important to place relative clauses next to the words they modify in order to avoid confusion of the meaning.

Remember: place relative clauses next to the word or words they modify. Also keep in mind that when it comes to punctuation in a complex sentence, if a dependent clause comes first in a complex sentence, place a comma after it.

Restrictive and Non-Restrictive Clauses

Restrictive and non-restrictive clauses were mentioned previously in this text. Do you recall what these two special cases of clauses mean? If a relative clause is *essential to the meaning* of a noun or the sentence itself, it is called a *restrictive clause*. You would not use commas around it.

However, if a relative clause is *not essential to the meaning* of a noun or the sentence itself, it is called a *non-restrictive clause*. You would use commas around it.

Here is another hint for you: Use the relative pronoun *that* to begin restrictive clauses.

None of the birds that were found in that region were infected by the West Nile virus.

The chairs that had been sold to Mr. Singh are missing from the storage area.

Several out-of-the-way places in Ontario, which we enjoyed very much, are featured in the magazine *Travel Ontario*.

Exercise 10 Relative Clauses and Complex Sentences

Use the following as relative clauses to make good complex sentences. Use separate paper. Your instructor may ask to see your work.

who worked at the department store (relative clause)

Sentence containing the relative clause: The woman who worked at the department store won the lottery.

1. that was incorrect
2. who invented the SnoreMaster
3. which was fun
4. who wore the leather jacket
5. which is being torn down
6. who is tall and thin
7. that we bought
8. which they are investigating

Exercise 11 Group Activity: Review of Complex Sentences

Form a group of three to five students. Below are sets of simple sentences. Combine each set into one good complex sentence. Rewrite your sentences. Be prepared to share your answers.

The television was too loud.

The television belonged to my neighbour.

The television annoyed me.

The television that belonged to my neighbour annoyed me because it was too loud.

1. The students were busy.

   The students were finishing.

   The teacher talked to the students.

   _____

   _____

2. My uncle owns a horse.

   The horse is a champion.

   _____

   _____

3. Eggs are expensive.

   Cheese is expensive.

   Eggs are a good source of protein.

   Cheese is a good source of protein.

   _____

   _____

4. The house was for sale.

   The house was rundown.

   The house sold last week.

   _____

   _____

5. The man was a millionaire.

   The man owned property.

   The property was on Prince Edward Island.

   _____

   _____

6. The woman had an interview.

   The woman was nervous.

   The woman wore a red suit.

   _____

   _____

7. The farmer lost money on his crops.

   His crops were ruined by the drought.

   _____

   _____

8. The elevator door slid open.

   I heard music inside the elevator.

   _____

   _____

9. A letter arrived.

   The letter was in a pink envelope.

   The letter was addressed to Peter.

   _____

   _____

10. The mayor made an announcement.

    The citizens of the town were shocked.

    _____

    _____

11. The newspaper was on strike.

    The management called a meeting.

    _____

    _____

12. Unusual patterns of stars can be seen.

    Unusual patterns of stars are best seen in the fall.

    In the fall earth's atmosphere is clear.

    _____

    _____

13. He enjoys shopping.

    He enjoys buying items on sale.

    Sale items are often bargains.

    _____

    _____

14. The wall was freshly painted. Ed leaned on the wall.

    Ed left a mark on the wall.

    _____

    _____

15. The family bought a jeep.

    The family rented camping gear.

    The family went on a camping trip to Alaska.

    _____

    _____

Exercise 12 Independent Clauses, Dependent Clauses, and Commas

Underline independent clauses. Put parentheses ( ) around dependent clauses. Insert commas wherever you think they are needed in the sentences.

1. Salvatore is the best Italian chef in town because he cares about the quality of food in his restaurant.

2. The actress answered the reporter's questions after the filming was over.

3. Since you have decided to stop drinking have you noticed any change in your outlook?

4. Several of the students were from Argentina where they had been political prisoners.

5. While the teacher was reading a story to the class a student gave each child at the Valentine's party a book of cut-out valentines some scissors and some glue.

6. When he was in the navy Ted learned many skills in electronics.

7. Because Rick prefers to work alone he is often assigned to the night shift.

8. Rose and her sister opened a ladies' fashion store in the small mall although neither of them had any experience in operating a business.

9. Albertina stood on the deck watching the seabirds while her children played below on the beach.

10. Red orange green and purple peppers were used in the salad because the colours looked wonderful on the buffet table.

11. As the cat studied the bird in the tree the bird in the tree studied the cat.

12. Roger read the magazine article until it was time to go for the appointment.

13. Because the pedlar did not have a licence the police officer arrested him.

14. Biologists from Cape Breton report a drop in the number of songbirds because dangerous pesticides are getting into their food source and making the birds sterile.

Exercise 13 Review of Simple, Compound, and Complex Sentences

Read each sentence carefully. Write **S** after all simple sentences. Write **C** after all compound sentences. Write **CX** after all complex sentences. Check your answers in the Answer Key at the back of the book.

1. The Rangers have won most of their games, but the Oilers are not far behind them. _____

2. Although the salesclerk tempted me into buying the new appliance, I was not convinced it was a bargain. _____

3. Several of the lettuce heads and a few of the spinach plants had been damaged by insects. _____

4. Thirty dollars is not enough to buy a ticket, but you may be able to get a better deal from the other ticket booth. _____

5. Randolph is worried about his looks and is concerned over his thinning hair. _____

6. The library is closed on Sundays, and it is often closed holiday Mondays, too. _____

7. Delicious and nutritious meals can be made for very little money if you are willing to spend the extra time on preparation. _____

8. Canada is a country made up of many cultures and beliefs. _____

9. We travelled for three long hours, but we were unable to find a motel. _____

10. Since he has been elected president, he has been hard to contact. _____

11. The members of the jury could not reach a verdict in the difficult trial. _____

12. She decided to go back to school after her children had left home. _____

13. Some television shows are utterly stupid; they are often insulting to the viewers. _____

14. While the teams were on the field, a fan threw a chicken at the umpire. _____

15. She rested for an hour, and then she read. _____

Exercise 14 Review of Simple, Compound, and Complex Sentences

1. Write a simple sentence using the word *refrigerator*.

2. Write a complex sentence using the word *flowers*.

3. Write a compound sentence using the word *honest*.

4. Write a complex sentence using the word *several*.

5. Write a compound sentence using the word *pamphlet*.

6. Write a simple sentence using the words *hot dog*.

7. Write a complex sentence using the word *terrifying*. Be sure the sentence has one restrictive clause.

8. Write a simple sentence using the word *chief*.

9. Write a complex sentence using the word *office*.

_____

_____

10. Write a compound sentence using the word *forecast*.

_____

_____

Compound and Complex Sentences

The final pattern of sentence you will see in the English language is the *compound-complex sentence*. This sentence combines one or more dependent clauses with a compound sentence. This pattern of sentence is not as common as the other three mentioned earlier in the chapter. However, as an academic reader you will see the pattern. As an academic writer, you should try to write a compound-complex sentence once in a while in your writing. Doing so will help your writing style.

> The parents of the child who had been chosen for the part in the commercial were ecstatic, and they planned to celebrate with their family that evening.

> Eating too much of a good thing could be harmful if you think about items like butter or cheese, and this excess could lead to heart disease.

In the first example, you can see a compound sentence made up of two independent clauses or simple sentences:

> The parents were ecstatic, and they planned to celebrate with their family that evening.

You also see a relative clause (restrictive, by the way, to define which child won).

> who had been chosen for the part in the commercial

The combination of the compound sentence with the relative (dependent) clause makes up a compound-complex sentence.

In the second example, the compound sentence is *eating too much of a good thing could be harmful, and this excess could lead to heart disease*. The dependent clause is *if you think about items like butter or cheese*. The combination of a compound sentence with a dependent clause gives you a compound-complex sentence.

Exercise 15 Compound-Complex Sentences

All of the following sentences are compound-complex. Underline the compound sentence. Put the dependent clause or clauses in parentheses ( ).

1. After the terrible storm was over, the villagers assessed their buildings for damage, and they tried to rescue their animals.

2. Some of the people who were applying for the position were waiting in the main foyer of the building; they wanted to speak to the recruiting officer.

3. Neither Sheffield nor his partners would answer the enquiries that the government tax inspector was asking; moreover, they appeared to snub him in the hallway.

4. Of all the creatures on earth that she could want for a pet, why would she be interested in purchasing a boa constrictor, and where would she keep it?

5. The smuggler who was importing heroin was caught on an impaired driving charge, and he was also alleged to have been speeding at the time.

6. Work on this until you have completed it, and then you can go home.

Exercise 16 Group Activity: Writing Compound-Complex Sentences

Forms groups of three to five people. Write compound-complex sentences using each of the following words. Be prepared to share your answers with the rest of the class.

1. turnip
2. the weather
3. one player
4. believes
5. the parents
6. smiled
7. worries
8. the Internet
9. stuffy
10. his dog

Chapter 14: Review Test

Part 1: Identifying Patterns of Sentences

Read each sentence carefully. Write **SIMPLE** after each simple sentence. Write **COMPOUND** after each compound sentence. Write **COMPLEX** after each complex sentence. (2 points each, 30 points)

1. If I work hard, I'll pass the course. _____
2. The painter dipped his brush, and then he considered the canvas. _____
3. Too much sugar is not good for children's health. _____
4. He worked for the Red Cross; he was a volunteer. _____
5. Will you be over for supper tonight? _____
6. Beat this batter until it is smooth. _____
7. Because the flood had washed away the bridge, the road was closed. _____
8. The puppy tugged at the tablecloth, but he could not pull it down. _____
9. My sister-in-law and her friend took a trip to Greece last spring. _____
10. Many new techniques are used in medicine today, but many ways are still traditional. _____
11. The race was over although the fans were still cheering. _____
12. Tomatoes and citrus fruits are high in vitamin C. _____
13. We ate and drank together. _____
14. As the baby slept, the family played a board game. _____
15. He works out every day, and he feels better for it. _____

Part 2: Identifying Clauses

Underline every independent clause (simple sentence). Put parentheses around every dependent clause. (½ point for each main clause and ½ point for each dependent clause, 20 points)

1. After you read the book, give me your opinion of it.
2. Although we had chopped all the wood, we were too exhausted to stack it.
3. Arnie does best when he works alone.
4. The kindergarten class gave a concert because they wanted to raise money for a field trip.
5. Wipe your feet before you come in.
6. Wait until the red light comes on.
7. If I watch the baby for you, will you buy me a coffee?
8. Before the class was over, he had left.

9. The sailor wanted to know if he could buy me a drink.

10. He acted in movies until he was 80 years old.

Part 3: Combining Sentences

Combine these sentences into one good complex sentence. (5 points each, 20 points, to be marked by the instructor or the marker.)

1. We cleaned the carpet.

    We painted the wall.

    We were exhausted.

    _____

    _____

2. The car was new.

    The car was expensive.

    We bought the car anyway.

    _____

    _____

3. She bought a lottery ticket.

    The lottery ticket cost $20.

    She wanted to win.

    _____

    _____

4. The bears were dangerous.

    The bears were getting into garbage.

    The wildlife workers moved the bears.

    _____

    _____

Part 4: Your Own Sentences

In the spaces provided, write your own sentences, but be sure to follow directions carefully. (5 points each, 30 points, to be marked by the instructor or the marker.)

1. Write a good complex sentence using the word *bicycle* in your sentence.

2. Write a good simple sentence using the word *cigarette* in your sentence.

3. Write a good compound sentence using the word *plane* in your sentence.

4. Write a good simple sentence using the word *politician* in your sentence.

5. Write a good complex sentence using the word *supper* in your sentence.

6. Write a good compound sentence using the word *elephant* in your sentence.

ESL POINTER

Conditional Sentences Using the Conjunction *If*

Although *if* is a little word, it can cause big confusion because the conditions it can express can be complicated. *If* is a subordinate conjunction used when you wish to state a conditional relationship of some sort. *If* may be used in three conditional cases:

Case 1: To express facts or generalizations that are true in the world

> If people do not drink enough water, they will die.
>
> If the plant is not given this fertilizer, it will not flourish.

Case 2: To express predications or to make inferences

> If this book is by Agatha Christie, it is probably a mystery novel.
>
> If Rini uses her mother's recipe, the pizza will be delicious.
>
> If the library is not open on Sunday, Josef cannot access the Internet.

Case 3: To express fantastic ideas—ones that cannot come true

> If I were you, I would leave him. (I cannot be another person; I can only be myself. Note the use of the verb *were* with the subject *I*.)
>
> If he were a prizefighter, he would be dangerous. (It is not likely the subject will ever be a prizefighter. Notice the use of the verb *were* again.)
>
> If cats could fly, there would be fewer birds. (Cats cannot fly.)

Exercise 1 Identifying Conditions

Read each sentence. Decide whether *if* expresses case **1, 2,** or **3.** Write your answer after each sentence. Check your answers in the Answer Key.

1. If the employee bought the company, he would fire all of us. ____
2. If ice melts, it leaves a puddle of water. ____
3. If the game is against the team from Oshawa, we might win. ____
4. If rainbows had pots of gold at the ends of them, most people would be rich. ____
5. If the sulphuric acid is placed in this plastic container, it will dissolve it. ____
6. If a mouse were to have a credit card, its house would be full of cheese. ____

7. If the train arrives at midnight, the passengers will be unable to take public transit in our city. _____

8. If the food contains too many additives, I will get a migraine. _____

9. If people sleep in too often, they will find it difficult to get up early. _____

10. If they offer us a good price, we will sell our condominium. _____

11. If the traffic is heavy at three o'clock, I will miss my meeting. _____

12. If she were 10 years younger, she would marry him. _____

13. If I were a witch, I'd cast a spell on you. _____

14. If you leave the butter out, it will go rancid in the warm room. _____

Exercise 2 Constructing Sentence Patterns

Work in pairs. Construct sentences according to the directions given below. Use separate paper. Be prepared to share your answers with others.

1. Write a compound sentence using *but* as the coordinating conjunction.

2. Write a compound-complex sentence using *who* in a relative, restrictive clause.

3. Write a simple sentence containing a compound verb.

4. Write a complex sentence using *because* as the subordinate conjunction.

5. Write a simple sentence with a compound subject.

6. Write a compound-complex sentence using *that* in a relative, restrictive clause.

7. Write a complex sentence using *which* in a relative clause.

8. Write a complex sentences using *when* as a subordinate conjunction.

9. Write a compound-complex sentence using a semicolon effectively.

CHECKOUT

1. What makes sentence patterns different from one another is how the clauses in each pattern relate.

2. Relative clauses must be placed next to the words they describe in a sentence.

3. Compound sentences contain two S-V sets joined by a coordinating conjunction.

4. Try varying your own writing style by using different patterns of sentences.

chapter 15

Sentence-Level Errors

Chapter Objectives

What will you have learned when you have completed this chapter? You will be able to

1. identify and repair sentence faults—run-on sentences, comma splices, sentence fragments, pronoun reference errors, parallelism faults, and faulty shifts.
2. use semicolons correctly in compound sentences.
3. distinguish conjunctive adverbs from joiners.

Introduction: Six Types of Sentence Faults

A number of sentence errors occur frequently in student writing. In this chapter you will find several types: run-on sentences, comma splices, sentence fragments, pronoun errors, parallelism faults, and faulty shifts. These sentence-level errors are faults which are considered serious because they disrupt meaning.

These sentence-level errors are often subtle. In other words, as a writer you must keep them in mind when you edit, revise, and proofread. Here are some tips:

1. Think about what you want to say. Write your sentence and then reread it carefully.
2. Concentrate on getting your ideas into words.
3. Read and reread your sentences as many times as needed to make sure the sentences are saying what you want them to say. Read your sentences out loud to "hear" them.
4. Concentrate on the grammatical aspects of your sentence after you are satisfied the sentence means what you want it to mean.
5. Check for spelling and punctuation errors.
6. Now check for the subtle sentence-level errors discussed in this chapter.
7. It is important to refer to an English handbook from time to time. Look up something when you are uncertain about it, for looking something up is a good way to learn.
8. Discuss structural sentence errors with others; you will find this method also enhances your learning.
9. You should be aiming constantly and consistently to improve the standards of your academic writing and to edit your own work better. Aim for improvement.

Try writing the self-test on sentence-level errors that follows. Check your answers the Answer Key at the back of the book.

Chapter 15: Self-Test

Part 1: Identifying Fragments and Sentences

Read the following groups of words. Some are correct sentences; others are not. Write **S** after the groups of words that are correct sentences. Write **FRAG** after the groups of words that are fragments. (1 point each, 10 points)

1. Paid attention during the whole lecture. _____
2. Pamela battling a serious illness. _____
3. Because we noticed three seals on the beach. _____
4. An orchid is a delicate flower. _____
5. Murray will be right over with the pizza. _____
6. With frustration and a heavy heart. _____
7. Interviews the clients for the company. _____
8. Donna locking the garage by remote control. _____
9. Since I picked up a *Globe and Mail* at the newsstand. _____
10. Learning to water-ski can be fun. _____

Part 2: Identifying Run-ons and Sentences

Read the following groups of words. Some are correct sentences; others are not. Write **S** after the groups of words that are correct sentences. Write **RO** after the groups of words that are run-on sentence faults. (1 point each, 10 points)

1. Hardly a word had been spoken during the dinner, everyone was deep in thought. _____
2. Owen was nervous on his first date with Kathy because it was the first since his divorce. _____
3. Some species of wildlife must be placed under protection, otherwise, their natural habitat would disappear with land development. _____
4. Marcie will write a proposal for starting a new program at the college, but she will have difficulty convincing the Ministry of Forests and Land Resources to give her funds. _____
5. The rescue attempt was set back because of the wind on the water; however, a crew will try again when the weather breaks. _____
6. The engineering department will set its exam for next week, consequently, students will be studying hard. _____

7. The carpenter measured the closet wall then he began making notes. _____
8. The TV movie was so melodramatic; we couldn't bear to watch it. _____
9. Patchwork quilting can be done by anyone, however, a person has to have patience with the sewing. _____
10. Del's prescription was very expensive he said it cost over $100. _____

Part 3: Identifying Fragments and Run-on Faults

Read each of the following word groups. If the word group is a correct sentence, write **S** after it. If the word group is a fragment, write **FRAG** after it. If the word group is a run-on, write **RO** after it. (1 point each, 10 points)

1. On occasion, Bill visits the museum, he is very interested in natural sciences. _____
2. Clark seems preoccupied with fixing his car this evening, therefore, he will not be going to class. _____
3. Several of the women were taking prenatal classes to help them with their first births; many were accompanied by their partners. _____
4. Having many preparations to make for the journey into space. _____
5. Our family does not enjoy packaged foods, and we rarely buy them at the grocery store. _____
6. There were more than 16 chess players in the room all were deeply concentrating. _____
7. Since she was elected to the legislature in Winnipeg. _____
8. Describing the treatment he had received as a hostage. _____
9. Jeremy, sick with the flu, stayed in bed all weekend. _____
10. The anxious group preferred to speak with the manager of the mall immediately, on the other hand, they were willing to make an appointment to see him. _____

Part 4: Finding and Repairing Fragments and Run-ons

Read each of the following groups of words. If the word group is a fragment, write **FRAG** after it. Then correct the fragment error, and write the correction in the spaces provided. If the word group is a run-on, write **RO** after it. Then correct the run-on error, and write the correction in the spaces provided. (1 point for each correct identification, 1 point for each correction of error, 20 points to be marked by the instructor or the marker.)

1. Worrying and having low self-esteem. _____

_____

_____

2. Heather really enjoying her summer at Lake of the Woods. _____

3. The pitcher bent down to pick up the ball, then he stretched a little and walked to the mound. _____

4. The committee decided the supervisor's action was not ethical, consequently, the group recommended his removal from the company. _____

5. Slow down when you come to the hospital zone the police monitor the area carefully. _____

6. Under the stars in the little tent the boy. _____

7. Tent caterpillars spin cocoons, then, in this state, they can safely and slowly change into adults. _____

8. Although the microwave was purchased last Tuesday. _____

9. Wondering whether she should brake or not. _____

10. Matt refinished the rocking chair, Sarah built the futon frame. _____

_____

_____

Part 5: Repairing Sentence Faults

The following sentences contain one of the following sentence faults: fragment, run-on, pronoun reference error, shift in person/number, or shift in verb tense. First, read each sentence. Then repair the error and write the corrected version of the sentence in the space provided. You do not need to tell what kind of error the sentence contains. (2 points each, 30 points, to be marked by the instructor or the marker)

1. Several of the girls at camp were missing her mother back home.

_____

_____

2. If one wants to argue, you should get your facts straight.

_____

_____

3. Tony looks upset, but he wasn't talking to anyone.

_____

_____

4. Artichokes a little hard to clean.

_____

_____

5. Because the bank is closed for the holiday.

_____

_____

6. She works out at the gym, then she goes to lunch with her friends.

7. Alexis was a wonderful stage actor. Who died at age 50.

8. All of the women enjoyed herself.

9. He completes the assignments, then he goes to Rome.

10. There was a huge mess and several complaints about the party, this made the landlord angry.

11. Kevin is studying decimal fractions in his math class, however he doesn't understand it.

12. Wayne told Rudy that he was fired.

13. Because the staples don't fit the staple gun.

_____

_____

14. Everybody should vote according to his conscience.

_____

_____

15. Jennifer informed Georgia that she was the better singer of the two.

_____

_____

Sentence Fragments

A sentence is a whole idea. It carries meaning to a listener or a reader because it makes sense. A fragment, on the other hand, is incomplete. It does not express a whole idea. A sentence fragment is a piece of a sentence that poses as a complete sentence. A fragment may begin with a capital letter and end in a period or a question mark; however, it does not make sense on its own. Often sentence fragments begin with conjunctions like *because, since, as, although, when,* or *unless*. Here are some examples of sentence fragments:

Because he was not invited.

Worried after the long illness.

Her family in which there are two girls and one boy.

Since the weather has been cloudy.

Standing alone waiting for the bus.

Notice that pieces of information are missing from all of the above examples. Sometimes an independent clause might be missing as in the first example. At other times, the subject may be missing as in the second example. In the third example, the writer has not included a verb for the subject. In the last example, it is not certain who is standing alone; in other words, you may say the subject is missing.

Some situations may allow for a writer's or speaker's use of fragments. In conversation, for example, listeners can complete the meaning of a speaker's fragment by simply asking the speaker what he means, or they may feel they understand what the speaker means because both speaker and listener have been engaged in a quick, back-and-forth communication. In formal academic writing, however, you do not expect to have to ask the writer what he or she meant. Of course, many famous writers have used fragments in their writing, but in academic writing, *fragments are considered errors because they are imprecise and potentially confusing*. Sentence fragments are considered a type of sentence fault or sentence-level error.

Read the following piece of writing. Can you spot the many fragments that make the meaning difficult to follow in an effective and precise manner?

Riding around in his new car last Saturday night. Bruno felt really happy. He had promised his friend, Frankie, to pick him up at seven. The thrill. The speed. Suddenly, arriving at his favorite Greek restaurant. Because he loved to go there every Saturday. Bruno remembered. Thinking Frankie was probably angry at him. After all. He has forgotten to pick up his best friend. Who had been waiting for two hours! Embarrassing!

Tips: How to Correct Fragment Errors

1. **If the subject or verb is missing, add one.**

    Fragment: Working all weekend.
    Correction: Marcel is working all weekend.

    Fragment: Mrs. Lomas on the escalator.
    Correction: Mrs. Lomas is on the escalator.

2. **If a fragment gives partial information, add the necessary information to make it complete.** Sometimes it is effective to join the fragment to the sentence in front of it.

    Fragment: A traffic jam occurred near the bridge. Because only one lane was open.

    Correction: A traffic jam occurred near the bridge because only one lane was open.

3. **Sometimes it works to join the fragment to the sentence after it.**

    Fragment: Although he had not spoken at the meeting. We knew he had something to say.

    Correction: Although he had not spoken at the meeting, we knew he had something to say.

4. **If the fragment does not closely relate to the sentence before or after it, place it in a separate and complete sentence by adding more words.**

    Fragment: Louis was always a musical person. Since he was three.
    Correction: Louis was always a musical person. Since he was three, he has played the piano and the violin.

Semicolon Use

Remember: compound sentences may contain a semicolon.

Often, if a semicolon is used in a sentence, the semicolon indicates that the two parts of the sentence are independent clauses. Each part of the compound sentence is really like a simple sentence that makes sense on its own. Do not write a complete sentence on one side of the semicolon and a fragment on the other. For example:

                       complete idea   fragment
Incorrect: Mrs. McVitie lost her purse; became frantic.

                       complete idea   complete idea
Correct: Mrs. McVitie lost her purse; she became frantic.

                       complete idea   fragment
Incorrect: Children should be taught street safety; knowing how to react to strangers.

                               complete idea   complete idea
Correct: Children should be taught street safety; they should know how to react to strangers.

Exercise 1 Fragments

Read the following groups of words. Some are complete sentences; others are not. Write **S** after the correct complete sentences. Write **FRAG** after the groups of words that are not complete. Check your answers in the Answer Key.

1. Gardening, a pastime enjoyed by many people. ____

2. Sarah leaving the class before the others. ____

3. Shopping for bargains is difficult in 2005. ____

4. Because he was unable to complete his project on time. ____

5. Fishing as a way of life is dying out. ____

6. Although the roads are slippery in the winter. ____

7. Because the teachers were on strike. ____

8. Andy found a part-time job in sales. ____

9. The police will investigate the matter over the next few weeks. ____

10. Soybeans are rich in protein. ____

11. Shivering, huddling together for warmth, the stranded hikers. ____

12. Stay calm. ____

13. Rocky is expert at diving and swimming. ____

14. The academy opening in the winter of 2005. ____

15. Despite the heavy protests and the threats of violence. ____

16. Some diseases are transmitted through the air. ____

17. She fought against depression. ____

18. With balloons and face painting in the main tent. ____

19. Do you think because he was caught? ____

20. Building boats is an expensive hobby. ____

Exercise 2 Repairing Fragments

Work in pairs. Find all sentence fragments. Rewrite each sentence in order to correct errors. Note: not all word groups in the following exercise are fragment errors. Some may be correct sentences. Use separate paper.

1. A woman working for minimum wage in Canada today.

2. Three seals were spotted off Mervin's Point last night.

3. Then stopped to chat with his friend.

4. Under the tree near the old oak was a chest full of money.

5. The pony ridden only on Saturdays.

6. The unfriendly serviceperson sorting through the pile of bills.

7. Because she had forgotten her wallet, she could not pay for her groceries.

8. Since she was appointed to the position.

9. In the tool shed at the back of the yard.

10. Cruising along the highway, we saw many visitors who were taking pictures of the elk.

11. The pharmacist talking to a customer about some medication.

12. The dog under the porch of one of the old buildings.

13. Alex and Mike sitting on the lawn eating their lunches.

14. Cartons of beer were delivered to the wrong store.

15. All of the ingredients for the special cake.

16. Laurence and Caroline took their parents out for an Italian dinner. Lorenzo's the best Italian restaurant in the city.

17. Greeted her enthusiastically at the airport.

18. I used to be frightened of the dark when I was little; even had to have a night light in my room.

19. Children were running amuck in the mall. Because Santa was to arrive soon.

Run-on Sentences

A run-on sentence is a fault because the writer has written two, perhaps even three, sentences as a single sentence *without using the correct punctuation or correct conjunction to connect the sentences*. Once again, meaning becomes confused because of the sentence fault.

Run-on: Their idea was to complete their computer graphics courses and get good jobs new hope was on their horizon.

Correction 1: Their idea was to complete their computer graphics courses and get good jobs: new hope was on their horizon.

Correction 2: Their idea was to complete their computer graphics courses and get good jobs; new hope was on their horizon.

Correction 3: Their idea was to complete their computer graphics courses and get good jobs. New hope was on their horizon.

Correction 4: Their idea was to complete their computer graphics courses and get good jobs for new hope was on their horizon.

Notice that in the example above the run-on fault has been corrected in four different ways. In the first correction, a full colon is used to join one sentence to the other. In the second, a semicolon is used to connect ideas. In the third, the sentence has been separated into two smaller sentences. In the fourth, the conjunction *for* is used to connect clauses. All four repair methods are good ones. You might be able to think of others, too.

Exercise 3 Run-on Sentences

Read each sentence. If the sentence is a run-on sentence, write **RO** after it. Then correct the error and rewrite your corrected sentence in the space provided. If the sentence is correct as given, write **CORRECT** after it. Check your answers in the Answer Key.

1. The young couple was arguing about the rent money, however, they seemed to settle their differences. _____

_____

_____

2. Two of the bank managers were fired from their positions the government inspectors had found serious errors in their accounting systems. _____

3. Daisy loves to play baseball in the spring her husband, Arnold, likewise loves the game. _____

4. The teacher was avoiding discussion about AIDS many students, on the other hand, were interested in talking about it. _____

5. I found the shoes very uncomfortable, however, I could not return them because the store had gone out of business. _____

6. On election night, the crowd gathered around the favoured candidate, they cheered her every word. _____

7. Each worker had to take a cut in pay, according to the manager of the mill. _____

8. Can you help me with this account, or will I have to solve this problem myself? _____

9. After the severe rains, most of the plains were flooded, as a result, the farmers could not sow their crops until late spring. _____

10. Despite his gruff manner, he is a gentle person who tries to mind his own business and stay out of trouble. _____

11. The garden store in the new mall was a success, the bookstore located near it was not successful, however. _____

12. The magician turned to us with a smile then he disappeared. _____

13. Crystal loves to collect antique coins and jewellery she travels all over Canada making her purchases. _____

Comma Splice

When you use a comma to join two sentences, you have committed another kind of run-on sentence fault called a *comma splice*. According to today's rules of punctuation, a comma is not used to join items; in fact, its function in sentences is quite the opposite—to separate items. Use the semicolon to join related sentences.

Comma Splice: The students investigated the possibility of starting a newspaper, several volunteers wanted to organize the first meeting.

Correction: The students investigated the possibility of starting a newspaper; several volunteers wanted to organize the first meeting.

Correction: The students investigated the possibility of starting a newspaper, and several volunteers wanted to organize the first meeting.

Correction: The students investigated the possibility of starting a newspaper. Several volunteers wanted to organize the first meeting.

Conjunctive Adverbs

As you will recall from Chapter 12, some adverbs may look as if they can join clauses in a sentence, but they cannot. This group of adverbs is called *conjunctive adverbs* because they look like conjunctions, or joiners. As a writer or reader, you can tell whether a word is working like a conjunction in a sentence or not.

Simply attempt to move the word you think is a conjunction to another position in the sentence. If you can move the word to another position and the sentence or clause still makes sense, then the word you have moved is not a true joiner or conjunction.

Marvin wanted to get the new position in the firm; however, he felt anxious about submitting his résumé.

Marvin wanted to get the new position in the firm; he felt anxious about submitting his résumé, however.

Does the sentence still make sense? Can *however* be moved to other positions in the clause? Will the clause still make sense? You can conclude, then, that *however* cannot be a conjunction because it can be moved to various positions.

However is an example of a conjunctive adverb. It relates the ideas of the second clause back to the ideas of the first clause. True conjunctions are fixed in their positions. Notice, too, that when *however* is moved in the example, the semicolon is the punctuation mark doing the work of joining.

Try to move the italicized word in the following sentence to another position.

Paul was annoyed with his selection in the cafeteria *because* he found the snack stale and salty.

Can you move *because* to any other position in the clause so that the clause still makes sense? The word *because* is a true conjunction or joiner: it is fixed into position.

It is important, then, that you ensure conjunctions or semicolons are used in your compound sentences.

Incorrect:	Polly put the kettle on consequently we all had tea. (Run-on fault)
Correct:	Polly put the kettle on; consequently, we all had tea.
Correct:	Polly put the kettle on, and consequently, we all had tea.
Correct:	Polly put the kettle on. Consequently, we all had tea.
Incorrect:	Tara was upset by the meeting therefore she plans to complain to the supervisor. (Run-on fault)
Correct:	Tara was upset by the meeting; therefore, she plans to complain to the supervisor.
Correct:	Tara was upset by the meeting, and therefore, she plans to complain to the supervisor.
Correct:	Tara was upset by the meeting. Therefore, she plans to complain to the supervisor.

Here is a list of common conjunctive adverbs. You will see these words used often in sentences. Remember: they do not join independent clauses.

Conjunctive Adverbs

moreover	still
therefore	nevertheless
however	likewise
otherwise	furthermore
then	consequently

Exercise 4 Run-on Sentences

Read each of the following sentences. Write **RO** after the word group if you think it is a run-on sentence. Write **S** after the word group if you think it is a correct sentence. Check your answers in the Answer Key found at the end of the book.

1. Learning more about helicopter flying was Adam's dream. _____

2. The racket kept us up all night consequently we feel a bit grumpy today. _____

3. Warner Brothers has been in the business of making Hollywood movies for over 70 years they are still producing some blockbusters. _____

4. Her garden was a small paradise with a tiny pool full of fish, lush ferns and shrubs, and flowers of many colours. _____

5. Brian had never been to the opera surprisingly, he enjoyed the performance. _____

6. Montague Stately was an eccentric millionaire who decided to retire to one of the smallest islands in the St. Lawrence. _____

7. If you do your own house renovations, be sure to get all the proper permits and inspections. _____

8. They were expecting lots of customers for the Christmas rush, they were stocked up on items in September. _____

9. Cuddles, her prize Doberman pinscher, was trained to guard the property, furthermore, he was expected to alert the household about any suspicious activities. _____

10. *Oliver Twist* is my favourite Dickens book, however, my sister insists *Martin Chuzzlewit* is better. _____

11. The dispatch came from Colonel Upstart, but the lieutenant refused to acknowledge it. _____

12. At one time, almost everyone's intelligence was measured by a test called an IQ, or intelligence quotient, test. _____

13. These vegetables need to be pared, then they need to be steamed for dinner service at six. _____

14. A small meteor struck the earth just outside Calgary and left a crater seven metres across. _____

15. The sculpture was placed on exhibit just outside city hall; it became an object of interest to visitors. _____

16. He shouted for assistance, then he lay still. _____

17. The shaman of the tribe came forward he wanted to assist the RCMP in their search for the lost child. _____

18. Those pesticides are toxic; please refrain from using them. _____

Exercise 5   Fragments and Run-ons

Read each of the following sentences. If the sentence is correct as it stands, write **CORRECT** after it. If the sentence is a run-on sentence, write **RO** after it. Then repair the sentence and rewrite the correct sentence in the space provided. If the sentence is not a sentence but a fragment, write **FRAG** after it. Then repair the fragment and rewrite the correct sentence in the space provided. You may work in pairs. Be prepared to share your answers.

1. The city had become a sprawling megalopolis the citizens found themselves choking in the exhaust-filled air. _____

_____

_____

Chapter 15   Sentence-Level Errors   **301**

2. The young cougar seemed irritated by the heat. Yowling as it slowly clambered up a small, rocky hill. _____

3. We are sorry to inform you that you did not win the contest your drawing however was noted by the judges to be exemplary. _____

4. If Eddie calls later. Tell him I'll be home around eight. _____

5. Justin was appointed to the Order of Canada because of the work he had done with Southeast Asian immigrants since 1965. _____

6. Organizing a club for older women returning to formal education. _____

7. Her youngest, a child of four, has been selected to appear in a commercial for Canadian Tire. _____

8. The family discussing politics over the evening meal. _____

302   Part 2   Sentence Foundations

9. Juanita, Esther, and Estella are sisters from Mexico who recently arrived in Canada, they are not familiar with Canadian slang. _____

10. Although the can did not have a label. _____

11. He waved through the window, then he entered the restaurant. _____

12. The protest ended peacefully. Although some people on the roadblock had been slightly injured. _____

13. Most teenagers love to be independent; they enjoy the feeling of being in charge. _____

14. The propeller of the motor had been damaged by the rocks. No damage to the boat itself. _____

15. My Uncle Rufus is an excellent tailor; as a matter of fact, he sews most of my clothes. _____

Pronoun Reference Problems

Sometimes errors occur in sentences because writers make incorrect or unclear pronoun references. You must pay particular attention to the *antecedent* of a pronoun in order to determine what the meaning of a sentence is. *The word the pronoun refers to* in a sentence is called an antecedent. Furthermore, you must make sure that a pronoun agrees with its antecedent; otherwise, you will make a grammatical or sentence-level error called a *pronoun reference fault*.

Vague or Ambiguous Pronoun Reference

If there is no clear antecedent for your pronoun, you will have a *vague pronoun reference* problem. If your pronoun could refer to more than one antecedent, you have a pronoun reference problem called *ambiguous pronoun reference*. Remember: a reader may misinterpret the meaning of a whole sentence because the antecedent of the pronoun is not clear or not stated.

Incorrect: Several large herons were fishing in the shallow lagoon; it was moving so slowly that we could not tell when it had actually moved. (vague pronoun reference. What is the antecedent for *it*?)

Correct: Several large herons were fishing in the shallow lagoon; they were moving so slowly that we could not tell when they had actually moved. (*herons* is the antecedent of *they*)

Incorrect: The dispute between the workers and the managers did not end until they invited them to a weekend retreat. (ambiguous pronoun reference)

The problem is ambiguity because the antecedent could be *workers* or *managers*. Who invited whom?

Correct: The dispute between the workers and the managers did not end until the workers invited the managers to a weekend retreat.

Correct: The dispute between the workers and the managers did not end until the managers invited the workers to a weekend retreat.

Incorrect: Donald told Alfie he had won the championship. (ambiguous)

Who told whom?

Correct: Donald told Alfie, "I have won the championship."

Correct: Donald told Alfie, "You have won the championship."

Correct: Donald who had won the championship told Alfie about it.

Correct: Alfie who had won the championship told Donald about it.

Each of the above corrections has a different meaning. Be clear about what it is you want to say, and choose your correction carefully.

Problems with the Pronoun *This*

One of the worst offenders when it comes to creating vague pronoun reference is the use of the word *this*. Usually, *this* has no clear antecedent in the sentence. If you want to use *this*, then use a noun right after it.

Incorrect: My friend Elmore loves to hang glide in foreign countries and to fly wherever he wants to practise his sport; this has cost him quite a bit of money over the years.

What exactly does *this* refer to? Can you tell? Is there a clear antecedent?

Correct: My friend Elmore loves to hang glide in foreign countries and to fly wherever he wants to practise his sport; these activities have cost him quite a bit of money over the years.

Pronoun Agreement

In addition, be sure that the pronoun agrees with other parts of the sentence in number and in gender.

Incorrect: Every woman was given their assignments at the meeting.

Correct: Every woman was given her assignment at the meeting.

The understanding is that *assignment* should reflect back to *every woman* since that is the subject. *The pronoun must agree with its antecedent in gender and number.* The subject is a singular, feminine subject; therefore, the pronoun must also be a singular, feminine noun—*her*.

Incorrect: Some of the men brought his own transportation.

Correct: Some of the men brought their own transportation.

The indefinite pronoun *some* refers to a count noun—a plural—*men*. The pronoun must also be in the third person plural—*their*.

Incorrect: All of the boys wanted his own bicycle.

Correct: All of the boys wanted their own bicycles.

The indefinite pronoun *all* refers to a count noun (*boys*). Since it is in the plural, the pronoun must also be in the plural—*their*.

Incorrect: Everyone has to make up his own mind.

Correct: Everyone has to make up his or her own mind.

Also Acceptable: Everyone has to make up their own minds.

Everyone is also an indefinite pronoun. You may structure your sentence to avoid sexism as shown by the second correction—*Everyone has to make up their own minds*. You may notice it is now becoming accepted practice to use the word *their* when referring to indefinite pronoun expressions such as *everyone, everybody, every person, all*, and so forth in order to refer to people in general. The use of *their* in these cases avoids sexism in the language; in other words, using *their* with indefinite pronouns helps you avoid naming a specific gender. It is important, however, to find out if your instructor welcomes this practice. Some instructors do not allow the use of *their* with indefinite pronouns.

Exercise 6 Pronoun Reference

Work in pairs. Find the pronoun reference problems in each of the following sentences. Then repair the error by rewriting the sentence correctly in the given space. Share your answers with others in the class, and check your answers in the Answer Key.

1. Erica told Janice she was coming to lunch.

2. People could get a special pass to see the clipper ship; this made them very enthusiastic.

3. Everyone must do his best.

4. When Elvis' first song was recorded in 1955, he quickly became popular.

5. Hal told Roger about his new investment.

6. The boy was caught speeding and driving without a licence, and this shocked his parents.

7. Every boy can have their own racquets on the court.

_____

_____

8. Melissa sent Tina to pick up the team uniforms after she returned from the game.

_____

_____

9. Every woman was given their own set of documents for the meeting.

_____

_____

10. Some of the girls brought her own lunch.

_____

_____

11. Mrs. Norman asked her if she would sing at the reception.

_____

_____

12. No one really knew who the missing man was, but everyone had a theory about it.

_____

_____

Shifts in Sentences

A *shift* in a sentence is a *sudden change in tense, mood, voice, person, or number.*

Tense has to do with the times of the verbs. If you write more than one verb with more than one tense, be sure the times seem logically possible. *Voice* has to do with verbs. *Active voice* means that the subject does the action in the sentence. *Passive voice* means that the subject receives the action of the verb.

Active Voice: I washed the sink with disinfectant.
Passive Voice: The sink was washed with disinfectant by me.

Try to use the active voice whenever you can in your writing. It makes your ideas (subjects) more direct for the reader. It also makes plain who the agents are and what actions they are responsible for.

Person has to do with subject and point of view. You may recall the earlier discussion on point of view:

Person and Point of View

I	first person point of view
you	second person point of view (singular)
he	third person point of view
she	third person point of view
it	third person point of view
we	first person point of view (plural)
you	second person point of view (plural)
they	third person point of view (plural)

Number has to do with the subject and whether it is plural or singular. For example, *he*, *she*, and *it* are singular pronoun subjects, while *we* and *they* are plural.

Person and Number Shifts

A *change from one subject to another* or *from one verb tense to another* in the same sentence are *two common types of shifts* that make sentences confusing to read. Look over the following examples.

SHIFTS IN PERSON

Incorrect: The spectators jumped up excitedly from their seats; we were thrilled by the power play.

The first part of the sentence has *spectators* as the subject. The second part of the sentence has *we* as the subject. A reader would expect to read *they* as the second subject because *they* agrees in number with *spectators*.

Correct: The spectators jumped up excitedly from their seats; they were thrilled by the power play.

Correct: We spectators jumped up excitedly from our seats; we were thrilled by the power play.

Incorrect: A worker in a large organization often feels as if they have been overlooked.

The subject of the first clause is *a worker*; the subject of the second clause is *they*.

Correct: Workers in large organizations often feel as if they have been overlooked. (non-sexist)

Incorrect: If one wants to learn about birds, you should take part in nature walks.

One is the subject of the first clause, and *you* is the subject of the second clause.

Correct: If you want to learn about birds, you should take part in nature walks.

Shifts in Tense

Be sure that the tenses you use in various part of your sentence make sense. If they are illogically sequenced, your reader will have trouble following your idea.

Incorrect: Marlon walked along the beach, and then he goes in.

The first verb *walked* is past tense; the second verb *goes* is present tense.

Correct: Marlon walked along the beach, and then he went in.

Correct: Marlon walks along the beach, and then he goes in.

Incorrect: Hannah goes to the flea market every Saturday and hunts for bargains; she loved showing off her purchases.

The verbs in the first part of the sentence, *goes* and *hunts*, are in the present tense. The verb in the second part of the compound sentence, *loved*, is in the past tense. The verbs are inconsistent in the sequence of tense. It seems that the writer wants to talk about Hannah's habit of going to flea markets, so the present tense seems preferable; after all, Hannah probably still enjoys hunting for bargains.

Correct: Hannah goes to the flea market every Saturday and hunts for bargains; she loves showing off her purchases.

Exercise 7 Group Activity: Shift Errors

Form a group of three to five people or work in pairs. Read each of the following sentences. Each contains an error in shifts: person, number, or tense. Rewrite your correction in the space provided. After you have agreed, check your answers in the Answer Key found at the back of the book.

1. Helen is pleased with the promotion; she intended to do well in her new position as manager.

   _____

   _____

2. The epidemic spread throughout the countryside, and the doctors attempt to inoculate all residents.

   _____

   _____

3. If one wants to learn about fruit farming, you should talk to an orchardist.

4. Lola had never tried parachute jumping before; she listens carefully to the instructor's directions.

5. Several children were playing hopscotch and skipping, but we did not hear the sound of the siren.

6. The stunt crew was setting up outside the Empress Hotel, and he had some expensive technical equipment.

7. If you don't know about it, one should ask.

8. Because it was the long weekend, the trailer park is packed with vehicles.

9. Everyone should be careful about getting too much sun exposure if you do not want to increase the risk of skin cancer.

10. After we discussed the idea, we leave.

_____

_____

Parallelism Problems

Perhaps the most subtle error of all for you to spot in your own sentences is a *parallelism fault*. Faulty parallelism means that *all grammatical structures in a series are not in the same form*. For example, if a verb phrase is set up in the first part of the sentence, for instance, other verbs in further parts of the sentence must match the first verb structure.

Imagine you have written the following sentence in an essay or research paper:

The economy was slowed because of poor production, loss of workers, and many people were getting too greedy.

Does the sentence sound incorrect to you?

The problem with the sentence is that the grammatical structures do not match in form. It contains faulty parallelism.

In the first case, you see an adjective noun combination.

poor production

In the second case, you see a noun followed by a prepositional phrase.

loss of workers

In the third case, you see a clause.

many people were getting too greedy.

To repair the faulty parallelism, make all of the phrases have the same grammatical feature.

The economy was slowed because of *poor production, worker loss,* and *many people's excessive greed.* (All parts are now adjective and noun combinations.)

The economy was slowed because *production was slower, workers were lost,* and *many people were getting too greedy.* (All parts are now in clause form.)

The economy was slowed because of *slow production, worker loss,* and *excessive greed.* (This version tidies up the adjective and noun combinations.)

Here are some examples of *correct* sentence parallelism:

She is an excellent student, a loyal mother, and a helpful reader in the library.
(adj noun, adj noun, adj noun)

The general manager of marketing **was planning** to visit all the plants in the Stouffville region in the coming year, **was scheduling** meetings with new managers in October, and **was organizing** a planning session for the month of June.
(verb phrase, verb phrase, verb phrase)

Here are more examples of *faulty parallel* structure:

The new park is quiet, well-maintained, and has low landscaping costs.

Emile loves to dance, cook, and playing the classical guitar.

Morris can draw just as well as, if not better, than Trudy.

Why are the three sentences above not parallel in structure? Can you figure out where the faulty parallelism lies in each sentence?

Hints to Finding Parallelism Faults

How can you decide if a sentence has faulty parallelism?

1. **Grammatical structures must match in all parts of the sentence.**

    Examine the structure in the first part of the sentence; then check to see whether the structures following are in balance.

    Correct: Tilling the soil, planting a variety of seeds, and weeding the garden took up most of Vaughn's long weekend.
    (gerund, gerund, gerund)

2. **Balance comparisons.**

    Incorrect: The report showed that boys spend more money on items in the computer store than girls.

    Why is the preceding sentence incorrect? Do you notice how illogical it is?

    Correct: The report showed that boys spend more money than girls do on items in the computer store.

3. **Balance the modifiers.**

    Incorrect: They requested a plumber and poet.

    Why is the above incorrect?

    Correct: They requested a plumber and a poet.

4. **Verb forms should be balanced for all parts of the sentence.**

    Incorrect: He has been writing songs, thinking about producing an album, and is happy to receive any interest in his project.

    Correct: He has been writing songs, thinking about producing an album, and has been happily waiting to receive any interest in his project.

5. **Balance *neither–nor, either–or, not only–but also* constructions.**

   Incorrect: She not only finished the typing but also the filing.

   Place *not only* and *but also* next to the similar grammatical structures in the parts of the sentence. Such positioning will make a smoother sentence.

   Correct: She *not only* finished the typing *but also* completed the filing.

   Correct: She finished *not only* the typing *but also* the filing.

Exercise 8 Parallelism Errors

Each of the following sentences contains faulty parallelism errors. Find the errors and then rewrite the sentences to eliminate the parallelism problems. Use separate paper for your work.

1. Thinking through the problem, discussing its possible solutions, and to want to change the situation contributed to the new policy.
2. My dog has, and will continue to attempt, to beg for food.
3. The student survey showed that women own more computers than men.
4. The company hired a security expert and priest.
5. She not only likes chocolate but also marshmallows.
6. The gorilla was large, hated his owners' poodles, and scared them daily.
7. The eagle had been circling for hours and waited for salmon in the stream.
8. Penny is attractive, rich, and a penny-pincher.
9. Not only did the artist paint with oils, but also the properties of acrylics intrigued her.
10. Playing the harmonica, to do carving, and being a volunteer occupy my grandfather's time.

Exercise 9 Sentence Faults

The sentences contain one of the following sentence faults:

a. fragment

b. run-on

c. shift in person/number

d. shift in verb tense

e. pronoun reference error

f. parallelism error

Work in pairs. First, read each sentence. Decide what the error is within each sentence. Then repair the error and write the corrected version of the sentence in the space provided. Check your answers in the Answer Key.

1. All of the girls wanted to get her camping gear at the same sporting goods store.

   _____

   _____

2. Although he knew the shed really needed an undercoat. Bobby felt too lazy to do the job properly.

   _____

   _____

3. Some foods rich in beta carotene.

   _____

   _____

4. At the registration desk, Alan rented a locker and pays for it for one term at the college.

   _____

   _____

5. My friend Janet is very photogenic, however, she does not like having her picture taken.

   _____

   _____

6. One could safeguard against accidents in the home if we just paid attention to safety details.

   _____

   _____

7. Sodium fluoride has been added to the water system of the city. Despite the fact that many claim this chemical is poisonous.

8. Walter really wanted to build a solar house, he checked the building regulations with the regional planning office.

9. The family bought a tandem bicycle; we particularly want to use it on vacation.

10. The weary visitors were so exhausted after their long flight from Taiwan that they fall asleep immediately.

11. Her testimony at the trial necessary to the defence.

12. Walking, riding, and to climb were her exercise manias.

Exercise 10 Sentence Faults

The sentences contain one of the following sentence faults:

a. fragment

b run-on

c. shift in person/number
d. shift in verb tense
e. pronoun reference error
f. parallelism error

First, read each sentence. Then repair the error and write the corrected version of the sentence in the space provided. Check your answers in the Answer Key.

1. It seems the whole world fearful of terrorist attacks.

2. Everyone should decide what is best for his own children.

3. Woody Allen started out as a popular stand-up comic, moreover, his fame earned him a job as a screenwriter.

4. Since that terry cloth robe was so expensive. It should look better after only three washings.

5. Because Lord Peakinloft managed his estate well, one was left with no debt.

6. The Morgan brothers had a contract to do all the plumbing in the new housing development, then their company went bankrupt.

7. The selector on our stereo was broken, and they couldn't fix it.

8. With all the self-assurance of a king. Marmaduke entered the ballroom.

9. The soggy tomato sandwiches did not make an appetizing lunch when we go on the picnic.

10. The tea tastes bitter perhaps it has been brewed too long.

11. The proprietor of the bed and breakfast wanting to please all of her guests.

12. Some people enjoy sewing because they found sewing their own clothes saved money.

13. Although the condo is small. There is plenty of storage space in the basement.

14. One ought to check with the head server before you make a complaint.

_____

_____

15. He and his brother Manny bought a cottage near Bala, and he loves going to it on weekends.

_____

_____

Exercise 11 Group Activity: Some Final Editing Practice

This final editing exercise is made up of three paragraphs, each containing specific grammatical or mechanical errors. Try working on each one in a group, so that you can help each other and share ideas. Be prepared to provide answers to the whole class. Check your answers in the Answer Key.

The following editing practice contains these common faults:

punctuation (comma, semicolon, colon) errors

fragments

run-ons

S-V disagreement

parallelism errors

possessive (the apostrophe) errors

adverb and adjective usage errors

Paragraph 1: Punctuation and the Use of the Apostrophe in Possessives

The following paragraph contains errors in the following:

comma use (including comma splices)

semicolon use

colon use

apostrophe use with possessive case

Read the paragraph. Underline all errors you spot. Correct each error.

318   Part 2   Sentence Foundations

No one knew who was to inherit Mrs. Blethershotts estate and her enormous fortune, it remained a great mystery to everyone. Because Ethyl the maid had remained in Mrs. Blethershotts service for so long all of the staff expected her to receive some small compensation for her years of loyalty. The butler Archibald felt certain he was to win something as well he had served the Blethershott Manor for over 40 years, he had not had one days absence from his duties. It was the cooks opinion that she should receive the most, she had done three things in her opinion that counted the most, served fresh nutritious food to the Mistress kept a tight budget and made herself available to the Mistress every whim. The chauffeur Kendrick did not agree that the other members of staff were worthy of receiving any more than a few dollars. Since he had arrived at Blethershott Manor he had given the Blethershotts his devoted attention not once had he complained about their unreasonable demands. In fact Kendrick had said very little, moreover, he now believed he was the most likely to inherit. Everyone's suspicion had begun to create peculiar tension in the household no one seemed able to sleep the night before the reading of the will.

Paragraph 2: Fragments, Run-ons, Comma Splices

Read the paragraph Underline all errors you spot. Correct each error.

Taking children to their first daycare can be an unnerving experience for new parents, the day of tearful and loud protests of a child can make even the most calm parent feeling flustered and guilty. Weeks in advance, many parents try to explain to their children what wonderful places daycares are. Because the parents are trying to avoid the "big scene" on the daycare steps. Some children seem to listen carefully. To understand what their parents are telling them. Some children seem to understand their parents' explanation fully, these children seem relaxed and happy about the new arrangement. Of course, once the new parents and their new daycare students arrive at the destinations, it becomes another matter entirely, teachers, students, parents, assistants, and children all seem to be talking at once. Frightened and anxious faces tell the tale. Because no one seems to want to leave and no one seems to want to stay! It is hard to imagine. That in just a few short weeks. Most children seem to love their new "schools" and welcome each day's activities.

Paragraph 3: Parallelism and Adjective and Adverb Use

Read the paragraph. Underline all errors you spot. Correct each error.

According to *Monday Magazine*, Victoria is Canada's "city of poisons" because of the overuse of pesticides and herbicides by residential gardeners and sellers are enthusiastic to sell these chemicals. The situation has naturalists and environmentalists real upset. *Monday Magazine*, April 24–30, 1997, states that "some of these compounds are tested for their cancer-causing potential, but most have been introduced without any of assessment of their effects on the immune and nervous systems" (8). To ensure that gardening chemicals are being used good, to eliminate their overuse, and controlling garden pests and diseases will take better management on the part of the industry and government. There are still few laws which are real effective and can be enforced. For example, although many residential gardeners in Victoria feel badly about the harm that garden chemical agents create, these same citizens continue to use agents such as malathion, propoxur, captan, and 2,4-D. These chemicals act very slow on the environment, and years later, dangerous traces can be found in the soil and the drinking water supply. Beneficial insects, songbirds, garter snakes, and amphibians are also sure harmed by the abuse and we tend to overuse commonly available garden chemicals.

Chapter 15: Review Test

Part 1: Identifying Fragments and Sentences

Read the following groups of words. Some are correct sentences; others are not. Write **S** after the groups of words that are correct sentences. Write **FRAG** after the groups of words that are fragments. (1 point each, 10 points)

1. Experiencing the great outdoors. _____
2. Marjorie photographing the new totem pole. _____
3. After his late shift was over. _____
4. Speeding causes accidents. _____
5. The Calgary Stampede was a huge success this year. _____
6. If we telephone after midnight. _____
7. Forecasts the weather accurately. _____
8. Connie tying the dried flower wreath. _____
9. When the course was offered through the Access Network. _____
10. Making mistakes is part of learning. _____

Part 2: Identifying Run-ons and Sentences

Read the following groups of words. Some are correct sentences; others are not. Write **S** after the groups of words that are correct sentences. Write **RO** after the groups of words that are run-on sentence faults. (1 point each, 10 points)

1. The new telescope lens was delivered to the observatory the scientists supervised the unloading of the expensive lens. _____
2. Because he was out at third, we lost the game. _____

3. That little sparrow has a beautiful song, however, it is not spectacular in appearance. _____

4. The racehorse stood in its stall, and it tried to watch the pedestrians in front of the stables. _____

5. The best vegetable stew is made with root vegetables, dill dumplings make a tasty addition to the meal, too. _____

6. The striking workers would not yield on any of the issues, consequently, management locked out the workers. _____

7. He got a substantial inheritance, then he quit his job and retired to Costa Rica. _____

8. The dessert squares were unusually rich and sweet; each of us could eat only a tiny piece. _____

9. The substitute teacher was exhausted at the end of the day, the Grade 7 class had worn her out. _____

10. Some illnesses are hereditary, others are caused by poor diets. _____

Part 3: Identifying Fragments and Run-on Faults

Read each of the following word groups. If the word group is a correct sentence, write **S** after it. If the word group is a fragment, write **FRAG** after it. If the word group is a run-on, write **RO** after it. (1 point each, 10 points)

1. In Greek mythology, Hades was the underworld, it was ruled by Pluto and Persephone. _____

2. The council did not pass the motion to expand bus service to the campus, therefore, many students had to find alternate forms of transportation. _____

3. Colour therapy is a technique used for stress relief and relaxation purposes. _____

4. Deciding which letter to answer first. _____

5. Nintendo seems to be a world leader in video game production, but competition to stay on top is demanding. _____

6. Nathan decided not to apply for the job he believed he would not get it anyway. _____

7. Since Dawn has taken her training in pediatric nursing. _____

8. Debating the bill in Parliament. _____

9. Kenneth, troubled by her letter, gave Ruth a call. _____

10. The commercial advertised a handy tool for peeling apples, however, I sent away for the gadget and found it did not work as demonstrated. _____

Part 4: Finding and Repairing Fragments and Run-ons

Read each of the following groups of words. If the word group is a fragment, write **FRAG** after it. Then correct the fragment error, and write the correction in the space provided. If the word group is a run-on, write **RO** after it. Then correct the run-on error, and write the correction in the space provided) (1 point for each correct identification, 1 point for each correction of error, 20 points, to be marked by the instructor or the marker.)

1. Delivering furniture for a summer job. _____

2. Trudi wanting a change in scenery. _____

3. The trainer spoke to the athletes on the field, then she posted their training schedule in the locker room. _____

4. The frost in California destroyed the citrus crop, consequently, prices for oranges skyrocketed in Canadian supermarkets. _____

5. Rock climbing is a popular sport today, however, everyone needs some training before setting out. _____

6. Beside the old school grounds near a Garry oak a baseball glove. _____

7. The blackberries grew in dense thickets, walkers enjoyed picking the berries in early fall. _____

_____
_____

8. Although the player was interested in the trade. _____

_____
_____

9. Practising her dancing every day after school. _____

_____
_____

10. The women made rag dolls from the old clothes the children made stick toys. _____

_____
_____

Part 5: Repairing Sentence Faults

The following sentences contain one of the following sentence faults: fragment, run-on, pronoun reference error, shift in person/number, or shift in verb tense. First, read each sentence. Then repair the error and write the corrected version of the sentence in the space provided. You do not need to tell what kind of error the sentence contains. (2 points each, 30 points)

1. Everybody cheered and got to his feet.

_____
_____

2. If one becomes negative in attitude, your health suffers.

_____
_____

3. Randy owns a car, but he walked to work.

4. Growing some vegetables in rocky soil.

5. Because the customer is angry.

6. She grooms her dog, Pokey, then she plays ball with him.

7. Manuel was a marvellous painter. Who died in a prison camp.

8. All of the men brought his own ideas.

9. Kim counts all the day's cash, then she makes a deposit.

10. Rodney was spending too much money, staying out late, and sleeping in every day, this made his parents angry.

11. Buying lottery tickets is his passion, however, his wife doesn't understand it.

12. Marla told Patsy she got a raise.

13. Because the accounts aren't in order.

14. Everybody should decide for himself.

15. Malcolm informed Todd that he was the better athlete of the two.

ESL POINTER

Verbals and Parallelism

A *verbal* is a word or phrase constructed from verbs but acting as other parts of speech.

1. **Gerunds are verbals that act as nouns.**

   Exercising in the gym can be lacklustre.

   Exercising is a gerund, a verbal that ends in *-ing* and acts as a noun. *Exercising* is the subject of the sentence.

   Hunting for mice and dust balls keeps my cat occupied.
   Hunting is a gerund in a special phrase: *Hunting for mice and dust balls*. The whole gerundial phrase is the subject of the sentence.

2. **Participles are verbals that often end in *-ing* or *-ed*.** They usually act as adjectives in sentences.

   Walking to work, Wilma lost her new silk scarf.
   Walking to work is a participial phrase describing Wilma. It acts as an adjective.

   Playing with matches, Little Bratso set the wood shed on fire.

   Playing with matches is a participial phrase modifying *Little Bratso*.

   Worried about his money, Leroy decided to make a budget.

   Worried about his money is a participial phrase describing *Leroy*.

3. **Infinitives are verbs that consist of *to* + the present simple tense of a verb (usually).** Infinitives can function as nouns, adjectives, or adverbs.

   To win was Theo's goal.
   To win is an infinitive. It is acting as a noun subject of the sentence.

   The dog to groom is waiting for your attention.
   To groom is an infinitive. It describes which dog, so it functions as an adjective.

Finding parallelism faults is rather difficult at times. Sometimes, you can be guided by examining the verbals. All verbals must be in the same form if the sentence has parallel structure.

Exercise 1 Verbals and Parallelism Faults

In each of the following sentences, underline the verbals. Then identify them. Finally, be sure the verbals in the sequence are the same (parallel); if they are not, make the sentence parallel by making the verbals all the same type. Check your answers in the Answer Key.

1. Smoking, reading, and to cook were Aunt Lulu's passions.

2. Trudging up the hill, pulling his little red wagon, and reddened in the face, the little boy continued his paper route.

3. Yuni wanted to sing, to dance, and drinking on her anniversary.

4. Catching flies, to sit in the sun, and to move very little are how a frog spends its day.

5. Earning a salary as an engineer, paying off his student loans, and to have a family of his own were the young student's dreams.

6. Staring out the window, brushing her hair, and talked on the cellphone, Phillis noticed a raccoon in the garbage can in the neighbour's back yard.

7. The manager told the two workers that having long breaks, being late for work, and to be glib with the customers were the reasons they were fired.

8. The ballet teacher taught her students to be enthusiastic, free, and to be energetic.

Exercise 2 Eliminating Parallelism Faults

These sentences have parallelism problems. Find the errors and repair them. Work in pairs. Decide on correct answers together.

1. Working with children is stimulating, challenging, and has its rewards.

2. Not being able to speak the language causes confusion, is frustrating, and it's sometimes embarrassing.

3. To prevent crime, attending to victims of accidents and crimes, and how to apprehend safely those suspected of crime are a police officer's responsibilities.

4. Being sound of mind and physically strong, the elderly man was able to live quite happily by himself.

5. Three of the issues the committee will have to deal with right away are camp maintenance, how to get staff for the camp, and promoting camp.

6. His doctor advised him to eat less, exercise more, and no smoking at all.

7. For many people, attending AA meetings is first embarrassing, possibly even humiliating, then helpful, and finally it is a success.

8. A high level of motivation, experience in problem solving, and you should not be concerned about your every decision are necessary if you hope to run a successful business.

9. Influential factors in any nation's economic regression are bad management of natural resources, policies regarding national debt might be unwise, and the unions' inflationary demands.

10. Although the first applicant seemed scared and showed shyness, the second was a composed person and outgoing.

CHECKOUT

1. Sentence-level errors—fragments, run-ons, shifts in person/number, shifts in verb tense, pronoun reference errors, and parallelism faults—are considered serious faults because they disrupt meaning.

2. Try to use the active voice whenever you can in your writing.

part 3

readings

chapter 16

Paragraph Readings

Chapter Objectives
What will you have learned when you have completed this chapter? You will be able to
1. recognize how rhetorical modes have been used to organize ideas.
2. spot key words and phrases which indicate the rhetorical pattern.
3. make note of the vocabulary, evidence, and purpose in readings.
4. think critically while reading other writers' work.

Introduction

This chapter provides readings for you to read and analyze. The paragraphs are organized according to the rhetorical modes you have been studying. These professional pieces are excerpts from longer selections; however, each still stands on its own as a good example of writing according to a mode of development. You will also notice a wide range of topics discussed in the readings. These readings should help you focus on modes, but at the same time, they should assist you in thinking about and discussing other more global ideas that relate to people, their interactions, and the issues in their lives and environments.

Your instructor may ask you to read the paragraphs and then work in groups to answer the questions. As you read, pay attention to how the writers have structured their ideas, what evidence they use, what vocabulary they have selected, and what purpose they may have had in writing the pieces. Also observe your own reactions to the ideas the writers present.

Time-Order, or Process, Mode

Reading 1: A Pill to Make You Thin
Jacqueline Swartz

In one of the few major studies done in Canada, Wellesley Hospital studied 60 obese patients who took fen-phen for a year. At first the subjects ate less. Unlike amphetamines, which kill appetite, the new diet pills cause satiety. "Appetite is what makes you go to the table; satiety is what makes you leave it," says Dr. Ezzat, who monitored the study. But several months after the subjects stopped taking the pills, their weight crept back up. By two years, 60 per cent had gained back all the weight they had lost; 40 per cent kept some off. (D5)

"A Pill to Make You Thin" by Jacqueline Swartz, The Globe and Mail, *September 6, 1997, D5.*

1. How is Swartz's piece an example of time-order development?
2. What are some of the transitions she uses?
3. What evidence does she supply?
4. Do you find her argument compelling? Why or why not?
5. Why do you think Swartz wrote this paragraph?
6. Is this article timely in your opinion?
7. Why are diet drugs so popular?

Reading 2: Keeping Your Sanity

Student Writer: Desirée Stevens

Keeping your sanity and getting out of the house at 7:30 a.m. with four kids is not as easy as it looks. The first and most important thing I have to do is get up at least one hour before the kids at about 4:30 to 5:00 a.m. I use this time to gather my thoughts about what has to be accomplished throughout the day while having my coffee and getting myself ready. At 6:00 a.m., if I don't have my head on straight, it's too late! Now it's time to wake my 8-year-old, Ashleigh. She has to be woken first because she needs to have the room dark for a while and it takes her the longest to get ready. Ashleigh always has books to look at and things to think about. Next, I go to the boys' room to give Rory, my 7-year-old, his clothes and start convincing him to "rise and shine." The whole time I'm persuading Rory to wake up, I get my year old and youngest, Christian, up and dressed. Hopefully by this time Rory is on the move. I now head back to the girl's room to dress Shayneigh, my 5-year-old who can do it herself but sometimes needs Mommy to spend that time with her. Now we head downstairs for breakfast; hopefully I have at least three kids following me. Breakfast is usually served with bickering, fighting and "don't look at me" on the side. This is when I make snacks and get together everything we will all need for our day. If Ashleigh hasn't sauntered down by this time, I have to remind her about the time. While Ashleigh is eating, we move to the TV room for cartoons while I do hair. Finally, it's time to start the car and while it's warming, I call the kids to get on their coats and shoes—it's usually a tangle of arms and legs while I check faces and ensure that nothing is inside out. This is when Ashleigh finally comes to life with a fit of fury. She insists that there's something she needs for school or something she forgot to tell me I was to help her with, and it's due today. I call this my "at the door torment," and I really try not to "lose it" at this point; I'm so close to victory. I do what I can for Ashleigh, and at long last, get everyone to the car. When the last child is dropped off, I'm wide awake and more than ready for a day with my nose in the books.

Reprinted by permission of the author.

1. How can you tell that this is an example of time-order mode?
2. What are some of the transitions used?
3. What evidence does the author provide?
4. Do you think the ordering of events in Stevens' piece mirrors the way a parent keeps his or her sanity?
5. What does the author's expression, "have my head on straight," mean?
6. Do you find that there is humour in Stevens' view?

Reading 3: Optical Microscope and Electron Microscope
Dr. R. C. Brooks

Invented in 1591, the optical microscope uses light and lenses to magnify objects. By 1870 scientists realized that the nature of light would limit magnification to only 2000 times. In 1932, the first electron microscope was invented. It replaced light with streams of electrons and used magnets instead of lenses. Albert Prebus and James Hillier built Canada's first electron microscope at the University of Toronto in 1939. Today, electron microscopes can magnify an object by over 500 million times.

"Optical Microscope and Electron Microscope," Dr. R. C. Brooks, Curator Physical Sciences and Space, Canada Science and Technology Museum, What Does It Do?, 2003, **www.science-tech.nmstc.ca/english/collection/lab_equipment.cfm**.

1. Is there a topic sentence or a main idea in this piece of writing?
2. Are transitions used which show a chronological relationship? Which ones are used?
3. What problem may have motivated scientists to invent the electron microscope?
4. What are some differences between optical and electron microscopes?
5. Can you explain how lenses work in an optical microscope?
6. Do you think electron microscope images would be rendered black and white or colour?
7. Can an electron microscope enable you to see the movements of living cells?
8. For what purpose would it be useful to magnify an object 500 million times?

Reading 4: Site Preparation, Planting and Care
The Canadian Rose Society

Roses will grow in any good soil but do poorly in high alkaline soils, which should be amended, possibly with sulphur. For best results, and to allow the soil time to settle, prepare the beds at least 3 weeks before planting in April, or as soon as the soil is workable for spring planting, or in September for fall planting. Double digging is recommended, if at all possible. Where this is not possible, improve the existing soil by adding generous amounts of well-rotted manure, compost and peat moss. Mix these well into the soil to a depth of at least 30 cm (12 inches). Where the soil depth is not sufficient, or to improve drainage where soil contains excessive amounts of clay, using beds built up to a depth of 15 to 20 cm (6 to 8 inches) with good top soil will provide suitable growing conditions.

"Site Preparation, Planting and Care," The Canadian Rose Society, 2003, **www.mirror.org/groups/crs/**.

1. What shows a time-order method of organizing ideas in this piece?

2. Is there a topic sentence in the paragraph?

3. How does the closing sentence bring the writer's ideas together?

4. What does the author mean by the expression "good soil"?

5. Are you familiar with the gardening term "double digging"?

6. Do you think most plants grow best in acid soil or alkaline soil?

7. If soil is high alkaline, rather than lower the pH, could it be less expensive to grow acid-loving plants in containers?

Reading 5: Mackenzie House, Historic Buildings of Toronto
Sandra Alexandra

Mackenzie House is located at 82 Bond St. and was the home of William Lyon Mackenzie from 1859 until 1861, the year he died. Mackenzie came to York in 1820 from Scotland and was the driving force behind the reform movement in Upper Canada. He gave reformers a voice through his newspapers, the *Colonial Advocate* and the *Constitution*. Mackenzie won the first mayoralty race in the newly formed city in 1834. In 1837 he led the largely unsuccessful rebellion which culminated in a brief clash at Toronto, after which Mackenzie fled to the United States. In 1849 he returned to Toronto after an amnesty was proclaimed for those who had participated in the rebellion. This building, built in 1857, would have been part of a terrace (several adjoining buildings of the same design). Today it is a museum, restored to the period.

"Mackenzie House, Historic Buildings of Toronto," Sandra Alexandra, History of Toronto and County of York, Ontario, Canada, **www3.sympatico.ca/stillh2o/history/buildings3.html**, Stillwater Productions, 2001, 2002, p. 3.

1. What shows that chronological order is used as a method of organizing ideas in this piece?

2. Is there a topic sentence in the paragraph?

3. How long did William Lyon Mackenzie live in Mackenzie House?

4. What is meant by the expression "restored to the period"?

5. What is meant by the architectural term "terrace"?

6. Do you think a Canadian rebel leader could find sanctuary in the United States today?

Comparison and Contrast Mode

Reading 6: The Devil in Ms. Griffiths
R. M. Vaughan

Indeed, a closer look at the paintings reveals an almost fanatical attention to the gradation of skin tone, to all the smudges and streaks underneath even the healthiest glow. Griffiths' new paintings are also markedly softer than her previous works. Hair sits atop heads like glowing haloes, in diaphanous counterpoint to the finely etched faces it encircles. Clothing is rendered as a series of watery folds, more like damp seaweed than constructed garments. And her backgrounds, formerly detailed vistas packed with biographical, character-defining details, have dissolved into soupy visions of innocuous trees and empty, monochromatic fields—the kind you see before you in a dream.

"The Devil in Ms. Griffiths," R. M. Vaughan, Canadian Art, *Spring 2002, Volume 19, Number 1, p. 40.*

1. Has Vaughan used both comparison and contrast in this piece?
2. Can you find differences and similarities that are highlighted by Vaughan?
3. Has Vaughan used block form or point-by-point organization?
4. What do you think Vaughan means by "details have dissolved into soupy visions"?
5. Do you think Griffiths has changed the way she paints? Why or why not?

Reading 7: The Liontamer
David Elliott

Questions of moral weight and identity politics apply even to her mechanics of painting. When she talks about the development of her craft, she acknowledges a career-long struggle between two very different ways of rendering. On the one hand there is the detailed busywork of earnestly copying what you see and the pleasure of patient, meditative labour. This is realism, but it also has links to the decorative arts and to folk tradition, which connect it, in her mind, to women's work. Think van Eyck, the Pre-Raphaelites, Klimt, but think also weaving and embroidery. Then there is the grand style of European oil painting, in which the world is translated through the virtuosic shorthand of the artist's brush. Dramatic naturalism, full of bravado, it is the more exalted approach. Or at least it used to be. It also carries heavy-duty white, male connotations. Think Rubens, Degas, de Kooning. This is the kind of painting that Wagschal was both honouring and challenging in her *Cyclops* self-portrait.

"The Liontamer," by David Elliott, Canadian Art, *Fall 2001, Volume 18, Number 3, p. 92.*

1. How can you tell David Elliott's piece is an example of comparison and contrast development?
2. Can you find similarities and differences pointed out by Elliott?

3. What does Elliott mean by the expression "questions of moral weight"?
4. What is identity politics?
5. What would you expect feminists' paintings to look like?

Reading 8: Winter Tick on Different Host Species
F. A. Leighton

Mooring and Samuel (1998a, b, c) studied the response of moose, elk and bison to Winter Tick and concluded that the high susceptibility of moose to high levels of parasitism and severe disease compared to the much lower susceptibility of the other ungulate species studied could be explained, in large measure, by the grooming behaviour of moose compared to that of other species. Winter Ticks infest their ungulate hosts in September and October, but moose do not respond to the presence of the larvae or nymphs with intensive grooming. It is only when adult ticks begin to feed, in February and March, that moose groom intensively and in proportion to the number of ticks on their skin. Thus, moose go into winter carrying most of the Winter Ticks that infested them in the fall, and may have vast numbers of adult ticks on their skin, beginning to feed, before they start to respond to them in any protective way, by grooming. In contrast, white-tailed and mule/black-tailed deer, bison and elk groom more intensively in fall and early winter. This early grooming effectively removes a substantial proportion of the Winter Tick larvae and nymphs before they can become adults. Thus, these species seldom have large numbers of adult Winter Ticks on their skin and, therefore, seldom suffer significant disease.

"Winter Tick on Different Host Species," Grooming Behaviour and Winter Ticks, Winter Tick in Moose and Other Ungulates, F. A. Leighton, Reviewer: W. M. Samuel (August 2000),
http://wildlife.usask.ca/bookhtml/Winter%20Tick/wintertick3.htm.

1. What ideas are compared and contrasted in Leighton's piece?
2. Which sentence is the topic sentence?
3. What does the term "ungulate hosts" mean?
4. What is meant by "lower susceptibility"?
5. Can you think of a reason why winter ticks infest their hosts in September and October but begin feeding in February and March?
6. Can you suggest a theory to explain why the grooming behaviour of some ungulates is different from that of others?

Reading 9: General Overview, Research: Theoretical Chemistry
Joshua Wilkie

Theoretical chemists, unlike theoretical physicists, are generally unable to predict the outcome of the cutting edge experiments in their discipline. Computers are not yet fast enough to solve the Schrödinger equation exactly for the many atoms participating in a typical chemical reaction. The origin of this computational problem can be traced to the indeterministic nature of quantum mechanics. Newtonian mechanics predicts a unique outcome for any computer experiment, so classical calculations are easy. Quantum mechanics can only specify the relative probabilities of an enormous number of possible outcomes, and since all of these possibilities must be calculated and stored in computer memory the computational costs of quantum calculations increase exponentially with the number of participating atoms. Since Newtonian theory is incorrect at the molecular level we cannot avoid solving the Schrödinger equation if we wish to make accurate predictions.

"General Overview, Research: Theoretical Chemistry," Joshua Wilkie, Chemical and Structural Biology, Computational Chemistry, *Simon Fraser University, Canada, 2003,* **www.sfu.ca/chemistry/faculty/Wilkie.htm**.

1. What ideas are compared and contrasted in this piece of writing?
2. Does the paragraph have a topic sentence?
3. What details are provided to support the main idea?
4. What is an equation used for?
5. What is meant by the term "computational problem"?
6. Do you know what the expression "increase exponentially" means?
7. Can you give an example of a "typical chemical reaction"?
8. In addition to theoretical chemistry, can you name some branches of chemistry?

Cause and Effect Mode

Reading 10: Give Girls a Chance
Cheryl Embrett

Homemaker's believes that every girl child in every country around the world has the right to an education. Lack of basic education is at the root of poverty, sickness and conflict. Last year the World Bank identified education of girls as the key to effective development, saying countries that promote women's rights and increase their access to schooling have lower poverty rates, faster economic growth and less corruption than countries that do not. But in developing countries today almost 900 million adults are illiterate, two-thirds of them women and girls. There are 42 million fewer girls in primary schools than boys, and gender disparities exist at all levels of education. Meanwhile, in Canada, aboriginal girls are 16 percent less likely to complete high school and 20 percent less likely to complete university than non-native girls.

"Give Girls a Chance," Cheryl Embrett, Homemaker's, *May 2002, p. 77.*

1. Why is Cheryl Embrett's piece an example of cause and effect development?

2. What are some of the transitions the writer uses?
3. What evidence does the writer supply?
4. Do you find the author's argument compelling? Why or why not?
5. Does Embrett think that some boys should not have the right to an education?
6. What is the topic sentence?
7. What issue is the author raising?
8. Should Canadians be concerned about the issue? Why or why not?

Reading 11: Halifax, Nova Scotia's Eclectic Ol' Capital by the Sea

Allan Lynch

More than a million immigrants, refugees, war brides, Home Children and troops first glimpsed Canada at Halifax. Pier 21, in the last remaining immigration shed on the waterfront, serves as the country's memorial to these newcomers. The heritage centre features emotional videos of immigrant experiences, interactive displays and a huge archive for searching family and ship history. One in five Canadians can trace their roots to this facility.

"Halifax, Nova Scotia's Eclectic Ol' Capital by the Sea," Allan Lynch, Westworld, Summer 2000, p. 63.

1. How is Allan Lynch's piece an example of cause and effect development?
2. What evidence does Lynch supply?
3. What function do memorials serve in society? Do you agree that they are necessary? Why or why not?
4. What is meant by the expression "trace their roots"?
5. Why did Home Children come to Canada?
6. What is the meaning of "immigration shed" in Lynch's paragraph?

Reading 12: A Look at Barrier-free Design

Maureen Sherlock-Glynn and Brenda Millar

Perhaps the greatest motivating factor for the use of barrier-free design has been the growing voice of people with disabilities across Canada. The work of a host of consumer groups over time has resulted in the emergence of some truly committed and progressive employers, designers, builders and landlords who appreciate the importance of universal design to securing their position in today's markets. Through lobbying and the sharing of their expertise, people with disabilities have done more than any other group to advance the philosophy of barrier-free design.

"A Look At Barrier-free Design," Maureen Sherlock-Glynn and Brenda Millar, Abilities Magazine, January 2003.

1. How is Sherlock-Glynn and Millar's piece an example of cause and effect writing development?

2. What is the topic sentence?

3. What is meant by "barrier-free design"?

4. Do you think that universal design can benefit everyone?

5. What consumer group has done most to promote barrier-free design?

6. What perk do builders, landlords, designers, and employers receive if they embrace barrier-free design?

Reading 13: Caring for Wildlife Habitat at Home
Susan Campbell and Sylvia Pincott

If you care for woodland, stream, or wetland habitat on your property, your best course of action is to do nothing at all. Manicuring, cleaning up, creating pathways, and clearing underbrush harms existing habitat and destroys the younger growth necessary to form future habitat. It also makes the area vulnerable to predators. The only potentially beneficial interference with natural areas is the removal of human-made garbage or the addition of native plants to complement existing vegetation.

"Caring for Wildlife Habitat at Home," Susan Campbell and Sylvia Pincott, Naturescape British Columbia, 1995, p. 13.

1. How is this Campbell and Pincott piece an example of cause and effect writing development?

2. What is meant by "habitat"?

3. Are Campbell and Pincott giving readers sound advice?

4. Do you think that popular urban landscaping practices might be harmful?

5. How do you think bylaw enforcement officers decide which neighbourhood yards are unsightly?

6. Might fire, health, and insurance officials be concerned that natural areas too close to population centres create hazards?

7. What moral principles, if any, should direct gardening and landscaping activities?

Definition Mode

Reading 14: Letter to the Editor
Kevin Neish

How do you define "terrorism"? In the 1960s, I marched and protested to support a person the U.S. government then defined as a dangerous subversive who supported terrorism, and now Martin Luther King has a national holiday in his name. In the 1970s, I took part in civil disobedience in the name of a man [sic] the U.S. and Canadian governments considered a dangerous subversive and now Rigoberta Menchu has a Nobel Peace Prize. Had the state back then had the power of this new "anti-terrorism" bill, I would have been jailed for my support of many people they then defined as terrorists, but who are now heroes. This bill will do nothing to address the true causes of "terrorism," Third World inequality and injustice, but it will be used to attack and hamper Canadian activists in their quest to create a just and terror-free world.

Letter to the Editor, Kevin Neish, Times-Colonist, *October 25, 2001, p. A11.*

1. What is the writer saying about the definition of "terrorist"?
2. What is the writer's diction like?
3. What point of view does the writer express?
4. What does the writer use as evidence?
5. Do you agree with the writer? Why or why not?
6. What do you think the author's purpose is in writing a letter to the editor?

Reading 15: Dracula Without Kitsch
John Arkelian

Vampires have been with us for as long as we have been telling stories. Just as they mesmerize their victims, vampires transfix their audiences, holding us spellbound by an irresistible power. Their power is their ability to inspire what Coleridge called "desire with loathing strangely mix'd." We may envy the vampire's earthly immortality, not to mention his potent sexuality and seductive charm, but we recognize and abhor the essential emptiness of his existence. To survive, the vampire must steal the blood, and hence the life, of others. The new Canadian musical *Dracula,* written by Richard Ouzounian with music by Marek Norman and now playing at the Stratford Festival, brings fresh blood to an oft-told tale.

"Dracula Without Kitsch," John Arkelian, The Canadian Forum, *July 1999, p. 26.*

1. How is John Arkelian's piece an example of definition development?
2. What ideas are supplied by the author?
3. Do you find the author's definition complete—why or why not?
4. Who was Coleridge?
5. What does Arkelian mean by the expression "earthly immortality"?

Reading 16: What Is a Megathrust Earthquake?
Ralph G. Currie

A megathrust earthquake is a very large earthquake that occurs in a subduction zone, a region where one of the earth's tectonic plates is thrust under another. The Cascadia subduction zone is located off the west coast of North America. From mid Vancouver Island to northern California the Juan de Fuca Plate is subducting beneath the North American Plate. The two plates are continually moving towards one another, yet become "stuck" where they are in contact. Eventually the build-up of strain exceeds the friction between the two plates and a huge megathrust earthquake occurs.

"What Is a Megathrust Earthquake?," Ralph G. Currie, Head, Pacific Geoscience Centre, All About Earthquakes, 2003, Geological Survey of Canada, Frequently Asked Questions, **www.pgc.nrcan.gc.ca/seisomo/equinfo/q-a.hem#mega-what**.

1. Is there a topic sentence in Currie's piece of writing?
2. To what general class of things does a megathrust earthquake belong?
3. What is the main distinguishing feature of a megathrust earthquake?
4. What is meant by "subducting beneath the North American Plate"?
5. How long is the Cascadia subduction zone?
6. Why do tectonic plates become "stuck"?
7. Can you suggest how a megathrust earthquake could be predicted?

Classification and Division Mode

Reading 17: Tomatoes, Tomatoes
Lois Hole

Many times I am asked which is my favourite tomato variety, and my answer always is that I have many tomato favourites. Every year I grow at least one and a half dozen varieties in my garden. I must have paste tomatoes for sauces, cherry tomatoes for salads and snacks, and larger tomatoes for sandwiches, soups and every other imaginable use. To ensure that I have fresh tomatoes for the longest period, I grow my favourite early variety, which ripens about mid-July, and my favourite small tomato, which ripens a couple of weeks earlier. I also grow a selection of my favourite later-maturing varieties, so that I have plants still bearing fruit when fall frosts arrive.

"Tomatoes, Tomatoes," Lois Hole, Tomato Favorites, 1996, p. 44.

1. Why is Lois Hole's piece an example of classification development?
2. Can you find ideas that are clustered?
3. Why do you think Hole grows so many varieties of tomatoes?
4. What is a paste tomato?

Reading 18: Participation, Participants, and Providers
Gordon Selman, Mark Selman, Michael Cooke, and Paul Dampier

Research into non-participation has found that it is possible to divide barriers into three categories: situational, dispositional, and institutional. The situational barriers are the circumstances of the potential learner and include such describable items as disposable income, means of transportation, and availability of child-minding services. The dispositional barriers likewise belong to the learner, but in this case are a function of the individual's personality. Psychological factors such as fear of returning to the evaluative attention of a teacher, the feeling of intellectual inadequacy after being away from schooling for a long time, or a general disinterest in learning once a good job has been secured are three examples of dispositional barriers. The last category of barrier, institutional barriers, are those put up by the institutional sponsor of the learning activity. These barriers are not seen as being intentionally erected by the institution to discourage participation; rather they reflect the operating practices of the particular institution which have adverse consequences. Thus the decisions taken by the institution in offering an adult education course, such as scheduling, class location, pre-requisites, instructor selection and so on, will for some potential participants become reasons for their not participating. Of the three barriers to participation, then, it is evident that "ownership" of the situational and dispositional barriers resides with the individual while the institutional barriers resides with the provider. Thus any attempts to lower these barriers to the point where participation is enabled requires understanding and communication between the non-participant and the provider.

"Participation, Participants, and Providers," Gordon Selman, Mark Selman, Michael Cooke, and Paul Dampier, The Foundations of Adult Education in Canada, *Second Edition, 1998, pp. 138–139.*

1. Why is Selman, Selman, Cooke, and Dampier's piece an example of classification and division development?
2. What are some of the transitions the writers use?
3. What evidence is supplied by the authors?
4. Do you find the authors' argument compelling? Why or why not?
5. Why do you think they wrote this paragraph?

Reading 19: Chosen Peoples: Aboriginals Are Now Being Courted by Universities Across the Country
Brian Bergman

The Naziel siblings are part of UNBC's Northern Advancement Program, one of several initiatives offered by universities across Canada that help aboriginal students make the transition to higher education—both mature ones like Patricia and Warner, as well as those coming directly from high school. The Naziels both felt dead-ended in their jobs and eager for a new challenge. But they were also intimidated by the prospect of returning to school. In that regard, UNBC's program, which takes in about 25 first-year aboriginal students annually, proved a godsend. A key element is a two-week orientation, held every August. This year's session included a weekend wilderness retreat, culminating in a five-hour "talking circle" that saw students share their personal histories around a campfire. "I found that extremely powerful," says Warner Naziel, a father of two who is majoring in anthropology. "It helped us identify classmates who are having problems in their lives, so we can keep an eye on them and make sure they don't fall through the cracks."

"Chosen Peoples: Aboriginals Are Now Being Courted by Universities Across the Country," Brian Bergman, Maclean's, *January 14, 2002, p. 39.*

1. How does the writer use classification and division to develop his ideas?
2. What is the Northern Advancement Program?
3. What do you think the writer means when he says, "initiatives offered by universities across Canada that help aboriginal students make the transition to higher education"?
4. Do you think this program will prove to be effective? Why or why not?
5. What is a "talking circle"?
6. Do you think such an initiative would work on your campus?

Reading 20: Engineering Rice Plants with Trehalose-Producing Genes Improves Tolerance to Drought, Salt, and Low Temperature
Ray Wu and Ajay Garg

Rice is a major source of food for more than 2.7 billion people on a daily basis. Rice is planted on about one-tenth of the earth's arable land and is the single largest source of food energy to half of humanity. Of the 130 million hectares of land where rice is grown, about 30 percent contain levels of salt too high to allow normal rice yield. Another 20 percent of this land is periodically subject to drought conditions that routinely affect food production. About 10 percent of the locations where rice is grown occasionally experience temperatures that are too low for healthy plant development. It is difficult to improve rice tolerance against these abiotic stresses because they involve not a single gene but a network of genes. Fortunately, recent developments in transgenic approaches offer new opportunities to elucidate the functions of many useful candidate genes from different organisms and to improve the resilience and yield of rice plants. Moreover, developing salt-tolerant transgenic rice plants can introduce new areas of land that currently contain salt too high to grow rice. It is expected that genetically engineered, improved rice varieties will help combat world hunger and poverty.

"Engineering Rice Plants with Trehalose-Producing Genes Improves Tolerance to Drought, Salt, and Low Temperature," Ray Wu and Ajay Garg, AgNet, Information Systems for Biotechnology, March 4, 2003, **www.c-ciarn.uoguelph.ca/whats_in_the_news.html**.

1. Can you see a cluster of points that supports an idea?
2. What does the term "abiotic stress" mean?
3. Why is it difficult to improve rice tolerance?
4. Will genetic engineering increase rice production? How?
5. Do the authors of this piece support genetic modification of rice plants? Why or why not?
6. From what "different organisms" might "useful candidate genes" be obtained?
7. What is meant by the expression "elucidate the functions"?
8. Are you convinced by this piece of writing? Why or why not?

Reading 21: Urban Oil Spills as a Non-Point Pollution Source in the Golden Horseshoe of Southern Ontario
James Li and Peter McAteer

Being the economic engine of Canada and the home of 5 million people, the environmental health of the Golden Horseshoe is very important. Among various pollution sources into the lake, urban oil spills as a non-point pollution source have not caught the attention of most residents. These spills can cause terrestrial impacts by poisoning animals and plants, groundwater contamination by infiltration, and surface water pollution by algal bloom and fish kills and destruction of freshwater invertebrates and vertebrates. In order to investigate the significance of this pollution source, 10 years of spill records in the Golden Horseshoe have been compiled. On the average, about 1050 L per day of oil escaped to the land, water and air environment in this region. About one-third of these spills eventually entered Lake Ontario. Among various types of spilled oil, gasoline, diesel fuel, aviation fuel and furnace oil accounted for the highest reported volume. The former Metropolitan Toronto led the frequency and volume of spills, while Hamilton-Wentworth followed closely. Spills frequently occur on roads, at service stations and at electrical transformers, while the highest spill event volumes occur at bulk plants/terminals/depots and at refineries. The predominant causes of spills are related to leaks from containers, pipes and hoses, and cooling systems. However, the principal reasons for oil spills are human error and equipment failure. The transportation, public and petroleum sectors are responsible for 60% of the reported spill cases, while the petroleum sector alone accounts for nearly 50% of the reported spill volume. Given the significant volume of spilled oil, it is important that all levels of government and private industries increase their effort to promote pollution prevention such as preventive maintenance, improved employee training and/or retraining, and proper vigilant supervision. Additionally, control devices such as oil-water interceptors should be sized properly and implemented at strategic locations across the Golden Horseshoe.

"Urban Oil Spills as a Non-Point Pollution Source in the Golden Horseshoe of Southern Ontario," James Li and Peter McAteer, Department of Civil Engineering, Ryerson Polytechnic University, Toronto, Ontario M5B 2K3, Water Quality Research Journal of Canada, *Vol. 35(3): 313–340 (2000). Theme issue: Stormwater Pollution,* **www.cciw.ca/wqrjc/35-3/35-3-331.htm**.

1. How are ideas clustered in this piece of writing?

2. How can you tell the use of division as an organizing device in this paragraph?

3. How are transitions used to help the flow of writing in this paragraph?

4. What do you think is meant by the expression "non-point pollution source"?

5. What are some examples of animals scientists class as invertebrates?

6. Do small pollution incidents contribute significantly to environmental degradation? Is this idea supported in the paragraph?

7. Are you convinced by this piece of writing? Why or why not?

chapter 17

Longer Readings

Chapter Objectives
What will you have learned when you have completed this chapter? You will be able to
1. recognize rhetorical modes in longer readings.
2. be more aware of writers' specialized vocabulary.
3. read and think critically while reading.
4. respond analytically to focussed questions requiring interpretation.

Introduction

The following readings contain several paragraphs and are written about a variety of subjects. They have been grouped under one of four themes and each reading is assigned to one of five rhetorical patterns.

Your instructor will decide with the class which readings will be assigned. Read each assigned reading carefully. After you read each selection, answer the questions that follow it. Your instructor may ask you to complete these and be prepared to discuss your ideas with others in the class.

Along with what each writer is saying, try to pay attention to how each is saying it. Here are some tips for reading longer selections:

1. Read the entire article in order to get the gist of it. (The gist is the general idea.)
2. Read the article again, paying attention to the specific content. Write down the main ideas as you come across them.
3. Pay attention to words that you do not understand. Look up these words in a dictionary, or ask someone else what they mean.
4. Look at the way the author has arranged his or her ideas. Do you see one rhetorical pattern that seems to influence the piece in general?
5. Pay attention to the writer's argument. Can you list the arguments the writer is making?

Family and Relationships

Reading 1: Bad Boys
Mordecai Richler

Finding the "right" partner seems to preoccupy people of all cultures. In his selection, Richler takes a humorous look at these encounters from the days of his youth by classifying date types. He chooses the rhetorical pattern of classification and division to drive his points home. Richler, born and raised in Montreal and author of ten novels, several collections of essays and screenplays, is best known for the biting satire and social commentary in his writing. Richler was awarded with many prizes for his writing, including the Giller Prize in 1997 for *Barney's Version*. Prior to his death on July 3, 2002, he was made a Companion of the Order of Canada.

When we were horny teenagers, me and my bunch dreaded the coming of Saturday nights. Our anxieties, such as they were, struck as we left high school on Friday afternoons, loping home to begin to work the phones. Would we manage to get a date for the following night or would we be humiliated yet again? We were sixteen years old at the time, grade 11 students in Montreal, and the ungrateful girls we had invested in selflessly for years—treating them to double features at the Rialto, followed by toasted tomato and mayo sandwiches, washed down with Cokes or milkshakes at Ben Ash's, never mind the cost—had suddenly turned against us. Upwardly mobile in their nifty sweaters, tight skirts, nylons, and high heels, reeking of some cheap perfume shoplifted at Woolworth's, they now preferred the company of older guys, later to prosper as dentists or accountants, who were already at McGill. This being the case we often had to put up with being men without women, as Mr. Hemingway had it, on Saturday nights, settling for going out together to shoot pool at the Park Billiards. However, there were Saturday nights when we did make out, repairing to neck on a bench in Outremont Park after the movie.

Be that as it may, I'm glad dating is no longer a problem for me and my bunch, because we would now all be classified as either the Show-Off, Know-It-All, Cheater, Sex Guzzler, Mr. Ego, Bug-Eyed Boy, or Boozer, dismissed as Losers to Watch Out For. I am indebted for this information to a fascinating book which recently came my way, RED *FLAGS! How to Know When You're Dating a LOSER*, published by Plume, the down-market imprint of Penguin Books. It is the seminal work of two eminent shrinks, doctors Gary S. Aumiller and Daniel A. Goldfarb. Aumiller is an "internationally known" lecturer and Goldfarb serves as Webmaster to several psychology self-help sites on the Internet. Both authors have put in time as the prez of the Society of Police and Criminal Psychology and helped some 4,000 patients solve problems and make better decisions before combining to warn women about the 25 Losers to Watch Out For and How to Dump Them and Move On.

Consider, for instance, the Show-Off. In an idiom refreshingly free of academic prose, the authors warn, "If the man you are dating does more strutting than a rooster on Viagra in a brand-new hen house," this guy's a turkey. Cook his goose. The Show-Off, according to the prescient authors, can easily be recognized. He is a braggart, and a sharp dresser, who flexes his muscles a lot, and looks at himself frequently in the mirror, and, um, "other reflective substances" but is very insecure underneath his plumage. Reminds me of Hershel Greenbaum. Show him the Red Flag, girls.

"The Game for the Know-It-All is Jeopardy! Beat Him to the Buzzer," say Aumiller and Goldfarb. Signals to watch out for: his eyes dart, he namedrops, puts his friends down, and insists on ordering dinner for you. Yes, but like Arnie Debrofsky of blessed memory, he also showers a lot, and reads lots of non-fiction, which don't strike me as such bad things. But the doctors also adjudge him a Loser and highly recommend a clean break, goodbye: "Then go home and turn on the Discovery Channel and learn about the mating rituals of the giant Galapagos turtles. You too can know it all."

The Sex-Guzzler, as you might have expected, is very bad news. "The Way to Your Heart is Not Through Your Pants." Happily such villains can be easily spotted. They tend to wear gold jewellery, neck chains, bracelets, touch you very quickly on the first date, and talk about life being an adventure and about the need to take risks. Watch out, girls. If the sex is great, you could end up a Guzzler yourself.

With equal ease the doctors dispose of Mr. Ego ("If He Thinks He's God's Gift, Exchange Him!"); the Cheater, who tends to look at your breasts or legs and to invade personal space; the Bug-Eyed Boy, yet another eye-darter, who looks at body parts, not faces, when he is talking to you or other women (gosh, I used to know guys like that); and the Boozer, no eye-darter he, but he does tend to be restless, and at times has a rumpled look. Worse news. He has more than two drinks on the first date. Aumiller and Goldfarb recommend boozers to rely on the three Ms: meetings with Alcoholics Anonymous, meditation, and masturbation, "because he should not have a woman around."

RED FLAGS! takes no prisoners. It provides women with further good advice against Neglecters, Pleasers, Possessors, Abusers, and Loners, taking in just about all of my cherished male friends. Girls, beware of these two shrinks. Dump Them. Cook Their Goose. Lest you end up old maids.

Richler, M. (2000, March). Bad boys. Saturday Night, *115(2), 78. Copyright of* Saturday Night *is the property of the National Post.*

1. Richler uses a lot of slang in his article. Can you spot some? Can you explain what some of the terms mean?

2. What, according to Richler, was a typical date when he was a teenager?

3. What does Richler mean by "upwardly mobile" (underlined in your text)?

4. What classifications does the article mention for the person called "a date"?

5. What are some of the characteristics of each type of date?

6. What is the tone of Richler's article? (The tone has to do with the author's attitude to his or her topic or reader.) Why do you think Richler wrote the article?

7. What is the difference, in your opinion, between dating in Richler's time (during the 1950s) and dating today?

8. Do you agree with the classifications of a date mentioned in the article? Why or why not?

Reading 2: A Personal Journey through Genetics and Civil Rights

David Suzuki

Famous for his work in popularizing science through his long-running television program, *The Nature of Things*, David Suzuki, also a renowned geneticist, author, professor of genetics at the University of British Columbia and passionate environmentalist, provides a perspective on his life story and how it helped to shape him as a scientist and as a person. Suzuki uses a time order, or process mode to express his views. He also asks his readers to consider what responsibility science has to society.

The most powerful force shaping society today is science applied by industry, medicine, and the military. New scientific ideas and techniques pervade every aspect of our lives, changing the way we do things and how we perceive the world, thus altering our aspirations and notions of who we are, why we are here, and where we are going. Yet, with rare exceptions, scientists are virtually invisible in the popular media and in debates and reports on economic, social, and even environmental issues. As a geneticist and a journalist, I am constantly reflecting on the nature of the relationship between science and society. Here I recount the path that I have followed as a means to convey my experiences around, and opinions on, this complex relationship.

My grandparents emigrated to Canada early in this century, driven from their homeland by terrible poverty. Both of my parents were born in Vancouver, British Columbia, as was I in 1936. Insulated from widespread racism and the ravages of the Great Depression by my parents and childish innocence, my earliest memories are of a happy childhood. On 7 December 1941, when Japan attacked Pearl Harbor, my life was changed forever. The racism that had festered in British Columbia ever since Japanese and Chinese began coming to the province in the late 1800s could now be vented openly under the guise of self-defense and patriotism. My family and I felt completely Canadian because we had never been to Japan, and at home English was our spoken language. In the months following Pearl Harbor, the Canadian government moved to control the feared treachery of its Japanese population by invoking the War Measures Act against all people of Japanese descent.

The War Measures Act was a heinous piece of legislation that failed to recognize that while it is easy to guarantee civil rights and freedoms when times are good, those guarantees only matter when times are difficult. Twenty-two thousand Japanese, most Canadian citizens by birth, were rounded up and sent to internment camps in abandoned mining settlements deep in the Rocky Mountains. My father was separated from our family and shipped to a different camp for one year before being reunited with us. We were impoverished by the loss of our savings, our home, and almost all of our possessions (each person was allowed to take 70 pounds of luggage to the camps). When the war drew to a close, we were expelled from British Columbia and my family ended up working as farmhands in southern Ontario. As a child I learned that hard work and a good education were the only means to extricate myself from this poverty. Pearl Harbor, incarceration, and expulsion from British Columbia shaped my psychic demons—a knee-jerk aversion to any perceived discrimination or bigotry—and I developed a compulsive need to excel at whatever I did to prove my worth as a human being.

I did well in high school and received a scholarship to Amherst College, where I majored in biology. In embryology and genetics courses, I was enthralled by the exquisite beauty and elegance of development and heredity. After graduating in 1958, I enrolled in the doctoral program in zoology at the University of Chicago. The launch of Sputnik by the Soviet Union electrified the world and stimulated a frantic rush to bolster science, mathematics, and engineering in North America. It was a golden period of enthusiasm and expansion in all of the natural sciences, including genetics. As a graduate student during this exuberant time, I acquired the belief that science could eliminate superstition and ignorance by providing us with an understanding of the underlying mechanisms of all the cosmic forces impinging on our lives. In genetics, I believed that through a better understanding of mutation, recombination, and gene activity, we would eventually be able to manage, and possibly even eliminate, the hereditary problems that afflict humankind.

In the early 1960s there were numerous job opportunities in the United States as universities expanded their science departments. Nevertheless, I chose to return to Canada. Even though Canada had incarcerated my family during the war and expelled us from British Columbia, it was still my home and I wanted to contribute and work to make it a nation that could live up to its boast of being a place where all of its citizens were treated equally. I returned in 1962 as an assistant professor in the Department of Genetics at the University of Alberta in Edmonton.

As the most junior member of the department, I was assigned to teach genetics to students majoring in agriculture. They constantly pushed me to explain the agricultural implications of genetics with questions about the green revolution, about ways to improve milk output or weight gain by gene engineering, and about the possibility of the perpetuation and amplification of highly productive animals by cloning. As a snobby scientist who reveled in basic research, I had not paid attention to the practical consequences of genetics research and was now forced by students to read more widely on this topic, whereupon I discovered a vast and interesting literature.

In 1963 I moved to the University of British Columbia. Most students in my classes hoped to go to medical school, so they would quiz me about medical genetics, human heredity, and the possibility of genetically altering people. I gave a talk about genetic engineering to students at a campus dorm in which I discussed the techniques of DNA transfer by transformation and transduction, the possibility of cloning, and the implications for people. At the end of my talk a student demanded to know why, if such terrible possibilities come from new ideas and techniques, was I still doing research in genetics. I glibly answered that I was doing basic research into mechanisms of cell division and chromosome behaviour in fruit flies, not applied work. The student rejected my answer. Knowledge, he pointed out, was like a huge pool of information. Like water added to a lake, any scientific result becomes diffused throughout the pool of information. So when someone comes up with a practical application, there is no way to identify the specific studies that made it possible. Ideas are built on the collective base of accumulated knowledge, thereby blurring any distinction between practical and basic science. The student had a point, and I was spurred to read more about applied genetics.

To my shock, I discovered that eugenics, the attempt to apply hereditary principles to improve the human genetic condition, was not some weird aberration, but had been created and supported by leading geneticists. Eugenics was considered a legitimate scientific discipline. Eugenicists made pronouncements about the supposed hereditary nature of tuberculosis, syphilis, indolence, sloth, drunkenness, criminality, and deceit. Indeed, Edward East, a distinguished Harvard professor and president of the Genetics Society of America, once wrote: "In reality, the negro is inferior to the white. This is not hypothesis or supposition; it is a crude statement of actual fact."

As geneticists discovered principles governing heredity and showed that most were universal, there was an understandable sense of excitement. Geneticists believed that they had their hands on the levers of life and were on the verge of elucidating principles that could be applied to eliminate hereditary disease and abnormalities while increasing the level of intelligence and ability. Extrapolating readily from studies on inheritance of physical traits like flower colour in plants or wing shape in flies, geneticists jumped to conclusions about the inheritance of intelligence and behaviour, often confusing their beliefs and values with scientifically meaningful categories. By invoking the word "inferior"—like the words "better" or "worse"—East, too, was treating a value judgment as if it was not something that could be measured scientifically.

To my horror, I found that Josef Mengele, the infamous "angel of death" at Auschwitz, was a human geneticist who held peer-reviewed research grants to carry out studies on twins at the death camp. Race purification, an element of Nazi policy, was in part justified by the climate of optimism surrounding genetics as a means to improve the human condition. By the end of the war, when the horrors of the Holocaust were revealed, the accepted wisdom was that human behaviour and intelligence were primarily an expression of environmental factors. Even though I had received an outstanding liberal arts education and a thorough training in genetics, I had not been taught this aspect of the history of my discipline.

To add to my discomfort, I began to understand that genetics had been the underlying rationale that had justified the incarceration of Japanese-Canadians. Parliamentary transcripts indicate that a British Columbian member of Parliament, A. W. Neill, stated in 1937: "To cross an individual of the white race with an individual of a yellow race, is to produce in nine cases out of ten a mongrel wastrel with the worst qualities of both races." While not quite a Mendelian ratio, it was, nevertheless, an apparently quantified claim. In February 1941, Neill told the Prime Minister: "We in British Columbia are firmly convinced that once a Jap, always a Jap." Implicit in Neill's statement was a belief in the hereditary nature of perceived racial traits, such as perfidy and deceit. Thus, bigotry was cloaked by the legitimizing claims of scientists. At the very least, this lesson from recent history can warn us about the hazards of extending the boundaries of scientific claims beyond immediate experiments.

This grotesque intersection of two great passions in my life-genetics and civil rights was an agonizing confrontation with the intersection of science and society. I concluded that, above all, scientists are fallible human beings with all of the foibles, idiosyncrasies, talents, and shortcomings of any other group. Our perspective is shaped by professional self-interest, training, and ambition, and it is easy to become so enthralled with our work that, without reflection, we make grand claims about the potential of our discoveries and ideas. Moreover, in the flush of research and its exciting results, it is easy to forget that science progresses by conjecture and supposition, and that hypotheses will be evidentially modified, corroborated, or discarded. The ideas about gene and chromosome structure and regulation that excited me when I graduated in 1961 seem laughably far from what we believe today, and most of today's cutting-edge notions will be just as far off the mark 20 or 30 years from now. So what is the hurry to apply our notions so quickly? Often we make discoveries simply because our knowledge base is so tiny that we are bound to learn new things. This means that our ignorance is so great that we have virtually no capacity for prescription, that is, little capacity to recommend ways to correct problems that we encounter.

Scientists need to learn more about the social ramifications of their activity as revealed by history. We need to understand more intimately the nature of scientific knowledge, its strengths, weaknesses, limits, and how it differs from other ways of knowing. Above all, we must encourage public discourse about the interface between science and society and support those among our students and colleagues who enter this arena.

Suzuki, D. (1998). A personal journey through genetics and civil rights. Science, 281(5384), 1796. Copyright of Science is the property of American Association for the Advancement of Science.

1. What does Suzuki mean when he says "scientists are virtually invisible in the popular media"?

2. What is the War Measures Act? Why does Suzuki mention it? How did it affect him personally?

3. What was the "launch of Sputnik" Suzuki mentions, and why do you think he believes the event was such a turning point for science?

4. What does Suzuki say about how he first perceived the role of science when he was a graduate student?

5. What is the metaphor for knowledge used in the article? (A metaphor is an implied comparison between two things or ideas so that one illuminates the imagined common qualities of the other.)

6. What is "eugenics"? Why was Suzuki upset when he discovered this area of study?

7. Does the article contain an important irony? (Irony is a development that is oppositie to, or a mockery of, an expected result.)

8. In your opinion, what is Suzuki's purpose in writing this article? Was he successful?

Environment and the Outdoors

Reading 3: Betrayal of Trust
Once again, Canadians are asking, "How could this happen?"
Sharon Butala

Due to the serious events in Walkerton, Ontario and North Battleford, Saskatchewan, Canadians have taken a sober look at the safety of their public drinking water. Sharon Butala, a writer and thinker concerned about the environment of the Canadian prairies, was born and raised in rural Saskatchewan. She worries about the conditions of rural life, particularly for women. Her essay describes how the difficulties she experienced in finding safe drinking water on her first ranch connected with her beliefs that governments must act responsibly in regard to the safety of its citizens. She employs a cause and effect mode to outline her views on that relationship.

I was raised in rural and small-town Saskatchewan. We children used to raft every spring on sloughs swollen by meltwater, falling in and splashing one another, and swam—our parents poised to grab us, so swift was the current—in the Saskatchewan River. I remember narrow, hilly, sandy roads lined with a thick deciduous forest that we used to take instead of highways for sheer pleasure in the beauty. We didn't have indoor plumbing until the early 1950s when we moved to Saskatoon. Like us, most small-town or rural people had pumps in the kitchen and outdoor biffies. We bathed once a week in tin tubs of water—melted snow in winter—heated on the cookstove. Yet we were more likely to suffer from gas poisoning from our coal-fired furnaces, or from a fall downstairs, than from illnesses caused by drinking or bathing in the water.

In the mid-'70s, when I moved from Saskatoon to the Butala ranch near the Montana and Alberta borders, I soon developed a problem with diarrhea. I didn't notice it had become chronic until one day I realized I had a half-dozen bottles of anti-diarrhea medication sitting on windowsills and shelves in every room of the old ranch house. I went to the doctor, who, despite testing, was unable to find a cause. But through happenstance, I discovered the origin of my ailment. It was the ranch water, which, in this semi-arid region of southwestern Saskatchewan, came from a well, the blessed presence of which decided where the Butalas would put their house and ranch buildings, in fact, whether they could live there at all.

My husband, Peter, and his family had always used that water. Their bodies had adapted to it, but mine, accustomed to better quality urban water, couldn't handle it. Testing showed the well water was so hard it was barely fit for human consumption. I weighed only 98 lb. at the time and the accompanying pain, fatigue and dehydration could conceivably have killed me, if my husband hadn't immediately begun bringing me water from elsewhere.

Then, in the late 1970s, we built our new house only 20 m from the small Frenchman River, which supplied our household, our cattle and horses, and our local flood irrigation system. I was warned against using this water for cooking or drinking. A number of families, nevertheless, drank it as it was, without any attempt to filter or purify it. We, however, put nearly $10,000 into a seepage filtration well beside the river, plus various other paraphernalia to provide us with safe, clean water. No government helped us to pay for this, although if help had been available we would have accepted it. When it came to water, like most rural families, we were pretty much on our own.

When I was born, Saskatchewan had been a province for only 35 years. I think we all had a sense of "roughing it" in a raw, new place, and that in the years to come everything would improve. Well, yes and no. In a country the United Nations has declared for several years running to be the best in the world to live in, how can we not feel it a betrayal that the water running from taps in homes, not just in North Battleford, Sask., but all over Canada, is no longer safe to drink. Worse, the agencies established to provide clean, safe water apparently can't be relied on to do the job properly. And as residents of Walkerton, Ont., and North Battleford would probably say, they can't be trusted either to warn us when equipment breaks down, or when floods or other non-usual sources of pollution render the water supply questionable. Premier Lorne Calvert has announced an independent judicial inquiry into the failure of the North Battleford system, so we're also being treated to the sight of officials scrambling to distance themselves from blame for the presence of Cryptosporidium, the parasite that caused illnesses in the city's water supply. In the year 2001, in the darkest part of the night, North Battleford residents must have been wondering what happened. Why, when we are so advanced compared to 50 years ago, could the things we trusted in most completely fail us, so that suddenly we feel no safer than the much-pitied poor of developing countries?

I think that one answer lies in the reluctance of governments to provide money for projects that lack glamour. All over Canada, infrastructure for cleaning and purifying water is archaic in design and/or decaying, and the repair or replacement of such equipment hasn't paid off in political capital, and thus, has been neglected. Also, we are suffering from the effects of governments buying into the odd idea that less government is better, and from the odious notion of user pay, an erosion of the most basic democratic principle of equality of opportunity for rich and poor, rural and urban alike.

The result, as the residents of Walkerton and North Battleford know all too well, has been that governments began to pare services and to charge individuals for others that had been free. In Saskatchewan, for example, rural folk didn't pay the provincial laboratory to test our water until about five years ago. And such testing has never been, and isn't now, mandatory. Now people are asking, if governments refuse to be responsible for the provision of safe water, just what are our governments for? Are they there only to satisfy the demands of the corporate fat cats while the vast majority, the so-called ordinary people, must fend for themselves?

Each province sets it own water quality guidelines for Cryptosporidium—and these can vary widely. But our whole idea of what constitutes a safe and adequate water supply has to be rethought. With a huge increase in human populations, and in animals held in giant feedlots and barns, all producing vast amounts of waste, water pollution is more likely to occur. And we continue to drain wetlands and mow down forests, our natural filtration systems, as if we didn't know that doing so lessens our precious water supply and destroys its quality.

Today, just about everything has become a commodity, from trips into space to human embryos. In such a milieu, having to buy our drinking water, an idea that 50 years ago would have horrified people, has become normal. In all this uproar about water contamination in North Battleford, and in the rapid backpedalling of officials, we seem to have lost sight of the basic, unadulterated fact that water is not merely nice to have, or pretty when in lakes or rivers: water is life itself.

Sadly, the great beauty that was once Saskatchewan is disappearing at a frightening pace. The trees that lined our country roads have been cut down; the fields of wildflowers plowed under; the sloughs drained and filled to make room for farms or urban sprawl. The wild, dangerous Saskatchewan River of my childhood is dammed, its once pristine waters no longer safe. Along with its purity, something else equally vital has been destroyed: the trust of people, far from the centres of power, in the ideal we were all raised with—that in a democracy, the government is not them, but that it is us.

Butala, S. (2001, May 21). Betrayal of trust. Maclean's, 114(21), 28. Copyright of Maclean's *is the property of Rogers Media.*

1. Butala's article begins with several terms that are specific to the Canadian prairies. In the first paragraph, you will see "sloughs", "meltwater", and "biffies". What do these terms mean?

2. What implications are to be derived from Butala's statement: "When it came to water, like most rural families, we were pretty much on our own"?

3. What contrast does Butala use in her article?

4. What are Butala's views on why the safety of our drinking water has declined?

5. How is the title, "Betrayal of Trust" appropriate in your opinion?

6. What environmental damage has contributed to the state of unsafe drinking according to Butala?

7. What does the concept of trust mean in regard to democracy?

8. Do you agree with Butala's position? What do you think should be done to rectify the problem of adequate and safe drinking water?

Reading 4: The Worst Kind of Ice-Breaker

I felt totally incapable of thought, possessed by the purest form of panic. The instinct to save is solid and can obliterate common sense.

Judy Plaxton

Personal and almost tragic experiences can cause us to appreciate more fully who we are and what other people in our lives mean to us. In the next selection, Judy Plaxton remembers an accident on the ice that almost claimed the life of her husband and her dog. She recalls the feeling of helplessness she experienced in trying to rescue them from the freezing waters. Plaxton relates her story in a time order, or process mode so that the events feel more immediate to the reader. She considers how fragile life really is.

There was a time when my sleep was disturbed by anxious dreams. I would see deep, dark water surrounded by sharp ice and feel its numbing cold. To dispel these images, I would replace them with others. Fields of grass, running brooks and shimmering sunlight would help me return to sleep.

The desire to live in a country setting drew my husband and me out of the city. After retirement, we bought a small farm. We settled in effortlessly. Frogs croaking from our pond and murmuring breezes replaced the intrusive drone of city air-conditioners. Summer flies were the only pests. Colourful autumn became winter. The breeze became a fierce wind that howled around the house. The snow sparkled with sunlight and scrunched underfoot. We were delighted with it all.

But one quiet winter afternoon, we experienced a dark side to our pastoral Eden. I had returned from a short trip to town to find that my spouse had been searching the sideroads; his words "I've lost the dog" were distinctly ominous, conjuring pictures of speeding cars or dog-nappers.

Our Labrador Retriever is very playful and friendly but after our move from the city had demonstrated a distinct desire to stay close to us. On this day, with my spouse busy in the barn, she slipped away. She may have seen his concentration on his work as an absence of fun, but also as a chance to investigate a wider world.

We dressed warmly and began the search. Soon we heard a distant barking and headed in the direction of the sound. As we got closer, the barking had a howling, desperate sound. We found her in the middle of a neighbouring pond, only her soaking wet, seal-like head visible; surrounded by ice, unable to climb out.

Seeing her in that state launched us immediately into a rapid no-time-to-think mode. This proved to be our undoing. There was a small boat near the edge of the pond. We quickly turned it upright, untied it and pushed it towards the edge of the ice. My husband climbed in and began to scoot his way towards the open water, intending to reach out and pull the dog into the boat. When he tried to haul her out, the boat tipped over under his leaning weight, and he was in the water!

My heart immediately went into overload. I slid and shuffled my way rapidly to the edge of the ice, hearing it creak beneath me, and grabbed his hands. I noticed that they were bleeding from holding onto the edge of the ice. We held on hard to each other, the phrase "for dear life" acutely meaningful. He laboured to try and get his breathing under control, then tried to heave himself out of the water but, weighted with soaking-wet winter clothing, was unable to do so.

I continued to feel totally incapable of thought, possessed by the purest form of panic. I called for help but we were alone in our struggle on this beautiful winter afternoon. Somehow we managed a rhythmic effort as, with each attempt to launch himself out, my spouse broke some more ice and I nimbly stepped back out of the way, still managing to grimly hold on. He was afraid of pulling me in and I was afraid to let go. Finally, with one huge exertion, the inevitable happened and I crashed through the ice into the water. This mishap proved to be helpful. By breaking a larger amount of ice with that force, we were closer to shore. Moments later, he could touch bottom for the first time and by continuing to smash the ice with our hands, we were finally able to clamber up onto the bank, dog included.

There followed a numbing race through fields of snow to our house. Towels, blankets and hot tea eventually restored our circulation and calmed us. I had difficulty sleeping that night because of the recurring vision of my husband neck-deep in icy water, gasping for breath. We talked about the experience a great deal afterward, imagining terrible conclusions that might have been. If we had not found the dog within the time frame that we did, she would have slipped under the water and we would never have known what had happened to her. We wondered how long she would have been able to stay afloat. If my shopping trip had kept me longer in town, and if my husband had found and attempted to rescue the dog by himself, he also would have struggled alone. This was a thought too horrible to pursue. We were amazed, too, that I had been able to hold onto him as I am approximately half his weight. Simple buoyancy was probably one reason, and grim determination fuelled by masses of adrenaline another.

Our children, upset by our story, chided us for our lack of logic. Our son's vehement "You do not risk your life for the dog!" expressed their alarm. Attempted pet rescues with terrible results, sadly, do occur, but the instinct to save is solidly there and can obliterate common sense.

Like any other near-fatal accident, it has been a powerful learning experience. We now have at our pond a long rope with a wooden handle, which could be thrown to someone struggling in the water. We also placed at the site an extension ladder to use to reach out across an icy surface.

We continue to find immense pleasure in the beauty of our surroundings, our home, but perhaps with a little less romanticism and a dollop more of caution. I no longer have bad dreams, but when I hear our dog whimper in her sleep, I wonder if she is chasing a rabbit or dreaming that she is drowning.

Plaxton, J. (2003, March 7). The worst kind of ice-breaker. *The Globe and Mail*, p. A16.

1. What rhetorical mode does Plaxton use?

2. What does "pastoral Eden" (underlined in your text) mean? How is the expression fitting?

3. What is the contrast Plaxton describes between urban and rural life?

4. How does Plaxton make use of description?

5. What do you think Plaxton means when she says "the instinct to save is solidly there and can obliterate common sense"?

6. Why are such incidents as Plaxton describes "powerful learning experiences"?

7. Why do you think Plaxton wrote the article?

8. Have you ever had a trying experience similar to Plaxton's? In a few sentences, can you describe it?

Reading 5: Sonar Surveillance Despite Whale Injuries
Peter Carter

Concerned environmentalists point out that orca whale populations in the Pacific Northwest are on the decline. Some specialists argue that decreases in fish populations, exposure to toxins like PCBs in the water, and the increase of surface and underwater boat traffic are all contributing factors in the dropping numbers of orca whales off the coast of Vancouver Island and the state of Washington. Peter Carter is a physician and environmental activist living on the Gulf Islands of British Columbia. His claim is that testing by American naval experts is also adding to the harm of coastal water orcas, and he utilizes a cause and effect rhetorical pattern to establish that link.

For the last several years the US Navy has been moving ahead with plans to deploy Low Frequency Active Sonar, or LFA—a new extended-range submarine-detection system that will introduce into the world's oceans noise billions of times more intense than that known to disturb large whales. Now the National Marine Fisheries Service has proposed issuing a permit that would allow the navy to proceed with LFA deployment and, in the process, to harass, injure, or even kill marine mammals while flooding the ocean with intense noise.

Undeniable evidence that high-power "active" sonar systems can and do kill marine animals emerged in March 2000, when beach strandings of four different species of whales and dolphins in the Bahamas coincided with a Navy battle group's use of extremely loud active sonar there. Despite efforts to save the whales, seven of them died; a National Marine Fisheries Service and US Navy investigation established with virtual certainty a connection between the strandings and the sonar—and that active sonar system put out mid-frequency sound, which generally does not travel as far as LFA.

Although active sonar has been suspected in previous strandings, analysis of the heads of several dead whales enabled scientists to confirm, for the first time, the dangerous role of active sonar to a level of certainty that even the Navy could not ignore. All but one of the whales suffered hemorrhages in and around the ear, almost certainly the result of <u>acoustic trauma</u>. And in February 2001, a marine scientist observed that at least one of the whale species that stranded in the Bahamas had virtually disappeared from the area, raising questions about impacts well beyond the initial strandings and deaths.

According to the Navy, LFA functions much like a floodlight, scanning the ocean at vast distances with intense sound. Each transmitter in the system's long array can generate 215 decibels of sound, a level millions of times more intense than is considered safe for human divers. Worse yet, not far from the array of transmitters the signals begin to combine, and the result as the signals travel is sound as forceful as if as much as 240 decibels had been transmitted at the source. (To understand just how powerful these sounds are, keep in mind that the decibel scale used for measuring noise is like the Richter scale used for measuring earthquakes—both use small differences to express increasing orders of magnitude.) Thanks to the combined power of all these sound waves, LFA can illuminate hundreds of thousands of square miles of ocean at one time. In 1991, scientists produced a loud, low-frequency signal off the coast of Heard Island in the southern Indian Ocean, and found that it was still detectable off the West Coast of the United States. That signal was effectively 100 times less powerful than LFA's.

For years the Navy had been testing the LFA system in complete secrecy and in violation of environmental laws. In 1995, Natural Resources Defence Council (NRDC) brought the sonar tests to light and demanded that the Navy comply with federal and state statutes and disclose how the sonar would affect marine mammals, sea turtles and other ocean species. As a result, the Pentagon agreed to conduct a full-scale study of environmental impacts before putting the LFA system into use across an estimated 80% of the world's oceans.

In late January 2001, the Navy released its Environmental Impact Statement, which according to law should be a "rigorous and objective evaluation" of environmental risks. Yet the US Navy's study fails to answer the most basic questions about its controversial system: How will LFA affect the long-term health and behaviour of whales, dolphins and hundreds of other species? Taking place as it does over an enormous geographic area, what effect might it have on marine populations?

According to the US Navy's study, scientists briefly exposed a 32-year-old US Navy diver to LFA sonar at a level of 160 decibels—a fraction of the intensity at which the LFA system is designed to operate. After 12 minutes, the diver experienced severe symptoms, including dizziness and drowsiness. After being hospitalized, he relapsed, suffering memory dysfunction and seizure. Two years later he was being treated with anti-depressant and anti-seizure medications.

Whales use their exquisitely sensitive hearing to follow migratory routes, locate one another over great distances, find food and care for their young. Noise that undermines their ability to hear can threaten their ability to function and survive. As one scientist succinctly put it: "A deaf whale is a dead whale." But what concerns marine scientists even more than short-term effects on individual animals is the potential long-term impact that the Navy's LFA system might have on the behaviour and viability of entire populations of marine mammals.

Sound has been shown to divert bowhead and gray whales and other whales from their migration paths, to cause sperm and humpback whales to cease vocalizing, and to induce a range of other effects, from distressed behaviour to panic. A mass stranding of beaked whales off the west coast of Greece in 1996 has been associated with an LFA-type system being tested by NATO. And last year's whale deaths in the Bahamas add further evidence of the risks of intense active sonar. Leading marine experts say the Navy's limited assessment cannot tell us how long-term exposure to LFA sonar will affect the breeding, feeding, and migration of whales and other marine species. It is exactly such long-term effects on vital activities, say the experts, that pose the greatest risk of pushing endangered species over the brink into extinction.

The National Marine Fisheries Service announced its proposal to permit LFA even as its own investigations into the Bahamas strandings continue. In the wake of the recent dramatic confirmation of the dangers of active sonar, NRDC is calling on the Fisheries Service to withdraw its proposed permit and deny the Navy's application to deploy LFA.

Carter, P. (2002, August 15–28). Sonar surveillance despite whale injuries. Island Tides, 14(16), 2.

1. How does LFA work?
2. How does LFA disrupt whales' hearing?
3. What is "acoustic trauma" (underlined in your text)?
4. Why would this article be seen to have a cause and effect arrangement of ideas?
5. What examples does Carter use to prove his point?
6. Why do you think Carter wrote this article?
7. According to Carter, why is hearing so critical to whales?
8. What is your opinion of military testing? Should it be kept secret? Why or why not?

Reading 6: Whose Trail Is It Anyway?
Tom Cruickshank

The clash between those who wish to be stewards of the land and those who wish to develop it is an issue frequently raised in the media and newspapers. In the next selection, Tom Cruickshank provides a pointed example of such a conflict in a beautiful and popular region of Quebec. One group wishes to keep the area peaceful and natural for walking, horseback riding, and hiking while another group wants to use the trail for recreational vehicles and sport. Cruickshank divides the issue by classifying the users of the trail system, and this classification and division rhetorical pattern works effectively to outline the problems entailed by the conflict.

Things came to a head in St-Lazare last summer. Accusations flew and fingers were pointed as two factions argued over who has access to the much-beloved trail system in this growing bedroom community just west of Montreal. On one side was the horsy set, for whom St-Lazare has been a refuge for generations. On the other were enthusiasts of a different kind: dirt bikers and ATV owners. At issue was the extent to which motorized vehicles should be allowed to use town pathways.

And what great pathways they are. The trail system, hundreds of kilometres long, winds through pine woods and open meadows surrounding this town of 13,000, linking various neighbourhoods to each other and to the great outdoors. For years, horseback riders had them to themselves, but as St-Lazare evolved from hobby farm community to commuter town, the riders were soon joined by legions of newcomers. At first the new users—joggers, birdwatchers, hikers, cyclists and cross-country skiers—seemed to co-exist without incident. It wasn't until the arrival of motor-enthusiasts that things turned ugly.

Last spring, equestrians were aghast at the number of ATVs on local paths, particularly a four-kilometre stretch through a corner of a pine forest, which provided a much-needed link in the regional network of ATV trails. Not only did the presence of motorized vehicles shatter the peace, they argued to town council, but it also posed a safety hazard because, as every rider knows, a horse can easily spook when confronted with unexpected noise. As the summer progressed, tensions mounted, reaching a boiling point at not one, but two council meetings, where the police were called to keep the peace. Meanwhile, a local ATV club did nothing to defuse the situation when it purchased an ad in a French-language newspaper and decried the equestrians as a bunch of Anglo elitists bent on preserving the trails as their exclusive domain. Sensing a clash of cultures, the *National Post* picked up the story and ran it on its front page.

The battle for the bridle path in St-Lazare is a microcosm of an issue dogging trail development across Canada. Although enthusiasts of all stripes agree that trails are a wonderful asset to country living, there is no consensus over who should be allowed to use them. Invariably, the lines are drawn when the issue of motorized vehicles arises and the argument goes much further than spooked horses. It's a classic showdown between those who equate the outdoor experience with peace and quiet and those who favour the roar of an engine with the call of the wild. It seems the twain shall never meet: Safety is often voiced as the main objection to motor bikes, ATVs and snowmobiles, but at the root of it all is a general disdain for anything noisy in what is supposed to be an unspoiled setting. For its part, the motorized crowd—snowmobilers especially—is far more numerous and apt to be better organized. In fact, they support and maintain more trails than all the other users combined.

The debate has even affected the Trans Canada Trail, the 18,000 kilometre cross-country route currently under development. Acknowledging the importance of snowmobilers to its long-term viability, it has no problem with motorized use in winter, but ATVs are so far banned in light of potential conflicts with other summertime users. Meanwhile in other locales, the most common solution has been separate trails for separate functions. The debate in St Lazare was resolved this way, with a new four-kilometre link through the woods reserved for ATV use. Meanwhile, motorized vehicles have been banned from other local paths. However, there is still the nagging question of policing. Volunteers from ATV and equestrian clubs alike are patrolling for violators, but all it will take is one stray vehicle and one startled horse and you can bet the battle will heat up all over again.

Cruickshank, T. (2003, June). Whose trail is it anyway? *Harrowsmith Country Life, 27*(170), 34.

1. What is an ATV?

2. Cruickshank uses the expression "a horse can easily spook" (underlined in your text). What does this expression mean?

3. What does Cruickshank mean when he says "decried the equestrians as a bunch of Anglo elitists" (underlined in your text)?

4. What is the issue that Cruickshank outlines in his article?

5. How might the issue have been seen as a "clash of cultures," as Cruickshank says?

6. Why is Cruickshank's article a good example of classification and division?

7. Who is right in the debate in your opinion? Why?

8. How should trails be developed in your view?

Business and Marketing

Reading 7: The Trouble with "How's it going, ladies?"
Don Cherry's opening line in the Molson Bubba commercial mars an otherwise hilarious ad.

Richard Rotman

Richard Rotman examines language use and advertising in the next reading. He points out how strongly influenced viewers are by the sometimes sexist language used in commercials. Viewers can be persuaded or dissuaded because icons such as Don Cherry are employed as key figures in the advertiser's message. Rotman chooses a comparison and contrast mode to convey his distinctions on the subject.

In beer advertising, sexism often rears its ugly head, but a recent lesson that my 12-year-old daughter taught me showed how ingrained it is in the daily imagination. Not just ingrained but part of the negative messages with which sports-minded young girls like her are bombarded every day.

It happened watching one of our favourite TV spots: Don Cherry, the hockey sage of "Coach's Corner" fame, meets up with beer-loving sports fans featured in a series of Bensimon·Byrne spots. The cast later dresses in Cherry's trademark <u>vertiginous</u> sport jackets and buys the new Molson Canadian Bubba beer keg emblazoned with the outspoken coach's image.

In the spot, he walks into the apartment with the beer-guzzling guys and derisively says: "Hey, how's it going, ladies?" Any male who has ever been on a sports team has heard that one before. When the game or the play is going badly, the coach will employ reverse psychology by goading the players with the terms "girls" or "ladies." To a young man, this is the ultimate emasculating insult.

But my bright, engaging daughter viewed that and said, "Why does he call them 'ladies'?" On her soccer teams (one of which I coach), the coach never uses that term. Her female basketball coach never calls the girls "boys" or something like that. In fact, her coaches probably call the girls "guys" more often than not.

She asked me to explain and I was at a loss; she had me cold. I fumbled through stuttering attempts to rationalize a male in-group term. Truthfully, there was no reasonable explanation that would hold water with my daughter. The whole thing was so lame—lame because Cherry, the Coach of All Coaches, used the term exactly as it is tossed off in countless locker rooms all across North America. "How's it going, ladies?" expresses to young men that they are beneath contempt and are therefore described as girls, the most provocative derogatory term possible.

But looking at it another way, Molson has made a monumental mistake, hidden in a small line of dialogue. Starting the action with a well-known sports figure, who is a kind of perverse role model, contemptuously referring to young men as "ladies" is a breach of corporate responsibility. With its cavalcade of bouncing busty bimbos, beer advertising is the last time-honoured refuge of sexist values. The prototypical young men in the

Molson spot, the future husbands and fathers of the world (if that seems imaginable), take their social cues from these ads. Sadly, the consumption of beer is presented as the key to good times (of course in moderation, as the brewers would respond) and winning over the opposite sex. Even more sinister is the placement of the women in this series of spots: When the beer is poured and the party starts, the most buxom woman is positioned next to the main character, as if he's won the prize. In this spot, coach Cherry is standing next to the vavoomy woman at the happy conclusion.

I am mad at myself for enjoying this clever series of spots, for they have shown my sports-enthusiast daughter that being described as a girl is what boys fear most. They have given her a window into the misogynistic world of men's sports, which is a different universe than the one women experience. In men's sports, to be inadequate is to be a girl. That message is particularly traumatic when many studies report that girls' self-image declines following the onset of maturity.

Brewers and other companies entwined in promoting sports should be more careful. This is a time of female empowerment, and a small phrase such as "How's it going, ladies?" creates a larger ripple effect. Are there not other derogatory terms that coach Cherry could have said to this gaggle of geeky losers? How about "Hello, little boys" or "Hi, turkeys." Or simply, "Well, who do we have here?" All of which would adequately convey the coach's scorn for this crew of Molson-loving jellyfishes.

It's always remarkable what does seep through in ads, given how many people vet them, from agencies to focus groups and clients. One would give much to be a fly on the wall to hear the debate about the spot. Was there some young woman at the client or the agency, perhaps a sports participant herself, who heard "How's it going, ladies?" and remained silent, not daring to protest the insult in what surely must be a macho-charged, Hockey Night in Canada atmosphere?

Moreover, this is not to try to censor an ad that fits into network standards, was mostly in good taste and downright hilarious. (Kudos to Don Cherry for letting himself be parodied.) Instead, it's to advocate that advertisers, especially those influencing young males, rise above the milieu in which they work.

Pandering to all the usual prejudices in beer advertising is more passé than one can imagine. What's worse, it's bad public relations to continue to spread those tired old macho attitudes to the easily influenced. Surely the creative minds that produced the funny idea of the boys with the Bubba garbed like Don Cherry can come up with something less insidious than "How's it going, ladies?"

Rotman, R. (2003, May 26). The trouble with "How's it going, ladies?" *Marketing Magazine, 108*(20), 8. Copyright of Marketing Magazine is the property of Rogers Media.

1. What is sexism?

2. In your opinion, why did Rotman write the article?

3. Who is Don Cherry?

4. What does "in beer advertising, sexism often rears its ugly head" mean?

5. Can you give examples of sexism in beer advertising?

6. What do "vertiginous" and "misogynistic" mean (underlined in your text)?

7. Who should advertising serve? Do advertisers also have a social responsibility? Why or why not?

8. Have you seen some ads on television lately which you consider sexist? What were they? Why do you consider them sexist?

Reading 8: Reinventing Our Food for Fun and Profit
Pam Freir

The food industry is a multi-billion dollar enterprise that is constantly looking for ways to re-package its food products. In her article, Pam Freir takes an amusing look at ways in which products are "reinvented" to appear to be new to the consumer. She uses many examples to prove her point that companies and advertisers will go to any means possible to sell something, and her use of the comparison and contrast mode keeps the reader in tune with her thinking.

If what we eat is any indication of who we are, we've got a lot of explaining to do. Two recent stories, one from Paris, the other from the U.S., tell us all we need to know.

On the uncomfortably-close-to-home front, the *Wall Street Journal* reports that H.J. Heinz Co. has "transformed one of the planet's most mundane food products . . . into a star." (Note that familiar weasel, *food product*, which means, of course, it's not actually food at all). Anyway, the reinvented "star" on the ersatz food horizon is ketchup. And its new claim to fame is its colour. Green.

People are eating it up.

But that's not all. There's been a packaging breakthrough too. Green ketchup comes in a user-friendly, easy-squeeze container cunningly contoured to fit a child's hands. And children love it. With every happy squirt and splat they are unleashing a flood of ketchup on a scale never seen before.

Green, of course, looks especially good on the corporate bottom line. Which explains the current euphoria at ketchup headquarters. Heinz has created a marketing phenomenon: Increased sales are no longer a reflection of increased consumption. People aren't necessarily eating more ketchup. They're just emptying the containers faster.

"As long as they're putting it on their plates, we're happy," says spokesman Michael Mullen.

Waste not, profit not. That's the dictum.

The Heinz success story has got others scrambling for a toehold in this kiddie-food play land. Quaker Oats has children digging through their oatmeal in search of edible jewels, gold coins and treasure chests. Parkay has just unveiled two new margarines—in shocking pink and electric blue. These too are packed for squeezability and fun.

"They're good for drawing pictures," we are told. Whether anyone actually eats the stuff is of no particular interest. It's selling. Things are different in Paris. John Henley wrote this in a report to the *Guardian Weekly*:

> "For lunch yesterday my son had cream of spinach soup, gigot d'agneau accompanied by petits pois and puree of new potatoes, and a slice of tarte tatin topped off with a dollop of creme fraiche."
> "All that was missing was a glass or two of Burgundy and a nice fat cigar."

Henley is quick to concede the appropriateness of this seeming lapse. His son, Nathan, is nine months old.

The menu is a typical one at the day-care his son attends. And although it employs a fulltime chef, it is not, as Henley points out, "a posh crèche stuffed full of toffee-nosed little Pierre-Henris." This is your standard, urban neighbourhood day-care and the kids are just regular kids.

The French, you see, like their children to get "an early start on the important things in life;" Henley explains. When Nathan was barely three months old his pediatrician suggested introducing a little Roquefort cheese into his diet. "Taste development is essential," she advised. So even if Nathan turns up his little nose at the offering, his world is richer for the encounter.

So what'll it be? Green ketchup on a Velveeta slice? Or creme fraiche on a tarte, tatin? And another question: Who cares? Does it matter? If that oft-quoted gastronome, Brillat-Savarin, is to be believed, it does: "The destiny of nations depends on what and how they eat."

It's an unsettling thought. Personally, I'm reluctant to throw in my lot with a culture defined by green ketchup and electric blue margarine. I'm uneasy with a generation that plays with its food, profits from the leftovers, and has forgotten that apples grow on trees. Besides, I have a hunch that a nation preoccupied with diving for treasure in its breakfast cereal could wind up choking on its own party favours.

No, I'm betting on Nathan. Not just because of the food that's set in front of him but because of the values that food embodies. Nathan will grow up knowing the difference between a Happy Meal and a joyous one. He will approach his food with a keen palate, an open mind and what M.F.K. Fisher calls "inquisitive gusto." And chances are he will approach his life and the larger world with the same curiosity, acceptance and enthusiasm.

I think Nathan's going to turn out O.K. He may never acquire a taste for Roquefort cheese but he'll at least recognize it as food, not play dough.

Freir, P. (2001, November 14). Reinventing our food for fun and profit. *Times Colonist*, p. D1.

1. What do "mundane", "ersatz", and "euphoria" mean (underlined in your text)?

2. What do you think Freir means when she says, "a posh crèche stuffed full of toffee-nosed little Pierre-Henris" (underlined in your text)?

3. What do you think "weasel" means? (Freir says: "that familiar weasel, food product.")

4. Can you name other "weasel words" advertisers like to use in descriptions of their products?

5. What does Freir mean when she says "green, of course, looks good on the corporate bottom line"? What does it mean when a company is "in the red" or "in the black"?

6. What is the tone of Freir's article? Why do you think that?

7. How can some products be a "packaging breakthrough" as Freir suggests? Can you name other "packaging breakthroughs"?

8. In your opinion, why do advertisers aim their ads at children?

Reading 9: Cirque du Soleil
Jason Kirby

The world-famous Cirque du Soleil, more like a spectacle than a traditional circus, had relatively humble beginnings in the province of Quebec, according to Jason Kirby in the following article. Kirby uses a time order, or process mode to trace the Cirque du Soleil's development. From Kirby's piece the reader can see that from one small idea a gigantic enterprise can emerge.

If you've never been to one of Cirque du Soleil's performances, you're probably wondering how a bunch of penniless street performers from Quebec juggled their acrobatic act into a global entertainment giant with almost a billion dollars in annual revenue. Even if you have, you have to admit it's a stunning achievement. No other Canadian entertainment company can match Cirque's clout. The movers and shakers of Las Vegas bent over backward to lure Cirque to the Strip in 1998; it now has two permanent shows there. Disney forked out $25 million to build a theatre for the troupe in Orlando, Fla. Today, Cirque employs more than 2,500 people, with three permanent shows and five on tour. Some six million people worldwide took in a performance in 2002, making Cirque arguably Canada's best-known company abroad.

Cirque du Soleil is definitely not the kind of circus you remember as a kid. The troupe got its start in the early 1980s, when Daniel Gauthier and Guy Laliberte, a fire eater and stilt-walker, and a few other street entertainers created a unique show that combined mind-bending acrobatics and original music, wrapped around weighty themes (*Varekai*, Cirque's latest show, is based on Icarus's fall from grace). In 1984, Rene Levesque caught a performance in Quebec City and wrote the struggling troupe a cheque for $1.5 million. Three years later, after some disappointing reviews in Canada, Laliberte and Gauthier spent their last dollars on a series of shows in Los Angeles. The audience, packed with celebrities, loved it.

Today, the private company generates revenue of roughly $800 million a year, landing Laliberte and Gauthier (now retired) on the Canadian Business Rich 100 list. While for years it received money from the Quebec government (and really, what company in that province doesn't?), Cirque has funded its growth almost completely through its impressive cash flow.

But Cirque has done some backpedaling on its expansion plans of late. Over the past couple of years, the company has periodically proposed a plan to open Cirque-themed complexes around the world. To their credit, CEO Laliberte and his team nixed the idea after considering the state of the global economy. The move did, however, raise the question: Is there a limit to how big Cirque du Soleil can get? It has had mixed success with its multimedia initiatives, including a 13-part documentary that aired last year to lukewarm audiences. Still, Cirque has plenty of room to grow in Europe, Asia and Latin America.

By all indications, Cirque has proven its ability to generate original, leading-edge shows. And with ticket prices creeping ever higher—at about US$100, tickets for the Cirque's sell-out show "O" are among the most expensive in Las Vegas—it's clear people are as eager as ever to be wowed.

Kirby, J. (2003, February 3). *Cirque du Soleil.* Canadian Business, *76(2), 82. Copyright of* Canadian Business *is the property of Rogers Media.*

1. What is the history of Cirque du Soleil? Use a timeline to draw in significant dates or events.

2. What does the expression "Cirque has done some backpedaling on its expansion plans of late" mean (underlined in your text)?

3. In your opinion, what is Kirby's purpose in writing this article?

4. What does "clout" mean (underlined in your text)?

5. Kirby refers to "movers and shakers" in his article (underlined in your text). What do you think this expression means and where do you think it comes from?

6. The article refers to Icarus. Who is he, and why do you think people are fascinated by his story?

7. What, in your opinion, is unique about Cirque du Soleil?

8. What do you think is meant by "the global economy"? In your opinion, how can artists and performers fit into the new scheme of things?

Reading 10: CD Pirates Drive Down the Music Volume

Sales slump, stars rebel. Can the industry survive?

Edward Helmore

The various uses of the Internet lead to questions about what are ethical or fair practices. Some individuals believe that downloading music from the Net is a form of theft because recording artists and music companies own the songs and are not being paid for their products. Other people think that if something is on the Internet it is in the public domain because the Internet is not regulated. Helmore examines the issue by dividing it into its constituent parts, using the rhetorical mode of classification and division. Evaluate what side of the issue you are on as you read.

Until Michael Greene, president of the Recording Industry of America, took to the stage at the end of the Grammy awards ceremony in February, the proceedings had all but managed to ignore the elephant in the room that everyone pretended not to notice.

In his address Greene only partially addressed the main concern of the industry chiefs there: the survival of the business in its present form.

"Many of the nominees tonight, especially the new and less established artists, are in immediate danger of being marginalised out of our business," he warned the audience in Los Angeles. He might have added that the loss of young artists would ultimately ensure the collapse of the music industry itself.

The specific threat to which Greene was referring is rampant electronic music swapping—now estimated at 3.6 billion songs a month—among consumers, most of whom no longer need to pay for their pleasure. Worse still, CD-burning technology allows unlimited copies to be made of copyright material.

But few people think illegal copying fully explains why music sales dropped by more than 10 per cent last year, making them worth a staggering $1.5 billion less than those in 2000. The top 10 albums sold 60 million copies in the United States in 2000. Yet last year the total was only 4 million. The industry says the effects of September 11 and the recession have compounded its woes, but many argue that the sales slump is a sign of a deeper malaise. Industry analysts talk of a series of problems: a rebellion by artists against recording contracts, the soaring costs of marketing and promotion, and competition from DVDs and video games.

Yet the analysts point to the industry's failure to adapt its business model to new technologies. "They're still fighting technology, and as long they're fighting it they're going to lose," says Michael Goodman, media and entertainment analyst at the Yankee Group. "The labels can say they want control, but they've lost it and it's not coming back. Until they come up with a new model, whereby the consumer has the control, they're going to continue to see sales decline."

In a business in which only about 5 per cent of artists and groups are successful in the marketplace, margins for error are slim. The head of one major record label told the *New York Times* that in 1994 the profit margin on a successful artist was 30%. Spiralling costs have cut this to around 8 per cent.

Moreover the sales cushion that sustained profits in the 90s is disappearing. Consumers were then replacing vinyl albums with CDs, providing a <u>cash cow</u>. These catalogue sales are down by between 20 per cent and 30 per cent. As a result, labels are slashing staff numbers. Fewer new bands are being signed, and older stars such as Mariah Carey, David Bowie, Sinead O'Connor and Rod Stewart are leaving or being dropped.

Not everyone believes the music industry's claim that it is the innocent victim of technology. Many fault it for valuing quick profits on instant but unenduring hits over the importance of nurturing high-quality acts for the long term. The result, say the critics, is a legion of one-hit wonders.

A rebellion against the industry is being launched by some of those that have profited most from it. The evening before the Grammys, a series of concerts featuring Beck, Courtney Love, the Eagles, Billy Joel, Stevie Nicks, Sheryl Crow, the Dixie Chicks, No Doubt and Pearl Jam's Eddie Vedder sought to promote a battle to change the structure of record contracts. Angry artists complain that they are little more than indentured servants to labels that hold them to restrictive, seven-album deals and short-change them on royalties. The artists want to change California's contract laws. But the record companies say holding artists to long-term contracts is the only way they can afford to develop untested talent, and if the law is changed they will move from Los Angeles, with the loss of around 25,000 jobs.

Some record company executives argue, with good reason, that the rebel artists, and most of the recording industry itself, are fighting the wrong battles. "Instead of arguing about contracts, which only affect superstars, or technology, they should be fighting independent promotion costs," says one executive.

The real problem, they say, is the expense of marketing music to the consumer. Beyond the cost of signing acts, recording their music and making videos, the labels' biggest expense is getting a song on radio, still king when it comes to making a hit. One firm, San Antonio-based Clear Channel Communications, owns 1,225 radio stations, about 10 per cent of the nation's total, plus the country's biggest live-concert promotions firm, 19 TV stations and 770,000 poster sites. It also owns SFX, the nation's biggest concert promoter. To get a song added to the playlist of a radio station costs $1,000 in independent promotion fees. There are thousands of stations in the US, so it costs at least $100,000 to get a song a limited hearing, and more like $500,000 for it to be played across the country.

Unless some of these problems are solved quickly, the business's economics will get even worse. Whether there are good songs that the public don't get to hear, or bad ones they can listen to, the effect is the same: no sales.

"The greatest issue the industry faces is coming to terms with developing artists," says Don Gorder, a music business academic. "Artists say the reason there is not a lot of good music out there is because large corporations are calling too many of the shots. Record labels say it's because everyone is stealing our music."

Helmore, E. (2002, April 4–10). *CD pirates drive down the music volume.* Guardian Weekly, 14.

1. What is the article mainly about?

2. How is the article a good example of a classification and division arrangement?

3. What does Helmore mean when he says, "the proceedings had all but managed to ignore the elephant in the room that everyone pretended not to notice"?

4. What specific reasons are given to explain why music sales are dropping in the past few years?

5. What is a "cash cow" (underlined in your text)?

6. According to Helmore, how is the recording industry responsible for falling sales?

7. What arguments do you find convincing in the article? Why?

8. Should consumers be prevented from downloading music from the Internet? Why or why not?

Culture and Communications

Reading 11: Phone Calls Are Futile

A new study finds most business professionals prefer to communicate digitally. Whither the telephone?

Charles Whaley

When it comes to technology in the workplace, everyone seems to have an opinion about what works best. In the next selection, Charles Whaley claims that using e-mail is far more effective than picking up a telephone. The writer defines what a "telephone bigot" is; he organizes the article by a definition rhetorical pattern.

I've been accused of being a "telephone bigot" and won't deny it. In fact I'm proud of it.

I rarely place a call to a friend or stranger if I have an e-mail address to use instead. I won't answer the phone if you call me unless you've made an appointment by e-mail (my mother knows this—she's booked a recurring slot Sunday afternoons).

Even if someone does have an appointment to speak with me by telephone, I'll have the ringer turned off, so I won't hear you trying to get through.

What's more, I'll reply to every single mail I feel deserves attention before I'll even begin to listen to my voice mail. And if your voice message doesn't include a damn good reason for me to call you back, forget it.

I haven't spoken to the editor of this fine publication by phone since she assumed the role (nor the editor before her for that matter). It would be a waste of time for both of us. If we really need to talk, I'll buy her lunch (at a time and place to be determined by e-mail). After all, I'm not anti-social. I just prefer to be sociable in a social setting, not when I'm trying to get work done.

For some time I thought I was fairly unique in this regard, and attributed much of what others have called "arrogance" with the fact I run my own business and set my own rules.

It turns out I'm not alone. META Group recently conducted a study of business professionals in 387 organizations and discovered 80 per cent of respondents prefer e-mail to phone. I take this to mean most people consider it unprofessional to phone someone when you can e-mail them instead. I heartily agree.

In fact, about three-quarters of respondents believe being without e-mail would be more of a loss than being without phone service (I get uneasy when that many people agree with me).

These numbers are particularly impressive in light of the fact we've all seen our e-mail volumes (and the time we need to spend on them) increase significantly. Apparently the annoyances of e-mail are inconsequential compared to the intrusiveness and productivity loss associated with telephone conversations.

Another joint study by Legato Systems and Osterman Research found 79 per cent of IT professionals are now using e-mail for mission-critical operations, so you can't raise the argument e-mail is being preferred because of its frivolous side (joke of the day, picking the bar for this Friday's get together, etc.).

So where does this leave the humble telephone? Will it eventually go the way of the dodo or the buggy whip? Of course not. We still keep horses around, although they're a pretty useless form of transportation by today's standards. We've found <u>niche applications</u> for equine technology (racing, jumping, glue, natural fertilizers, etc.), and no doubt we'll find niche applications for the telephone as well.

Whaley, C. (2003, May 23). Phone calls are futile. Computing Canada, *29(10), 13.*

1. What is a "telephone bigot"?
2. What results did the studies discussed show? Are the studies the writer mentions convincing? Why or why not?
3. Identify the points to Whaley's argument.
4. What is a "niche application" (underlined in your text)?
5. Why do you think Whaley wrote this article?
6. Do you agree with the writer's statement: "I just prefer to be sociable in a social setting, not when I'm trying to get work done"? What do you think is suggested by this statement?
7. In your opinion, what significant differences are there between being able to work from home or having to go to another place to work?
8. Which do you prefer—phone or e-mail? Why do you think you prefer one over the other?

Reading 12: The Simplification of Culture
Neil Bissoondath

Neil Bissoondath was born in Trinidad and came to Canada where he was educated at York University. He is a well-known writer and television host. The following selection is an excerpt from Chapter 5 of Bissoondath's controversial book, *Selling Illusions: The Cult of Multiculturalism in Canada*, which criticized the Canadian government's policy on multiculturalism. In the excerpt, Bissoondath examines language and culture, and argues that acquiring a new language does not necessarily mean letting go of one's culture and its traditions. The rhetorical mode he uses is comparison and contrast because he distinguishes his experiences and beliefs about language from those of his grandparents.

> In Canada, I don't think we've really explored how the <u>immigration experience</u> changes people, when they move from one country to another. It's easier just to comment on different foods and folkloric dances than to really understand what people go through when they emigrate.... In Canada, there has been a tendency to trivialize.
> —*Nino Ricci, quoted in Profiles, February 1994 (underlining added)*

It is at times strange to me that for my great-grandparents English was a second language. They were Brahmins, members of the learned caste, but poor. In Trinidad they led <u>tenuous</u> lives working the land, going about their daily tasks—cutting sugar-cane stalks, tending rice paddies—mostly in Hindi. That I find this strange says much about the change that the years have brought. Both the lives they led and the language they spoke have now grown impossibly remote, their faces, even their names, long drifted, for my generation at least, into an irretrievable anonymity.

Change, made inevitable by time and space and Bible-toting missionaries from another British colony called Canada, marked itself on their children. In the schools that <u>bartered</u> education for religious conversion (the bargain always kept, my paternal grandfather and one of his brothers remaining loyal to the old faith, while two other brothers embraced the new), a greater facility in English was acquired. In an agrarian society, this could not have been easy—but forever after, my grandfather ritually read his daily newspaper, lips soundlessly forming the words.

For both my grandfathers, the new language offered escape from the <u>enervating</u> labours of the field. My paternal grandfather found success in commerce, while my mother's father, less practical, more of a dreamer, engaged what little literary life the island had to offer by becoming a newspaper reporter who wrote short stories in his spare time.

Success, though, exacted a price. For my father's parents (my mother's father died before I was born), Hindi eventually became little more than a language of religion and secrets, spoken only in prayer and for privacy between themselves. In both families, English, the language of success, was the language of communication with the children, the result being that my parents spoke no Hindi save a word here and there, mostly terms of endearment or disparagement infrequently uttered.

Within three generations, then, the language of my great-grandparents had all but disappeared, and along with it had gone a way of life: dependence on the land and religious belief. We felt no sense of loss, no <u>tincture</u> of regret, no romantic attachment to a language that no longer served the purposes of our circumstance. And those of my parents' generation who still clung to the distant past—the few women who wore only saris, the few men who went to India in search of wives—came to be viewed as eccentric and foolish.

My own world was very different from the one in which my parents had grown up. While, for them, going abroad to study remained a grand and lengthy journey—farewells at the docks, the slow progression of the ship towards the horizon—for my generation it was one more step in a normal progression. Like my contemporaries', my mode of travel was jet-powered, the trip a few short hours. My only language was English, my popular cultural influences in an island independent only ten years less British or Indian than American: not Ravi Shankar or Laurence Olivier but the Temptations and Clint Eastwood. Through schooling, I acquired French, Spanish and the cultural influences they entailed, including an enduring love of the poetry of the Spanish poet Federigo García Lorca.

When, at the age of eighteen, I left Trinidad for Canada, the journey that had begun in India a century before—and here I mean not just the physical journey—was simply proceeding to its next logical step. Members of my family now live not only here but in England and the United States as well. After twenty years, this country now claims all of my loyalty, intellectual and emotional.

India and many things Indian have been left behind. Trinidad and many things Trinidadian have been left behind. Much else, though, has been assumed along the way. In a way, then, time and circumstance have succeeded where the Canadian missionaries failed—not in terms of religion but in terms of culture. It is a change that can be viewed as a loss to be mourned but there is, too, a less nostalgic way of looking at it.

In his novel *A Bend in the River*, V. S. Naipaul writes: "The world is what it is; men who are nothing, who allow themselves to become nothing, have no place in it." Making a place for ourselves is what my families have long been good at: it is one of the effects of the fear of becoming nothing. Both families are now replete with doctors and lawyers, teachers and writers. All this has come, in great part, through a refusal to brood over the loss of one language and its cultural baggage and a willingness to fully embrace another. English, then, is not for us a borrowed language but an acquired one, as fully part of my families today as Hindi was a hundred ago: the distinction is vital.

The languages I speak are central to me. My attachment to them is strong and passionate. They have made me what I am; have provided me with a way of looking at the world, of exploring and understanding it. Perhaps most important of all, they have given me the means of expressing what I see. For in being a writer, in engaging through my imagination the varied elements of familial experience, I am linked to my maternal grandfather and to all of the faceless, nameless people who came before.

Bissoondath, N. (2002). Selling illusions. Excerpt from Chapter 5, "The simplification of culture" (pp. 72–75). Toronto: Penguin Books Canada. Copyright Neil Bissoondath, 2002.

1. What do "tenuous", "bartered", "enervating", and "tincture" mean (underlined in your text)?

2. What tone has the writer chosen? Why do you think so?

3. What do you think is meant by "the immigration experience" (underlined in your text)?

4. What is irony? Are there some examples of irony in Bissoondath's article? What are they?

5. What comments do you suppose Bissoondath is making about language and cultural ties?

6. What contrasts does Bissoondath mention?

7. In your opinion, what does Bissoondath mean when he says, "Making a place for ourselves is what my families have long been good at: it is one of the effects of the fear of becoming nothing"?

8. What is "multiculturalism"? A policy promoted by provincial and federal governments in Canada? Can multiculturalism exist if people are not willing to give up some cultural ties of their own?

Reading 13: Rink Rage
The Economist, November 1, 2003

Hockey is considered by many to be Canada's national sport. The game, however, may be taking some unexpected turns. In the following selection, the writer likens "road rage" to the anger some parents feel when their children are on the ice playing hockey and how this fury has turned into verbal and physical abuse. The writer builds the argument through the use of a cause and effect rhetorical pattern.

Canadians like to say that their national religion is ice hockey. The sport bridges English- and French-speakers, native and non-native, east and west—and marks national identity by helping to distinguish them all from Americans. Such is its importance that John Manley, the finance minister, had no qualms about lobbying a bank last week to help out a cash-strapped professional team—and suffered little criticism for doing so.

Not long ago, hockey was said to be "in crisis." In 1967, 97 per cent of players in the National Hockey League (NHL), the top professional league in North America, were Canadians; a generation later, that figure had slipped towards 60 per cent, and many of the league's more graceful and skilled players were Swedes, Czechs or Russians. When Canada's men failed to win a medal in hockey at the 1998 winter Olympics, that seemed to underline the slide. So a <u>revival</u> campaign was launched—and succeeded. At last year's Olympics, Canada's men and women both won hockey golds.

Ironically, this success has come at the cost of a new fear. Could it be that Canadians have been encouraged to try too hard at hockey? Two lawsuits suggest that they have. In one, a ten-year-old Toronto boy sued the coach of an opposing team for C$10,000 ($6,400); the coach, he alleged, had said that he planned to "put a bounty" on him. The coach denied this, and the suit was dismissed. Now a teenage player in New Brunswick is suing his league for $300,000, saying he should have won its Most Valuable Player trophy.

Trivial as these cases may be, they highlight a character recognizable to most Canadians: the "<u>hockey dad</u>," who <u>goads</u> and <u>chastises</u> his child to play better, heckles referees, and then berates the coach—all in the hope that his skating sprog will grow up to earn an NHL salary of $1m or more.

Cases of "rink rage," from verbal abuse to physical assault, are rising. One in three of the 33,000 referees in minor-league hockey leaves each year. "The number one reason is the abuse they take from parents, players and coaches," says Willi Saari, of the Canadian Hockey Association. Many players and coaches drop out too. So the Association has begun a new anti-crisis campaign. The message this time: "Relax, it's just a game." If only it were.

Rink rage. (2003, January 11). The Economist, *366(8306), 32. Copyright of* The Economist *is the property of Economist Newspaper Limited.*

1. What is the argument the article proposes? Can you summarize it in a few sentences, using your own words?

2. What do "revival", "goads" and "chastises" mean (underlined in your text)?

3. What do you think the statement "Canadians like to say that their natural religion is ice hockey" means?

4. Why do you think the writer chose the title "rink rage"?

5. Why does the writer see an irony in the recent Canadian success of Olympic gold in both men and women's hockey?

6. What is a "hockey dad" (underlined in your text)? What characteristics does a "hockey dad" possess?

7. Should the Government of Canada subsidize professional sports teams when teams are in financial trouble? Why or why not?

8. Why do you think Canadians take their hockey so seriously in general?

Reading 14: Intellectual Property: A Different Kind of Inuit Ownership

Denise Rideout

Businesses' and corporations' copyright protect their company logos; the use of one without the appropriate permission and payment can cost someone a lot of money in legal fees. In the next reading, Denise Rideout explores how an Inuit cultural symbol has been co-opted as a marketing tool by business and government. Using the rhetorical pattern of definition, Rideout investigates the characteristics of a cultural icon.

The inuksuk, a symbol of Inuit culture that appears on the Nunavut flag and directs hunters on the tundra, is somewhat of a marketing device in southern Canada. Its image is popping up on t-shirts and key chains, found on company logos and is even used to sell brands of beer.

And Inuit groups across the country don't like the way non-Inuit businesses are exploiting the inuksuk to make a profit.

"The inuksuk is a big item when it comes to it being misappropriated by other individuals, non-Inuit or non-Aboriginals, for business purposes," said John Cheechoo, a director at Inuit Tapiriit Kanatami (ITK) who has been looking into ways to protect Inuit cultural symbols.

"It's a problem and it's been there for a while," Cheechoo said in an interview in Ottawa.

The major Inuit organizations in Canada sent representatives to Ottawa last week to brainstorm ways to prevent Qallunaat businesses and companies from using Inuit symbols to promote and sell their products.

The Inuit groups want the law to protect what is known as their "intellectual property rights." Current federal legislation designed to protect intellectual property covers art, trademarks, and technologies—but only if they are new or original. This makes it difficult to protect old designs, such as the traditional inuksuk symbol.

Along with ITK, Pauktuutit, Nunavut Tunngavik Inc., the Inuvialuit Regional Corp., the Labrador Inuit Association and the Avataq Cultural Institute attended the discussions with officials from the federal department of foreign affairs who specialize in intellectual property laws. Since this was a gathering of policy advisors, and not a meeting of politicians, the discussions weren't open to the public.

Robert McDougall of the department of foreign affairs said the aim of the National Roundtable on Intellectual Property and Traditional Knowledge was to get the perspective of Inuit and First Nations groups.

It turned out they had much to say. Inuit organizations worry their cultural icons are being exploited. Sometimes that misuse is happening in their own communities.

In Labrador, for instance, some Qallunaat are making and selling soapstone carvings—an artform usually mastered by Inuit carvers.

"We were always concerned with the Japanese making plastic carvings. Now it seems we've got a fight on the other front. We're now competing with non-Inuit soapstone carvers, especially in Labrador," said Gary Baikie, a representative of the Labrador Inuit Association.

Baikie recounted how these soapstone carvings are being mistaken for genuine Inuit pieces. "A buddy of mine went into an art gallery and bought a carving and he was all happy about how he'd gotten this Inuk carving. I looked at the bottom of it and the name wasn't even an Inuk one."

Another sore spot for Labrador Inuit is when Qallunaat get access to traditional knowledge and then make money off it, Baikie said.

"The one thing that we noticed is that when we [published] our 'Footprints are Everywhere,' which is the basis of our land claim, it contained a lot of traditional knowledge talking about the best hunting areas and best fishing areas. All of sudden, after that was published, we see lodges popping up in the best hunting and fishing spots," he said.

"So we became aware of how sensitive this information is."

Since then, the LIA has adopted guidelines outlining how outside researchers can conduct studies in Labrador and what they can do with the information gathered.

Incidents like this prompt Inuit organizations to take a look at how they can protect their intellectual property and traditional knowledge. Five years ago, Pauktuutit, the national Inuit women's association, laid the groundwork. Pauktuutit made it its mission to protect the design of the traditional women's parka, the amauti.

Veronica Dewar, Pauktutiit's president, said Inuit women didn't want to see fashion designers appropriate the design of the amauti.

"We've already lost our kayak design many years ago and we don't want to go that route with the amauti," Dewar said. "Inuit own that. But how do we protect it?"

In May 2001, Pauktuutit brought a group of Inuit seamstresses and intellectual property rights experts to Rankin Inlet for a workshop on current laws and regulations.

Indigenous women from Panama also attended, telling the Inuit seamstresses that their government has laws to protect their traditional clothing designs from exploitation.

Pauktuutit has invited the Panamanian women to another such workshop in Ottawa this fall. "We are really pushing this issue now," Dewar said.

"We may not adopt their legislation, but we want some ideas on how to go about it."

Rideout, D. (2003, May 30). Intellectual property: A different kind of Inuit ownership. *Nunatsiaq News*. Retrieved May 30, 2003, from http://www.nunatsiaq.com/archives/030530/news/nunavut/30530_04.html

1. Who are the Inuit?

2. What is the "inuksuk" and, according to Rideout, why is it so important to the Inuit?

3. What is Rideout's argument? Summarize it in a few sentences.

4. What is a "cultural icon" (underlined in your text)? Can you think of other examples of "cultural icons" besides the inuksuk?

5. How have some groups organized to protect traditional knowledge and cultural objects?

6. In your opinion, how can groups protect their traditions from exploitation?

7. In what ways are governments responsible for the protection of groups against exploitation by business interests? Do you agree they should be responsible? Why or why not?

8. In your opinion, are cultural symbols a form of intellectual property? Why or why not?

answer key

Chapter 1: Preparing and Planning to Write

Exercise 7 Creating Outlines from Paragraphs

PARAGRAPH 1

Topic Sentence: People should not be allowed to smoke in public places.

Major point 1: tobacco smoke irritating and offensive

Proof (explanation or example): respiratory health problems

Proof (explanation or example): allergies

Proof (explanation or example): unpleasant smell

Major point 2: damage to physical property

Proof (explanation or example): furniture and rugs

Proof (explanation or example): wallpaper and paint

Major point 3: public risk of fire

Proof (explanation or example): tossed lit cigarette

Proof (explanation or example): flammable fabrics

Proof (explanation or example): crowded places

Wrap-up sentence: People should show respect for other patrons and their safety by not smoking in public places.

PARAGRAPH 2

Topic Sentence: Consumers can "food-shop" wisely.

Major point 1: think and plan

Proof (explanation or example): weekly menu

Proof (explanation or example): store "specials"

Proof (explanation or example): grocery list

Major point 2: convenience foods

Proof (explanation or example): costly items

Proof (explanation or example): ingredients

Proof (explanation or example): additives

Major point 3: nutritional value

Proof (explanation or example): complex carbohydrates

Proof (explanation or example): available choices

Proof (explanation or example): food preparation

Proof (explanation or example): fresh produce

Wrap-up sentence: With some planning and attention, consumers can do some careful shopping in the grocery store, while saving money and avoiding unnecessary trips to the store.

ESL Pointer Exercise 2 Count and Non-Count Nouns

1. freedom
2. work
3. (correct)
4. traffic
5. garbage
6. (correct)
7. popcorn
8. (correct)
9. housework
10. (correct)

Chapter 2: Analyzing Paragraph Development

Exercise 2 Identifying Rhetorical Mode in Paragraphs

1. Definition
2. Comparison/contrast
3. Comparison/contrast
4. Definition
5. Time-order/process
6. Classification/division

ESL Pointer Exercise 1 Indefinite Articles

1. a
2. an
3. a
4. a
5. a
6. an
7. a
8. a
9. a
10. an
11. an
12. an
13. a
14. a
15. an
16. an

ESL Pointer Exercise 2 Articles

1. an
2. The
3.
4.
5. an
6.
7. a
8.
9.
10. the, the
11.
12. an, the
13. An
14. a
15. the
16. an
17. The
18. the, a *or* the
19. the
20. the

Chapter 3: Analyzing Detail Organization

Exercise 1 Locating the Topic Sentence

1. Main idea? Who was F. H. Varley?
2. Main idea? The establishment of the UN.
3. Main idea? The problematic history of tree cutting in Canada or technical difficulties in the pioneer days of lumbering in Canada.
4. Topic Sentence: Rowing is a sport that is gaining in popularity.

ESL Pointer Exercise 1 Expressions of Quantity

1. some, any, most, more, all, a lot of, many, several, a few, a couple of, both
2. some, much, more, less, a lot of, very little, no
3. each, every, any, one, some, most, more, all, a lot of, many, several, a few, a couple of, both
4. some, most, more, all, a lot of, no
5. some, any, most, more, all, a lot of, many, several, a few, a couple of, both, few, fewer
6. a little, some, any, much, more, all, less, a lot of, very little, no

7. some, any, more, all, few, fewer, a lot of, no, many, several, a few, a couple of, both
8. each, every, any, one, some, most, more, all, a lot of, a little, much, less, very little, no
9. any, some, most, more, a lot of, a little, much, all, less, very little, no
10. some, any, most, more, all, a lot of, many, several, a few, a couple of, both, no
11. some, any, most, more, all, a lot of, a little, much, no
12. each, every, any, one, no
13. some, any, most, more, all, a lot of, many, several, a few, a couple of, both, no
14. each, every, any, one, no

Chapter 4: Time-Order or Process Development

ESL Pointer Exercise 1 *Transitions*

1. Blank 1 (First, To begin with, In the first place)
   Blank 2 (Next, After that, Later, Secondly, Afterward, Soon, After a while, In due time, Then, Meanwhile, Following that, Finally, Lastly)
2. Blank 1 (First, To begin with, In the first place)
   Blank 2 (Next, After that, Later, Secondly, Afterward, Soon, After a while, In due time, Then, Meanwhile, Following that)
   Blank 3 (Then, After that, Later, Meanwhile, Afterward, Finally, Soon, Following that, After a while, Thirdly, In due time, Next)
   Blank 4 (next, after that, later, fourthly, afterward, soon, after a while, in due time, then, meanwhile, following that)
   Blank 5 (Next, After that, Later, Fifthly, Afterward, Soon, After a while, In due time, Then, Meanwhile, Following that, Last, Finally)
3. Blank 1 (First, To begin with, In the first place)
   Blank 2 (Next, After that, Later, Secondly, Afterward, Soon, After a while, In due time, Then, Meanwhile, Following that)
   Blank 3 (Next, After that, Later, Thirdly, Afterward, Soon, After a while, In due time, Then, Meanwhile, Following that, Last, Finally)
4. Blank 1 (First, To begin with, In the first place)
   Blanks 2 and 3 (Next, After that, Later, Secondly, Thirdly, Afterward, Soon, After a while, In due time, Then, Meanwhile, Following that)
   Blank 4 (Next, After that, Later, Fourthly, Afterward, Soon, After a while, In due time, Then, Meanwhile, Following that, Last, Finally)
5. Blank 1 (First, To begin with, In the first place)
   Blank 2 (next, after that, later, secondly, afterward, soon, after a while, in due time, then, meanwhile, following that, last, finally)
6. Blank 1 (First, To begin with, In the first place)
   Blank 2 (Next, After that, Later, Secondly, Afterward, Soon, After a while, In due time, Then, Meanwhile, Following that)
   Blank 3 (Next, After that, Later, Thirdly, Afterward, Soon, After a while, In due time, Then, Meanwhile, Following that, Last, Finally)
7. Blank 1 (first, to begin with, in the first place)
   Blanks 2 and 3 (Next, After that, Later, Secondly, Thirdly, Afterward, Soon, After a while, In due time, Then, Meanwhile, Following that)
   Blank 4 (Next, After that, Later, Fourthy, Afterward, Soon, After a while, In due time, Then, Meanwhile, Following that, Last, Finally)

8. Blank 1 (first, to begin with, in the first place)
Blank 2 (next, after that, later, secondly, afterward, soon, after a while, in due time, then, meanwhile, following that)
Blank 3 (next, after that, later, thirdly, afterward, soon, after a while, in due time, then, meanwhile, following that, last, finally)

Chapter 5: Comparison and Contrast Development

ESL Pointer Exercise 2 Expressions of Comparison and Contrast

1. similar to
2. different from
3. but
4. different from
5. similar to
6. the same as
7. but
8. different from *or* similar to
9. similar to / but
10. similar to

Chapter 6: Classification and Division Development

ESL Pointer Exercise 1 Transitions

Other answers may also be suitable. Please see your instructor.

1. one kind of / one type of
2. one kind of / one type of
3. One part of
4. one kind of / one type of
5. one part of / one component of
6. One part of
7. one kind of / one type of
8. one part of
9. One kind of / One type of
10. One part of / One component

ESL Pointer Exercise 2 Practice with Transitions

Other answers may also be suitable. Please see your instructor.

1. One sort of / One kind of
2. The first part / The second part / etc.
3. One kind / The second sort / The first type
4. Blank 1—The first part / The second part
   Blank 2—To illustrate / Accordingly / Specifically
   Blank 3—Another part / The second part
5. one kind / one type / one sort
6. one kind / another type / the last type

7. for example,
8. one group / one kind / the third group
9. one sort of / the fourth type of
10. one category / one kind
11. Blank 1—category / sort / etc.
    Blank 2—for example
12. the sixth type / another kind
13. Blank 1 (one kind / the third type)
    Blank 2— also
    Blank 3—the second kind / another type
14. Blank 1—the first kind
    Blank 2—a second sort
    Blank 3—the third type
15. Furthermore / Accordingly / Besides that / Specifically

Chapter 8: Definition Development

ESL Pointer Exercise 1 Clauses

1. D / I	6. D / I	11. D / I
2. I / D	7. I / D	12. D / I
3. I / D	8. I / D	13. D / I
4. D / I	9. D / I	14. I / D
5. I / D	10. I / D	15. D / I

ESL Pointer Exercise 3 Clauses

If you have another answer you think is correct, please see your instructor.

1. Although he is shy about performing publicly, Salim writes his own songs.
2. The owl sat silently watching from the highest branch of the tree while the mouse scurried through the grasses below, *or* While the mouse scurried through the grasses below, the owl sat silently watching from the highest branch of the tree.
3. Does Yasmina visit you when she is in town?
4. After slicing the mushrooms, heat the butter. *or* After you slice the mushrooms, heat…
5. The choreographer spends his time rehearsing until the show starts.
6. Harpreet was delighted because her relatives arrived from India.
7. Since Marina is having a baby in April, she is looking at baby clothing in the flyers.
8. Though she won't admit it, Zoe hates cooking.
9. Wherever the cat goes, her kittens follow.
10. Before he went to Cuba, he went to Spain. *or* He went to Cuba before he went to Spain.
11. Do not turn off the computer unless you will be away for more than one day.
12. Kira went to the marketplace where she bought eggplant for the stew.

Chapter 9: Beginning Essays

ESL Pointer Exercise 1 Voice

1. passive
2. active
3. active
4. passive
5. passive
6. passive
7. active
8. active
9. passive
10. passive
11. active
12. active
13. passive
14. passive

ESL Pointer Exercise 2 Voice

1. Its owner leashed the poodle to the bike rack.
2. Chef Bonhomme prepared a feast.
3. The station master found the umbrella.
4. Margaret Atwood wrote the novel.
5. The ranch hand placed the saddle on the horse.
6. Detective Goodley solved the murder.
7. The board held him responsible.
8. My children arranged my party.
9. The accident upset her.
10. My brother convinced me to quit smoking.

Chapter 10: Nouns, Pronouns, and Verbs

Self-Test: Part 1 Nouns, Pronouns, and Verbs

1. Mr. Miller, property, lake
2. representative, moment
3. workers, petition
4. doctor, pills, depression

Self-Test: Part 2 Nouns as Subjects or Objects

1. Mary Jane (S) Peter (S)
2. machine (S)
3. Malcolm (S) Bob (O)
4. crows (S)
5. group (S) fries (O) sandwiches (O) coffee (O)

Self-Test: Part 3 Verbs

1. had been waiting
2. will be singing
3. Have worked
4. is
5. started

Self-Test: Part 4 Verb Tenses

1. P
2. F
3. PT
4. P or F
5. PT
6. P
7. P
8. PT
9. PT
10. PT

Self-Test: Part 5 Verb Forms

1. eaten
2. sworn
3. saw; did see; was seeing
4. began; had begun; did begin; were beginning
5. done
6. brought
7. choosing
8. worked
9. written
10. drive

Self-Test: Part 6 Identification

1. pronoun
2. noun
3. verb
4. verb
5. verb
6. pronoun
7. noun
8. verb
9. noun
10. pronoun

Self-Test: Part 7 Verb Identification

1. decided (A)
2. are (NA)
3. stopped (A)
4. thought (A)
5. is (NA)

Exercise 1 Classifying

1. dogs
2. cooking *or* kitchen utensils
3. cars *or* vehicles
4. furniture
5. animals *or* mammals

Exercise 2 Nouns

foot	examination	end	hour
wagon	planet	paint	skip
rum	hate	community	person
apricot	love	law	ghetto
joke	harbour	tent	television
sauce	hero	kitchen	

Exercise 3 Concrete and Abstract Nouns

1. passengers (C) bus (C) rain (C)
2. Ronnie (C) models (C) collection (C or A)
3. artist (C or A) paper (C) scissors (C) glue (C) pencil (C)

4. children (C) games (C or A) boss (C or A)
5. ship (C) coat (C) paint (C)
6. prince (C) guests (C) party (A)
7. hotel (C) gunshots (A) fire (A) silence (A)
8. carpenter (C) nails (C) trim (C) window (C)
9. eggs (C) pavement (C)
10. program (A)
11. company (C or A) order (C) van (C)
12. skunk (C) bushes (C) path (C) shed (C)
13. wasp (C) woman (C)
14. Paul (C) truck (C) farm (C)
15. fight (A) bar (C) rule (A) hockey (C)

Exercise 5 Subject Nouns

1. Marie	4. Terry	7. Wally	10. car
2. dog	5. Sylvia	8. dancers	11. team
3. boxer	6. workers	9. wolf	12. train

Exercise 6 Subject Nouns

1. actor	4. dog	7. soup	10. lamp
2. Margaret	5. Tom	8. lawn	11. Philip
3. paper	6. Yogurt	9. cookies	12. children

Exercise 7 Subject Nouns and Object Nouns

1. Rodd (S) plywood (O)
2. students (S) rules (O)
3. man (S) money (O)
4. puppy (S) rag (O)
5. Mrs. Pobsby (S) rug (O)
6. chef (S) salad (O)
7. boy (S) ankle (O)
8. cousin (S) pizza (O)
9. Ozzie (S) rocks (O) stones (O)
10. Madame Lem (S) disaster (O)

Exercise 8 Subject Nouns and Object Nouns

1. child (S) picture (O)
2. coffee (S) (no object)
3. crow (S) garbage (O)
4. girl (S) novel (O)
5. supervisor (S) party (O)
6. family (S) picnic (O)
7. Francis (S) parrot (O)
8. Charlie (S) time (O)
9. gentleman (S) sandwich (O) beer (O)
10. Harvey (S) sauce (O)

Exercise 10 Pronouns

1. it
2. he and she, him and her, they *or* them
3. it *or* she *or* he *or* him *or* her
4. he *or* she *or* him *or* her
5. it *or* they *or* them
6. it
7. he *or* him
8. they *or* them
9. He *or* She; it
10. They; her
11. They; them
12. She; him or her
13. He; it
14. He; it
15. They

Exercise 11 Subject and Object Nouns and Pronouns

1. We (S) cream (O)
2. Rhonda (S) poem (O)
3. mayor (S) gallery (O)
4. he (S) reports (O)
5. I (S) parade (O)
6. Books (S) papers (S) (no object)
7. we (S) voices (O)
8. John (S) I (S) charge (O)
9. She (S) it (O)
10. Al (S) meat (O)
11. You (S) cold (O) chills (O)
12. I (S) Joe (O) her (O)
13. We (S) program (O)
14. dogs (S) cat (S) squirrel (O)
15. He (S) window (O)
16. They (S) kite (O)
17. I (S) rocks (O)
18. doctor (S) nurse (S) progress (O)
19. She (S) strawberries (O)
20. students (S) (no object)

Exercise 13 Action Verbs

1. rang
2. caught
3. (no action verb)
4. swims
5. seeded
6. cooked
7. went
8. stopped
9. traded
10. understood
11. wrote
12. fixed
13. bought
14. read
15. saw

Exercise 14 Action and Non-Action Verbs

1. lay — ACT
2. is — NO ACT
3. has — NO ACT
4. smells — NO ACT
5. were — NO ACT
6. is — NO ACT
7. interviewed — ACT
8. are — NO ACT
9. purchased — ACT
10. will be — NO ACT
11. was — NO ACT
12. is — NO ACT
13. felt — NO ACT
14. smokes — ACT   drinks — ACT
15. sounded — NO ACT

Exercise 16 Identifying Verb Tense

1. present perfect progressive
2. past perfect
3. present perfect progressive
4. past perfect
5. present progressive; simple present
6. simple past; past progressive
7. past perfect; simple past
8. simple present; simple future
9. past progressive
10. future perfect; simple present
11. present perfect
12. simple past; past progressive

Exercise 18 Adding Verb Forms

1. written	6. known	11. spoken	16. saw
2. forgiven	7. saw	12. fallen	17. torn
3. taken	8. given	13. became	18. written
4. broken	9. ridden	14. taken	19. gone
5. thrown	10. began	15. chosen	20. given

ESL Pointer Exercise 1 Working with Verb Tenses

1. They had not listened.
2. Felicia will go on Tuesday.
3. The dog barked all day.
4. Those roses will be dying.
5. He invites me.
6. Sandra has been playing the accordion.
7. The clown will do card tricks.
8. Vicky cuts her hand.
9. The cat was catching mice.
10. I am taking my time.
11. Lisa was not tolerating it.
12. I will clear my desk on Thursday.
13. Pamela inflated the story.
14. We will collect bottles.
15. Terry has closed the case.
16. The schedule is out of date.
17. Joanne will scan the headlines. Joanne is going to scan the headlines.
18. The sheriff notes your new address.
19. The child had been tearing her jacket.
20. He spins the wheel.

Chapter 11: Subjects and Verbs

Self-Test: Part 1 Subject and Verb Identification

1. Amy (S) Lowell (S) booked (V)
2. druggist (S) filled (V)
3. Lucinda (S) comes (V)
4. flies (S) were (V) buzzing (V)
5. Several of the customers (S) were (V)
6. child (S) seemed (V)
7. Have (V) you (S) had (V)
8. we (S) spotted (V)
9. ice cream (S) is (V)

Self-Test: Part 2 Subject–Verb Agreement

1. wants
2. were
3. is
4. pours
5. perform
6. is
7. are
8. make
9. Is
10. Have

Self-Test: Part 3 Identification of Subjects

1. Dawn (S) niece (S)
2. One (S)
3. case (S)
4. manager (S)
5. Marcus (S) Leo (S)
6. hoot (S)
7. instructor (S)
8. one (S)

Self-Test: Part 4 Subject–Verb Identification

1. judge (S) jury (S) looked (V)
2. [You] (S)
3. are (V) children (S)
4. Machines (S) buzzed (V) hummed (V)
5. burst (S) came (V)
6. Bonnie (S) was (V) writing (V)
7. Randy (S) clipped (V) weeded (V)

Self-Test: Part 5 Subject–Verb Agreement

1. was
2. are
3. Has
4. is
5. (correct)
6. goes
7. were
8. (correct)
9. was
10. owns
11. was
12. checks
13. have
14. are
15. harmonizes

Exercise 1 Subjects and Verbs

1. children (S) are (V)
2. We (S) whispered (V)
3. daughter (S) is (V)
4. Maxwell (S) worked (V)
5. I (S) phoned (V)
6. She (S) is (V)
7. You (S) are (V)
8. friend (S) was (V)
9. They (S) drank (V)
10. Margaret (S) lives (V)

Exercise 3 Verb Phrases

1. is working
2. has been driving
3. might rain
4. must write
5. should go
6. are deciding
7. was picking
8. can leave
9. has had
10. may have been writing

Exercise 5 Prepositional Phrases

1. Across the valley
2. along the river; near some rocks
3. of bears; at the park gate
4. among the papers
5. with a loud voice
6. on the stage; of the show
7. against the odds
8. Near the swamp; beside a clump; of weeds
9. through the crowd; of protesters
10. behind the counter

Exercise 7 More about Prepositional Phrases

1. from a dealer (where) in Edmonton (where)
2. in the woods (where)
3. of snakeskin (what)
4. against the strong winter wind (how)
5. After the game (when)
6. from Jamaica (where) until Sunday (when)
7. on the floor (where)
8. of magpies (what) in the trees (where)
9. of flowers (what)
10. under the bridge (where)

Exercise 8 Verbs, Verb Phrases, and Subjects

1. I (S) <u>met</u> (At the party) (from Yellowknife)
2. One (S) <u>escaped</u> (of the horses) (from the corral)
3. driver (S) <u>fell</u> (of the commercial truck) (at the wheel)
4. raise (S) <u>was</u> (of $30)
5. bunch (S) <u>arrived</u> (of flowers) (for you)
6. winners (S) <u>stayed</u> (of the race) (at the racetrack)
7. marks (S) <u>were</u> (for his mechanics exams)
8. game (S) <u>continued</u> (after the storm)
9. ducks (S) loons (S) <u>were feeding</u> (near the shore)
10. master (S) <u>tripped</u> (of ceremonies) (on his way) (to the podium)

Exercise 9 Subject–Verb Agreement and Detail Phrases

1. are (on the desk)
2. is (to the doors) (on the wall)
3. drives (from Flin Flon)
4. is (of men) (in pay)
5. have (of the students)
6. are (in the fridge)
7. was (Up the hill) (over the bridge)
8. prepares (In the mornings) (for her family)
9. irritates (of cigarettes)
10. go (of those items)

Exercise 11 Verbs and Commands

1. You (S) stack (V)
2. you (S) offer (V)
3. You (S) distribute (V)
4. you (S) remove (V)
5. you (S) arrange (V)
6. You (S) stop (V)

Exercise 12 One *and* Each

1. goes
2. was
3. gives
4. is
5. needs
6. has

Exercise 14 Subject–Verb Agreement

1. is
2. were
3. is
4. goes
5. makes
6. are
7. have
8. have
9. were
10. is

ESL Pointer Exercise 1 Agreement and Indefinite Pronouns

1. A few of the people were
2. Some of the movie was
3. Most of the children love
4. One of his marriages was
5. None of the wine in the antique bottle tastes
6. (correct)
7. All of the furniture was
8. Alistair and most of his friends drink
9. no one wants
10. (correct)
11. All of the paint was
12. Some of the evidence is

ESL Pointer Exercise 2 More Subject–Verb Agreement

1. The audience . . . was throwing
2. there were piles
3. (correct)
4. (correct)
5. Students or the professors vote
6. (correct)
7. Most of the photographs are
8. Nobody questions
9. there are extra computers
10. (correct)
11. No one . . . has been notified
12. Each of the missing reports has been
13. Neither of the departments . . . has
14. The committee makes
15. None of the conference was
16. The CD or the memos contain
17. two-thirds . . . was destroyed
18. flock . . . was gathering

Chapter 12: Punctuation and Capitalization

Self-Test: Part 1 Comma Use

1. beaver, eagle, bulldog,
2. finished,
3. soil, lumps, seedlings, labels, wagons, site,
4. 10, 1871,
5. (correct)
6. bang, understand,
7. (correct.)
8. day, garden,
9. 12, 1988, 16,
10. course, sarcastic, stupid,

Self-Test: Part 2 Semicolon Use

1. hutch;
2. tourist;
3. (correct)
4. broken;
5. hospital;
6. green;
7. myself;
8. (correct)
9. electronics;
10. treasure;
11. night;
12. classics;
13. pulpit;
14. (correct)

Self-Test: Part 3 Colon Use

1. parts:
2. secret:
3. gifts:
4. ridiculous:
5. (correct)
6. material:
7. orders:

Self-Test: Part 4 Commas, Colons, and Semicolons

1. students; level, schedules,
2. (correct)
3. payment, rent, limit;
4. communication; is, functions,
5. He, hand, platform
6. Page, Atwood, Canada; States, Britain,
7. circle;
8. secret:

Self-Test: Part 5 Capitalization

1. Monday Uncle Robert Four Roads Motel
2. Toronto
3. Royal Canadian Mounted Police Port Renfrew
4. We Swiss French
5. Credit Union Saturdays Fridays
6. Mrs. Walsh Department Mines Resources
7. Safeway Coke Lansdowne Junior High School

Exercise 1 Using Commas

1. town, Dylan, Cohen,
2. baby, wash, calls, dinner,
3. (correct)
4. (correct)
5. Alberta, Columbia, Saskatchewan,
6. (correct)
7. Barbara, California, Portland,
8. cakes, cookies, juice,
9. sugar, butter,
10. dough, batter, buns, breads, baked, sorted,
11. pink, red, orange, blue,
12. breakfast, egg, toast, jam,
13. Baden Baden, 22, 6,
14. Winnipeg, Manitoba, Edmonton, Alberta, Current,
15. Rice, wheat, lentils,

Exercise 3 Using Commas

1. glue, nails, bits,
2. anxiety, marks,
3. Sydney, Australia, Tuesday, 23,
4. (correct)
5. Squirrels, chipmunks, rats,
6. ham, bacon,
7. beads, blocks, drawing, painting, whispering, listening,
8. psychology, philosophy,
9. (correct)
10. jalapeño, vinegar,
11. Hamilton, Ontario,
12. roll, blues,
13. sugar, milk,
14. Maureen, Alice, Amanda,
15. Saturday, 1,
16. Vancouver, Oshawa,
17. Apples, quinces,
18. interesting, informative,
19. stairs, bedroom, doors,
20. wage, conditions,
21. Poodles, terriers, spaniels,
22. refrigerator, steps, fence,
23. Valencia, Mandarin,
24. 11, 1918,
25. résumés, interviews, techniques,

Exercise 5 Complex Sentences

1. (Since he fought with his sister),
2. (While Ronald was baking the bread),
3. (no comma)
4. (because the wind was so strong) (no comma)
5. (Unless I win the chess game),
6. (until her boyfriend picked her up) (no comma)
7. (As Mario opened the library book),
8. (Since my uncle is a nervous fellow),

9. (if she wanted to bury the bone or not) (no comma)
10. (While her parents were on vacation),
11. (if there is any work) (no comma)
12. (As Rodney turned to get the box of cereal from the store shelf),
13. (Because the snowstorm blew down some heavy trees),
14. (because he is a tremendous organizer) (no comma)

Exercise 6 Group Activity: The Semicolon

1. dogs;
2. OK
3. up;
4. OK
5. OK
6. project;
7. lot,
8. (no semicolon)
9. (no semicolon)
10. OK
11. OK
12. church,
13. OK
14. OK
15. state,

Exercise 7 Colon Use

1. (no colon)
2. (no colon)
3. OK
4. OK
5. (no colon)
6. OK
7. (no colon)
8. (no colon)
9. worsening:
10. OK

Exercise 10 Using Apostrophes

1. Zoe's she's
2. children's
3. men's
4. golfer's
5. cat's
6. Anna's
7. ship's passengers'
8. They'll
9. hospital's he'd Dad's
10. We're you're sheep's

Exercise 11 Capitalization

1. Has Uncle Fred Doctor Robinson
2. Did I Uncle Seth
3. The Mr. Eng
4. Early Superintendent Davis
5. Inspector Gladeau Chief Beckley

Exercise 12 Capitalization

1. *A Whale Killing* Farley Mowat Canadian
2. Many Indo-Canadian India
3. My I Christmas Halifax
4. Last Tuesday March April
5. Did Gwen English Italian Spanish
6. Mark *Twelve Days Better Body*
7. A Dr. Johnson Red Deer
8. New Year's Day Canadian
9. The French Moncton
10. Chef Schneider German

ESL Pointer Exercise 2 Practice with Direct and Indirect Speech

1. The clerk replied that the cost of mailing the package was $20.00.
2. My sister-in-law said, "I am afraid of mice and spiders."
3. One television reporter said, "I am shocked by the damage to the building."
4. Chula explained that, in about two months' time, she would be on a train in the Sudan.

5. The president stated that one of the things he (or she) disliked the most was being misquoted by the press.
6. The two students complained to Professor Nguyen, "Our marks are incorrect on the economics exam."
7. Tara remarked that she would not work on week nights any longer unless she got a raise.

Chapter 13: Modifiers

Self-Test: Part 1 Finding Adjectives

1. (no adjectives)
2. impatient convenience
3. fresh lemon
4. historic wonderful beautiful
5. excited light-fingered bustling
6. young imposing dinosaur
7. thick blueberry
8. shaggy stone
9. strong
10. (no adjectives)

Self-Test: Part 2 Finding Adverbs

1. quietly
2. Today usually
3. desperately quite dangerously
4. intensely now
5. certainly unexpectedly tomorrow
6. excitedly not
7. extremely just
8. (no adverbs)
9. tightly then
10. commonly rather well

Self-Test: Part 3 Finding Prepositional Phrases

1. (Despite the weather) (in the rain)
2. (about the exam) (on Monday) (with anyone)
3. (in your garden)
4. (in the lunch room)
5. (for a beer) (at the hotel)
6. (in a short time)
7. (of students) (on the platform)

Self-Test: Part 4 Identifying Adjective and Adverb Prepositional Phrases

1. (from Brazil) ADJ (to immigration officials) ADV
2. (of pumpkins) ADJ (of sunflowers) ADJ (of the hall) ADJ
3. (of the planks) ADJ (from the deck) ADV
4. (through the mall) ADV (about their plans) ADV
5. (in her arms) ADV

Self-Test: Part 5 Using Comparisons

1. better
2. most
3. worst
4. better
5. least
6. most
7. more
8. better
9. More
10. better

Self-Test: Part 6 Your Own Sentences

Please show your work to your instructor.

Self-Test: Part 7 Usage

1. really
2. badly
3. well
4. well
5. bad

Exercise 3 Adjectives That Compare

1. bad, worse *or* good, better
2. best
3. worst
4. better *or* worse
5. worst
6. most
7. most
8. more *or* less
9. most
10. more *or* less
11. more *or* less
12. most *or* least
13. more *or* less
14. more *or* less
15. better *or* worse

Exercise 5 Adverbs

1. often really freely
2. lazily just
3. seldom too
4. sadly slowly weakly
5. very usually happily
6. never quite
7. usually almost
8. often somewhat
9. always very generously
10. scarcely strangely
11. perfectly fluently
12. unhappily just too
13. furiously then
14. beautifully almost never
15. somewhat so loudly

Exercise 6 Adverbs

1. really carefully yesterday
2. neatly outside
3. noisily over there
4. clumsily
5. most
6. here recently
7. Seldom intentionally
8. ferociously
9. Yesterday quietly happily
10. rarely anywhere
11. Bravely back
12. early later
13. shyly
14. Immediately
15. Slowly quietly
16. less
17. Today brightly
18. too
19. more
20. extremely
21. Honestly rarely
22. more always
23. down calmly clearly
24. softly
25. Tomorrow quite
26. loudly angrily
27. so blankly
28. certainly strongly
29. casually immediately
30. hardly extremely well

Exercise 8 Prepositional Phrases

1. (Between you and me) (in honour) (of their parents' wedding anniversary)
2. (of flames and melted rock)
3. (of embroidery) (in many cultures) (of the world)
4. (in a bog) (near Copetown, Ontario)
5. (In case) (of an emergency)
6. (in the waters) (around Vancouver Island)
7. (for children) (of their homes and parents) (behind them)
8. (Inside the tunnel) (from beneath them)
9. (for their great beauty) (despite their irritating voices)
10. (of clay) (in the centre) (of her wheel) (with her foot)
11. (Along the edges) (of the field) (of a red-brown mineral)
12. (of jewels) (without a trace)
13. (Across the open meadows) (through the thickets and forests) (to safety)
14. (in my notebook) (on Wednesday)
15. (Below the surface) (of the water) (of tiny blue fish)

16. (in the scene) (except Vicki) (with the nature hike)
17. (of wine) (for me)
18. (in a tangle) (of old fishing line) (below the wharf)
19. (into my business) (about me)

Exercise 10 Adjective or Adverb Prepositional Phrases

1. (On Sunday afternoon) ADV (on the grounds) ADV (for a reunion) ADV
2. (of the dogs) ADJ (in the playground) ADV (on tricycles) ADJ
3. (in the city) ADJ (for better wages) ADV
4. (in the sun hat) ADJ (for the finest carnations) ADJ
5. (Inside the house) ADV (around the kitchen) ADV (for their dinner) ADV
6. (of salmon) ADJ (from the chemical spill) ADV (of garden fertilizer) ADJ
7. (at the large, decorated table) ADV (about the celebration) ADV (of her eightieth birthday) ADJ
8. (from the American ship) ADJ (on Government Street) ADJ
9. (from that region) ADJ (of the globe) ADJ (of their new Canadian home) ADJ
10. (during the Gulf War) ADV (by various countries) ADV
11. (on the upper deck) ADV (of the large ferry) ADJ
12. (with this heavy couch) ADV (to the other side) ADV (of the room) ADJ
13. (by the other man's threats) ADV (within a few minutes) ADV
14. (in the little blue sneakers) ADJ (of chocolate ice cream) ADJ
15. (of biscuits) ADJ (from Britain) ADV
16. (On an evening) ADV (during the winter) ADV (in the fourth quadrant) ADV (of the galaxy) ADJ
17. (On Laugh Night) ADV (on Tuesday) ADV (at the downtown bar) ADV (to a silent audience) ADV
18. (of campers) ADJ (along the beach) ADV (at low tide) ADV
19. (of blackbirds) ADJ (in the treetops) ADV
20. (of crunchies) ADJ (of milk) ADJ
21. (of books) ADJ (up the stairs) ADV (down the hall) ADV (into my room) ADV (on the shelf) ADV (over my bed) ADJ
22. (of roses) ADJ (inside the basket) ADV (of chocolates) ADJ
23. (Despite my protests) ADV (on the trip) ADV

Exercise 13 Adjective and Adverb Usage

1. really *or* badly
2. really
3. badly—good *or* real
4. badly
5. really bad
6. well *or* badly
7. bad *or* real *or* good
8. bad—really *or* badly
9. really
10. real
11. really
12. well
13. really—badly *or* well
14. good *or* real—badly
15. bad—real *or* good
16. well *or* badly
17. well *or* badly
18. well *or* badly
19. real

ESL Pointer Exercise 1 Prepositions of Place and Time

1. in
2. at
3. At
4. at
5. in
6. In
7. at
8. in
9. in
10. On
11. at
12. in
13. On
14. In
15. on

ESL Pointer Exercise 2 Adjectives + Prepositions

1. pleased with
2. opposed to
3. popular with
4. capable of
5. suspicious of
6. aware of
7. attached to
8. capable of
9. suitable to *or* for
10. similar to
11. related to
12. satisfied with
13. proud of
14. afraid of
15. accustomed to

Chapter 14: Patterns of Sentences

Self-Test: Part 1 Identifying Patterns of Sentences

1. complex
2. compound
3. simple
4. compound
5. simple
6. complex
7. complex
8. compound
9. simple
10. compound
11. complex
12. simple
13. simple
14. complex
15. compound

Self-Test: Part 2 Identifying Clauses

1. (While you were at the store) <u>the office supervisor called you</u>
2. (Although the wind was strong) <u>no property was damaged</u>
3. <u>Please ask Meg</u> (if she is coming with us)
4. <u>Ronald played the violin</u> (until he was 12 years old)
5. <u>Call me</u> (when you get home)
6. <u>We're having a celebration</u> (after our last exam is over)
7. (Since she left) <u>I've been lonely</u>
8. <u>The fisherman caught some fish</u> (when he went out yesterday)
9. (As the child walked) <u>he whistled</u>
10. (When we were away last weekend) <u>the power was off at our house</u>

Exercise 4 Simple and Compound Sentences

1. S
2. S
3. S
4. C
5. C
6. S
7. C
8. S
9. C
10. C
11. S
12. S
13. C

Exercise 5 Two Types of Clauses

1. Because we had a party last night (D), we're exhausted today (I).
2. A salesperson will help you (I) if you ring the bell (D).
3. When Joan was in Europe (D), she visited Rome (I).
4. The kids were watching television (I) as we were playing cards (D).
5. Although Maxine is a qualified welder (D), she can't find work (I).
6. Before you go to bed (D), let the cat out (I).
7. After his family telephoned (D), Bob was depressed (I).
8. Since Aileen won't be able to be in class tomorrow (D), I'll collect the assignment for her (I).
9. The plant died (I) because it was left in the hot sun (D).
10. If I tell you about it (D), will you keep it a secret (I)?
11. Because her son had the measles (D), Dorothy missed a week of classes (I).

12. When he went for the interview (D), he lost his glasses (I).
13. He twisted his ankle (I) while he was waterskiing (D).
14. If the baby cries (D), pick her up (I).
15. I wanted to go to Montreal (I) although I couldn't afford the trip (D).
16. The game was exciting (I) because the two teams were very competitive (D).
17. I can't go home (I) until I finish this work (D).
18. After the new manager was appointed (D), the employees became suspicious (I).
19. Most of the students were nervous (I) because they'd been away from school for a long time (D).
20. While I was driving down Blakely Road (D), I saw a family of deer near the roadside (I).

Exercise 6 Clauses and Complex Sentences

1. CONDITION	6. CONDITION	11. CONDITION	16. CONDITION
2. TIME	7. CONDITION	12. TIME	17. TIME
3. TIME	8. TIME	13. TIME	18. TIME
4. CONDITION	9. CONDITION	14. CONDITION	19. TIME
5. TIME	10. CONDITION	15. TIME	20. CONDITION

Exercise 9 Simple, Compound, and Complex Sentences

1. SIMPLE	6. SIMPLE	11. SIMPLE	16. COMPLEX
2. COMPLEX	7. COMPLEX	12. COMPOUND	17. COMPLEX
3. COMPLEX	8. SIMPLE	13. SIMPLE	18. COMPOUND
4. SIMPLE	9. COMPOUND	14. COMPOUND	19. SIMPLE
5. COMPOUND	10. SIMPLE	15. COMPOUND	20. SIMPLE

Exercise 13 Review of Simple, Compound, and Complex Sentences

1. C	6. C	11. S
2. CX	7. CX	12. CX
3. S	8. S	13. C
4. C	9. C	14. CX
5. S	10. CX	15. C

ESL Pointer Exercise 1 Identifying Conditions

1. case 3	6. case 3	11. case 2
2. case 1	7. case 1	12. case 3
3. case 2	8. case 2	13. case 3
4. case 3	9. case 2	14. case 1
5. case 1	10. case 2	

Chapter 15: Sentence-Level Errors

Self-Test: Part 1 Identifying Fragments and Sentences

1. FRAG	6. FRAG
2. FRAG	7. FRAG
3. FRAG	8. FRAG
4. S	9. FRAG
5. S	10. S

Self-Test: Part 2 Identifying Run-ons and Sentences

1. RO
2. S
3. RO
4. S
5. S
6. RO
7. RO
8. S
9. RO
10. RO

Self-Test: Part 3 Identifying Fragments and Run-on Faults

1. RO
2. RO
3. S
4. FRAG
5. S
6. RO
7. FRAG
8. FRAG
9. S
10. RO

Self-Test: Part 4 Finding and Repairing Fragments and Run-ons

Please show your work to the instructor.

Self-Test: Part 5 Repairing Sentence Faults

Please show your work to the instructor.

Exercise 1 Fragments

1. FRAG
2. FRAG
3. S
4. FRAG
5. S
6. FRAG
7. FRAG
8. S
9. S
10. S
11. FRAG
12. S
13. S
14. FRAG
15. FRAG
16. S
17. S
18. FRAG
19. FRAG
20. S

Exercise 3 Run-on Sentences

1. The young couple was arguing about the rent money; however, they seemed to settle their differences.
2. Two of the bank managers were fired from their positions; the government inspectors had found serious errors in their accounting systems.—*or*—Two of the bank managers were fired from their positions because the government inspectors had found serious errors in their accounting systems.
3. Daisy loves to play baseball in the spring; her husband, Arnold, likewise loves the game.—*or*—Daisy loves to play baseball in the spring, and her husband, Arnold, likewise loves the game.
4. The teacher was avoiding discussion about AIDS, many students; on the other hand, were interested in talking about it.—*or*—The teacher was avoiding discussion about AIDS. Many students, on the other hand, were interested in talking about it.
5. I found the shoes very uncomfortable; however, I could not return them because the store had gone out of business.—*or*—I found the shoes very uncomfortable. However, I could not return them because the store had gone out of business.
6. On election night, the crowd gathered around the favoured candidate; they cheered her every word.—*or*—On election night, the crowd gathered around the favoured candidate. They cheered her every word.
7. CORRECT
8. CORRECT
9. After the severe rains, most of the plains were flooded; as a result, the farmers could not sow their crops until late spring.—*or*—After the severe rains, most of the plains were flooded. As a result, the farmers could not sow their crops until late spring.

10. CORRECT
11. The garden store in the new mall was a success; the bookstore located near it was not successful, however.—or—The garden store in the new mall was a success. The bookstore located near it was not successful, however.
12. The magician turned to us with a smile; then he disappeared.—or—The magician turned to us with a smile, and then he disappeared.—or—The magician turned to us with a smile. Then he disappeared.
13. Crystal loves to collect antique coins and jewellery; she travels all over Canada making her purchases.—or—Crystal loves to collect antique coins and jewellery. She travels all over Canada making her purchases.—or—Crystal loves to collect antique coins and jewellery, and she travels all over Canada making her purchases.

Exercise 4 Run-on Sentences

1. S
2. RO
3. RO
4. S
5. RO
6. S
7. S
8. RO
9. RO
10. RO
11. S
12. S
13. RO
14. S
15. S
16. RO
17. RO
18. S

Exercise 6 Pronoun Reference

1. Erica told Janice, "I am coming to lunch."
   Janice told Erica, "I am coming to lunch."
   Janice was coming to lunch, and she told Erica about it.
   Erica was coming to lunch, and she told Janice about it.
2. People could get a special pass to see the clipper ship; this possibility made them very enthusiastic.
3. Everyone must do their best.
   Everyone must do his or her best.
4. When Elvis recorded his first song in 1955, he quickly became popular.
5. Roger bought a new investment, and he told Hal all about it.
   Hal bought a new investment, and he told Roger all about it.
   Hal told Roger, "You should hear about my new investment."
   Roger told Hal, "You should hear about my new investment."
6. The boy was caught speeding and driving without a licence, and this behaviour shocked his parents.
7. Every boy can have his own racquet on the court.
8. Melissa sent Tina to pick up the team uniforms after Tina returned from the game.
   Melissa sent Tina to pick up the team uniforms after Melissa returned from the game.
9. Every woman was given her own set of documents for the meeting.
10. Some of the girls brought their own lunches.
11. Mrs. Norman asked Bernice (or another name) if she would sing at the reception.
12. No one really knew who the missing man was, but everyone had a theory about who he was.
    No one really knew who the missing man was, but everyone had a theory about what had happened to him.

Answer Key   401

Exercise 7 Group Activity: Shift Errors

1. Helen is pleased with the promotion; she intends to do well in her new position as manager.
2. The epidemic spread throughout the countryside, and the doctors attempted to inoculate all residents.
3. If you want to learn about fruit farming, you should talk to an orchardist.
   If one wants to learn about fruit farming, one should talk to an orchardist.
4. Lola had never tried parachute jumping before; she listened carefully to the instructor's directions.
5. Several children were playing hopscotch and skipping, but they did not hear the sound of the siren.
6. The stunt crew was setting up outside the Empress Hotel, and they had some expensive technical equipment.
7. If you don't know about it, you should ask.
   If one doesn't know about it, one should ask.
8. Because it was the long weekend, the trailer park was packed with vehicles.
9. Everyone should be careful about getting too much sun exposure if they do not want to increase the risk of skin cancer. *or* " . . . if he or she does not want to increase the risk . . . "
10. After we discussed the idea, we left.
    After we discuss the idea, we leave.

Exercise 9 Sentence Faults

1. All of the girls wanted to get their camping gear at the same sporting goods store.
2. Although he knew the shed really needed an undercoat, Bobby felt too lazy to do the job properly.
3. Some foods are rich in beta carotene.
   Some foods rich in beta carotene are said to be very healthful in our diets.
4. At the registration desk, Alan rented a locker and paid for it for one term at the college.
5. My friend Janet is very photogenic; however, she does not like having her picture taken.
   My friend Janet is very photogenic. However, she does not like having her picture taken.
6. We could safeguard against accidents in the home if we just paid attention to safety details.
   One could safeguard against accidents in the home if one just paid attention to safety details.
7. Sodium fluoride has been added to the water system of the city, despite the fact that many claim this chemical is poisonous.
8. Walter really wanted to build a solar house; he checked the building regulations with the regional planning office.
   Walter really wanted to build a solar house, so he checked the building regulations with the regional planning office.
   Walter really wanted to build a solar house. He checked the building regulations with he regional planning office.
9. The family bought a tandem bicycle; they particularly wanted to use it on vacation.
10. The weary visitors were so exhausted after their long flight from Taiwan that they fell asleep immediately.
11. Her testimony at the trial is necessary to the defence.
    Her testimony at the trial was necessary to the defence.
12. Walking, riding, and climbing were her exercise manias. *or* "To walk, to ride, and to climb . . . "

Exercise 10 Sentence Faults

1. It seems the whole world is fearful of terrorist attacks.
   It seems the whole world was fearful of terrorist attacks.
   It seems the whole world, fearful of terrorist attacks, is heightening security measures.

402 Answer Key

2. Everyone should decide what is best for their own children.
   Everyone should decide what is best for his or her own children.
3. Woody Allen started out as a popular stand-up comic; moreover, his fame earned him a job as a screenwriter.
   Woody Allen started out as a popular stand-up comic. Moreover, his fame earned him a job as a screenwriter.
4. Since that terry cloth robe was so expensive, it should look better after only three washings.
5. Because Lord Peakinloft managed his estate well, he was left with no debt.
   Because Lord Peakinloft managed his estate well, his heirs were left with no debt.
   Because Lord Peakinloft managed his estate well, his estate was left with no debt.
6. The Morgan brothers had a contract to do all the plumbing in the new housing development; then their company went bankrupt.
   The Morgan brothers had a contract to do all the plumbing in the new housing development, and then their company went bankrupt.
   The Morgan brothers had a contract to do all the plumbing in the new housing development. Then their company went bankrupt.
7. The selector on our stereo was broken, and the technician couldn't fix it.
8. With all the self-assurance of a king, Marmaduke entered the ballroom.
9. The soggy tomato sandwiches did not make an appetizing lunch when we went on the picnic.
10. The tea tastes bitter; perhaps it has been brewed too long.
11. The proprietor of the bed and breakfast wants to please all of her guests.
12. Some people enjoy sewing because they find sewing their own clothes saves money.
13. Although the condo is small, there is plenty of storage space in the basement.
14. You ought to check with the head server before you make a complaint.
    One ought to check with the head server before one makes a complaint.
15. He and his brother Manny bought a cottage near Bala, and they love going to it on weekends.

Exercise 11 Group Activity: Some Final Editing Practice

Paragraph 1: Punctuation and the Use of the Apostrophe in Possessives

> No one knew who was to inherit Mrs. Blethershotts' estate and her enormous fortune; it remained a great mystery to everyone. Because Ethyl maid had remained in Mrs. Blethershotts' service for so long, all of the staff expected her to receive some small compensation for her years of loyalty. The butler Archibald felt certain he was to win something as well; he had served the Blethershott Manor for over 40 years, and he had

not had one day's absence from his duties. It was the cook's opinion that she should receive the most. She had done three things in her opinion which counted the most: served fresh nutritious food to the Mistress, kept a tight budget, and made herself available to the Mistress' every whim. The chauffeur Kendrick did not agree that the other members of staff were worthy of receiving any more than a few dollars. Since he had arrived at Blethershott Manor, he had given the Blethershotts his devoted attention. Not once had he complained about their unreasonable demands. In fact, Kendrick had said very little; moreover, he now believed he was the most likely to inherit. Everyone's suspicion had begun to create peculiar tension in the household; no one seemed able to sleep the night before the reading of the will.

Paragraph 2: Fragments, Run-ons, Comma Splices

Taking children to their first day of daycare can be an unnerving experience for new parents. The tearful and loud protests of a child can make even the most calm parent feeling flustered and guilty. Weeks in advance, many parents try to explain to their children what wonderful places daycares are because the parents are trying to avoid the "big scene" on the daycare steps. Some children seem to listen carefully to understand what their parents are telling them. Some children seem to understand their parents' explanation fully; these children seem relaxed and happy about the new arrangement. Of course, once the new parents and their new daycare students arrive at the destination, it becomes another matter entirely. Teachers, students, parents, assistants, and children all seem to be talking at once. Frightened and anxious faces tell the tale because no one seems to want to leave and no one seems to want to stay! It is hard to imagine that in just a few short weeks, most children seem to love their new "schools" and welcome each day's activities.

Paragraph 3: Parallelism and Adjective and Adverb Use

According to *Monday Magazine,* Victoria is Canada's "city of poisons" because of the overuse of pesticides and herbicides by residential gardeners. Sellers are enthusiastic to sell these chemicals. The situation has naturalists and environmentalists really upset. *Monday Magazine,* April 24–30, 1997, states that "some of these compounds are tested for their cancer-causing potential, but most have been introduced without any assessment of their effects on the immune and nervous systems" (8). To ensure that gardening chemicals are being used well, to eliminate their overuse, and to control

> garden pests and diseases will take better management on the part of the industry and government. There are still few laws which are really effective and enforceable. For example, although many residential gardeners in Victoria feel bad about the harm that garden chemical agents create, these same citizens continue to use agents such as malathion, propoxur, captan, and 2,4-D. These chemicals act very slowly on the environment, and years later, dangerous traces can be found in the soil and the drinking water supply. Beneficial insects, songbirds, garter snakes, and amphibians are also surely harmed by the abuse and overuse of commonly available garden chemicals.

ESL Pointer Exercise 1 Verbals and Parallelism Faults

1. Smoking, reading, and cooking were Aunt Lulu's passions.
   To smoke, read, and cook were Aunt Lulu's passions.
   To smoke, to read, and to cook were Aunt Lulu's passions.
2. Trudging up the hill, pulling his little red wagon, and reddening in the face, the little boy continued his paper route.
3. Yuni wanted to sing, to dance, and to drink on her anniversary.
   Yuni wanted singing, dancing, and drinking on her anniversary.
   Yuni wanted to sing, dance, and drink on her anniversary.
4. Catching flies, sitting in the sun, and moving very little are how a frog spends its day.
   To catch flies, to sit in the sun, and to move very little are how a frog spends its day.
   To catch flies, sit in the sun, and move very little are how a frog spends its day.
5. Earning a salary as an engineer, paying off his student loans, and having a family of his own were the young student's dreams.
   To earn a salary as an engineer, (to) pay off his student loans, and (to) have a family of his own were the young student's dreams.
6. Staring out the window, brushing her hair, and tallking on the cell phone, Phillis noticed a raccoon in the garbage can in the neighbour's backyard.
7. The manager told the two workers that having long breaks, being late for work, and being glib with the customers were the reasons they were fired.
8. The ballet teacher taught her students to be enthusiastic, free, and energetic.
   The ballet teacher taught her students to be enthusiastic, to be free, and to be energetic.

index

A

academic writing. *See* writing tips; essay
adjectives. *See* modifiers
adverbs. *See* modifiers
agreement. *See* pronouns; verbs; sentence-level errors; check-out; ESL pointers
apostrophe. *See* punctuation
argument
   academic writing conventions 4, 65
   cause and effect 88
   essay 110, 116, 117, 127
   evidence 117
   paragraphs 44
   tips for constructing 117
assignments
   academic students 180
   evaluation 4
   expository writing 114
   presentation 58, 70

B

because 94
brainstorming 7–9
   paragraph writing 9

C

capitalization
   books 214
   buildings 215
   cultures, nationalities, languages 213
   days of the week, months of the year, holiday names 214
   geographical names 215
   I, the pronoun 213
   names and titles of people 212
   occupations; ranks 212
   organizations and institutions 215
   places in addresses 214
   products, registered trademarks 215
   relatives 213
   rivers, lakes, mountains 215
   seasons 214
   sentences 212
case. *See* pronouns
cause and effect 87–96
   See also methods of writing development
   complexity of the topic 90
   conclusions 88
   convincing clarity needed 23, 116
   describes relationship between ideas 23, 87, 96
   establish the relationship between ideas 87
   influences 87
   link cause to effect 23, 87, 88, 359
   oversimplification 88
   paragraphs 23, 90–91
   reading; background research 88
   readings 337
   transitions 90
   using details 23
   writing assignment; cause and effect 92–93
   writing techniques 87
   writing tips, 88–90
checkout
   academic writing 193, 221
   active voice 327
   adjectives; adverbs 252
   analyze writing 74
   brainstorming 17
   cause and effect 34, 96
   chart method; generate writing ideas 74
   classification and division 34
   classification of words 163
   clustering 17
   comma; clauses 221
   comparison; analogy 74
   comparison and contrast 34
   complete sentences 192
   compound sentences 284
   compound subjects; verbs 193
   conjunctive adverbs 221, 299
   definition 34
   drafting process 62

407

English handbook 221
essay writing 127
evaluation; conventions of presentation 85
explanation 17
freewriting 17
getting started writing 127
grammar 163
interesting sentences 252
key words 61
memorization 192
method; perspective; purpose 85
modals 193
outlining 17
paragraph composition 17, 34
prepositional phrases 252
prewriting 17
proof 17
punctuation 221
relative clauses 284
rhetorical methods of development 34
sentence-level errors 327
sentence patterns 284
subject-verb agreement
starting writing 108
subject of sentence 163
table; organize writing ideas, 85
thesis statement 127
thinking notes; mapping ideas 108
time-order or process 34
title page 62
topic sentence 17
transitional words as clues 74
verb phrases 193
words of description 252
wrap-up sentence 17
your reader 127
chronological. *See* time-order
classification and division 21, 75
   See also methods of writing development
   classification 21
   cluster or categorize ideas using classification 21, 75, 345
   division 22
   organization of information 78
   paragraphs 22, 28, 46, 78–79
   readings 341
   scientific writing 22
   topics, classification paragraph 80
   topics, division paragraph 81
   transitions 76, 84–85
   use of 22
   writing, classification paragraph 80
clauses
   adding conditions 263
   comma usage 108, 203, 221, 271, 275
   complex sentences 106, 205, 262, 269, 271
   compound sentences 94, 269
   compound-complex sentences 278
   conjunctions 257
   conjunctive adverbs 299
   dependent clause 94, 106, 108, 221, 262, 269, 275
   independent clause 94, 106, 205
   introductory phrases; clauses 200
   main clause 205
   non-restrictive 203, 271
   parenthetical expression 203
   position in sentence 94
   relative 270, 271, 278, 405
   restrictive clause 204, 271
   semicolon 94, 206, 293
   sentence fragment 262
   simple sentences 256, 269
   subject-verb sets 253, 256, 257
   subordinate clause 106
   subordinating conjunction 94
clustering 10
   block form 21
   classification, analysis 21, 75
   framework 21
   organizing knowledge 75
   paragraph outline 10
   writing technique, mapping ideas 10
comma splices 285, 298
comparison and contrast 34, 63
   See also methods of writing development
   analogy, special comparisons 65, 74
   chart the distinguishing features 64
   comparison, development 65
   establish measurements 65
   comparison and contrast, together 19
   contrast differences; compare similarities 20, 63
   paragraph development 25, 68
   readings 335
   transitions 66
   writing assignment, comparison paragraph 70
   writing assignment, contrast paragraph 70
conclusion. *See* paragraph; essay
conjunctions
   See also clauses

    coordinating 94, 257, 262, 284
    subordinate 94, 264, 265, 283
conjunctive adverbs 206, 298, 299
contrast. *See* comparison and contrast

D

definite article 30
definition 21, 97
    See also methods of writing development
    complex method 24
    explain, distinguish, examine 24
    division and definition 97
    formal definition 97
    paragraphs 101
    readings 339
    stipulative definition 97
    thinking notes 99, 100, 108
    topics, definition 105
    writing assignment, paragraph 104
    writing, generating ideas 98
definitions
    extended 97
    forming 97
    stipulative 97
details; organization 35–50
    See also topic sentence
    block form 63
    cause and effect 23
    chronological order 20
    classification and division 22
    clustering 12
    comparison and contrast 20
    paragraphs; support 35
    point form 63
    prepositional phrases 173, 223, 236
    rhetorical modes 35
    subject-verb agreement 177
development. *See* methods of writing development

E

editing
    editing exercises 317
    essay essentials 110
    expectations 109
    paragraphs 4
    punctuation 195
    sentence-level errors 285
    writing techniques 118

ESL pointers
    adjectives and prepositions 250
    articles, use of 30
    because 94
    cause and effect 95
    clauses 108
    comma, in sentences 95
    conditional sentences, conjunction *if* 283
    conditions, identification 283
    count and non-count nouns 15
    direct and indirect speech 221
    indefinite pronouns 189
    modifiers 251
    nouns; quantity words 49
    parallelism; verbals 325, 326
    parallelism faults 326
    plurals. *See* plurals
    prepositions, place and time 249
    quantity, expressions of 47
    quotation marks 219
    sentence patterns 284
    since 94
    so 94
    subordinate conjunctions 106, 265
    therefore 94
    transitions, time-order 60
    verb agreement 189, 191
    verb tense 161
    voice, passive and active 124
essay
    See also writing tips; freewriting
    academic essay 109
    argument, tips for constructing 117
    brainstorm for ideas 113–114
    cause and effect transitions 90
    classification and division transitions 76
    comparison transitions 66
    concluding paragraph 120
    controlling idea 113
    conventions of essay writing 3, 4, 85, 109, 116
    editing 109, 118, 168, 195, 285, 317
    essentials of the essay 110
    evidence, how to choose it 110, 116, 117, 118
    expository essay 114
    how to write an essay 110
    introduction 116
    ideas, organizing them
    opportunities of essay writing 110
    overgeneralization 114
    overview of the parts 111–112

organization 110, 116, 127
point of view 109
points; proof; support 110, 116, 117, 120, 127
presentation 4, 51, 85, 110, 116
proofreading 56, 57, 59, 109
standards 4, 57, 285
summary statement 120
thesis statement 109, 111, 114, 115, 116
time-order transitions 52
topic 7, 109, 111, 112–113, 114, 116
transitional devices 118
transitional sentences 111
transitional words and phrases 53
vocabulary, essay writing terms 112
writing, getting started 9, 39, 65, 89, 108, 113, 127
writing the body of an essay 41, 109, 111, 116
writing the conclusion 111, 120
writing the introduction 109, 111, 116
evidence 116, 117
  See also paragraph; essay
expository writing 114

F

freewriting 9–10

G

grammar 131–327

I

if 283
indefinite article 30
interrupters. *See* parenthetical expressions

M

main idea. *See* topic sentence
marking scheme sheet 56
methods of writing development
  cause and effect 23, 87–94
  classification and division 21, 75–85
  comparison and contrast 20, 63–74
  definition 24, 97–108
  time-order and process 20, 51–62
modifiers 223–252
  adjectives 226
    comma use 199
    comparison 229, 230, 311
    creating interesting sentences 226
    bad; badly 242
    describers 227
    forms 229
    good; well 242
    infinitives 325
    intensifiers 244
    misplaced modifiers 241
    mixed forms 230
    more; most 230
    parallelism 310, 311
    participial phrase 325
    participle 125, 152, 154, 325
    placement, usage 241
    prepositional phrases 225, 236
    prepositions, arrangements 250
    real; really 242
    that compare; regular, irregular 229–230
    verbals 325
  adverbs 231
    bad; badly 242
    conjunctive adverbs 94, 206, 285, 298, 299
    describers 231
    good; well 242
    infinitives 325
    intensifiers 244
    -ly ending 232
    real; really 242
    telling when, how, why, where 233
    placement, usage 241
    prepositional phrases 173, 223, 236
    when 233
  prepositional phrases; prepositions
    adjectives, arrangements 250
    common prepositions 174
    describers 236
    detail phrases 173, 236
    introductory words of direction 173, 236
    list of prepositions 236
    nouns, pronouns 236
    object of preposition 131, 139, 141, 173, 236
    phrases; adjective, adverb 236, 238
    place and time 249
    placement; sentences 173, 175, 182, 236
    prepositional phrases 173, 175, 236–241
    subject-verb sets 236
    telling how, where, when, what 173, 236
    verb phrases 173
    words of direction 236

Index 411

N

nouns
  a; an 31
  antecedent of pronoun 304
  concrete and abstract nouns
  compound
  count and non-count 15, 304
  definition of a noun 135
  detail phrases
  function in sentences 137
  gerund 325
  infinitive acting as noun 325
  modifiers and nouns 223, 236
  plurals. *See* plurals
  prepositional phrases 173
  pronouns, substitution for nouns 141
  restrictive and non-restrictive clauses 271
  subjects and objects 137, 138, 141
  this 304

O

organization
  academic writing conventions 4
  cause and effect 88, 96
  classification 75
  clear ideas 4, 116
  detail organization 35
  dominant pattern 46
  editing assignments
  essay 110, 116, 127
  library and internet 78
  method of writing 85
  paragraphs 55
  time-order or process 51
outlines 7, 10, 12, 17, 99

P

paragraphs 1–127
  See also essay
  block form 68
  body of the paragraph 41
  brainstorming 9
  cause and effect 87–96
  classification and division 21, 75
  clustering 10, 21
  comparison and contrast 20, 63
  compositions 131, 132
  conclusion of the paragraph 44
  definition 24, 97
  detail organization 35–50
  details 23
  drafting process 55
  editing exercises 317
  effective topic sentences 37
  explanation; proof, points 17
  five rhetorical modes 19
  freewriting 9, 17
  identifying rhetorical modes 28
  in essays 4, 131
  key words or phrases 54
  location of topic sentence 35
  marking scheme, paragraphs 56
  methods of writing development 19
  organization of 4, 19, 35, 46, 55, 85, 88
  outlines 10, 17
  paragraph compositions, examples 5
  paragraph, definition of 4, 17
  paragraph development 34
  paragraph organization, how to set it up 55
  parts of a paragraph composition 17
  patterns in topic sentences 39
  point by point 68
  points in the paragraph body 41
  proof, evidence, support for the point 41
  proofreading marks 57
  reading for modes 25
  time-order or process 20, 51
  title page 59
  topic sentence 35, 54
  transitions 52, 60, 76
  wrap-up sentence 17, 44, 53
parallelism. *See* sentences; sentence-level errors;
    ESL pointers; modifiers
parenthetical expressions 203
participles. *See* modifiers
patterns. *See* methods of writing development
person. *See* sentence lever errors
phrases
  topic sentence 54, 61
  transitions 52, 118
plurals 47, 210, 304
possessives 210
practice writing to improve your skills 55, 285
prepositional phrases. *See* modifiers
presentation
  See also writing tips

academic writing conventions 4
   computer paper 59
   font 59
   marking scheme sheet 56
   proofreading 55, 57, 59, 109, 195, 285
   title page 51, 59
   writing assignments 85, 110, 116
pronouns
   agreement, number and gender 304
   antecedent, pronoun reference fault 303, 304
   capitalization 220
   case 180
   form, changes of 141
   function in sentences 141
   gender and number 304
   indefinite pronouns 189, 304
   one; *each* 180
   prepositional phrases 173, 236
   pronoun case; subject-verb agreement 180
   pronoun use; noun use 141
   reference fault 303, 304
   relative clauses 270
   relative pronoun, restrictive clause 271
   sentence fault, reference errors 285, 303
   sexism 304
   subject form, object form 141, 163, 168
   subject-verb agreement 180, 189
   substitutes for nouns 141
   take the place of nouns 141, 180
   that 271
   this 304
   vague or ambiguous reference 303, 304
proofreading marks 57
punctuation
   apostrophe; possession, contraction 210
   colon 197, 295
      use and misuse 208
   comma
      category 1 198
      category 2 203
      commas in complex sentences 205
      compound sentence 94
      coordinating conjunction 94
      conjunctive adverbs 206, 221
      definition of 198
      dependent clause 221
      parenthetical expressions 203
      punctuating sentences 95
      quotations 220
      semicolon with comma 199
   subordinate clause 94, 108
   transitions 76
semicolon 206, 293, 295
   compound sentences 259, 293
   conjunctive adverbs 94, 206, 298
   independent clauses 94, 206, 293
quotation marks 219
   open, closed 220

Q

quotation marks. *See* punctuation

R

readings
   business and marketing
      The Trouble With: "How's it going ladies?" Richard Rotman 363
      Reinventing Our Food for Fun and Profit, Pam Freir 365
      CD Pirates Drive Down the Music Volume, Edward Helmore 368
      Cirque du Soleil, Jason Kirby 367
   cause and effect paragraph readings 337–339
   classification and division paragraph readings 341–345
   comparison and contrast paragraph readings 335–337
   culture and communications
      Intellectual Property, Denise Rideout 376
      Rink Rage, The Economist 375
      Phone Calls Are Futile, Charles Whaley 371
      The Simplification of Culture, Neil Bissoondath 372
   definition paragraph readings 339–341
   environment and the outdoors
      Betrayal of Trust, Sharon Butala 354
      Sonar Surveillance Despite Whale Injuries, Peter Carter 359
      Whose Trail Is It Anyway?, Tom Cruickshank 361
      The Worst Kind of Ice-Breaker, Judy Plaxton 356
   family and relationships
      Bad Boys, Mordecai Richler 347
      A Personal Journey Through Genetics, David Suzuki 350
   finding points in body paragraphs 41–42
   five modes of paragraph development 20–25

identifying rhetorical modes in
    paragraphs 28–30
locating the topic sentence 36
time-order or process paragraph
    readings 331–334
reading for modes 25–27
reading like a writer 3, 19, 35, 68
what is a paragraph 4
review tests
    Chapter 10, nouns, pronouns, and verbs 156
    Chapter 11, subjects and verbs 187
    Chapter 12, punctuation and capitalization 217
    Chapter 13, modifiers 246
    Chapter 14, patterns of sentences 279
    Chapter 15, sentence-level errors 319
revising 4, 109, 285
rhetorical modes. *See* methods of writing
    development
run-on sentence. *See* sentence faults

S

self-tests
    Chapter 10, nouns, pronouns, and verbs 131
    Chapter 11, subjects and verbs 165
    Chapter 12, capitalization and punctuation 195
    Chapter 13, modifiers 223
    Chapter 14, sentence patterns 254
    Chapter 15, sentence-level errors 286
sentences
    See also topic sentence; clauses
    analyze whole sentences 168–169
    capitalization 212
    cause and effect 94
    colon 208
    comma use 94, 95, 198, 205, 298
    complex sentences 94, 106, 108, 205, 262
    compound sentences 94, 178, 257, 258
    compound subject and object 140, 204
    compound-complex sentences 278
    concluding sentence 12, 45
    conditional sentences 283
    conjunctive adverb 206, 298
    coordinating conjunctions 257
    definite and indefinite articles 30
    fragments. *See* sentence-level errors
    grammar and sentences 131, 134, 165
    modifiers add detail and colour 223
    objects 138, 140, 163
    parallelism 310–312, 325

parts of speech 135
patterns of sentences 253–284
person and point of view 307
prepositional phrases in sentences 173–176, 236
pronoun references 303–304
questions 182
quotations 220
run-on sentences 295
semi-colon 206, 293
sentence fragments 268
sentence-level errors 285–327
sentence of description 137, 145
shifts in sentences 306
simple sentences 256
study the whole sentence 137
subjects 137, 138, 140, 144, 169, 182
subject-verb agreement 180–184
subject-verb sets 205, 236, 253, 256, 262
subordinate conjunctions 265
thesis statement. *See* essay
transitional sentences 111, 118
understood subjects 179
wrap-up sentence 4, 12, 45
sentence fragments. *See* sentence-level errors
sentence-level errors
    comma splice 298
    fragment 291–292
    parallelism problems 310–312
    person and point of view 307
    pronoun agreement 304
    pronoun reference problems 303–304
    run-on sentences 295
    shifts in sentences 306
sexist language, avoiding 304
since 94
so 94
subordinating conjunctions 106, 265

T

tense
    future perfect 150
    future perfect progressive 151
    future progressive 150
    past perfect 150–151
    past perfect progressive 151
    past progressive 150
    present 149
    present perfect 150, 151
    present perfect progressive 151

present progressive 150
simple future 149
simple past 149
to be 169
to have 169
that 271
therefore 94
thesis statements. *See* essay
time-order and process
   See also methods of writing development
   chronological order 20, 51
   describing a sequence 20, 51
   essay, writing assignment 123
   method of development 20, 51–62
   order of events 20
   paragraph writing composition 57
   readings, paragraphs 331–334
   sequence of events 51, 53
   steps and stages 20
   time-order transitions 52
   writing a story from your life 51
   writing about how to do something 20, 51
title page
   essentials of an essay 110
   example of a title page 59
topics
   See also writing assignments
   cause and effect 93
   classification, division 80, 81
   comparison, contrast 70, 71
   definition 105
   time-order 58
topic sentence
   developing an effective topic sentence 37
   locating the topic sentence 35–36
   paragraph composition 4
   placement of the topic sentence 35
   reveals mode of development 54
   shaping topic sentences 37–39

V

verbs
   action verbs 144, 146, 148, 173, 176, 192
   auxiliary verbs 146–149, 154, 182, 192
   compound verbs 173, 180
   has, *have*, and *had* 154
   helping verbs 147, 192
   irregular verb forms 152
   linking verbs 145
   modals 193
   non-action 144, 145, 147
   subject-verb agreement 166, 177, 180
   verb phrases 171, 193
   regular verb forms 152
voice 124, 327

W

writing assignments
   #1 time-order paragraph 57
   #2 contrast paragraph 70
   #3 comparison paragraph 70
   #4 classification paragraph 80
   #5 division paragraph 81
   #6 cause and effect paragraph 92
   #7 definition paragraph 104
   #8 time-order or process essay 123
writing tips
   academic writing 3
   building self-confidence 131
   drafting process 55
   English handbooks 195, 221
   formal and informal 180
   marking scheme sheet 56
   presentation of assignments 85
   proofreading 55, 56
   proofreading marks 57
   read other writers' works 35
   rules and conventions 3
   title page 59
   writing conference 55
   write for your reader 34, 44, 52

MARQUEE SERIES

Microsoft®

PowerPoint®
365
2019 Edition

Nita Rutkosky

Audrey Roggenkamp
Pierce College Puyallup
Puyallup, Washington

Ian Rutkosky
Pierce College Puyallup
Puyallup, Washington

PARADIGM
EDUCATION SOLUTIONS

St. Paul

Vice President, Content and Digital Solutions: Christine Hurney
Director of Content Developmen: Carley Fruzzetti
Testers: Desiree Carvel; Ann E. Mills, Ivy Tech Community College of Indiana, Evansville, IN
Director of Production: Timothy W. Larson
Production Editor/Project Manager: Jen Weaverling
Cover and Text Design: Valerie King
Senior Design and Production Specialist: Julie Johnston
Copy Editor: Deborah Brandt
Indexer: Terry Casey
Vice President, Director of Digital Products: Chuck Bratton
Digital Projects Manager: Tom Modl
Digital Solutions Manager: Gerry Yumul
Senior Director of Digital Products and Onboarding: Christopher Johnson
Supervisor of Digital Products and Onboarding: Ryan Isdahl
Vice President, Marketing: Lara Weber McLellan
Marketing and Communications Manager: Selena Hicks

Care has been taken to verify the accuracy of information presented in this book. However, the authors, editors, and publisher cannot accept responsibility for web, email, newsgroup, or chat room subject matter or content, or for consequences from the application of the information in this book, and make no warranty, expressed or implied, with respect to its content.

Trademarks: Microsoft is a trademark or registered trademark of Microsoft Corporation in the United States and/or other countries. Some of the product names and company names included in this book have been used for identification purposes only and may be trademarks or registered trade names of their respective manufacturers and sellers. The authors, editors, and publisher disclaim any affiliation, association, or connection with, or sponsorship or endorsement by, such owners.

Paradigm Education Solutions, is independent from Microsoft Corporation and not affiliated with Microsoft in any manner.

Cover Photo Credit: © whitehoune/Shutterstock.com; © manzrussali/Shutterstock.com.

We have made every effort to trace the ownership of all copyrighted material and to secure permission from copyright holders. In the event of any question arising as to the use of any material, we will be pleased to make the necessary corrections in future printings.

ISBN 978-0-76388-694-3 (print)
ISBN 978-0-76388-688-2 (digital)

© 2020 by Paradigm Publishing, LLC
875 Montreal Way
St. Paul, MN 55102
Email: CustomerService@ParadigmEducation.com
Website: ParadigmEducation.com

All rights reserved. No part of this publication may be adapted, reproduced, stored in a retrieval system, or transmitted in any form or by any means, electronic, mechanical, photocopying, recording, or otherwise, without prior written permission from the publisher.

Printed in the United States of America

28 27 26 25 24 23 22 21 20 19   1 2 3 4 5 6 7 8 9 10 11 12

Contents

Introducing PowerPoint iv
Getting Started GS-1

Section 1 Preparing a Presentation 1
1.1 Opening, Saving, and Closing a Presentation; Running a Slide Show 2
1.2 Applying a Design Theme; Inserting Slides; and Inserting Text 6
1.3 Opening and Navigating in a Presentation; Choosing a Slide Layout 10
1.4 Changing Views 12
1.5 Changing the Slide Layout; Selecting and Moving a Placeholder 14
1.6 Rearranging, Deleting, and Hiding Slides 16
1.7 Using the Tell Me and Help Features 18
1.8 Checking Spelling; Using the Thesaurus 20
1.9 Navigating in a Slide Show; Using Ink Tools;
    Using Options on the Slide Show Toolbar 22
1.10 Adding Slide Transitions and Transition Sounds 26
1.11 Previewing Slides and Printing 28
     Features Summary 30

Section 2 Editing and Enhancing Slides 31
2.1 Increasing and Decreasing Indent; Cutting, Copying, and Pasting Text 32
2.2 Applying Font Formatting and Font Effects 34
2.3 Applying Font Formatting at the Font Dialog Box; Replacing Fonts 36
2.4 Formatting with Format Painter 38
2.5 Changing Alignment and Line and Paragraph Spacing 40
2.6 Changing Slide Size and Design Themes; Formatting Slide Background 42
2.7 Inserting, Sizing, Positioning, and Formatting an Image 44
2.8 Inserting and Formatting a Screen Clipping 48
2.9 Inserting and Formatting SmartArt 50
2.10 Applying Animation to Objects and Text 54
     Features Summary 56

Section 3 Customizing a Presentation 57
3.1 Using the Clipboard Task Pane 58
3.2 Finding and Replacing Text 60
3.3 Inserting and Formatting WordArt 62
3.4 Drawing and Customizing Shapes 64
3.5 Displaying Gridlines; Inserting a Text Box; Copying and Rotating Shapes 66
3.6 Creating and Formatting a Table 68
3.7 Inserting Action Buttons and Hyperlinks 70
3.8 Formatting with a Slide Master 72
3.9 Inserting Headers and Footers 74
3.10 Adding Audio and Video 76
3.11 Setting and Rehearsing Timings for a Slide Show 78
     Features Summary 80

Integrating Programs Word, Excel, and PowerPoint 81
3.1 Exporting a PowerPoint Presentation to Word 82
3.2 Exporting a Word Outline to a PowerPoint
    Presentation 84
3.3 Linking an Excel Chart with a Word Document and a PowerPoint Presentation 86
3.4 Editing a Linked Object 88
3.5 Embedding and Editing a Word Table in a PowerPoint Slide 90

Index 93

Introducing

PowerPoint® 365

Create colorful and powerful presentations using PowerPoint, Microsoft's presentation program that is included in the Office suite. Use PowerPoint to organize and present information and create visual aids for a presentation. PowerPoint is a full-featured presentation program that provides a wide variety of editing and formatting features as well as sophisticated visual elements such as images, SmartArt, WordArt, and drawn objects. While working in PowerPoint, you will produce presentations for the following six companies.

First Choice Travel is a travel center offering a full range of traveling services from booking flights, hotel reservations, and rental cars to offering travel seminars.

The Waterfront Bistro offers fine dining for lunch and dinner and also offers banquet facilities, a wine cellar, and catering services.

Worldwide Enterprises is a national and international distributor of products for a variety of companies and is the exclusive movie distribution agent for Marquee Productions.

Marquee Productions is involved in all aspects of creating movies from script writing and development to filming. The company produces documentaries, biographies, as well as historical and action movies.

Performance Threads maintains an inventory of rental costumes and also researches, designs, and sews special-order and custom-made costumes.

The mission of the **Niagara Peninsula College** Theatre Arts Division is to offer a curriculum designed to provide students with a thorough exposure to all aspects of the theatre arts.

In Section 1 you will learn how to

Prepare a Presentation

Prepare a presentation using a template provided by PowerPoint or create a presentation and apply formatting with a design theme. Preparing a presentation consists of general steps such as creating and editing slides; adding enhancements to slides; and saving, previewing, printing, and closing a presentation and running a slide show. When running a slide show, the way in which one slide is removed from the screen and the next slide is displayed is referred to as a *transition*. Interesting transitions and transition sounds can be added to slides in a presentation.

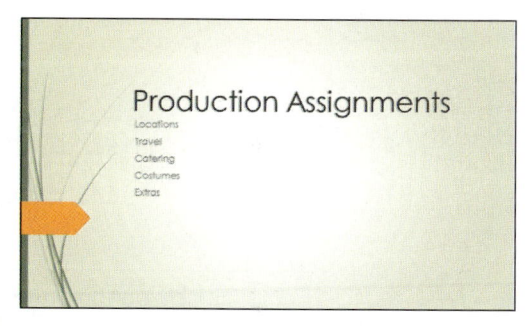

Create presentations using PowerPoint design themes and apply various slide layouts to change the appearance of slides.

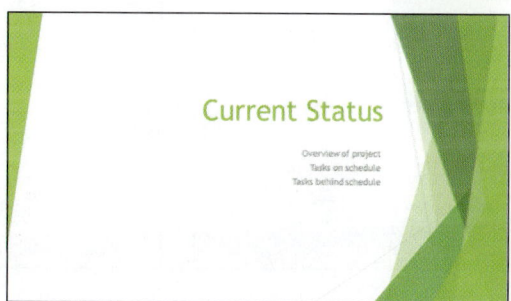

Introducing POWERPOINT

In Section 2 you will learn how to

Edit and Enhance Slides

Edit slides and slide elements in a presentation to customize and personalize the presentation. Editing can include such functions as rearranging and deleting slides; cutting, copying, and pasting text; changing the font, paragraph alignment, and paragraph spacing; and changing the design theme, theme color, and theme font. Add visual interest to a presentation by inserting images, pictures, and SmartArt organizational charts and graphics.

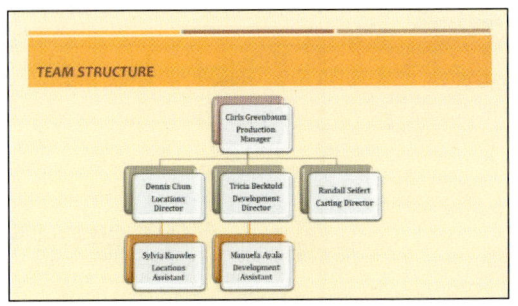

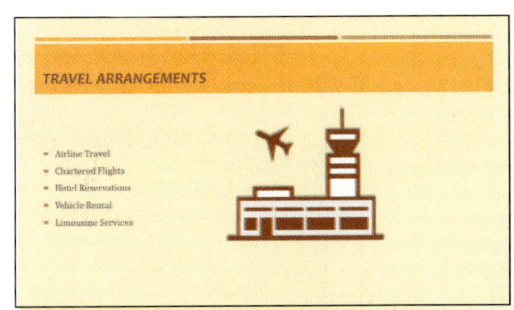

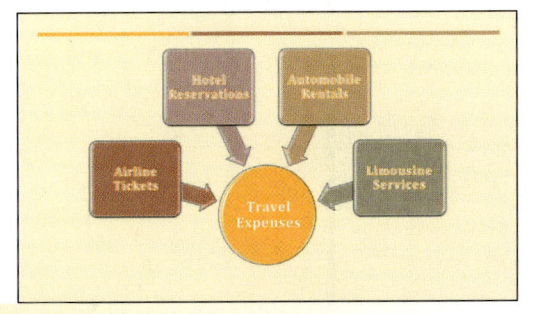

Edit slides by performing such actions as rearranging and deleting slides and changing slide size. Perform editing tasks on text in slides such as changing the font, paragraph alignment, and spacing. Enhance the visual interest of a presentation by inserting such elements as a company logo, image, an organizational chart, and a graphic.

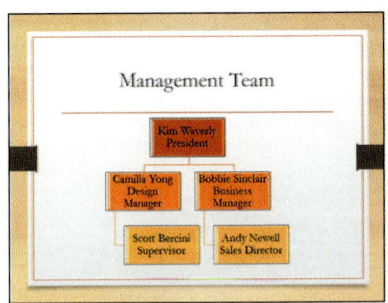

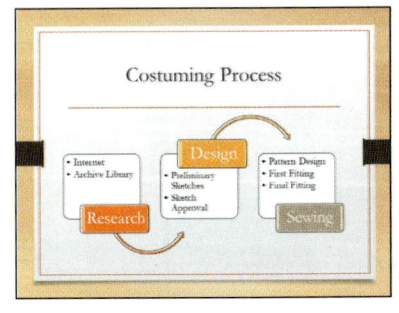

Introducing POWERPOINT

In Section 3 you will learn how to

Customize Presentations

Customize a presentation with the WordArt feature and by drawing and formatting objects and text boxes. Additional features for customizing a presentation include using the Clipboard; inserting and formatting a table; inserting actions buttons, hyperlinks, and headers and footers; and inserting audio and video files.

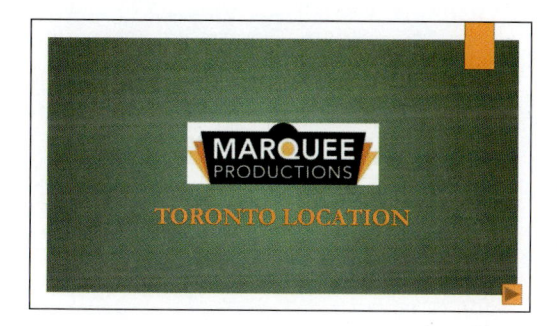

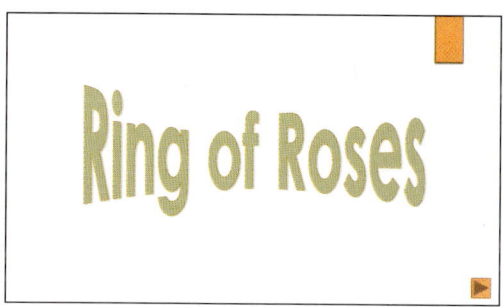

Further customize presentations with features such as headers and footers, audio and video files, WordArt, shapes, text boxes, and tables.

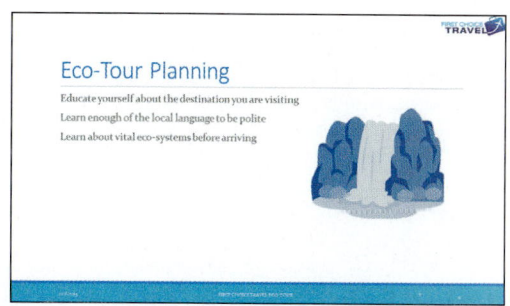

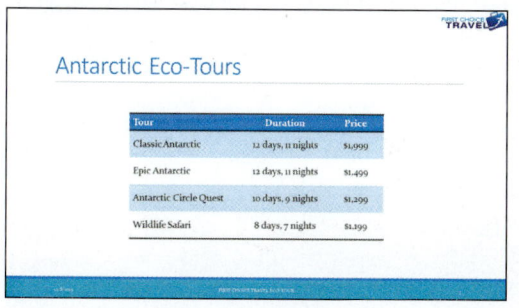

Introducing POWERPOINT

Getting Started

Adjusting Monitor Settings, Copying Data Files, and Changing View Options

Skills

- Set monitor resolution
- Modify DPI settings
- Retrieve and copy data files
- Change view options

This textbook and the accompanying eContent were written using a typical personal computer (tower/box, monitor, keyboard and mouse) or laptop. Although you may be able to perform some of the activities in this textbook on a different operating system or tablet, not all the steps will work as written and may jeopardize any work you may be required to turn in to your instructor. No matter what computer you use, you can access the content using the virtual Office experience in Cirrus. If you are unable to access Cirrus or a compatible computer, explore what options you have at your institution such as where and when you can use a computer lab.

One of the evolutions of the Microsoft Office product is that it is offered in a subscription-based plan called Microsoft Office 365. An advantage of having an active Microsoft Office 365 subscription is that the subscription includes and incorporates new features or versions as they are released. This method of providing the Microsoft Office product may impact section activities and assessments. For example, new features and adjustments made to Office 365 may alter how some of the steps discussed in the Marquee Series are completed. The Marquee eContent and online course will contain the most up-to-date material and will be updated as new features become available.

In Activity 1 you will customize your monitor settings so that what you see on the screen should match the images in this textbook. In Activity 2 you will obtain the data files you will be using throughout this textbook from your Cirrus online course. Activity 3 includes instructions on how to change the view settings so that your view of files in a File Explorer window matches the images in this textbook.

Activity 1 Adjusting Monitor Settings

Before beginning activities in this textbook, you may want to customize your monitor's settings. Activities in the sections in this textbook assume that the monitor display is set at 1920 x 1080 pixels and the DPI is set at 125%. Adjusting a monitor's display settings is important because the ribbon in the Microsoft Office applications adjusts to the screen resolution setting of your computer monitor. A monitor set at a high resolution will have the ability to show more buttons in the ribbon than a monitor set to a low resolution. Figure GS1 at the bottom of the page shows, the Word ribbon: at the screen resolution featured throughout this textbook and in the virtual office experience (1920 × 1080).

What You Will Do   Adjust the monitor settings for your machine to match the settings used to create the images in the textbook. If using a lab computer, check with your instructor before attempting this activity.

1 Right-click a blank area of the desktop and then click the *Display settings* option at the shortcut menu.

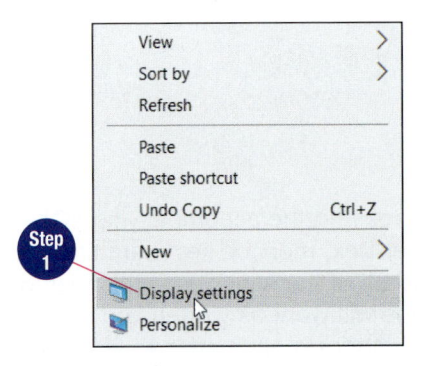

2 At the Settings window with the *Display* option selected, scroll down and look at the current setting displayed in the *Resolution* option box. If your screen is already set to 1920 × 1080, skip ahead to Step 5.

> Screen resolution is set in pixels. *Pixel* is the abbreviation of *picture element* and refers to a single dot or point on the display monitor. Changing the screen resolution to a higher number of pixels means that more information can be seen on the screen as items are scaled to a smaller size.

Figure GS1 Word Ribbon Set at 1920 x 1080 Screen Resolution

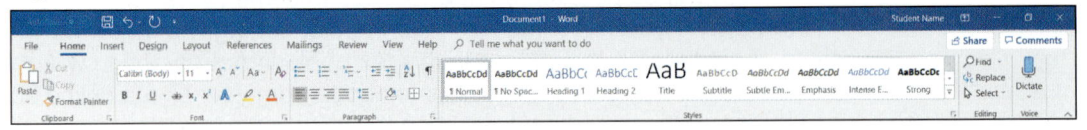

GS-2 GETTING STARTED

3. Click the *Resolution* option box and then click the *1920 × 1080* option. **Note: Depending on the privileges you are given on a school machine, you may not be able to complete Steps 3–7. If necessary, check with your instructor for alternative instructions.**

> If the machine you are using has more than one monitor, make sure the proper monitor is selected. (The active monitor displays as a blue rectangle in the Display pane of the Settings app.)

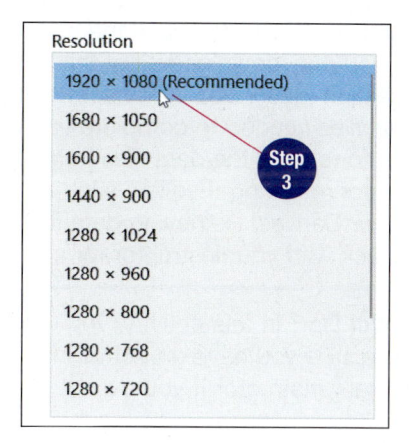

Resolution
1920 × 1080 (Recommended)   ← Step 3
1680 × 1050
1600 × 900
1440 × 900
1280 × 1024
1280 × 960
1280 × 800
1280 × 768
1280 × 720

4. Click the Keep changes button at the message box asking if you want to keep the display settings.

> Some monitor settings will render the computer unusable because objects on the desktop or in a window will become inaccessible and hidden. In this case, Windows will automatically revert the settings to the previous configuration after 30 seconds.

5. At the Settings window with the *Display* option active, look at the percentage in which the size of text, apps, and other items currently display (also known as the DPI setting). For example, items on your screen may display at 100%. If the percentage is 125%, skip to Step 12.

> The computers used to create the images in this textbook uses the 125% DPI setting, which slightly increases the size of text, applications, buttons, and options.

6. Click the option box below the text *Change the size of text, apps, and other items*, and then click the *125%* option in the drop-down list.

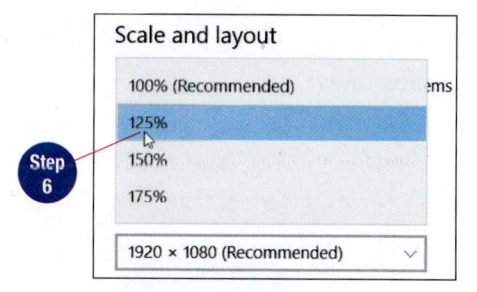

Scale and layout
100% (Recommended)
125%   ← Step 6
150%
175%

1920 × 1080 (Recommended)

7. The message *Some apps won't respond to scaling changes until you sign out.* appears in the *Scale and Layout* section of the dialog box. You may need to sign out of Windows and restart your computer for the scaling options to apply.

Activity 2   Retrieving and Copying Data Files

While working through the activities in this book, you will often be using data files as starting points. These files need to be obtained from your Cirrus online course or other locations such as your school's network drive. All the files required to complete the coursework are provided through Cirrus. You have the ability to access all of the data files from the Course Resources. You may download all of the files at once or only download the files you need for a specific section (described in the activity below). Cirrus online course activities also provide the individual files needed to complete each activity. Make sure you have internet access before trying to retrieve the data files from Cirrus. Ask your instructor if alternate locations are available for retrieving the files, such as a network drive or online resource such as D2L, BlackBoard, or Canvas. Retrieving data files from an alternate location will require different steps, so check with your instructor for additional steps or tasks to complete.

What You Will Do   In this activity, you will download data files from your Cirrus online course. Make sure you have an active internet connection before starting this activity. Check with your instructor if you do not have access to your Cirrus online course.

1. Insert your USB flash drive into an available USB port.

2. Navigate to the Course Resources section of your Cirrus online course. *Note: The steps in this activity assume you are using the Chrome browser. If you are using a different browser, the following steps may vary.*

3. Click the Student Data Files link in the Course Resources section.

    A zip file containing the student data files will automatically begin downloading from the Cirrus website.

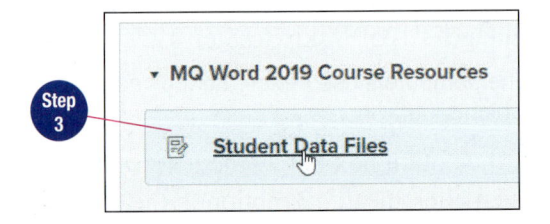

4. Click the button in the lower left corner of the screen once the files have finished downloading.

    Clicking the button in the lower left corner of the screen will open File Explorer and the StudentDataFiles folder displays in the Content pane.

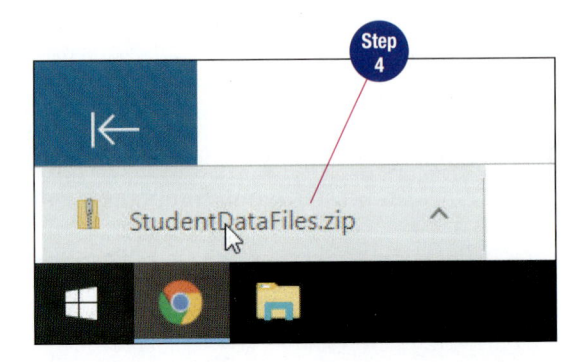

5 Right-click the *StudentDataFiles* folder in the Content pane.

6 Click the *Copy* option at the shortcut menu.

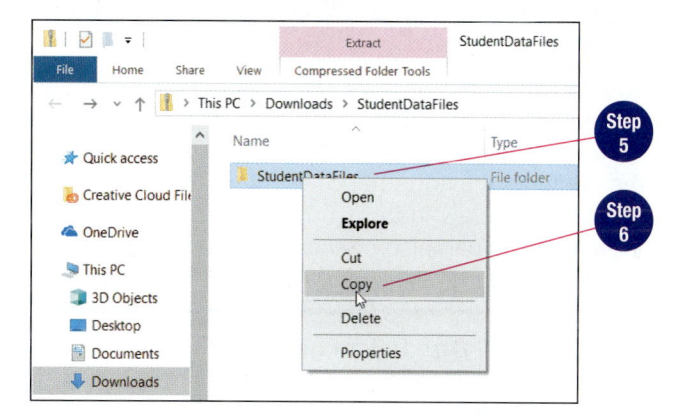

7 Click your USB flash drive that displays in the Navigation pane at the left of the File Explorer window.

8 Click the Home tab and then click the Paste button in the Clipboard group.

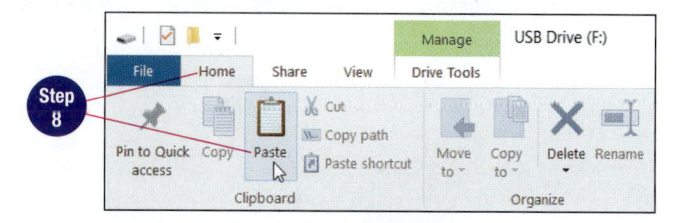

9 Close the File Explorer window by clicking the Close button in the upper right corner of the window.

Activity 2 **GETTING STARTED** GS-5

Activity 3 Changing View Options

You can change the view of the File Explorer window to show the contents of your current location (drive or folder) in various formats, including icons, tiles, or a list, among others. With the Content pane in Details view, you can click the column headings to change how the contents are sorted and whether they are sorted in ascending or descending order. You can customize a window's environment by using buttons and options on the File Explorer View tab. You can also change how panes are displayed, how content is arranged in the Content pane, how content is sorted, and which features are hidden.

What You Will Do Before getting started with the textbook material, you need to adjust the view settings so that items in the File Explorer window appear the same as the images in the textbook.

1. Click the File Explorer button on the taskbar.

    By default, a File Explorer window opens at the Quick access location, which contains frequently-used folders such as Desktop, Documents, Downloads, Pictures and so on. It also displays recently used files at the bottom of the Content pane.

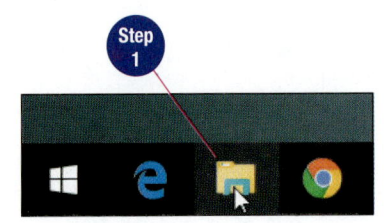

2. Click the drive letter representing your storage medium in the Navigation pane.

3. Double-click the *ExcelS2* folder in the Content pane.

4. Click the View tab below the Title bar.

5. Click the *Large icons* option in the Layout group.

    After you click an option on the View tab, the View tab collapses to provide more space in the File Explorer window.

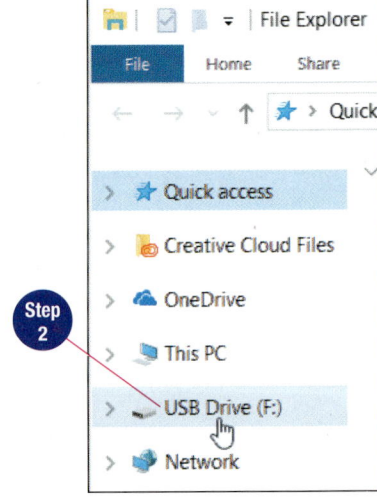

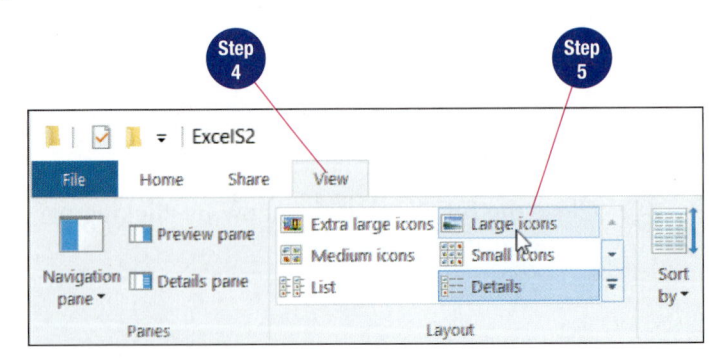

GS-6 GETTING STARTED

6 Click the View tab.

7 Click the *Details* option in the Layout group.

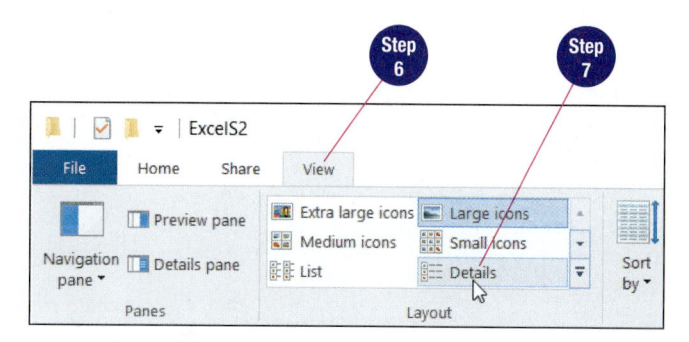

8 With files now displayed in Details view, click the *Name* column heading to sort the list in descending order by name.

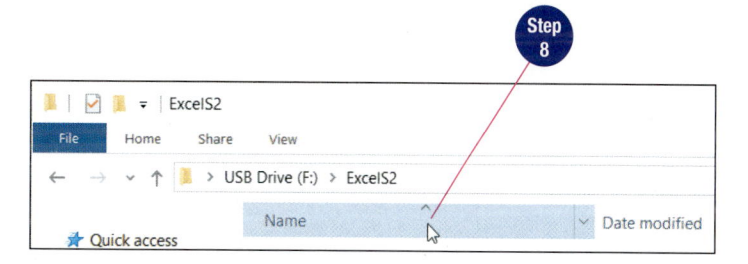

9 Click the *Name* column heading again to restore the list to ascending order by name.

10 Close the File Explorer window by clicking the Close button in the upper right corner of the window.

In Addition

Changing the Default View for All Folders

You can set a view to display by default for all folders of a similar type (such as all disk drive folders or all documents folders). To do this, change the current view to the desired view for the type of folder that you want to set. Next, click the Options button on the View tab and then click the View tab at the Folder Options dialog box. Click the Apply to Folders button in the Folder views section and then click OK. Click Yes at the Folder Views message asking if you want all folders of this type to match this folder's view settings.

Turning on File Extensions

By default, file extensions do not display. Turning on file extensions is helpful in identifying the type of file. Turn on file extensions at the File Explorer window by clicking the View tab and then clicking the *File name extensions* check box to insert a check mark.

PowerPoint

SECTION 1

Preparing a Presentation

> **Data Files**
> Before beginning section work, copy the PowerPointS1 folder to your storage medium and then make PowerPointS1 the active folder.

Skills

- Open, save, and close a presentation
- Run a slide show
- Choose a design theme
- Insert a new slide in the presentation
- Navigate in a presentation
- Change the slide layout
- Change the presentation view
- Rearrange, delete, and hide slides
- Use the Tell Me and Help features
- Check spelling in a presentation
- Use Thesaurus to display synonyms for words
- Run a slide show and use the Pen button options during a slide show
- Use ink tools
- Add slide transitions and transition sounds to a presentation
- Print and preview a presentation

Projects Overview

Marquee Productions — Use a predesigned template to prepare a presentation about the new features in PowerPoint; prepare a movie production meeting presentation; prepare a location team meeting presentation.

Worldwide Enterprises — Prepare an executive meeting presentation for Worldwide Enterprises.

The Waterfront Bistro — Prepare a presentation containing information on the accommodations and services offered by The Waterfront Bistro.

First Choice Travel — Prepare a presentation on Toronto, Ontario, Canada.

Performance Threads — Prepare a presentation for a costume meeting.

The online course includes additional training and assessment resources.

1

Activity 1.1 Opening, Saving, and Closing a Presentation; Running a Slide Show

PowerPoint is a presentation graphics program used to organize and present information. Use PowerPoint to create visual aids for a presentation and then print copies of the aids as well as run the slide show. To open a predesigned PowerPoint template, open the PowerPoint program, click the template, and then click the Create button. The presentation screen contains a variety of features for working with a presentation, such as the Title bar, Quick Access Toolbar, ribbon, and Status bar. After creating a presentation, save the presentation so it is available for future use. Save a presentation at the Save As backstage area.

What You Will Do You are an employee of Marquee Productions and Microsoft Office has just been installed on your computer. You need to prepare a presentation in the near future so you decide to open a PowerPoint file and experiment with running the slide show.

Tutorial
Opening a Presentation Based on a Template

Tutorial
Exploring the PowerPoint Screen

Tutorial
Running a Slide Show

Tutorial
Saving to a Removable Disk

Tutorial
Closing a Presentation and Closing PowerPoint

1 At the Windows desktop, click the Start button and then click the PowerPoint tile at the Start menu.

Depending on your system configuration, these steps may vary.

2 At the PowerPoint opening screen, click the *Welcome to PowerPoint* template.

If this template is not visible, you will need to search for it. To do this, click in the search text box, type Welcome to PowerPoint, and then press the Enter key.

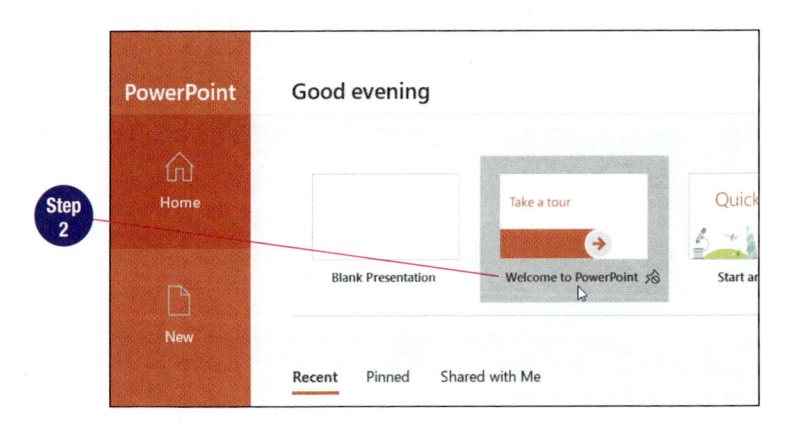

3 Click the Create button.

The Welcome to PowerPoint template opens in the PowerPoint window. What displays in the PowerPoint window will vary depending on what type of presentation you are creating. However, the PowerPoint window contains some consistent elements such as those identified in Figure 1.1. Refer to Table 1.1 for a description of the window elements.

4 Run the slide show by clicking the Start From Beginning button on the Quick Access Toolbar.

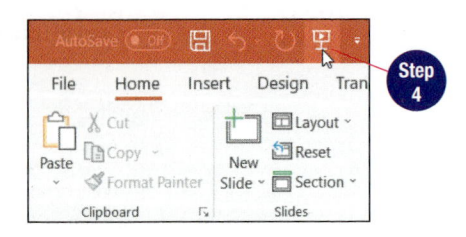

2 **POWERPOINT** Section 1 Preparing a Presentation

5 When the first slide fills the screen, read the information and then click the left mouse button. Continue reading the information in each slide and clicking the left mouse button to advance to the next slide. When a black screen displays, click the left mouse button to end the slide show.

FIGURE 1.1 PowerPoint Window

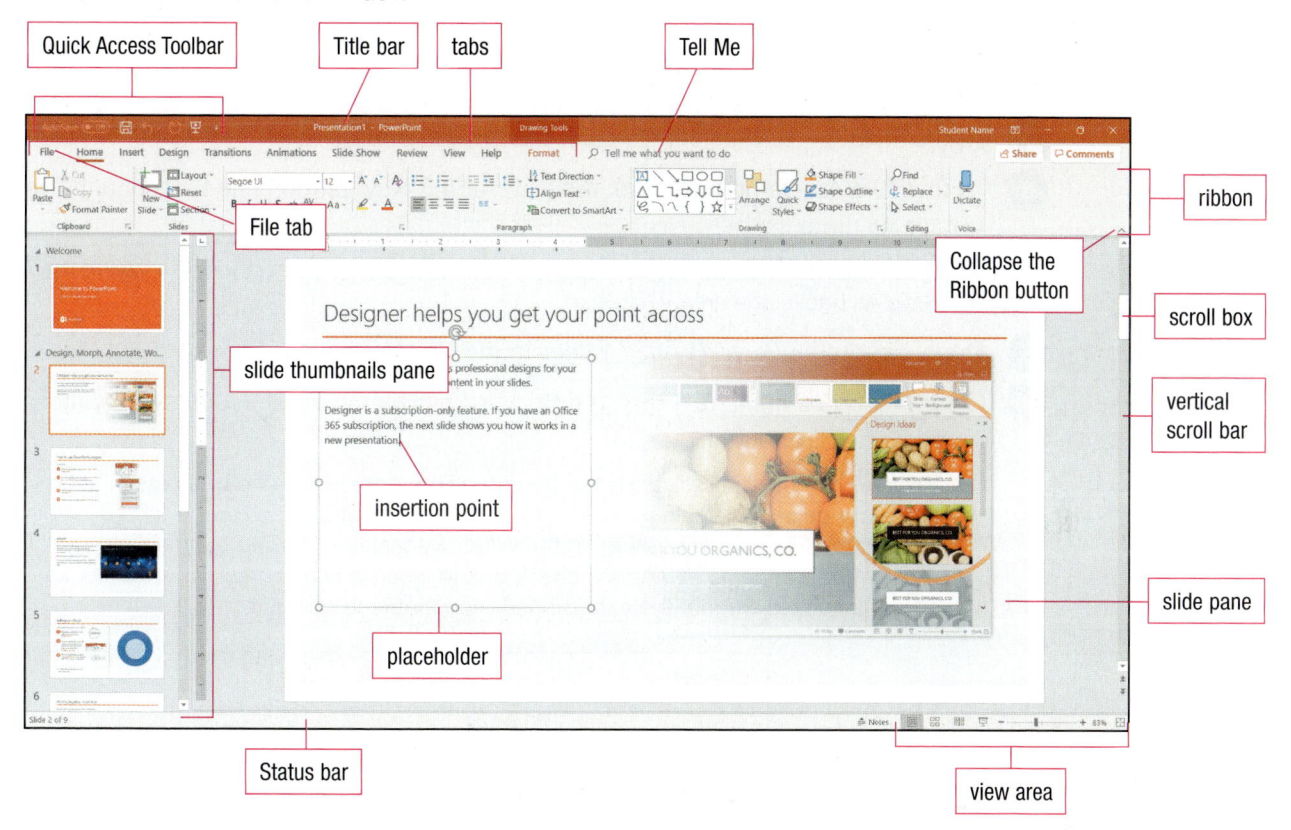

Table 1.1 PowerPoint Window Elements

Feature	Description
Collapse the Ribbon button	when clicked, removes ribbon from screen
File tab	when clicked, displays backstage area that contains options for working with and managing presentations
I-beam pointer	used to move insertion point or to select text
insertion point	indicates location of next character entered at the keyboard
placeholder	location on slide with dotted border; holds text or objects
Quick Access Toolbar	contains buttons for commonly used commands
ribbon	area containing tabs with options and buttons divided into groups
scroll box	used to scroll through slides in presentation; click and hold down mouse button on scroll box to indicate slide number and title
slide pane	displays slide and slide contents
slide thumbnails pane	left side of screen; displays slide thumbnails
Status bar	displays slide number, view buttons, and Zoom slider bar
tabs	contain commands and buttons organized into groups
Tell Me	used to look up a feature and provide options for using the feature
Title bar	displays presentation name followed by program name
vertical scroll bar	used to display specific slides
view area	location on the Status bar that contains buttons for changing presentation view

6. Save the presentation by clicking the Save button 🗎 on the Quick Access Toolbar.

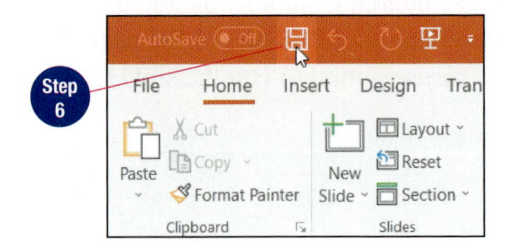

7. At the Save As backstage area, click the *Browse* option.

8. At the Save As dialog box, click the drive in the Navigation pane that contains your storage medium.

   Press the F12 function key to display the Save As dialog box without displaying the Save As backstage area.

9. Double-click the *PowerPointS1* folder in the Content pane.

10. Click in the *File name* text box, type 1-MPPowerPoint, and then press the Enter key (or click the Save button).

    PowerPoint automatically adds the file extension *.pptx* to the end of a presentation name. By default, file extensions do not display. File extensions can be turned on by clicking the File Explorer button on the Windows taskbar, clicking the View tab, and then clicking the *File name extensions* check box to insert a check mark. This textbook will show file names without the extensions, since that is the default.

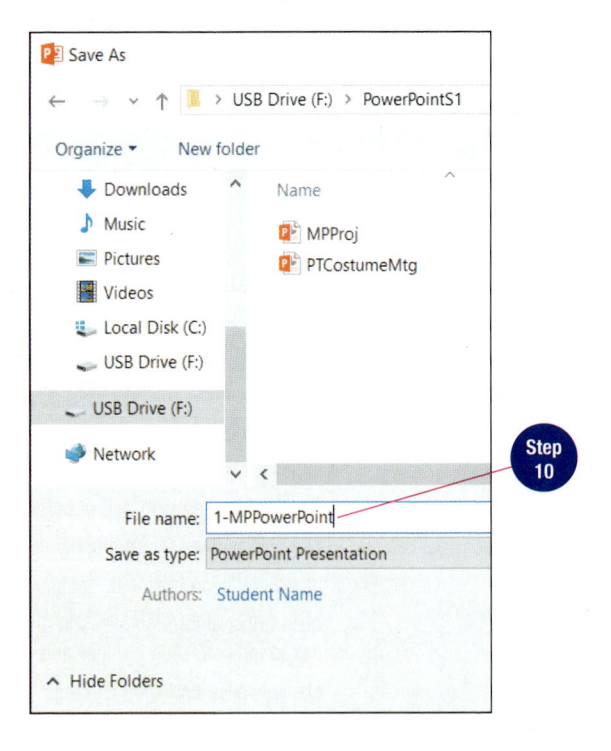

4 **POWERPOINT** Section 1 Preparing a Presentation

In Brief

Create Presentation with Predesigned Template
1. Click File tab.
2. Click *New* option.
3. Click template.
4. Click Create button.

Save Presentation
1. Click Save button on Quick Access Toolbar.
2. Click *Browse* option.
3. Navigate to location.
4. At Save As dialog box, type presentation file name.
5. Press Enter key.

Run Slide Show
1. Click Start From Beginning button on Quick Access Toolbar.
2. Click left mouse button to advance slides and to end slide show.

Print Presentation in Outline Layout
1. Click File tab.
2. Click *Print* option.
3. Click second gallery in *Settings* category.
4. Click *Outline*.
5. Click Print button.

Close Presentation
1. Click File tab.
2. Click *Close* option.

---

11. At the PowerPoint window, print the presentation information in outline layout by clicking the File tab and then clicking the *Print* option.

    The File tab is in the upper left corner of the screen at the left of the Home tab. When you click the File tab, the backstage area displays with options for working with and managing presentations.

12. At the Print backstage area, click the second gallery in the *Settings* category (the gallery containing the text *Full Page Slides*) and then click *Outline* in the *Print Layout* section of the drop-down list.

13. Click the Print button. *Note: If working in a lab, check with your instructor before printing.*

14. Close the presentation by clicking the File tab and then clicking the *Close* option.

    If a message displays asking if you want to save the presentation, click Yes.

15. Close PowerPoint by clicking the Close button in the upper right corner of the screen.

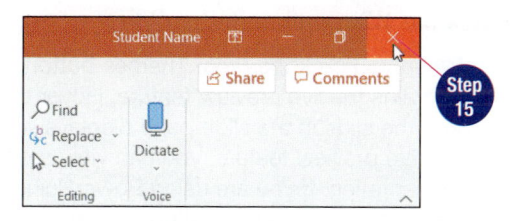

Check Your Work Compare your work to the model answer available in the online course.

In Addition

Using Tabs

The ribbon area displays below the Quick Access Toolbar. The buttons and options in the ribbon area vary depending on the tab selected and the width of the window displayed on the screen. PowerPoint features are organized into tabs that display in the ribbon area. Commands and buttons are organized into groups within a tab. For example, the Home tab, which is the default tab, contains the Clipboard, Slides, Font, Paragraph, Drawing, and Editing groups. Hover the mouse pointer over a button to display a ScreenTip with the name of the button, a keyboard shortcut (if any), and a description of the purpose of the button.

Activity 1.1 **POWERPOINT** 5

Activity 1.2 Applying a Design Theme; Inserting Slides; and Inserting Text

Create a PowerPoint presentation using an installed template similar to the previous activity, or begin with a blank presentation and apply personalized formatting or a slide design theme. To display a blank PowerPoint presentation, use the keyboard shortcut Ctrl + N, or click the File tab (or the File tab and then the *New* option), and then click the *Blank Presentation* template at the backstage area. A PowerPoint presentation screen displays in Normal view with the slide pane in the center and the slide thumbnails pane at the left side of the screen.

What You Will Do Chris Greenbaum, production manager for Marquee Productions, has asked you to prepare slides for a movie production meeting. You decide to prepare the presentation using a design template provided by PowerPoint.

Tutorial — Opening a Blank Presentation

Tutorial — Applying a Design Theme

Tutorial — Inserting and Deleting Text in Slides

Tutorial — Inserting a New Slide

1. Open PowerPoint.
2. At the PowerPoint opening screen, click the *Blank Presentation* template.
3. At the PowerPoint window, click the Design tab.
4. Click the More Themes button in the Themes group.

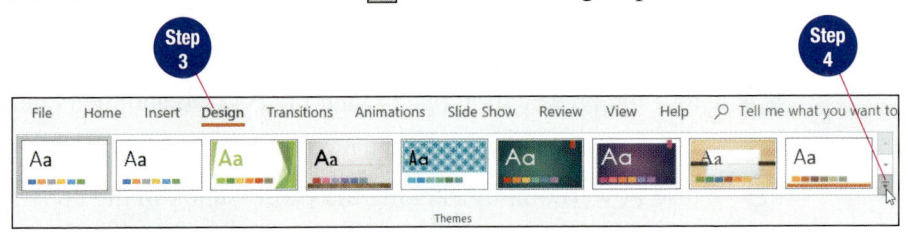

5. Click the *Wisp* option in the *Office* section of the drop-down gallery.

   When you click the More Themes button, a drop-down gallery displays. This gallery contains the live preview feature. Hover the mouse pointer over one of the design themes and the slide in the slide pane displays with the design theme formatting applied. With the live preview feature, you can view a design theme before actually applying it to the presentation. If you are using PowerPoint 365, the Design Ideas task pane opens at the right side of the screen with additional options for the selected design theme. Apply an option by clicking the option thumbnail in the task pane. Close this task pane by clicking the Design Ideas button in the Designer group on the Design tab.

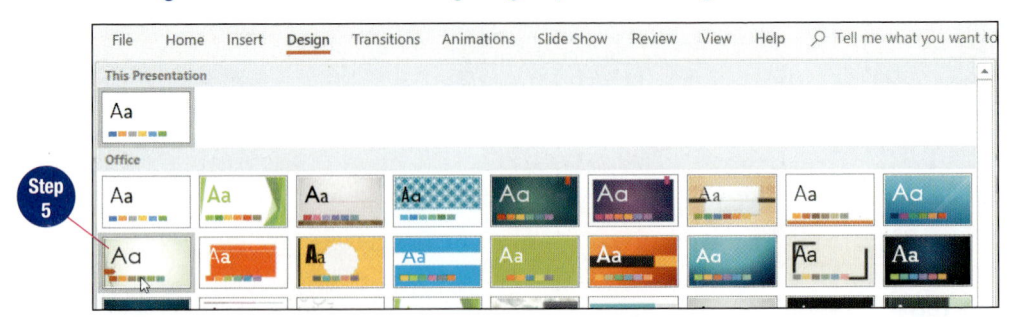

6. Click the second option from the left in the Variants group.

   This changes the tab at the left of the slide to a dark gold color.

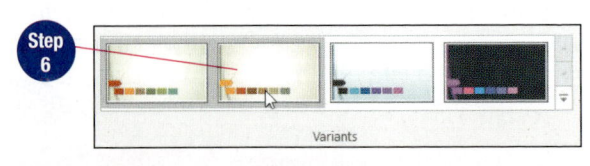

7 Click in the *Click to add title* placeholder in the slide and then type Marquee Productions.

> A *placeholder* is a location on a slide that is marked with a border and holds text or an object.

8 Click in the *Click to add subtitle* placeholder in the slide and then type Movie Production Meeting.

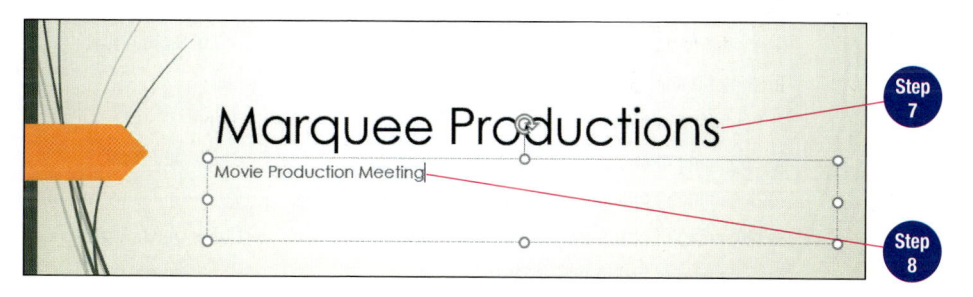

9 Click the Home tab and then click the New Slide button in the Slides group.

> When you click this button, a new slide displays in the slide pane with the Title and Content layout. You will learn more about slide layouts in Activity 1.3.

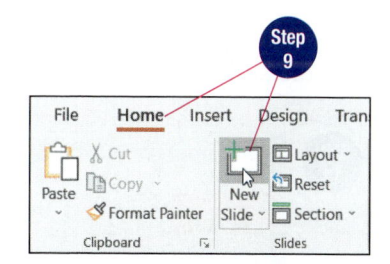

10 Click in the *Click to add title* placeholder in the slide and then type Agenda.

11 Click in the *Click to add text* placeholder in the slide and then type Production Team.

12 Press the Enter key and then type the following agenda items, pressing the Enter key after each item except the last one: Production Assignments, Production Schedule, Locations, and Summary.

> You can use keys on the keyboard to move the insertion point to various locations within a placeholder in a slide. Refer to Table 1.2 on the next page for a list of insertion point movement commands.

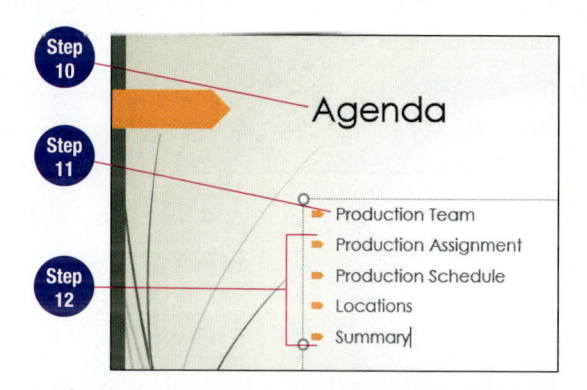

13 Click the New Slide button in the Slides group on the Home tab.

Activity 1.2   **POWERPOINT**   7

Table 1.2 Insertion Point Movement Commands

To move insertion point	Press
One character left	Left Arrow
One character right	Right Arrow
One line up	Up Arrow
One line down	Down Arrow
One word to the left	Ctrl + Left Arrow
One word to the right	Ctrl + Right Arrow
To end of a line of text	End
To beginning of a line of text	Home
To beginning of current paragraph in placeholder	Ctrl + Up Arrow
To beginning of previous paragraph in placeholder	Ctrl + Up Arrow two times
To beginning of next paragraph in placeholder	Ctrl + Down Arrow
To beginning of text in placeholder	Ctrl + Home
To end of text in placeholder	Ctrl + End

14. Click in the *Click to add title* placeholder in the slide and then type Department Reports.

15. Click in the *Click to add text* placeholder in the slide and then type the bulleted text as shown in the slide below. Press the Enter key after each item except the last one.

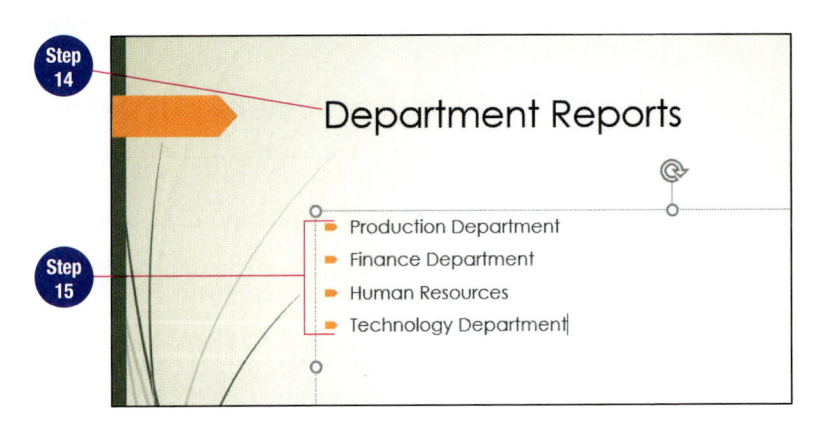

16. Click the New Slide button in the Slides group on the Home tab.

17. Click in the *Click to add title* placeholder in the slide and then type Locations.

18. Click in the *Click to add text* placeholder in the slide, type Studio Shoots, and then press the Enter key.

19. Press the Tab key, type Vancouver Studio, and then press the Enter key.

    Pressing the Tab key demotes the insertion point to a second-level bullet, while pressing Shift + Tab promotes the insertion point back to the first level.

20. Type Los Angeles Studio and then press the Enter key.

In Brief

Choose Design Theme
1. Click Design tab.
2. Click More Themes button.
3. Click theme at drop-down gallery.

Insert New Slide
1. Click Home tab.
2. Click New Slide button.
OR
Press Ctrl + M.

21. Press Shift + Tab, type Location Shoots, and then press the Enter key.
22. Press the Tab key, type Stanley Park, and then press the Enter key.
23. Type Downtown Streets.

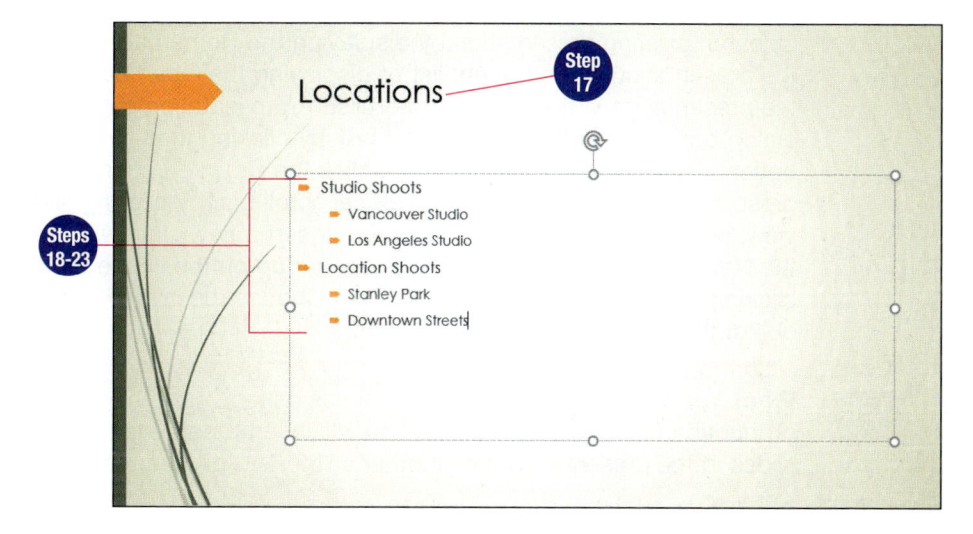

24. Click the Save button on the Quick Access Toolbar.
25. At the Save As backstage area, click the *Browse* option.
26. At the Save As dialog box, click the drive in the Navigation pane that contains your storage medium.
27. Double-click the *PowerPointS1* folder in the Content pane.
28. Click in the *File name* text box, type 1-MPProdMtg, and then press the Enter key (or click the Save button).
29. Close the presentation by clicking the File tab and then clicking the *Close* option.

Check Your Work Compare your work to the model answer available in the online course.

In Addition

Planning a Presentation

Consider the following basic guidelines when preparing content for a presentation:

- **Determine the main purpose.** Do not try to cover too many topics. Identifying the main point of the presentation will help to stay focused and convey a clear message to the audience.
- **Determine the output.** To help decide the type of output needed, consider the availability of equipment, the size of the room where the presentation will be held, and the number of people who will be attending the presentation.
- **Show one idea per slide.** Each slide in a presentation should convey only one main idea. Too many ideas on a slide may confuse the audience and cause the presenter to stray from the purpose of the slide.
- **Maintain a consistent design.** A consistent design and color scheme for slides in a presentation will create continuity and cohesiveness. Do not use too much color or too many images or other graphic elements.
- **Keep slides uncluttered and easy to read.** Keep slides simple to make them easy for the audience to understand. Keep words and other items, such as bullets, to a minimum.
- **Determine printing needs.** Will the audience members require handouts? If so, will these handouts consist of a printing of each slide? an outline of the presentation? a printing of each slide with space for taking notes?

Activity 1.2 **POWERPOINT** 9

Activity 1.3 Opening and Navigating in a Presentation; Choosing a Slide Layout

Open an existing presentation by displaying the Home backstage area and then clicking the presentation in the Recent list or displaying the Open backstage area and then clicking the presentation in the *Recent* option list. A presentation can also be opened at the Open dialog box. Display the Open dialog box by clicking the File tab and then clicking the *Open* option. At the Open backstage area, click the *Browse* option. Navigate through slides in a presentation with buttons on the vertical scroll bar, by clicking slide thumbnails in Normal view, or by using keys on the keyboard. Insert a new slide with a specific layout by clicking the New Slide button arrow in the Slides group on the Home tab or the Insert tab and then clicking the layout at the drop-down list. Choose the layout that matches the type of text or object that will be inserted in the slide.

MARQUEE PRODUCTIONS

What You Will Do Chris Greenbaum has asked you to add more information to the movie production meeting presentation. You will insert a new slide between the second and third slides in the presentation and another at the end of the presentation.

Tutorial
Opening from a Removable Disk

Tutorial
Navigating to Slides

Tutorial
Choosing a Slide Layout

Tutorial
Saving with the Same Name

1. Click the File tab and then click the *Open* option.
2. At the Open backstage area, click the *Browse* option.
3. In the Navigation pane of the Open dialog box, click the drive where your USB flash drive is located (such as *Removable Disk (F:)*).

    You can also display the Open dialog box without displaying the Open backstage area by pressing Ctrl + F12.

4. Double-click the *PowerPointS1* folder in the Content pane.
5. Double-click *1-MPProdMtg* in the Content pane.
6. With **1-MPProdMtg** open, click the Next Slide button ▼ at the bottom of the vertical scroll bar.

    Clicking this button displays the next slide, Slide 2, in the presentation. Notice that *Slide 2 of 4* displays at the left of the Status bar.

7. Click the Previous Slide button ▲ above the Next Slide button to display Slide 1.

    When you click the Previous Slide button, Slide 1 displays in the slide pane and *Slide 1 of 4* displays at the left of the Status bar.

8. Display Slide 2 in the slide pane by clicking the second slide in the slide thumbnails pane (the slide titled *Agenda*).

9. Insert a new slide between Slides 2 and 3 by clicking the New Slide button in the Slides group on the Home tab.

    When you select a slide in the slide thumbnails pane and then click the New Slide button, the new slide is inserted after the selected slide.

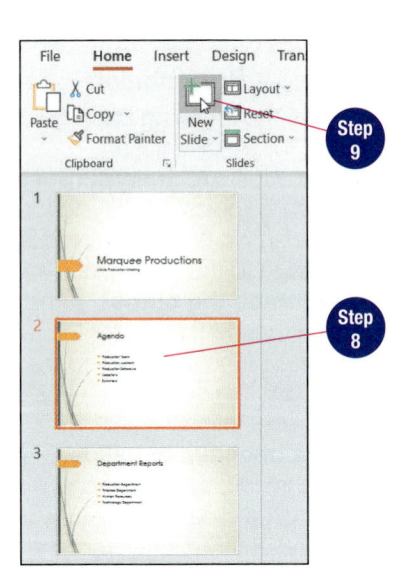

10 **POWERPOINT**   Section 1   Preparing a Presentation

In Brief

Open Presentation from Removable Disk
1. Press Ctrl + F12.
2. In the Navigation pane of the Open dialog box, click the drive containing the removable disk.
3. Double-click folder in Content pane.
4. Double-click presentation in Content pane.

10. Click in the *Click to add title* placeholder in the slide in the slide pane and then type Production Schedule.

11. Click in the *Click to add text* placeholder in the slide and then type the bulleted text as shown at the right. Press the Enter key after typing each item except the last one.

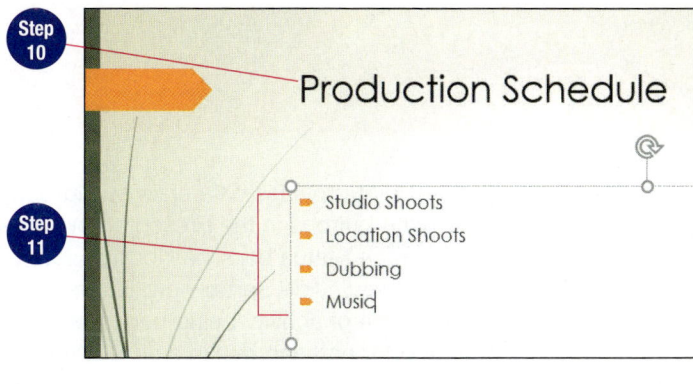

12. Click below the last thumbnail in the slide thumbnails pane. (You may need to scroll down the slide thumbnails pane to display the last slide.)

   When you click below the slide thumbnail, an orange horizontal line displays below Slide 5.

13. Click the New Slide button arrow on the Home tab and then click the *Title Slide* layout in the drop-down list.

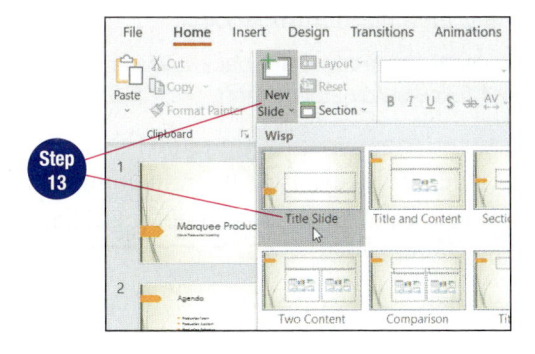

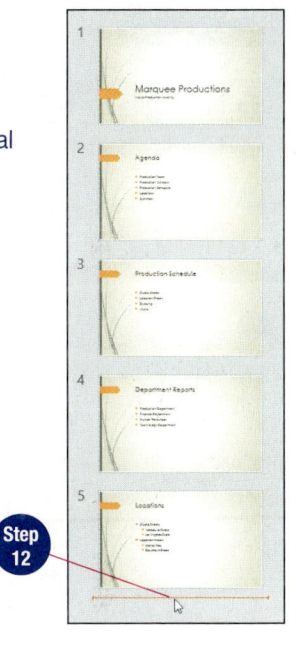

14. Click in the *Click to add title* placeholder and then type Production Leader.

15. Click in the *Click to add subtitle* placeholder and then type Chris Greenbaum.

16. Click the Save button on the Quick Access Toolbar to save **1-MPProdMtg**.

Check Your Work Compare your work to the model answer available in the online course.

In Addition

Opening a Presentation from the Recent or *Recent* Option List

The Home backstage area contains a list of the most recently opened presentations. In addition to the Home backstage area, the Open backstage area with the *Recent* option selected displays a list of the most recently opened presentations. The presentations in the *Recent* option list at the Open backstage area are grouped into categories such as *Today*, *Yesterday*, and possibly *This Week* and *Older*. To open a presentation from the Recent list at the Home backstage area or the *Recent* option list at the Open backstage area, click the presentation name in the list.

Activity 1.3 **POWERPOINT** 11

Activity 1.4   Changing Views

PowerPoint provides different viewing options for a presentation. Change the presentation view with buttons in the Presentation Views group on the View tab or with buttons in the view area on the Status bar. The Normal view is the default view, and this view can be changed to Outline view, Slide Sorter view, Notes Page view, or Reading view. Choose the view based on the type of activity being performed in the presentation. The Outline view provides another method for entering text in a slide. When Outline view is active, the slide thumbnails pane changes to an outline pane for entering text. Insert speaker's notes into a presentation using the notes pane, which can be displayed by clicking the Notes button on the Status bar.

What You Will Do   After reviewing the movie production presentation, Chris Greenbaum has asked you to add a new slide and edit an existing slide.

Tutorial
Changing Views

Tutorial
Entering Text in the Outline Pane

Tutorial
Changing the Display Percentage

1. With **1-MPProdMtg** open, click the View tab and then click the Outline View button in the Presentation Views group.

2. Click immediately right of the text *Music* in the third slide (near the middle of the outline pane), press the Enter key, and then press Shift + Tab.

   This moves the insertion point back a level and inserts the number *4* followed by a slide icon.

3. Type Production Assignments, press the Enter key, and then press the Tab key. Type the remaining text for Slide 4 as shown at the right. Do not press the Enter key after typing *Extras*.

4. Click immediately right of the text *Location Shoots* in the third slide.

5. Press the Enter key and then type Editing.

   This inserts *Editing* between *Location Shoots* and *Dubbing*.

6. Make Slide 6 (*Locations*) the active slide in the slide pane, click in the *Click to add notes* placeholder in the notes pane (if the text is not visible, click the Notes button on the Status bar to display the notes pane), and then type Camille Matsui will report on the park location.

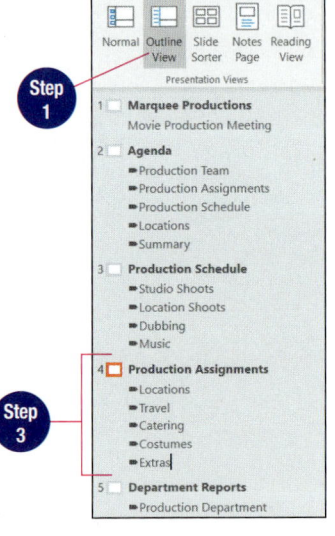

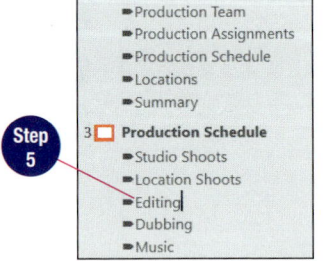

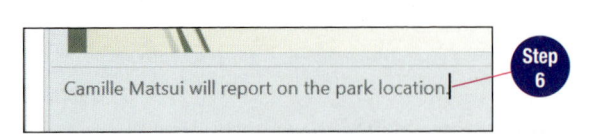

7. Display the slides in Notes Page view by clicking the Notes Page button in the Presentation Views group.

   In Notes Page view, an individual slide displays on a page with any added notes displayed below it. Notice that the note you created about Camille Matsui displays below the slide on the page.

8. Click the Previous Slide button on the vertical scroll bar until Slide 1 displays.

In Brief

Display in Normal View
1. Click View tab.
2. Click Normal button.
OR
Click Normal button on Status bar.

Display in Outline View
1. Click View tab.
2. Click Outline View button.

Display in Slide Sorter View
1. Click View tab.
2. Click Slide Sorter button.
OR
Click Slide Sorter button on Status bar.

Display in Notes Page View
1. Click View tab.
2. Click Notes Page button.

9. Increase the zoom by clicking the Zoom button in the Zoom group on the View tab, clicking *100%* at the Zoom dialog box, and then clicking OK.

10. You can also change the zoom using the Zoom slider bar. Change the zoom by positioning the mouse pointer on the Zoom slider button at the right side of the Status bar. Click and hold down the left mouse button, drag to the right until the zoom percentage at the right of the Zoom slider bar displays as approximately *138%*, and then release the mouse button.

11. Click the Zoom Out button at the left of the Zoom slider bar until *70%* displays at the right of the slider bar.

    Click the Zoom Out button to decrease the zoom display and click the Zoom In button to increase the display.

12. View all slides in the presentation as slide thumbnails by clicking the Slide Sorter button in the view area on the Status bar.

13. View the presentation in Reading view by clicking the Reading View button in the Presentation Views group.

    Use Reading view to show the presentation to someone viewing the presentation on his or her own computer. You can also use Reading view to view a presentation in a window with controls that make the presentation easy to view. In Reading view, navigation buttons display in the lower right corner of the screen immediately left of the view area on the Status bar.

14. View the slides in the presentation in Reading view by clicking the left mouse button on the slides until a black screen displays. At the black screen, click the mouse button again.

    This returns the presentation to the previous view—in this case, Slide Sorter view.

15. Return the presentation to Normal view by clicking the Normal button in the Presentation Views group.

16. If necessary, close the notes pane by clicking the Notes button on the Status bar.

17. Save **1-MPProdMtg**.

Check Your Work Compare your work to the model answer available in the online course.

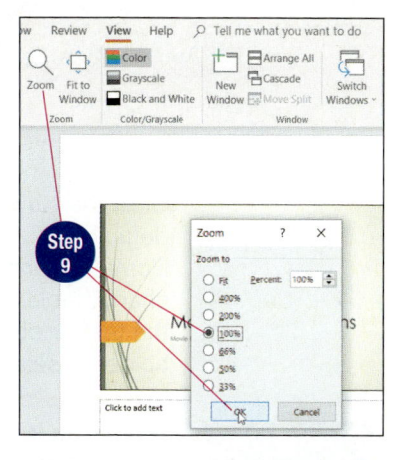

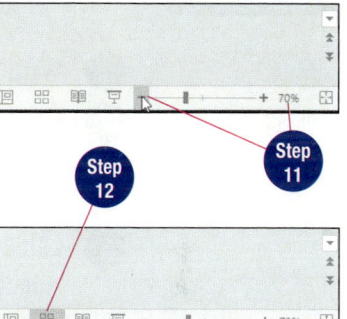

In Addition

Navigating Using the Keyboard

Use the keyboard to display slides in a presentation. In Normal view, press the Down Arrow or Page Down key to display the next slide or press the Up Arrow or Page Up key to display the previous slide in the presentation. Press the Home key to display the first slide in the presentation and press the End key to display the last slide in the presentation. Navigate in Outline view and Slide Sorter view by using the arrow keys on the keyboard. Navigate in Reading view by using the Right Arrow key to move to the next slide or the Left Arrow key to move to the previous slide.

Activity 1.4   **POWERPOINT**   13

Activity 1.5   Changing the Slide Layout; Selecting and Moving a Placeholder

Click the New Slide button and a slide is inserted with the Title and Content layout. This default layout can be changed by clicking the Layout button in the Slides group on the Home tab and then clicking a layout at the drop-down list. Objects in a slide, such as text, charts, tables, and other graphic elements, are generally positioned in placeholders. Click the text or object to select the placeholder and a dashed border will surround the placeholder. A selected placeholder can be moved, sized, and/or deleted.

What You Will Do   You have decided to make a few changes to the layout of slides in the movie production presentation.

Tutorial
Modifying Placeholders

Tutorial
Changing a Slide Layout

1. With **1-MPProdMtg** open, make Slide 7 active in the slide pane.

2. Click the Home tab, click the Layout button in the Slides group, and then click the *Title and Content* layout at the drop-down list.

3. Click immediately right of the *r* in *Leader* (this selects the placeholder), press the Backspace key until *Leader* is deleted, and then type Team.

    Sizing handles display around the selected placeholder. Use these sizing handles to increase and/or decrease the size of the placeholder.

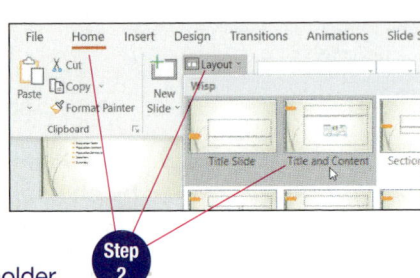

4. Click immediately right of the *m* in *Greenbaum*.

5. Type a comma (,), press the spacebar, and then type Production Manager.

6. Press the Enter key and then type the remaining names and titles shown in the slide above. (Do not press the Enter key after typing *Josh Hart, Locations Director*.)

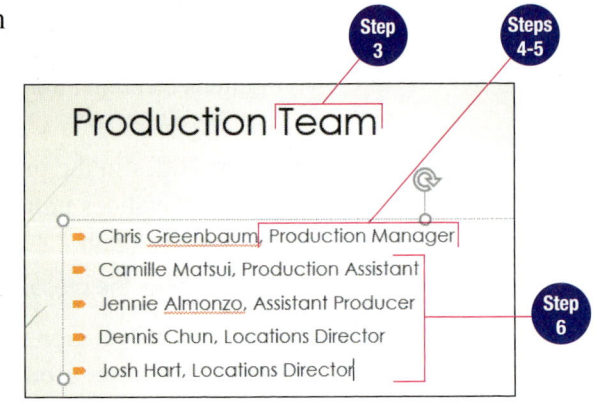

7. Click the Previous Slide button on the vertical scroll bar until Slide 4 displays.

8. Change the slide layout by clicking the Layout button in the Slides group and then clicking the *Title Slide* layout at the drop-down list.

9. Click in the title *Production Assignments*.

    This selects the placeholder.

10. Decrease the size of the placeholder by positioning the mouse pointer on the middle sizing handle at the top of the placeholder until the pointer turns into an up-and-down pointing arrow. Click and hold down the left mouse button, drag down to the approximate location shown at the right, and then release the mouse button.

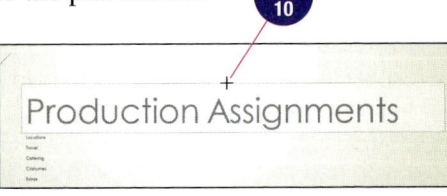

14   **POWERPOINT**   Section 1   Preparing a Presentation

In Brief

Change Slide Layout
1. Make slide active.
2. Click Home tab.
3. Click Layout button.
4. Click layout.

Move Placeholder
1. Click inside placeholder.
2. Drag with mouse to new position.

Size Placeholder
1. Click inside placeholder.
2. Drag sizing handles to increase/decrease size.

11. Move the title placeholder so it positions the title as shown in Figure 1.2. To do this, position the mouse pointer on the placeholder border until the mouse pointer displays with a four-headed arrow attached, click and hold down the left mouse button, drag to the approximate location shown in the figure, and then release the mouse button.

12. Increase the size of the subtitle placeholder (and the size of the text). Begin by clicking in the word *Locations*.

    This selects the placeholder containing the text.

13. Position the mouse pointer on the middle sizing handle at the top of the placeholder until the pointer turns into an up-and-down-pointing arrow. Click and hold down the left mouse button, drag up approximately one inch, and then release the mouse button.

    Increasing the size of the placeholder automatically increases the size of the text in the placeholder. This is because, by default, PowerPoint automatically sizes the contents to fit the placeholder. Read the In Addition at the bottom of this page for information on the AutoFit Options button.

14. Move the content placeholder so it positions the text as shown in Figure 1.2. To do this, position the mouse pointer on the placeholder border until the mouse pointer displays with a four-headed arrow attached, click and hold down the left mouse button, drag to the approximate location shown in the figure, and then release the mouse button.

Figure 1.2 Slide 4

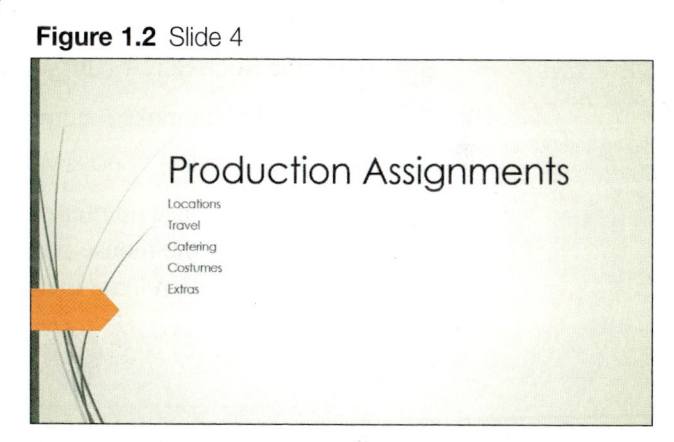

Production Assignments
Locations
Travel
Catering
Costumes
Extras

15. Click outside the placeholder to deselect it.

    If you are not satisfied with the changes you make to a placeholder, click the Reset button in the Slides group on the Home tab. This resets the placeholder's position, size, and formatting to the default settings.

16. Save **1-MPProdMtg**.

Check Your Work Compare your work to the model answer available in the online course.

In Addition

Using the AutoFit Options Button

If the size of a placeholder is decreased so the existing text does not fit within it, PowerPoint will automatically decrease the size of the text so it fits in the placeholder. Click in the text that has been decreased in size and an AutoFit Options button displays at the left of the placeholder. Click the AutoFit Options button and a list of choices displays for positioning objects in the placeholder, as shown at the right. The *AutoFit Text to Placeholder* option is selected by default and tells PowerPoint to fit text within the boundaries of the placeholder. Click the middle choice, *Stop Fitting Text to This Placeholder*, and PowerPoint will not automatically fit the text or object within the placeholder. Choose the last option, *Control AutoCorrect Options*, to display the AutoCorrect dialog box with the AutoFormat As You Type tab selected. Additional options may display depending upon the placeholder and the type of data it contains.

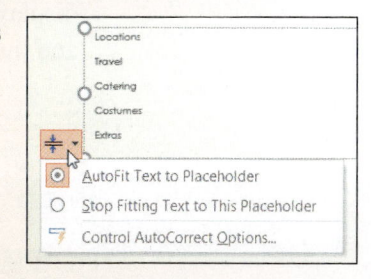

Activity 1.5 **POWERPOINT** 15

Activity 1.6   Rearranging, Deleting, and Hiding Slides

Editing a presentation may include such tasks as rearranging, deleting, or hiding specific slides. PowerPoint provides various views for creating and managing a presentation. Manage slides in the slide thumbnails pane or in Slide Sorter view. Switch to Slide Sorter view by clicking the Slide Sorter button in the view area on the Status bar or by clicking the View tab and then clicking the Slide Sorter button in the Presentation Views group.

What You Will Do   Chris Greenbaum has asked you to make some changes to the presentation, including rearranging the slides, deleting a slide, and hiding a slide.

Tutorial
Rearranging Slides

Tutorial
Deleting Slides

Tutorial
Hiding and Unhiding Slides

1. With **1-MPProdMtg** open, click Slide 5 in the slide thumbnails pane and then press the Delete key on the keyboard.

   You can also delete a slide by right-clicking the slide in the slide thumbnails pane and then clicking *Delete Slide* at the shortcut menu.

2. Click the Slide Sorter button in the view area on the Status bar.

3. Click Slide 6 to make it active.

   A selected slide displays with an orange border.

4. Position the mouse pointer on Slide 6, click and hold down the left mouse button, drag the slide (the mouse pointer will display with a square attached) to the left of Slide 3, and then release the mouse button.

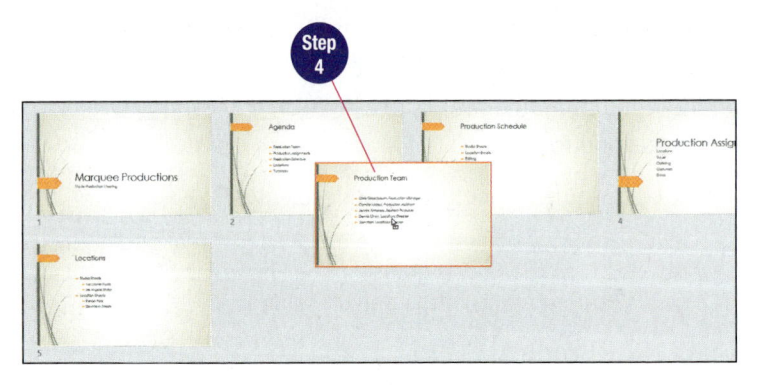

5. Click the Normal button in the view area on the Status bar.

6. Position the mouse pointer on the Slide 5 thumbnail in the slide thumbnails pane, click and hold down the left mouse button, drag up until the slide displays immediately below the Slide 3 thumbnail, and then release the mouse button.

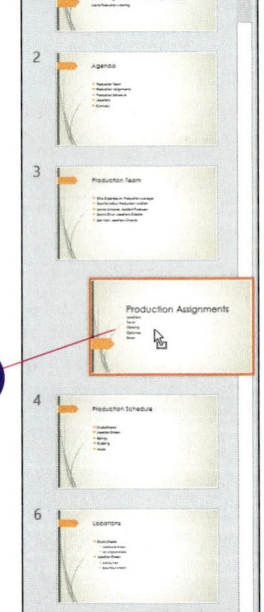

16   POWERPOINT   Section 1   Preparing a Presentation

In Brief

Delete Slide
1. Right-click slide thumbnail.
2. Click *Delete Slide*.
OR
1. Click slide in slide thumbnails pane.
2. Press Delete key.

Move Slide
1. Click Slide Sorter button on Status bar.
2. Click slide.
3. Drag to new position.
OR
1. Click slide in slide thumbnails pane.
2. Drag to new position.

Hide Slide
1. Click slide thumbnail.
2. Click Slide Show tab.
3. Click Hide Slide button.

7 With the Slide 4 thumbnail selected in the slide thumbnails pane (thumbnail displays with an orange border), hide the slide by clicking the Slide Show tab and then clicking the Hide Slide button in the Set Up group.

When a slide is hidden, the slide thumbnail displays dimmed and the slide number displays with a diagonal line across the number.

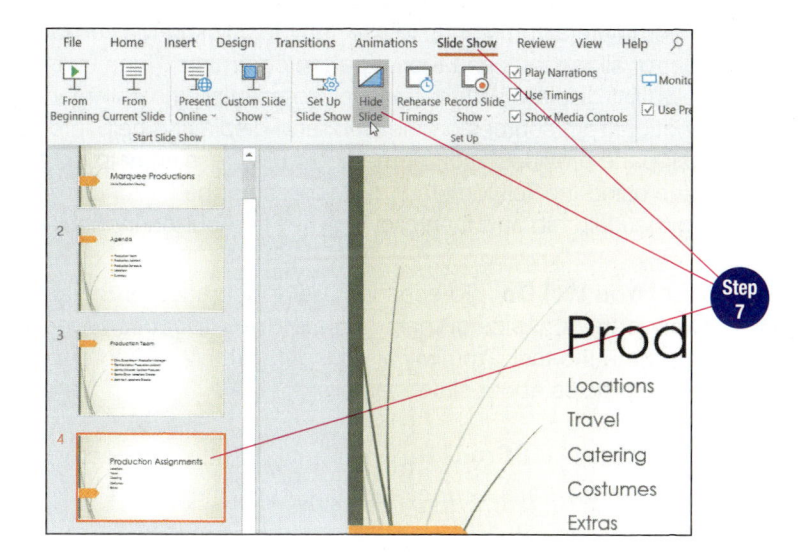

8 Run the slide show by clicking the From Beginning button in the Start Slide Show group. Click the left mouse button to advance each slide until a black screen displays. At the black screen, click the left mouse button again.

9 After running the slide show, you decide to redisplay the hidden slide. To do this, make sure the Slide 4 thumbnail is selected in the slide thumbnails pane and then click the Hide Slide button in the Set Up group.

10 Save **1-MPProdMtg**.

Check Your Work Compare your work to the model answer available in the online course.

In Addition

Copying Slides within a Presentation

Copying a slide within a presentation is similar to moving a slide. To copy a slide, position the mouse pointer on the desired slide, press and hold down the Ctrl key, and then click and hold down left mouse button. Drag to the location where you want the slide copied, release the left mouse button, and then release the Ctrl key. When you drag with the mouse, the mouse pointer displays with a square and a plus symbol attached.

Activity 1.6 **POWERPOINT** 17

Activity 1.7 Using the Tell Me and Help Features

PowerPoint includes the Tell Me feature, which provides information and guidance on how to complete a command. To use Tell Me, click in the *Tell Me* text box on the ribbon to the right of all the tabs and then type the command. Type text in the *Tell Me* text box and a drop-down list displays with options for completing the command, displaying information on the function from sources on the web, and displaying help information on the function. The Help task pane provides another method for accessing help on a command. Display the Help task pane using the Tell Me feature, by pressing the F1 function key on the keyboard, or by clicking the Help tab and then clicking the Help button in the Help group.

What You Will Do To enhance the appearance of Slide 1 in the presentation, you will change the font size of the subtitle *Movie Production Meeting*, using the Tell Me feature to complete the task. You will also use the Tell Me feature to access the Help task pane and locate articles about slide masters.

Tutorial
Using the Tell Me Feature

Tutorial
Using the Help Feature

1. With **1-MPProdMtg** open, make Slide 1 the active slide, click in the subtitle *Movie Production Meeting*, and then click the border of the placeholder to select it.

2. Click in the *Tell Me* text box.

    The *Tell Me* text box is on the ribbon at the right of the Drawing Tools Format tab and contains the text *Tell me what you want to do*. When you click in the text box, the last five functions entered will display in a drop-down list.

3. Type font size in the *Tell Me* text box.

    A drop-down list displays with options such as *Font Size*, *Decrease Font Size*, *Font Settings*, and *Increase Font Size*.

4. Click the arrow at the right of the *Font Size* option at the drop-down list.

    When you click the arrow at the right of the *Font Size* option, a side menu displays.

5. At the side menu that displays, click *28*.

    The 28-point font size is applied to the selected subtitle. The Tell Me feature guided you through the process of changing font size without having to learn how to change font size using a button on the ribbon or an option at a dialog box.

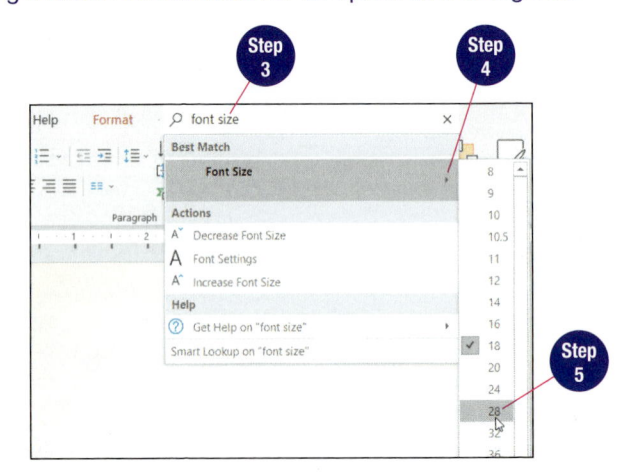

18 **POWERPOINT** Section 1 Preparing a Presentation

In Brief

Use Tell Me
1. Click in *Tell Me* text box.
2. Type search phrase.
3. Click option.

Use Help
1. Position mouse over button.
2. Click Tell me more link.
OR
1. Press F1 function key.
2. Type search text.
3. Press Enter key.
OR
1. Click Help tab.
2. Click Help button.
3. Type search text.
4. Press Enter key.

6 The Tell Me feature also includes access to the Help task pane. To display the Help task pane with information on slide masters, click in the *Tell Me* text box and then type slide master.

7 At the drop-down list, point to *Get Help on "slide master"*.

8 At the side menu that displays, click the first option.

Clicking an option in the side menu displays the Help task pane at the right side of the screen. Read the information in the task pane. You can also display the Help task pane by pressing the F1 function key or clicking the Help tab and then clicking the Help button.

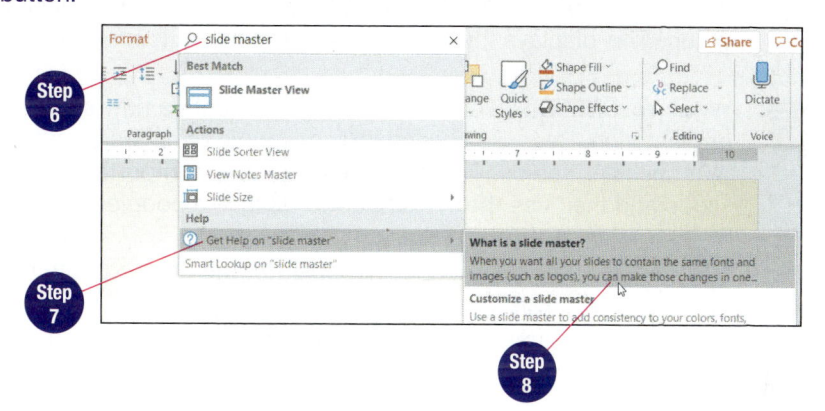

9 Close the Help task pane by clicking the Close button in the upper right corner of the task pane.

Check Your Work Compare your work to the model answer available in the online course.

In Addition

Accessing Smart Lookup

Use the Smart Lookup feature to access information on a function from a variety of sources on the web such as Wikipedia, Bing, and the Oxford Dictionary. The Tell Me feature is one way to access Smart Lookup. To use Tell Me for Smart Lookup, click in the *Tell Me* text box, type the function, and then click the *Smart Lookup* option in the drop-down list. Clicking the *Smart Lookup* option displays the Smart Lookup task pane at the right side of the screen with information on the function from a variety of locations on the internet. Smart Lookup can also be accessed with the Smart Lookup button in the Insights group on the Review tab or by selecting text, right-clicking the selected text, and then clicking *Smart Lookup* at the shortcut menu.

Getting Help on Specific Functions

Some dialog boxes and backstage areas contain a help button that, when clicked, will display the Microsoft Office Support website with information about the functions in the dialog box or backstage area. Hover the mouse over some buttons and the ScreenTip that displays may include a help icon and the text *Tell me more*. Click this hyperlinked text and the Help task pane displays with information about the button feature. Hover the mouse pointer over a button and then press F1 to display the Help task pane with information about the button feature.

Activity 1.8 Checking Spelling; Using the Thesaurus

Use PowerPoint's spelling checker to find and correct misspelled words and duplicated words (such as *and and*). The spelling checker compares words in slides with words in its dictionary. If a match is found, the word is passed over. If no match is found, the spelling checker stops, selects the word, and offers possible replacements. Use the Thesaurus to find synonyms, antonyms, and related words for a particular word. To use the Thesaurus, click in a word, click the Review tab, and then click the Thesaurus button in the Proofing group. This displays the Thesaurus task pane with information about the word.

MARQUEE PRODUCTIONS

What You Will Do You have decided to create a new slide in the movie production presentation. Because several changes have been made to the presentation, you know that checking the spelling of all the slide text is important. Complete a spelling check of all slides and then use the Thesaurus to replace a couple of words with synonyms.

Tutorial
Checking Spelling

Tutorial
Using the Thesaurus

1 With **1-MPProdMtg** open, position the mouse pointer on the scroll box on the vertical scroll bar at the right side of the screen. Click and hold down the left mouse button, drag the scroll box to the bottom of the scroll bar, and then release the mouse button.

This displays Slide 6 in the slide pane. As you drag the scroll box on the vertical scroll bar, a box displays indicating the slide number and slide title (if the slide contains a title).

2 Click the Home tab and then click the New Slide button in the Slides group.

This inserts a new slide at the end of the presentation.

3 Click in the *Click to add title* placeholder and then type *Summary*.

4 Click in the *Click to add text* placeholder and then type the text shown in the slide at the right.

Type the words exactly as shown. You will check the spelling in the next steps.

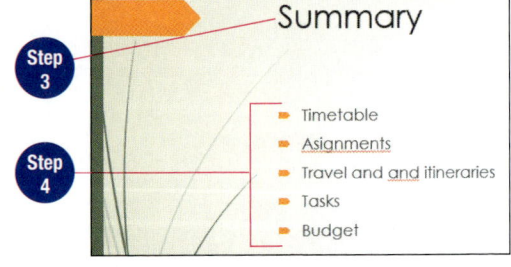

5 Complete a spelling check by moving the insertion point to the beginning of the word *Timetable*, clicking the Review tab, and then clicking the Spelling button in the Proofing group.

6 When the spelling checker selects *Asignments* in Slide 7 and displays *Assignments* in the list box in the Spelling task pane, click the Change button.

Refer to the In Addition for a description of the Spelling task pane buttons.

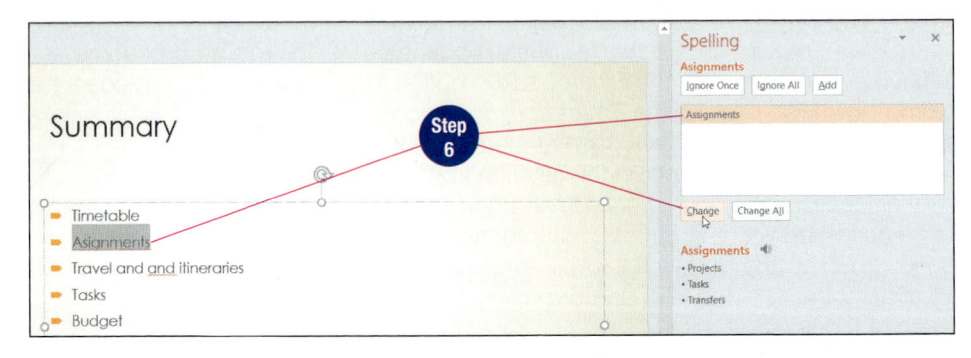

20 POWERPOINT Section 1 Preparing a Presentation

In Brief

Complete Spelling Check
1. Click Review tab.
2. Click Spelling button.
3. Change or ignore highlighted words.
4. When spelling check is completed, click OK.

Use Thesaurus
1. Click in word.
2. Click Review tab.
3. Click Thesaurus button.
4. Position mouse pointer on replacement word in Thesaurus task pane, click down arrow at right of word, click *Insert*.

7. When the spelling checker selects the second *and* in the slide, click the Delete button.

8. If the spelling checker selects *Greenbaum* in Slide 3, click the Ignore All button.

   Greenbaum is a proper name and is spelled correctly. Clicking the Ignore All button tells the spelling checker to leave the name as spelled.

9. If the spelling checker selects *Almonzo* in Slide 3, click the Ignore All button.

10. At the message stating that the spelling check is complete, click OK.

11. Display Slide 7 in the slide pane and then click in the word *Timetable*.

12. Look up synonyms for *Timetable* by clicking the Thesaurus button in the Proofing group.

    The Thesaurus task pane displays at the right side of the screen and contains lists of synonyms for *Timetable*. Depending on the word you are looking up, the words in the Thesaurus task pane list box may display followed by *(n.)* for *noun*, *(v.)* for *verb*, *(adj.)* for *adjective*, or *(adv.)* for *adverb*. Antonyms may display in the list of related synonyms, usually near the end and followed by *(Antonym)*.

13. Position the mouse pointer on the word *Schedule* in the Thesaurus task pane, click the down arrow at the right of the word, and then click *Insert* at the drop-down list.

    This replaces *Timetable* with *Schedule*.

14. Close the Thesaurus task pane by clicking the Close button in the upper right corner of the task pane.

15. Right-click in the word *Tasks*, point to *Synonyms*, and then click *Responsibilities*.

    The shortcut menu offers another method for displaying synonyms for words.

16. Save **1-MPProdMtg**.

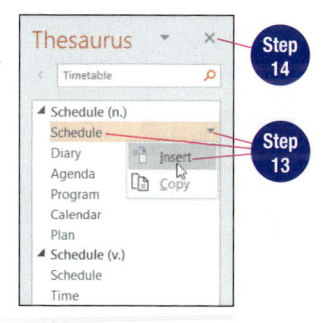

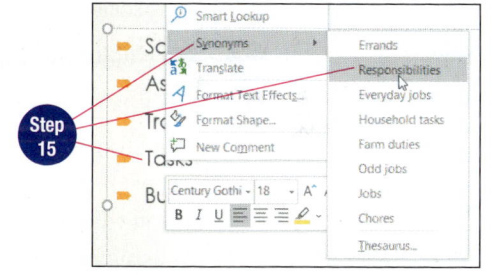

Check Your Work Compare your work to the model answer available in the online course.

In Addition

Using Spelling Task Pane Buttons
This table displays descriptions of the Spelling task pane buttons.

Button	Function
Ignore Once	skips that occurrence of the word and leaves currently selected text as written
Ignore All	skips that occurrence of the word and all other occurrences of the word in the presentation
Add	adds the selected word to the main spelling check dictionary
Delete	deletes the currently selected word(s)
Change	replaces the selected word with the selected word in the suggestions list box
Change All	replaces the selected word and all other occurrences of the word in the presentation with the selected word in the suggestions list box

Activity 1.8 **POWERPOINT** 21

Activity 1.9 Navigating in a Slide Show; Using Ink Tools; Using Options on the Slide Show Toolbar

Run a slide show in PowerPoint manually, advance the slides automatically, or set up a slide show to run continuously for demonstration purposes. In addition to the Start From Beginning button on the Quick Access Toolbar, run a slide show with the From Beginning button on the Slide Show tab or the Slide Show button on the Status bar. Run the slide show beginning with the currently active slide by clicking the From Current Slide button in the Start Slide Show group or clicking the Slide Show button in the view area on the Status bar. Use the mouse or keyboard to advance through the slides. Buttons on the Slide Show toolbar can also be used. These buttons display when the mouse pointer is moved while running a slide show. Use the pen tool to emphasize major points or draw the attention of the audience to specific items in a slide. The pen tool contains options such as a laser pointer, drawing pen, highlighter, and eraser. Write and highlight on a slide in Normal view with options on the Ink Tools Pens tab. Display this tab by clicking the Start Inking button in the Ink group on the Review tab. This feature is useful when using a pen, stylus, or finger to draw on a tablet. If the Draw tab displays on the ribbon, the Start Inking button will not display on the Review tab. However, the Draw tab contains options for drawing and highlighting on a slide. (This activity assumes the Start Inking button is available.)

What You Will Do   You are now ready to run the movie production meeting slide show. You will use the mouse to perform various actions while running the slide show and use the pen tool and ink tools to emphasize points in slides.

Tutorial
Navigating in a Slide Show

Tutorial
Changing the Display when Running a Slide Show

Tutorial
Displaying Slide Show Help and Hiding Slides during a Slide Show

Tutorial
Using Pen Button Options during a Slide Show

Tutorial
Using Ink Tools

1. With **1-MPProdMtg** open, click the Slide Show tab and then click the From Beginning button in the Start Slide Show group.

    Clicking this button begins the slide show, and Slide 1 fills the entire screen.

2. After viewing Slide 1, click the left mouse button to advance to the next slide.

3. At Slide 2, move the mouse pointer until the Slide Show toolbar displays dimmed in the lower left corner of the slide and then click the Previous button (displays with a left arrow) on the toolbar to display the previous slide (Slide 1).

    Use buttons on the Slide Show toolbar to display the next slide, the previous slide, or a specific slide; use the pen, laser pointer, and highlighter to emphasize text on the slide; display slide thumbnails; and zoom in on elements of a slide. You can also display the Slide Show Help dialog box, shown in Figure 1.3, which describes all the navigation options available while running a slide show. Display this dialog box by clicking the More slide show options button on the Slide Show toolbar and then clicking *Help*.

4. Click the Next button (displays with a right arrow) on the Slide Show toolbar to display the next slide (Slide 2).

5. Display the previous slide (Slide 1) by right-clicking anywhere in the slide and then clicking *Previous* at the shortcut menu.

    Right-clicking displays the shortcut menu with a variety of options including options to display the previous or next slide.

22   POWERPOINT   Section 1   Preparing a Presentation

Figure 1.3 Slide Show Help Dialog Box

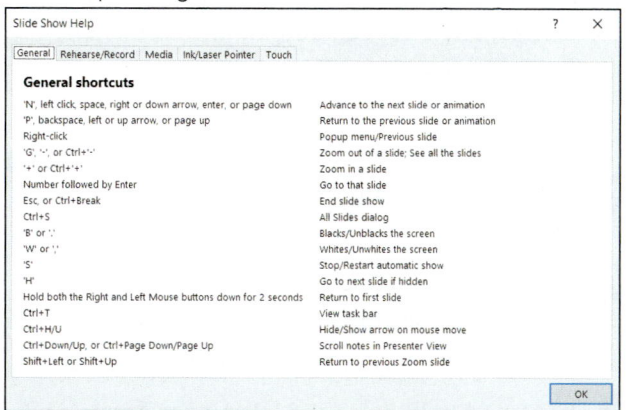

6. Display Slide 4 by pressing the number 4 key and then pressing the Enter key.

   Move to any slide in a presentation by typing the slide number and then pressing the Enter key.

7. Change to a black screen by pressing the letter B key.

   When you press the letter B key, the slide is removed from the screen and the screen displays black. This might be useful in a situation where you want to discuss something with your audience that is unrelated to the slide.

8. Return to Slide 4 by pressing the letter B key.

   Pressing the letter B key switches between the slide and a black screen. Press the letter W key if you want to switch between the slide and a white screen.

9. Zoom in on the bulleted items in Slide 4 by clicking the Zoom into the slide button (displays as a magnifying glass) on the Slide Show toolbar, hovering the magnification area over the bulleted items, and then clicking the left mouse button.

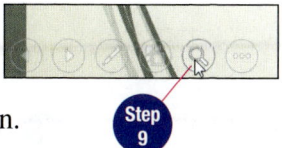

10. Right-click on the screen to display Slide 4 without magnification.

11. Display thumbnails of all the slides in the presentation while viewing the slide show by clicking the See all slides button on the Slide Show toolbar.

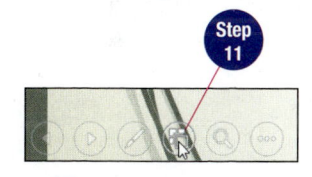

12. Click the Slide 3 thumbnail on the screen.

    This displays Slide 3 in the slide show.

13. Click the left mouse button to display Slide 4. Continue clicking the left mouse button until a black screen displays. At the black screen, click the left mouse button again.

    This returns the presentation to the Normal view.

14. Make Slide 1 active.

15. Display Slide 2 by clicking the Next Slide button at the bottom of the vertical scroll bar.

16. Click the From Current Slide button in the Start Slide Show group on the Slide Show tab.

    Clicking this button begins the slide show with the active slide.

17. Run the slide show by clicking the left mouse button at each slide until Slide 5 is active (contains the title *Production Schedule*).

Activity 1.9 **POWERPOINT** 23

18. Move the mouse to display the Slide Show toolbar, click the Pen button, and then click *Laser Pointer*.

    This turns the mouse pointer into a red, hollow, glowing circle.

19. Practice moving the laser pointer around the screen.

20. Click the Pen button on the Slide Show toolbar and then click *Pen*.

    This turns the mouse pointer into a small circle.

21. Click and hold down the left mouse button and draw a circle around the text *Location Shoots*.

22. Using the mouse, draw a line below *Dubbing*.

23. Erase the pen markings by clicking the Pen button on the Slide Show toolbar and then clicking *Erase All Ink on Slide*.

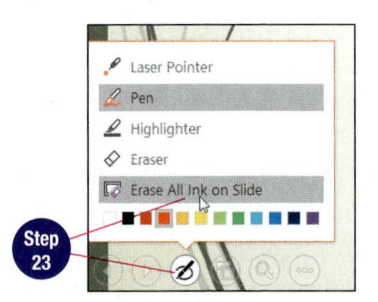

24. Change the color of the ink by clicking the Pen button and then clicking the *Blue* color (ninth color option).

25. Using the mouse, draw a blue line below the word *Music*.

26. Return the mouse pointer back to an arrow by pressing the Esc key.

27. Click the left mouse button to advance to Slide 6.

28. Click the Pen button and then click *Highlighter*.

29. Using the mouse, drag through the words *Studio Shoots*.

30. Using the mouse, drag through the words *Location Shoots*.

31. Return the mouse pointer back to an arrow by pressing the Esc key.

32. Press the Esc key on the keyboard to end the slide show without viewing the remaining slides. At the message asking if you want to keep your ink annotations, click the Discard button.

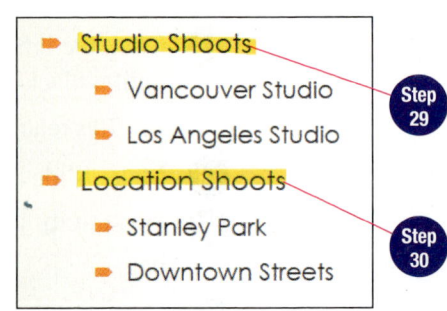

POWERPOINT Section 1 Preparing a Presentation

In Brief

Run Slide Show
Click Start From Beginning button on Quick Access Toolbar.
OR
1. Click Slide Show tab.
2. Click From Beginning button or From Current Slide button.
OR
Click Slide Show button on Status bar.

Use Pen Tool When Running Slide Show
1. Run slide show.
2. Move mouse.
3. Click Pen button on Slide Show toolbar.
4. Click *Pen* option.
5. Draw in slide with pen.

Use Ink Tools
1. Click Review tab.
2. Click Start Inking button.
3. Draw or highlight on slide using pen or highlighter options.
4. Click Stop Inking button.

---

33. With Slide 6 displayed in Normal view, draw a circle around text to display when running a slide show. Begin by clicking the Review tab and then clicking the Start Inking button in the Ink group.

    The Ink Tools Pens tab will display with options for writing or highlighting on a slide. This feature is particularly useful for tablets. The mouse pointer will display as a small circle. If the Review tab does not contain the Start Inking tool, remove the Draw tab from the ribbon. To do this, click the File tab and then click *Options*. At the PowerPoint Options dialog box, click the *Customize Ribbon* option in the left panel. Click the *Draw* check box in the list box at the right to remove the check mark and then click OK to close the dialog box.

34. Click the *Dark Green Pen (0.35 mm)* option in the Pens gallery (fourth column, first row).

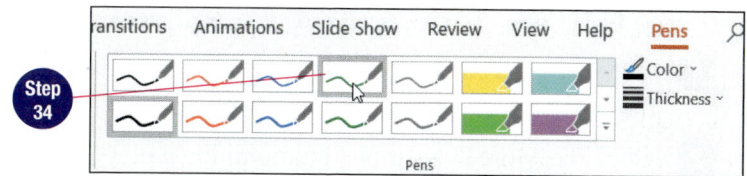

35. Using the mouse, draw a rectangle around the text *Studio Shoots*.

    If you are not satisfied with the appearance of the rectangle, click the Undo button on the Quick Access Toolbar, and then draw the rectangle again.

36. Click the *Aqua Highlighter (4.0 mm)* option in the Pens gallery (seventh column, first row).

37. Using the mouse, drag through the words *Los Angeles Studio*.

38. Click the Stop Inking button in the Close group to turn off the inking feature.

39. Click the Slide Show button in the view area on the Status bar.

40. Notice that the green rectangle and aqua highlighting display on the slide and then press the Esc key to return the presentation to Normal view.

41. Save **1-MPProdMtg**.

Check Your Work Compare your work to the model answer available in the online course.

In Addition

Hiding and Displaying the Mouse Pointer

When running a slide show, the mouse pointer is set, by default, to be hidden after three seconds of inactivity. The mouse pointer will appear again when the mouse is moved. Change this default setting by clicking the More slide show options button on the Slide Show toolbar, clicking *Arrow Options*, and then clicking *Visible* if the mouse pointer should always be visible or *Hidden* if the mouse pointer should not display at all when running the slide show. The *Automatic* option is the default setting.

Viewing in Presenter View

When running a slide show using two monitors, the presentation can display in Presenter view on one of the monitors. Use this view to control the slide show. For example, in Presenter view speaker notes are visible, all the Slide Show toolbar options are available, and slides can be advanced and slide timings can be set. Press Alt + F5 to display the presentation in Presenter view.

Activity 1.10 Adding Slide Transitions and Transition Sounds

A variety of transitions and transition sounds can be applied to a presentation. When running a presentation, a transition is how one slide is removed from the screen and the next slide is displayed. Interesting transitions such as fades, dissolves, push, cover, wipes, stripes, and bar can add interest to your presentation. In addition to a transition, a transition sound can be applied that will play as one slide is removed from the screen and the next slide is displayed. Add transitions and transition sounds with options on the Transitions tab.

What You Will Do You have decided to enhance the movie production meeting presentation by adding transitions and transition sound to the slides.

Tutorial
Adding Slide Transitions

Tutorial
Adding Sound to Slide Transitions

1. With **1-MPProdMtg** open, click Slide 1 in the slide thumbnails pane and then click the Transitions tab.

2. Click the More Transitions button in the gallery in the Transition to This Slide group.

3. Click the *Ripple* option in the *Exciting* section at the drop-down list.

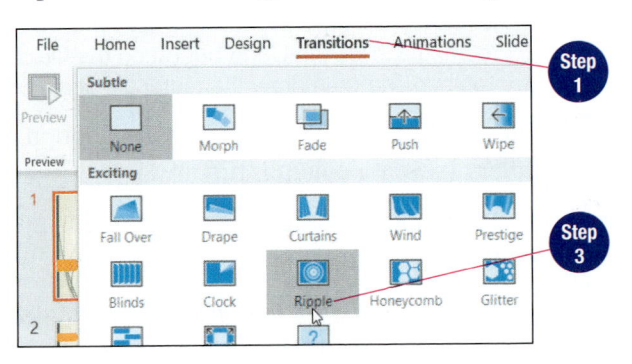

4. Click the Effect Options button in the Transition to This Slide group and then click *From Top-Left* at the drop-down list.

   The effect options change depending on the transition selected.

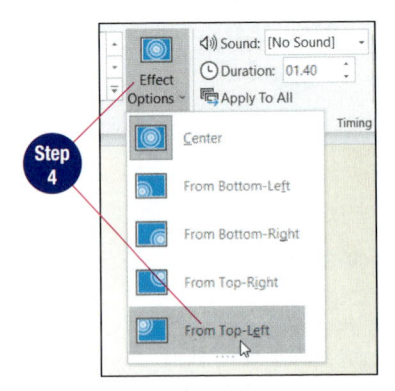

5. Click the *Sound* option box arrow in the Timing group.

6. Click the *Breeze* option at the drop-down list.

26 POWERPOINT Section 1 Preparing a Presentation

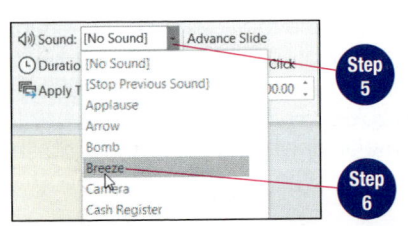

In Brief

Add Transition to All Slides in Presentation
1. Click Transitions tab.
2. Click More Transitions button in gallery in Transition to This Slide group.
3. Click transition.
4. Click Apply To All button.

Add Transition Sound to All Slides in Presentation
1. Click Transitions tab.
2. Click *Sound* option box arrow.
3. Click sound option.
4. Click Apply To All button.

7. Apply three seconds to each slide transition by clicking in the *Duration* measurement box, typing 3, and then pressing the Enter key.

8. Click the Apply To All button in the Timing group.

   Notice that Play Animations star icons display below the slide numbers in the slide thumbnails pane.

9. Click the Slide 1 thumbnail in the slide thumbnails pane.

10. Run the slide show by clicking the Slide Show button in the view area on the Status bar.

11. Click the left mouse button to advance each slide.

12. At the black screen after the last slide, click the left mouse button again to return the presentation to the Normal view.

13. Click the More Transitions button in the gallery in the Transition to This Slide group.

14. Click the *Curtains* option in the *Exciting* section of the drop-down list.

15. Click the *Sound* option box arrow and then click *Whoosh* at the drop-down list.

16. Click the *Duration* measurement box down arrow until *02.50* displays.

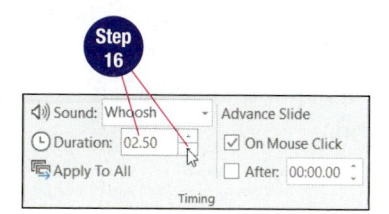

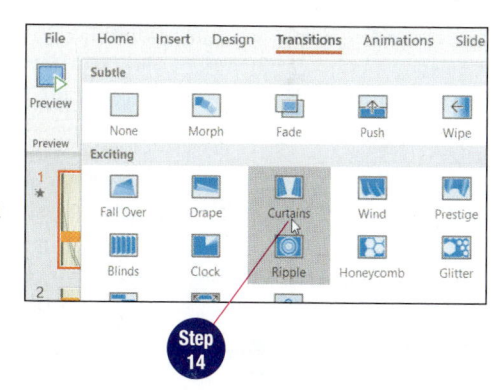

17. Click the Apply To All button in the Timing group.

18. With Slide 1 active, run the slide show.

19. Save **1-MPProdMtg**.

In Addition

Running a Slide Show Automatically

Slides in a slide show can be advanced automatically after a specific number of seconds by inserting a check mark in the *After* check box in the Timing group and removing the check mark from the *On Mouse Click* check box. Change the time in the *After* measurement box by clicking the *After* measurement box up or down arrow or by selecting the number in the measurement box and then typing the specific time. If the transition time should affect all slides in the presentation, click the Apply To All button. In Slide Sorter view, the transition time displays below each affected slide. Click the Slide Show button to run the slide show. The first slide displays for the specified amount of time and then the next slide automatically displays.

Activity 1.10   **POWERPOINT**   27

Activity 1.11 Previewing Slides and Printing

A presentation can be printed with each slide on a separate piece of paper; each slide at the top of the page, leaving the bottom of the page for notes; up to nine slides or a specific number of slides on a single piece of paper; or the slide titles and topics in outline form. Before printing a presentation, consider previewing it. Choose print options and display a preview of the presentation at the Print backstage area. Display this view by clicking the File tab and then clicking the *Print* option. Click the Back button or press the Esc key to exit the backstage area without choosing an option.

What You Will Do Staff members need the movie production meeting slides printed as handouts and as an outline. You will preview and print the presentation in various formats.

Tutorial
Previewing Slides and Printing

1. With **1-MPProdMtg** open, display Slide 1 in the slide pane.

2. Click the File tab and then click the *Print* option.

    Slide 1 of the presentation displays at the right side of the screen as it will when printed. Use the Next Page button (right-pointing arrow) below and at the left of the slide to view the next slide in the presentation, click the Previous Page button (left-pointing arrow) to display the previous slide in the presentation, use the Zoom slider bar to increase or decrease the size of the slide, and click the Zoom to Page button to fit the slide in the preview area in the Print backstage area. The left of the Print backstage area displays the Print button and *Copies* measurement box along with two categories—*Printer* and *Settings*. Click the Print button to send the presentation to the printer. Specify the number of copies to print with the *Copies* measurement box. Use the *Printer* gallery to specify the printer. The *Settings* category contains a number of galleries that describe how the slides will print.

3. Click the Next Page button below and at the left of the preview slide to display the next slide in the presentation.

    This displays Slide 2 in the preview area.

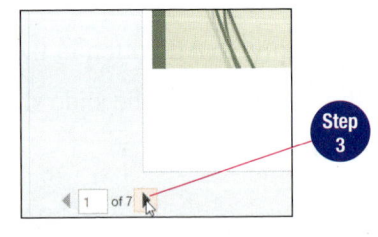

4. Click the Zoom In button ➕ at the right of the Zoom slider bar two times.

    Click the Zoom In button to increase the size of the slide or click the Zoom Out button (displays with a minus symbol) to decrease the size of the slide.

5. Click the Zoom to Page button at the right of the Zoom slider bar.

    Click the Zoom to Page button to fit the entire slide in the viewing area in the Print backstage area.

28 **POWERPOINT** Section 1 Preparing a Presentation

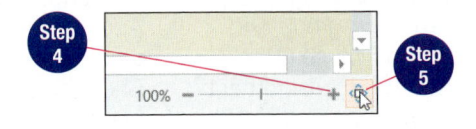

6. You decide to print the slides on two pages and you want to preview how the slides will display on the pages. To do this, click the second gallery in the *Settings* category (contains the text *Full Page Slides*) and then click *4 Slides Horizontal* in the *Handouts* section.

   Notice how four slides display on the preview page.

7. Click the Print button at the top of the Print backstage area.

8. You want to print all slide text on one page to use as a reference during your presentation. To do this, click the File tab and then click the *Print* option.

9. At the Print backstage area, click the second gallery in the *Settings* category (contains the text *4 Slides Horizontal*) and then click *Outline* in the *Print Layout* section.

10. Click the Print button at the top of the Print backstage area.

    With the *Outline* option selected, the presentation prints on one page with slide numbers, slide icons, and slide text in outline form.

11. You want to print only Slide 6. To do this, click the File tab and then click the *Print* option.

12. At the Print backstage area, click the second gallery in the *Settings* category (contains the text *Outline*) and then click *Full Page Slides* in the *Print Layout* section.

13. Click in the *Slides* text box below the first gallery in the *Settings* category, type 6, and then click the Print button.

14. Save **1-MPProdMtg**.

15. Close the presentation by clicking the File tab and then clicking the *Close* option.

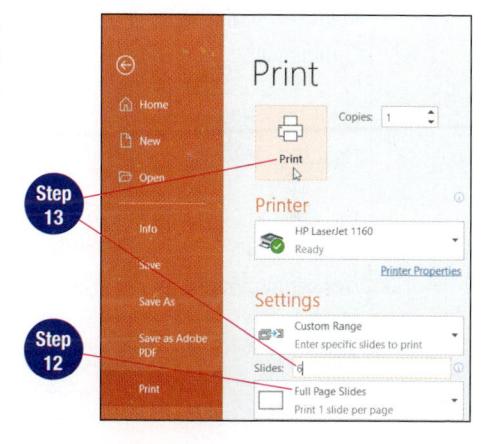

Check Your Work Compare your work to the model answer available in the online course.

In Addition

Using Options at the Slide Size Dialog Box

Change slide orientation with options at the Slide Size dialog box, shown at the right. Display this dialog box by clicking the Design tab, clicking the Slide Size button in the Customize group, and then clicking *Customize Slide Size* at the drop-down list. Use options at this dialog box to specify how slides should be sized; page width and height; orientation for slides; and orientation for notes, handouts, and outlines.

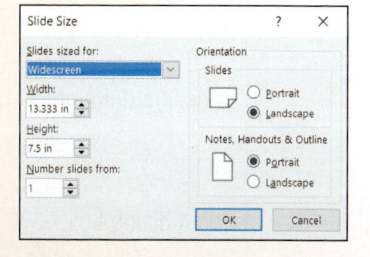

Activity 1.11 **POWERPOINT** 29

Features Summary

Feature	Ribbon Tab, Group	Button/Option	File Tab Option	Keyboard Shortcut
apply transitions and sound to all slides	Transitions, Timing			
close a presentation			Close	Ctrl + F4
close PowerPoint				
display Presenter view				Alt + F5
Help task pane	Help, Help			F1
hide slide	Slide Show, Set Up			
ink tools	Review, Ink			
layout	Home, Slides			
new slide	Home, Slides OR Insert, Slides			Ctrl + M
Normal view	View, Presentation Views			
Notes Page view	View, Presentation Views			
Open backstage area			Open	Ctrl + O
open blank presentation				Ctrl + N
Outline view	View, Presentation Views			
Print backstage area			Print	Ctrl + P
Reading view	View, Presentation Views			
run slide show from current slide	Slide Show, Start Slide Show			Shift + F5
run slide show from Slide 1	Slide Show, Start Slide Show			F5
save			Save	Ctrl + S
Save As backstage area			Save As	
Slide Sorter view	View, Presentation Views			
spelling checker	Review, Proofing			F7
themes	Design, Themes			
Thesaurus	Review, Proofing			Shift + F7
transitions	Transitions, Transition to This Slide			
transition duration	Transitions, Timing			
transition sound	Transitions, Timing			
Zoom dialog box	View, Zoom			

PowerPoint

SECTION 2

Editing and Enhancing Slides

Data Files

Before beginning section work, copy the PowerPointS2 folder to your storage medium and then make PowerPointS2 the active folder.

Skills

- Increase and decrease the indent of text
- Select, cut, copy, and paste text
- Apply font and font effects
- Find and replace fonts
- Apply formatting with Format Painter
- Change alignment and line and paragraph spacing
- Change the slide size and format design themes and slide background
- Insert, size, position, and format images
- Insert and format a screen clipping
- Insert and format a SmartArt graphic
- Apply animation to objects and text in a slide

Projects Overview

Marquee Productions — Open an existing project presentation, save the presentation with a new name, and then edit and format the presentation. Open an existing annual meeting presentation for Marquee Productions and then save, edit, and format the presentation.

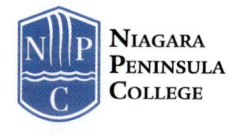

Niagara Peninsula College — Open an existing presentation for the Theatre Arts Division and then save, edit, and format the presentation.

First Choice Travel — Open an existing presentation on vacation specials and then save, edit, and format the presentation.

The Waterfront Bistro — Prepare and format a presentation on the services offered by The Waterfront Bistro.

Performance Threads — Prepare and format a presentation on company structure, policies, and benefits.

Worldwide Enterprises — Prepare and format a presentation for a planning meeting of the distribution department.

The online course includes additional training and assessment resources.

31

Activity 2.1 Increasing and Decreasing Indent; Cutting, Copying, and Pasting Text

Text that is formatted as a bulleted list in a slide can have multiple levels. Click the Decrease List Level button in the Paragraph group on the Home tab or press Shift + Tab to promote text to the previous level. Click the Increase List Level button or press the Tab key to demote text to the next level. Text levels can also be promoted (decrease the text indent) and/or text levels can be demoted (increase the text indent) in the slide in Outline view. Select text in a slide and then delete the text from the slide, cut text from one location and paste it into another, or copy and paste the text. Use buttons in the Clipboard group on the Home tab to cut, copy, and paste text.

What You Will Do   Chris Greenbaum, production manager for Marquee Productions, has prepared a documentary project presentation and has asked you to edit the presentation by increasing and decreasing text levels and selecting, deleting, moving, copying, and pasting text in slides.

Tutorial
Increasing and Decreasing Indent

Tutorial
Selecting Text

Tutorial
Cutting, Copying, and Pasting Text

1. Open **MPProj** from your PowerPointS2 folder and then save the presentation with the name **2-MPProj**.

2. Display Slide 5 in the slide pane.

3. You decide to promote the names below *Script Authors* so that they display as second-level bullets. To do this, position the mouse pointer immediately left of the *D* in *Dana*, click the left mouse button, and then click the Decrease List Level button in the Paragraph group on the Home tab.

    Clicking the Decrease List Level button will promote text to the previous tab position, while clicking the Increase List Level button will demote text to the next tab position.

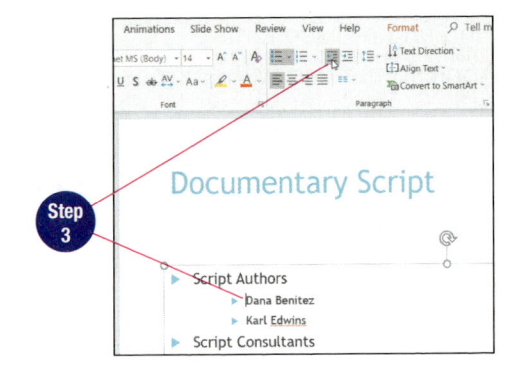

4. Position the insertion point immediately left of the *K* in *Karl* in Slide 5 and then promote the text to the previous level by pressing Shift + Tab.

5. Demote two of the names below *Script Consultants*. Begin by clicking immediately left of the *J* in *Jaime* and then clicking the Increase List Level button in the Paragraph group on the Home tab.

6. Position the insertion point immediately left of the *G* in *Genaro* and then press the Tab key.

7. Display Slide 6 in the slide pane.

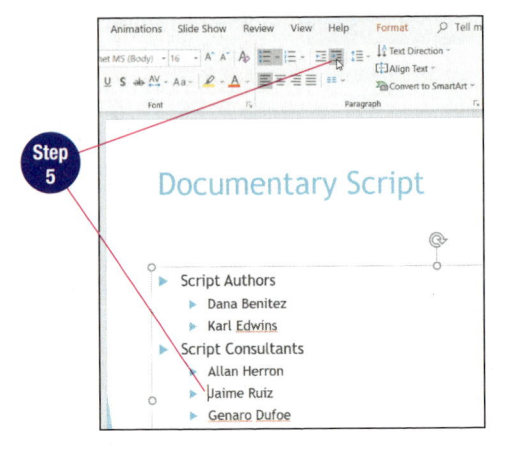

32   POWERPOINT   Section 2   Editing and Enhancing Slides

In Brief

Decrease Text Level Indent
Click Decrease List Level button or press Shift + Tab.

Increase Text Level Indent
Click Increase List Level button or press Tab.

Cut and Paste Text
1. Select text.
2. Click Cut button.
3. Position insertion point.
4. Click Paste button.

Copy and Paste Text
1. Select text.
2. Click Copy button.
3. Position insertion point.
4. Click Paste button.

---

8. Position the mouse pointer on the bullet before *Script Rewriting* until the mouse pointer turns into a four-headed arrow and then click the left mouse button.

    This selects the text *Script Rewriting* and displays the Mini toolbar, which provides easy access to formatting options and buttons. Refer to the In Addition for additional information on selecting text.

9. Press the Delete key.

    This deletes the selected text.

10. Display Slide 5 in the slide pane.

11. Position the mouse pointer on the bullet before *Genaro Dufoe* until the mouse pointer turns into a four-headed arrow and then click the left mouse button.

12. Click the Cut button in the Clipboard group on the Home tab.

    The keyboard shortcut to cut text is Ctrl + X.

13. Position the mouse pointer immediately left of the *A* in *Allan Herron*, click the left mouse button, and then click the Paste button in the Clipboard group.

    The keyboard shortcut to paste text is Ctrl + V.

14. Using the mouse, drag to select the text *Script Authors* and then click the Copy button in the Clipboard group.

    The keyboard shortcut to copy text is Ctrl + C.

15. Make Slide 2 active, position the insertion point immediately left of the *S* in *Scouting*, and then click the Paste button in the Clipboard group.

    If *Script Authors* and *Scouting* display on the same line, press the Enter key.

16. Save **2-MPProj**.

    Check Your Work Compare your work to the model answer available in the online course.

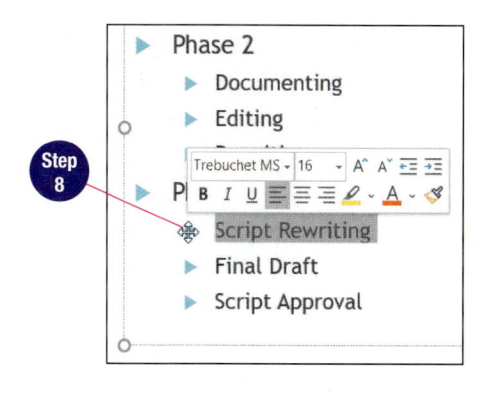

In Addition

Selecting Text

To select	Perform this action
entire word	Double-click word.
entire paragraph	Triple-click in paragraph.
text mouse pointer passes through	Click and drag with mouse.
all text in selected object box	Click Select button in Editing group and then click Select All; or press Ctrl + A.

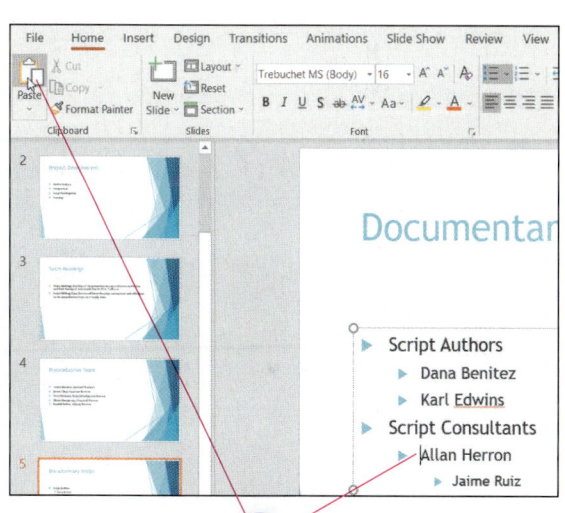

Activity 2.1 **POWERPOINT** 33

Activity 2.2 Applying Font Formatting and Font Effects

The Font group on the Home tab contains two rows of options and buttons. The top row contains options and buttons for changing the font and font size and a button for clearing formatting. The bottom row contains buttons for applying font effects such as bold, italics, underlining, text shadow, strikethrough, and character spacing, as well as buttons for changing the case and/or font color of selected text.

What You Will Do Certain text elements on slides in the documentary project presentation need to be highlighted to make them stand out. You decide to apply font effects to and change the font size of specific text.

Tutorial
Applying Font Formatting

1. With **2-MPProj** open, display Slide 1 in the slide pane.

2. Select the title *Marquee Productions* and then click the Italic button I in the Font group on the Home tab.

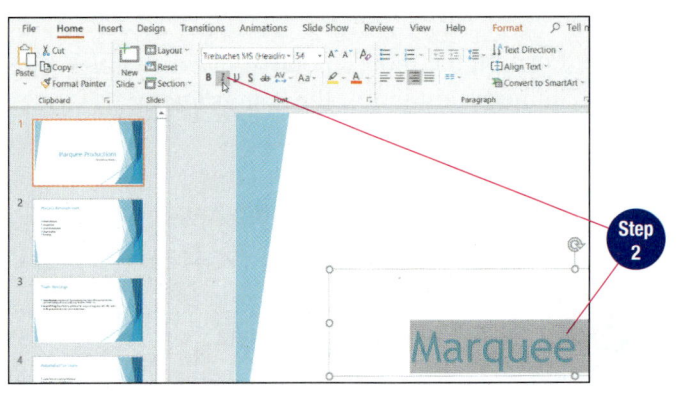

3. Select the subtitle *Documentary Project*, click the Increase Font Size button $A^˄$, and then click the Bold button B in the Font group.

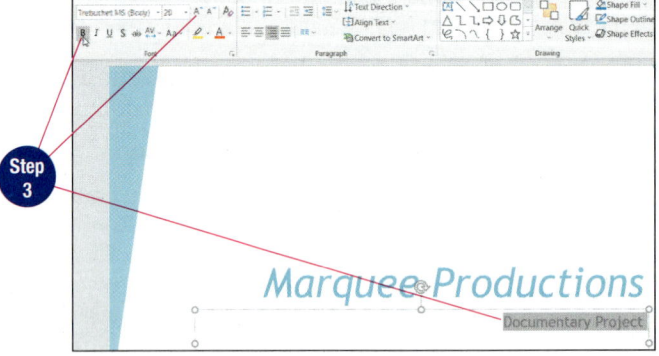

4. Make Slide 6 active in the slide pane, select the text *Phase 1*, and then click the Underline button U in the Font group.

5. Select and then underline the text *Phase 2*.

6. Select and then underline the text *Phase 3*.

7. Make Slide 1 active.

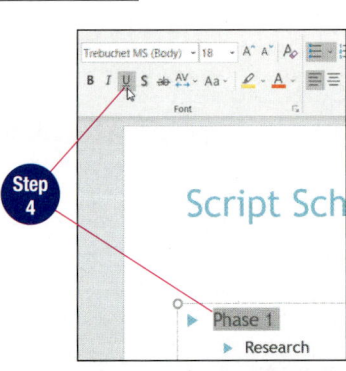

34 POWERPOINT Section 2 Editing and Enhancing Slides

In Brief

Apply Font Effects with Font Group
1. Select text.
2. Click appropriate button in Font group.

8. Select the title *Marquee Productions*, click the *Font* option box arrow in the Font group, scroll down the drop-down gallery (fonts display in alphabetical order), and then click *Cambria*.

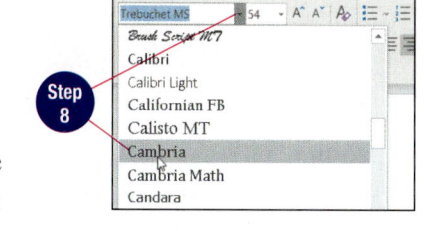

9. Select the subtitle *Documentary Project*, click the *Font* option box arrow, and then click *Cambria* at the drop-down gallery.

   The drop-down gallery displays the most recently used fonts at the top of the gallery.

10. Make Slide 6 active, select the text *Phase 1*, click the Underline button to remove underlining, and then click the Bold button to apply bold formatting.

11. With *Phase 1* still selected, click *Trebuchet MS* in the *Font* option box, type cam, and then press the Enter key.

    An alternative method for selecting a font is to type the first few letters of the font name in the *Font* option box until the entire font name displays and then press the Enter key.

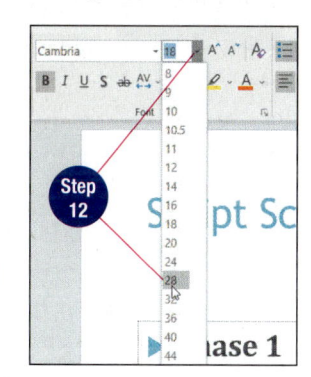

12. Click the *Font Size* option box arrow and then click *28*.

13. Select the text *Phase 2*, remove the underlining, apply bold formatting, change the font to Cambria, and then change the font size to 28 points.

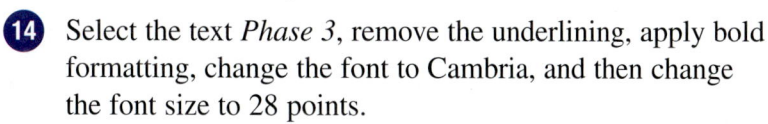

14. Select the text *Phase 3*, remove the underlining, apply bold formatting, change the font to Cambria, and then change the font size to 28 points.

15. Print Slides 1 and 6. Begin by clicking the File tab and then clicking the *Print* option.

16. At the Print backstage area, click in the *Slides* text box (below the first gallery in the *Settings* category) and then type 1,6.

17. Click the second gallery in the *Settings* category (contains the text *Full Page Slides*) and then click *2 Slides* in the *Handouts* section of the drop-down list.

18. Click the Print button.

    The two slides print on the same page.

19. Save **2-MPProj**.

Check Your Work Compare your work to the model answer available in the online course.

In Addition

Choosing Fonts

A typeface is a set of characters with a common design and shape. PowerPoint refers to a typeface as a *font*. Fonts can be decorative or plain and are either monospaced or proportional. A monospaced font allots the same amount of horizontal space for each character, while a proportional font allots a different amount of space for each character. Fonts are divided into two main categories: serif and sans serif. A serif is a small line at the end of a character stroke. Consider using a serif font for text-intensive slides, because the serifs can help move the reader's eyes across the text. Use a sans serif font for titles, subtitles, headings, and short lines of text.

Activity 2.2 **POWERPOINT** 35

Activity 2.3   Applying Font Formatting at the Font Dialog Box; Replacing Fonts

In addition to options and buttons in the Font group on the Home tab, font formatting can be applied with options at the Font dialog box. Use options at this dialog box to change the font, as well as its style and size; change the font color; and apply formatting effects such as underline, strikethrough, superscript, subscript, small caps, and all caps. To change the font for all slides in a presentation, use the Replace Font dialog box to replace all occurrences of a specific font in the presentation.

What You Will Do   You are still not satisfied with the fonts in the documentary project presentation, so you decide to change the font for the title and subtitle and replace the Trebuchet MS font on the remaining slides.

Tutorial
Applying Font Formatting at the Font Dialog Box

Tutorial
Replacing Fonts

1. With **2-MPProj** open, make Slide 1 active.

2. Select the title *Marquee Productions*.

3. Display the Font dialog box by clicking the Font group dialog box launcher on the Home tab.

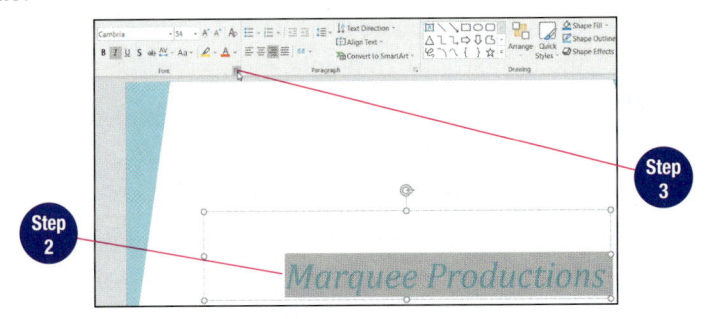

4. At the Font dialog box, click the *Latin text font* option box arrow and then click *Candara* at the drop-down list.

5. Select the current measurement in the *Size* measurement box and then type 60.

6. Click the Font color button in the *All text* section and then click the *Blue, Accent 2, Darker 25%* option (sixth column, fifth row in the *Theme Colors* section).

7. Click OK to close the Font dialog box.

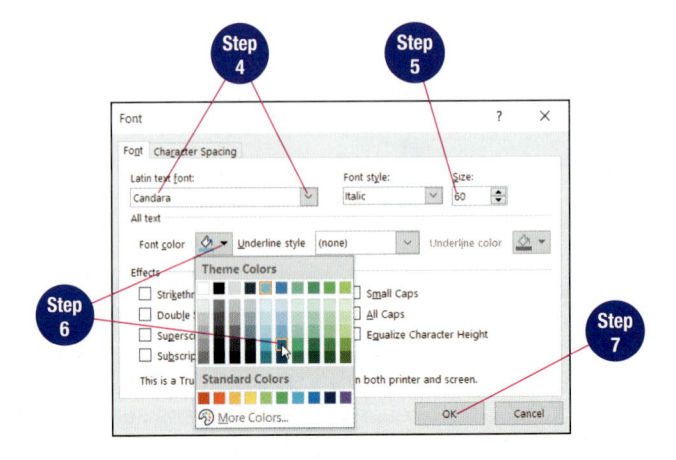

36   POWERPOINT   Section 2   Editing and Enhancing Slides

In Brief

Change Font at Font Dialog Box
1. Select text.
2. Click Font group dialog box launcher.
3. Click options at Font dialog box.
4. Click OK.

Change All Occurrences of Font
1. Click Replace button arrow.
2. Click *Replace Fonts*.
3. Make sure appropriate font displays in *Replace* text box.
4. Press Tab.
5. Click *With* option box arrow.
6. Click new font.
7. Click Replace button.
8. Click Close button.

8. Select the subtitle *Documentary Project*.

9. Click the Font group dialog box launcher.

10. At the Font dialog box, click the *Latin text font* option box arrow and then click *Candara* at the drop-down list.

11. Click the *Font style* option box arrow and then click *Bold Italic* at the drop-down list.

12. Select the current measurement in the *Size* measurement box and then type 30.

13. Click the Font color button in the *All text* section and then click the *Turquoise, Accent 1* color option (fifth column, first row in the *Theme Colors* section).

14. Click OK to close the Font dialog box.

15. Make Slide 2 active.

16. You decide to replace all occurrences of the Trebuchet MS font in the presentation with the Cambria font. To begin, click the Replace button arrow in the Editing group on the Home tab and then click *Replace Fonts* at the drop-down list.

17. At the Replace Font dialog box, click the *Replace* option box arrow and then click *Trebuchet MS* at the drop-down list.

18. Click the *With* option box arrow, scroll down the drop-down list and then click *Cambria*.

19. Click the Replace button and then click the Close button.

20. Save **2-MPProj**.

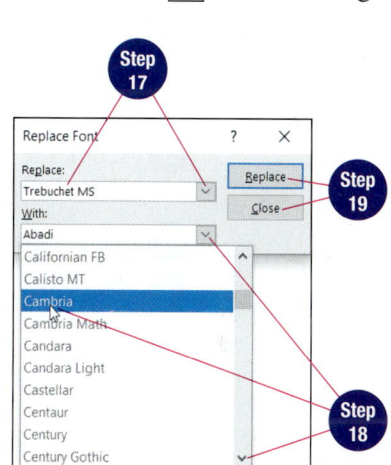

Check Your Work Compare your work to the model answer available in the online course.

In Addition

Choosing Fonts

Choose a font for a presentation based on the tone and message the presentation should convey. For example, choose a more serious font such as Constantia or Cambria for a conservative audience and choose a less formal font such as Comic Sans MS, Lucida Handwriting, or Mistral for a more informal or lighthearted audience. For text-intensive slides, choose a serif font such as Cambria, Constantia, Garamond, or Bookman Old Style. For titles, subtitles, headings, and short text items, consider a sans serif font such as Calibri, Candara, Arial, or Trebuchet MS. Use no more than two or three different fonts in each presentation. To ensure text readability in a slide, choose a font color that contrasts with the slide background.

Activity 2.3 **POWERPOINT** 37

Activity 2.4 Formatting with Format Painter

Use the Format Painter feature to apply the same formatting in more than one location in a slide or slides. To use Format Painter, apply formatting to text, position the insertion point anywhere in the formatted text, and then double-click the Format Painter button in the Clipboard group on the Home tab. Using the mouse, select the additional text to which the formatting is to be applied. After applying the formatting in the specific locations, click the Format Painter button to deactivate it. If formatting is to be applied in only one other location, click the Format Painter button just once. The first time text is clicked or text is selected, the formatting will be applied and the Format Painter button will be deactivated.

MARQUEE PRODUCTIONS

What You Will Do   Improve the appearance of slides in the documentary project presentation by applying a font and then using Format Painter to apply the formatting to other text.

Tutorial
Formatting with Format Painter

1. With **2-MPProj** open, make sure Slide 2 is active.
2. Select the title *Project Development*.
3. Click the Font group dialog box launcher.
4. At the Font dialog box, click in the *Latin text font* option box, type can, and then press the Tab key.

    As you type letters, fonts that match the letters display in the option box.

5. Click the *Font style* option box arrow and then click *Bold Italic* at the drop-down list.
6. Select the current measurement in the *Size* measurement box and then type 40.
7. Click the Font color button in the *All text* section and then click the *Blue, Accent 2, Darker 25%* color option (sixth column, fifth row in the *Theme Colors* section).
8. Click OK to close the Font dialog box.

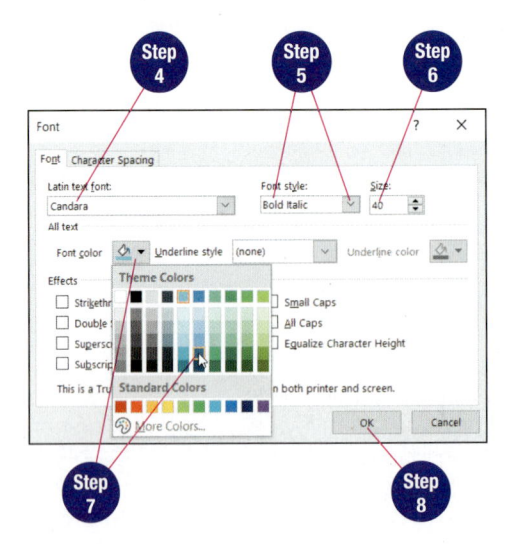

9. Deselect the text by clicking in the slide in the slide pane.

38   POWERPOINT   Section 2   Editing and Enhancing Slides

In Brief

Format with Format Painter
1. Click in formatted text.
2. Double-click Format Painter button.
3. Click in or select text to be formatted.
4. Click Format Painter button.

10 Click in the title *Project Development*.

11 Double-click the Format Painter button in the Clipboard group on the Home tab.

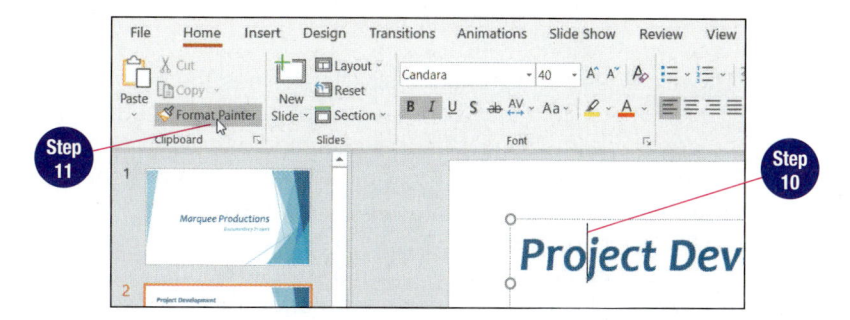

12 Click the Next Slide button to display Slide 3.

13 Triple-click *Team Meetings* to select the title.

> The mouse pointer displays with a paintbrush attached. This indicates that Format Painter is active. You can also apply the formatting by clicking individual words in the title, but doing so will not format the spaces within titles that consist of more than one word. If the paintbrush is no longer attached to the mouse pointer, Format Painter has been turned off. Turn it back on by clicking in a slide title with the desired formatting and then double-clicking the Format Painter button.

14 Click the Next Slide button to display Slide 4.

15 Using the mouse, select the title *Preproduction Team*.

16 Apply formatting to the titles in the remaining three slides.

17 When formatting has been applied to all slide titles, click the Format Painter button in the Clipboard group on the Home tab.

> Clicking the Format Painter button turns off the feature.

18 Save **2-MPProj**.

Check Your Work Compare your work to the model answer available in the online course.

In Addition

Choosing a Custom Color

Click the Font color button at the Font dialog box and a palette of color choices displays. Click the *More Colors* option and the Colors dialog box displays with the Standard tab selected, showing a honeycomb of color options. Click the Custom tab and the dialog box displays as shown at the right. Use options on this tab to mix your own color. Click a color in the *Colors* palette or enter the values for the color in the *Red*, *Green*, and *Blue* measurement boxes. Adjust the luminosity of the current color by dragging the slider at the right side of the color palette.

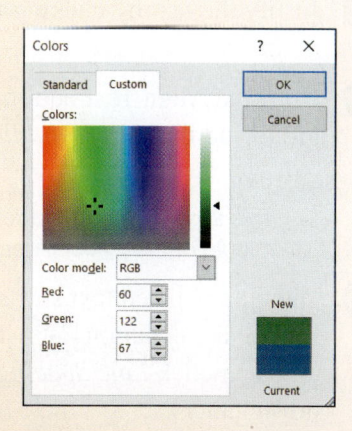

Activity 2.4 **POWERPOINT** 39

Activity 2.5 Changing Alignment and Line and Paragraph Spacing

The slide design theme generally determines the horizontal and vertical alignment of text in placeholders. Text may be left-aligned, center-aligned, right-aligned, or justified in a placeholder as well as aligned at the top, middle, or bottom of the placeholder. Change alignment for specific text with buttons in the Paragraph group on the Home tab or with options from the Align Text button drop-down gallery. Use options at the Line Spacing button drop-down gallery or the *Line Spacing* option at the Paragraph dialog box to change line spacing. The Paragraph dialog box also contains options for changing text alignment and indentation as well as spacing before and after text.

What You Will Do Change the alignment and improve the appearance of specific text in slides by adjusting the vertical alignment and paragraph spacing of text.

Tutorial
Changing Alignment

Tutorial
Changing Line Spacing

Tutorial
Changing Paragraph Spacing

1. With **2-MPProj** open, make Slide 1 active.

2. Click in the text *Marquee Productions* and then click the Center button in the Paragraph group on the Home tab.

   You can also change text alignment with the keyboard shortcuts shown in Table 2.1.

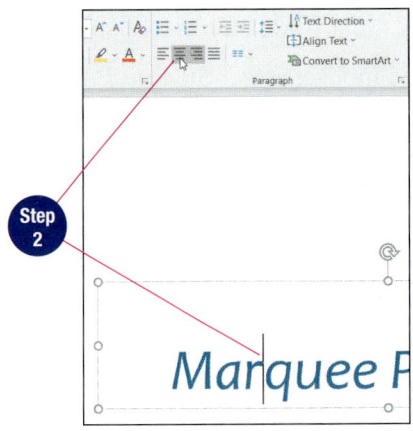

3. Click in the text *Documentary Project* and then click the Center button.

4. Make Slide 3 active (contains the title *Team Meetings*), click in the bulleted text, and then press Ctrl + A to select all of the bulleted text.

   Ctrl + A is the keyboard shortcut for selecting all text in a placeholder.

5. Justify the text by clicking the Justify button in the Paragraph group.

6. Click the Align Text button in the Paragraph group and then click *Middle* at the drop-down gallery.

   This aligns the bulleted text vertically in the middle of the placeholder.

7. With the bulleted text still selected, click the Line Spacing button in the Paragraph group and then click *Line Spacing Options* at the drop-down gallery.

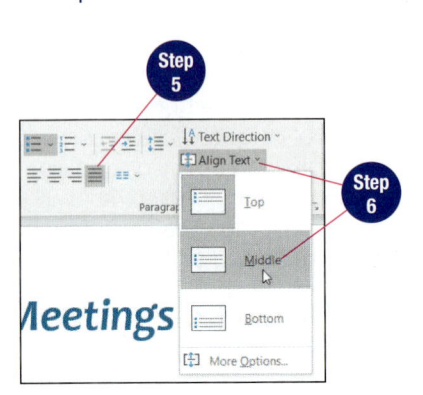

40 POWERPOINT Section 2 Editing and Enhancing Slides

In Brief

Change Horizontal Text Alignment
1. Select text or click in paragraph.
2. Click alignment button in Paragraph group.

Change Vertical Text Alignment
1. Click Align Text button.
2. Click alignment.

Change Line Spacing
1. Click Line Spacing button.
2. Click spacing.
OR
1. Click Line Spacing button.
2. Click *Line Spacing Options*.
3. At Paragraph dialog box, specify spacing.
4. Click OK.

8. At the Paragraph dialog box, click the *After* measurement box up arrow two times.

   This inserts *12 pt* in the *After* measurement box.

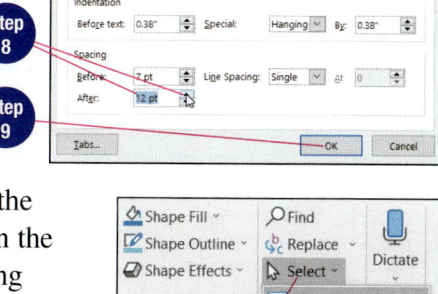

9. Click OK to close the dialog box.

10. Make Slide 4 active (contains the title *Preproduction Team*).

11. Click in the bulleted text and then select all of the bulleted text by clicking the Select button in the Editing group on the Home tab and then clicking *Select All* at the drop-down list.

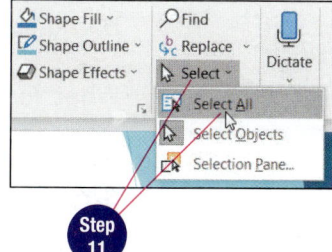

12. Click the Line Spacing button in the Paragraph group and then click *1.5* at the drop-down gallery.

13. Make Slide 7 active (contains the title *Preproduction Assignments*).

14. Click in the bulleted text and then press Ctrl + A.

15. Click the Line Spacing button in the Paragraph group and then click *Line Spacing Options* at the drop-down gallery.

16. At the Paragraph dialog box, click the *After* measurement box up arrow two times.

    This inserts *12 pt* in the *After* measurement box.

17. Click OK to close the dialog box.

18. Print only Slide 1 of the presentation as a handout.

19. Save **2-MPProj**.

Table 2.1 Alignment Keyboard Shortcuts

Alignment	Keyboard Shortcut
left	Ctrl + L
center	Ctrl + E
right	Ctrl + R
justify	Ctrl + J

Check Your Work Compare your work to the model answer available in the online course.

In Addition

Inserting a New Line

When creating bulleted text in a slide, pressing the Enter key causes the insertion point to move to the next line, inserting another bullet. Situations may occur where a blank line should be inserted between bulleted items without creating another bullet. One method for doing this is to use the New Line command, Shift + Enter. Pressing Shift + Enter inserts a new line that is considered part of the previous paragraph. Press the Enter key to continue the bulleted list.

Activity 2.5 **POWERPOINT**

Activity 2.6 Changing Slide Size and Design Themes; Formatting Slide Background

By default, the slide size in PowerPoint is Widescreen (16:9), but slide size can be changed with options in the Slide Size button drop-down list in the Customize group on the Design tab. Change the design theme applied to slides in a presentation or change the color, font, or effects of a theme with options on the Design tab. Format the slide background with options in the Format Background task pane. Display this task pane by clicking the Format Background button in the Customize group on the Design tab.

What You Will Do   You are not pleased with the design theme for the documentary project presentation and decide to apply a different theme and then change the colors and fonts for the theme.

Tutorial
Changing Slide Size

Tutorial
Modifying Design Themes

Tutorial
Formatting the Slide Background

1. With **2-MPProj** open, click the Design tab.

2. Click the Slide Size button in the Customize group and then click *Standard (4:3)* at the drop-down list.

3. At the Microsoft PowerPoint dialog box, click the Maximize button.

   Click the Maximize button to maximize the size of the content on the new slide. Click the Ensure Fit button to scale down the contents of the slide to fit on the new slide.

4. Run the slide show beginning with Slide 1 and notice any changes to the layout of the slides.

5. Click the Slide Size button and then click *Custom Slide Size* at the drop-down list.

6. At the Slide Size dialog box, click the *Slides sized for* option box arrow and then click *Widescreen* at the drop-down list.

7. Click OK.

8. Click the More Themes button in the Themes group.

9. Click *Dividend* at the drop-down gallery.

10. Click the More Variants button in the Variants group.

11. Point to *Colors* and then click *Yellow Orange* at the side menu.

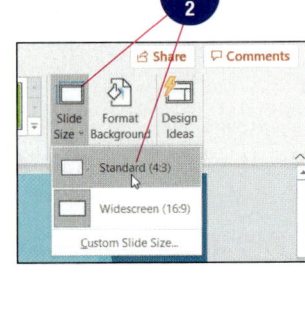

42   **POWERPOINT**   Section 2   Editing and Enhancing Slides

In Brief

Change Slide Size
1. Click Design tab.
2. Click Slide Size button.
3. Click slide size.

Change Design Theme
1. Click Design tab.
2. Click More Themes button.
3. Click theme.

Change Theme Colors
1. Click Design tab.
2. Click More Variants button.
3. Point to *Colors*.
4. Click option.

Change Theme Fonts
1. Click Design tab.
2. Click More Variants button.
3. Point to *Fonts*.
4. Click option.

Format Slide Background
1. Click Design tab.
2. Click Format Background button.
3. Make changes in task pane.

12. Make Slide 2 active.

13. Click the More Variants button in the Variants group.

14. Point to *Fonts*, scroll down the side menu, and then click *Cambria*.

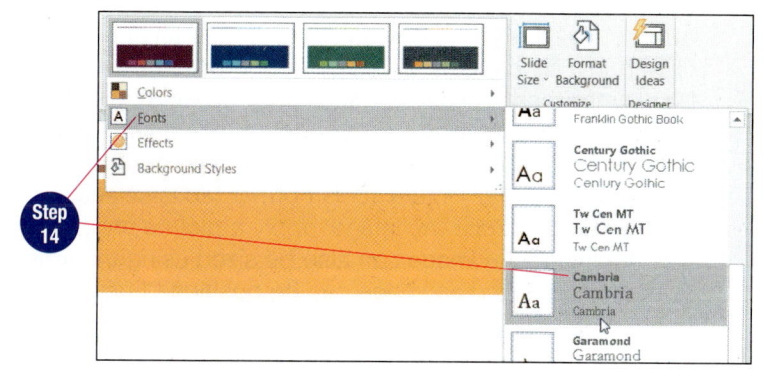

15. Apply a background style by clicking the More Variants button in the Variants group, pointing to *Background Styles*, and then clicking *Style 9* at the side menu (first column, third row).

16. Run the slide show beginning with Slide 1.

17. Customize the background by clicking the Format Background button in the Customize group on the Design tab.

    This displays the Format Background task pane with a number of options for customizing slide backgrounds.

18. At the Format Background task pane, if necessary, click *Fill* to display fill options.

19. Click the *Solid fill* option, click the Color button, and then click the *Light Yellow, Background 2* color option (third column, first row in the *Theme Colors* section).

20. Click the Apply to All button at the bottom of the task pane.

21. Close the task pane by clicking the close button in the upper right corner.

22. Save **2-MPProj** and then print Slide 1 of the presentation.

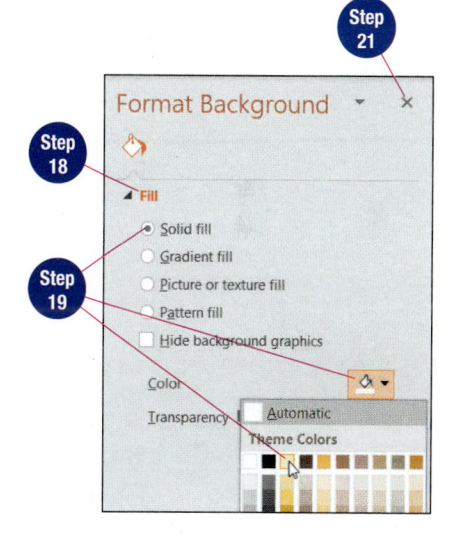

Check Your Work Compare your work to the model answer available in the online course.

In Addition

Inserting an Image as a Slide Background

Insert an image as the background of an entire slide by clicking the Design tab and then clicking the Format Background button in the Customize group. At the Format Background task pane, click *Fill* to display fill options, and then click the *Picture or texture fill* option. Click the File button in the *Insert picture from* section, navigate to the folder containing the image, and then double-click the image. The image will automatically be inserted as the current slide's background.

Activity 2.6 **POWERPOINT** 43

Activity 2.7 Inserting, Sizing, Positioning, and Formatting an Image

Add visual interest to a presentation by inserting an image such as a logo, picture, or clip art in a slide. Insert an image from a drive or folder with the Insert Picture dialog box. Display the Insert Picture dialog box by clicking the Pictures button on the Insert tab or clicking the picture image in the content placeholder. At this dialog box, navigate to the drive or folder containing the image and then double-click the image. The image is inserted in the slide and the Picture Tools Format tab is selected. Use buttons on the Picture Tools Format tab to recolor the image, apply a picture style, arrange the image in the slide, and size the image. An image can also be sized using the sizing handles that display around the selected image and an image can be positioned using the mouse.

What You Will Do   Chris Greenbaum has asked you to insert the company logo on the first slide of the presentation and insert and format an image on a new slide at the end of the presentation.

Tutorial
Inserting, Sizing, and Positioning an Image

Tutorial
Formatting an Image

1. With **2-MPProj** open, make sure Slide 1 is active.

2. Click in the title *Marquee Productions*, click the title placeholder border (border turns into a solid line when selected), and then press the Delete key.

   The title text will be deleted but the placeholder will not.

3. Delete the title placeholder by clicking the title placeholder border again and then pressing the Delete key.

4. Complete steps similar to those in Steps 2 and 3 to delete the subtitle text and placeholder.

5. Insert the company logo in the slide as shown in Figure 2.1. To begin, click the Insert tab and then click the Pictures button in the Images group.

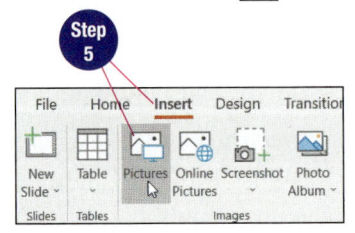

6. At the Insert Picture dialog box, navigate to your PowerPointS2 folder and then double-click the **MPLogo** image file.

   The image is inserted in the slide, selection handles display around the image, and the Picture Tools Format tab is active. If the Design Ideas task pane displays at the right side of the screen, close the task pane by clicking the Close button in the upper right corner of the task pane.

7. Increase the size of the logo by clicking in the *Width* measurement box in the Size group, typing 6.5, and then pressing the Enter key.

   When you change the width of the logo, the height automatically adjusts to maintain the proportions of the logo. You can also size an image using the sizing handles that display around the selected image. Use the middle sizing handles to change the width of an image. Use the top and bottom handles to change the height, and use the corner sizing handles to adjust both the width and height of the image at the same time.

44   **POWERPOINT**   Section 2   Editing and Enhancing Slides

8. Move the logo so it is positioned as shown in Figure 2.1. To do this, position the mouse pointer on the image until the pointer displays with a four-headed arrow attached, click and hold down the left mouse button, drag the image to the position shown in the figure, and then release the mouse button.

9. With the image selected, click the Color button in the Adjust group and then click the *Saturation 200%* option (fifth option in the *Color Saturation* section).

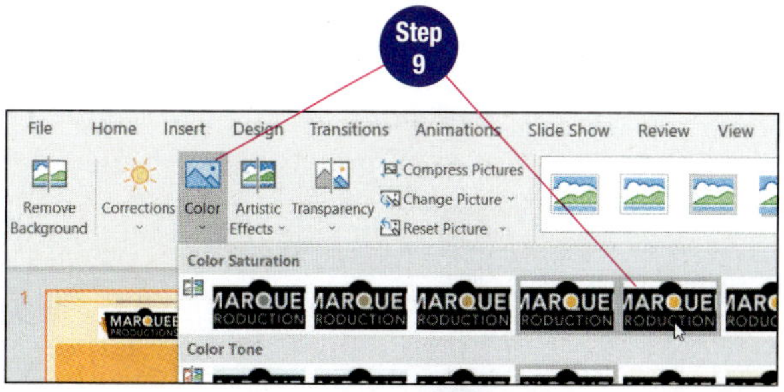

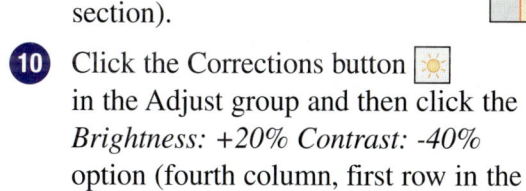

10. Click the Corrections button in the Adjust group and then click the *Brightness: +20% Contrast: -40%* option (fourth column, first row in the *Brightness/Contrast* section).

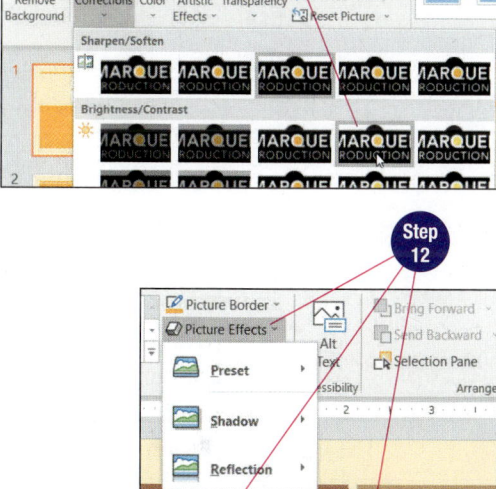

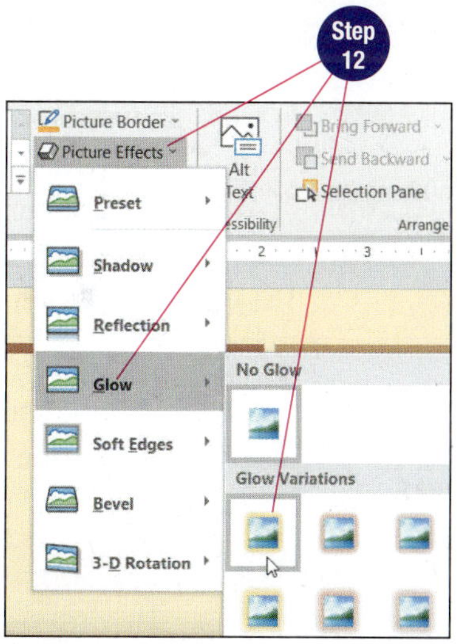

11. Click the *Drop Shadow Rectangle* option in the Picture Styles gallery (fourth option).

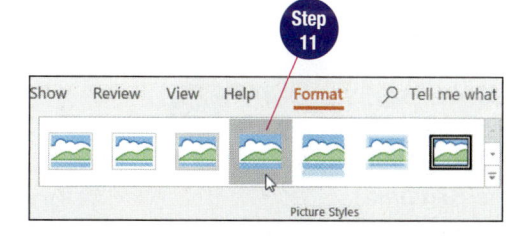

12. Click the Picture Effects button in the Picture Styles group, point to *Glow*, and then click the *Glow: 5 point; Orange, Accent color 1* option (first column, first row in the *Glow Variations* section).

13. Click outside the logo to deselect it.

Figure 2.1 Slide 1

Activity 2.7 **POWERPOINT** 45

14. Make Slide 7 active.

15. Insert a new slide by clicking the New Slide button in the Slides group on the Home tab.

16. Click in the *Click to add title* placeholder and then type Travel Arrangements.

17. Click in the *Click to add text* placeholder and then type the bulleted text shown in Figure 2.2.

18. Click the Insert tab and then click the Pictures button in the Images group.

19. At the Insert Picture dialog box, navigate to your PowerPointS2 folder and then double-click the **Airport** image file.

20. Click in the *Height* measurement box in the Size group on the Picture Tools Format tab, type 3.5, and then press the Enter key.

    When you change the height measurement, the width measurement changes automatically to maintain the proportions of the image.

21. Using the mouse, drag the image so it is positioned as shown in Figure 2.2.

22. Click the Color button in the Adjust group on the Picture Tools Format tab and then click the *Brown, Accent color 2 Light* option (third column, third row in the *Recolor* section).

23. Click the Corrections button in the Adjust group and then click the *Brightness: 0% (Normal) Contrast: +40%* option (third column, fifth row in the *Brightness/Contrast* section).

24. Click the Picture Effects button in the Picture Styles group, point to *Shadow*, and then click the *Offset: Top Right* option (first column, third row in the *Outer* section).

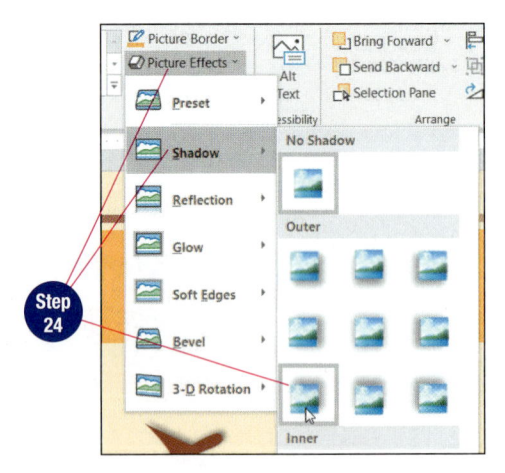

46 **POWERPOINT**   Section 2   Editing and Enhancing Slides

In Brief

Insert Image
1. Click Insert tab.
2. Click Pictures button.
3. At Insert Picture dialog box, navigate to folder.
4. Double-click image file.

㉕ Click the Rotate button in the Arrange group and then click *Flip Horizontal* at the drop-down gallery.

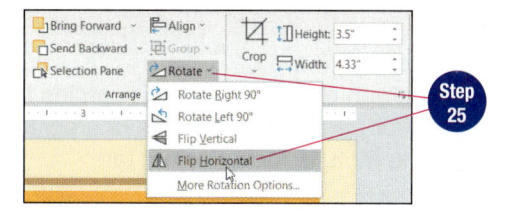

㉖ Make Slide 7 active and then click the Home tab.

㉗ Click in the title *PREPRODUCTION ASSIGNMENTS* and then click the Format Painter button in the Clipboard group.

㉘ Make Slide 8 active and then select the entire title *TRAVEL ARRANGEMENTS*.

This applies 40-point Candara bold italic formatting in a brown accent color.

㉙ Save **2-MPProj**.

Figure 2.2 Slide 8

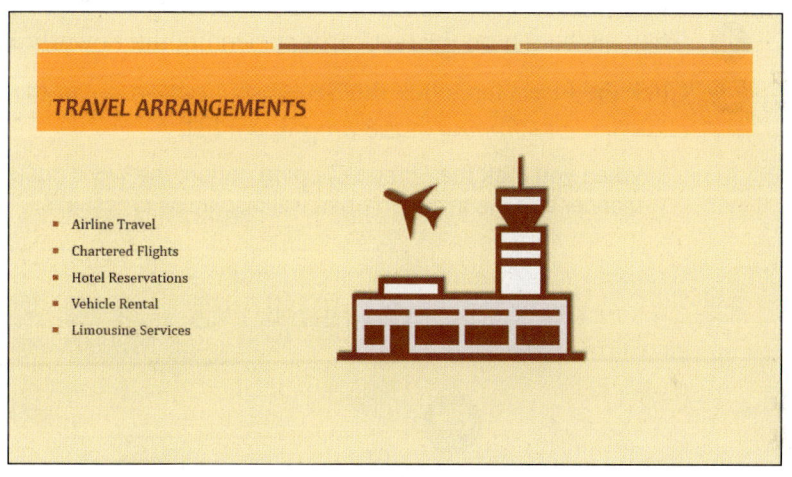

Check Your Work Compare your work to the model answer available in the online course.

In Addition

Formatting with Buttons and Options on the Picture Tools Format Tab

Format images in a slide with buttons and options on the Picture Tools Format tab. Use buttons in the Adjust group to adjust the brightness and contrast of the image; change the image color or change to a different image; reset the image to its original size, position, and color; and compress the image. (Compress an image to reduce the resolution or discard extra information to save room on a hard drive or to reduce download time.) Use buttons in the Picture Styles group to apply a pre-designed style, insert a picture border, or apply a picture effect. The Arrange group contains buttons for positioning the image and aligning and rotating the image. Use options in the Size group to crop the image and specify the height and width of the image.

Inserting an Online Image

Click the Online Pictures button on the Insert tab and the Online Pictures window displays. Use options in this window to search for images using Bing. At the window, click a category or type a category in the search text box and then press the Enter key. In the list of images, double-click the desired image. The image is inserted in the slide and the Picture Tools Format tab is active.

Activity 2.7 **POWERPOINT** 47

Activity 2.8 — Inserting and Formatting a Screen Clipping

The Images group on the Insert tab contains the Screenshot button, which can be used to capture all or part of the contents of a screen as an image. Format a screenshot with options on the Picture Tools Format tab.

What You Will Do Chris Greenbaum has asked you to include a screen clipping of the title page of a script document in a slide.

Tutorial
Inserting and Formatting Screenshot and Screen Clipping Images

1. With **2-MPProj** open, make Slide 6 active.

2. Insert a screenshot image from a Word document into the slide. Begin by opening Word and then opening **MPScript** from your PowerPointS2 folder.

   Make sure 2-MPProj and MPScript are the only open files.

3. Click the Zoom Out button at the left of the Zoom slider bar until *50%* displays at the right of the slider bar.

4. Click the button on the taskbar representing the PowerPoint presentation **2-MPProj**.

5. Click the Insert tab, click the Screenshot button in the Images group, and then click *Screen Clipping* at the drop-down list.

   When you click the *Screen Clipping* option, the Word document will display in a dimmed manner and the insertion point will display as crosshairs.

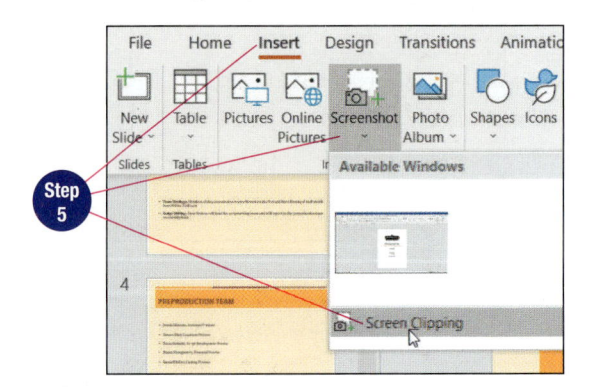

6. With the Word document displayed in a dimmed manner, position the crosshairs in the top left corner of the Word document and then drag down and to the right to select the entire document.

   Once you have created a screenshot of the Word document, the image will be inserted into Slide 6 of 2-MPProj.

7. With the screenshot selected, click in the *Shape Height* measurement box in the Size group on the Picture Tools Format tab, type *5*, and then press the Enter key.

48 POWERPOINT Section 2 Editing and Enhancing Slides

In Brief

Insert Screenshot
1. Click Insert tab.
2. Click Screenshot button.
3. Click *Screen Clipping*.
4. Select image or text.

⑧ Click the Picture Border button arrow in the Picture Styles group and then click the *Orange, Accent 1* option at the drop-down list (fifth column, first row in the *Theme Colors* section).

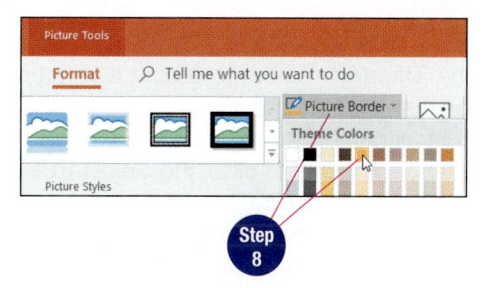

Step 8

⑨ Position the screenshot in the slide as shown in Figure 2.3.

⑩ Click the Word button on the taskbar, close the document, and then close Word.

If a message displays asking if you want to save changes made in the document, click the Don't Save button.

⑪ Save **2-MPProj**.

Figure 2.3 Slide 6

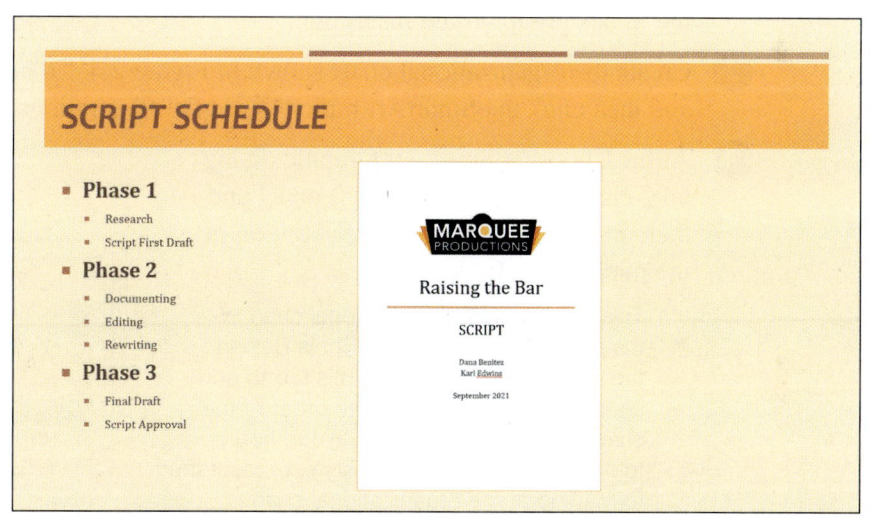

Check Your Work Compare your work to the model answer available in the online course.

In Addition

Inserting a Screenshot

To capture the entire screen, open a file, click the Insert tab, click the Screenshot button in the Images group, and then click the screen thumbnail at the drop-down list. The currently active file does not display as a thumbnail at the drop-down list—only any other files that are open.

Activity 2.8   **POWERPOINT**   49

Activity 2.9 Inserting and Formatting SmartArt

Use the SmartArt feature to create a variety of graphic diagrams, including process, cycle, relationship, matrix, and pyramid diagrams. SmartArt can also be used to visually illustrate hierarchical data in an organizational chart. To display a menu of SmartArt choices, click the Insert tab and then click the SmartArt button in the Illustrations group. This displays the Choose a SmartArt Graphic dialog box. At this dialog box, click the type of organization chart or graphic in the left panel and then double-click the graphic in the middle panel. This inserts the organizational chart or graphic in the slide. Some SmartArt graphics are designed to include text. Type text in a graphic shape by selecting the shape and then typing text in the shape. Use buttons on the SmartArt Tools Design tab and the SmartArt Tools Format tab to customize a graphic.

What You Will Do Chris Greenbaum has asked you to create a slide containing an organizational chart that illustrates the hierarchy of the people involved in production and a slide containing a SmartArt graphic of travel expenses.

Tutorial
Inserting, Sizing, and Positioning SmartArt

Tutorial
Formatting SmartArt

1. With **2-MPProj** open, make Slide 2 active and then click the New Slide button in the Slides group on the Insert tab.

2. Create the organizational chart shown in Figure 2.4. To begin, click the Insert tab and then click the SmartArt button in the Illustrations group.

3. At the Choose a SmartArt Graphic dialog box, click *Hierarchy* in the left panel and then double-click the *Hierarchy* option in the middle panel.

   This displays the organizational chart in the slide with the SmartArt Tools Design tab active. Use buttons on this tab to add additional boxes, change the order of the shapes, choose a different layout, apply formatting with a SmartArt style, or reset the formatting of the organizational chart.

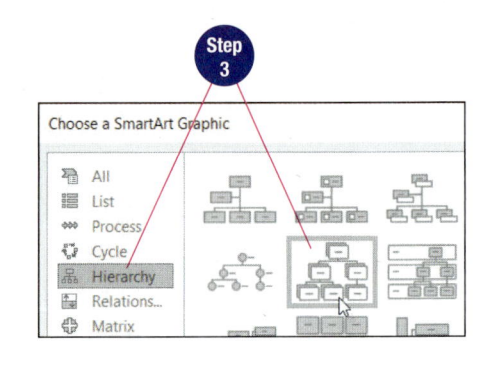

4. If a *Type your text here* window displays at the left of the organizational chart, close it by clicking the Text Pane button in the Create Graphic group.

   You can also close the window by clicking the Close button in the upper right corner of the window.

5. Delete one of the boxes in the organizational chart. Begin by clicking the border of the second text box from the top at the left side of the chart.

   Make sure the box containing the *[Text]* placeholder is selected.

6. Press the Delete key.

7. With the second box from the top at the right selected, click the Add Shape button in the Create Graphic group.

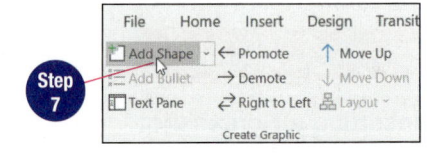

   This inserts a box to the right of the selected box.
   Your organizational chart should contain the same boxes shown in Figure 2.4. (The new box does not contain a *[Text]* placeholder, but you can still type text in the box.)

50 POWERPOINT Section 2 Editing and Enhancing Slides

8. Click the *[Text]* placeholder in the top box, type Chris Greenbaum, press the Enter key, and then type Production Manager. Click in each of the remaining boxes and type the text as shown in Figure 2.4.

9. Click the Change Colors button in the SmartArt Styles group on the SmartArt Tools Design tab and then click the *Colorful Range - Accent Colors 4 to 5* option (fourth option in the *Colorful* section).

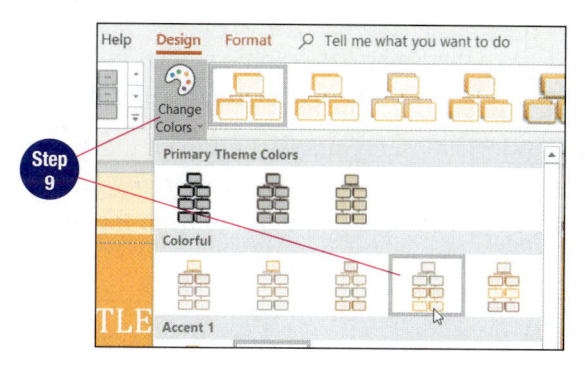

10. Click the More SmartArt Styles button at the right of the gallery in the SmartArt Styles group.

11. Click the *Inset* option at the drop-down gallery (second option in the *3-D* section).

12. Click the SmartArt Tools Format tab.

13. Click inside the SmartArt graphic border but outside any shape.

14. Click in the *Height* measurement box in the Size group, type 5, click in the *Width* measurement box, type 10, and then press the Enter key.

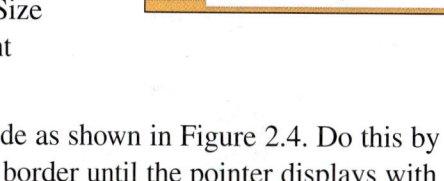

15. Move the graphic so it is positioned in the slide as shown in Figure 2.4. Do this by positioning the mouse pointer on the graphic border until the pointer displays with a four-headed arrow attached, clicking and holding down the left mouse button, dragging the graphic to the specific location, and then releasing the mouse button.

16. Click in the *CLICK TO ADD TITLE* placeholder and then type Team Structure.

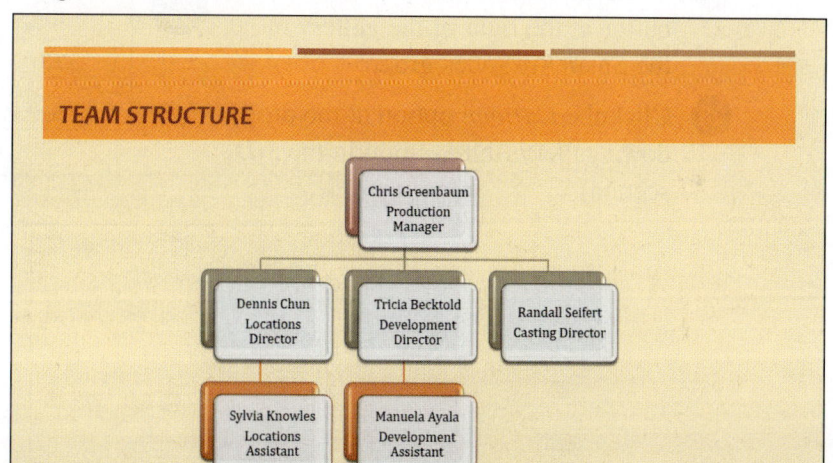

Figure 2.4 Organizational Chart

Activity 2.9 **POWERPOINT** 51

17. Make Slide 2 active, click in the title *Project Development*, click the Home tab, and then click the Format Painter button in the Clipboard group.

18. Make Slide 3 active and then select the entire title *Team Structure*.

19. Make Slide 9 active.

20. Click the New Slide button arrow in the Slides group on the Home tab and then click the *Blank* layout at the drop-down list.

21. Create the SmartArt graphic shown in Figure 2.5. To begin, click the Insert tab and then click the SmartArt button in the Illustrations group.

22. At the Choose a SmartArt Graphic dialog box, click *Relationship* in the left panel and then double-click the *Converging Radial* option in the middle panel. (This option may be the first option from the right in the sixth row or the first option from the left in the seventh row.)

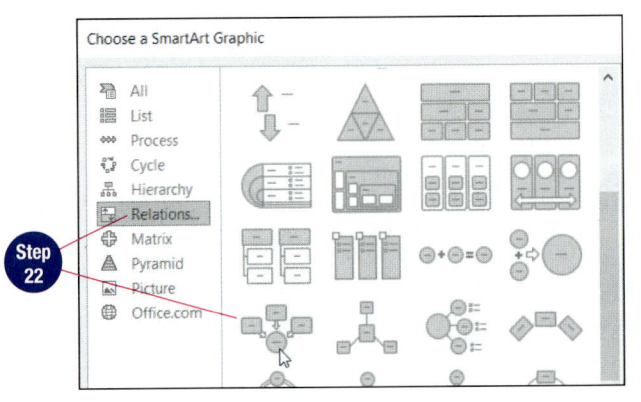

23. If necessary, close the *Type your text here* window by clicking the Close button in the upper right corner of the window.

24. Click the Add Shape button in the Create Graphic group.

25. Click in each of the shapes and insert the text shown in Figure 2.5.

26. Click the Change Colors button in the SmartArt Styles group and then click the *Colorful - Accent Colors* option (first option in the *Colorful* section).

27. Click the More SmartArt Styles button at the right of the gallery in the SmartArt Styles group.

28. Click the *Cartoon* option at the drop-down gallery (third option in the *3-D* section).

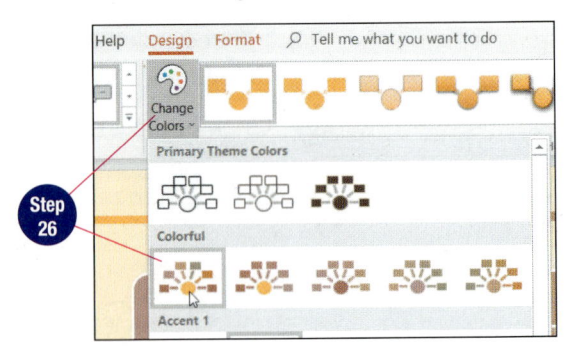

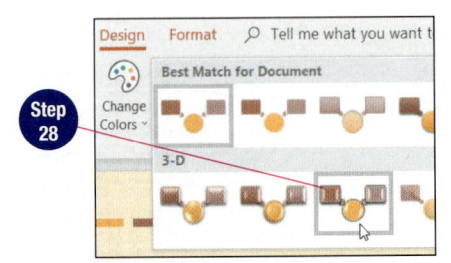

52   **POWERPOINT**   Section 2   Editing and Enhancing Slides

In Brief

Create Organizational Chart
1. Click Insert tab.
2. Click SmartArt button.
3. Click *Hierarchy*.
4. Double-click organizational chart.

Create SmartArt Graphic
1. Click Insert tab.
2. Click SmartArt button.
3. Click category in left panel.
4. Double-click graphic.

29. Click the SmartArt Tools Format tab.

30. Click inside the SmartArt graphic border but outside any shape.
    This deselects the shapes but keeps the graphic selected.

31. Click the More WordArt Styles button at the right of the gallery in the WordArt Styles group and then click the option in the fourth column, second row (white fill with orange outline).

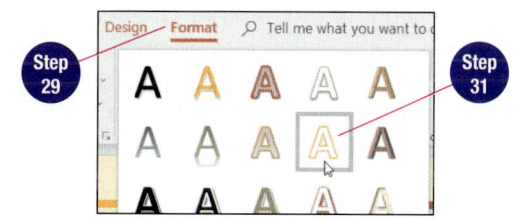

32. Click in the *Width* measurement box in the Size group, type 9.5, and then press the Enter key.

33. Click the Align button in the Arrange group and then click *Align Center* at the drop-down list.

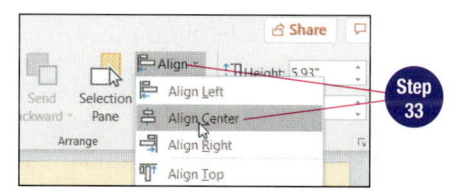

34. Save **2-MPProj**.

Figure 2.5 SmartArt Graphic

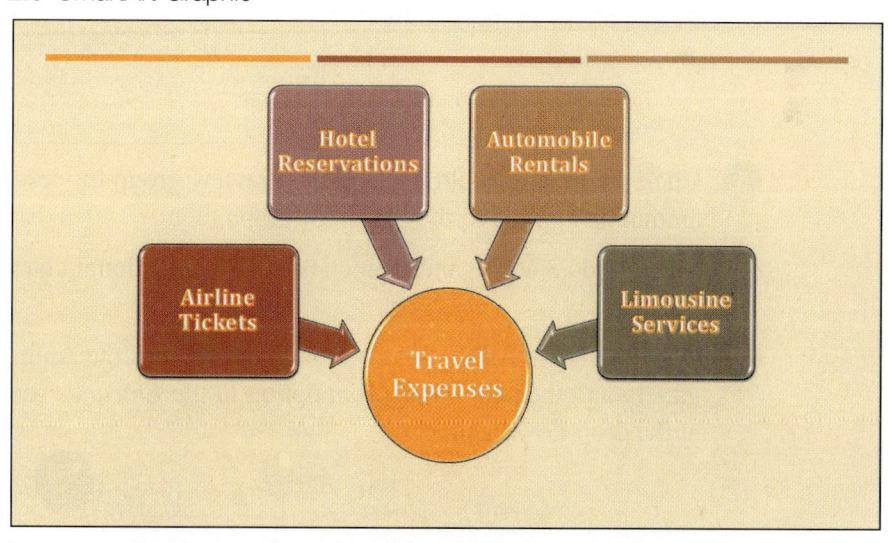

Check Your Work Compare your work to the model answer available in the online course.

In Addition

Inserting Text in the Text Pane

Enter text in a SmartArt shape by clicking in the shape and then typing the text. Text can also be inserted in a SmartArt shape by typing text in SmartArt's text pane. Display the text pane by clicking the Text Pane button in the Create Graphic group on the SmartArt Tools Design tab.

Activity 2.9 **POWERPOINT** 53

Activity 2.10   Applying Animation to Objects and Text

Animate individual objects and text in a slide with options on the Animations tab. Click the Animations tab and the tab displays with a variety of animation styles and with options for customizing and applying times to animations in a presentation. Click the More Animations button at the right of the gallery in the Animation group and a drop-down gallery of animation styles displays that can be applied to objects and text as they enter a slide, exit a slide, and/or follow a motion path. Animations can also be applied to emphasize objects in a slide. If the same animation is to be applied to other objects in a presentation, use the Animation Painter button in the Advanced Animation group on the Animations tab.

What You Will Do   To finalize the presentation, Chris Greenbaum has asked you to apply animation to objects and text in the presentation.

Tutorial
Applying and Removing Animations

Tutorial
Modifying Animations

1. With **2-MPProj** open, make sure Slide 10 is active and the SmartArt graphic is selected.

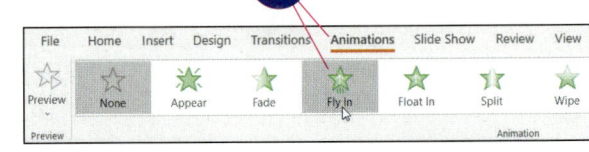

2. Click the Animations tab and then click the *Fly In* option in the Animation gallery in the Animation group.

3. Click the Effect Options button in the Animation group and then click *One by One* in the *Sequence* section at the drop-down gallery.

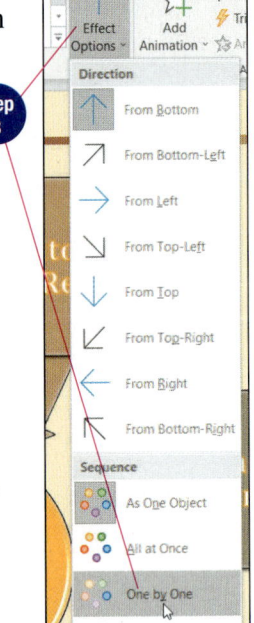

4. Click the *Duration* measurement box up arrow in the Timing group two times.

   This inserts *01.00* in the measurement box.

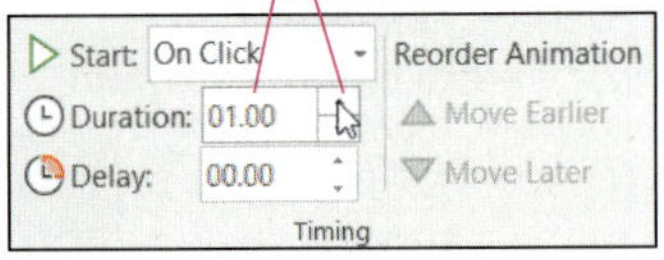

5. Click the Preview button in the Preview group to view the animation applied to the SmartArt graphic.

6. Make Slide 3 active and then click the organizational chart to select it.

7. Click the More Animations button at the right of the Animation gallery and then click the *Zoom* option in the *Entrance* section at the drop-down gallery.

8. Click the Effect Options button in the Animation group and then click *One by One* in the *Sequence* section at the drop-down gallery.

54   POWERPOINT   Section 2   Editing and Enhancing Slides

In Brief

Apply Animation to Object
1. Click object.
2. Click Animations tab.
3. Click animation option.

9. Click Slide 2 to make it active and then click in the bulleted text to select the placeholder.

10. Click the *Fly In* option in the gallery in the Animation group.

    Applying this animation creates a *build* for the bulleted items. A build displays important points in a slide one point at a time and is useful for keeping the audience's attention focused on the point being presented rather than reading ahead.

11. Click the *Duration* measurement box up arrow in the Timing group two times.

    This inserts *01.00* in the measurement box.

12. Apply the same animation to the bulleted text in Slides 4 through 9. To begin, click in the bulleted text to select the placeholder and then double-click the Animation Painter button in the Advanced Animation group.

13. Make Slide 4 active and then click in the bulleted text. (This selects the placeholder and applies the Fly In animation and the duration time.)

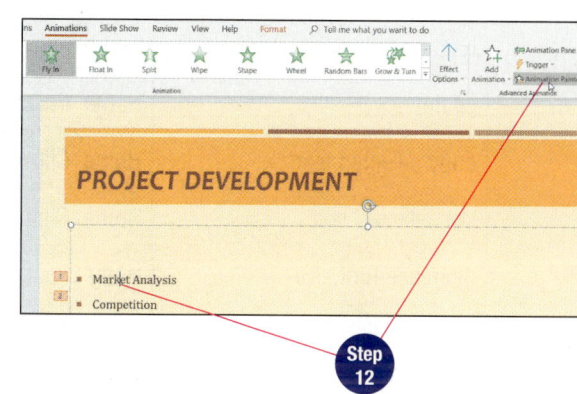

14. Make Slide 5 active and then click in the bulleted text.

15. Make Slide 6 active and then click in the bulleted text. Repeat this action for Slides 7–9.

16. Click the Animation Painter button to turn off the feature.

17. Make Slide 1 active and then run the slide show. Click the mouse button to advance slides and to display the individual organizational chart objects, bulleted items, and SmartArt graphic objects.

18. Print the presentation as handouts with six slides displayed horizontally on one page. To do this, click the File tab and then click the *Print* option.

19. At the Print backstage area, click the second gallery (contains the text *Full Page Slides*) in the *Settings* category and then click *6 Slides Horizontal* at the drop-down list.

20. Click the Print button.

21. Save and then close **2-MPProj**.

Check Your Work Compare your work to the model answer available in the online course.

In Addition

Applying Custom Animation

Apply custom animation to selected objects in a slide by clicking the Animation Pane button in the Advanced Animation group on the Animations tab. This displays the Animation task pane at the right of the screen. Use options in this task pane to control the order in which objects appear on a slide, choose animation direction and speed, and specify how objects will appear in the slide.

Activity 2.10 **POWERPOINT** 55

Features Summary

Feature	Ribbon Tab, Group	Button	Keyboard Shortcut
align left	Home, Paragraph		Ctrl + L
align right	Home, Paragraph		Ctrl + R
align vertically	Home, Paragraph		
animation effect options	Animations, Animation		
bold	Home, Font		Ctrl + B
center	Home, Paragraph		Ctrl + E
copy selected text	Home, Clipboard		Ctrl + C
cut selected text	Home, Clipboard		Ctrl + X
decrease font size	Home, Font		Ctrl + Shift + <
decrease list level	Home, Paragraph		Shift + Tab
font	Home, Font		
font color	Home, Font		
Font dialog box	Home, Font		Ctrl + Shift + F
font size	Home, Font		
format background	Design, Customize		
Format Painter	Home, Clipboard		
increase font size	Home, Font		Ctrl + Shift + >
increase list level	Home, Paragraph		Tab
insert image	Insert, Images		
insert screenshot	Insert, Images		
insert SmartArt	Insert, Illustrations		
italic	Home, Font		Ctrl + I
justify	Home, Paragraph		Ctrl + J
line spacing	Home, Paragraph		
paste selected text	Home, Clipboard		Ctrl + V
preview animation	Animations, Preview		
slide size	Design, Customize		
underline	Home, Font		Ctrl + U

PowerPoint

SECTION 3

Customizing a Presentation

Data Files
Before beginning section work, copy the PowerPointS3 folder to your storage medium and then make PowerPointS3 the active folder.

Skills

- Copy and paste items using the Clipboard task pane
- Find and replace text
- Insert and format WordArt
- Draw and customize objects
- Display gridlines
- Insert a text box
- Copy and rotate shapes
- Create and format a table
- Insert action buttons
- Insert a hyperlink
- Format with a slide master
- Insert headers and footers
- Add audio and video
- Set and rehearse timings for a slide show

Projects Overview

Marquee Productions Add visual appeal to a presentation on filming in Toronto by inserting WordArt, shapes, text boxes, and a table. Improve a presentation on a biography project by inserting WordArt, shapes, text boxes, an image, a logo, and a footer. Update a presentation on the annual meeting by applying a design theme, theme colors, and theme fonts and formatting using a slide master. Prepare and format a project schedule presentation.

Performance Threads Format a presentation on costume designs for Marquee Productions and add visual appeal by inserting a logo, WordArt, shapes, text boxes, a table, and a footer.

First Choice Travel Add a video clip and audio file to a presentation on eco-tour adventures. Format a presentation about a vacation cruise and add visual appeal by inserting a logo and audio clip, setting and rehearsing timings, and setting up the slide show to run continuously. Enhance a presentation on tours in Australia and New Zealand by inserting WordArt, a footer, and an audio clip; setting and rehearsing timings; and setting up the slide show to run continuously. Prepare a presentation on a Moroccan tour.

The online course includes additional training and assessment resources.

57

Activity 3.1 Using the Clipboard Task Pane

Use the Clipboard task pane to collect up to 24 different items and then paste them in various locations in slides. To display the Clipboard task pane, click the Clipboard group task pane launcher in the Clipboard group on the Home tab. The Clipboard task pane displays at the left side of the screen. Select text or an object to be copied and then click the Copy button in the Clipboard group. Continue selecting text or items and clicking the Copy button. To paste an item into a slide in a presentation, position the insertion point in the desired location and then click the item in the Clipboard task pane. (If the copied item is text, the first 50 characters display in the Clipboard task pane.) After inserting all items into the presentation, click the Clear All button to remove any remaining items from the Clipboard task pane.

What You Will Do In preparation for a meeting about the Toronto location shoot, you will open the Toronto presentation and then copy and paste multiple items into the appropriate slides.

Tutorial
Using the Clipboard Task Pane

1. Open **MPToronto** and then save it with the name **3-MPToronto**.

2. Display the Clipboard task pane by clicking the Clipboard group task pane launcher. If items display in the Clipboard task pane, click the Clear All button in the upper right corner of the task pane.

3. Make Slide 2 active and then select the name *Chris Greenbaum*. (Do not include the space after the name.)

4. With *Chris Greenbaum* selected, click the Copy button in the Clipboard group.

   When you click the Copy button, the name *Chris Greenbaum* is inserted as an item in the Clipboard task pane.

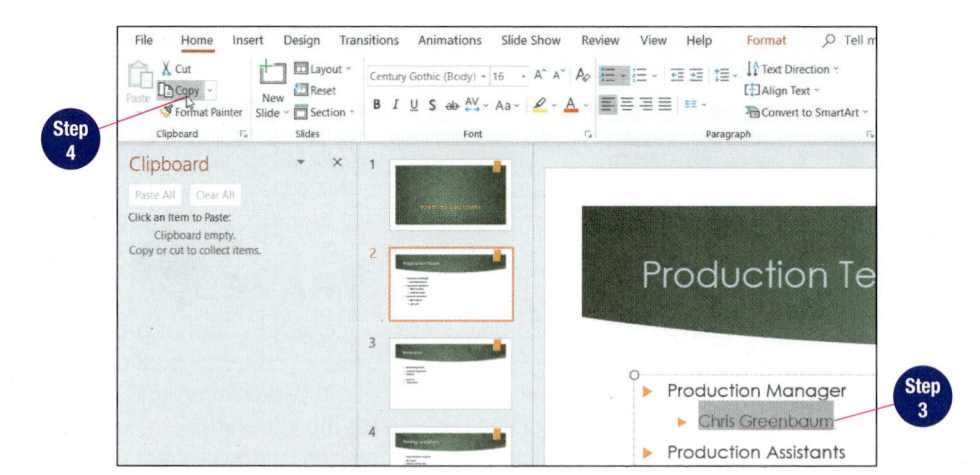

5. Select the name *Camille Matsui* (do not include the space after the name) and then click the Copy button. Select the name *Dennis Chun* (without the space after) and then click the Copy button. Select the name *Josh Hart* (without the space after) and then click the Copy button.

6. Make Slide 3 active, position the insertion point immediately right of *Location Expenses*, press the Enter key, and then press the Tab key.

In Brief

Use Clipboard Task Pane
1. Click Clipboard group task pane launcher.
2. Select text, click Copy button.
3. Continue selecting text and clicking Copy button.
4. Position insertion point.
5. Click item in Clipboard task pane.
6. Insert additional items.
7. Click Clear All button.
8. Close Clipboard task pane.

7. Click *Chris Greenbaum* in the Clipboard task pane.

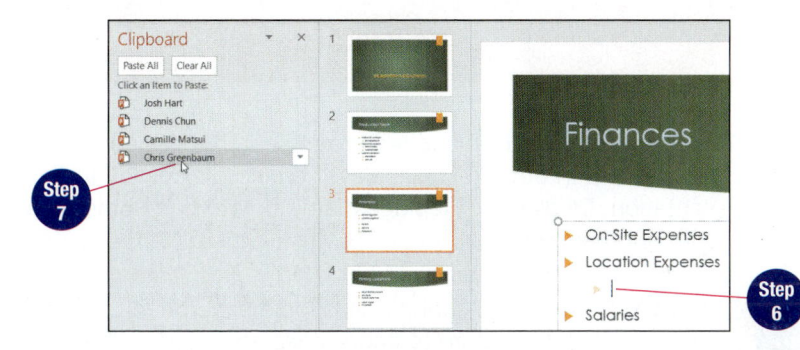

8. Position the insertion point immediately right of *Production*, press the Enter key, press the Tab key, and then click *Camille Matsui* in the Clipboard task pane.

9. Make Slide 4 active, position the insertion point immediately right of *Royal Ontario Museum*, press the Enter key, press the Tab key, and then click *Dennis Chun* in the Clipboard task pane.

10. Position the insertion point immediately right of *Island Airport*, press the Enter key, press the Tab key, and then click *Dennis Chun* in the Clipboard task pane.

11. Position the insertion point immediately right of *King Street*, press the Enter key, press the Tab key, and then click *Josh Hart* in the Clipboard task pane.

12. Click the Clear All button in the Clipboard task pane and then click the Close button ⊠ in the upper right corner of the task pane.

13. Make Slide 1 active and then insert the **MPLogo** image. To begin, click the Insert tab and then click the Pictures button in the Images group. Make your PowerPointS3 folder active and then double-click **MPLogo**.

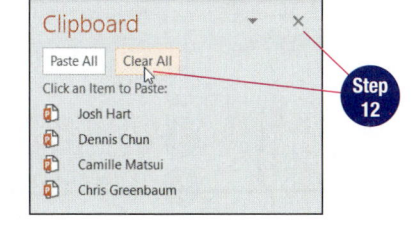

14. Size and move the logo so it better fills the slide.

15. Save **3-MPToronto**.

Check Your Work Compare your work to the model answer available in the online course.

In Addition

Using Clipboard Task Pane Options

Click the Options button at the bottom of the Clipboard task pane and a drop-down list displays with five options, as shown at the right. Make an option active by inserting a check mark before the option. With the options, the Clipboard task can can be displayed automatically when text is cut or copied, the Clipboard can be displayed by pressing Ctrl + C two times, text can be cut or copied without displaying the Clipboard task pane, the Office Clipboard icon can be displayed on the taskbar when the Clipboard is active, or a status message can display when copying items to the Clipboard.

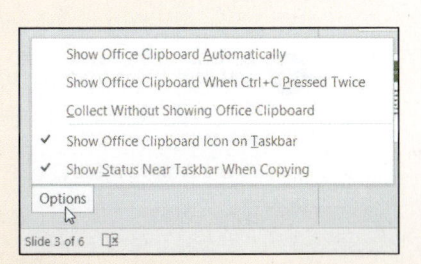

Activity 3.1 **POWERPOINT** 59

Activity 3.2 Finding and Replacing Text

Use the Find and Replace feature to search for specific text in slides in a presentation and replace it with other text. Display the Find dialog box to find something specific in a presentation. Display the Replace dialog box to find something in a presentation and replace it with another item.

MARQUEE PRODUCTIONS

What You Will Do A couple of people have been replaced on the Toronto location shoot. Use the Replace feature to find names and replace them with new names in the Toronto presentation.

Tutorial
Finding and Replacing Text

1. With **3-MPToronto** open, make sure Slide 1 is active.

2. Camille Matsui has been replaced by Jennie Almonzo. Begin the find and replace by clicking the Replace button in the Editing group on the Home tab.

   This displays the Replace dialog box with the insertion point positioned in the *Find what* text box.

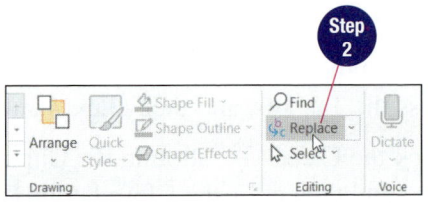

3. Type Camille Matsui in the *Find what* text box.

4. Press the Tab key and then type Jennie Almonzo in the *Replace with* text box.

5. Click the Replace All button.

   Clicking the Replace All button replaces all occurrences of the *Find what* text in the presentation. If you want control over which occurrences are replaced in a presentation, click the Find Next button to move to the next occurrence of the text. Click the Replace button if you want to replace the text, or click the Find Next button if you want to leave the text as written and move to the next occurrence.

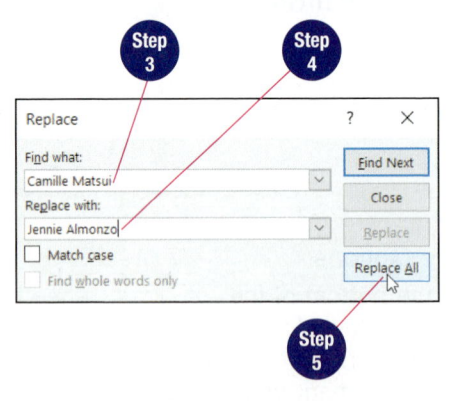

6. At the message stating that two replacements were made, click OK.

   The Replace dialog box remains on the screen.

60 **POWERPOINT** Section 3 Customizing a Presentation

In Brief

Find and Replace Text
1. Click Replace button.
2. At Replace dialog box, type find text.
3. Press Tab and then type replace text.
4. Click Replace All button.
5. Click Close button.

7 Josh Hart had to leave the project and is being replaced by Jaime Ruiz. At the Replace dialog box, type Josh Hart in the *Find what* text box.

When you begin typing the name *Josh Hart*, the previous name, *Camille Matsui*, is deleted.

8 Press the Tab key, type Jaime Ruiz in the *Replace with* text box, and then click the Replace All button.

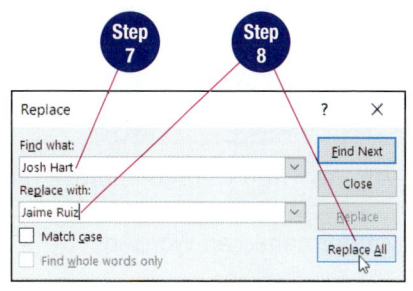

9 At the message stating that two replacements were made, click OK.

The Replace dialog box remains on the screen.

10 The title *Manager* has been changed to *Director*. At the Replace dialog box, type Manager in the *Find what* text box.

11 Press the Tab key, type Director in the *Replace with* text box, and then click the Replace All button.

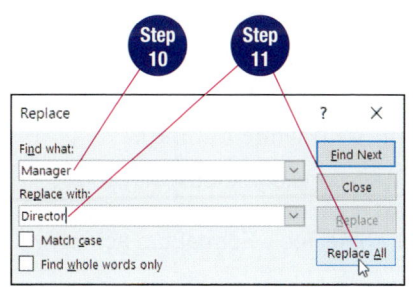

12 At the message stating that one replacement was made, click OK.

13 Close the Replace dialog box by clicking the Close button in the upper right corner of the dialog box.

14 Save **3-MPToronto**.

Check Your Work Compare your work to the model answer available in the online course.

In Addition

Using Replace Dialog Box Options

The Replace dialog box, shown at the right, contains two options for completing a find and replace. Choose the *Match case* option to exactly match the case of the find text. For example, if *Company* is entered in the *Find what* text box, PowerPoint will stop at *Company* but not *company* or *COMPANY*. Choose the *Find whole words only* option to find a whole word, not a part of a word. For example, if *his* is entered in the *Find what* text box and *Find whole words only* is not selected, PowerPoint will stop at *this*, *his*tory, *chis*el, and so on.

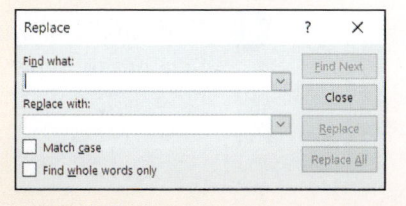

Activity 3.2 **POWERPOINT** 61

Activity 3.3 Inserting and Formatting WordArt

Use the WordArt feature to create text with special formatting that makes it stand out. WordArt can be formatted in a variety of ways, including conforming it to a shape. To insert WordArt, click the Insert tab, click the WordArt button in the Text group, and then click a WordArt style at the drop-down list. When WordArt is selected, the Drawing Tools Format tab displays. Use options and buttons on this tab to modify and customize WordArt.

What You Will Do You want to improve the appearance of the slide containing information on exterior shots by changing text to WordArt. You also want to insert a new slide with the title of the film formatted as WordArt.

Tutorial
Inserting and Formatting WordArt

1. With **3-MPToronto** open, make sure Slide 1 is active.

2. Click the New Slide button arrow in the Slides group on the Home tab and then click the *Blank* layout (first column, third row).

3. Insert WordArt by clicking the Insert tab, clicking the WordArt button in the Text group, and then clicking the option in the third column, third row (tan fill with white outline).

   This inserts a text box with *Your text here* inside and makes the Drawing Tools Format tab active.

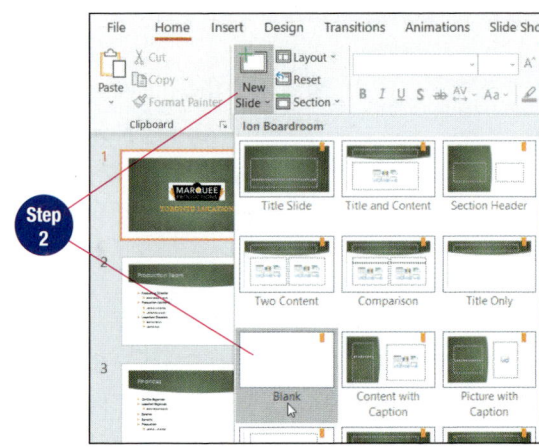

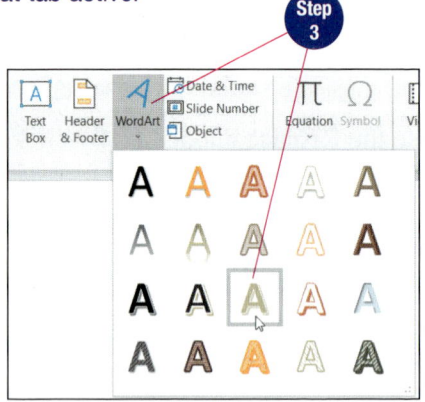

4. Type Ring of Roses.

5. Click in the *Shape Height* measurement box in the Size group, type 4, and then press the Enter key.

6. Click in the *Shape Width* measurement box in the Size group, type 9, and then press the Enter key.

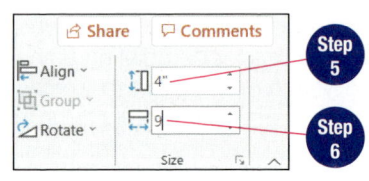

62 POWERPOINT Section 3 Customizing a Presentation

In Brief

Insert WordArt
1. Click Insert tab.
2. Click WordArt button.
3. Click WordArt option.
4. Type WordArt text.
5. Apply formatting.

7. Click the Text Effects button in the WordArt Styles group, point to *Transform* at the drop-down list, scroll down the side menu, and then click *Deflate* (second column, sixth row in the *Warp* section).

8. Click the border of the WordArt (border will display as a solid line), click the Text Outline button arrow, and then click the *Orange, Accent 1* color option at the drop-down gallery (fifth column, first row in *Theme Colors* section).

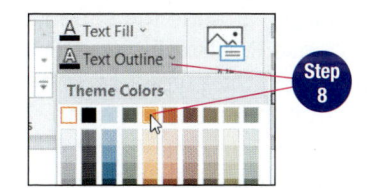

9. Position the WordArt in the middle of the slide as shown in Figure 3.1 by clicking the Align button in the Arrange group and then clicking *Distribute Horizontally* at the drop-down list. Click the Align button again and then click *Distribute Vertically* at the drop-down list.

10. Make Slide 4 active and then insert the **DollarSymbol** image from your PowerPointS3 folder. You determine the size, position, and color of the image.

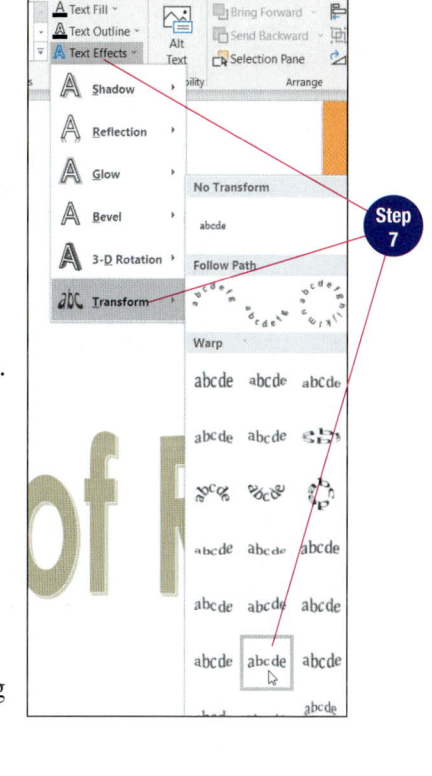

11. Save **3-MPToronto**.

Figure 3.1 Slide 2

Check Your Work Compare your work to the model answer available in the online course.

In Addition

Using the Drawing Tools Format Tab

When WordArt is selected in a slide, the Drawing Tools Format tab displays as shown below. Use options in the Insert Shapes group to draw a shape or text box. Apply a style, fill, outline, and/or effects to the WordArt text box with options in the Shape Styles group. Change the style of the WordArt text with options in the WordArt Styles group, specify the layering of the WordArt text with options in the Arrange group, and identify the height and width of the WordArt text box with measurement boxes in the Size group.

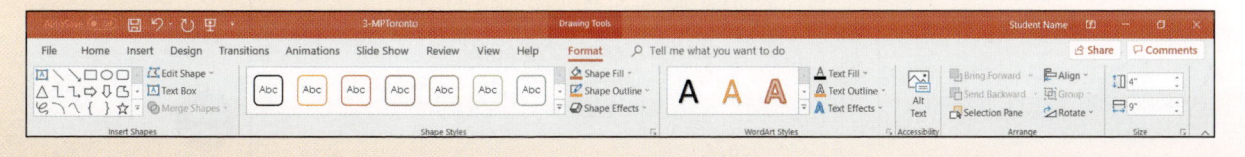

Activity 3.3 **POWERPOINT** 63

Activity 3.4 Drawing and Customizing Shapes

Use the shape options in the Drawing group on the Home tab or the Shapes button on the Insert tab to draw shapes in a slide, including lines, rectangles, basic shapes, block arrows, equation shapes, flowchart shapes, stars, banners, and callout shapes. Click a shape and the mouse pointer displays as crosshairs (plus sign). Click in the slide to insert the shape or position the crosshairs where the image is to begin, click and hold down the left mouse button, drag to create the shape, and then release the mouse button. This inserts the shape in the slide and also displays the Drawing Tools Format tab. Use buttons on this tab to change the shape, apply a style to the shape, arrange the shape, and change the size of the shape. Type text directly into a shape or use the Text Box button in the Text group on the Insert tab to draw a text box inside a shape and then type text in the box. The Drawing Tools Format tab also provides a Text Box button that can be used to draw a text box in a slide.

What You Will Do You will create a new slide for the Toronto site presentation that includes the Toronto office address inside a shape.

Tutorial
Inserting, Sizing, and Positioning Shapes

Tutorial
Formatting Shapes

1. With **3-MPToronto** open, make Slide 2 active.

2. Click the New Slide button in the Slides group on the Home tab. (Make sure the slide layout is Blank.)

3. Click the More Shapes button in the Drawing group on the Home tab.

   If the Illustrations group contains a Shapes button, click the Shapes button to display the drop-down list.

4. Click the *Scroll: Horizontal* shape at the drop-down list (sixth column, bottom row in the *Stars and Banners* section).

5. Position the mouse pointer in the slide, click and hold down the left mouse button, drag to create the shape as shown below, and then release the mouse button.

   If you are not satisfied with the size and shape of the image, press the Delete key to remove the image, select the shape, and then draw the image again.

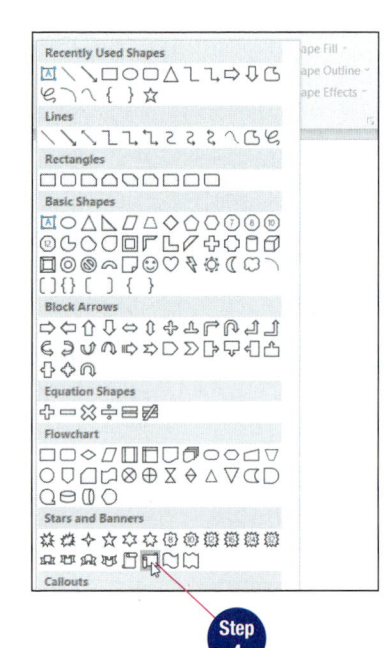

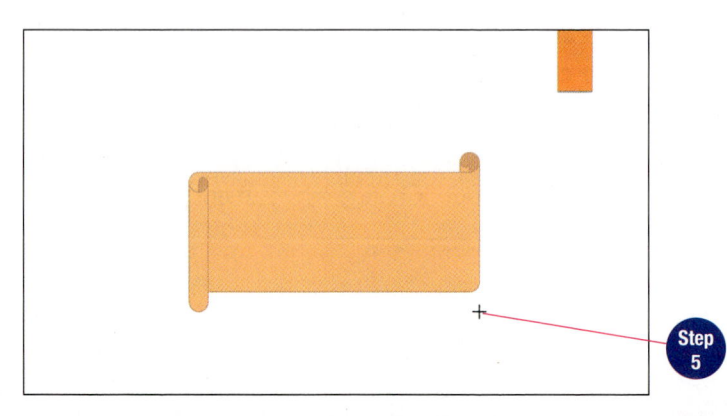

64 **POWERPOINT** Section 3 Customizing a Presentation

In Brief

Draw Shape
1. Click Home tab.
2. Click More Shapes button in gallery in Drawing group.
3. Click shape.
4. Click or drag in slide to draw shape.
OR
1. Click Insert tab.
2. Click Shapes button.
3. Click shape.
4. Click or drag in slide to draw shape.

6 With the shape selected, click the Drawing Tools Format tab and then change the shape style by clicking the More Shape Styles button in the Shape Styles group and then clicking the *Subtle Effect - Green, Accent 6* option at the drop-down gallery (seventh column, fourth row in the *Theme Styles* section).

7 Click the Shape Effects button in the Shape Styles group, point to *Glow*, and then click the *Glow: 18 point; Orange, Accent color 1* option (first column, fourth row in the *Glow Variations* section).

8 Click the Home tab.

9 Click the Font Size option box arrow and then click *24* at the drop-down gallery.

10 Click the Bold button in the Font group.

11 Click the Font Color button in the Font group and then click the *Orange, Accent 1, Darker 25%* color option (fifth column, fifth row in the *Theme Colors* section).

12 If the paragraph alignment is not set to center, click the Center button in the Paragraph group.

13 Type the following text in the shape:

MARQUEE PRODUCTIONS
Toronto Office
905 Bathurst Street
Toronto, ON M4P 4E5

14 Distribute the shape horizontally and vertically on the slide using options in the Arrange button drop-down list in the Drawing group on the Home tab.

15 Save **3-MPToronto**.

Check Your Work Compare your work to the model answer available in the online course.

In Addition

Displaying the Selection Task Pane

To select an object or multiple objects in a slide, consider displaying the Selection task pane. Display the task pane by clicking the Selection Pane button in the Arrange group on the Drawing Tools Format tab. Select an object by clicking the object name in the Selection task pane (see example at right). Select multiple objects by pressing and holding down the Ctrl key and then clicking objects. Click the button at the right of the object name to turn on/off the display of the object.

Activity 3.4 **POWERPOINT** 65

Activity 3.5 Displaying Gridlines; Inserting a Text Box; Copying and Rotating Shapes

To help position elements such as shapes and images on a slide, consider displaying gridlines. Gridlines are intersecting horizontal and vertical dashed lines that display on the slide in the slide pane. Display gridlines by clicking the View tab and then clicking the *Gridlines* check box in the Show group to insert a check mark. Create a text box in a slide by clicking the Text Box button in the Text group on the Insert tab. Click or drag in the slide to create the text box. Draw a shape in a slide and the selected shape displays with sizing handles and a rotation handle. Rotate a shape with the rotation handle or with the Rotate button in the Arrange group on the Drawing Tools Format tab. If a slide contains more than one object, multiple objects can be selected at once so they can be worked with as if they were a single object. Selected objects can be formatted, sized, moved, flipped, and/or rotated as a single unit.

MARQUEE PRODUCTIONS

What You Will Do You need to create a new slide for the Toronto presentation that displays the date for the last day of filming in Toronto. To highlight this important information, you will insert an arrow shape and then copy and rotate the shape.

Tutorial
Displaying Rulers, Gridlines, and Guides

Tutorial
Inserting and Formatting Text Boxes

Tutorial
Copying and Rotating Shapes

1. With **3-MPToronto** open, make Slide 8 active and then click the Insert tab.
2. Click the New Slide button arrow and then click *Title Only* at the drop-down list.
3. Click in the *Click to add title* placeholder and then type Last Day of Filming.
4. Turn on the display of gridlines by clicking the View tab and then clicking the *Gridlines* check box in the Show group to insert a check mark.
5. Click the Insert tab and then click the Text Box button in the Text group.
6. Position the mouse pointer in the slide and then draw a text box similar to what you see below. Use the gridlines to help you position the mouse when drawing the text box.
7. Change the font size to 24 points, apply bold formatting, apply the Orange, Accent 1, Darker 25% font color (fifth column, fifth row in the *Theme Colors* section), change to center alignment, and then type August 28. Click outside the text box to deselect it.
8. Click the Insert tab, click the Shapes button in the Illustrations group, and then click the *Arrow: Notched Right* shape (sixth column, second row in the *Block Arrows* section).

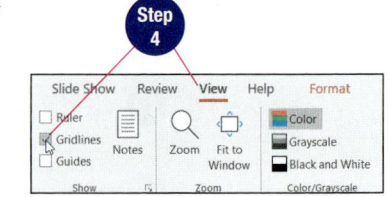

66 POWERPOINT Section 3 Customizing a Presentation

In Brief

Display Gridlines
1. Click View tab.
2. Click *Gridlines* check box.

Insert Text Box
1. Click Insert tab.
2. Click Text Box button.
3. Click in slide or drag to create text box.

⑨ Position the mouse pointer at the left side of the slide, click and hold down the left mouse button, drag to create the arrow shape as shown at the right, and then release the mouse button.

   Use the gridlines to help position the arrow.

⑩ With the arrow shape selected, copy the arrow by positioning the mouse pointer inside the shape until the mouse pointer displays with a four-headed arrow attached. Press and hold down the Ctrl key and then click and hold down the left mouse button. Drag the arrow to the right of the date, release the left mouse button, and then release the Ctrl key.

⑪ Click the Drawing Tools Format tab and then flip the copied arrow by clicking the Rotate button in the Arrange group and then clicking *Flip Horizontal* at the drop-down list.

⑫ Using the mouse pointer, draw a border around the three objects.

   When you release the mouse button, the three objects are selected.

⑬ With the Drawing Tools Format tab active, center-align the three grouped objects by clicking the Align button in the Arrange group and then clicking *Align Middle* at the drop-down list.

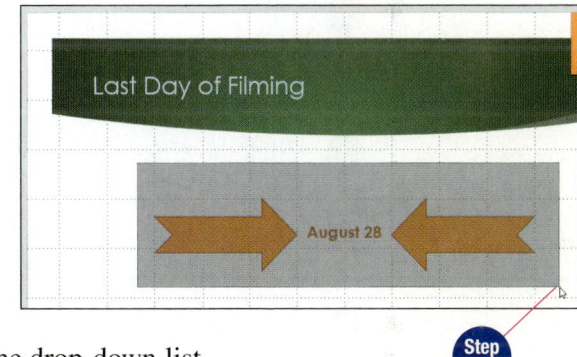

⑭ With the three objects still selected, horizontally distribute them by clicking the Align button and then clicking *Distribute Horizontally* at the drop-down list.

⑮ Turn off the display of gridlines by clicking the View tab and then clicking the *Gridlines* check box to remove the check mark.

⑯ Click outside the objects to deselect them.

⑰ Save **3-MPToronto**.

Check Your Work Compare your work to the model answer available in the online course.

In Addition

Rotating Objects

Use the rotation handle near a selected object to rotate the object. Position the mouse pointer on the rotation handle until the pointer displays as a circular arrow, as shown at the right. Click and hold down the left mouse button, drag in the desired direction, and then release the mouse button.

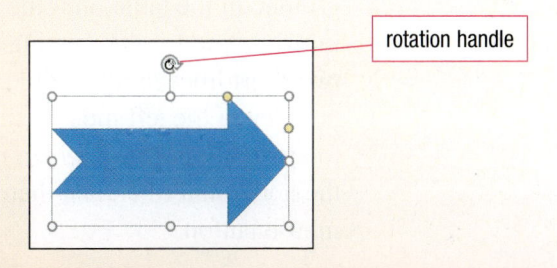

Activity 3.5 **POWERPOINT** 67

Activity 3.6 Creating and Formatting a Table

PowerPoint includes a Table feature that can be used to display columns and rows of data. Insert a table in a slide with the Table button on the Insert tab or with the Insert Table button in a content placeholder. When a table is inserted in a slide, the Table Tools Design tab is active. Use buttons on this tab to enhance the appearance of the table. With options in the Table Styles group, apply predesigned colors and border lines to a table. Maintain further control over the predesigned style formatting applied to columns and rows with options in the Table Style Options group. Apply additional design formatting to cells in a table with the Shading and Borders buttons in the Table Styles group. Draw a table or draw additional rows and/or columns in a table with options in the Draw Borders group. Click the Table Tools Layout tab and display options and buttons for inserting and deleting columns and rows; changing cell size, alignment, direction, and margins; changing the table size; and arranging the table in the slide.

What You Will Do After reviewing the slides, you decide to include additional information on the location timeline. To do this, you will insert a new slide and then create a table with specific dates.

Tutorial
Creating a Table

Tutorial
Changing the Table Design

Tutorial
Changing the Table Layout

1. With **3-MPToronto** open, make Slide 8 active and then click the Insert tab.

2. Click the New Slide button arrow and then click the *Title and Content* layout at the drop-down list.

3. Click the *Click to add title* placeholder in the new slide and then type Timeline.

4. Click the Insert Table button in the content placeholder.

5. At the Insert Table dialog box, press the Delete key and then type 2 in the *Number of columns* measurement box.

6. Press the Tab key and then type 9 in the *Number of rows* measurement box.

7. Click OK to close the Insert Table dialog box.

8. Turn on the display of the horizontal and vertical rulers. To do this, click the View tab and then click the *Ruler* check box in the Show group to insert a check mark.

9. Column 1 needs to be widened to accommodate the project tasks. To do this, position the mouse pointer on the middle gridline in the table until the pointer turns into a left-and-right pointing arrow with two short lines in the middle. Click and hold down the left mouse button, drag to approximately the 6-inch mark on the horizontal ruler, and then release the mouse button.

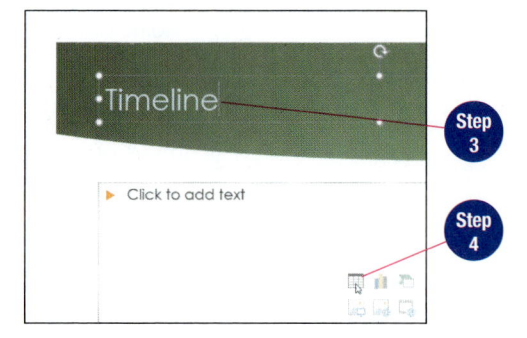

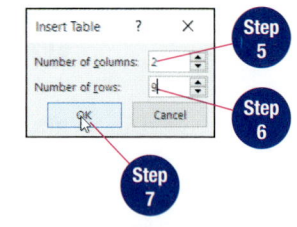

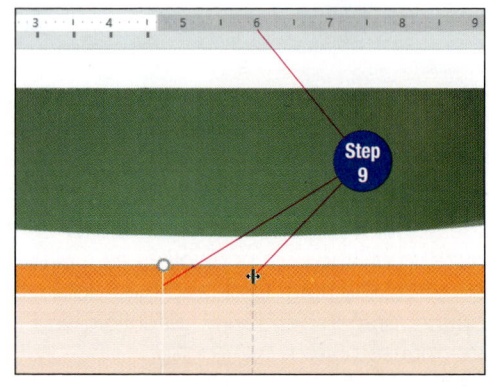

In Brief

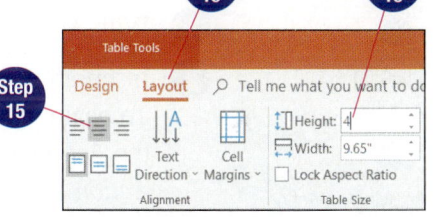

Create Table
1. Click Insert Table button in content placeholder.
2. At Insert Table dialog box, type number of columns and rows.
3. Click OK.

10. Starting with the insertion point positioned in the first cell, type all of the text shown in Figure 3.2. Press the Tab key to move the insertion point to the next cell. Press Shift + Tab to move the insertion point to the previous cell.

11. Click the More Table Styles button in the gallery in the Table Styles group on the Table Tools Design tab.

12. Click the *Medium Style 1 - Accent 1* option in the drop-down gallery (second column, first row in the *Medium* section).

13. Click the Table Tools Layout tab.

14. Select the first row in the table by positioning the mouse pointer at the left of the first row in the table until the pointer turns into a black, right-pointing arrow and then clicking the left mouse button.

15. Click the Center button in the Alignment group.

16. Click in the *Height* measurement box in the Table Size group, type 4, and then press the Enter key.

17. Distribute the table horizontally on the slide.

18. Save **3-MPToronto**.

Figure 3.2 Slide 9 Table

Activity	Date
Open Toronto Office	May 11
Costume Delivery	July 6
Van Rental	May 11, May 21
Car Rental	May 21, June 1
Royal Ontario Museum Filming	June 15 to June 25
Exterior Shots: Downtown Streets, CN Tower	June 26 to July 1
Toronto Island Park Filming	July 6 to July 12
Casa Loma Interior and Exterior Filming	July 20 to August 7

Check Your Work Compare your work to the model answer available in the online course.

In Addition

Moving and Sizing a Table

Increase or decrease the size of a table by typing the measurements in the *Height* and *Width* measurement boxes in the Table Size group on the Table Tools Layout tab. Another method is to drag the sizing handles that display around a table border to increase or decrease the size. When the insertion point is positioned in a table, a border containing white sizing handles surrounds the table. Position the mouse pointer on one of the sizing handles until the pointer displays as a two-headed arrow, click and hold down the left mouse button, and then drag to increase or decrease the size. Drag a corner sizing handle to change the size of the table proportionally. To move the table, position the mouse pointer on the table border until the pointer displays with a four-headed arrow and then drag to the desired position.

Activity 3.6 **POWERPOINT** 69

Activity 3.7 Inserting Action Buttons and Hyperlinks

Action buttons are drawn objects on a slide that have a routine attached to them. The routine is activated when the presenter clicks the action button. For example, an action button can be inserted to display a specific web page, a file in another program, or the next slide in the presentation. Creating an action button is a two-step process. The first step is to draw the button in the slide, and the second step is to define the action that will take place using options in the Action Settings dialog box. An action button can be customized in the same way a drawn shape is customized. A hyperlink can be inserted in a slide that, when clicked, will display a website or open another slide show or file. Insert a hyperlink with the Link button on the Insert tab.

What You Will Do To facilitate the running of the slide show, you decide to insert an action button at the bottom of each slide that will link to the next slide or the first slide. You also decide to insert a hyperlink to a website.

Tutorial
Inserting Action Buttons

Tutorial
Applying an Action to an Object

Tutorial
Inserting Hyperlinks

1. With **3-MPToronto** open, make Slide 1 active.

2. Insert an action button that, when clicked, will display the next slide. To begin, click the Insert tab, click the Shapes button, and then click the *Action Button: Go Forward or Next* option (second button in the *Action Buttons* section).

3. Position the mouse pointer (displays as crosshairs) in the lower right corner of Slide 1, click and hold down the left mouse button, drag to create a button that is approximately one-half inch square, and then release the mouse button.

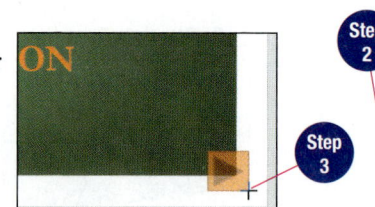

4. At the Action Settings dialog box, click OK. (The default setting for the *Hyperlink to* option is *Next Slide*.)

5. With the button selected, if necessary, click the Drawing Tools Format tab.

6. Select the current measurement in the *Shape Height* measurement box, type 0.5, and then press the Enter key. Select the current measurement in the *Shape Width* measurement box, type 0.5, and then press the Enter key.

7. Instead of drawing the button on each slide, you decide to copy it and then paste it in the other slides. To do this, make sure the button is selected, click the Home tab, and then click the Copy button in the Clipboard group.

8. Make Slide 2 active and then click the Paste button in the Clipboard group. Continue pasting the button in Slides 3 through 9. (Do not paste the button on the last slide, Slide 10.)

9. Make Slide 10 active and then insert an action button that will display the first slide. To begin, click the Insert tab, click the Shapes button, and then click *Action Button: Go Home* (fifth option in the *Action Buttons* section).

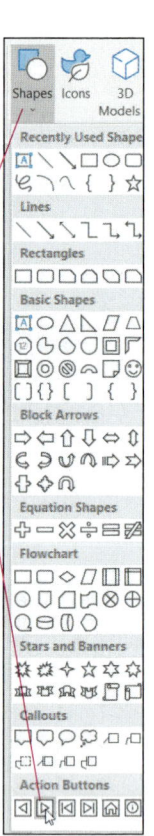

70 POWERPOINT Section 3 Customizing a Presentation

In Brief

Insert Action Button
1. Click Insert tab.
2. Click Shapes button.
3. Click action button.
4. Click or drag in slide to create button.
5. At Action Settings dialog box, click OK.

Insert Hyperlink
1. Click Insert tab.
2. Click Link button.
3. Make changes at Insert Hyperlink dialog box.
4. Click OK.

10. Position the mouse pointer in the lower right corner of Slide 10 and then click the left mouse button.

   When you click in the slide, a small square shape with a home icon in the center is inserted in the slide.

11. At the Action Settings dialog box, click OK. (The default setting for the *Hyperlink to* option is *First Slide*.)

12. With the button selected, click in the *Shape Height* measurement box on the Drawing Tools Format tab, type 0.5, and then press the Enter key. Click in the *Shape Width* measurement box, type 0.5, and then press the Enter key.

13. Make Slide 6 active and then create a hyperlink to the museum website. To begin, select *Royal Ontario Museum*, click the Insert tab, and then click the Link button in the Links group.

14. At the Insert Hyperlink dialog box, type www.rom.on.ca in the *Address* text box and then press the Enter key.

   PowerPoint automatically inserts *http://* at the beginning of the web address. The hyperlink text displays underlined and in a different color in the slide.

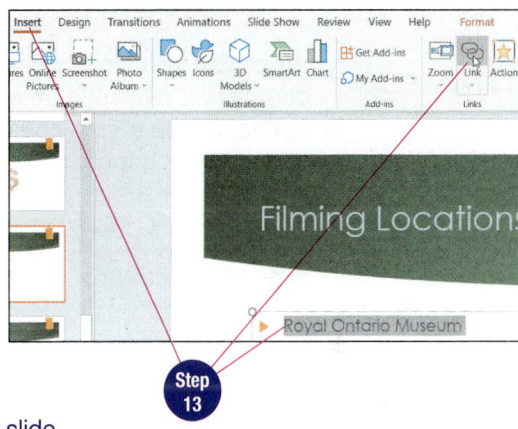

15. Run the slide show, beginning with Slide 1. Navigate through the slide show by clicking the action buttons. When Slide 6 (*Filming Locations*) displays, click the Royal Ontario Museum hyperlink.

16. After viewing the museum website, close the browser. Continue running the slide show. After viewing the slide show at least two times, press the Esc key to end the slide show.

17. Print the presentation as handouts with six slides displayed horizontally per page.

18. Save and then close **3-MPToronto**.

   Check Your Work Compare your work to the model answer available in the online course.

In Addition

Linking with Action Buttons

An action button can be created that links to a website during a slide show. To do this, draw an Action button. At the Action Settings dialog box, click the *Hyperlink to* option, click the *Hyperlink to* option box arrow, and then click *URL* at the drop-down list. At the Hyperlink to URL dialog box, type the web address in the *URL* text box and then click OK. Click OK to close the Action Settings dialog box. Other actions that can be linked to using the *Hyperlink to* option drop-down list include: *Next Slide, Previous Slide, First Slide, Last Slide, Last Slide Viewed, End Show, Custom Show, Slide, URL, Other PowerPoint Presentation*, and *Other File*. The Action Settings dialog box can also be used to run another program when the action button is selected, to run a macro, or to activate an embedded object.

Activity 3.7 **POWERPOINT** 71

Activity 3.8 Formatting with a Slide Master

When customizing formatting in a presentation, PowerPoint's slide master can be very helpful in reducing the steps needed to format slides. A presentation contains a slide master for each of the various slide layouts. To display slide masters, click the View tab and then click the Slide Master button in the Master Views group. The available slide masters display in the slide thumbnails pane at the left side of the screen. Apply formatting to the slide masters and then click the Close Master View button in the Close group to return to the Normal view.

What You Will Do   Melissa Gehring, manager at First Choice Travel, has asked you to complete a presentation on upcoming eco-tours offered by First Choice Travel. You decide to change the theme colors and fonts of the presentation in a slide master, as well as insert the company's logo in the upper right corner of all slides except the title slide.

Tutorial
Formatting with a Slide Master

1. Open **FCTEcoTours** and then save it with the name **3-FCTEcoTours**.

2. Click the View tab and then click the Slide Master button in the Master Views group.

   Hover the mouse pointer over a slide master in the slide thumbnails pane at the left side of the screen to display a ScreenTip with information about the slide layout and the number of slides in the presentation that use the layout.

3. Click the Theme Colors button in the Background group and then click *Blue* at the drop-down gallery.

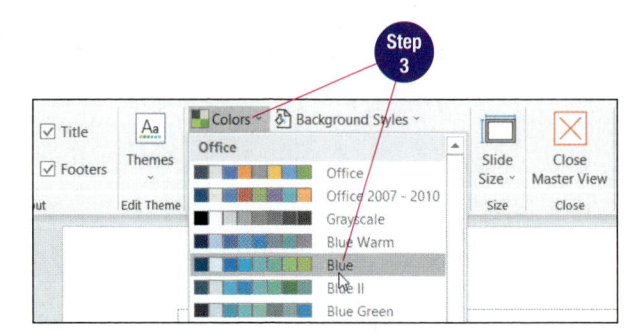

4. Click the Theme Fonts button in the Background group, scroll down the drop-down gallery, and then click *Calibri Light-Constantia*.

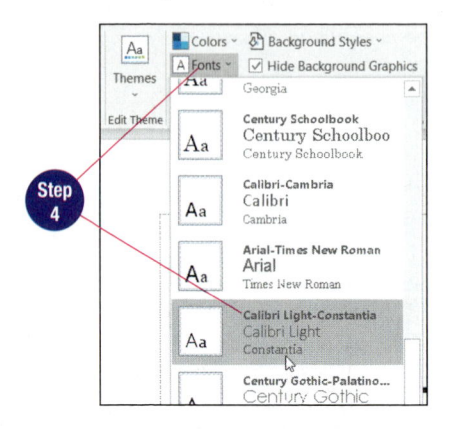

72   POWERPOINT   Section 3   Customizing a Presentation

In Brief

Format in Slide Master View
1. Click View tab.
2. Click Slide Master button.
3. Make changes.
4. Click Close Master View button.

5. Select the *Click to edit Master title style* placeholder text in the slide in the slide pane (the *Title Slide Layout* slide master is active in the slide thumbnails pane), click the Home tab, click the Font Color button arrow, and then click the *Blue* color option (eighth option in the *Standard Colors* section).

6. Click the top slide master (*Retrospect Slide Master*) in the slide thumbnails pane at the left side of the screen.

7. Select the *Click to edit Master title style* placeholder text, click the Home tab, and then click the Font Color button.

   This applies the Blue font color.

8. Insert the First Choice Travel logo in the slide master (so it prints on all slides except the first one). Begin by clicking the Insert tab and then clicking the Pictures button in the Images group.

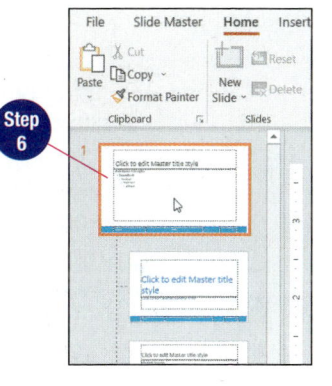

9. Navigate to your PowerPointS3 folder and then double-click **FCTLogo**.

10. Make sure the logo is selected.

11. Click in the *Height* measurement box, type 0.5, and then press the Enter key.

12. Click the Align button in the Arrange group and then click the *Align Right* option at the drop-down list.

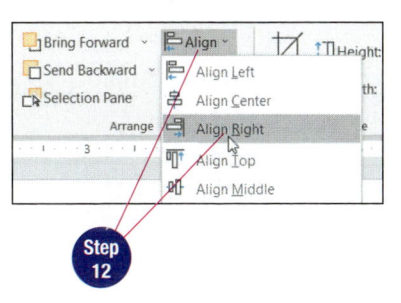

13. Click the Align button and then click the *Align Top* option.

14. Click the Slide Master tab.

15. Click the Close Master View button in the Close group on the Slide Master tab.

16. Save **3-FCTEcoTours**.

Check Your Work Compare your work to the model answer available in the online course.

In Addition

Applying More Than One Slide Design Theme
Each design theme applies specific formatting to slides. More than one design theme can be applied to slides in a presentation. To do this, select the specific slides and then choose the design theme. The design theme is applied only to the selected slides. If more than one design theme is applied to a presentation, multiple slide masters will display in Slide Master view.

Formatting Changes in Slide Master View
If the formatting of text is edited in a slide in Normal view, the link to the slide master is broken. Changes made to a slide master in Slide Master view will not affect the individually formatted slide. For this reason, make formatting changes in Slide Master view before editing individual slides in a presentation.

Activity 3.8 **POWERPOINT** 73

Activity 3.9 Inserting Headers and Footers

Insert information that should appear at the top or bottom of individual slides or at the top and bottom of individual printed notes and handouts pages using options at the Header and Footer dialog box. If the same type of information is to appear on all slides, display the Header and Footer dialog box with the Slide tab selected. Use options at this dialog box to insert the date and time, insert the slide number, and create a footer. To insert header or footer elements that print on all notes or handouts pages, choose options at the Header and Footer dialog box with the Notes and Handouts tab selected.

What You Will Do   Melissa Gehring has asked you to insert the current date and slide numbers in the slides and to create a header for notes pages.

Tutorial
Inserting Headers and Footers

1. With **3-FCTEcoTours** open, insert a footer that prints at the bottom of each slide. To begin, click the Insert tab and then click the Header & Footer button in the Text group.

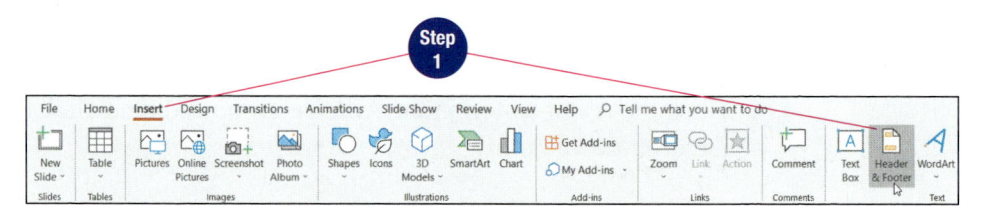

2. At the Header and Footer dialog box with the Slide tab selected, click the *Date and time* check box to insert a check mark. If necessary, click the *Update automatically* option to select it.

3. Click the *Slide number* check box to insert a check mark.

4. Click the *Footer* check box to insert a check mark, click in the *Footer* text box, and then type First Choice Travel Eco-Tours.

5. Click the Apply to All button.

6. Make Slide 7 active.

7. Display the notes pane by clicking the Notes button on the Status bar.

8. Click in the notes pane and then type Include additional costs for airfare, local transportation, and daily tours.

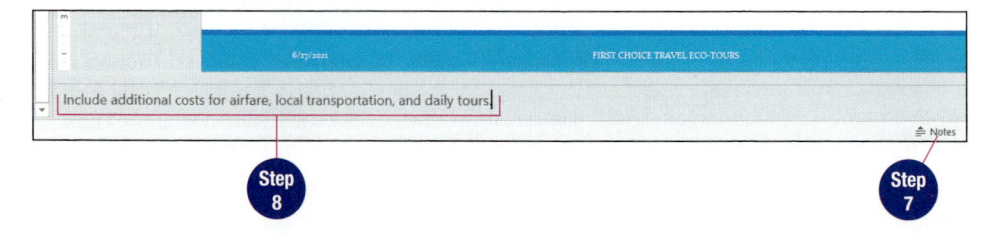

In Brief

Insert Header/Footer in Slide
1. Click Insert tab.
2. Click Header & Footer button.
3. At Header and Footer dialog box with Slide tab selected, choose options.
4. Click Apply to All button.

Insert Header/Footer in Notes and Handouts
1. Click Insert tab.
2. Click Header & Footer button.
3. At Header and Footer dialog box, click Notes and Handouts tab.
4. Choose options.
5. Click Apply to All button.

9. Insert a header that will display on notes and handouts pages by clicking the Header & Footer button on the Insert tab.

10. At the Header and Footer dialog box, click the Notes and Handouts tab.

11. Make sure a check mark does not display in the *Date and time* check box. If a check mark does display, click the check box to remove the check mark.

12. Click the *Header* check box to insert a check mark and then type First Choice Travel in the *Header* text box.

13. Click the *Footer* check box to insert a check mark and then type Eco-Tours in the *Footer* text box.

14. Click the Apply to All button.

15. Print the presentation as handouts with nine slides displayed horizontally per page.

16. Print Slide 7 as a notes page. To do this, click the File tab, click the *Print* option, click the second gallery (contains the text *9 Slides Horizontal*) in the *Settings* category, and then click *Notes Pages* in the *Print Layout* section.

17. Click in the *Slides* text box (below the first gallery in the *Settings* category) and then type 7.

18. Click the Print button.

19. Click the Notes button on the Status bar to close the notes pane.

20. Save **3-FCTEcoTours**.

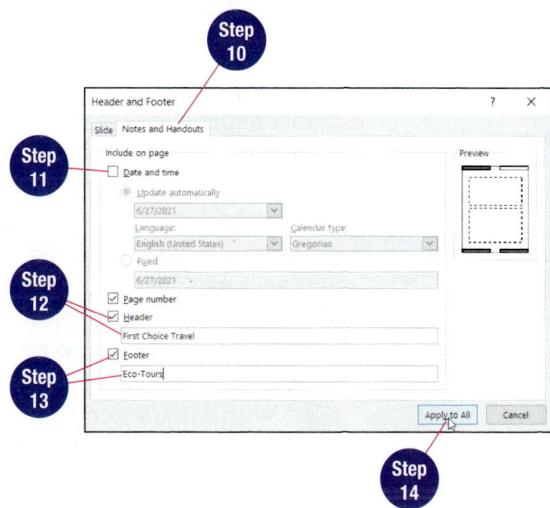

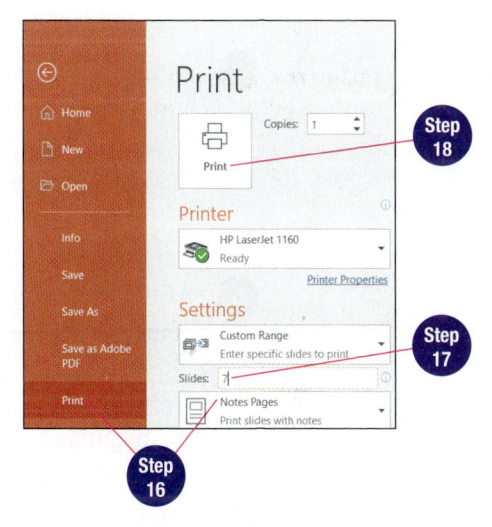

Check Your Work Compare your work to the model answer available in the online course.

In Addition

Using the Package for CD Feature

The safest way to transport a PowerPoint presentation to another computer is to use the Package for CD feature. With this feature, a presentation can be copied onto a CD or to a folder or network location and all of the linked files and fonts, as well as the PowerPoint Viewer program, can be included in case the destination computer does not have PowerPoint installed on it. To use the Package for CD feature, click the File tab, click the *Export* option, click the *Package Presentation for CD* option, and then click the Package for CD button. At the Package for CD dialog box, type a name for the CD and then click the Copy to CD button.

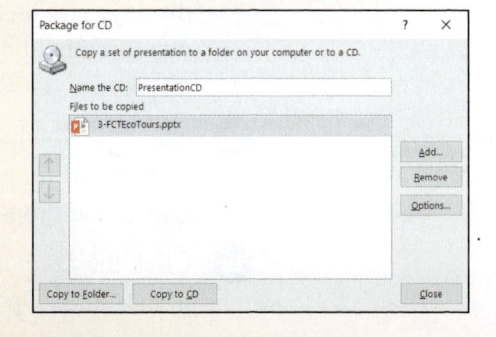

Activity 3.9 **POWERPOINT** 75

Activity 3.10 Adding Audio and Video

Adding audio and/or video effects to a presentation will turn a slide show into a true multi-media experience for the viewing audience. Including a variety of elements in a presentation will stimulate interest in a slide show and keep the audience engaged. Insert an audio file or video file from a folder or from the Insert Video window.

What You Will Do To add interest, you decide to experiment with adding a video file and an audio file to the presentation. The last slide of the slide show will display the video file and play an audio file. This will allow the presenter time to answer questions from the audience while the video and audio files play.

Tutorial
Inserting and Modifying an Audio File

Tutorial
Inserting and Modifying a Video File

1. With **3-FCTEcoTours** open, make Slide 7 active, click the Insert tab, and then click the New Slide button.

2. Click in the title placeholder and then type Let the adventure begin!

3. Click the Insert Video button in the content placeholder.

4. At the Insert Video window, click the Browse button to the right of the *From a file* option.

   You can also display the Insert Video dialog box by clicking the Insert tab, clicking the Video button in the Media group, and then clicking *Video on My PC*.

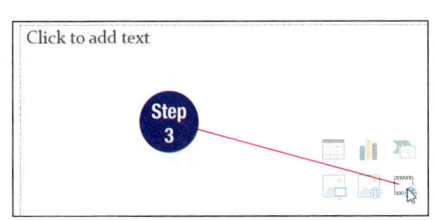

5. At the Insert Video dialog box, navigate to your PowerPointS3 folder and then double-click the **Wildlife** video file.

   This inserts the video file in a window in the slide and the Video Tools Format tab is selected. Use options and buttons on this tab to preview the video file; change the brightness, contrast, and color of the video; apply a formatting style to the video window; and arrange and size the video in the slide.

6. Click the Play button in the Preview group to preview the video file.

   The video plays for approximately 30 seconds.

7. After viewing the video, click the Video Tools Playback tab.

8. Click the *Fade In* measurement box up arrow in the Editing group until *01.00* displays and then click the *Fade Out* measurement box up arrow until *01.00* displays.

9. Click the Volume button in the Video Options group and then click *Low* at the drop-down list.

10. Click the *Loop until Stopped* check box in the Video Options group to insert a check mark.

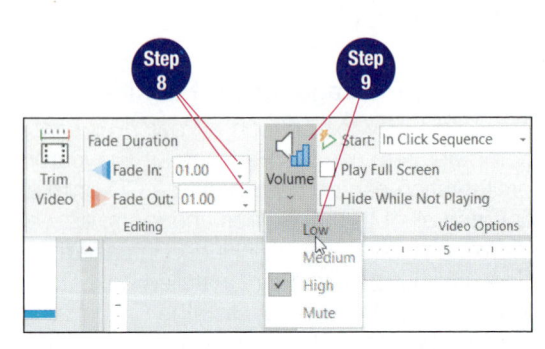

76 POWERPOINT Section 3 Customizing a Presentation

In Brief

Insert Video File
1. Click Insert Video button in placeholder.
2. Navigate to folder.
3. Double-click video file.
OR
1. Click Insert tab.
2. Click Video button.
3. Click *Video on My PC*.
4. Navigate to folder.
5. Double-click video file.

Insert Audio File
1. Click Insert tab.
2. Click Audio button.
3. Click *Audio on My PC*.
4. Navigate to folder.
5. Double-click audio file.

11. Make Slide 1 active and then run the slide show. When the slide containing the video file displays, move the mouse pointer over the video file window and then click the Play button at the bottom left of the window.

12. After viewing the video a couple of times, press the Esc key two times.

13. You decide that you want the video window to fill the slide, start automatically when the slide displays, and play only once. To do this, make sure Slide 8 is active, click the video file window, and then click the Video Tools Playback tab.

14. Click the *Play Full Screen* check box in the Video Options group to insert a check mark and then click the *Loop until Stopped* check box to remove the check mark.

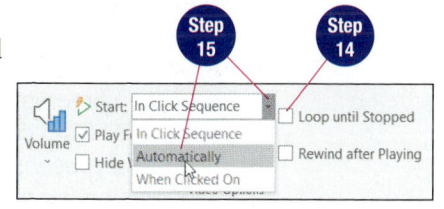

15. Click the *Start* option box arrow in the Video Options group and then click *Automatically* at the drop-down list.

16. Make Slide 1 active and then run the slide show. When the slide containing the video displays, the video will automatically begin. When the video is finished playing, press the Esc key to return to Normal view.

17. You decide that you want music to play after the presentation. Begin by making sure Slide 8 is the active slide, clicking the Insert tab, clicking the Audio button in the Media group, and then clicking *Audio on My PC* at the drop-down list.

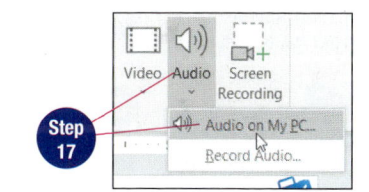

18. At the Insert Audio dialog box, navigate to your PowerPointS3 folder and then double-click the audio file named *FCTAudioClip-01*.

    This inserts the audio file in the slide, with the Audio Tools Playback tab selected.

19. If necessary, click the Audio Tools Playback tab.

20. Click the *Start* option box arrow in the Audio Options group and then click *Automatically* at the drop-down list.

21. Click the *Hide During Show* check box in the Audio Options group to insert a check mark and then click the *Loop until Stopped* check box to insert a check mark.

22. Make Slide 1 active and then run the slide show. When the last slide displays, watch the video, listen to the audio file for about a minute or two, and then press the Esc key to return to the Normal view.

23. Save **3-FCTEcoTours**.

Check Your Work Compare your work to the model answer available in the online course.

In Addition

Changing the Video Color

Use the Color button in the Adjust group on the Video Tools Format tab to change the video color. If the video is to play in black and white, click the Color button and then click the *Grayscale* option at the drop-down gallery. Click the *Sepia* option and the video will have an old-fashioned appearance when played.

Activity 3.11 Setting and Rehearsing Timings for a Slide Show

A slide show can be set up to run automatically with each slide displaying for a specific number of seconds. To set times for slides, click the Slide Show tab and then click the Rehearse Timings button in the Set Up group. The first slide displays in Slide Show view and the Recording toolbar displays. Use buttons on this toolbar to specify times for each slide. Use options at the Set Up Show dialog box to control the slide show. Display this dialog box by clicking the Set Up Slide Show button in the Set Up group. Use options in the *Show type* section to specify the type of slide show to be displayed. For the slide show to be totally automatic and run continuously until the show is ended, click the *Loop continuously until 'Esc'* check box to insert a check mark. In the *Advance slides* section, the *Using timings, if present* option should be selected by default. Select *Manually* to advance the slides using the mouse instead of the preset times.

What You Will Do Melissa Gehring has asked you to automate the slide show so it can be run continuously at the upcoming travel conference.

Tutorial
Setting Timings for a Slide Show

Tutorial
Looping a Slide Show Continuously

1. With **3-FCTEcoTours** open, save it with the name **3-FCTEcoTours-Rehearsed**.

2. Make Slide 8 active, click the audio icon to select it, and then press the Delete key. Click the video window to select it and then press the Delete key.

3. Type the following information in the content placeholder:

    Call today to schedule your exciting eco-tour adventure:
    ○ 1-888-555-1330
    Or visit our website:
    ○ https://ppi-edu.net/fc-travel

4. Select the content placeholder (make sure the border is a solid line) and then click the Bold button in the Font group on the Home tab.

5. Make Slide 1 active, click the Slide Show tab, and then click the Rehearse Timings button in the Set Up group.

    The first slide displays in Slide Show view, the Recording toolbar displays as well. The timing for the first slide begins automatically. Refer to Figure 3.3 for the names of the Recording toolbar buttons.

6. Wait until the time displayed for the current slide reaches four seconds and then click the Next button.

    If you miss the time, click the Repeat button to reset the clock back to zero for the current slide.

7. Set the following times for the remaining slides:
    - Slide 2: 5 seconds
    - Slide 3: 5 seconds
    - Slide 4: 4 seconds
    - Slide 5: 6 seconds
    - Slide 6: 8 seconds
    - Slide 7: 7 seconds
    - Slide 8: 8 seconds

8. After the last slide has displayed with the total slide show time, click Yes at the message asking if you want to keep the new slide timings.

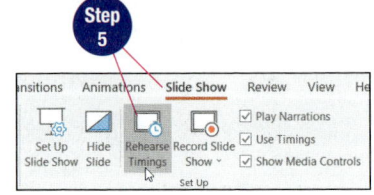

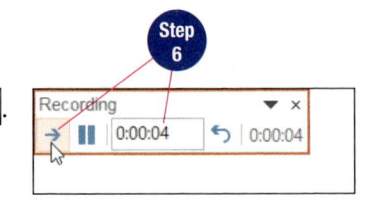

Figure 3.3 Recording Toolbar Buttons

Next — Pause — slide time — Repeat — total slide show time

In Brief

Set and Rehearse Timings
1. Click Slide Show tab.
2. Click Rehearse Timings button.
3. When correct time displays, click Next button.
4. Continue until times are set for each slide.
5. Click Yes at message.

Set Up Slide Show to Run Continuously
1. Click Slide Show tab.
2. Click Set Up Slide Show button.
3. Click *Loop continuously until 'Esc'* check box.
4. Click OK.

9 Click the Slide Sorter button on the Status bar. Notice the slides display with the times listed below. (The times that display include the transition duration time so the times may display with approximately one additional second added.)

You can adjust the timings manually with options in the Timing group on the Transitions tab. See the In Addition below.

10 Double-click Slide 1 to change to Normal view.

11 Set up the slide show to run continuously by clicking the Set Up Slide Show button in the Set Up group on the Slide Show tab.

12 At the Set Up Show dialog box, click the *Loop continuously until 'Esc'* check box.

13 Click OK to close the dialog box.

14 Insert an audio file in Slide 1 that will play continuously throughout the slide show. To begin, click the Insert tab, click the Audio button in the Media group, and then click the *Audio on My PC* option.

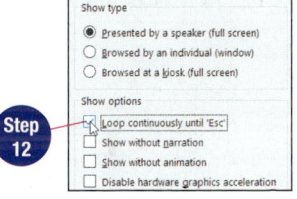

15 At the Insert Audio dialog box, navigate to your PowerPointS3 folder and then double-click the audio file named ***FCTAudioClip-02***.

16 If necessary, click the Audio Tools Playback tab. Click the *Start* option box arrow in the Audio Options group and then click *Automatically* at the drop-down list.

17 Click the *Play Across Slides* check box in the Audio Options group to insert a check mark, click the *Loop until Stopped* check box to insert a check mark, and then click the *Hide During Show* check box to insert a check mark.

18 Drag the audio icon to the bottom center of the slide.

19 Run the slide show, beginning with Slide 1. The slide show will start and run continuously. Watch the presentation until it starts for the second time and then end the show by pressing the Esc key.

20 Print the presentation as handouts with nine slides displayed horizontally per page.

21 Save and then close **3-FCTEcoTours-Rehearsed**.

Check Your Work Compare your work to the model answer available in the online course.

In Addition

Setting Times Manually

The time a slide remains on the screen during a slide show can be manually set using options in the Timing group on the Transitions tab. To set manual times for slides, click the *On Mouse Click* check box to remove the check mark and then click the *After* check box to insert a check mark. Click in the *After* text box, type the specific number of seconds the slide is to display on the screen when running the slide show, and then press the Enter key. Click the Apply To All button to apply the time to each slide in the presentation.

Activity 3.11 **POWERPOINT** 79

Features Summary

Feature	Ribbon Tab, Group	Button	Keyboard Shortcut
action button	Insert, Illustrations		
audio file	Insert, Media		
Clipboard task pane	Home, Clipboard		
draw shape	Insert, Illustrations OR Home, Drawing		
gridlines	View, Show		Shift + F9
header and footer	Insert, Text		
hyperlink	Insert, Links		Ctrl + K
rehearse timings	Slide Show, Set Up		
replace	Home, Editing		Ctrl + H
slide master	View, Master Views		
table	Insert, Tables		
text box	Insert, Text		
video file	Insert, Media		
WordArt	Insert, Text		

Integrating Programs | SECTION 3

Word, Excel, and PowerPoint

Data Files

Before beginning section work, copy the IntegratingS3 folder to your storage medium and then make IntegratingS3 the active folder.

Skills

- Export a PowerPoint presentation to a Word document
- Export a Word outline document to a PowerPoint presentation
- Link an Excel chart with a Word document and a PowerPoint presentation
- Edit a linked object
- Embed a Word table in a PowerPoint presentation
- Edit an embedded object

Projects Overview

MARQUEE PRODUCTIONS Create presentation handouts in Word for use in an annual meeting PowerPoint presentation.

Worldwide Enterprises Prepare a PowerPoint presentation for the Distribution Department of Worldwide Enterprises using a Word outline. Copy an Excel chart and link it to the Distribution Department meeting presentation and to a Word document and then edit the linked chart. Copy a Word table containing data on preview distribution dates, embed it in a PowerPoint slide, and then update the table.

FIRST CHOICE TRAVEL Export a PowerPoint presentation containing information on vacation specials offered by First Choice Travel to a Word document.

NIAGARA PENINSULA COLLEGE Link an Excel chart containing Information on department enrollments to a PowerPoint slide and then update the chart in Excel. Embed a Word table in a PowerPoint slide and then edit the table in the slide.

The online course includes additional training and assessment resources.

81

Activity 3.1 — Exporting a PowerPoint Presentation to Word

One of the benefits of a suite like Microsoft Office is that data in one program can be sent to another program. For example, send PowerPoint content to a Word document. To send presentation content to a document, click the File tab, click the *Export* option, click the *Create Handouts* option, and then click the Create Handouts button. At the Send to Microsoft Word dialog box, specify the layout of the content in the Word document and whether to paste content or link content and then click OK. One of the advantages to sending PowerPoint presentation content to a Word document is that the content can be formatted using the Word formatting options.

NIAGARA PENINSULA COLLEGE

What You Will Do   Create a Word document handout that contains slides from a PowerPoint presentation on the Theatre Arts Division at Niagara Peninsula College.

1. Open PowerPoint and then open **NPCDivPres**.

2. Save the presentation with the name **3-NPCDivPres**.

3. Click the File tab, click the *Export* option, click the *Create Handouts* option, and then click the Create Handouts button.

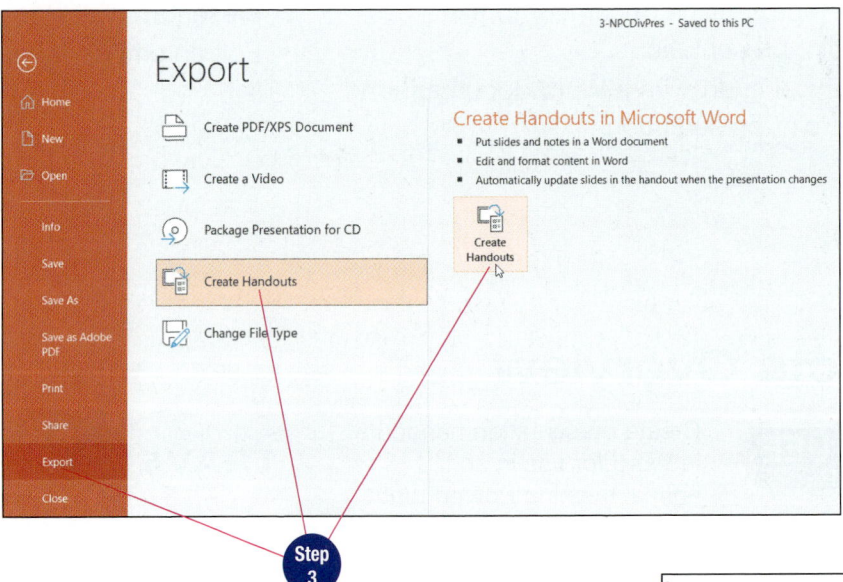

4. At the Send to Microsoft Word dialog box, click the *Blank lines next to slides* option.

5. Click the *Paste link* option in the *Add slides to Microsoft Word document* section and then click OK.

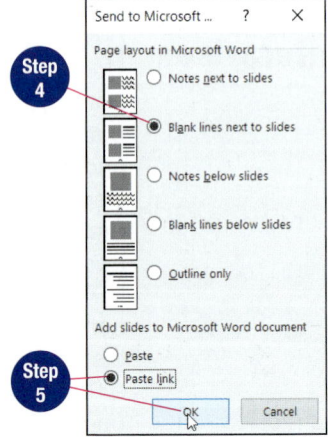

82   INTEGRATING PROGRAMS   Section 3   Word, Excel, and PowerPoint

In Brief

Export PowerPoint Presentation to Word
1. Open presentation.
2. Click File tab.
3. Click *Export* option.
4. Click *Create Handouts* option.
5. Click Create Handouts button.
6. Choose options at Send to Microsoft Word dialog box.
7. Click OK.

6. If necessary, click the Word button on the taskbar.

   The slides display in a Word document as thumbnails followed by blank lines.

7. Save the Word document in your IntegratingS3 folder and name it **3-NPCDivPresHandout**.

8. Print and then close **3-NPCDivPresHandout**.

9. Click the PowerPoint button on the taskbar.

10. Make Slide 3 active and then change *$750* to *$850*, *$350* to *$450*, and *$250* to *$300*.

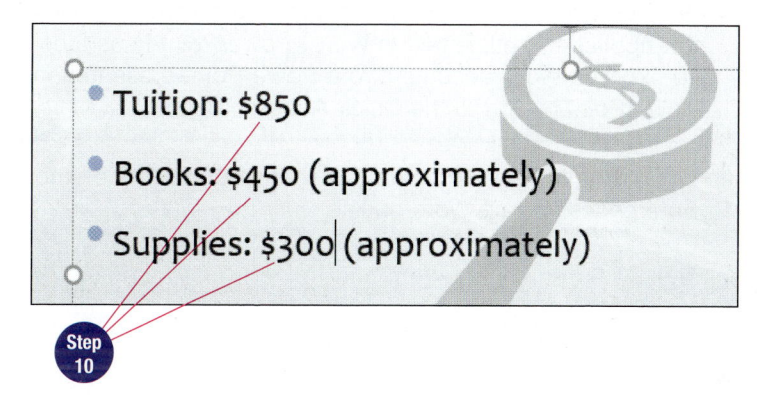

    - Tuition: $850
    - Books: $450 (approximately)
    - Supplies: $300 (approximately)

    Step 10

11. Save **3-NPCDivPres**.

12. Click the Word button on the taskbar and then open **3-NPCDivPresHandout**. At the message asking if you want to update the document with the data from the linked files, click the Yes button.

13. Scroll through the document and notice that the dollar amounts in Slide 3 reflect the changes you made to Slide 3 in the PowerPoint presentation.

14. Save, print, and then close **3-NPCDivPresHandout**.

15. Make PowerPoint active and then close **3-NPCDivPres**.

Check Your Work Compare your work to the model answer available in the online course.

In Addition

Pasting and Linking Data

The *Paste* option at the Send to Microsoft Word dialog box is selected by default and is available for all of the page layout options. With this option selected, the data inserted in Word is not connected or linked to the original data in the PowerPoint presentation. If the data in the presentation is updated and the data should be updated in the Word document as well, select the *Paste link* option at the Send to Microsoft Word dialog box. This option is available for all of the page layout options except the *Outline only* option.

Activity 3.1 **INTEGRATING PROGRAMS**

Activity 3.2 Exporting a Word Outline to a PowerPoint Presentation

As learned in the previous activity, the Microsoft Office suite allows users to send content in one program to another program. For example, send Word content to a PowerPoint presentation. Create text for slides in a Word outline and then export that outline to PowerPoint. PowerPoint creates new slides based on the heading styles used in the Word outline. Text formatted with a Heading 1 style becomes slide titles. Heading 2 text becomes first-level bulleted text, Heading 3 text becomes second-level bulleted text, and so on. If styles are not applied to outline text in Word, PowerPoint uses tabs or indents to place text on slides. To export a Word document to a PowerPoint presentation, first add the Send to Microsoft PowerPoint button to the Quick Access Toolbar.

Worldwide Enterprises

What You Will Do Prepare a presentation for the Distribution Department of Worldwide Enterprises using a Word outline.

1. Make sure both Word and PowerPoint are open.

2. Make Word active and then open **WEOutline**.

   Text in this document has been formatted with the Heading 1 and Heading 2 styles.

3. Add the Send to Microsoft PowerPoint button to the Quick Access Toolbar. Begin by clicking the Customize Quick Access Toolbar button at the right of the Quick Access Toolbar.

4. Click *More Commands* at the drop-down list.

5. At the Word Options dialog box, click the *Choose commands from* option box arrow and then click *All Commands* at the drop-down list.

6. Scroll down the list box below the *Choose commands from* option box and then double-click *Send to Microsoft PowerPoint*.

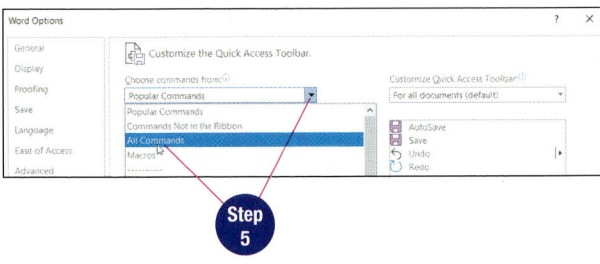

   Items in the list box display in alphabetical order.

7. Click OK to close the Word Options dialog box.

   Notice that the Send to Microsoft PowerPoint button has been added to the Quick Access Toolbar.

8. Send the outline to PowerPoint by clicking the Send to Microsoft PowerPoint button on the Quick Access Toolbar.

9. When the presentation displays on the screen, make sure Slide 1 is active. If necessary, click the Enable Editing button located below the ribbon. (If the presentation does not display, click the PowerPoint button on the taskbar.)

   The presentation is created with a blank design template.

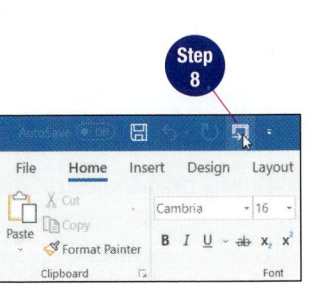

84 INTEGRATING PROGRAMS Section 3 Word, Excel, and PowerPoint

In Brief

Add Send to Microsoft PowerPoint Button to Quick Access Toolbar
1. Click Customize Quick Access Toolbar button on Quick Access Toolbar.
2. Click *More Commands*.
3. Click *Choose commands from* option box arrow.
4. Click *All Commands*.
5. Scroll down *Choose commands from* list box, double-click *Send to Microsoft PowerPoint*.
6. Click OK.

Send Word Outline to PowerPoint Presentation
1. Open Word document.
2. Click Send to Microsoft PowerPoint button on Quick Access Toolbar.

10. With Slide 1 active, change the layout by clicking the Layout button in the Slides group on the Home tab and then clicking the *Title Slide* option at the drop-down list.

11. Make Slide 4 active and then apply the Title Only layout. Apply the Title Only layout to Slides 5 and 6 as well.

12. Apply a design theme by clicking the Design tab, clicking the More Themes button in the Themes group, and then clicking the *Retrospect* option.

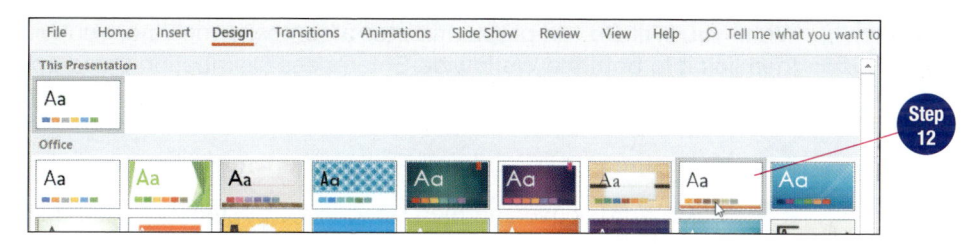

13. Click the second variant option in the Variants group (white with green).

14. Save the presentation and name it **3-WEDistDeptMtg**.

15. Close **3-WEDistDeptMtg**.

16. Click the Word button on the taskbar.

17. Right-click the Send to Microsoft PowerPoint button on the Quick Access Toolbar and then click *Remove from Quick Access Toolbar* at the shortcut menu.

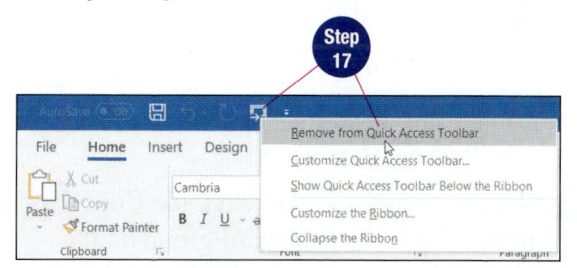

18. Close **WEOutline** without saving the changes.

Check Your Work Compare your work to the model answer available in the online course.

In Addition

Applying a Style in Word

Heading styles were already applied to the text in **WEOutline**. If an outline is created in Word that is to be exported to PowerPoint, apply styles using options in the Styles group on the Home tab. A Word document contains a number of predesigned formats grouped into style sets. Click the Design tab to display the available style sets in the Document Formatting group. Choose a style set and the styles visible in the Styles group on the Home tab change to reflect the selection. To display additional available styles, click the More Styles button (contains a horizontal line and a down-pointing triangle) at the right of the gallery in the Styles group on the Home tab. To apply a heading style, position the insertion point in the text, click the More Styles button, and then click the specific style at the drop-down gallery.

Activity 3.2 **INTEGRATING PROGRAMS**

Activity 3.3 — Linking an Excel Chart with a Word Document and a PowerPoint Presentation

An object, such as a table or chart, can be copied and linked to files created in other programs. For example, copy an Excel chart and link it to a Word document and/or a PowerPoint presentation. The advantage to copying and linking over copying and pasting is that when an object is edited in the originating program, called the *source program*, the object is automatically updated in the linked file in the other program, called the *destination program*. When an object is linked, it exists in the source program but not as a separate object in the destination program. Since the object is located only in the source program, changes made to the object in the source program will be reflected in the destination program. An object can be linked to more than one destination program or file.

Worldwide Enterprises

What You Will Do In preparation for a company meeting, you will copy an Excel chart and then link it to both the Worldwide Enterprises Distribution Department meeting presentation and to a Word document.

1. Make sure PowerPoint and Word are open and then open Excel.

2. Make Word active and then open **WERevDoc**. Save the document with the name **3-WERevDoc**.

3. Make PowerPoint active, open **3-WEDistDeptMtg**, and then make Slide 6 active.

4. Make Excel active and then open **WERevChart**. Save the workbook with the name **3-WERevChart**.

5. Copy and link the chart to the Word document and the PowerPoint presentation. Start by clicking in the chart to select it.

   Make sure you select the entire chart and not a specific chart element. To do so, try clicking just inside the chart border.

6. With the chart selected, click the Copy button in the Clipboard group on the Home tab.

7. Click the Word button on the taskbar.

8. Press Ctrl + End to move the insertion point to the end of the document.

9. Click the Paste button arrow and then click *Paste Special* at the drop-down list.

10. At the Paste Special dialog box, click the *Paste link* option, click the *Microsoft Excel Chart Object* option in the *As* list box, and then click OK.

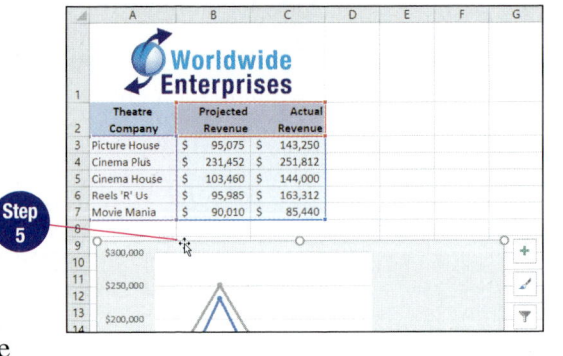

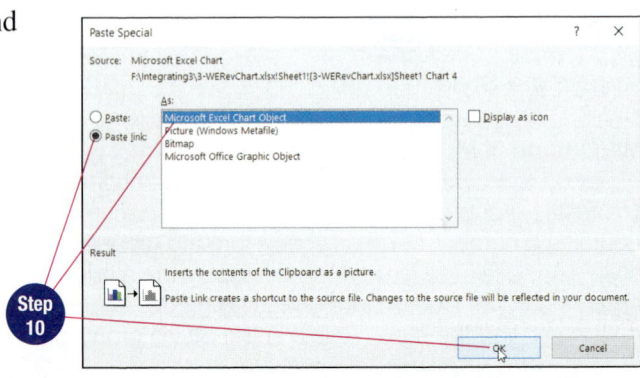

86 INTEGRATING PROGRAMS   Section 3   Word, Excel, and PowerPoint

In Brief

Link Object between Programs
1. Open source program, open file containing object.
2. Select object, click Copy button.
3. Open destination program, open file into which object will be linked.
4. Click Paste button arrow, click *Paste Special*.
5. At Paste Special dialog box, click *Paste link*.
6. Click object in *As* list box.
7. Click OK.

11. Select the chart and then center it by clicking the Center button in the Paragraph group on the Home tab.

12. Save, print, and then close **3-WERevDoc**.

13. Click the PowerPoint button on the taskbar.

14. With Slide 6 active, make sure the Home tab is selected, click the Paste button arrow, and then click *Paste Special* at the drop-down list.

15. At the Paste Special dialog box, click the *Paste link* option, make sure *Microsoft Excel Chart Object* is selected in the *As* list box, and then click OK.

16. Increase the size of the chart so it better fills the slide and then center it on the slide, as shown in Figure 3.1.

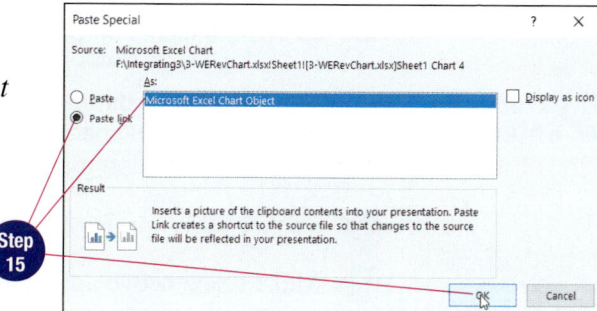

17. Click outside the chart to deselect it.

18. Save the presentation, print only Slide 6, and then close **3-WEDistDeptMtg**.

19. Click the Excel button on the taskbar.

20. Click outside the chart to deselect it.

21. Save, print, and then close **3-WERevChart**.

Figure 3.1 Step 16

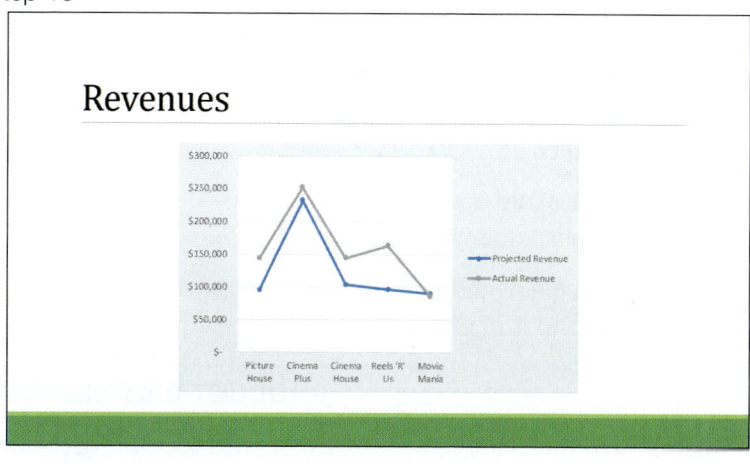

Check Your Work Compare your work to the model answer available in the online course.

In Addition

Linking Data or an Object within a Program

In this activity, an object was linked between programs using the Paste Special dialog box. An object can also be linked in Word using options at the Object dialog box. To do this, click the Insert tab and then click the Object button in the Text group. At the Object dialog box, click the Create from File tab. At the dialog box, type the file name in the *File name* text box or click the Browse button and then select the file from the appropriate folder. Click the *Link to file* check box to insert a check mark and then click OK.

Activity 3.3   **INTEGRATING PROGRAMS**   87

Activity 3.4 Editing a Linked Object

The advantage to linking an object over simply copying it is that editing the object in the source program will automatically update the object in the destination program(s) as well. To edit a linked object, open the file containing the object in the source program, make edits, and then save the file. The next time the document, workbook, or presentation is opened in the destination program, the object will be updated.

Worldwide Enterprises

What You Will Do Edit the actual and projected revenue numbers in the Worldwide Enterprises Excel worksheet and then open and print the Word document and the PowerPoint presentation that contain the linked chart.

1. Make sure Word, Excel, and PowerPoint are open.

2. Make Excel active and then open **3-WERevChart**.

3. You discover that one theatre company was left out of the revenues chart. Add a row to the worksheet by clicking in cell A6 to make it active. Click the Insert button arrow in the Cells group on the Home tab and then click *Insert Sheet Rows* at the drop-down list.

4. Type the following data in the specified cells:
    - A6: Regal Theatres
    - B6: 69550
    - C6: 50320

5. Click in cell A3.

6. Save, print, and close **3-WERevChart** and then close Excel.

7. Make Word active and then open **3-WERevDoc**. At the message asking if you want to update the linked file, click the Yes button.

8. Notice how the linked chart is automatically updated to reflect the changes you made to it in Excel.

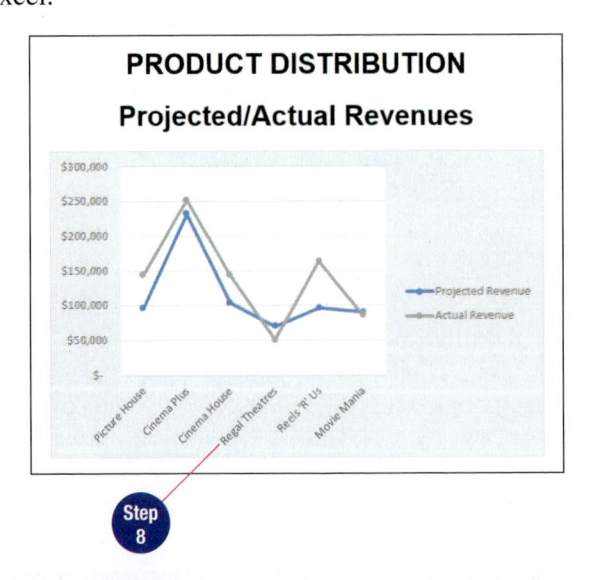

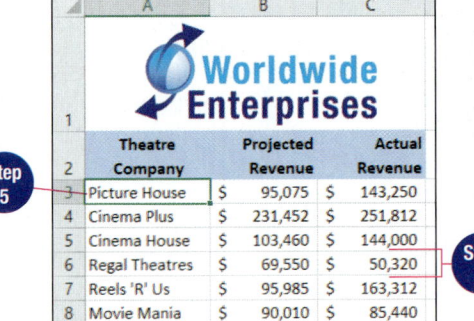

	A	B	C
1	Worldwide Enterprises		
2	Theatre Company	Projected Revenue	Actual Revenue
3	Picture House	$ 95,075	$ 143,250
4	Cinema Plus	$ 231,452	$ 251,812
5	Cinema House	$ 103,460	$ 144,000
6	Regal Theatres	$ 69,550	$ 50,320
7	Reels 'R' Us	$ 95,985	$ 163,312
8	Movie Mania	$ 90,010	$ 85,440

PRODUCT DISTRIBUTION
Projected/Actual Revenues

88 INTEGRATING PROGRAMS Section 3 Word, Excel, and PowerPoint

9. Save, print, and then close **3-WERevDoc**.

10. Make PowerPoint active and then open **3-WEDistDeptMtg**.

11. At the message stating that the presentation contains links, click the Update Links button.

12. Make Slide 6 active and then notice how the linked chart has been automatically updated to reflect the changes you made to it in Excel.

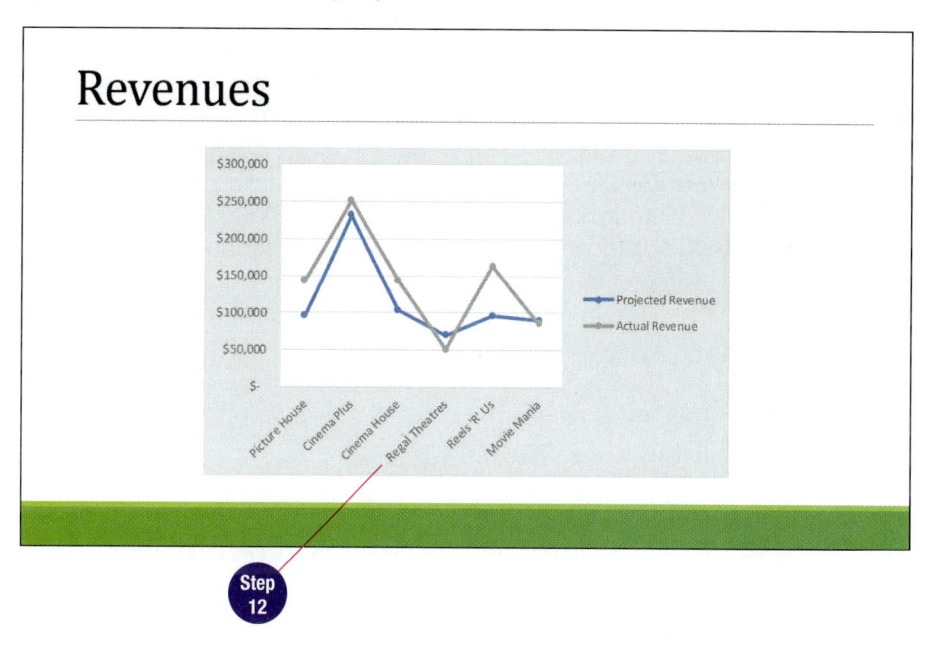

13. Save the presentation and then print only Slide 6.

14. Close **3-WEDistDeptMtg**.

Check Your Work Compare your work to the model answer available in the online course.

In Addition

Updating a Link Manually

A link can be updated manually in the destination program. To do this, open a Word document containing a linked object. Right-click the object, point to *Linked (type of object) Object*, and then click *Links*. At the Links dialog box, click the *Manual update* option and then click OK. With *Manual update* selected, the link will only be updated by right-clicking the linked object and then clicking *Update Link* or at the Links dialog box by clicking the link in the list box and then clicking the Update Now button.

Activity 3.4 **INTEGRATING PROGRAMS** 89

Activity 3.5 Embedding and Editing a Word Table in a PowerPoint Slide

An object can be copied and pasted, copied and linked, or copied and embedded from one file into another. A linked object resides in the source program but not as a separate object in the destination program. An embedded object resides in the source program as well as in the destination program. If a change is made to an embedded object in the source program, the change will not be made to the object in the destination program. The main advantage to embedding rather than simply copying and pasting is that an embedded object can be edited in the destination program using the tools of the source program.

Worldwide Enterprises

What You Will Do Copy a Word table containing data on preview distribution dates for Worldwide Enterprises and then embed the table in a slide in a PowerPoint presentation. Update the distribution dates for the two embedded tables.

1. Make sure both Word and PowerPoint are open.

2. Make PowerPoint active and then open **3-WEDistDeptMtg**.

3. At the message stating that the presentation contains links, click the Update Links button.

4. Make Slide 4 active.

5. Make Word active and then open **WEPrevDistTable**.

6. Click in a cell in the table and then select the table. To do this, click the Table Tools Layout tab, click the Select button in the Table group, and then click *Select Table* at the drop-down list.

7. With the table selected, click the Home tab and then click the Copy button in the Clipboard group.

8. Click the PowerPoint button on the taskbar.

9. With Slide 4 active, click the Paste button arrow and then click *Paste Special* at the drop-down list.

10. At the Paste Special dialog box, click *Microsoft Word Document Object* in the *As* list box and then click OK.

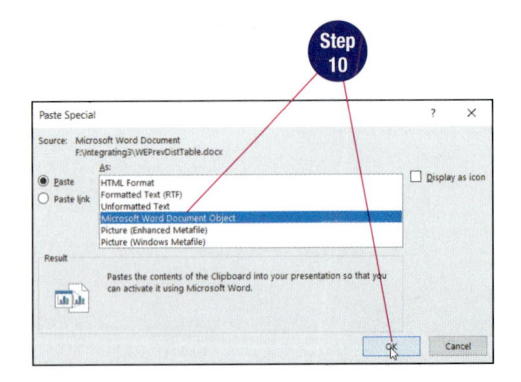

11. With the table selected in the slide, use the sizing handles to increase the size and change the position of the table as shown in Figure 3.2.

12. Click outside the table to deselect it.

90 INTEGRATING PROGRAMS Section 3 Word, Excel, and PowerPoint

Figure 3.2 Step 11

In Brief

Embed Object
1. Open source program, open file containing object.
2. Select object, click Copy button.
3. Open destination program, open file into which object will be embedded.
4. Click Paste button arrow, click *Paste Special*.
5. At Paste Special dialog box, click object in *As* list box.
6. Click OK.

Edit Embedded Object
1. Open file containing embedded object.
2. Double-click object.
3. Make edits, click outside object to deselect it.

Preview Distribution

Theatre Company	Location	Date
Cinema House	Montreal, Toronto	May 18
Cinema House	Vancouver	May 11
Cinema Plus	Los Angeles, San Diego	May 4
Cinema Plus	New York, Newark	May 11
Movie Mania	Wichita	May 25
Picture House	St. Louis	May 25
Picture House	Denver	May 18
Picture House	Salt Lake City	May 25

13. Save the presentation and then print only Slide 4.

14. Click the Word button on the taskbar and then close the document.

15. Click the PowerPoint button on the taskbar and then make Slide 5 active.

16. Make Word active and then open **WEGenDistTable**.

17. Click in a cell in the table and then select the table. To do this, click the Table Tools Layout tab, click the Select button in the Table group, and then click *Select Table* at the drop-down list.

18. Click the Home tab and then click the Copy button in the Clipboard group.

19. Click the PowerPoint button on the taskbar.

20. With Slide 5 active, click the Paste button arrow and then click *Paste Special* at the drop-down list.

21. At the Paste Special dialog box, click *Microsoft Word Document Object* in the *As* list box and then click OK.

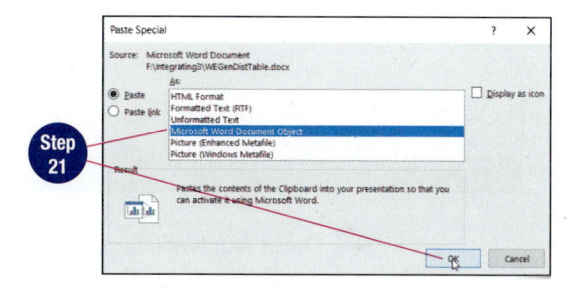

Step 21

22. Increase the size and position of the table in the slide so it displays as shown in Figure 3.3 on the next page.

23. The distribution date to Cinema Plus in Sacramento and Oakland has been delayed until June 1. Edit the date by double-clicking the table in the slide.

Double-clicking the table displays the Word tabs and ribbon at the top of the screen. Horizontal and vertical rulers also display around the table.

Activity 3.5 **INTEGRATING PROGRAMS** 91

24 Using the mouse, select *May 25* in the *Sacramento, Oakland* row and then type **June 1**.

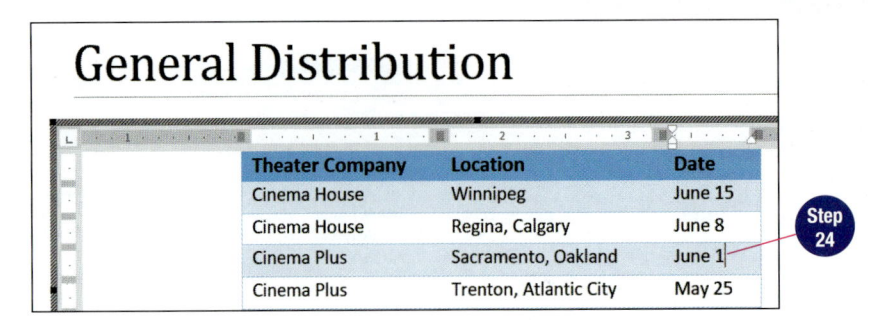

General Distribution

Theater Company	Location	Date
Cinema House	Winnipeg	June 15
Cinema House	Regina, Calgary	June 8
Cinema Plus	Sacramento, Oakland	June 1
Cinema Plus	Trenton, Atlantic City	May 25

Step 24

25 Click outside the table to deselect it.
  Notice that the Word tabs disappear.

26 Print Slide 5 of the presentation.

27 Apply a transition and transition sound of your choosing to all slides in the presentation and then run the slide show.

28 Save and close **3-WEDistDeptMtg** and then close PowerPoint.

29 Click the Word button on the taskbar, close the document, and then close Word.

Figure 3.3 Step 22

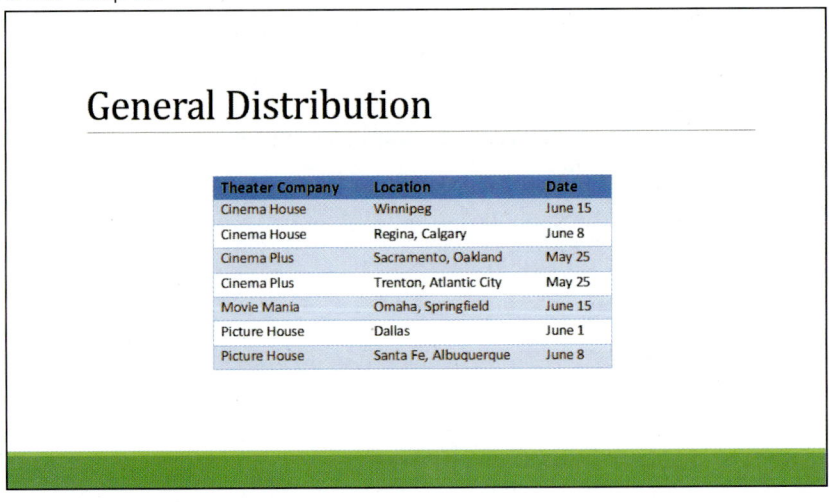

General Distribution

Theater Company	Location	Date
Cinema House	Winnipeg	June 15
Cinema House	Regina, Calgary	June 8
Cinema Plus	Sacramento, Oakland	May 25
Cinema Plus	Trenton, Atlantic City	May 25
Movie Mania	Omaha, Springfield	June 15
Picture House	Dallas	June 1
Picture House	Santa Fe, Albuquerque	June 8

Check Your Work Compare your work to the model answer available in the online course.

In Addition

Working with a Cropped Object

Some embedded or linked objects may appear cropped on the right or bottom side even if enough room is available to fit the image on the page or slide. A large embedded or linked object may appear cropped because Word converts the object into a Windows metafile (.wmf), which has a maximum height and width. If the embedded or linked object exceeds this maximum size, it appears cropped. To prevent an object from appearing cropped, consider reducing the size of the data by reducing the font size, column size, line spacing, and so on.

INDEX

A
action buttons
  inserting, 70–71
  linking, 71
Action Settings dialog box, 70
adding
  audio file, 76–77
  slides, 7–9
  sound, 26–27
  transitions, 26–27
  video, 76–77
alignment
  changing, 40–41
  shortcut keys, 41
animation
  applying custom, 55
  applying to objects and text, 54–55
Animation Pane button, 55
Animations tab, 54
antonyms, 20–21
audio file, adding, 76–77
AutoFit Options button, 15

B
backstage area, 4, 5
bold, 34
bulleted text, creating in slide, 41

C
chart, organizational
  inserting and formatting in SmartArt, 50–53
clip art images. See images
Clipboard task pane
  options on, 59
  using, 58–59
closing, PowerPoint, 5
Collapse the Ribbon button, 3
color
  changing theme, 42–43
  changing video clip color, 77
  choosing custom, 39
Colors dialog box, 39
copying
  Clipboard task pane, 58–59
  shapes, 66–67
  slides within presentation, 17
  text, 32–33
Create Handouts button, 82
creating
  presentation, with installed template, 2–5
  slides, 6–9
  table in a slide, 68–69
cropped objects, working with, 92
custom animation, applying, 55
custom color, choosing, 39

customizing, shapes, 64–65
cutting, text, 32–33

D
data
  linking within program, 87
  pasting and linking, 83
decreasing, indent, 32–33
deleting, slides, 16–17
design theme
  applying more than one, to presentation, 73
  changing, 42–43
  choosing, 6–9
design thumbnails, 6
destination program, 86, 88
drawing, shapes, 64–65
Drawing Tools Format tab, 62, 63
  using buttons and options in, 63

E
editing
  linked object, 88–89
  while checking spelling, 20–21
Excel chart, linking with Word document and PowerPoint presentation, 86–87
exporting
  presentation to Word, 82–83
  Word outline to PowerPoint presentation, 84–85

F
File tab, 3, 5
Find and Replace feature, 60–61
finding, text, 60–61
Font dialog box, changing fonts at, 36–37
font effects, applying, 34–35
Font group, applying font effects with, 34–35
fonts
  applying formatting, 34–35
  changing
    all occurrences of, 37
    at Font Dialog box, 36–37
    theme, 42–43
  defined, 35
  replacing, 36–37
footers, inserting, 74–75
Format Painter, formatting with, 38–39
formatting
  with buttons in Picture Tools Format tab, 47
  with Format Painter, 38–39
  with slide master, 72–73
  SmartArt graphic, 50–53
  WordArt, 62–63

G
gridlines, displaying, 66–67

H
handouts
  inserting headers/footer on, 74–75
  Word document that contains PowerPoint slides, 82–83
Header and Footer dialog box, 74
headers, inserting, 74–75
Help feature
  on specific functions, 19
  using, 18–19
hiding
  mouse pointer, 25
  slides, 16–17
Home tab, 5
  Font group in, 34
horizontal text alignment, changing, 40–41

I
I-beam pointer, 3
images
  compress, 47
  formatting with buttons in Picture Tools Format tab, 47
  inserting, 44–47
  moving, 44–47
  sizing, 44–47
indent
  decreasing, 32–33
  increasing, 32–33
Ink Tools, using during presentation, 25
inserting
  action buttons, 70–71
  footers, 74–75
  headers, 74–75
  hyperlinks, 70–71
  image, 44–47
  new line, 41
  online image, 47
  screenshot, 48–49
  slides in presentation, 10–11
  SmartArt graphic, 50–53
  text box, 66–67
  WordArt, 62–63
insertion point, 3
  movement commands for, 8
italic, 34

K
keyboard, for navigating presentation, 13

L
line, inserting new, 41
line spacing, changing, 40–41
linked object, editing, 88–89
linking
  action buttons, 71
  data, 83
  data/object within program, 87

Excel Chart with Word document/PowerPoint presentation, 86–87
  updating link manually, 89
Links dialog box, 89
live preview, 6

M
monospaced typeface, 35
More Themes button, 6
mouse pointer, 16–17
  hiding/displaying, 25
moving
  image, 44–47
  placeholder, 14–15
  slides, 16–17
  table, 69

N
navigating, in presentation, 10–11, 13
New Slide button, 7–8
Next Slide button, 10
Normal view, 12–13
notes, inserting headers/footer on, 74–75
Notes Page view, 12–13

O
objects
  editing linked, 88–89
  embedded, 90–92
  linked, 88–89
  linking within program, 87
  rotating, 67
  working with cropped, 92
objects, applying animation to, 54–55
Online Pictures button, 47
Open dialog box, 10
opening, presentation, 10–11
organizational chart, inserting and formatting in SmartArt, 50–53
Outline View, 12–13

P
Package for CD feature, 75
paragraph, changing spacing, 40–41
pasting
  data, 83
  text, 32–33
pen, using during presentation, 22–25
Picture Effects button, 45
pictures
  compress, 47
  formatting with buttons in Picture Tools Format tab, 47
  insert in slide background, 43
Picture Tools Format tab,
  formatting with buttons in, 47

Index **POWERPOINT** 93

placeholder, 3, 7
  AutoFit Options button, 15
  selecting and moving, 14–15
  sizing, 15
PowerPoint
  closing, 5
  opening, 2
  Package for CD feature, 75
  window elements in, 3
presentation
  adding audio/video, 76–77
  applying more than one design theme to, 73
  blank presentation, 6
  choosing typeface for, 37
  closing, 9
  copying slides within, 17
  creating with installed template, 2–5
  design theme, choosing, 6–9
  editing, 20–21
  embedding and editing Word table in, 90–92
  exporting to Word, 82–83
  exporting Word outline to PowerPoint, 84–85
  inserting slides in, 10–11
  keyboard for navigating, 13
  linking Excel chart with, 86–87
  main purpose of, 9
  navigating in, 10–11, 13
  opening, 10–11
  Package for CD feature, 75
  planning, 9
  Presenter view, 25
  previewing, 28–29
  printing, 28–29
  running, 22–25
    automatically, 27
    from current slide, 22–25
  saving, 9
  setting and rehearsing timing for, 78–79
  sound, 26–27
  transitions, 26–27
  using Ink Tools during, 25
  using pen during, 22–25
presentation cycle, completing, 2–5
Presenter view, 25
previewing, presentation, 28–29
Previous Slide button, 10
Print backstage area, 28–29
printing
  determining needs for, 9
  presentation, 28–29
  presentation in outline layout, 5
proportional typeface, 35

Q
Quick Access toolbar, 3

R
Reading view, 12–13
rearranging, slides, 16–17
Recent option list
  opening presentation from, 11
Rehearse Timings feature, 78–79
Replace dialog box, 60–61
Replace Font dialog box, 37
replacing
  fonts, 36–37
  text, 60–61
ribbon, 3, 5
rotating
  objects, 67
  shapes, 66–67
rotation handle, 66, 67

S
san serif typeface, 35
Save As dialog box, 4
Save button, 4
saving, presentation, 9
screenshot, inserting, 48–49
ScreenTip, 5
scroll bar, vertical, 3, 10
Selection task pane, 65
Send to Microsoft Word dialog box, Paste option at, 82, 83
serif typeface, 35
Set Up group, 78
Set Up Slide Show button, 79
shapes
  copying, 66–67
  customizing, 64–65
  drawing, 64–65
  rotating, 66–67
sizing
  image, 44–47
  placeholder, 15
  table, 69
slide design, maintaining consistent, 9
slide layout
  changing, 14–15
  choosing, 10–11
slide master, formatting with, 72–73
Slide Master view, 73
slide orientation, 29
slide pane, 3, 6
slides
  adding, 7–9
  changing size, 42–43
  consistent design for, 9
  copying within presentation, 17
  creating, 6–9
  deleting, 16–17
  formatting background, 42–43
  hiding, 16–17
  inserting headers/footer on, –75
  inserting in presentation, 10–11
  keeping easy to read, 9
  moving, 16–17
  navigating through, 10–11
  new, 7–8
  one idea per slide, 9
  picture in background, 43
  rearranging, 16–17
  running from current, 22–25
  tables in, 68–69
slide show
  running, 22–25
    automatically, 27
    continuously, 79
    manually, 22
  setting and rehearsing timings for, 78–79
  setting times manually, 79
Slide Size dialog box, 29
Slide Sorter View, 12–13
slide thumbnails pane, 3
SmartArt graphic
  formatting, 50–53
  inserting, 50–53
  inserting text, 53
  organizational chart in, 50–53
SmartArt graphic dialog box, 50–52
Smart Lookup feature, 19
sound, adding, 26–27
source program, 86, 88
spacing, changing line and paragraph, 40–41
spelling
  editing while checking, 20–21
  options in, 21
spelling checker, 20–21
Status bar, 3
strikethrough, 34
style, applying in Word, 85
synonyms, 20–21

T
table
  creating, in a slide, 68–69
  embedding and editing Word table in presentation, 90–92
  moving, 69
  sizing, 69
tabs, 3
  using, 5
Tell Me feature, 3
  using, 18–19
template, creating presentation with installed, 2–5
text
  applying animation to, 54–55
  copying, 32–33
  creating bulleted, 41
  cutting, 32–33
  finding and replacing, 60–61
  horizontal text alignment, 40–41
  inserting, in SmartArt graphic, 53
  pasting, 32–33
  selecting, 33
  vertical text alignment, 40–41
text box, inserting, 66–67
text pane, inserting text in, 53
Text Pane button, 53
theme color, changing, 42–43
theme font, changing, 42–43
thesaurus, 20–21
timings
  setting and rehearsing for presentation, 78–79
  setting manually, 79
Title bar, 3
transitions, adding, 26–27
typefaces
  choosing, 35, 37
  defined, 35
  monospaced, 35
  proportional, 35
  san serif, 35
  serif, 35

U
underline, 34

V
vertical scroll bar, 3, 10
vertical text alignment, changing, 40–41
video
  adding, 76–77
  changing color of, 77
view area, 3
views, changing, 12–13
View tab, 12

W
Word
  applying style in, 85
  embedding and editing table in PowerPoint presentation, 90–92
  exporting outline to PowerPoint presentation, 84–85
  exporting presentation to, 82–83
  linking Excel chart with, 86–87
WordArt, inserting and formatting, 62–63

Z
Zoom button, 13
Zoom dialog box, 13
Zoom slider bar, 13